THE POLITICS OF INEQUALITY

THE POLITICS OF INEQUALITY

South Africa Since 1948

GWENDOLEN M. CARTER

REVISED EDITION

FREDERICK A. PRAEGER, *Publisher*
NEW YORK

TO

LOUISE, PHYL

AND JIM

BOOKS THAT MATTER

Published in the United States of America in 1958 by
Frederick A. Praeger, Inc., *Publisher*
64 University Place, New York 3, N. Y.

Revised edition published in 1959

Second printing, 1962

Library of Congress Catalog Card Number: 58-8170

Printed in the United States of America

CONTENTS

ACKNOWLEDGMENTS

In preparing the form of this book, certain somewhat arbitrary decisions were made in the interest of clarity, or in response to its transatlantic publication. The spelling within quotations follows English usage, that in the body of the text is American. Moreover, although South Africans sometimes use the words 'Afrikaner' and 'Afrikaans' in a special sense, in this work Afrikaner refers to the people and Afrikaans only to the language.

Several small sections of this book have appeared elsewhere in the same or similar form and I appreciate the publisher's permission to use them in this work. Some parts of the introductory chapter were incorporated in *South Africa*, Foreign Policy Association Headline Book, January-February 1955; much of the historical material in the same chapter was used in the South African section of 'The Commonwealth Overseas: Variations on a British Theme', in *Modern Political Parties*, edited by Sigmund Neumann, and published by the University of Chicago Press 1956. Some of the description of United Nations consideration of the treatment of Indians which is in Chapter 15 first appeared in 'The Discrimination against Indians in South Africa' in *Problems in International Relations* edited by Andrew Gyorgy and Hubert S. Gibbs and published by Prentice-Hall in 1955. Also used are parts of 'Union of South Africa: Politics of White Supremacy', in *Contemporary Africa: Trends and Issues* edited by W. O. Brown, *The Annals*, March, 1955. The material which has appeared in print is only a very small fraction, however, of what the present work contains.

Particular thanks are extended to the Rockefeller Foundation for the study grant which enabled me to be in South Africa from August 1952 to September 1953, a period which included the 1953 election. My earlier three-month visit to South Africa during a year-long study tour of the Commonwealth in 1948-49 was made possible by the generosity of the Social Science Research Council, the Canadian Social Science Research Council and the International Secretariat of the Institute of Pacific Relations. The Rockefeller Foundation and the Social Science Research Council also contributed towards the preparation of the material for publication.

So many South Africans helped me in varied ways that I cannot name them all individually, but I hope they will realize how much their generosity was appreciated. I think with special gratitude of those who hold or have held important party offices like Dr. D. F. Malan, the Hon. J. G. Strijdom, Dr. T. E. Dönges, N. C. Havenga, Field-Marshal Jan Christian Smuts, J. H. Hofmeyr, J. G. N. Strauss, Sir de Villiers Graaff, Alec Hepple, and Mrs. Margaret Ballinger, who were willing to devote time from busy schedules to discuss policies and answer questions, and of the large number of other Members of Parliament including Harry Oppenheimer, P. A. Moore, Senator Carelius, Harm Oost, Hyman Davidoff, Mrs. Bertha Solomon, and Senator William Ballinger, who also shared their knowledge and experience. Party officials, in particular, Marais Viljoen, Senator M. P. A. Malan and P. W. Botha of the National Party, J. L.

Horak, F. J. van Biljon, Mrs. Cornelia van den Bos, and Miss Jacqueline de Villiers of the United Party, and Miss D. Ritchie of the Labour Party were unfailingly helpful through long series of interviews. The editors, and/or their chief assistants, of all the major newspapers in South Africa were generous with their time and information. Special thanks are due to P. Weber of *Die Bürger* for the many contacts which he made for me both with Nationalist Members of Parliament and National Party officials at every level, while the United and Labour Parties were equally helpful in facilitating my contacts with party workers at the constituency and ward levels. For material on the Torch Commando, I am particularly grateful to Ralph Parrott, Louis Kane-Berman, and Guy Braithwaite. I would also like to express my special appreciation to the leaders of the non-European organizations who so generously shared material and information with me. Among the many university colleagues who were of great assistance in gaining perspective on the current South African scene as well as increasing my store of knowledge were Drs. E. G. Malherbe, Arthur Keppel-Jones, Kenneth Kirkwood, Chris Coetzee, Gey van Pittius, Michael Louw, Monica Wilson, Leo and Hilda Kuper, Kenneth Heard, Edgar Brookes, I. D. MacCrone, Edward Roux, J. S. Marais, Eileen J. Krige, H. R. Burrows, A. H. Murray, Mabel Palmer, L. H. Samuels, and Michael Roberts, while other well informed individuals who contributed helpfully included Leo Marquard, Ellen Hellmann, Winifred Hoernlé, Sheila Patterson, Maurice Webb, Quintin Whyte, J. R. Neame, the Rev. Ben Marais, Father Trevor Huddleston, C. A. Michalson, I. C. Alva-Wright, and D. H. van Gend.

To those who read the manuscript in whole or in part goes a special word of thanks. The former include Professors Kenneth Kirkwood, William O. Brown, and Vernon McKay. Jeffrey Horton of the University of Witwatersrand added to a careful reading the heroic service of seeing the manuscript to the press while I was making my third visit to South Africa. National and United Party officials very kindly read the chapters on their respective parties to ensure their accuracy. Leo Marquard read a considerable part of the manuscript. The points which these kindly critics raised have been handled to the best of my ability and, of course, I assume full responsibility for what appears in print. Warm appreciation is also expressed to those who assisted me in the collection or preparation of material, notably Miss Brooks Parkman (now Mrs. Cal Woodard), Mrs. Ruth Dvorkin, Miss Bette Knapp, Mrs. Gloria Duran, Miss Margaret Meyer, Miss Lily Rabkin and Mr. Charles Brookes.

Above and beyond individuals stand out in my mind the hospitable warmth of the South African community and the beauty of the South African landscape. Not only interest but affection has led me to study South African problems. My background of training and experience has been in Canada, Great Britain and the United States and to them I owe my primary allegiance. But to South Africa I owe experiences never duplicated elsewhere. If one can express gratitude to a whole country, I should like to do so to South Africa and all its people.

GWENDOLEN M. CARTER

October, 1957
Northampton, Massachusetts

INTRODUCTION

Few countries have been so subject to publicity and criticism since World War II as has South Africa. It is a rare year in which no writer uses that colorful country as a subject. And yet, for all this publicity, there is remarkably little understanding in other countries either of the complexity of the problems which South Africa confronts or of the character of the forces which are shaking it.

Even South Africans themselves, sharply divided as they are by race and color, are largely unaware of the forces at work among them. Perhaps my greatest advantage in studying South Africa was that because I was a foreigner I was able to move from group to group as no native-born South African can do. Hardly less of an advantage was that I came to South Africa with no preconceived ideas and that throughout most of my two substantial periods of investigation in that country I was far more concerned with understanding the points of view and character of action of the different groups in the community than in judging them. No one who goes to South Africa for a serious study of the situation can ultimately avoid judgments. But to the best of my ability I have tried to separate facts and analysis from such judgments, and to let the former speak for themselves.

This book is primarily a political study of South Africa in the crucial period after the National Party came into office in 1948. I visited South Africa for the first time late in that year and it was my particular privilege to meet and talk with the dominant political figures of that moment, in particular with Field-Marshal Jan Christian Smuts, who had been defeated politically so short a time before, and Jan Hendrik Hofmeyr, his potential successor who tragically predeceased his leader, as well as with the new Prime Minister, Dr. Daniel F. Malan, and several members of the Nationalist Cabinet. When I returned in 1952 for more than a year of field study, my principal aim was to underpin my general impressions with first-hand knowledge of South African political parties and groups, not only through their records—which in any case are sparse and often poorly kept—but in particular through personal investigation. At all times I received extremely generous help from the officials and members of all the South African political parties and it was only through their cooperation that I was able to bring together the detailed material on their organization and functioning which forms a substantial part of this book.

Having long been interested in the party systems of Canada, Australia and New Zealand which, with South Africa, form the original overseas members of the Commonwealth of Nations, I had been puzzled as to why there was no comparable literature on political parties in South Africa. I found that neither in the universities nor elsewhere was there serious study of political parties or what in the United States is called 'political dynamics'. Nor had there been any careful analysis of a South African election. With limited resources I attempted therefore to secure as wide a range of information as possible on the 1953 general election, taking as my model the studies of the British general elections from 1945 to the present which have been prepared under the auspices of Nuffield College, Oxford. I had anticipated that it might be difficult to secure biographical material on the candidates for the election and indeed this proved to be the most time-consuming and costly enterprise on which I embarked. Much more surprising was the difficulty that I encountered in securing such apparently public information as election statistics, and the records of expenditures in elections. Electoral returns are printed in the *Government Gazette*, but without party designations, and it took a long search before I was able to determine the number of votes cast for particular parties. Despite provisions in the electoral law providing for public scrutiny of certain material for a year after an election, I was not able to see such records as those of expenditures in elections, though I was ultimately provided with this information by the Electoral Office.

But if it was often difficult to secure material on elections and on the political parties and groups of European South Africans (with the notable exception of the Torch Commando) it was virtually impossible to do so for non-European groups. During the first half of my 1952-53 period of study in the Union, the non-European passive resistance campaign was at its height. I listened to the trial of the first non-European leaders who were convicted of 'statutory Communism'. I attended the one public session of the African National Congress in December 1952. I talked to most of the leaders of African, Indian and Coloured groups. But typical of my difficulty in securing printed material was the time when I called for a collection of documents which an African lawyer had agreed to lend me only to find that it had been carried away with miscellaneous other papers on a casual police raid the night before.

In sharp contrast to the paucity of material in some spheres is the overwhelming bulk in others, notably parliamentary debates, the South African press, and United Nations discussions and reports on South African affairs. To cull these sources for salient points of view and indications of fundamental political philosophies was still more time-consuming, and often far more tedious than to piece together the scraps of information I tracked down on party organization and quasi-political groups. Yet I believe that only by quarrying this raw material has it been possible to perceive accurately the underlying and therefore all-important assumptions on which policy rests, or is attacked. As far as the 1953 election campaign was concerned I used the daily press, both Afrikaans and English. Apart from this period, I depended largely on press digests, of which by far the most comprehensive is the one prepared in the offices of the Jewish Board of Deputies in Johannesburg.

Since I used press material so much I needed to know circulation figures, type of readership and other relevant information so as to be able to estimate the effect of particular publications. But, like many other facts which are easy to secure elsewhere, this particular type of information is a closely guarded secret of the Audit Bureau of Circulation in Johannesburg. In this field, too, I conducted my own surveys. The information I secured is in Appendix I on the South African press.

If it were easier to secure the type of factual material on which this book is based, I should not have needed to incorporate so much detail in the text. If there were a more substantial literature of political analysis on South Africa, I would not have made the book so comprehensive. But because serious studies of South Africa are almost always specialized or historical I have aimed deliberately at a broad coverage in the hope of providing in a single volume the material necessary for understanding the political factors and forces operating in the Union today. I have done so with the conviction that these factors and forces are significant not only because of the complexity of the issues within the borders of South Africa but even more because South Africa has become a symbol of oppression to the peoples of color throughout the world. It is vital for those who care for the future of freedom to be able to gauge correctly whether or not this judgment is correct.

The second printing of this book has made it possible to include a brief appendix on voting returns in the 1958 election and to refer to the election of Dr. H. F. Verwoerd as leader of the National Party on September 2, 1958, following the death of Prime Minister J. G. Strijdom.

Section I: The Setting

CHAPTER I

WHAT THE NATIONALISTS INHERITED

Of all countries in the world, South Africa most fully mirrors within itself the crucial political, economic and social strains which rack the international community. Above all, it faces acutely within its own borders the most difficult question of our age: What should be the relation between the long established, dominant white minority throughout the world and the developing masses of the peoples of color?

Plural or White Society?

To most people, South Africa is a classic example of a plural society. In this view, each of South Africa's diverse racial groups—its nearly 3 million whites, over 9 million Africans, more than a million Coloured (mixed blood) and over a third of a million Asians—has legitimate claims through history and through its contributions to South African development to share in the control as well as the returns of the community. But white South Africans think of their country as Americans, Canadians and Australians think of theirs—as a white society dedicated to the values of Western civilization except for racial equality. To most white South Africans, the fact that four-fifths of the people who live in South Africa do not belong to this Western white society simply creates problems with which the whites have to wrestle, but not a need to change either their way of life or the assumptions on which rest their monopoly of political and economic power and social prestige.

The fact that white South Africans are so far outnumbered within their country by peoples of color has always made the relations between white and non-white or, as South Africans say, between Europeans and non-Europeans, the great motif of the South African story. But there are also two other themes which interact with this dominant issue and sometimes overshadow it. One of these themes is the struggle between Afrikaners and English South Africans for position and power within the dominant white group. In this struggle the Afrikaners have had the advantage of numbers; the English South Africans of wealth and of international connections. So it is not surprising that this second theme of South African history is closely bound with the third one: the effort, led by nationalistic Afrikanerdom, to resist or to free South Africa from outside influences, first those of British imperial power and economic control, and now of the United Nations.

None of these issues might have become so acute if South Africa had remained the simple agricultural society of the nineteenth century. But ever since 1886, when gold was found in payable quantities on the southern slopes of the Witwatersrand (Ridge of White Waters) in the Transvaal, South Africa has moved steadily into the industrial revolution. Before World War I it was chiefly the gold mines which needed heavy capitalization and large scale equipment to handle the vast quantities of gold-bearing rock which lie deep below the surface of the land. Between the two wars South Africa built an iron and steel industry which today provides for most of its own needs. During and after World War II, its secondary industries expanded so that today almost everything needed by an advanced civilization can be produced within the Union. In the process all of South Africa's people have been brought into ever closer contact with one another. And, as in other countries which have undergone the industrial revolution, this dynamic economic situation has encouraged economic and social mobility and thus threatened traditional racial and social divisions.

There are two obvious, though sharply contrasted answers to these developments. One is to permit the economic process to blur, and ultimately eradicate the customary political, economic and even social divisions within the community. The other is to reinforce these divisions so strongly that they can resist the economic pressures. The first answer is supported by almost all non-Europeans except fully tribalized Africans, but by only a tiny majority of Europeans, chiefly those enrolled in the Liberal Party which came into existence in May 1953. The latter objective is endorsed by the overwhelming majority of South African Europeans, but they differ amongst themselves as to how it can be achieved.

Some of the most idealistic among nationalistic Afrikaners support the idea of ultimately establishing a separate territorial entity for the Africans who form over three-fifths of South Africa's present population. Thus the African would have a home of his own as has the European, and all (rather than most) African labor in 'European' South Africa would be migratory labor. A basic problem with so neat a solution, however, is that all aspects of the South African economy depend so greatly on African labor. Still more serious is the fact that the 11 per cent of South African territory which is at present reserved solely for African occupancy (and thus known as the Native Reserves) cannot even support at subsistence level the 50 per cent or less of the Union's Africans who are now resident within them. The most obvious source of additional land, at least to a South African, is the High Commission Territories of Basutoland, Swaziland and Bechuanaland which form enclaves within or abut on South African territory; but British public opinion, which is sharply critical of South African Native policy, strongly opposes any suggestion of transferring these areas to that country. Moreover, it is the considered judgment of the official Commission on the Socio-Economic Development of the Reserves, commonly known as the Tomlinson Commission, that, even with the addition of the High Commission territories (not likely to be ceded in any case), it would require great sums of money and a long-term program to make the Native Reserves capable of supporting even three-quarters of the African population of this area of Southern Africa.[1] So far the Nationalist Government has not been prepared to commit itself to so long range a plan.[2]

Since practical politics do not now admit of either of the two more extreme solutions of South Africa's problems—the gradual economic and political integration of all South Africa's people on the one hand, or progressive territorial separation (often called ideal, or total apartheid) on the other—the present choice of means for maintaining the customary character of South African life narrows to those endorsed by the governing National Party and by the official Opposition, the United Party.

The United Party, as befits its conservative nature, would prefer to depend on tradition and custom rather than legislation to retain the segmented character of South African society. Strongly involved as are its members in the industrial advance of the country, the United Party is somewhat more flexible than the Nationalists in endorsing the advance of non-Europeans in the economy, and the provision of stable living centers for them near European towns and cities. Its policy is an empirical one, however, which is conditioned by circumstance and therefore more difficult to define than is that of the Nationalists.

The succeeding chapters of this book analyse in detail the programs of apartheid, or racial segregation defined by law, which the National Party put into force in the decisive period after it achieved power in 1948. Ever since that moment, the major attention of the Government has focused upon what it clearly regards as the chief issue in South African affairs: how to maintain European supremacy in every sphere of life and at the same time advance the industrial revolution in South Africa which helps to make that country independent of outside influences. Side by side with this objective has gone the Nationalist program of separate development for the African in line with what most Nationalists maintain to be the innate differences between Africans and Europeans. In both respects, the Nationalists have acted decisively and forcefully, enacting their programs through legislation which they have been prepared to put into force in the face of the most bitter criticism, often from Europeans as well as non-Europeans.

But the Nationalists, with their almost exclusively Afrikaner membership, have also been concerned with the power position of their own group within the white community. The great significance of the Nationalists' victory in the general election of 1953 was that they not only gained a secure parliamentary majority but also polled a relative increase in votes as compared with their opponents. It is true that no Nationalist Government in South African history has yet received a majority of the votes cast in a general election, but 1953 indicated a Nationalist swing which augured well for their continued political success.

The Nationalists have used legislation, as well as politics, to strengthen their own authority and their particular tenets within the white community in South Africa. This was particularly the case with the Citizenship Act of 1949 and with the Suppression of Communism Act of 1950, which has been used against Europeans as well as non-Europeans. It is true that the sharpest of all controversies between the Nationalists and their parliamentary opponents and outside critics (notably the Torch Commando, and the Black Sash women) has been over the means by which the Nationalists tried to remove the male Coloured voters in Cape Province from the common roll, where they had long voted for the same representatives as did Europeans, to a separate or communal roll from which to elect four Europeans to represent them in the House of Assembly. These means were attacked as unconstitutional inside Parliament, in the courts, and through public demonstrations; on this issue non-Nationalist Europeans in South Africa stood together, at least temporarily, to a degree unique in a period of peace. But the issue for most of the Nationalists' opponents was not the rights of the Coloured but the sanctity of the Constitution. And in the end the Nationalist success in achieving their purpose through the Senate Act (which added enough members to the second chamber to give the Nationalists the two-thirds majority of the two chambers necessary for a constitutional amendment) was the capstone of their dominance within the European community.

What way of life is it that the Nationalists seek so forcibly to ensure? What are the motive forces of Afrikaner nationalism? But also what is the character of the land which has shaped it, and the people who are moved so intensely by its fire? And what of other South Africans, white, African, Coloured, Asian? How do they live, and what are their ambitions? What is the political past of South Africa which has molded its present political configurations? What are the means of communication between South Africans? Does the press help the varied South African groups to understand one another better, or only intensify the barriers between them? These are questions to which we must seek answers before we take up in detail the form and justifications for Nationalist legislation, why the Nationalists won in 1953, the character of the National Party and its supporting groups, and those of its opposition inside and outside South Africa.

The Country

The setting within which South Africans grapple with their problems is of great natural beauty and variety, very unlike the common stereotype of Africa. Lying at the southern end of that continent well outside the tropics, it is 'white man's country', with an invigorating and healthful climate. The only independent State in Africa which is the home of people of European ancestry, South Africa is one-sixth the size of the United States and is over twice the size of France. Its most southerly area, Cape Province, is slightly larger than France. The northerly Transvaal, which shares borders with Southern Rhodesia and Portuguese East Africa, is the size of Germany; Natal on the Indian Ocean approximates Austria; while the Orange Free State in the center of South Africa has the area of Czechoslovakia.

In climate the Cape is like the Mediterranean or southern California and, similarly, includes fruit-growing areas. In the northeast the land rises in steps to the high veld, the grassy plateau of the interior, which nearly everywhere is 4,000 to 6,000 feet above sea level. East of the high veld are the spectacular mountains of the Drakensberg, with their sheer 5,000 foot wall above subtropical Natal. Between the mountains and Natal's coastal strip, on which the Indian Ocean crashes incessantly, lie a succession of softly rounded valleys whose lush green vegetation and twisting streams are not rivalled anywhere.

Lack of water is South Africa's greatest natural handicap. Eighty-six per cent of the land is semi-arid, with six months of winter drought alternating with six months of summer rains. Only one-third of the country receives more than 25 inches of rain a year, a minimum requirement for crops in most parts of the Union. There are no arterial rivers or lakes, and during the dry season both the Vaal and Orange rivers, on which so much of the central part of the country depends for its water supply, may run low. It is a byword that 'if you fall in a stream in the Orange Free State, get up and dust yourself off'.

Moreover, when the rains come, it is with a violence that swells the water courses to torrents, makes all but the modern roads impassable, and sometimes sweeps away even the most carefully prepared contour plowing. The deep-cut dongas (gullies), bare hillsides in the interior, and heavy red stains in the ocean at the outlets of the rivers mark the tragic progress of erosion in a land whose soil, at best, is none too good.

For over 300 years, almost as long in fact as in New England, there has been European settlement at the Cape. In 1652 the Dutch East India Company established a halfway revictualing station for their ships at Cape Town. The company was not disposed to foster immigration, however, and by 1708—55 years later—there were only 1,700 white settlers, of whom a little more than half were Dutch and the rest Germans and Huguenot French. About an equal number of slaves had been brought in to provide labor, and some of the local Hottentots were also pressed into service.

In 1717 the fateful decision was made to continue slavery as the basis of the country's economy rather than encourage more Dutch immigrants. Freehold land was no longer granted. The settlers, often at odds with officialdom, began to trek east, grazing their cattle on land beyond the jurisdiction of the Government. In their impatience at authority, and their belief that plenty of land was their natural right, they resembled Americans during the westward expansion.

Today it is not difficult to find in South Africa many of the same urges and traits of earlier days: the attachment to the land; the racial superiority of Europeans long in contact with primitive people of color; the tendency of the whites to take the law into their own hands, especially when dealing with non-Europeans. But in place of the relatively simple society of the eighteenth century, modern South Africa possesses a racial complexity which is greater than that found in any other country. Moreover, its racial diversity is matched by widely differing cultural backgrounds and ways of life.

The People

A salient fact for South African politics is that the country's Europeans are themselves divided by history, language and tradition. The majority of the whites, the Afrikaners, are an independent people whose strongly cherished Calvinism has marked overtones of fundamentalism and authoritarianism. Out of the classical Dutch, the Afrikaners have developed a vigorous, earthy language—Afrikaans—which they prize not only as an expression of their individuality but also as an effective literary medium. Originally farmers (this is the meaning of the term *Boers*, by which they were long known), Afrikaners have been increasingly drawn into industry in the last 30 years, largely because of the lack of productivity of the land. They still feel, however, that the *platteland* (rural areas) is the source of their distinctive characteristics. For all their accession to political power, nationalistic Afrikaners, now by far the majority, still have a *laager* (stockade) approach to life which induces in them an intense clannishness and also a suspicion of ideas which seem alien to their native culture.

The minority of the Europeans, the English South Africans, came later to the country, mainly from 1820 on, and have never won the majority position which the English-speaking enjoy in Canada, Australia and New Zealand. They have a strong influence, however, because the Cape became British after the Napoleonic wars, Natal was annexed in 1843, and the Boer republics of the

Free State and Transvaal were permanently brought under the British flag after the Anglo-Boer war of 1899-1902. Except in predominantly English-speaking Natal and parts of the eastern Cape Province, where many of them are on the land, the English in South Africa have worked chiefly in mining, industry, commerce and the professions. Thus they have exercised a predominant influence on the economic development of the country.

Their close economic and financial ties with Britain, coupled with a certain dependence on its cultural life, have led nationalistic Afrikaners to charge that the English are not true South Africans. Today, however, there is little justification for the accusation. In contemporary South Africa many Afrikaners still feel estranged from the English, however, by memories from the past: the way in which 'the imperial factor' (i.e., the British Government) pursued the Boers who had trekked into the interior to escape English influence; the experience of defeat in the Anglo-Boer war; the discrimination against Afrikaans until the 1920's; and the economic difficulties of the Afrikaners.

Moreover, the English and many Afrikaners differed sharply over South Africa's participation in the two world wars, one of which followed closely on the coming into effect of the South African Union in 1909 and the other saw a considerable section of nationalistic Afrikanerdom actively favoring Germany. But, above all, perhaps, their differences arise from different traditions and attitudes which have led to separate Afrikaans and English school systems; a separate Afrikaans and English press, where reporting of the news is often so divergent as to give the impression of totally different countries; and separate networks of voluntary societies. Moreover, although the major opposition party—the United Party—holds together most of the English and perhaps 15 per cent of the more liberally inclined Afrikaners, the National Party is almost exclusively Afrikaner.

One of the major differences of attitude between English and Afrikaners in the early nineteenth century was with regard to the non-Europeans. Under the influence of the English missionaries the Cape Government in 1828 extended to free people of color, mainly Hottentots, the same legal status as Europeans; in 1833 slavery was abolished throughout the British Empire. The impact of the first of these decisions was no less than the impact of the second. Slaves had been brought from Madagascar, West and East Africa, Ceylon, India and Malaya from the earliest days of the colony and, although there was a good deal of open miscegenation at first (the more so because there were originally few white women), color feeling hardened quickly.

The original distinction was between Christian and heathen. It was not long, however, before color became the index of status. Nothing was more bitterly resented by the established landowners of the Cape, with their fixed racial prejudices, than the British Government's attempt to make the law color-blind. From 1836 on, 10,000 Dutch families trekked North and East to escape this 'tyranny' and to base their political societies, like their churches, on the principle that there is no equality between white and black.

Over the years the descendants of slaves and Hottentots, with their admixture of European blood, merged to form the Cape Coloured, a distinctive people now numbering over a million and centered mainly in the western Cape areas. Many are dark skinned; some are so light they can, and do, pass as Europeans. With no distinctive language or culture of their own, the Coloured have in the past been treated as 'an appendage to the white race'. When the Cape received representative government in 1853, the franchise, like the law, was color-blind; and Coloured males who could meet certain educational and property tests voted on the same roll as Europeans until the long continued efforts of the National Party to remove them from the common to a separate roll succeeded in 1956.

Although many of the Coloured are still farm labourers, they also include numerous artisans and some professional people, mainly teachers and doctors. On the whole, however, their economic status is low. Socially, as well as politically, they are perhaps in the most difficult position of any group in the Union, being caught between the exclusiveness of the whites, with whom they would like to associate themselves, and the rising power of the African, with whom they feel little in common.

It is important to remember that the Dutch settlers did not come in contact with the Bantu-speaking Africans until late in the eighteenth century and that some African tribes are as recent immigrants to South Africa as are the Europeans. Driven by land hunger, as were the European trekkers, Bantu tribes had drifted slowly down from East and Central Africa. By 1775, when the Boers had expanded eastward to the Great Fish River, the Bantu had arrived at approximately the same point on the other side of the river. Their closely knit tribal structure gave the Bantus much greater cohesive force than the Hottentots had had. For nearly a century frontier settlers and Bantu tribes clashed in a long series of conflicts. Ultimately the Africans were subdued and pinioned on Reserves in the eastern Cape (the Transkei and Ciskei), northern and southern Natal and in parts of the Tranvaal. Moreover, they were already being drawn into the employment of the Europeans.

Today the more than 9 million Africans of the Union (who belong to scores of different tribes and represent four major linguistic groups and one minor) are found scattered throughout the country, providing its basic labor force in every field of activity. Probably only some 4 million are normally in the Reserves. Moreover most of these are women, children and older men, for 50 to 70 per cent of the able-bodied men whose families are in the Reserves are themselves working in the mines, industry or domestic employment in urban centers. Well over 2 million Africans live on European farms, either as paid laborers or as squatters who provide 90 to 180 days of labor a year in return for the right to graze cattle and raise their small subsistence crops. More than another 2 million are in European urban areas, some as migratory labor but an increasing number in municipally provided locations, or squatter towns.

About half a million of the Africans in urban areas are employed by the mines and housed in compounds close to their work; less than half of these are Union Natives, the rest being drawn from the British High Commission Territories (Basutoland, Swaziland and Bechuanaland), Portuguese East Africa, and the Rhodesias. Mine boys are given fixed contracts of 9 to 15 months and are expected to return to their families in the Reserves if they do not sign on for another period of service. Over 600,000 work in industry, for which the African shows considerable aptitude. A third of a million, including both men and women, are in personal service, many of them providing Europeans with the domestic help lacking in most other countries. Another 100,000 or so are in transport, public service and more rarely, the professions, mainly teaching but occasionally in law or medicine.

All these groups face or create their own particular difficulties. Farm employment is generally unpopular. Despite the fact that on farms the family unit can be kept intact, the low and sometimes worsening standard of living of farm labor makes it difficult for farmers to satisfy their demand for workers. Although, in contrast, the mines pay and feed their labor well, they too have difficulty with recruitment because the men must live in compounds separated from their families and work underground. Thus the mines and, to some extent, the farms turn perforce to 'foreign natives', that is, those from the High Commission Territories, the Rhodesias and even Nyasaland.

African males prefer to work in industry, but the problems here are housing and the social tensions arising out of the strains of urban life. A series of Urban Areas Acts from 1923 on have given municipalities power to control the influx of Natives.[3] Moreover, no male African can leave the Reserves without a pass from a European official. In spite of these provisions Africans surge increasingly into the Native locations outside the European towns and cities where they can combine family life with urban jobs. Especially since World War II this steady stream of Africans from the Reserves has overstrained the limited housing provided by the municipalities and led to shanty towns and *pondokkies* (shelters) of sacking or galvanized iron. Moreover with their parents working, with few facilities for education, poor conditions and no tribal restraints, young African boys often form gangs of *tsotsis* (ruffians), which terrorize their own people. These unsettled circumstances and the fact that there are still far more African men than women in the urban areas lead to promiscuity and to an illegitimacy rate running as high as 70 per cent in the Johannesburg area. An added problem is the continuous friction between the police and the location dwellers, partly over petty offences, such as those connected with the making and drinking of beer, partly because of police arbitrariness.

Europeans in South Africa often dismiss criticisms of the conditions of the locations by pointing out that the Africans have the Reserves, to which they can return. This argument overlooks two factors: that many Africans are now detribalized and have no foothold in the Reserves, and that even those who are still based in the Reserves have but a tenuous life there. At least 25 per cent of what is needed to keep the people of the Reserves at bare subsistence level comes from the earnings of those outside. Despite Government-aided efforts at rehabilitation of the land, some of which is among the best watered in the Union, most of the land in the Reserves is badly eroded and inefficiently cultivated. This is partly due to the absence of the men who are in urban areas so much of the time. Also, in general, the African is not a good agriculturist and is suspicious of Government efforts to teach him new techniques.

Even more serious, perhaps, is the extensive overgrazing of the lands that results from the African's pride in his cattle, which he considers his wealth. One of the most important of African social institutions is *lobola*, the giving of cattle by the bridegroom to the father of the bride, not in payment, as was first thought by Europeans, but as the cementing of the marriage bond. The Government has tried to convince the Africans that 'culling' of poor stock will enrich them. Partly, this has outraged tribal traditions; partly, it goes against their sense of value. One old Native pulled a crumpled ten-shilling note out of his pocket after such a lecture and asked, 'Is this worth less than a new note?' When assured that it was not, he replied smartly, 'Then why is my old cow less valuable than the young one?'

In the Reserves, tribal organization is still a reality, but the former authority of the chiefs is greatly diminished. This is partly because the Europeans broke it in the days of the Native wars, partly because chiefs are now somewhat torn between their responsibilities as leaders of their tribes and as paid Government officials, and partly because of the growth of an African nationalism transcending tribal barriers. The vast movement between the Reserves and urban areas accelerates the latter process; education, which over 40 per cent of the Africans now receive in lesser or greater degree, tends even more to dissolve tribalism. Nevertheless, the existence of separate languages and cultures means that the Bantu-speaking African retains a distinctiveness and racial pride quite different from those to which the Cape Coloured can aspire.

There is still one other group in the South African racial pattern—the Asians. Brought to South Africa from India in the 1860's to cultivate the sugar plantations of Natal, in which war-like African tribes such as the Zulus were reluctant to work, the Asians were at first indentured labor (i.e., in South Africa on temporary contracts) but after their terms expired, they often stayed on. Except for a few wives and children brought from India in recent years, South Africa's Asians, now numbering over a third of a million, have been for several generations in that country and look on it as their home. Many of them are shopkeepers, artisans, market gardeners or small farm owners; some are wealthy, but a great many are poor.

Indians have always suffered restrictions, and Mahatma Gandhi's first campaigns of passive disobedience (*satyagraha*) were organized against racial discrimination in South Africa. Indians have never been allowed to trade or farm in the Orange Free State, and less than a score live there; they may live and trade in the Transvaal but cannot legally own property. In Natal Indians may own property but lost the franchise when that colony gained responsible government near the end of the last century. The 15,000 to 20,000 Indians who live in the Cape lost their vote on the common roll along with the Cape Coloured in 1956.

The overwhelming majority of South African Asians live in Natal and the 'Indian problem' is Natal's most serious concern. More skilful and enterprising than the African, the Indians are disliked by the Europeans in that province because of their generally low standard of living, the way in which some of them do business and, in some instances, because of their success. The African, particularly the tribalized African, resents what he regards as exploitation by the Indian middleman. This was strikingly shown by the Durban riots of January 1949, when bands of largely tribalized Africans murdered a number of Indians in Durban and looted or burned Indian property following a chance incident in which an Indian struck an African boy. Yet it is also true that Indian and African nationalist leaders toured the mob-stricken areas of Durban together in the effort to end the violence and that they still maintain a working alliance based on their common opposition to discrimination.

The position of the Indian in South Africa presents the same obvious difficulties as that of the Cape Coloured. In Natal the entrenched position of the

European denies the Asian the middle-class status he possesses in East Africa. The degree to which Africans provide the basic labor force in Durban, as elsewhere, limits the opportunities of the Indian at the other end. Racially proud, the Indians are not only more concerned with political rights, but possess fewer of them than any other non-European group in South Africa. Moreover, continued efforts to persuade them to accept repatriation to India (with which most of them have few, if any, ties), plus considerable propaganda describing them as a 'foreign' element, give the South African Asian a constant sense of insecurity.

Even so brief a survey of the racial patterns in South Africa makes it obvious that the situation varies in different areas of the country. The simplest pattern is that in the Orange Free State, where the population is overwhelmingly Afrikaner, there are few Coloured and almost no Indians, and the Africans live mainly on European farms with a small sprinkling in the urban locations.

In Natal the people are chiefly English-speaking, although the north-western coal-mining areas have attracted many Afrikaner workers. There are almost no Coloured but practically all of the country's Indians and a large number of tribalized Africans living on Reserves, including the Zulus, who were once the aristocracy among them. Interestingly enough, Natal is the one area in South Africa where it is common for Europeans to speak a native language, Zulu, and in consequence there is probably a warmer, more personal contact between Africans and Europeans in Natal than elsewhere.

In the two more heavily populated provinces—the Cape and the Transvaal—the picture is still more complicated. In both, English- and Afrikaans-speaking are intermingled in the urban centers, although the commonly better standard of living of the English provides some residential separation. Partly as a result of historical developments, English-Afrikaner relations seem at their best in the Cape and at their worst in the Transvaal. The Cape has almost all the Coloured, largely in the western areas, a huge group of Africans in the East in the Transkei and Ciskei Native Reserves, and many others in its urban centers.

The Transvaal also has Native Reserves, although less extensive than those of the Cape, but its mining and industry attract the largest number of Africans of any province. There, too, are found some Coloured and more Indians, including some of the most forceful, advanced and radical in the latter group. Pressing ahead more quickly than any other area in South Africa, the southern Transvaal has by now attracted the largest percentage of the country's population. Moreover, in its intermingling of peoples, it provides the most potentially explosive area, but also the one which demonstrates the essential interdependence of all of South Africa's peoples.

Economic Structure and Change

Behind the political tensions of the Union lies the dynamic of an industrial revolution which is shaking the very foundations of a formerly simple agricultural and pastoral society. The exploitation of natural resources, and the stimulus of active governmental intervention in the economy have pushed South Africa with unusual rapidity through the stages leading to a relatively mature and balanced economy. Only a small proportion of South Africa's people, however, have shared actively either in the promotion, or the returns of this growth.

By far the most important of all agricultural activities in the Union is the raising of sheep for the production of wool. Ninety per cent of this wool goes abroad, representing South Africa's most important export commodity other than gold. Mohair from Angora goats was once a major export, but is now largely replaced by wool. Cattle farming is less important than might be expected, partly because of the limited local market.

Drought and soil erosion are the most serious handicaps of both pastoral and agricultural workers. The amount of cultivated land in the Union is relatively small; three-quarters of it lies in the high veld's so-called 'maize triangle', where there has been so much concentration on the production of corn in the past as to make it virtually a one-crop area. Ground corn—or mealie meal, as it is commonly called—is the staple diet of the African; it is also needed to supplement the fodder of stock.

On the whole, the yield of farming in the Union is low compared to that of the United States or South America. Although mixed farming is much more common than in the past, fertilizers are used sparingly and equipment is less advanced than in countries like Australia and New Zealand, partly, of course, because of South African dependence on cheap unskilled Native labor. Moreover, the natural grasses of the veld appear to lack phosphate, resulting in low-quality beef and mutton. To increase agricultural production would require more irrigation, better handling of soil erosion and more scientific farming on the part of many Afrikaner and some English farmers and nearly all Native African cultivators.

South Africa's wealth is not its soil but what lies below it. The country is known throughout the world for its gold and diamonds, but it also has the largest coal deposits in the Southern Hemisphere, much iron ore, chrome and manganese, some tin, copper, platinum ore, mica and asbestos. Titanium deposits have been found near the coast. Most spectacular of its recent developments are the building of an oil-from-coal industry and the processing of gold-mine dumps for the recovery of uranium.

Only for a short time was surface mining sufficient on the Witwatersrand, commonly called the Rand. Steadily the mines went deeper and deeper, following the ore-bearing rocks. Some of the mines of the Rand are now cutting rock two miles under the surface of the ground, that is, well below sea level. At 9,000 feet underground in the Crown mines outside Johannesburg the temperature is 109° F., and the air forced down to these levels has to be saturated with moisture to keep the miners from contracting silicosis and phthisis. Only heavy capital investment and highly modern equipment can handle operations of such complexity.

Gold is the basis of the Union's prosperity, for approximately one-half of the world's supply is mined there (17 million fine ounces in 1957, valued at £196 million). Almost all the gold was mined on the Rand until recently, when the new gold fields of the Orange Free State began to come into production. Experts have estimated that the Rand could have maintained South Africa's production levels by itself for at least another quarter century; the new fields add greatly to the country's potentialities.

A vast amount of rock must be crushed in order to produce any sizable amount of gold. In 1898 a ton of reef produced ·489 ounce of gold; by 1948 the amount had fallen to ·2005 ounce. The great flattened pyramids of rock and waste seen near the head of every mine on the 70-mile extent of the Rand bear testimony to the vast operations of rock-crushing and processing with cyanide, both needing huge quantities of water. To watch each stage from the initial breaking of the rocks brought up in huge lifts from the underground workings until the final payoff, when molten gold is poured into molds in the most heavily guarded section of the mines, entails walking through building after building, each equipped with the most elaborate machinery. Underground, of course, there is much more dependence on hand labor, for it is here that the mines' basic labor force of Africans hew out the materials which are then processed by the machinery.

Gold not only transformed the South African economy, but also its political future. When gold was discovered, the Transvaal had a simple agricultural economy, and its Afrikaner people under Paul Kruger, pioneer settler in the Transvaal and several times its president, wanted nothing so much as to be left alone. When Britishers and Continentals (the *Uitlanders*, or foreigners) flooded into the Rand seeking their fortunes, Kruger and his supporters excluded them from the franchise for fear they might add political influence to their economic power.

Many of Kruger's own people, especially the younger ones, grew impatient with his rule, and it is possible that he might have been peacefully ousted from power except for the unjustifiable and ill-fated Jameson Raid, an invasion of the Transvaal by a small private British force late in 1895. Rightly angered by this evidence that English interests were seeking by force to overthrow Afrikaner rule in the Transvaal, Afrikaners everywhere drew together against both Cecil Rhodes, the great empire-builder, then Prime Minister of the Cape, and the British Government in London. The Jameson Raid led to the Anglo-Boer war, 1899-1902. It also widened the division between English and Afrikaners in South Africa, which has not yet been bridged.

It is true that the British made a generous act of statesmanship after the Anglo-Boer war by offering the Transvaal and Orange Free State responsible government under the British flag. The most far-sighted of the Afrikaner leaders—General Louis Botha and General Jan Christian Smuts—accepted the offer in the spirit in which it was made. These steps paved the way for the decision in 1909 by statesmen of the two former Afrikaner States, as well as of the Cape and Natal, to form the South African Union. But the memory of defeat has always rankled in the minds of some Afrikaners, making it difficult, if not impossible, for them to work with the English in South Africa. Moreover, the fact that the gold mines have remained closely linked with overseas, and chiefly British financial interests, has been a source of irritation.

Not only is South Africa the world's largest producer of gold; it was until 1908 virtually the only source of diamonds in the world and is still rich in gem stones. Diamonds were discovered at Kimberley in Cape Province as early as 1867, nearly 20 years before gold was found on the Witwatersrand. Diamond mining, like gold mining, has become the monopoly of large companies like De Beers, for capital and technical equipment are necessary to follow the 'blue ground' volcanic pipes in which the diamonds are found. Much of the mining is now underground, although the earlier open digging has its memorial in the 'big hole' at Kimberley and another at the Premier mine, near Pretoria, where the world's largest diamond, the Cullinan, was found in 1905.

Today productive industries also occupy a sizable sector of the South African economy. The most important is the iron and steel industry, established in 1926 soon after South Africa's first Afrikaner Nationalist Prime Minister, General J. B. M. Hertzog, came into office. Afrikaner nationalists endorse industry because they want the Union to become as self-sufficient as possible. By 1952, 64 per cent of South Africa's steel needs were met by its own resources. Moreover, there has been a phenomenal increase in manufactured products for South African use, rising in value from £91·5 million in 1925-26 to £492 million in 1946-47 and over £1,200 million in 1955-56.

Another no less important reason than self-sufficiency for nationalist Afrikaner support of industry is that it provides a great many jobs for former rural Afrikaners, who can no longer make a living on the farms and have come to the cities to find employment. In the 1920's this flow of relatively unskilled Afrikaners into urban centers created what was proportionally the world's worst 'poor white' problem. The jobs for which these Afrikaners were fitted were being performed in most instances at that time by non-Europeans; the managerial positions to which they would have liked to aspire were in the hands of the long-urbanized, more prosperous English South Africans. Few experiences have seared so deep into nationalistic Afrikanerdom. Though today there are relatively few poor whites in the country, few Afrikaners forget that as late as the 1920's almost 60 per cent of their people were in or close to so degrading a status. Thus they support, with a vehemence often incomprehensible from outside, the means to which they attribute their rescue: the extended color bar in industry and commerce which protects white labor from the competition of Africans, Indians and even Coloured through laws or the action of white trade unions; Government-sponsored industries like the Iron and Steel Corporation (Iscor) with its numerous jobs at European pay scales for relatively unskilled Europeans; their entrenched position in the administration and the police; and Nationalist political power.

Power and transport have been bottlenecks in South Africa's economic development. The Electricity Supply Commission was established in 1922, but has never kept abreast of the demand. The railways are also State-owned and are often accused, with some justice, of inefficiency and poor service. A tremendous strain is placed on rail haulage, however, by the great distances of the major industrial area of the Witwatersrand from the ports—1,000 miles from Cape Town and over 500 from Durban—and the fact that the Rand's best supplies of coal are at Witbank, 70 miles away. The railway gauge is only 3 feet 6 inches, and despite considerable electrification, many trains are still coal-burning.

Road haulage offers a good supporting service between major centers; but the railways have been loath to relinquish any of the advantages of their former monopoly, and this has limited the use of trucks. Water transport is impossible because of the nature of the terrain and absence of navigable rivers and thus can be used as a supplement to rail and road only between the ocean ports.

A further problem arises from the concentration of industry in the Witwatersrand area and a few other places, notably Durban and near-by Pinetown,

East London, Port Elizabeth and the Cape Peninsula. Eighty per cent of the country's manufacturing is found in about 2·8 per cent of the land surface. This not only creates unhealthy concentrations of population but also serious problems of supply, in particular of water. The Vaal River, for example, which provides for the needs of the Witwatersrand, will be tapped to capacity in less than 20 years at present rates of growth.

Beyond these particular problems, however, lies the more general issue of whether the South African economy can, and should, support so high a proportion of secondary and service industries. Gold production has long provided the basic underpinning of its economy. Ever since South Africa went off the gold standard in 1932 the country has enjoyed an era of prosperity unrivalled by other advanced States. The reason is that depressions elsewhere tend to be cushioned for South Africa because of the strong position under such circumstances of its primary product, gold.

This period of prosperity was also one of industrial expansion, particularly between 1947 and 1952. The net result is that whereas mining contributed 19·5 per cent of the gross national product in 1938 as compared with 17·5 per cent for secondary and service industries, the comparable figures in 1952 were 12·9 per cent for mining and 23·6 per cent for manufacturing and service industries. It is true that 1952 marked a transition stage in industrial production, with certain sectors slowing the rate of expansion and a general trend towards review and adjustment. Some outside observers feel, however, that the extent of industrial development has created an imbalance in the Union's economic structure.

The most serious problems, however, are human ones. South Africa has a relatively small number of skilled workers (only about 1 per cent of the population), yet its industrial expansion creates demands for many more. Thus there is a constant pressure, particularly in industries like cotton manufacture, to use non-European and particularly African labor in semi-skilled and even skilled positions. Africans now constitute more than 50 per cent of the labor force of secondary industry, outnumbering white workers by more than 200,000, and perhaps as many as 40 per cent of all the semi-skilled and 6 per cent of the skilled workers in the Union are African. Such a development is often concealed by down-grading the position in terms of wages and description to avoid violating the industrial color bar in form, despite these breaches of it in fact.

The color bar is maintained far more rigidly in monetary returns for the job than in degree of skill and responsibility. The wide differential between the wages paid to white workers, whether skilled or unskilled, and non-European workers is sometimes as great as seven to one, and nearly always as high as three to one. The relatively high wages for Europeans are justified by the necessity of protecting their standard of living. Moreover, much of South African industry insists that it cannot maintain itself profitably if it pays higher wages to Africans. There are penalties, however, even for the European community in not doing so. Practically all housing provided for Africans is perforce sub-economic, that is, subsidized by the European tax-payer. Beyond this, the potential market provided by some 11 million non-Europeans has not yet materialized.

But even with the relatively low return for their labor compared with Europeans, there are thousands of Africans who are advancing economically.

In part, this satisfies their aspirations; in part, it creates new wants, new demands, and new bitterness. One of the most interesting features of current African nationalism in the Union is that its traditional leaders, the African school teachers, have now been joined by a new and articulate group coming out of secondary industry. Moreover, this latter group potentially possesses a type of power which Africans have never previously known, the power to cripple South African industry through a general strike. To bring this about would seem to require far more contact between different non-European groups, and a much higher degree of organization than now exists, but few Europeans in the Union are unaware that it is a long range possibility.

The dynamic expansion of its economy has helped to free South Africa from economic dependence on other countries, in particular Great Britain, and for this reason has been stimulated by Nationalists whether under Hertzog, Malan or Strijdom. But economic development of this type, particularly in a country with a relatively small white population, and shortage of skilled labor, tends to intermingle the different population elements, make for social mobility and, at the least, for strong economic and social aspirations by the depressed groups. These processes run counter to traditional South African *mores*. It is largely because the Nationalists, with their policy of apartheid, i.e., rigid racial separation defined in law, seem to offer the best chance of maintaining these traditional *mores* in the face of current economic development that its program has been so appealing to the average Afrikaner. In other words, apartheid, as the Nationalist sees it, is the means for preserving, and even intensifying racial and social divisions in a dynamic economic situation.

Politics prior to 1948

That Afrikaner nationalism has come only gradually, however, to see the relations between European and non-European as the crucial issue of South African politics is evident in the history of political parties prior to Dr. D. F. Malan's accession to political power in 1948. When the South African Union was created in 1910, the memory of the Anglo-Boer War was so immediate that the supreme question was whether mutual respect and compromise would govern the relations of Afrikaners and English South Africans, or whether the one or the other would try to force its pattern of life upon the whole country. In large measure, in fact, the shifting alignments of South African political parties have always reflected this issue, rather than specific questions of economic, social or foreign policy. The advantage, in so far as there is one, is that issues of race and nationalism have been debated in the tempering atmosphere of parliament and that the need to secure political power has sometimes helped to aid compromises. The danger is that every issue in the country has been injected with Afrikaner or English South African nationalism, thereby intensifying the threat of these forces to the unity of the State, and to South Africa's relationship to the Commonwealth.

Moreover, even before union had been achieved, two factors had operated to create an exclusive Afrikaner nationalism; their self-consciousness created in the effort to free themselves from British influence in the late nineteenth century, and their belief that a party represents a whole people, and exists to defend that people's traditions. This is a belief which finds no parallel in

French Canada, for example, where the solid support for a single party has arisen out of the feeling of need to protect contractual and minority rights. Yet though this sense of exclusive Afrikanerdom has constantly animated some of the Afrikaans-speaking, there have always been others who repudiated so narrow a nationalism in favor of a South Africa built on the united efforts of two peoples. Thus the basic division in South African politics has been between the party which, for one reason or another, reflected an exclusive Afrikaner nationalism, and that which held together members of both the English and Afrikaner communities in pursuit of internal and external goals on which both peoples could agree.

Political parties had taken shape in South Africa even before union was consummated. On the eve of union, the Afrikaners were working together as a group in each colony except Natal, with suggestive names like *Het Volk* (the people). The English South Africans who most opposed them, like the mining magnates of the Transvaal, formed their own political party. But most of the moderate English-speaking in the Transvaal and Cape were unsympathetic with the narrow aims of this exclusively 'pro-British' group. Aware that as a minority they could not themselves secure political power in any area except Natal, they chose rather to work with the Afrikaners. Thus, initially, the alignment in the Transvaal and Cape was between the Afrikaners and moderate English-speaking on the one hand, and the intransigent English South Africans on the other. In the Free State, the Afrikaners were dominant. In Natal, where the English South Africans formed the vast majority, there were only rudimentary parties roughly divided on economic issues between the trading and sugar interests of the coast and the farming interests of the interior.

The first alignments in the Union Parliament followed the pattern which had emerged in the Transvaal and the Cape. General Louis Botha, the wisest, most far-sighted of Afrikaner statesmen, and the first Prime Minister of the Union, aimed to build a united South Africa animated by common ideals. His first cabinet united the ministries from the former colonies, bringing together in the South African Party the Afrikaners and moderate English South Africans. Ranged against them was a purely English-speaking opposition known as Unionists, and a weak Labour Party consisting only of four members.

Within a short time, however, Botha's policy was challenged by General James Barry Hertzog, already known for his introduction of compulsory bilingualism in the Orange Free State. Hertzog's speeches, breathing a fervent Afrikaner nationalism, created a crisis, and he was dropped from the Cabinet. Thereupon, he created the National Party, dedicated, in external affairs, to placing the interests of South Africa before those of the Empire, and internally to the 'two-stream' concept: that Afrikaans- and English-speaking must develop separately until each reached its full realization. Hertzog believed that only then could a true South African nationalism arise, a nationalism embodying the Afrikaner tradition to which he felt the English would ultimately conform. Thus emerged almost from the beginning the split between the more moderate, more far-sighted Afrikaners, like Botha and Smuts, who accepted the spirit of the grant of self-government, and membership in the Commonwealth, and those Afrikaners like Hertzog and the more extreme Nationalists who were animated chiefly by their aspirations for their own group.

World War I, in a measure, strengthened both parties. Hertzog and his eleven followers opposed entry into the war, but held aloof from the abortive rebellion which broke out almost immediately. It was put down firmly but without retribution by Botha, who subsequently led South Africa in an honorable and united war effort which included capturing South-West Africa, a huge territory held by South Africa as a mandate ever since. Nonetheless, Hertzog had strengthened his position, especially in the Free State, where his party captured 16 out of 17 seats in the general election of 1915, bringing their total in the Assembly to 27. Though the South African Party decreased to 54 members, and thus lost its absolute majority, Botha secured an understanding with the English-speaking Unionists to support his war policy, which made it unnecessary to seek a coalition. On this basis, Botha remained as Prime Minister until his death in 1919.

Botha was succeeded as Prime Minister by General Jan Christian Smuts, whose distinguished services in the Imperial War Cabinet, and in drafting the Covenant of the League of Nations (of which South Africa became a charter member) had given him an international reputation but commended him less at home. Smuts' absence from South Africa during the war, and his lack of Botha's tact handicapped him in taking over the reins of office successfully. No less serious, he inherited the dissatisfaction resulting from a 23 per cent increase in the cost of living.

In the first election after the war, held in 1920, Smuts' South African Party won only 41 seats to the Nationalists 44; thus the English-speaking Unionists with 25 seats and Labour with 21 held the balance of power. Smuts turned first to the Nationalists, but their insistence on South Africa's right to secede from the Commonwealth violated his deep belief in the value of that association. Smuts then fused his party with the Unionists, and was returned to office in 1921 with a handsome majority. A new, and more or less permanent, alignment had appeared in which all the English-speaking South Africans, except those in the Labour Party, had merged their fortunes with the moderate Afrikaners, and stood opposed to militant Afrikanerdom.

Why did the predominantly English-speaking Labour Party act differently from other English-speaking elements in South Africa at this time? The reason was that its particular purpose—the protection of the interests of white labor not only in relation to the capitalists, but also against the competition of Native labor—ranked far higher with the South African Labour Party at that date than a division on racial lines. In the depression which struck South Africa after World War I, the interests of the farmers, who formed the bulk of Hertzog's followers, ran parallel to those of the urban workers who ousted so many Unionists in the towns in favor of Labour. Suspicious though Hertzog's Nationalists were of Labour's socialist objectives, they shared a hostility to big business similar to that which underlay American farmer-labor parties of the same period. Moreover, both parties were deeply concerned (as was Smuts too) about the poor-white problem, which soon threatened to engulf the white population as Afrikaners poured off their unproductive farms into the cities, only to find that the unskilled jobs, which were the only ones they were equipped to handle, were in the hands of non-Europeans.

The event which brought the Nationalists and Labour together was the great Rand strike of 1922. Both groups were already thinking seriously of the need to carve out an area in the economy in which white men even without skills could support a 'European standard of living', a standard which was, in fact, as high as that of comparable groups in the United States or Canada. At the end of 1921 the Chamber of Mines, the governing group of the gold mines and, in the eyes of Labour, of the South African Party, proposed to modify the color bar so that Africans could take semi-skilled jobs. Feelings on all sides ran high. In a situation of general confusion, gold and coal miners struck early in 1922 over the assumed threat to their livelihood of lower wages and the probable reduction in the number of their jobs. The situation flared into violence as a small group of Communists took up arms and seized strategic points on the Rand. As disorder spread, Smuts personally directed Government forces, which crushed the revolutionaries and forced the end of the strike. White labor thus lost its greatest mass effort, though it was to win its ultimate objective of maintaining its monopoly of skilled employment throughout South Africa. But out of its bitterness against both Smuts and South African capitalism, the Labour Party turned to the Nationalists and agreed to work with them at the next election. Two years later, in 1924, when for the only time in its history the Labour Party held the balance of power, it entered into a coalition with the Nationalists, which was known as the Pact Government. This alliance, which was always an uneasy one, was based on a common antagonism to Smuts, a common recognition of the needs of white labor, and an agreement by the Nationalists that they would not break the existing constitutional relationship between South Africa and the British Commonwealth.

For 15 years, from 1924 to 1939, Hertzog was Prime Minister of South Africa, depending first on this coalition with the Labour Party, then for 3 years with an absolute majority of his own, and from 1933 in coalition and ultimately fusion with Smuts' South African Party in what became known as the United Party. It was a period of great significance for South Africa, for it saw the working out of Hertzog's 'two-streams' concept to the point where he, himself, believed that the equality of the Afrikaner with the English South African had been achieved. Thus he was ready in the period after 1933 to concentrate upon united efforts. But he was to be no more successful than Botha had been in holding together Afrikanerdom and the moderate English-speaking in a common program of action.

The Nationalist-Labour coalition carried through two types of policies, characteristic for the future course of South African development. The one placed a legislative seal of approval on the so-called 'civilized labour policy', designed to protect white labor against African competition. Thus at a time when tariffs and the Government-sponsored iron and steel industry (Iscor) were creating a new series of skilled and semi-skilled jobs, the Colour Bar Act of 1926 extended widely the white monopoly of such positions which already existed in the mines. The Industrial Conciliation Act, two years earlier, set up machinery for establishing industrial councils, which had substantial authority in particular sectors of the economy, but specifically excluded 'pass bearing [i.e. male] Natives'.

The next year, 1925, the Wage Act set up means for fixing wages for unskilled and unorganized white and non-European workers, apart from laborers, domestic servants and Government employees. Underpinning this legislation, however, were the basic Master and Servant Acts and the Native Labour Regulation Act under which it is still a criminal offense in the Union for an

African to break his contract or refuse to obey an order, and the Urban Areas Act of 1923 limiting the influx of Natives to the towns. These restrictions, coupled with the economic need which was driving Africans (like Afrikaners) off the farms and out of the reserves, created pressures which Hertzog tried to deal with by policies of greater racial segregation—the forerunner of current apartheid policies.

The other policy of the Nationalist-Labour coalition emphasized the 'two streams' by reinforcing the position of the Afrikaner. Bilingualism was encouraged through requirements for Government service, etc. In another sphere, the process of adopting separate symbols of the nationalisms within South Africa resulted in *Die Stem van Sud Afrika* being given equal place with *God Save the King*. Subsequently, there was devised a separate South African flag (including, after a bitter struggle, a small Union Jack) which flew side by side with, and ultimately superseded, the Union Jack.

Internationally, Hertzog retained his nationalist aspirations though he shelved the idea of a republic as the price of Labour's support. But the course of development within the British Commonwealth was running with him. The Balfour Report of the Imperial Conference of 1926, with its assertion of the equality of status of the Dominions and Great Britain, satisfied Hertzog, who came home to tell his people that South Africa was now independent in fact and would soon be in form. The Statute of Westminster, 1931, which ensured the full legal sovereignty of Dominion Parliaments, was succeeded by the Status of the Union Act of 1934, which declared that the provisions of the Statute of Westminster were decreed by the Union Parliament itself. South Africa also acquired its own Great Seal and Signet, implying that all the authority of the Crown could be exercised within South Africa itself. Thus all doubts regarding full South African freedom and independence seemed laid to rest.

Yet though this was the purpose of these South African Acts, which formed the necessary prelude to the fusion of Hertzog's and Smuts' parties in 1934, there were, in fact, significant differences of interpretation between the two men about South Africa's relations with the Commonwealth. Hertzog emphasized the divisibility of the Crown, the right to secession (obviously now a legal possibility), and to neutrality in British wars; Smuts did not deny the constitutional points but repudiated the implication that they made for separateness. This would fit ill with his conception that membership in the Commonwealth with its mutual benefits and responsibilities was a greater freedom than insistence on narrow national purposes—a view which came from his philosophy of holism, which held that all entities tend to seek larger groupings within which to realize themselves. Thus fusion of Hertzog's and Smuts' parties meant, in fact, not a unity of approach in regard to Commonwealth relations, but an agreement to overlook differences in the interests of joining forces to deal with urgent internal issues.

The particular crisis which brought Hertzog and Smuts together in 1933 was economic. South Africa suffered severely in the depression, particularly after Great Britain, by far its best customer, went off the gold standard. Hertzog and N. C. Havenga, his Minister of Finance, insisted temporarily on keeping South Africa on the gold standard in what some people have suggested was an attempted declaration of economic independence of Great Britain. If it was, it backfired badly. As the crisis mounted, a former Nationalist minister threatened to stump the country in favor of leaving the gold standard; Smuts seemed within reach of political power again. On the eve of an election, Hertzog suddenly took the Union off the gold standard; more impressively, Smuts gave up the hope of winning the premiership and offered to serve under Hertzog in a coalition which was transformed into a fusion in 1934.

For a time, there seemed hope that the racial lines of division in South African party politics might be submerged in favor of concentration upon problems of development. This seemed the more likely because of the phenomenal economic advance of the Union after 1933. Many more gold mines came into production under the stimulus of increased American prices; demand for South African farm products brought prosperity to the *platteland*; secondary industries expanded. The city of Johannesburg grew more in four years than in the previous forty. Fusion and United Party leadership brought a new spirit of hope and confidence to the country.

Moreover, despite the misgivings of the more liberal members of the new United Party, a comprehensive Native policy was enacted in 1936 which embodied much of Hertzog's plans for greater racial segregation. Those Africans in the Cape who were eligible for the franchise were placed on a separate communal roll to elect three Europeans to the House of Assembly while provision was made for increasing the land available for the exclusive use of the Africans. Time was to prove how dangerous a precedent was this removal of the Africans from the common roll, but for the moment the so-called 'settlement' of the Native problem was hailed widely as one of the outstanding fruits of fusion.

Yet in sharp contrast to widespread manifestations of unity was the fact that the most extreme Afrikaners and the most extreme English-speaking elements both greeted fusion with hostility. A small minority of English-speaking from Natal left Smuts' South African Party before fusion and formed the Dominion Party, which busied itself in making speeches against the now fully accepted doctrine of the independent status of South Africa. More serious was Dr. Daniel F. Malan's break with Hertzog to form the 'Purified' National Party. This group preached a more virulent nationalism than Hertzog had ever done. Where Hertzog defended the equality of the English and Afrikaans languages, and the equal political rights of the two European peoples on which South Africa was built, Malan's group spoke at that time of a South Africa animated by Christian National Afrikaner ideals. In such a State, the English language would continue only as a convenience, and English South Africans would learn to cease yearning for 'home' and to 'live by the light of the moon' (i.e. standards and ideas from England) and be rooted as solely in South Africa as the *platteland* Afrikaner himself.

The most significant aspect of this 'purified' nationalism was the vigor with which it was promoted in every aspect of life, encouraging a new withdrawal of the Afrikaner people from the community as a whole. Afrikaner Boy Scouts seceded to form their own organization; Afrikaner student groups did likewise. In 1938, a country-wide commemoration of the Great Trek turned into an exclusively Afrikaner pageant. Out of it sprang the Ossewa Brandwag (the ox-wagon guard), a cultural organization which roused the widest, most fervent Afrikaner nationalist sentiment in generations.

For six years, from 1933 to 1939, Hertzog and Smuts worked together by concentrating on those questions on which they could agree, like economic and Native policy, and leaving on one side the tense issues of peace and war on which they were ultimately bound to differ. Hertzog had considerable sympathy for Hitler's attempt to re-establish Germany's position of equality among European nations, though not for his desire to re-acquire the former German colonies in Africa. In general, Hertzog found European maneuvers too remote to concern South Africa. Even Smuts was willing at the time of the Munich crisis to approve South African neutrality if war should break out. But by September 1939, Smuts and his followers believed that Nazi aggression was an international threat and not merely a European issue. Thus they advocated South African entry into the war. When fighting broke out in Europe Hertzog counselled neutrality. The cabinet split, and in a tense parliamentary session, in which opinions shifted to and fro, Smuts' stand was endorsed by 80 votes to 67. The Governor-General refused Hertzog a dissolution, and called Smuts to form a Government. One day after the British Parliament declared war on Germany, South Africa, too, was at war.

This time, there was no rebellion as in 1914. South Africa participated actively in the war through volunteer forces in which Afrikaners and English South Africans served side by side. But on the home front, party alignments gave grim evidence that separate nationalisms still held South Africans apart from one another.

Smuts formed a coalition consisting of about two-thirds of the members of the United Party—those from Natal, the Cape peninsula, eastern Cape province, and the Witwatersrand—the Dominion Party, and the Labour Party, now only a shadow of what it had been in the 1920's. Thus all English-speaking South Africans and a substantial group of moderate Afrikaners united behind him. Opposed to them stood Malan with his Purified National Party, and Hertzog and Havenga with about one-third of those who had formerly been members of the United Party, those from western Cape province, the Orange Free State, and northwestern Transvaal. Once again, as in 1921, English South Africans and moderate Afrikaners stood opposed to militant Afrikanerdom. This time the split was more dangerous for, as events would prove, it was Malan's concept of South Africa, not Hertzog's, which was to come into political power.

Not surprisingly, the fact that Hertzog and Malan were both on the Opposition benches after the outbreak of World War II led the rank and file of Afrikanerdom to demand that they re-establish the political unity broken in 1933, or, in Afrikaans, *Hereniging*. In fact, despite their apparent similarity, the two men stood for quite different political objectives. Hertzog believed that national unity would ultimately result in a republic; hence the republic as such was no longer an article of political faith to him. Malan believed that the republic, the Christian National Afrikaner republic, must first be established and that national unity would then ensue, since the English would ultimately see the necessity of accepting its tenets in order to maintain their influence within the community. Nonetheless, the pressure for unity was sufficient to result in an agreement between the two parliamentary parties in January 1940, and even into efforts to recast their organization into a single body, called *Die Herenigde Nasionale of Volksparty* (the Reunited National Party), and commonly known as the H.N.P.

But the most intransigent among the Nationalists, like Johannes G. Strijdom, then Nationalist leader in the Transvaal, and Charles R. Swart of the Orange Free State doubted the feasibility of the union. They never accepted the apparent expectation of Hertzog himself that the new party was based on his views. Moreover, they feared, particularly in the light of German victories in the middle of 1940, that the party was not dedicated sufficiently to a republic which could be instituted when Great Britain was defeated. In consequence, they worked to undermine Hertzog's influence.

The most vigorous attack came in the provincial Congress of the H.N.P. in Hertzog's own Orange Free State. Under Swart's leadership, Hertzog's statement of principles, which included full equality of rights for English South Africans, was rejected in favor of a platform which guaranteed them linguistic and cultural equality, but omitted civil and political rights. In protest, Hertzog resigned from the leadership of the nationalist movement in this province which he had held since the achievement of South African Union. A month later, he and his follower, Havenga, resigned their parliamentary seats. Unable to support the war which Smuts was fighting vigorously at the head of his coalition, or to accept the extremism of the H.N.P., Hertzog could find no place in political life for his policies. The small Afrikaner Party born formally in January 1941 to uphold Hertzog's policies was to prove more opportunistic than based on principle. The decisive fact was that the extremists of the H.N.P. had won their struggle to keep that party 'pure'.

But nationalistic Afrikanerdom had yet more challenges to its unity. The war gave great impetus to the Ossewa Brandwag but also turned that group from its cultural emphasis to an increasingly militaristic one, with Stormjaers (Storm-troopers), and by January 1941, a 'Kommandant-General', J. F. van Rensburg, who approved of Nazi political beliefs. The strength of the O.B. was its ability to fire the imaginations of young Afrikaners, to provide an outlet for individual contributions in a great nationalistic movement far more dramatic than a political party. Recognizing its value, but fearing its rivalry, the H.N.P., in October 1940, made the Craddock Agreement whereby the O.B. agreed to refrain from political activities. But as the emphasis of the O.B. became increasingly the one party State and van Rensburg challenged Malan's personal leadership of Afrikaner Nationalism, the latter determined to break the O.B.'s power. For Malan stood for two things: the universal allegiance of Afrikanerdom to his political party, the H.N.P., and the maintenance of what was the necessary milieu for his political party, the parliamentary system, through which Afrikaners had already won great successes and through which he believed they would continue to win still more striking ones.

The struggle to enforce the dominance of the H.N.P. lasted until the election of July 1943. During that time, there were four organs of Afrikanerdom, all more or less political: the H.N.P., the Afrikaner Party, the O.B., and the so-called New Order, a group of 18 members of Parliament who also dedicated themselves to Nazi political ideas and were led by Advocate Oswald Pirow, Hertzog's Minister of Defence in 1939 and a supporter of his neutrality policy. The H.N.P. and the Afrikaner Party were recognized political parties, both ostensibly based on principle. But as the Afrikaner Party lost members to Smuts' United Party it began to flirt with the O.B. for no discernible reason other than their joint opposition to Malan.

Though, as late as September 1942, Malan lent his name to the idea of a Christian National Republic in which the English might have a part but in which the Afrikaner would enjoy a position of ascendancy, his program for the election of July 1943 was more moderate. He offered full political, language and cultural rights to the English, and propounded a vague doctrine of trusteeship for the non-Europeans. The temper of his platform was anti-Communist, anti-capitalist, anti-imperialist, anti-war. The Afrikaner Party formulated much the same program except that where Malan called for a republic to ensure South African independence, the Afrikaner Party asserted that Hertzog had already secured this independence.

The results of the July 1943 election demonstrated that Smuts' policies commanded substantial support in the country. The United Party increased its seats from 70 to 89, and the coalition strength rose to 105 (110 with the Native representatives and some Independents). Everywhere, except in the Orange Free State, the U.P. had majorities.

But the election was equally significant for the H.N.P. In the first place, it decisively annihilated its rivals: the H.N.P. won 43 seats in place of its former 40; neither the Afrikaner Party nor the members of the New Order won a single seat. (The O.B. ran no candidates in this election.) Moreover, the H.N.P. not only kept its undisputed control of the hard core of Afrikanerdom; it increased its quantitative Afrikaner support. Thus though the Government gained 22 of the 24 seats previously held by the Afrikaner Party and New Order, while Malan only gained two of them, the H.N.P. cut down the percentage of the Afrikaner vote supporting Smuts from 40 per cent to 32 per cent.

With considerable political astuteness, Malan accepted the verdict of the voters on external policy, and turned his emphasis to internal issues. Moreover, he and other more flexible members of the H.N.P., like E. G. Jansen, Dr. Karl Bremer and Dr. T. E. Dönges, came to accept the fact that, if they wished to achieve political power, they would have to make their program more acceptable to English South Africans. Thus, despite the attitude of the intransigents like J. G. Strijdom, C. R. Swart, Eric Louw, and Hendrik F. Verwoerd, the H.N.P. began to place more emphasis on guaranteeing a place for the English within the society they envisaged, and even on membership in the British Commonwealth with a republican status like that of Eire. Thus the end of the war saw a certain moderating of official H.N.P. statements though little evidence that this meant any change in its fundamental ideas.

The issue which had the most serious effect on party politics immediately following World War II was the position of the Indians in South Africa. Relations between the Indians and Europeans in Natal had improved following the Cape Town Agreement of 1927 under which the Indian Government agreed to assist voluntary repatriation to India while the South African Government pledged itself to help those Indians who remained in South Africa to improve their standards of living and civilization. But since almost no Indians returned permanently to India and the Indian population grew steadily in size, pressure began to rise for residential segregation in Durban, Natal's chief city and port. In 1943, the Pegging Act made illegal inter-racial property transactions in Durban. Protests by South African Indians and the Indian Government led Prime Minister Smuts to attempt a compromise, but as it failed in the face of opposition both from Natal Europeans and the younger, more radical Indians in that province, he introduced a new and comprehensive measure, the Asiatic Land Tenure and Indian Representation Act, 1946. This measure coupled restrictions on land ownership and occupation by Indians with provisions for communal representation of Indians in both the Union Parliament and the Natal Provincial Council, in the latter by their own people. But only the former part of this legislation was implemented, since the Indians indignantly rejected the offer of political representation as long as they were discriminated against in other ways.

On the structure of South African political parties, the Act had a profound effect which bears testimony to the bitterness of feeling on the Indian issue. The Labour Party, now only a shadow of its former self, split on the question; its leader and a minority of its members opposed the grant of political rights to the Indians and were ejected; the majority accepted Smuts' proposal. The Dominion Party likewise split: its leader and the majority opposed the measure, ejected their liberals, and confusingly changed their name to South African Party. The United Party did not split so obviously, but its Natal members were particularly bitter about the measure and it heightened the tension between the conservative and liberal wings of the party, the leader of the latter group being Jan Hofmeyr. The only party benefiting from the tension arising out of the Asiatic legislation was the H.N.P., which successfully capitalized on the anti-Indian feeling in Natal and elsewhere to strengthen its position.

The attitude towards non-Europeans became the major political issue in the election of 1948. Jan Hofmeyr enunciated a program for the United Party which, though denying the essential equality of European and non-Europeans, yet asserted the necessity of giving every group in South Africa the chance for free development in terms of its potentialities. His words were torn from their context and translated into inflammatory phrases suggesting miscegenation. Even the liberal wing of the United Party was vaguely disturbed, and made little effort to fight back, while its most conservative group was antagonized. The H.N.P., in contrast, preached apartheid (racial segregation) without going into details about how it would be achieved. Coupled with its anti-Communist, anti-Indian propaganda, the H.N.P. succeeded, to everyone's surprise, in gaining political power.

The distribution of seats was strikingly even. Though the National and Afrikaner Parties got some 100,000 fewer votes than the United Party and Labour, the weighted rural vote worked to their advantage. The H.N.P. secured 70 seats; the Afrikaner Party, which had opened its ranks to members of the O.B. whom the H.N.P. refused to accept, won 9. The United Party had 65 seats, and Labour 6. The three Native representatives could be counted on to support Smuts. Thus Malan had temporarily to govern with the aid of N. C. Havenga, now leader of the Afrikaner Party.

The most striking aspect of the election was the degree to which it reflected national origins and sentiments. The two Afrikaner nationalist parties won practically every seat in the predominantly Afrikaans-speaking areas; the United Party and Labour, every seat in the English-speaking areas. Only about 20-25 per cent of the Afrikaans-speaking voted for Smuts' U.P. though that party had an equal number of Afrikaans- and English-speaking candidates. The H.N.P., in contrast, had not a single predominantly English-speaking candidate, and their Cabinet, naturally, was exclusively Afrikaner. For the first time in the history of the Union, the Government was composed of only one of its two European peoples. Moreover, the party in power was one which had gone through a long period in the wilderness for the sake of its convictions, and had emerged triumphant from opposition within the ranks of Afrikanerdom itself as well as from broader elements outside.

Politically, then, the year 1948 marks a watershed in South African politics. The possession of political power by the National Party since May 1948 has led to more sharply defined programs of racial segregation affecting all non-European groups, to efforts consciously to reinforce tribal divisions despite the continuous contacts of the Africans with Western patterns of action, and to a sustained attempt to mold European society in the Union to an Afrikaner nationalist pattern. Some of what the Nationalists are trying to do builds on programs which Hertzog had worked for, but most of it goes well beyond his objectives or his desires. Step by step through legislation and administration, present-day Nationalists are trying to put their own particular stamp on South African life.

How is it possible for the political leaders of less than 2 million people in a country of nearly 14 million inhabitants to be as effective as the Nationalists have been? Part of the answer lies in the divisions amongst non-Nationalist Europeans in South Africa; part of it in the weakness of the position of the non-Europeans, lacking as they are in economic resources and political influence. Part of the explanation must be sought in the driving force of a highly integrated, self-conscious Afrikanerdom whose urge for power rises no less from self-confidence in its own values and its own approach to a vastly complicated situation than from its fear of submergence, either by the atheistic liberalism it sees abroad, or by the overwhelming numbers of the non-Europeans within its own country.

Another factor in the situation is that to an extraordinary degree the different groups residing within South Africa lack meaningful communication with one another. The rarity of social contact on either a personal or an organizational level means that there are all too few opportunities for learning one another's point of view. Between European and non-European, of course, there is enforced social and residential segregation. But even between Afrikaner and English South African, there are commonly few interchanges of the type which might build up mutual understanding. Moreover, more than visible barriers impede communication. This is why it is so important to understand the structure of the South African press, which might be expected to be the supreme agent for encouraging understanding between South Africa's varied groups and, on the contrary, may even provide barriers to such understanding.

The Press

The distinctive feature of the South African press is that each group in the country has its own newspapers, and that these papers, in turn, write chiefly with that particular group in mind. The European press naturally has far more resources and wider circulation than the non-European press. It is more concerned with developments outside of South Africa. But the most important distinction is not between the European and non-European press but between the Afrikaans- and English-speaking newspapers. These form not only separate but also contrasting sets of daily and Sunday newspapers whose operations tend to intensify rather than moderate the differences between Afrikaners and English South Africans.

Most of the English-language newspapers are group-owned, heavily capitalized by overseas as well as South African funds, and linked to, though not dominated by, the big mining corporations. The Afrikaans dailies, in contrast, are a people's press, springing originally out of the same drive for self-expression as did Hertzog's National Party, and financed solely by local Afrikaans capital, much of it contributed by thousands of small shareholders.

More important, though not unrelated, are the differences in their interpretations of the function of the press, as well as in their sympathies. The English papers place a heavy emphasis on news (though they sometimes omit unpalatable facts), and normally restrict their views to the editorial columns. Their opposition to the Nationalists is often more obvious than their support of the United Party towards which, in practice, they are sometimes openly critical. In contrast, the Afrikaans dailies, with the exception of Cape Town's *Die Burger*, are opinion journals more than newspapers; all of them are strong propagandists for National Party attitudes and policies. In fact, the presentation of local affairs in the English and Afrikaans press is sometimes so affected by particular attitudes and sympathies as to make their accounts of a single event sound as if they referred to totally different countries.

This startling difference in presentation is the more serious because, by and large, English-speaking South Africans do not read the Afrikaans press, and thus are unaware of the interpretation of events provided for their Afrikaner neighbors. Many of the latter secure a wider view by reading both English and Afrikaans papers. Surveys in the Johannesburg area, for example, indicate that only 1 to 4 per cent of the English-speaking normally see an Afrikaans daily while 20 to 40 per cent of Afrikaners read an English paper. This is partly because there is more news in the English newspapers; partly because the urban Afrikaners, particularly on the Witwatersrand, are more bilingual than the English. In the Cape, a fair number of English-speaking people regularly read *Die Burger*. In general, however, the English and particularly the Afrikaans dailies serve their own communities to such a degree that they fail to play an integrating role in the country as a whole.[4]

There are four Afrikaans dailies in South Africa: *Die Burger* (Cape Town), *Die Transvaler* (Johannesburg), *Die Vaderland* (Johannesburg), *Die Volksblad* (Bloemfontein), and a bi-weekly, *Die Oosterlig* (Port Elizabeth). The oldest and also the most influential Afrikaans newspaper is *Die Burger*. Started in July 1915 with Dr. D. F. Malan as its editor and with little experience or capital to support it, *Die Burger* has grown into one of the outstanding papers in South Africa. Like the rest of the Afrikaans press, it secures most of its foreign news through the South African Press Association, which, in turn, depends on the facilities of the British press service, Reuters, but it was the first Afrikaans paper to have its own correspondent, E. A. Malga, abroad. *Die Burger* sets the tone for *Die Volksblad* and *Die Oosterlig* and all three are owned by *Die Nasionale Pers. Die Burger* is avowedly the organ of Cape nationalism, which likes to think of itself as more constant, less emotional and, in this sense, a more balanced and basic nationalism than that of the Transvaal.

Although all the Afrikaans dailies have a marked similarity in political tone, the two published in Johannesburg, *Die Transvaler* and *Die Vaderland*, differ in noticeable ways from each other and also from *Die Burger*. Where *Die Burger* represents Cape nationalism, *Die Transvaler* is the voice of Transvaal nationalism, with a still more strident and propagandistic tone. Where *Die Burger* commonly reflected Dr. Malan's attitude, *Die Transvaler* was known as Prime Minister Strijdom's paper, while *Die Vaderland* was long attuned to the views of N. C. Havenga.[5] *Die Burger* not only carries the most news of any of these papers, but has more news behind its views; *Die Transvaler's* unmistakable opinions shine through everything it publishes; *Die Vaderland* comes closest to a tabloid of any of the Afrikaans papers (perhaps modelled on the London *Evening Standard*), stresses feature articles and is often termed 'sensational' by its competitors.

The National Party and the Afrikaans press have an unusually close relation. While Dr. Malan and C. R. Swart, Minister of Justice, have long been on the board of *Die Nasionale Pers*, which owns *Die Burger*, J. G. Strijdom was chairman of *Die Voortrekker Pers Beperk*, which owns *Die Transvaler*, and C. R. Swart, F. C. Erasmus, T. E. Dönges and Dr. H. F. Verwoerd, all Cabinet Ministers, are on its board of directors. N. C. Havenga was chairman of *Die Afrikaanse Pers*, which owns *Die Vaderland*, and was also one of the directors of the Hertzog-Brebner Trust,[6] which helps to finance it. Moreover, a high proportion of Nationalist Ministers have had personal experience in press work before becoming full-time politicians.

The Afrikaans newspapers often insist that they are not a party press in the strict sense of the word both because of their large number of small shareholders, and the personal responsibility of their editors for what they write. Nonetheless, these dailies maintain an intimacy of contact with the politicians of their party which is rarely paralleled in other countries. This is particularly the case with *Die Burger* and *Die Transvaler*, which are closer to the Nationalist Government and better informed on its plans and policies than is *Die Vaderland*, which is nominally independent. The most remarkable evidence of the privileged position of the two chief Afrikaans papers is that the editor of *Die Burger* attends National Party caucus meetings, where he may speak especially on press and radio matters though he has no vote, while the editor of *Die Transvaler* similarly attends caucus when he is in Cape Town during the sessions. Nowhere else in the Commonwealth, or indeed in the United States or Western Europe, does such a practice exist.

There are two Afrikaans weekly newspapers of very different character, both from each other and from the Afrikaans dailies. *Dagbreek en Sondagnuus*, published in Johannesburg, is one of the most truly independent papers in South Africa. As between the Nationalists and the United Party, *Dagbreek* would undoubtedly support the former if it were essential to choose, but its inclinations are not strictly party ones. Its able and broad-minded editor, W. Van Heerden, believes in total apartheid, and also that the real political division in South Africa is between the Nationalists and the Liberals rather than along existing party lines. On the constitutional issue (see Chapter 4) *Dagbreek* was not slow to bring out what it recognized as strong points on the U.P. side, and it objected sharply to dragging the courts into the controversy over the Coloured vote. Even in the frenzy of the 1953 election campaign, *Dagbreek* made a conscious effort to present different points of view, seeking chiefly to clarify the issues under debate.

The other Afrikaans weekly newspaper is *Landstem,* published in Cape Town under the editorship of Piet Beukes. *Landstem* is a popular paper which has adopted such American devices as 'lonely heart' columns. *Landstem* makes a conscious effort to avoid committing itself politically, but is distinctive among Afrikaans papers in being obviously sympathetic to the United Party.

After the United Party's electoral defeat in 1953, many people blamed its lack of success on the absence of U.P. support of Afrikaans newspapers. This gap was, in fact, a new feature in the political situation, for prior to the 1948 election there had existed not only General Smuts' personal organ, a small daily in Pretoria called *Die Volkstem,* but also *Die Suiderstem* and certain other affiliated papers controlled by the politically ambitious chairman of the Cape United Party, Senator Conroy. The cost to the party of Senator Conroy's newspaper activities caused a revulsion among United Party supporters after the 1948 election, however, and was a major reason for establishing the United South Africa Trust Fund (see Chapter 11) to supervise the use made of contributions from corporations. Not only were the Conroy papers closed after the election as unsound business propositions but neither during the period between the 1948 and 1953 elections nor after the 1953 election was a serious attempt made to re-establish a press channel to the Afrikaners. While there seems little doubt that an obviously U.P.-inclined Afrikaans newspaper would have a very tough and probably unprofitable struggle for existence, it is also clear that the United Party is placed in a very disadvantageous position by having to depend solely on the English-language press to present its case sympathetically, and by having virtually no means of touching the more than 50 per cent of the Afrikaans-speaking who never read an English-language newspaper.[7]

As far as numbers and circulation are concerned, the English-language press far outstrips the Afrikaans press. There are 13 English-language papers appearing in the 4 South African provinces, only 1 of which, the *Diamond Fields Advertiser,* has a circulation lower than the least substantial of the Afrikaans dailies, *Die Oosterlig. The Star* and the *Rand Daily Mail* in Johannesburg, the *Cape Times* and the *Cape Argus* in Cape Town, and the *Natal Mercury,* each has a heavier circulation than the most widely read of the Afrikaans newspapers, *Die Vaderland.* The most striking figures are for total circulation, for the 5 Afrikaans dailies together sell only some 138,000 to 153,000 copies each day while the 13 English-language dailies sell 586,000 to 617,000 copies. The ratio for weekly newspapers is comparable with the 100,000 to 104,000 copies for *Dagbreek* being far outdistanced by the 487,000 to 494,000 copies of the 3 English-language Sunday newspapers. These ratios are the more surprising since there are nearly 1¾ million Afrikaans-speaking Europeans in South Africa to just under 1¼ million English-speaking. It is common knowledge, however, that the English press is read most heavily in the urban areas and that the Afrikaans press penetrates to a greater degree into the more sparsely populated *platteland.*

To a very considerable degree, the English-language press is group-owned and directed. The most far-reaching of the chains is the Argus Printing and Publishing Co. which controls the *Cape Argus* (Cape Town), *The Star* (Johannesburg), *The Diamond Field Advertiser* (Kimberley), *The Pretoria News,*

The Natal Daily News (Durban), *The Sunday Tribune* and *Sunday Post* (Durban), and has part ownership of *The Friend* (Bloemfontein). The other most important group is the Rand Daily Mail Ltd. which controls the *Rand Daily Mail, The Sunday Times* and *The Sunday Express.* While the total circulation of the Argus papers greatly exceeds that of the Rand Daily Mail Group, the latter controls by far the largest of South Africa's Sunday papers, *The Sunday Times,* and the largest of the country's morning papers, *The Rand Daily Mail,* whose circulation is almost twice that of the *Cape Times,* and nearly three times that of *Die Transvaler,* its Afrikaans competitor on the Witwatersrand.

Mining and industrial interests heavily predominate among the shareholders of both the Argus and the Rand Daily Mail groups; if there is a difference between them it is that the Rand Daily Mail group is more concerned with secondary industry than the Argus group and thus more apt to be interested in such issues as permanent housing and vocational training for Africans.

But despite their group affiliations, the Argus and Rand Daily Mail newspapers have much independence and distinctiveness. *The Star,* commonly looked on abroad as the outstanding paper in the Union, is moderate in tone, frequently champions social reforms for non-Europeans, and is often critical of the United Party, as well as of the Nationalists. *The Rand Daily Mail* is usually more outspokenly liberal on many issues, particularly those affecting Africans. *The Friend* provides consistently good analyses of current trends. None of them openly criticize the administration of the gold mines, but this is true of Afrikaans as well as English-language papers.

The most outstanding of the privately owned English-language papers is *The Natal Mercury,* which is independent in politics, though during the 1953 election it supported the United Party. Owned by the Robertsons, the head of whose family was the first Prime Minister of Natal, *The Natal Mercury* championed, if it did not create, the Dominion Party. It has a certain tenderness for the sugar interests in Natal and can be counted on to defend provincial interests. One of the *Mercury's* distinctive features is that it regularly publishes news in Zulu. Two other family owned papers are the East London *Daily Dispatch* and the *Eastern Province Herald* of Port Elizabeth, both of which have a provincial and local emphasis, and in the past shared a distrust of the Statute of Westminster with *The Mercury* and the Dominion Party.

All the English-language papers find themselves in a certain difficulty as far as politics are concerned. None of them are so avowedly partisan towards the United Party as the Afrikaans dailies are towards the Nationalists, nor do they have anything like the same intimate contact with its politicians. On the other hand, even those papers like the *Mercury,* which insist on their independence, or like *The Star,* which in the past had been openly critical of United Party vacillations on Native policy, were unwilling to do anything to handicap that party in its electoral contest with the Nationalists in the spring of 1953. This was the more so because the English-language press was blamed severely in some quarters for the 1948 defeat of the U.P. on the ground that its persistent criticism of that party had undermined the confidence of its supporters. Thus the English-language papers faced, and face a dilemma. Their general view is that newspapers should form a third estate exercising critical judgment, disclosing the weaknesses of friends as well as foes, and thus stimulating constructive action. At the same time, they hesitate to do anything which might weaken the only viable political opposition to the National Party which, as they well know, can depend at all times on the Afrikaans dailies to provide it with a solid phalanx of support.

Little change can be expected in the structure of the South African European press. It is always costly to start a newspaper, particularly against the competition of well-established ones. Two further factors limit or virtually prevent the establishment of new papers in South Africa: the franchises established by the South African Press Association, and the entrenched position of the Central News Agency both in publishing and in distribution.

The South African Press Association was formed in 1938 as an independent and non-profit-making news gathering agency, and has an agreement with Reuters for mutual supply of news. One by-product of this arrangement is that South African papers get a wide coverage of Commonwealth and Western European news but relatively less on the United States. The Press Association franchises, or closed areas, limit their distribution of news to one Afrikaans and one English newspaper issued at a particular time of day within a particular area. New franchises can be secured only with the approval of a three-quarters majority vote of the Press Association. Since the Argus group owns one-third of the shares of the Press Association it has a veto on new franchises, which, under any circumstances, would be difficult to secure. Moreover all the European dailies, except *Die Transvaler*, and many of the weeklies are published by the Central News Agency and distributed by its chain of bookshops and stalls throughout the country. Here again it is difficult for a new paper to break into the system.

These barriers to the establishment of new European papers exist as constant handicaps to the non-European press. Nonetheless, Africans, Coloured and Asians each have newspapers of their own, though commonly with small circulations and operating under great difficulties. The African, or Bantu press has received considerable support from Europeans, both financially and in editorial assistance; the Coloured and Indian papers much less so. But each of them makes an effort to express a distinctive attitude, and to represent the views of their community.

One paper which falls into none of these categories is *New Age*, which follows the Communist line, and, to a far greater degree than the rest of the party press,[8] influences more than the converted. *New Age* (formerly the *Guardian*, then *Clarion*, then *Advance*) is written in English, appears weekly in Johannesburg and in Cape Town, the chief centers of what is now illegal Communist activity, and includes far more news about African organizations than appears elsewhere. During the drive against Communism in the Union, which culminated in the Suppression of Communism Act, 1950, the *Guardian* was banned (see p. 70), but the paper soon appeared again in a different guise and *New Age* is still sold openly in the Union, despite the fact that its publishing company was a defendant in the 1957 'treason trials' (see p. 73), as was its controlling figure, Len Lee-Warden, Native representative for Cape Western. While it is always difficult to estimate the effect of a newspaper which appears under the handicap of potential illegality, the fact that *New Age* openly and vigorously expresses the demand for equality which every non-European cherishes gives it a power which should not be underestimated. At the same time, it is unlikely that educated Africans, Indians and Coloured have read the Communist press over the years to anything like the same degree as they read English or Afrikaans newspapers or their own section of the non-European press.

Within the non-European press, it is the Africans, as befits their numbers, for whom the largest number of papers, over 20 in all, are designed. Perhaps three-quarters of a million to a million Africans are now touched by these papers either as readers or, if illiterate, as listeners. While it has no immediate political importance, the African press is a mark of the growing Westernization and articulateness of its people, and an important means of developing a sense of cohesion amongst them which overrides tribal distinctions.

Apart from missionary papers, whose importance is largely restricted to their converts, the pioneers and most long-lived among Bantu newspapers were founded by Africans themselves: John Tengo Jabavu, whose *Imvo Zabantsundu* (*Native Opinion*) was first published in King Williamstown in 1884; and Dr. John Dube, whose *Ilanga lase Natal* (*The Natal Sun*) was founded in 1904. Both men and both papers established traditions of fearless discussion which were carried on by a number of other papers with less fortunate histories. Among these, the most vigorous and interesting was *Abantu-Batho* (*The People*), the organ of the Native National Congress, which was founded in 1912, and was the forerunner of the present African National Congress.

A significant modern development in the field of African newspapers came in 1931, when two imaginative Europeans, B. G. Paver and I. J. La Grange, established the Bantu Press. The Bantu Press, a non-profit-making organization centered in Johannesburg, which aims to become an independent national trust on the model of *The Times* (London), introduced group ownership and direction into the Native press, established sound business methods, and has vastly enlarged the scope and opportunities of African journalism.

The first publication of the Bantu Press was *Bantu World* (now called *The World*), a bi-weekly printed mainly in English, which first appeared in 1932, and rapidly gained popularity, in part because of experienced handling by its first editor and co-founder, R. V. Selope Thema, formerly editor of *Abantu-Batho*. Soon after the appearance of the *Bantu World*, the Bantu Press began to increase its holdings, purchasing the three major surviving Native papers, *Imvo Zabantsundu, Ilanga lase Natal,* and *Mochochonono* and subsequently a series of other publications in the Union and Rhodesia. By 1946, the Bantu Press owned 8 and printed 15 papers, all of which were edited by Africans. The printing staff was also wholly African though working under the direction of a European.

The World has a national circulation (though heaviest in the Transvaal and Swaziland) and relatively good standards of journalism. Conservative in tone (and recently sharply critical of the African National Congress), it restricts itself mainly to news, leaving comment to its signed contributions, letters and editorials. The second most widely read African newspaper, *Umteteli wa Bantu* (*The Mouthpiece of the African People*) is still more conservative, having been founded by the Native Recruiting Corporation of the Chamber of Mines after the Native strike in the gold mines in 1921, in the hope of influencing or even leading Native opinion. *Umteteli* also has a national circulation but largely because it is distributed in mine compounds on the Rand and Free State, and in the two large Native Reserves, the Transkei and the Ciskei. Growing increasingly in popularity is the African weekly, *Drum*, which was launched after World War II with European financial backing and an English editor and has much more openly tackled African grievances than either *The World* or *Umteteli*.

Only one important Bantu newspaper has been owned and operated wholly by Africans: *Inkundla ya Bantu* (*The Bantu Forum*). Like other Bantu papers, *Inkundla* was a weekly, published in Verulam, Natal, under an outstanding African editor, Jordan K. Ngubane. A journal of comment rather than news, *Inkundla* was remarkably balanced in its attitude, but with a shrewd pointedness to its comments. Strongly anti-Communist in attitude, *Inkundla* not only supported the African National Congress, but also favored cooperation between Africans and Indians in their mutual interest. Financial difficulties forced it to cease publication in 1951.

Though the Bantu press papers and *Umteteli* still maintain their circulation, the more independent attitude of *Inkundla* and now of *Drum* have tended to give the latter papers a greater position of leadership among African intellectuals. Thus influence in the African press seems not unnaturally to go hand in hand with the voicing both of grievances and of aspirations.

Because of the geographical concentration of the Coloured in the Western Cape, and particularly in and around Cape Town, the three Cape Town weeklies concerned with the interests of the non-Europeans—*The Sun*, the *Cape Standard* and the *Torch*—devote their attention chiefly to the interests, grievances, and aspirations of the Coloured community. In this sense the three papers are primarily political in character. Though 90 per cent of the Coloured speak Afrikaans as a home language, all three papers are chiefly in English partly because knowledge of this language is common among the urban Coloured, and partly because the papers hope to attract African and Indian readers.

The Sun is the oldest of the three papers, having been established in 1931; it is also the most conservative. It has consistently supported the Coloured Advisory Council established in 1943, which many Coloured bitterly oppose on the ground that it puts them in a separate category like the Africans. *The Sun* has a certain amount of European capital invested in it, and openly supports the United Party.

The Cape Standard, founded in 1935, opposes the Coloured Advisory Council, is more militant than *The Sun*, and also more sympathetic to African aspirations. Though it was never the organ of the Communist Party it has printed a great deal more news about that group over the years than ever appeared in *The Sun*. Most radical and bitter in tone of the three Coloured papers is *Torch*, which was started in 1946, has strong Trotskyite influences, and calls itself the organ of the Non-European Unity Movement, which opposes cooperation with Europeans.

The differences between the three Coloured weeklies reflect fundamental divisions among the Coloured people themselves. While all the Coloured resent discrimination, they differ sharply as to whether it is better to accept the status provided currently by Europeans in the hope of being at least in a more privileged position than other non-Europeans, or whether they should throw in their lot with the non-European group as a whole. Though *The Sun*, for example, proudly terms itself 'South Africa's Non-European Newspaper', the Coloured press does little, if anything, to draw the non-European or even the Coloured community together. Its chief usefulness may well be as a safety valve through which the current views and bitterness of the Coloured are aired freely without attracting the attention of the Europeans.

Most intensely political and communally-oriented of all the non-European papers are those belonging to the Indian press. It is also distinguished from the Bantu and Coloured press by its greater independence from European capital. Both factors arise out of the greater wealth and the earlier and more intense political consciousness of South Africa's Indians than of any of the other non-European groups in that country.

Mahatma Gandhi founded the first Indian paper in South Africa—*Indian Opinion*—in 1903, and it was edited by his son, Manilal Gandhi, until his death in 1956. *Indian Views* was started in 1914. Both papers are weeklies, published in Durban; both are opinion journals rather than newspapers, and such news as they print is linked directly with the Indian community at home or abroad; both are conservative in tone. *Indian Opinion* is Hindu-oriented, however, and favors the South African Indian Congress, though it retains much editorial independence of view. *Indian Views* is owned and edited by Moslems, many of whom belong to the wealthy merchant class, and it represents the Natal Indian Organization, which is more prepared to negotiate with the Nationalist Government than is the South African Indian Congress.

Both *Indian Opinion* and *Indian Views* circulate chiefly among rural Indians. In comparison, *The Leader*, a mass-type paper published in Maritzburg, Natal, since 1941, is the organ of the more radical working-class Indians of the South African Indian Congress. *The Leader* is often critical of Leftist tendencies among Indians and works deliberately to draw the Indian community together.

As with the Coloured weeklies, the Indian press reflects a wide range of opinions from conservatism to radicalism, the former more marked in the rural areas, the latter in the cities. Still more than the Coloured papers are the Indian papers self-centered and, in a sense, ingrown. Moreover, like the Coloured press, the Indian weeklies attract relatively little attention from Europeans. Because the Indian community is more purposeful than the Coloured group, however, and because the South African Indian Congress works far more closely with the Africans than does any Coloured organization, the ultimate influence of the Indian press is greater. Moreover, the much higher percentage of literacy among Indians than among either Coloured or, of course, Africans, gives the Indian press a greater importance amongst its own people.

One of the most serious difficulties of the non-European press is its inability to support a daily. The most frequent publication among non-European papers, oddly enough, is the one Chinese paper, *Chiao Sheng Tao* (*The Chinese Consular Gazette*), which serves South Africa's 3,000 Chinese three times a week. Printed in Chinese, the paper circulates mainly in Johannesburg and Port Elizabeth, where most of the Chinese live, but it is also found in other parts of the Union and even outside. *Chiao Sheng Tao* is mainly concerned with matters of communal interest, but it shares the resentment of the rest of the non-European press at the racial discrimination from which all non-Europeans suffer.

The non-European press in South Africa faces two major difficulties: the illiteracy and other handicaps of so many of its constituents; and the lack of capital and of the facilities which are enjoyed by European publications. The non-European press can make use of none of the services of the Central News Agency either for publishing or for distribution. Only the Bantu Press has the capital backing and the distribution facilities which enable it somewhat to overcome the handicaps to which more isolated papers are subject.

A newspaper commonly performs two distinct functions: to serve as a medium for local news, views and discussion; and to link its particular group of readers with the national and international community by bringing them news of outside events, attitudes and developments, and commenting intelligently upon them. Only *Die Burger* and the more outstanding among the English-language papers can be said to perform both tasks adequately. Much of the Afrikaans press and also the more locally oriented among the English papers fail to fulfil the second of these functions in much the same way as does almost all the non-European press. In other words, their orientation towards the special interests and predispositions of their own group narrows their horizons to the point where they become bearers of a message rather than expanding their readers' view.

There are good reasons why the non-European press suffers acutely from this latter difficulty. Only the members of the Bantu Press group and some of the Indian papers can use the South African Press Association news service to any extent, and then to a much more limited degree than the average European paper. Non-European journalists are handicapped in getting material by denial of library facilities, and by their inability to cover most public meetings, including parliamentary sessions. Inevitably, these papers must concentrate on what their journalists and editors know best, the aspirations and bitterness of their own particular group. By being forced in this way into the reiteration of communal views and attitudes, much of the potentially healthful effect of expressing opinion is transformed into an intensification of current reactions.

The high degree of non-European illiteracy, and the lack of a common language also handicap the growth of the non-European press. In recent years, Afrikaners are showing an increasing amount of concern at the degree to which English has become the *lingua franca* of South Africa's non-Europeans. This trend may be somewhat slowed by educational practices under the Bantu Education Act (Chapter 3), but the preponderance of the English-speaking in South African cities as well as in the province of Natal, where so many Africans and nearly all Indians live, will long continue the importance of English to non-Europeans. The most striking example of this importance is that the Coloured press uses English almost exclusively, though the Coloured are largely an Afrikaans-speaking group. Only the most conservative of the Indian papers, *Indian Views*, still uses Gujerati extensively. The Bantu Press, to be sure, uses Native languages freely and widely, but it usually also provides considerable material in English. Whether this dependence on English will be a help or a handicap for the non-European press in the long run will be influenced by future educational practices, but the steadily increasing literacy and political consciousness among non-Europeans ensures that their demands for reading material will increase.

Though they must not be pushed too far, there are some instructive parallels between the position of the Afrikaans papers and the non-European press. Both are strongly oriented towards their own communities, and are read hardly at all outside their own groups. Both place a strong emphasis on opinion, and less on news, unless the latter is directly concerned with the particular group. Both stress the particular aims of their own community rather than attempting to interpret the position of other groups in the country. Even the English-language press, for all its greater and more impartial coverage of national and international events, tends almost unconsciously to regard South Africa as an extension of the English-speaking group. All this is no doubt natural, and done also in other countries. The net result, however, is that the press in South Africa fails to perform the role of interpreting one group to another, and thus of building the bridges between them which might develop a more tolerant, even if not a more cohesive, national community.

Section II: Imposing the Nationalist Pattern

CHAPTER 2

THE NATIONALIST IMPACT ON EUROPEAN SOCIETY

Though the Nationalists are best known abroad for the way they have implemented their conception of racial separation, their primary concern, like that of other European South Africans, is the white society of their country. What is distinctive about the Nationalists is that they represent a well-defined community and ideology within European South Africa. Though they have said far less about shaping the character of European society in South Africa than about promoting apartheid, the particular stamp of Afrikaner Nationalism has become increasingly noticeable since 1948 in European life.

The fundamental differences of approach between the Nationalists and their political opponents are illustrated in their attitudes to the two laws analysed in this chapter: the South African Citizenship Act of 1949 and the Suppression of Communism Act of 1950. These are not only the most significant laws directly affecting Europeans passed after the Nationalists came to power, but also aroused deep controversy. The consideration of this legislation enables us to pick out matters of primary concern for South Africa in the first years of Nationalist control, and to see through their handling, their justification, and their effects, both what has been happening in that country and the reasons for it.

Parliament, and particularly the House of Assembly, is the forum which the Nationalists have chosen in good democratic style to present their program; legislation and administrative rulings are their highly flexible and effective means of securing their purposes. The way in which they have used them, however, has often been subject to sharp United Party criticism. Basically what the Nationalists have done is to use accepted institutions and practices in a doctrinaire spirit which weighs far higher the purposes of its own particular community than the mellow traditions of an historic parliamentarianism. Thus the view of Parliament as a place to talk (*parler*), to exchange views and, as far as possible, reach a consensus of opinion, gives place almost invariably to the business-like approach of getting legislation enacted. The Opposition from its side has sometimes contributed to Nationalist self-justification of their procedures by attempting to block legislation through obstructionist tactics rather than by well-founded and carefully reasoned arguments. Under all circumstances, however, the Nationalists drive through their bills, almost always without yielding changes. The result is that the true function of Parliament—to mirror community views, safeguard minority and individual rights, exert constant pressure on the Government to justify its policies and proposals, and provide the community at large with an understanding of the character and import of legislation—is often performed inadequately.

In the parliamentary system, each stage of a bill serves a particular purpose. In the introductory stage, the purpose is information. The introducer gives notice that he will introduce a bill which he describes by its short title. Next day, he asks leave to introduce it. This is rarely debated, though occasionally a full-scale debate ensues.[1] First reading follows immediately after introduction of the measure. There is no debate at that point and though amendments, or notice of later amendments, may be offered, they are rare. Only after first reading is the bill normally printed.

The second reading is the crucial stage of the bill because it is concerned with the principle underlying the measure. If the Opposition is not prepared to accept this principle of action, there are three ways in which it can act: it may move an amendment or, more technically, a 'reasoned negative', that is, that the House refuse to pass the measure unless such and such changes are made; it may try to vote the measure down; or it may seek to have the bill referred to a select committee on which all parties are represented. If a select committee is asked to consider the principle of the bill, the measure is discharged from second reading, referred to the committee and then brought back for second reading. If only details need consideration, the bill may be referred to the select committee after second reading. The Speaker determines the number of persons to serve on a select committee and notifies the whips (in charge of the party's business) who choose them.

The third, or committee, stage, unlike that in the United States, is concerned only with details, i.e., how to implement the principles accepted at second reading. At the next, or report stage, the purpose is solely to make the bill consistent, and pertinent amendments may be offered here which are relevant to other amendments already accepted. If the House gets hopelessly muddled in the report stage, as occasionally happens when too many amendments are accepted, the bill may be sent back to the committee stage. Lastly comes third reading, which is the final decision on the bill as amended.

If the Opposition accepts the principle of a bill, as the United Party often did with Nationalist legislation, but wants to change particular features of the measure, the customary procedure is to vote for second reading without a division, but to give formal notice of amendments to be introduced in the committee stage and to declare that the party will vote against the bill at third reading unless these amendments are accepted.

The Parliamentary battle in South Africa has been much hotter under the Nationalists than during the United Party régime. Smuts and Hofmeyr often showed contentious legislation to the Nationalist opposition before introducing it to the House, thus making it easier to get their views. Since the Nationalists have become the Government, they have never followed this practice. Moreover, as happened with the Citizenship bill, they sometimes act without consultation through the 'regular channels', i.e., the whips. This may lead to the breaking of relations, as it did at that time, which entails the ending of 'pairing', that is, the matching of a supporter and an opponent so that neither needs to be in the House to vote. Another means of exerting pressure on a Government is to threaten to call a series of divisions, which slows up the order of business. Any ten members can call a division, and it provides the most effective weapon a small party can use against the Government.

The whips normally make the arrangements for the order of speakers in a debate though, of course, the Speaker has the right to recognize any member he wishes. His task is facilitated, however, by the lists of speakers which the whips draw up. In the debate on the budget, the Nationalist whips pay special attention to the wishes of the Opposition but otherwise are less influenced by their desires than is true in a debate in the British House of Commons. In a no-confidence motion, the whips are normally in complete control of the debate in the South African House of Assembly and know which members will answer whom. One of their chief functions, particularly when their party is in office, is to keep their party leaders fully informed of the course of events in the House. While they are also responsible, of course, for seeing that members are on hand to vote, South African whips, unlike those in Great Britain, do not indicate the importance of particular votes by sending out as notices one, two, and three line whips, whose underscoring reflects the urgency of attending the meeting; because of the smaller number of members in their parties they keep close personal touch to ensure the requisite number of votes.

The most overworked persons in the House are the Afrikaans-speaking members of the United Party, who comprise about one-third of its representatives. In the Citizenship Bill debate, for example, they carried the burden of the discussion regarding inclusion of a phrase symbolic of South Africa's Commonwealth membership. The United Party leader,—J. G. N. Strauss, until late 1956, and Sir de Villiers Graaff thereafter,—often opens a debate in one language and closes it in another. The fact that relatively few English-speaking members of the United Party are completely bilingual is a serious handicap to the party, because of the strong stress which the Nationalists put on Afrikaans.

The division of time between the parties is in the hands of the Speaker. Some Speakers give the Government and the official Opposition the same amount of time and allot extra time to the minority parties. Speaker J. H. Conradie, however, who held this office from 1949 on, divides time evenly between the Government and the Opposition as a whole.

As in all deliberative bodies, the position of the Speaker in the South African House of Assembly is of great importance. At his best, a Speaker is the guardian of the liberties of individuals and minority groups in the House, administering the rules impartially and standing above the heat of politics. Perhaps the most outstanding of South African Speakers was Dr. E. G. Jansen, who served in this office from 1924 to 1929 and again from 1933 to 1943. Though Jansen opposed participation in the war, General Smuts asked him to continue as Speaker in 1939 when Smuts and Hertzog split and the former became Prime Minister. When Jansen stood openly as a Nationalist in 1943, however, the United Party withdrew its support from him and elected another speaker. Twice Minister of Native Affairs, in 1929 and again in 1948, Dr. Jansen became Governor-General in 1950.

The Nationalists broke with convention in selecting J. F. T. Naudé as Speaker in 1948 without consultation with Opposition whips. In 1949, Naudé was made Minister of Posts and Telegraphs and Conradie was selected as Speaker, again without consultation, a fact which led the Opposition, very reluctantly, to put up a candidate of its own. Here, as in other places, the United Party has found itself torn between its own strong sense of tradition and its reluctance to let the Nationalists break a parliamentary convention without retaliation. In office, Conradie has not displayed the quick, effective, and clear decisiveness of Jansen, and the Opposition feels he has sometimes used his office in a partisan fashion more to be expected in the American congressional than the parliamentary system. In 1953, however, the United Party decided not to contest his seat, partly to conform to the traditional restraint in this matter which they would like to see established firmly in South Africa, but perhaps also because it was a Nationalist stronghold in any case.

Not only is the Speaker master of the debate, he also is asked on occasions for important rulings on constitutional questions, e.g., on the necessity of a two-thirds vote on the Separate Representation of Voters' bill. (See Chapter 4). Traditionally, the Speaker has sought his advice in such issues from the clerk of the House, who is the technical expert on such matters.[2] Conradie, however, takes his advice from the law advisers of the crown. In the issue referred to above, the latter approved the majority procedure, which was subsequently declared unconstitutional by the Appeal Court and the Speaker followed their reasoning though he was also in possession of an opposing opinion by the parliamentary legal adviser. It is hardly surprising that the Opposition found this to be further evidence of Nationalist partisanship on the Speaker's part.

All these formalities and conventions may seem dull or unimportant to outsiders, but they provide the framework within which Parliament is able to operate. Nothing is more irritating to a conservative party like the United Party than to have them deliberately disregarded or broken. The Nationalists, from their side, found it difficult to understand, particularly at first, why the United Party put such emphasis on forms and in consequence tended to treat their protests as obstructionism. Thus to the very real differences in approach and objectives has been added this further irritant, never more marked than in the first of the measures on which the Nationalists sharply clashed with the United Party, the bill to define South African citizenship.

The South African Citizenship Act, 1949[3]

No Nationalist legislation created greater bitterness in the United Party and throughout non-Nationalist South Africa than did the South African Citizenship Act, partly for its provisions, but also because of the way and spirit in which it was pushed through Parliament. In the debates, moreover, appeared with disturbing clarity the contrasting views of the Nationalists and the United Party on the role of English and Afrikaners within South Africa. With their early militancy well to the fore, the Nationalists asserted their right to shape South Africa to their own pattern, not only because they had acceded to political office but also because the Afrikaner had been the first to open up the country. Thus behind the technicalities of citizenship definition, and the provisions whereby newcomers could acquire it, lay a deeper and more fundamental issue of what was to be the future character of the South African nation.

The South African Citizenship Act was one of a series of such measures passed by Commonwealth countries following World War II. These Acts shifted the emphasis from the older position under which citizens of Commonwealth countries enjoyed a common status because of a common British nationality to a newer one (more consonant with the accepted independent status of all Commonwealth members and its greater decentralization in the postwar period), in which citizenship was a local status to which special privileges were accorded by the other Commonwealth countries.

One of the historic advantages of being 'British', it should be noted, had been the possession of a common nationality which opened the way for those from any part of the Commonwealth to travel freely to all other parts of the Commonwealth and Empire and to gain the franchise and work permits more easily than was the case for citizens of foreign countries. In Great Britain (where the original common law ruling that everyone born in the King's Dominions is a natural-born subject has been interpreted most generously), persons from other Commonwealth countries were traditionally granted the franchise, held public office, and entered the civil service on approximately the same terms as those born within Britain itself. Other parts of the Commonwealth were somewhat more restrained in extending privileges to 'British subjects', particularly those from Asia whose entry was seriously restricted or stopped altogether by immigration laws. On the whole, however, overseas Commonwealth countries provided marked privileges for persons possessing the status of 'British subject', which was defined basically and by common agreement in the British Nationality and Citizenship Act of 1914 and amendments thereto. Each Commonwealth country naturally had its own provisions for naturalization—those for South Africa being embodied in the British Nationality in the Union and Naturalization and Status of Aliens Act, 1926 (No. 18 of 1926)—but relatively uniform provisions were retained since naturalization not only admitted a person to citizenship in a particular country but also to such marked advantages in other parts of the Commonwealth.

The process of defining citizenship in separate Acts was begun by Canada in 1947, and subsequently all other Commonwealth countries, including Great Britain, did likewise. The British Nationality Act, which became law on July 30, 1948, provides that any citizen of the United Kingdom, its colonies, or a country of the Commonwealth, has by virtue of that citizenship the status of 'British subject' or, since some people objected to the word 'subject', of 'Commonwealth citizen', the terms being interchangeable. This status still provides many material advantages in Great Britain, such as the right to enter or leave at any time, to qualify for the franchise after one year of residence, to be a member of Parliament or of the civil service (except in wartime). All other Commonwealth countries grant some, though not such broad privileges to persons (other than Asians and Africans) coming from other Commonwealth countries. All of them, except South Africa, include the phrase 'British subject' or 'Commonwealth citizen' in their legislation to indicate their maintenance of the concept of common status.

Up to the passage of the South African Citizenship Act, a person possessing the status of British subject, i.e., coming from Great Britain, Canada, Australia, or New Zealand, automatically acquired South African citizenship after two years' domicile in the Union. Persons from other Commonwealth countries, and the Republic of Eire, must now meet all the same provisions in acquiring citizenship as a non-British immigrant except that they need five instead of six years' residence or, if the wife of a South African citizen, two years instead of three. They must be able to read and write one of the two official languages and have 'an adequate knowledge of the responsibilities and privileges of South African citizenship', a phrase left undefined. The citizen of another

Commonwealth country does not become naturalized as do non-Commonwealth immigrants but receives South African citizenship by registration. Registration, however, like naturalization, is not automatic after a certain period of time but lies within the absolute discretion of the Minister of the Interior and may be withdrawn by executive action.

The debate[4] in the House of Assembly on the Citizenship bill proceeded in an atmosphere marked by tension and recrimination. Before second reading of the measure, the United Party broke off normal parliamentary relations because the Government moved the bill forward for earlier consideration without conferring with or even giving notice to the Opposition. The United Party called persistently for a select committee to consider so significant a measure; the Nationalists not only refused to agree, but imposed the guillotine procedure (under which all pending amendments automatically drop and the vote is taken after a specified number of hours of debate) for the committee, report, and third reading stages. In justification of this procedure, the Nationalists referred frequently and bitterly to the United Party's use of such parliamentary devices to pass wartime measures. The United Party denied that the situations were comparable and was openly resentful of what it considered a violation of parliamentary practice, the more so because of its opposition to certain features of the measure.

Basic to the controversy was a different interpretation of the subject at issue. The United Party felt that citizenship was a constitutional matter which should be considered with great care to reach the largest possible measure of unanimity. The Nationalists, in contrast, regarded citizenship as a political matter in which their own particular point of view should be decisive. Thus they saw no reason to provide the special procedure of a select committee or to seek an agreed measure. Moreover, they felt that despite the United Party's opposition to the measure at this time, it would ultimately come round or, as they felt, advance to the position expressed in their legislation. United Party objections thus were looked on either as delaying tactics or as reflecting outworn concepts. On few issues was there so little understanding or even attempt at understanding by the Nationalists of the Opposition point of view.

The controversy between the Government and Opposition centered round three points: the role of English and Afrikaner in the shaping of South Africa; the criteria for immigrants; and the importance of a symbolic gesture to the concept of a common status for citizens of the older Commonwealth countries. While the first issue was not, of course, a part of the legislation, the divergent views expressed on it not only caused much of the acrimony but also underlay the comments on the specific provisions of the Citizenship bill.

In this debate, English-speaking South Africans found themselves for the first time in the novel and uncomfortable role of a minority of late comers, accused of a dual allegiance which impaired their right to be considered full South Africans. 'Are we and those thousands who have been living here in a spirit of union to be an oppressed minority only permitted to live here provided we accept the ideas and ideology of the Hon. Minister?' asked a United Party member bitterly.[5] F. C. Erasmus, Minister of Defence, was quick to retaliate that Afrikaners were the majority and had been long offended by the British superiority complex. Jingoism had changed sides, remarked F. W. Waring of the United Party. Dr. B. Friedman, a United Party liberal, went still further to charge that Malan nationalism was 'narrow and exclusive', aiming at 'sectional domination', and to reduce 'all so-called unnational elements to the status of second-class citizenship'.[6]

Characteristic of a widely held Nationalist view was Dr. J. H. Loock's comment that it would be far better if the United Party 'which is today developing into an English party . . . [would] appoint English leaders to state their point of view' for then 'we will be able to fight openly against each other'. He understood that 'an Englishman in this country' would want to fight for 'his rights', but warned 'he must not use my fellow Afrikaners to do it'.[7] G. F. H. Bekker said the English would be given equal treatment but 'the country belongs, in the first instance, to those people who opened it up'.[8] Thus throughout the debate ran the notion of opposing rights and claims of the two European peoples of South Africa. A United Party Afrikaner, P. B. Bekker, put his finger on underlying motivations when he said of Malan nationalism that

> it drives inward all the time. It is a nationalism based on fear. It is a nationalism that lives in a house without windows but full of mirrors and there dwells self-adulation. . . It is born of fear, a legitimate fear, because the story of the past has been a very dark story in some respects.[9]

Against this background of accusations and counter-accusations, it is hardly surprising to find the granting of citizenship looked on as a party political tool. Two Labour Party members, H. Davidoff and A. Hepple, charged that the Nationalists wanted to lengthen the period for immigrants to get citizenship because of fear that the newcomers would vote Labour. United Party speakers put their emphasis on the need for immigrants to develop the country. C. R. Swart, Minister of Justice, countered that United Party-imported immigrants would vote against 'the nationalist-minded', and said that he was not prepared to let the future of South Africa be determined by people who got the franchise automatically. Dr. A. J. R. van Rhijn said openly that immigrants might determine 'which Government is going to govern the country' and that their choice was inevitably a matter of party policy.[10]

Behind this exchange lay also two different conceptions of the ideal immigrant. The United Party felt that familiarity with democratic procedures, the parliamentary system, and the values of Western civilization were the most important qualifications. The Nationalists looked instead at attitudes towards South Africa's most pressing problems: the Native question, and what they called 'national-mindedness', which they associated with bilingualism. Since Western civilization cherished equality, Nationalists foresaw that immigrants might be a dangerous influence. In any case to introduce them to South African ways and to imbue them with a sense of distinctive South Africanism would need time. When Dr. van Rhijn said caustically that the Nationalists wanted 'pure mothers' milk in our country, whereas the other side wants to have imported condensed milk', he meant pure in relation to Afrikaner Nationalist objectives, as he made clear by adding that those who did not want 'to join us in our trek to the future will simply fall by the way in the great path of South Africa'.[11]

The United Party claimed that it was a breach of faith with recent British immigrants to advance the length of time needed for their citizenship from two to five years, and warned that it would undermine overseas confidence so essential for investment to spur South African development. Capt. Henwood asked that recent immigrants be excluded from the provisions of the bill as 'a matter of honour'. Viljoen, Minister of Education, retaliated 'What's all the fuss?' It was an attitude to retroactive legislation as characteristic of the Nationalists as it was objectionable to the United Party.

The United Party also fought the provision that left the grant of citizenship to the discretion of the Minister. Particularly for those from other Commonwealth countries, they felt that the process should be automatic as long as the applicants met the provisions of the law. On this issue the Minister, Dr. T. E. Dönges, took refuge behind the similar provisions for executive discretion in the Australian Citizenship Act, though his surprisingly frequent citing of overseas precedents roused some of his own supporters, notably Dr. J. H. Steyn, to ask in irritation 'Must we eternally run after others; cannot we create anything original in this country?'[12] Moreover he felt that automatic citizenship was not consonant with South Africa's position as a sovereign independent nation. Dönges added that the franchise was not a right but a privilege. It was a view befitting the Nationalist conception of making the South African nation to their own pattern.

Similar attitudes appeared in the respective arguments about including the clause found in other Commonwealth citizenship acts providing for the term 'British subject' or 'Commonwealth citizen'. 'Why do I and all of us here, quite apart from sentiment, want to retain the idea of Commonwealth citizenship?' asked a United Party member. 'Because we consider it to be a symbol of the desire of South Africa for closer association with all that is best in our Western civilization.'[13] Others saw the affirmation of Commonwealth status as important for economic relations—'what is the good of nationhood, of citizenship, if we do not have a sound economic basis on which to build it and to maintain it?'[14]—and for South Africa's role in Africa.

On this issue, however, perhaps more than any other appeared the Afrikaner Nationalists' insistence that a united nation required a single loyalty. Dr. N. Diederich, former head of an Afrikaner aid society, the Reddingsdaadbond (see Chapter 10) felt that 'clinging to a hyphenated citizenship blocks the establishment of an unhyphenated nation'. A leading member of the Afrikaner Party foresaw that it would be necessary 'to break family bonds, hard as it is' to achieve free development and South African unity. Dr. van Rhijn took another line in asserting angrily that:

> On this side of the House we Afrikaners want unblemished title deeds. We no longer want an endorsement in red ink on our certificate of citizenship which suggests that there is still a sort of servitude of British nationality attached to our status.[15]

Those who cared more for being British than South African could make the choice.

Nationalist cabinet members were less belligerent but felt there was no content to the idea of common status. Dr. D. F. Malan called it 'a name without a meaning',[16] while Dönges declared that India's membership in the Commonwealth (as accepted at the Prime Minister's Conference in London, April, 1949) made a common status impossible. In some ways, however, the Nationalists showed as deep an understanding of the meaning and workings of the Commonwealth as did the Opposition. Viljoen, Minister of Education, spoke of it as 'an unwritten conception between friendly states', while Dr. J. H. Steyn called it 'an organism' which must develop out of its own 'centrifugal dynamic force'.[17]

The main point at issue remained the concepts and primary allegiance of the Government and the Opposition. The United Party envisaged a South Africa not only built on the basis of its two European peoples but working in close harmony with the other older members of the Commonwealth, receiving constant infusions of strength from them through immigration and investment and sharing, to the greatest extent considered possible in the South African context, in the values and attitudes of western democratic countries. In their view, close Commonwealth relationship and the reinforcement of the British tradition served not to detract from but to enrich South Africanism.

The Nationalists, in contrast, sought South African unity through the elimination of outside loyalties. Though they were quite prepared to maintain outside relationships on a basis of friendship and mutual advantage, they rejected the idea that it should be based on sentiment. The unity they sought was one patterned on their own experience and based on their values. Some Nationalists appealed for compulsory bilingualism for new citizens; others reiterated the plea for one flag and one anthem. They rejected the United Party charges of racialism by casting the accusation back at them.

'This measure will assist us to create our own South African nation,' said Mr. D. J. G. van den Heever, 'and that, of course, will ultimately wipe them and their party completely off the face of South Africa. By paralysing racial strife, you paralyse the United Party . . .'[18] Dönges' last remark on the bill was that it would 'weld together both peoples in a unified South Africa in one citizenship and one loyalty on the basis of a common love for our fatherland'.

What the Nationalists did not, or would not, see was that by opposing so adamantly the United Party position on the bill, they were reinforcing it. Major P. V. G. van der Byl, former United Party Minister of Native Affairs, pointed out that, if the measure was to be, as Dönges said, 'the foundation of our nationhood as an independent people', it should carry with it 'the good will of the vast majority of the Europeans in this country' and should not 'leave wounds that may take many years to heal'.[19] Yet the Nationalists' handling of the measure did exactly that. Throughout the course of the measure, the Opposition fought doggedly, forcing votes at every stage. The United Party proposed 41 amendments, of which 26 fell through the guillotine. All the votes marked unusually high totals on both sides because there was no pairing: second reading, 77-68; guillotine motion, 76-62; committee stage, 77-63; and third reading, 75-63. In the Senate, the measure passed on June 27 by 16 to 15. Moreover, both General Smuts and his subsequent successor, J. G. N. Strauss, asserted that the United Party would repeal the measure if it was returned to power. On a broad overall view, the divergencies reflected in the debate on the Citizenship bill arose out of history; the unfortunate fact was that the measure and its handling did nothing to promote the greater understanding of each other's point of view which can be the only sound basis of unity.

The United Party opposition to the Citizenship bill had been reinforced by a flood of protests throughout the country, especially from Natal, the British

Empire Service League, the Civil Rights League, and ex-servicemen's and voters' associations. Mass meetings of protest were held in Johannesburg, Springs, Cape Town, and Durban. The *Rand Daily Mail* endorsed the United Party's efforts to stave off what it called 'disaster, despotism and totalitarianism'.[20] The *Natal Daily News* said the measure attempted to create 'a new class of voteless "uitlanders" before the next election', and called the new nationalism 'top doggism with an ideology'.[21] The *Pretoria News* felt the measure resulted from the dislike of a Nationalist minority for 'anything "foreign", above all for the English-speaking and all things English'.[22]

The latter point and the implication that the Nationalists wanted to turn the United Party into an English-minority party were strongly repudiated by *Die Burger* on June 22, 1949.[23] A few days earlier, however, it used the defence of attack in declaring that 'English domination in South Africa' was 'still openly propagated' and that some people believed it was the motive behind earlier United Party plans for post-war immigration. Such domination would always be a possibility, it maintained, so long as there remained outside South Africa 'a pool of ten million Britons'.[24] On June 16, *Die Burger* charged that the United Party's actions against the bill amounted to 'sabotage of a nature which the Government chosen by the electorate dare not permit'. Regretting the use of the guillotine, it still found it a necessary evil to allow the Government to carry on its work. *Die Oosterlig* on June 17 spoke of 'jingo agitation and resistance'.[25] *Die Vaderland* wrote severely about 'men with Afrikaans names' who had undertaken to support the rights of the English-speaking 'with deplorable maliciousness' against Afrikaner Ministers. In what it called 'all seriousness', it suggested there be citizenship classes both for new arrivals and for others who needed 'revision courses for blunted Colonial memories'. Thus the press contributed no more than the parties to a better understanding or basis of unity on this fundamental issue of citizenship.

The effect of the Citizenship Act is almost impossible to determine. Returning from England, where he had been throughout the debate on the measure, General Smuts called the Act 'a great calamity for the country', causing 'greater racial division than I have seen for many a day'.[26] He added that 'damage has been done to fundamental unity and the good feeling which was arising in the country'. At the least, the measure made it possible for the Nationalists to make the future decisions about who should be added to the South African nation and on what terms.

The relation of the Citizenship bill to immigration had been stressed frequently on both sides during the debates. In practice, it would be hard to show that the Citizenship Act by itself had much effect on lessening immigration to South Africa, particularly from other Commonwealth countries. Even before introducing the measure, however, the Nationalists had withdrawn their support from the United Party-sponsored program of post-war immigration from Great Britain, and grave rumors about Nationalist policy also limited both immigration and investment. While, in 1947, nearly 29,000 immigrants were admitted and almost 36,000 in 1948, the number had dropped sharply by the latter part of 1949 to about half the 1947 rate. At the same time, a substantial number of South Africans, including Afrikaners, were moving north into the Rhodesias, partly seeking new economic opportunities, but partly also because of dislike of Nationalist policies.[27]

While it was commonly said for a long time that the Nationalists opposed immigration while the United Party sponsored it, the difference between the two parties was less about the need for immigrants than the question of what kind of immigrants. Both recognized the need to enlarge the white population, partly to lessen the great disparity in numbers between Europeans and non-Europeans, and partly to meet South Africa's great need for skilled workers. Because of its more cosmopolitan character, the United Party has been able to emphasize numbers as such; the Nationalists, in contrast, placed their emphasis, at least until 1954, on ease of assimilation in attitude as well as race.

In April, 1950, a new Nationalist attitude to immigration was heralded when the Dutch Reformed Church Congress proposed that immigrants be a means of replacing Native labor by white.[28] At the same moment, J. G. Strijdom publicly endorsed immigration from Holland,[29] and *Die Transvaler* echoed him in saying on April 10 that there could not be too many Calvinist Hollanders coming to South Africa.[30] On December 30, 1950, Dönges called for 25,000 immigrants in the next three years.[31] Yet the position of the Nationalists remained equivocal. They were committed to defend the position of the semi-skilled Afrikaner worker, the main source of their electoral strength in the cities, as well as the characteristic features of Afrikaner life. Dönges told Parliament in February, 1951, that immigration must fit not only the expanding requirements of the South African economy but also the needs of the settled white population.[32] When A. E. Robinson, of the United Party, called for 100,000 immigrants,[33] B. J. Schoeman, Minister of Labour, said the Union wanted 25,000 Germans,[34] and *Die Transvaler* echoed that immigrants must come from western European Protestant elements.[35] *Dagbreek* staged a debate on whether immigration offered a threat to Afrikaner culture: one side stressed the great assimilating powers of Afrikanerdom and the other warned that immigrants were less assimilable than they used to be.[36] *Die Burger* pointed out the crux of the general problem, however, by showing that there were more jobs than workers and that industrialization and apartheid could not be reconciled without immigration of skilled workers.[37]

The Nationalists' dilemma over immigration intensified throughout 1952. The *Star* reported on March 4, not without satisfaction, that 'the Government is trapped' as skilled immigrants did not want to come to South Africa.[38] The Minister of Education retaliated by saying South African adults should be trained as artisans to meet the urgent need and was heartily applauded by *Die Transvaler* and *Die Vaderland*.[39] When the United Party leader, J. G. N. Strauss, called for balanced and selective immigration in September,[40] *Die Transvaler* retorted angrily that it threatened to plough the Afrikaner under.[41] This was the line maintained through the 1953 election period as a counter balance to United Party propaganda in support of immigration. In that election, it should be noted, the United Party probably lost a good many votes because the period necessary for citizenship and the franchise had been lengthened from two to five years by the Citizenship Act. Yet as one of their own supporters pointed out, most if not all of these votes would have contributed to urban seats where the United Party already held majorities rather than to the marginal ones where the outcome was in doubt.

Not till 1954 did the Nationalists respond more openly to the goads, not only of their opponents, but also of the economic situation. *Die Volksblad* wrote of the need for immigration on January 9;[42] *Die Vaderland* picked up the cry on June 19,[43] the *Star* applauding that it had seen 'light at last'.[44] *Die Burger* suddenly, on June 24, blamed the Opposition and the frightening picture they painted of Nationalist-controlled South Africa for the small number of immigrants, and the *Cape Times* retaliated next day that the Government had deliberately tried to keep out potential anti-Nationalist voters.[45] By September, however, both the *Evening Post* and the *Rand Daily Mail* could see a 'clearly discernible' change in the Nationalist attitude towards immigration.[46] Even then, the Government could hardly be oblivious to the D. R. C. Congresses which had urged earlier in the year that immigrants should be adaptable to the Afrikaner religion and culture,[47] and to the problem raised by *Die Oosterlig* at the end of the year: 'How can we gain the necessary friends for national unity and the republic?'[48]

Few issues provide more difficult counter-pulls for the Nationalists than immigration. On the one hand, it is obvious that both the economic development they endorse and their apartheid policy demand a larger white population in South Africa, and a more skilled one. On these grounds, they have no disagreement with the United Party. But the political supremacy and cultural distinctiveness of the nationalist Afrikaner are no less significant goals to the Nationalists. The Citizenship Act and, in particular, some of the arguments used to support it, reflected their determination to build South Africa's Europeans into a nation unified in support of those ideals and objectives which the Nationalists themselves feel most fundamental. The same objective of homogeneity in their own pattern is reflected throughout Nationalist arguments and policies on immigration. But here too can be seen the problem implicit in the handling of the Citizenship bill that the very intensity of the effort to secure unity and the overemphasis on definitions may help to defeat its own or broader purposes.

Though the connection is more remote, something may be said here about the Nationalists' use of executive power in regard to entering or leaving the Union. Just as they regard the definition of citizenship as a political matter, so do the Nationalists look on the granting of visas or of passports. Thus they have not infrequently refused entry to the country by persons who were thought to be hostile in their attitude, or who were seeking information for purposes the Nationalists did not endorse. The Government refused, for example, to permit the United Nations Committee on Racial Discrimination in South Africa[49] to enter the country and also a student group which sought in 1954 to investigate conditions in the universities, as well as outspoken critics like the Rev. Michael Scott, champion of the South West Africa Herero tribe and director of the Africa Bureau in London. Moreover, European and non-European South Africans have been refused passports, e.g., Dr. T. Alper, a woman atomic scientist, in May 1951; two prominent leaders of the South African Indian Congress, Dr. Y. M. Dadoo and Dr. G. M. Naicker, to prevent them from going to the United Nations in September 1948; and a distinguished African, Professor Z. K. Matthews, of Fort Hare University, in mid-1954. The Nationalists take the position that a passport, like citizenship, is a privilege, not a right. In this matter, there is no recourse to the courts in the Union as in the United States. Moreover, it is now illegal to leave the Union without a passport. Thus travel to and from South Africa is subject to ministerial discretion, a matter of very great concern to many of the Government's European opponents and to all non-Europeans.

The Suppression of Communism Act, 1950[50]

To group the South African Citizenship Act with the Suppression of Communism Act may well seem unwarranted at first view. The general purpose of the latter measure found wide approval amongst the white population of South Africa; at no time was there an embittered opposition to its provisions which echoed the exchanges over the Citizenship bill. Nonetheless two features of the Suppression of Communism bill—the breadth of its definitions of Communism, and its wide grant of executive discretion—roused grave misgivings that the Act would be used not only against those who propagated the doctrines of Communism by word or deed but also against liberal critics of the Government as well as against non-Europeans who opposed apartheid policies. Thus behind the debates on the Suppression of Communism bill and the criticism of its subsequent use lurk the same fears that powered the opposition to the Citizenship Act: that the Nationalists would use the measure to enforce their own pattern of life and objectives throughout South Africa.

The racial pattern of South Africa explains in itself why South African Europeans are still more fearful of Communism than are other Western people. Since the days of Lenin, Communism has avowedly sought an alliance between the working class revolution and the masses in colonial or underdeveloped areas. Moreover, Communism has identified itself with racial equality, a concept which strikes at the roots of the assumptions on which white South Africans base their monopoly of political power, and the industrial color bar. British and American liberal democracy also endorses racial equality and therefore Afrikaner Nationalists mistrust liberals whether inside or outside their country. But non-European agitation against prevailing conditions in South Africa is much more commonly attributed to Communist than to liberal influences, though in many instances it stems in practice from neither of these sources, but from African and Indian nationalism.

The history of the South African Communist Party is an odd one but it has been closely enough linked to the organized efforts of non-Europeans to improve their conditions to provide some substance for the fears of South African Europeans. At the same time the story of its activities needs to be sketched in some detail in order to provide perspective on the significance of the Communist Party in the Union.

In its interest in and work with non-Europeans, the Communist Party has differed sharply from the South African Labour Party, which has always been a white workers' party and, until recently, maintained a highly conservative, even reactionary, attitude on race relations. The original split in the Labour Party, out of which came the South African Communist Party, however, was not over this issue but over South Africa's participation in World War I. S. P. Bunting[51] and some other prominent Labour figures who opposed the war effort resigned from the Labour Party or were expelled, and, in September, 1914, formed the International Socialist League. Not until a year later did Bunting develop the sincere concern for black workers which henceforth molded his life and activities. In 1921, the International Socialist League was merged in the newly founded South African Communist Party, in which black as well as white members were welcomed.

The crucial decision as to whether the Communist Party should strive to be the radical wing of the orthodox labor movement or the leader of the black workers was made in 1924. The Communist Party threw its weight behind the 1924 election of the Pact Government (see p. 30) believing that the alliance of the Labour Party and Hertzog's Nationalists, with their Afrikaner workers' support, would strengthen labor unity, the more so because both these parties had seemed to make overtures to the non-European voters in the Cape. Once in office, however, the Pact Government concentrated on its 'civilized labour policy' to defend white workers from the competition of non-Europeans. Some Communist Party leaders, like W. H. Andrews, felt that the future of the party lay with organized white labor; Andrews withdrew from active work in the Communist Party to concentrate on trade union activities when he was overborne by others like Bunting, who believed that black workers must be given equal attention.

The Communist Party found it far from easy, however, to win acceptance of its self-assigned role as the leader of the non-European workers. The largest mass organization of Africans in the history of South Africa, Clements Kadalie's Industrial and Commercial Workers' Union of Africa (I.C.U.), chose to align itself with the missionaries and other liberals and in December, 1926, expelled its Communists. But partly through its revived newspaper, the *South African Worker*, and through night schools for Africans, the Communists gradually won a number of new Native adherents, among them Moses Kotane, long an important figure in the Party.

A still more serious problem developed out of the local Party's relations with Moscow. Until 1927, the South African Communist Party was left very much on its own; from that year on, a series of 'directives' from Moscow battered the local Communists and ultimately broke the Party to shreds. At that point the Soviet Union saw Great Britain as its major world enemy, and decided to attack British finance capital and what it called 'its South African ally, Boer imperialism'.[52] Thus it declared that the objective for South Africa was 'an independent Native republic, as a stage towards a workers' and peasants' republic'. Bunting, horrified, tried vainly at the sixth World Congress of the Communist International in Moscow, mid-1928, to change the decision. He pointed out that white workers would be further alienated by such a slogan, and that it would harm rather than aid the Native movement, which was perpetually bordering on illegality.[53] Though defeated, Bunting returned to South Africa prepared to continue working in the Communist Party. In 1929, following a proposal of the Moscow conference, Bunting helped to launch the 'League of African Rights' as a mass organization under Communist Party guidance. Moscow immediately vetoed the move. In September, 1931, Bunting, W. H. Andrews, Solly Sachs and other prominent Communists were expelled from the Party for 'right deviationism'. Four years later, continued Moscow pressure resulted in Edward Roux and Moses Kotane being ejected from the Party's Political Bureau.

Within a limited time, however, Moscow switched to its new line of the 'united front'. The Communist Party, now without most of its able members, tried vainly to form a united front with the Labour Party. Roux dropped out of the Party in disgust at the obvious wire-pulling for the interests of Moscow alone. On the other hand, when the Soviet Union celebrated its twentieth anniversary, W. H. Andrews was welcomed in Moscow as a fraternal labor delegate. On his return to the Union, he re-entered the South African Communist Party on May 1, 1938, and subsequently became chairman of its Central Committee. At the outbreak of World War II, the Communist Party again shifted to the left. Dr. Y. M. Dadoo, a Johannesburg Indian, went to jail for speeches opposing the war and demanding full democratic rights for non-Europeans. As elsewhere, however, the South African Communist Party switched to full support of the Government's war effort when the Soviet Union was attacked by Nazi Germany. In consequence, Communist Party members had little further interference during the course of the war.

After the war, the most touchy point concerning the Communist Party was its relation with certain African trade unions. Since the traditional labor movement long ignored the African because he was both black and unskilled, it is hardly surprising that the first African trade unions were started by Communists. Though 'pass carrying' (that is, male) Africans are not recognized as 'employees' under the Industrial Conciliation Act of 1924 and thus have no guaranteed right either to demand collective bargaining or to strike, they had formed what may be called unofficial trade unions from 1927 on. These unions united in a Non-European Trade Union Federation in 1929, but it disintegrated between 1930-33 due to the depression and the splits in the Communist Party.

The Native Clothing Workers' Union under an able African, Gana Makabeni, an expelled Communist, helped to develop new African trade unions under African leadership. Another group of African trade unions under a white Trotskyite named Max Gordon was still more successful and developed into the Joint Committee in Johannesburg which, at its height in 1940, had 21 unions including laundry, commercial, baking, printing, dairy, chemical, and general workers' unions, and 23-26,000 members. The liberal-minded Institute of Race Relations (see p. 336) tried to unite the Makabeni and Joint Committee unions in 1938 but without success.

In 1942, however, a new Council of Non-European Trade Unions was formed in Johannesburg with 29 affiliated unions; by 1945, it claimed to represent 150,000 organized African workers. Communist support secured the election, as its chairman, of John Marks, the able, eloquent African secretary of the African Mine Workers' Union. Thus most of the 50-odd African trade unions on the Rand were under either Communist or Trotskyite influence, with the possible exception of a small group of unions under an African named Kosa.[54]

In the meantime, Communists had been busy organizing both in the Western Cape and Natal. In the latter province they organized some racially mixed industrial unions, including the Natal Sugar Industry Employees' Union with Indian and African members. In the Cape, due largely to the efforts of a young girl, Ray Alexander, a number of new unions were formed on an inter-racial basis, some of them with a majority of non-Europeans, mainly Coloured. The Communists also captured control of the Cape Federation of Trades, with which most unions in the Cape up to that time had been affiliated. Some of these unions, like the Garment Workers' Union, then broke away. Some other Cape unions were in a small independent group, while well-established craft unions like the Typographical and Engineers' Union were affiliated with the South

African Trades and Labour Council. The latter, under liberal leadership, admitted all *bona fide* trade unions regardless of their racial composition, but of its 46 affiliated unions in 1941 only 8 were non-European or mixed unions, representing some 400 out of 21,500 members.[55]

A sporadic outburst of strikes in 1942 by African workers, some but not all of whom were unionized, led General Smuts' United Party Government to promulgate War Measure 145, which made all strikes by Africans illegal under any circumstances. This measure was subsequently used in connection with the largest and, temporarily, most effective strike ever called by Africans, that of the African Mine Workers' Union in 1946, in which some 60,000 African mine-workers on the Johannesburg Reef struck for higher wages. After lasting about four days, the strike was broken by the police. Fifty Africans, Indians, and Europeans connected with the African Mine Workers' Union and the Communist Party were charged under War Measure 145 and sentenced to fines or imprisonment. Among them were Moses Kotane, then General Secretary of the Communist Party, Dr. Y. M. Dadoo, and Brian Bunting, son of S. P. Bunting, and subsequently a Native representative in the House of Assembly.

Police raids on Communist Party offices and its newspaper, the *Guardian*, as well as on many trade unions, did not produce enough evidence to proceed with charges of conspiracy initially coupled with those under War Measure 145. In November, 1946, however, the whole National Executive Committee of the Communist Party was charged with sedition and brought to Johannesburg for trial. Though the trial dragged on for more than a year, its results were inconclusive.

Almost as soon as the Nationalists came into office, they set up a Departmental Committee to investigate Communism in the Union. On the eve of the 1949 Provincial elections in which they sought a new mandate for their apartheid policy, C. R. Swart, Minister of Justice, told the House of Assembly on February 16, 1949, that the Committee's report disclosed 'a national danger' which made it imperative to combat 'the dangerous undermining' by the Communists of 'our national life, our democratic institutions, and our Western philosophy'. More specifically, Swart said the report disclosed that a number of 'supposedly independent organizations' were actually Communist-fronts, that this was particularly serious as far as trade unions were concerned, that there were lecturers and students in 'certain universities' who were 'enthusiastic' Communists and also teachers in non-European schools, and that there were evening classes teaching the principles of Communism. While unwilling to disclose the Government's plans, the Minister called for full Opposition support for whatever steps the Government might decide to take.[56]

The Opposition press showed considerable apprehension, however, that the Government planned to attack more than Communists. The *Rand Daily Mail*, on February 21, called the statement 'a red-herring to cross the trail of hard battering on financial and economic policy' and feared that the definition of Communist would be 'so widely drawn' as to include many people with no affiliation to that movement.[57] The *Pretoria News* saw it as 'a political move calculated to panic the voters on the eve of the Provincial elections'.[58] In fact, Dr. Malan, in an election meeting at Goodwood in the Cape on February 20, declared that the Communists would rather have the United Party in office than the Nationalists because they were not afraid of the former, and *Die*

Burger repeated this argument while openly charging that the Communists 'have thrown their full weight behind the United Party candidates'.[59] In answer, the United Party pledged itself in an open statement to oppose Communism and any other threat to democracy in South Africa. But the way to do so, it felt, was through constructive social and economic measures, and particularly through freedom of speech, religion, and press, since Communism could not flourish in a free society. 'The Nationalist approach to the problem,' it warned, 'like that of the Nazis, is to brand all its opponents as Communists.'[60]

When Fred Carneson of the Communist Party decisively defeated the United Party candidate in the election for a Native representative in the Provincial Council on December 7, 1949, as Sam Kahn, also of the Central Committee of the Communist Party, had similarly won a place as a Native representative in the House of Assembly the previous year,[61] the Nationalist press found it a reinforcement of their fears that Communism, 'with its promises of equality', had a strong hold among detribalized Africans. Only an apartheid policy 'which strives to give the Native a home in his own area and outside the white community where he can carry out his deepest desires', could be a satisfactory alternative to this appeal, in *Die Burger's* view.[62] *Die Vaderland* saw the Carneson election as a 'clarion call' to all Europeans to stand together on race relations policy.[63] The *Cape Times*, in contrast, feared this election would encourage the Nationalists to take repressive measures against the non-European, for example, to take this last direct vote away from them, while repressive measures in turn would help Communism to flourish.

Tension continued to build up over the Government's plans to curb Communism. The English-language press reiterated all its misgivings when the Speech from the Throne announced baldly that this would be a subject for legislation in the coming session. The *Evening Post* feared that the purpose was 'to swallow the liberal camel, not strain the Communist midget'.[64] From the other side, the Dutch Reformed Church was reported to be urging the Government to close the Soviet Consulate in Pretoria,[65] said to be a center for Communist propaganda throughout Africa,[66] and to tighten the law punishing incitement of non-Europeans against Europeans.[67] On March 6, its Church Congress called for State action against Communism.[68] The Ossewa Brandwag asked the Government to ban the Communist Party outright.[69]

The Nationalist measure, as first introduced on May 5, 1950, seemed singularly vague in the light of all this discussion. Entitled the 'Unlawful Organizations Bill', it prohibited 'certain activities detrimental to the interests of the Union', made it possible to declare that organizations promoting these activities were illegal, and to prohibit 'certain periodical and other publications'. Though Sam Kahn, the one Communist in the House of Assembly, immediately accused the measure of proscribing Communism, the Speaker pointed out that there was no mention of Communism in the bill. On May 19, however, the House was told that 'the one and only preconceived object' of the bill was 'to combat Communism'.[70] In the hope of securing 'a united front' on the measure, the Minister asked that it be referred for discussion to a Select Committee representative of all parties. Out of this Committee came a revised Nationalist proposal known as the Suppression of Communism Bill, presented to the House on June 5, 1950, and allotted 30 hours for its consideration under guillotine procedure.

The Suppression of Communism Act, which is very like the Bill which emerged from the Select Committee, declares the Communist Party to be an unlawful organization. It makes it possible to declare unlawful other organizations which promote Communist activities, to prohibit 'certain periodical or other publications' and also certain Communist activities. It appointed a Liquidator to take over the assets of organizations declared unlawful, which were to be distributed ultimately to charitable societies once all debts had been paid. Moreover, under the direction of the Minister of Justice, the Liquidator could (and did) compile a list of 'office-bearers, officers, members or active supporters' of any unlawful organization, after giving individuals a 'reasonable' chance to show why their name should not appear. The Minister could then forbid those 'named' to take part in any specified organization. But the 'naming' process is not essential before taking action, for the Minister can forbid 'any person' to take part in any specified organization or to enter or remain in a prescribed area, and he can also prohibit any gathering if it appears to aid the objects of Communism.

The crucial question was the definition of Communism and of a Communist. The Act defines Communism as the doctrine of Marxian Socialism as expounded by Lenin or Trotsky, the Comintern or the Cominform, or, still more broadly, as

> any related form of that doctrine expounded or advocated in the Union for the promotion of the fundamental principles of that doctrine

and, in particular, any doctrine or scheme aiming at one of the following four purposes. The first is to establish a one-party State based on the dictatorship of the proletariat. The second, which was subsequently termed 'statutory Communism' by the courts when used against leaders of the non-European defiance campaign, reads:

> which aims at bringing about any political, industrial, social or economic change within the Union by the promotion of disturbances or disorder, by unlawful acts or omissions or by the threat of such acts or omissions or by means which include the promotion of disturbance or disorder, or such acts or omissions or threat.

The third follows much the same wording as the second, but covers such attempts under the guidance or with the cooperation of a foreign Government (obviously the Soviet Union or other Communist State) for the purpose of promoting a system like that enumerated in the first section. The fourth section is linked to the objectives of section one or two if they are sought by 'the encouragement of feelings of hostility between the European and non-European races of the Union'. A Communist is said to be a person who professes to be such or after the right to make representations 'is deemed by the Governor-General' to be so on the basis of advocating 'any of the objects of Communism' or any act or mission to assist such an object.

From the first, there was a clear difference of approach to the measure between the Nationalists and the United Party.[71] The former constantly justified it on the ground that Communists aimed to destroy the democratic way of life in

South Africa and that therefore they must be outlawed and deprived of their means to 'contaminate' anyone. The United Party saw a serious danger that this bill itself might destroy the democratic way of life. A United Party member spoke of it as 'one of the most far-reaching and dangerous bills ever proposed'.[72] The United Party leader, Strauss, also bitterly opposed the restrictions of the guillotine procedure on so important a measure. He was supported by the Labour Party leader, John Christie, who warned fruitlessly that 'those who used the physical guillotine perished by that guillotine in the end',[73] while Kahn's quick tongue called it 'jet-propelled legislation'.[74]

The United Party made it obvious that it was as much opposed to Communism as were the Nationalists, but that it was deeply concerned about the breadth of the definition of Communism, the lack of adequate recourse to the courts, and the wide executive powers under the bill. In the Select Committee, Strauss had submitted an alternative measure which took care of these objections by providing a more precise definition of Communism, dissolving the Communist Party rather than declaring it illegal, and making it impossible to take action against any other organization unless it was found guilty by a court of committing the overt act of propagating Communism. Moreover, the Strauss proposal made it impossible to act against an individual unless he, too, was found guilty by a court of 'an act of Communism', or against a publication except by court judgment. While these provisions of the Strauss plan safeguarded individual and group liberty far better than the Nationalist bill, they were coupled with the disturbing proposal that the burden of proof of his innocence should be placed on the accused and that Communist activities be considered high treason leading to sentence of death. This last part of his proposal was used frequently by Strauss in the 1953 election campaign as evidence of United Party opposition to Communism.

Strauss' plan, it must be noted, was a personal, not a party one.[75] Most United Party members disliked the idea that the burden of proof be put on the accused[76] and tacitly agreed with C. R. Swart, who gleefully took the chance to charge that it was a departure from 'a sacred principle'.[77] United Party Senator A. M. Conroy specifically declared he would not have voted for the Strauss plan.[78] Tactically it seems to have been a mistake that Strauss did not secure party agreement to all aspects of his proposal before submitting it.

In the debates in the House, Strauss emphasized United Party opposition to wide executive powers and his party's constructive approach to Communism by killing its causes: depression, unemployment, poverty, slum conditions, and the high cost of living. Specifically he moved that the second reading of the bill should not be passed because

> in seeking to combat Communist totalitarianism it creates a Fascist despotism in that it clothes the executive with unnecessarily wide and despotic powers, fails to provide for full and effective access to the courts, and makes intolerable inroads upon the freedom of the citizen, including the power to violate the sanctity of his home.[79]

While wholly in favour of eliminating Communists from the trade unions, he pointed out the 'tremendous temptation to weed out political opponents' as well.[80] Nor were there adequate opportunities for rectifying mistakes under the bill once a person or organization had been 'named'. Particularly he challenged the Government powers of search, seizure and inquisition—'there is your Gestapo in all its nakedness'[81]—though Swart justifiably pointed out similar provisions in bills passed earlier under the United Party. Fundamentally, however, the United Party objections to the measure rested on the lack of any adequate recourse to the courts.

The Labour Party showed itself still more alarmed lest the measure be used (as it subsequently was) against trade union leaders. The Minister of Justice inserted a special provision in the bill (section 1(2)) to specify that a legitimate strike or lockout following a labor dispute did not fall under the definition of Communism, but Labour members found this no comfort. Alex Hepple, subsequently leader of the party, pointed out that removing key individuals in trade unions was almost tantamount to destroying the unions.[82] When Swart declared the trade unions were protected, Hyman Davidoff shouted, 'It's a bluff.'[83]

It was left to the senior Native representative, Mrs. Margaret Ballinger, to warn that the measure would be used 'to deprive the growing African national movement of their African leaders'.[84] With keen insight she declared, too, that

> the dangers inherent in the effort to suppress any political view by legislative means are too great a price to pay for a result which is itself entirely uncertain.[85]

Except for small concessions, however, for which they took great credit, the Nationalists insisted on keeping their bill in the form in which they brought it from the Select Committee. Implicit or explicit in their arguments was that Communism was responsible for Native unrest or demands. Swart emphasized that because of 'the peculiar conditions prevailing in this country', South Africa was 'one of the most fertile fields for Communism'.[86] To Mr. M. de W. Nel, a Nationalist backbencher, the legislation was a protection for the non-European. 'Now they will understand that Communism is an evil,' he declared, 'and that the Government is sincere in its desire to wipe it out.' Less justifiably, he warned that 'Bantu nationalism is the wooden horse in which Communism is hiding'.[87] Swart and Dr. Diederichs made great use of the 1928 Moscow directive to the Communist Party to work for a black republic, and Swart added that a recently seized Communist Party document proposed a general strike to be carried out by non-European organizations.[88] He spoke also of 'a secret military organization among the Natives led by a Communist' of which no more seems subsequently to have been heard.[89] J. H. Steyn, a backbencher, was not untypical when he said that far too much time had been spent on 'the ideological aspect of Communism because in the form in which we get it in South Africa it is purely and solely a racial issue'.[90]

The Opposition's demands for more recourse to the courts somewhat embarrassed the Nationalists, particularly at first. Swart said this would dry up the Government's confidential sources of information and only drive the Communists underground. To wait for an overt act of Communism and then use criminal procedures, as Strauss proposed, would open the way to lengthy delays. Moreover, the Communist Party might change its name after the bill was passed, as had happened in Canada, and then the Government would have to wait again for an overt act. Finally, Swart called Communism a snake and declared, 'if you want to kill a snake, you can't play with it'.[91] Another favorite line towards the end of the debate was to say that it was no more possible for the Nationalists to use democratic means against the Communists than it had been for the United Party when fighting the Nazis.[92]

Despite occasional breaks in the unity of the Opposition, as over the Strauss proposal, or some Labour amendments, it held firm on all major questions, fighting the measure on its own chosen ground. Perhaps the best statement of this was by Sir de Villiers Graaff, Strauss' chief lieutenant, who enumerated four simple points: everyone should know what the law is and how to avoid transgression; there must be recourse to the courts; executive powers must not be so wide that they are capable of abuse; and limits must be placed on Government rights of search, seizure, and inquisition.[93] The end result, however, hardly conformed to these criteria, and Labour's valiant attempts to write in a more orthodox definition of Communism were equally unsuccessful.[94] The measure was passed, 64-49, by the House of Assembly on June 20, the last day of the session, by the Senate, 19-18, through the casting vote of its president, on June 24, 1950, and became law two days later.

While the bill was discussed in the House, the press and public had not been quiet. The Johannesburg Bar saw the bill putting freedom in jeopardy,[95] and the Cape and Durban Bar Councils protested.[96] The South African Trades and Labour Council opposed it,[97] while Miss Anna Sheepers, a leader of the Garment Workers' Union, warned it meant the end of trade unionism.[98] Demonstrations against the bill were held in Cape Town and elsewhere. The English-language press constantly reiterated the dangers of giving such sweeping powers to the Minister and thus imperilling liberty. The *Rand Daily Mail* felt it embodied 'a futile principle that an idea can be crushed by legislation',[99] the *Cape Argus* that 'it goes to the foundations of our society',[100] and the *Friend* that the departure from court appeal was 'on the high road to totalitarianism'.[101]

Interesting was the perceptible shift in the Nationalist press from an original hesitation to widespread support. *Die Vaderland* greeted the Unlawful Organizations Bill with reservations and warned 'we must not create a boomerang for ourselves'.[102] On June 20, however, it reported the Afrikaner Party was supporting the measure wholeheartedly, and on June 23 commented with satisfaction that 'the gilt is now off Communism' as young and undeveloped liberal spirits would realize. People were at last awake to 'un-South African activities'.[103] *Die Burger* similarly hesitated at first, declaring that such legislation in a democratic country was an experiment.[104] On June 7, it remarked that a precise definition in such legislation was 'an ideal' which could never be fulfilled.[105] Six days later, it insisted the Minister could not deprive even a Communist 'of all his freedom', and that 'several loopholes' were left to the ordinary citizen.[106] By the end, however, *Die Burger* was convinced of the bill's merit though perhaps with some reservations. Already the bill had had a salutary effect, it declared on June 22, but it would rarely be needed after the original cleaning-up process.[107]

Die Transvaler was more wholehearted in its support of the bill, and exploited United Party opposition to it. On May 2 it accused the United Party and the Communist Party of having 'a harmful and unholy alliance'.[108] After

Swart charged in Parliament that numerous organizations were harboring Communists, *Die Transvaler* saw evidence of conspiracies 'which can unchain devils of terror'. 'There is no time to talk nonsense about legal points', it declared on June 15, 'and the obligation to let action drag out endlessly in the courts for the sake of meeting certain democratic requirements.' It believed an 'emergency situation' existed.[109] The *Evening Post*, in a sense, agreed on June 21, but because it believed that the powers under the bill would be used 'for a more gradual and stealthy encroachment on the rights of individuals and societies who do not see eye to eye with the Government'.[110]

One of the obvious purposes of the Suppression of Communism Act was to unseat the one Communist in the House of Assembly, a Native representative, Sam Kahn. Under a United Party amendment, the law provided for a hearing by a Committee of the relevant legislative body before a member could be expelled under this law unless he professed to be a Communist.[111] On June 20, 1950, four days before the Act came into effect, Sam Kahn dramatically announced in the House that the Communist Party had dissolved. This action created legal complications in removing Kahn from the House and Carneson from the Cape Provincial Council, as well as in dealing with the Communist Party itself.

To overcome these difficulties, the Government pushed through a further measure,[112] which tightened the anti-Communist machinery by inserting a much wider definition of 'Communist' capable of covering anyone who had ever professed Communism inside or outside the Union, or was deemed by the authorities to be a 'Communist' on the basis of his actions inside or outside the country, and made the operation of the Act retroactive. In long-winded clauses, the amendment also sought to prevent any further legal delays to fully liquidating the Communist Party and unseating Communist members of legislative bodies.[113] The *Friend* remarked wryly that South Africa would be the first democratic country to expel a man from Parliament because of his political convictions, while even *Die Volksblad* regretted that fighting Communism forced democracy to take up weapons it would rather not use.[114]

Typical of Opposition attitudes in Parliament were the Labour leader's denunciation of the new bill as 'wicked and dangerous', and the comment of the United Party expert on education, P. A. Moore, that it spread 'a net so wide that probably there was no intelligent citizen who couldn't be caught in it'. Equally characteristic was the rejoinder by a Nationalist that, in the cold war against Communism, any measure was justified.[115]

Though it had opposed the two Suppression of Communism Acts, the United Party approved the appointment of a select committee, early in 1952, to inquire into the positions of Sam Kahn and Fred Carneson. This was set up despite Mrs. Ballinger's protest that to unseat the two was an attempt to deprive Africans of their voice in the House and the Labour Party's amendment that the committee should only investigate these men's activities after the passage of the Suppression of Communism Act.

The *Rand Daily Mail* protested editorially:

> Naturally the Nationalists want to gag Mr. Kahn as soon as possible. What shocks us is that the United Party should also have lent itself to such a procedure.[116]

The *Star* felt this was 'unusually muddled thinking', however, both because the Suppression of Communism Act was the law and the select committee procedure had been due to United Party efforts. If 'fair and active inquiry' disclosed that persons were 'active Communists of actual or potential danger to the State', it pointed out, the United Party favored 'vigorous action' against them.[117]

The Select Committee exhaustively examined Mr. Kahn,[118] heard evidence on his case, and reported, 7 to 5, that he fell within the purview of the Suppression of Communism Act. When the report came to the House of Assembly, on May 20, 1952, there were many United Party and other protests, however, against exacting the full penalty under the law. Dr. C. F. Steyn, leader of the United Party in the Free State, pointed out that nowhere else in the world was such action taken against a man merely because he was a Communist at a time Communism was legal. Others felt the House should not disenfranchise several thousand voters who had sent their representative to the House in good faith. Kahn himself maintained that what he believed in was Socialism, Republicanism, and equal rights for Europeans and non-Europeans and asked for a trial before the law courts. But Dr. A. Hertzog's reply from the Nationalist benches expressed well his party's attitude. He declared it would be irresponsible to allow 'a man with spiritual smallpox to go among his electorate and spread that spiritual smallpox'.[119] The Select Committee report was accepted by 77 votes to 55, a straight party vote. On May 26, 1952, Kahn and Carneson were expelled from their respective legislative bodies.

Though well-known as a former Communist and on the Liquidator's list, Brian Bunting, son of S. P. Bunting, offered himself as a candidate in the by-election caused by Sam Kahn's expulsion. The Government moved too late to stop the election machinery from operating, and Bunting was elected overwhelmingly and took his seat in the House of Assembly in January, 1953. Failing to unseat him by any other means, another Select Committee was appointed on July 6, which heard evidence from Bunting and others. It voted on August 31, 1952, by 9-2 (with the 3 United Party members agreeing, but with Mrs. Ballinger and Leo Lovell of the Labour Party dissenting) that he fell within the provisions of the act.[120] One more attempt was made by the Communists when Ray Alexander, who had been so successful in organizing mixed unions in the Cape, tried to stand for the Cape Western seat, but she was prohibited from so doing. The Government thus made it impossible for a Communist to be chosen a Native representative by the Cape Africans. It is less sure that its victory was more than a surface one.

Another less successful effort was aimed at the once Communist-controlled newspaper, the *Guardian*. Its offices were raided late in November, 1950,[121] but not until May, 1952, was it officially banned.[122] The *Cape Times* commented on May 24 that it was the first time in the history of a non-totalitarian country that a newspaper had been put out of existence simply 'by the edict of a party politician', since it was not propagating Communism.[123] The English press also saw the ban as an attack on the freedom of the press. They need not have been so concerned, however, since, as the *Rand Daily Mail* announced on May 27,

> from the ashes of the dead newspaper, *The Guardian*, is to arise, phœnix-like, another newspaper, to be called *The Clarion*,

edited by Brian Bunting, who had edited the *Guardian*, and with some of its resources.[124] Faced with the necessity of going through the same procedure as used towards the *Guardian*, the Government decided to leave the *Clarion*, or, as it soon became, *New Age*, untouched.

Barely had the Suppression of Communism Act been passed when B. J. Schoeman, Minister of Labour, announced his determination to rid the trade unions of Communists and their supporters.[125] The South African Trades and Labour Congress announced in September that it would not defend avowed Communists.[126] It was seriously shaken, however, like other union groups, as the 'naming' and the expulsion processes were stepped up in May, 1952.

Particularly intense feeling was aroused when Solly Sachs, the vigorous and beloved leader of the Garment Workers' Union, who had been expelled from the Communist Party in 1930, was 'named' in May, 1952, and ordered to resign from his trade union. The Union, composed largely of women, with some non-Europeans among its 18,000 members, called a public meeting on the steps of the Johannesburg City Hall on May 24 which Sachs[127] addressed, though under ban not to attend such gatherings. As the police arrested and carried him off, a riot broke out. The police charged. Forty-one civilians were injured, according to C. R. Swart's report to the House, as well as a number of the police. *Dagbreek* estimated 58 injured in all,[128] but the *Sunday Times* figures were as high as 66 hospitalized and many treated privately. Most of those injured were women and many of them non-European. The *Star* and *Rand Daily Mail* strongly criticized the action of the police, while *Die Transvaler* and *Die Vaderland* defended it.[129] Davidoff, of the Labour Party, gave an eyewitness account in the House, in which he accused the police of deliberate provocation. Despite United Party urging, however, the Prime Minister refused to have a commission of inquiry. Few events in recent time have caused greater bitterness in the labor movement.

Deep concern about these developments led the British Trades Union Congress, the World Federation of Trade Unions, and the National Executive of the British Labour Party to respond forcefully to appeals sent by the South African Labour Party and the Trades and Labour Council. A unanimous resolution of the British Labour Executive expressed its 'profound concern' and stigmatized the Malan Government as 'a political despotism which merits the condemnation of the free peoples of the world'.[130] Dr. Malan responded bitterly in an interview in *Die Burger* on May 29 to what he termed 'untrue and insulting accusations', and accused the British Labour Party of being 'a disrupting factor in the Commonwealth' whose return to office would be 'a catastrophe'.[131] The Nationalist press rang all possible changes on this statement and also accused the United Front—the United Party, Labour Party, and Torch Commando[132]—of being the new 'uitlanders' appealing for overseas help.[133] The English-language press was also somewhat unhappy about the appeal abroad, and urged, in the words of the *Cape Times* on May 30, that the Opposition stand 'on its own South African feet'.[134]

What the South African Trades and Labour Council realized, however, was both its own inherent weakness and the lack of unity amongst trade unions at large. When the S.A.T.L.C. was established in 1930, it was as the official voice of labor in South Africa, and it was ready to act on behalf of all trade unions: European, mixed, and non-European. At no time were all unions affiliated with it, however, as it never included civil servants, teachers, most railway employees, nor any large number of non-Europeans. In April, 1947, the Trades and Labour Congress broke wide open over the issue of debarring Native trade unions from affiliation; when this effort was defeated, six Pretoria trade unions (of which the most important was the S.A. Iron and Steel Trades' Association of the Government-owned Iscor) withdrew and formed their own federation, called the Co-ordinating Council of South African Trade Unions, with 13,000 white members.

The struggle was not only over racial policy but also between the old craft unions and newer industrial unions. In 1950, more unions dis-affiliated from the S.A.T.L.C. to form the South African Federation of Trade Unions. By 1953 the latter had 23 unions with a membership of 100,000 as compared with the S.A.T.L.C.'s 50 unions with a membership of 83,000. The separateness of the Railway unions (70,000 members), Engineering union (19,000), and Western Province federation (25,000) further split South African labor. Some unions, in particular the Co-ordinating Council, strongly support Nationalist policies. Thus no united front could be maintained in response to Government pressure.

Systematically, the Government has acted against trade union officials. Swart announced on July 21, 1953, that the names of 53 trade union leaders were on the Liquidator's list; by September 18, 33 of these had been removed from their posts, and soon after a further 15 were removed.[135] These included nine national secretaries, a national organizer, a president, and a vice-president, and affected unions with a total membership of about 80,000.[136] All the trade union officials who lost their positions were also prohibited from attending meetings for two years; after September 1, 1953, they could also no longer attend a religious, recreational, or social gathering without securing from the Minister a special exemption from the ban. Alex. Hepple, the new leader of the Labour Party, told Parliament in September, 1953, that these wholesale removals had caused a reign of terror in the trade unions, and that some unions were having great difficulty in replacing those officials who had been removed. He also charged that action was being taken on the basis of secret reports and that those affected had no way of finding out how they had transgressed.[137]

The 'naming' process and removal from office are not necessarily connected. Probably some 500 persons have been 'named' over the years since the act was instituted, almost all of them members of the Communist Party at one time, but only about 100 of these have been removed from office. Only membership in Parliament is specifically refused to a person who has been 'named'. But of some 300 persons who have been removed from their offices, the majority have never been 'named'. Thus the act is a flexible and highly effective tool for acting not only against those whose membership in the Communist Party has been proved, but also against those whose activities are associated in the view of the executive with the purposes of Communism as defined in South Africa.

The Suppression of Communism Act has been used extensively not only against trade union leaders, but also against the leaders of non-European organizations.[138] Twenty African and Indian leaders in the defiance campaign (see Chapter 14) were convicted in the Johannesburg courts in October, 1952, of what the judge called 'statutory Communism', that is, of seeking to bring about 'political, industrial, social, or economic change within the Union by the promotion of disturbance or disorder, by unlawful acts or omissions or by the threat of such acts or omissions'. Put on suspended sentence, they were prohibited from attending gatherings of more than three persons for a period of two years; subsequently a number of Cape non-European leaders were similarly tried and sentenced. In 1953, a number of leading Africans were banned from membership in the African National Congress.[139] Few more effective means have been devised for limiting the growth and activities of organizations, at least in public.

Most far-reaching and spectacular of the actions taken under the Suppression of Communism Act were the so-called 'treason trials' which began with the arrest in December, 1956, of over 150 persons, including 100 Africans, 23 Europeans and 29 Indians and Coloured. Among those accused of high treason, sedition and offences under the Riotous Assemblies Act and the Suppression of Communism Act for their participation in the National Liberation Movement of the Congress of the People (see Chapter 14) were Mr. L. B. Lee-Warden, African representative for Cape Western, Dr. Z. K. Matthews, acting Principal at Fort Hare University, which is solely for non-Europeans, Chief Albert Luthuli and P. P. D. Nokwe, President and acting National Secretary of the African National Congress, and Dr. G. M. Naicker, President of the South African Indian Congress. Though the defendants were let out on bail, they were forbidden to attend any gathering other than of a social, religious, educational or recreational nature except that Mr. Lee-Warden was allowed to attend Parliament, and a Methodist minister, Mr. D. C. Thompson, was permitted to preach if the police were given advance copies of his sermons.

Regardless of their outcome, the treason trials have had a powerful impact on South Africa, and particularly on those who have been seeking to develop communication between Europeans and non-Europeans. As Father Trevor Huddleston, long a champion in South Africa of non-European rights, pointed out in a letter to *The Times*, December 10, 1956, the Suppression of Communism Act

> is peculiarly effective as a deterrent to those White South Africans who, liberal in their sympathies, yet dread the consequences of being identified in any way with Communism. It is effective also in silencing those Africans whose terribly limited freedom can vanish immediately they are involved in a police raid.

Few South African Europeans have felt the direct impact of Nationalist legislation. Many non-Nationalists would indignantly repudiate the suggestion that European society in the Union has changed noticeably since 1948. Yet the pressures to conformity are unmistakable to outsiders and to some South Africans themselves.

It would be surprising if this were not the case. Never before in the history of South Africa has so single-minded an administration been in power, or one which represents so intense an Afrikaner nationalism. Hertzog, it must be remembered, not only governed at first in company with the Labour Party, but also had a more limited goal in mind: to develop Afrikanerdom to the point where it could work on equal terms with English-speaking South Africa. Malan and Strijdom nationalism has its own conception of life, rooted in historic Calvinism, shaped in the isolation of the veld, and powered by a sense of special identity and mission. The Nationalists could well feel that they were betraying their trust if they slackened their efforts to shape South Africa to their own pattern.

By and large, non-Nationalist South Africans of European ancestry are occupied too much with their own affairs, occupational and social, to resist, or perhaps even to notice. They have put their stamp on life in the big cities where most of them live relatively isolated either from Nationalist South Africans or from the mass of detribalized non-Europeans about whom the Nationalists are so concerned. They share many of the same general conceptions regarding non-Europeans as do the Nationalists. They are anti-Communist. At only a few places, therefore, as in the Citizenship Act, have they felt directly affronted. In a sense, they provide the vacuum within which Nationalist efforts can have the greater effect. Even when they, or their political representative, the United Party, offer resistance to Nationalist moves, it is commonly on grounds of procedure rather than principle. Thus the process of attrition proceeds.

CHAPTER 3

SPELLING OUT APARTHEID

Far more obvious than the Nationalists' effect on European society is their impact on the non-European. With surprising rapidity, the implications of apartheid have been spelled out in legislation which provides fixed and definite provisions for what had almost always been customary practice. Initially apartheid legislation fell into the category of prohibitive, or negative apartheid, either seeking to reduce the contacts which industrialization and urbanization inevitably induce, or to remove such rights as non-Europeans possessed in European areas. Subsequently more radical measures of positive apartheid were introduced, like the Bantu Authorities Act and the Bantu Education Act, which seek to reinforce, or rather, at this late stage of contact, to re-create separate institutions, attitudes and values.

The group of non-Europeans which has felt the shock of negative apartheid legislation most acutely is the Coloured. This is because their status has been traditionally higher than that of the Bantu, and their relations with Europeans, particularly Afrikaners, closer. For the century or more before the Afrikaner came in contact with the African tribes slowly seeping down from the North and moving westward, the Coloured, or their ancestors, were the only non-Europeans with whom the Afrikaners were associated. When the Afrikaners trekked North to escape the English influence in the Cape, they took their Coloured servants with them. The language of 90 per cent of the Coloured is Afrikaans. But the very closeness of this historic relationship, and the differentness of the status accorded the Cape Coloured made it inevitable that the Nationalists should strike at them first. In a way, it was to affirm their color stand before the world, as one Nationalist put it.

Positive apartheid, on the other hand, is primarily for the Bantu. The Coloured have accepted European standards too completely to establish a distinctive culture amongst them, though the Nationalists would like to give them a separate sense of identity and self-respect.[1] The Indians have an ancient and distinctive culture, but the Nationalists seek only to rid the country of this group or, as this has not proved feasible, to restrict and culturally to ignore them. The Bantu are different, however—great in numbers, all-important as the basic labor force in every sphere of life, and thus in intimate contact with the Europeans throughout the country. For them, negative apartheid is mere legislative affirmation of traditional racial segregation except where it takes the more radical form of ideal or territorial apartheid. Positive apartheid seeks to make the African the separate person which theory declares him to be.

For many Nationalists positive apartheid measures give the Bantu his due, that is, the opportunity to evolve in his own pattern which European contact threatens so drastically to change. Other Nationalists, and some non-Nationalists, see positive apartheid programs as means to control the African in a highly dynamic economic situation by providing him with counter-directives to integration. Still other non-Nationalists believe, however, that positive apartheid, particularly the Bantu Education Act, strikes at the roots of the African's efforts to secure a fruitful return for the labor he contributes to European society by gaining full access to the rich heritage of Western civilization. Along with most non-Nationalist anthropologists, these people recognize that culture contact is already far advanced in South Africa, and believe that it is too late to attempt to reverse it, even if it were desirable to do so.

The United Party has been in a particularly difficult position in regard to most apartheid legislation because its members, for the most part, accept the same frame of reference in dealing with the non-European as do the Nationalists. The United Party's chosen methods for dealing with the non-European are typically conservative ones: to work empirically, adjusting to particular circumstances and laying down as few general principles as possible. The Nationalists, in contrast, are at their most doctrinaire in regard to the non-European. Since the Native problem is the one which evokes the most deeply felt fears among European South Africans, particularly *platteland* and working-class Afrikaners, it also serves best the purposes of propaganda. Thus the United Party has found itself threading its way unhappily between quicksands and mountains, between keeping the Nationalists from making capital out of its reactions to apartheid legislation and responding to the high rectitude of Nationalist theorizing, particularly in the face of the frequently divergent attitudes of its members on apartheid legislation.

The Prohibition of Mixed Marriages Act, 1949[2]

One of the earliest of the Nationalist measures struck at the marriages still taking place infrequently between Europeans and non-Europeans, that is, chiefly, the Coloured. These marriages could still be solemnized in the Cape and Natal, though no machinery for so doing existed in the Transvaal. Between 1943 and 1946, less than 100 mixed marriages a year were consummated in the Union, the figures running 92, 99, 92, and 77 for the respective years.[3] European marriages in 1945 and 1946, in contrast, amounted to 24,071 and 28,308, so the problem was a small if irritating one.

Miscegenation, out of which the Cape Coloured arose originally, has long been socially unacceptable in South Africa. As far back as 1685, Europeans were forbidden by law to marry freed slaves of full color, though marriages with half-breeds were allowed. In 1927, the Hertzog Nationalist-Labour coalition passed an Immorality Act penalizing extra-marital relations between Europeans and Africans. The Prohibition of Mixed Marriages Act, 1949, and an amended Immorality Act passed the following year, extended these provisions to the relations between Europeans and Coloured.

The difficulty here was not just of color, or even of shade. Because the Coloured are a very mixed people, no satisfactory definition has been reached by which to differentiate them. In the Liquor Act of 1927, for example, a Coloured was defined as one who is neither a European, an Asiatic nor a Native. Habitual association with and acceptance as Coloured was subsequently used as a distinguishing feature for the Population Register. The possibility, and indeed the prevalence, of light-skinned Coloured 'passing' as white, coupled with the fact that some of the oldest and most distinguished Afrikaner families in the Cape have some admixture of colored blood, made the issue both sensitive and, to the Nationalists, of pressing importance.

As the parliamentary debate[4] made clear, the Nationalists were not concerned so much with race purity in the biological sense as with strengthening the barriers against increasing infiltration by the Coloured. The special urgency of the problem, they emphasized, arose from the process of industrialization and consequent urbanization which inevitably brought Europeans and non-Europeans into closer contact both in their places of employment and their dwelling areas. The characteristic theme of self-preservation of the European race appears throughout the Nationalist speeches on the bill.

By introducing this particular measure before either the Immorality Amendment Bill or the Population Registration Bill, and also by presenting it in rather loose and careless wording, the Nationalists provided the United Party with an opportunity of which the latter took full advantage. United Party members pounced on the problems of defining a Coloured; the criteria to be used by marriage officers, whom the law made responsible for refusing to solemnize such marriages; the procedure for voiding a marriage; the consequences for the children; and the distasteful use of informants. So penetrating were they that Dr. T. E. Dönges was forced to accept a wide range of clarifications and improvements in the statute. For these the United Party smugly claimed so much credit that C. R. Swart finally countered with the remark that it was 'no disgrace' if the Opposition showed 'some intelligence' and assisted the Government in placing 'something better' in the bill.[5]

The atmosphere in this debate was much friendlier than in most discussions of apartheid measures, and no divisions were called in either the committee or report stages. But these facts hardly conceal the underlying dilemma which the United Party faced over the measure. Smuts had immediately expressed the United Party's opposition to mixed marriages, but strongly stated that this type of 'prohibiting legislation' did not provide 'a practical solution'. On the contrary, the elimination of mixed marriages was a matter for public opinion and race pride, he declared, voicing the typically empirical approach of the United Party to race relations. Others reinforced the point that this was no matter for law as in the comment that:

> This was a contest between the Minister of the Interior and the Creator. He is trying to lay down a definite line where no definite line can be drawn.[6]

A more basic approach to the problem, which several United Party members voiced, would be to eliminate the advantages of 'passing' by improving the status of the Coloured and to strengthen the white strain by immigration (to which a Nationalist backbencher, J. H. Abraham, objected characteristically that the hearts of these immigrants would be corrupted on arrival by the liberals).

Sharp divergencies thus existed, in fact, between the Nationalists and the United Party over whether the measure should be passed at all. In the background lay the contrasting approaches of their respective churches. Dönges declared the three Dutch Reformed Churches had asked for the measure.

Mrs. Ballinger, senior among the Natives' representatives, pointed out, on the other side, that neither the Anglican nor the Roman Catholic Church would recognize the State's right to interfere with the sacrament of marriage. Subsequently, the South African Anglican Synod protested the measure for this reason.[7]

Yet the United Party was not willing to push its dislike of the character of the legislation to the point where it opposed the measure as such. A United Party member accused the Government of deliberately attempting to embarrass his party with the legislation; a Nationalist backbencher, A. Steyn, underlined the point in saying:

> The party over there dare not go to the country and say that because here and there a person is not purely white or coloured, he may stand in the way of the whole people. You cannot do it. It is your duty to side with this party. The people will call you to account.[8]

Moreover, Dönges could point constantly to the example of the United States to justify incorporating such provisions in legislation (e.g., 30 American states with similar laws; 15 with a marriage officer to administer them).

Also, the press gave the United Party little incentive to fight. The *Natal Witness* said the bill was 'realistic', asserting that public opinion was not 'a sufficient safeguard'.[9] The *Natal Daily News* called the measure 'horrible' but did not elaborate.[10] The Convention of Coloured Organizations opposed it as useless. On the whole there was not much interest in the measure.[11]

The limited application of the law did not escape comment. One of the Nationalist experts on color questions, W. A. Maree, was joined by Labour's N. G. Eaton in asking why the provisions of the bill were not extended more widely to ban marriages between the three non-European groups: Africans, Coloured, and Asiatics. Dönges declared this was under consideration, though no action has ensued. In fact, the Mixed Marriages Act falls into the category of European protective legislation. Perhaps even more truly, however, its purpose was expressed by one of the Nationalists, Dr. J. H. Steyn, who felt the measure was neither practical nor necessary, but saw its worth as 'a documentation' of the South African way of life. Practical or not, it was an assertion of the special position of the white race.

Few prosecutions have taken place under the Mixed Marriages Act. No one obviously Coloured would attempt, henceforth, to marry someone obviously European. Most of the cases have come before the courts through informers and commonly the partners have been genuinely unaware that they fell within the purview of the Act.

One of the most talked of mixed marriages in recent times, that of Seretse Khama (titular chief of the Bamangwato tribe of Bechuanaland) to an Englishwoman, took place about the same time as the Mixed Marriages Bill was proceeding through Parliament. The tribe's decision to accept Seretse as chief despite his marriage touched the Protectorate's nearest neighbors, South Africa and Rhodesia, on a sensitive spot. The *Star* commented, on June 27, 1949, that if the British Government approved the tribe's decision, it would scandalize many whites in South Africa, whereas rejection might 'irretrievably' offend the Bantu; its own view, expressed next day, was to leave the situation to itself.[12]

Die Burger and *Die Transvaler* strongly disapproved the marriage, and the Dutch Reformed Church passed a resolution that Seretse should not be recognized as chief.[13] *Die Vaderland* called on the British Government 'to honour the principle of apartheid'.[14]

The British Government's decision, early in 1950, to withhold recognition from Seretse Khama for five years met enthusiastic Nationalist press reactions. *Die Transvaler* declared, on March 10, that Britain had given in to the demands of apartheid and two days earlier had commented with satisfaction that 'the time for expediency in colonial politics had passed'. *Die Vaderland* wondered why the ban was only for five years. *Die Burger* was more basic in its approach, noting that while 99 out of 100 whites in Africa would approve, an equal percentage in Britain would disapprove, indicating the serious gulf over racial problems between the British at home and white settlers in Africa.[15]

Yet the English language press was far from sure that the British decision was wise or justified. The *Cape Argus*, it is true, felt it to be the wisest thing to do in unusual and difficult circumstances. The *Star's* impression of the decision, however, was that it was 'unmitigatedly bad', while the *Cape Times* and *Daily Despatch* could not see any justification for it. The *Friend* declared it might be 'a pyrrhic victory for Dr. Malan', but felt the British would not depart from paths of justice and fair dealing. The *Forum*, a liberal monthly, thought the decision would do much harm to White-Black relations.[16] If South African opinion was a factor in the British decision, it was not that of the Opposition press.

As for the non-Europeans, the one formal protest was that of the South African Indian Congress made directly to Prime Minister Attlee.[17] For the others, the *Bantu World* wrote sadly that the Seretse issue had been 'confused by politics and emotion'.[18]

Amendment to the Immorality Act of 1927, 1950

The companion legislation to the Mixed Marriages Act was the amendment to extend to the Coloured the provisions of the Immorality Act of 1927 (Act No. 5, 1927) or, as its full title read, the Act to prohibit illicit carnal intercourse between Europeans and Natives and other acts in relation thereto. The purpose of the 1950 legislation, in fact, was not to check immorality as such but, as Dr. Dönges expressed it, 'to try to preserve some sort of apartheid in what one may call prostitution';[19] in other words, to prevent further admixture of European and Coloured blood.

The United Party was somewhat handicapped in opposing the amendment to the Immorality Act by the fact that it had agreed to the early measure and that Smuts had said in the debate on the Mixed Marriages Bill that illicit relations between Europeans and Coloured were the real evil. Nonetheless, they reiterated justifiably many of the same arguments they had used in debating the Mixed Marriages Bill, notably the difficulty of differentiating Europeans from Coloured in certain cases. In an amendment which condemned miscegenation but opposed the measure, Colin Steyn, leader of the United Party in the Orange Free State, argued, on March 1, 1950, that white civilization had maintained itself for 300 years without this prohibition, that the evil was on a small scale and the measure unworkable. He declared that the bill cast a slur on the Coloured and would create ill feeling between them and the Europeans.

The United Party was on particularly firm ground when it pointed out that if the bill was to be introduced at all, it should include prohibitions against illicit intercourse between all racial groups. P. A. Botha, Nationalist Secretary in the Cape, agreed that miscegenation between Coloured and Native should also be penalized so that the Coloured might gradually develop a 'sense of nationhood'.[20] Mrs. Ballinger went to the root of that particular problem, however, when she pointed out that prostitution was an inevitable result of African migratory labor, with its disastrous effect on the African family unit. Other points in the legislation which the United Party criticized were placing the onus of proving innocence on the accused, the power the measure gave to the police to enter and search private premises, and punishment by imprisonment rather than fines.

United Party opposition to the measure, in which it was joined tacitly but not actively by the Labour Party, proved unavailing, however, as second reading passed by 66 to 55. Thereafter the measure secured virtual unanimity. The committee stage was remarkable for its harmony, the Minister of the Interior accepting, on March 28, a United Party amendment that it would be sufficient defence if the accused had 'reasonable cause' to believe he was a person of the same race. The report stage passed unopposed, and the third reading without a vote.

Part of the reason for the rapid petering out of the United Party attack was that the Nationalists were not slow to point out inconsistencies in the United Party position as well as to engage in their customary frontal attacks. If the number of instances was small, they asked, how could the enforcement problem be large? If the measure was not necessary, why lighten the penalty? If, as the United Party felt, foreign sailors were to blame in most instances, how could public opinion help to prevent this? S. M. Loubser, a Nationalist backbencher, added in his customary vehement way that others than sailors responsible for miscegenation were the Communist Party, which accepted no line of demarcation between European and non-European, and liberals 'attending dances' and associating 'as equals' with the Coloured. Europeans in South Africa would have to work out their own salvation, he asserted, for world opinion believed in equality.[21]

The Nationalists were not hesitant to accuse the United Party of favoring the Coloured to gain their votes.[22] Another argument[23] was that under the influence of its liberals the United Party was no longer the champion of 'pure blood' and was prepared to let things slide until the white race perished. F. W. Waring, in reply, charged that the measure was a cheap political stunt so the Nationalists could go to the *platteland* and say the United Party favored miscegenation. In fact, as on so many other occasions, the United Party was outmaneuvered, partly because it had no answer to the problem of miscegenation except educating public opinion, partly because the Nationalists exploited so well their advantage in having a more clear-cut, simpler but not necessarily more valid approach to the problem.

A few prosecutions have taken place under the amendment to the Immorality Act, notably in instances where European and Coloured, though not married, have been living together over a period of time. In these instances, the family was broken up, and the customary penalty of three months in jail imposed. Whether the result justified the personal hardships involved depends upon the point of view. It has, moreover, been noted in Parliament and the press that, under the present act, Coloured or African females have been found guilty and sentenced, while their European male partners have, in a separate trial, been acquitted.

The Population Registration Act, 1950

The logical corollary to the Mixed Marriages Act and Amendment to the Immorality Act is the Population Registration Act, under which everyone in the Union is ultimately to have an identity certificate showing whether he is white, Native or Coloured. Logical though it might be, however, the United Party thoroughly disliked the legislation, in particular the idea that Europeans would have to carry the equivalent of a 'pass', long associated with the controlled movements of male Bantu outside the Reserves.

The Act provides that the Director of the Census is to compile a national register, based on the census of 1951, in which everyone is classified according to race. If anyone wishes to object to his own or anyone else's classification, he may do so on payment of £10, to be forfeited if the complaint is 'vexatious or unfounded'. The objection is heard by a board of three appointed by the Minister of the Interior; a further appeal to the Appeal Court is possible, but this is, of course, expensive and entails publicity.

The definitions of the Act illustrate the degree to which customary associations and community acceptance are decisive rather than color as such. A white person is one who is 'obviously white in appearance', or 'by general repute and acceptance'. But a person who is Coloured by general repute is ranked as such even if he is white in appearance.

The idea of a South African national register was not new. In 1935, a parliamentary Select Committee found the project impracticable, too costly and of little value unless it covered the whole population, including the 3 to 4 million African women and children in the Reserves for whom there are no vital statistics. The committee also opposed such a register on the ground that personal liberty should not be curtailed without important reasons.

Even before the Population Registration Bill was introduced, Dr. Malan had been quoted in *Die Burger*, on February 21, 1950, as saying that 'a national register is the basis of the whole policy of apartheid'. At second reading, Dönges stressed the practical administrative advantages of the measure for controlling illegal immigration, crime, or tax evasion, but made clear that the main purpose of securing 'the life story of every individual' was to create the machinery 'necessary to enforce social apartheid'. In an unusual understatement, Dönges declared that:

> We cannot expect any government to enforce the existing laws, which provide for a certain amount of discrimination, if we withhold the machinery necessary for the application of that form of discrimination.[24]

General Smuts immediately moved to refer the Bill to a Select Committee, charging that it gave expression to the policy of apartheid rather than providing for a national register. He pictured a white mistress with her identity card while her African maid had none. (Only African males carry passes and Dönges initially excluded women and children under 18.) More importantly, he pointed out the likelihood of friction and evasion and the unreliability of the register.

> I think all this probing into private affairs [he said], this listening to informers, this effort to classify what is unclassifiable, what is impossible to achieve, will create a situation which will hit this country hard in years to come.[25]

The stage had been set, and the debate proceeded along lines that could hardly be called fundamental. The United Party and Labour Party voiced grave suspicions that the Government's purpose in establishing the register was more sinister than appeared on the surface. 'Can we trust them to resist the temptation to use the pernicious machinery which they are creating under this bill?' asked a United Party backbencher.[26] Leo Lovell, of the Labour Party, charged that the bill's real purpose was to extend the Government's political control to Europeans since he could not see that it would aid apartheid: '. . . the Minister of the Interior's register will only be a duplicate of the good Lord's register.' Even if it was what it appeared, why subject white people to the shame of being treated like Natives? asked R. J. du Toit. De Villiers Graaff called the register 'a human stud book', and P. B. Bekker warned that white civilization could not be perpetuated by legislation, and that undue haste in setting limits created gulfs not goodwill. During third reading, a United Party member told the Nationalists that 'if this bill had been passed forty years ago many would be Coloured who are white today. Can you fix for all time a particular section in a particular group?' Most vehement was Dr. B. Friedman, who declared bitterly that

> . . . the epoch of the witch hunt is upon us. The search for the taint in the blood has become a major political preoccupation in this country.[27] . . . In the end, in order to avoid infinite trouble and vexation, it will be far more convenient to have some distinguishing mark tattooed on your forehead like some oriental caste. . . .[28]

The Nationalists picked up the United Party arguments with zest. J. J. Fouche told Smuts that if he found it impossible to draw a line of demarcation between European and non-European 'then we have lost or abandoned the struggle to maintain a white race in this country'.[29] Others charged that the United Party opposition was because it realized that the register was the foundation stone of apartheid. 'They are not sons of South Africa, and they do not want to be,' declared Colonel J. L. B. Döhne, 'they want doubts to exist as far as one's identity is concerned.'[30] Another Nationalist welcomed the idea of classifying human beings like animals, and cited the Old Testament injunction regarding distinguishing marks and not mingling with other races. It was, in sum, one of the least edifying of apartheid debates.

In an apparent effort to be conciliatory, Dönges referred the measure to a Select Committee after the Nationalists forced through second reading. The major change in the bill was its extension to everyone in the country (for which the United Party took great credit) though the Minister retained powers to exclude certain groups until it was administratively feasible to include them. Once the measure came into the committee of the whole house, however, a vast number of amendments were introduced (44 on the first 7 clauses) and frequent divisions called. In retaliation, the Government called for closures after shorter and shorter periods, until feelings were running high and charges were thrown around indiscriminately. Votes were close, and at one point the Government was defeated and had to recommit the measure and take another vote. The United Party rejected Dönges' distinction between a pass and an identity card, which he based chiefly on the ground that a pass must always be carried and an identity card could be produced later, and declared that 'we intend to fight this pass issue to the last ditch'.[31] One constructive proposal by J. G. N. Strauss was to repeal all existing passes and replace them with identity cards with photos or finger-prints. In practice, the multiplicity of Native passes was unified in a single document in 1953.

The United Party maintained its opposition to the end, Strauss opposing the third reading of the bill on the ground that the measure placed irritating and unnecessary burdens on South Africans, and opened the door to prying. Major P. V. C. van der Byl, former Minister of Native Affairs, warned it might increase the resentment of the Coloured, and that 'we may soon find ourselves living in a hostile camp . . . We cannot keep elemental emotions, once roused, permanently down by guns'. The comment seemed less called for by this measure than by others, but it was not without truth.

The English-speaking press provided less comment on the Population Registration bill than might have been expected. As early as January 20, 1950, the *Star* had suggested it might be the most controversial measure yet introduced, and quoted Senator Brookes, one of the Native representatives, as saying it would create a caste system.[32] The *Cape Argus* felt it might not be practicable in South Africa and the *Friend* wondered openly what the Government's intention was. When details became known, the *Star* and the *Rand Daily Mail* saw the measure as emphasizing 'the obsession with race',[33] and the *Cape Argus* as reflecting the trend of the Government towards more, rather than fewer passes.[34] The *Natal Witness* and *Mercury* displayed the greatest dislike of the measure, the former feeling that it reflected the 'appetite for more power' and provided 'one more interference with the negative freedom of the individual', while the latter found 'something abhorrent' about a 'compulsory "pass system"' and 'arbitrarily dividing the public into three distinct cells'.[35] The *Cape Times* ran two articles by Leo Marquard which declared that the bill was one of 'the most sinister pieces of legislation' yet introduced.[36] In the end, the *Star* summed up its reactions by pointing out that the Nationalists were often inconsistent and contradictory in their tactics, but yet had 'a dreadful and unnatural consistency in their ultimate aims'.[37]

The Afrikaans press was still less vocal on the subject. *Dagbreek* urged that the bill be treated on its merits[38] and *Die Transvaler*, backed by *Die Burger*, said indignantly that the provisions were not as bad as the United Party made out, since the card would not list political affiliations or, in effect, be a pass.[39] *Die Vaderland* felt the measure would end duplication of work, and *Die Volksblad* endorsed its 'clear dividing line between white and non-white'.[40] Late in the year, *Die Transvaler* quoted with satisfaction Minister of Education Viljoen's statement that the Population Registration Act was a step towards making the country safe.[41]

The Nationalist position, both in the debate and in the press, was characteristic of the party's belief in defined categories and a permanent settlement. The distinction which the United Party made between a population register in time of emergency (such as the Nationalists so often cited as a precedent) and the type the Nationalists were instituting made little sense of the latter. Nor did the abhorrence or suspicion with which some people greeted the whole conception. From the Nationalist point of view, it was a neat and tidy way of arranging an otherwise complicated and confused situation. If certain hardships were involved in the process,[42] that seemed to them a small price to pay for certainty, even if, as seemed likely, that certainty would take years to achieve.

The Group Areas Act, 1950[43]

The Group Areas Act is a still more striking example than the Population Registration Act of the Nationalist belief in categories. In many ways the most far reaching, and certainly the most complicated legislation instituted by the Nationalists, the Group Areas Act, according to Dr. Malan, is 'the kernel of the apartheid policy' and 'the most crucial for determining the future of race relations'. Dönges called it 'the cornerstone' of positive apartheid, though it bids fair to remove a great many people's rights before it provides any. In the meantime, during the long and arduous process of implementation, the Group Areas Act complicates land transfers throughout most of the Union.

The Group Areas Act builds on a long succession of segregation measures which have chiefly affected Africans and Indians. In each of the four areas which subsequently comprised the Union of South Africa, separate lands, or Reserves, were set aside for the Bantu during the nineteenth century; these were formally scheduled in the Natives' Land Act of 1913,[44] which froze the existing allocation of land between the Bantu and others. Recognizing the inadequacy of land available for the Africans, the Native Trust and Land Act of 1936,[45] which was part of Hertzog's general settlement of that year, provided that additional land could be acquired for the Native Reserves to bring them up to 13 per cent of the Union's total area. This goal has not yet been achieved because of the difficulties of persuading Europeans to sell land for this purpose.

Outside the Reserves, Africans are closely controlled in their movements and living places. Male Africans need passes from the Native Commissioner to leave the Reserves, and further passes to be in urban areas, and the Native (Urban Areas) Act of 1923[46] established Native locations and villages outside European residential centers as the only places where Africans can live, apart from hostels for single men or women, or the facilities for Native servants. A 1937 amendment to this Act virtually debarred Africans from buying property from non-Africans in cities or townships. In fact, there is relatively little land owned outright by Africans anywhere in the Union. Another amendment in 1949 placed further restrictions on Africans entering and living in European urban areas.

A still closer parallel to the Group Areas Act was provided by the long series of measures restricting Indians in the Transvaal and Natal in varying degrees in regard to property rights, occupancy and trading. (The apex of restrictions on Indians is the complete prohibition of their presence in the Orange Free State, which was enacted in 1891.) Increasing Indian penetration of European residential areas in Durban led to the temporary Natal Pegging Act of 1943 and, in an effort to produce a final settlement, to the controversial Asiatic Land Tenure and Indian Representation Act of 1946.[47] In 1949 the Nationalists repealed its provisions for the limited communal representation of Indians in the Natal Provincial Council and House of Assembly, which, in any case, the Indians had rejected and which had never been brought into operation. Under the Land Tenure section of the Act, which remained operative, areas could be divided between exempted and unexempted; in the latter no Asiatic could buy or occupy fixed property without a permit from the Minister of the Interior, who was assisted by a Land Tenure Advisory Board, two members of which could be Indian.

The objective of the Group Areas Act[48] is to extend the principle of residential segregation to its ultimate conclusions. For this purpose, it divides the inhabitants of South Africa into the familiar three categories of white, Native and Coloured. The white group includes those 'obviously' or 'generally accepted' as such, but not a white woman married to, or cohabiting with, a Native or Coloured person. The Native group similarly includes any person 'who in fact is, or is generally accepted as a member of an aboriginal race or tribe of Africa' and any woman married to or cohabiting with such a person. The Coloured take in the rest, including any woman married to, or cohabiting with, a Coloured person. The Group Areas Act, however, also makes it possible further to subdivide the category of Coloured into any 'ethnical, linguistic, cultural or other group of persons'. Three such groups were created on March 30, 1951: The Indian, Malay and Chinese groups. The first and last are defined as persons in the Cape, Natal and Transvaal who are or are generally accepted as being members of a race or tribe 'whose national home' is in India or Pakistan, or in China. The Malays are members of the 'race or class known as Cape Malays', but only those in specified districts in the Cape and Transvaal exist as far as the act is concerned. Thus the criteria for subdivision is numbers; where these are small, their members are lumped together with the general Coloured group.

The ultimate goal is to restrict each defined group to its own particular area as far as ownership, occupancy and trading are concerned. When this has been carried through, at least it will make a neat pattern on paper, even if it is not easy to keep human beings in watertight residential compartments. In the process of achieving this goal, however, the Union includes a bewildering maze of different categories, each with its own particular rules or restrictions.

Four categories may be distinguished on the way to what may be termed a 'full' group area, that is one in which ownership, occupancy and acquisition of land and premises are virtually restricted to a single enumerated group. (An enumerated group refers both to individuals and to companies controlled by particular racial groups, except big mining or industrial concerns.) The differences between these categories are intended to fit them to varying circumstances. A controlled area is one in which immovable property cannot be sold or, with certain exceptions, leased without a permit to a person who is not of the same ethnic group as the owner. In a specified area, the basis of control is present occupancy rather than ownership. The Transvaal and Natal were both proclaimed controlled and specified areas on March 30, 1951. A major result was to peg Indian occupancy as it then existed by eliminating the exempted areas under the 1946 act. The Cape was made simultaneously a controlled and, for two years, an 'open' area, that is, one in which occupation of land and premises were free from permit control during that period.

The other two categories are not concerned with restricting ownership or occupancy to the existing group but with moving toward the ultimate goal of residential 'purity'. In a defined area, the Minister specifies the group for which the area is reserved. In a group area for occupation, the latter is limited to the specified group, but there is one year of grace for someone from another group, and property may also be owned by someone of another group. In a group area for ownership, there are the same restrictions on occupancy as in controlled or specified areas, and it is impossible for a disqualified person or company, for whom that particular group area is not intended, to acquire property. Moreover, a company must dispose of any immovable property it possesses in that area within ten years, while a person retains only a life interest in anything immovable which he owns there. In all cases, exceptions are possible only by permit.

In making his decisions about group areas, the Minister draws on the advice of the Land Tenure Advisory Board, whose seven members were appointed by him on September 29, 1950. They do not have a fixed term, nor is there provision that the members of the board shall be representative of different racial groups. The Board hears testimony from all sides, and is supposed to take into account the availability of alternative accommodation, though without any obligation to provide it. After July 7, 1955, the establishment of group areas requires parliamentary approval; up until then it could be done by executive act.

The most bitter feeling in the debate over the Group Areas Act arose from the Prime Minister's motion to impose the guillotine from the very start of discussion.[49] Charging that it was a 'dictatorial curtailment' of the rights of the people and Parliament to bring up contentious detailed legislation at the end of the session and thrust it through in this fashion, Strauss laid the responsibility at the door of the 'relentless driving force' behind Dr. Malan, 'the cold, aloof and sinister' Dr. Dönges. He asked for consultation and an agreed measure. Major Piet van der Byl felt it was essential to investigate the problem carefully before proceeding with legislation, and the United Party justifiably made much of this point in the succeeding debates. Others warned that the measure would be imposed on provincial and municipal authorities. Despite Opposition protests, however, the guillotine was instituted for all stages, while Dr. J. H. Steyn did not improve the atmosphere by saying airily, 'It's all in the political game'.

The Nationalists maintained that the Group Areas bill was necessary both to maintain white paramountcy, and to give other races a chance for their own development. Dönges felt that residential segregation would eliminate friction between the races, and that it was endorsed by 'a public opinion which is nurtured by the instinct for survival'. At the same time, he said that:

> there is no reason why the majority of the services in particular areas should not be conducted for certain groups by members of that particular group.[50]

Recognizing the difficulties inherent in the measure, he declared:

> It is the price we have to pay in order to achieve certainty as to the future environment of our homes and places of business. It is the sacrifice we will have to make in order to bring about conditions most favourable for inter-racial harmony.

Dönges' supporters were more concerned with stressing white paramountcy and the insidious effects of racial contact. J. E. Potgieter called mixed residential areas 'deathbeds of the European race', and D. C. H. Uys said they led to 'loss of colour sense'. Firmest on this point was Dr. Malan, who declared that education and civilization for the non-European narrowed 'the natural gulf' to the European and made it more difficult in mixed communities 'for the white man to maintain himself as white'. Others called for an end to the 'barren aping of the white man that is replacing the Natives' spiritual life', and charged that the United Party would turn the Coloured into 'imitation Europeans'.

From the Opposition side, the United Party was insistent on its dedication to the principle of residential and social segregation. But such a 'massive, ill-digested bill with tremendous implications' should have a public inquiry, said Strauss in moving his amendment to second reading, for it grossly interfered with vested rights, threatened South Africa's model system of land registry, lacked adequate protection for individuals and local authorities, and provided serious inroads on the rule of law and the power of Parliament. Both Strauss and D. E. Mitchell stressed the problem that no compensation was provided under the bill. The Labour Party presented a still stronger amendment, providing for alternative housing and financial compensation, which the United Party later virtually adopted as its own. In general, the United Party approved the principle of voluntary segregation, at least for the Coloured, but it was constantly in difficulties with its own Natal members who were more outspokenly antagonistic to Indian penetration than even the Nationalists.

Dr. D. L. Smit, former Secretary for Native Affairs, was one of the few to point out how much the bill would work to the advantage of Europeans, since they already owned most of the land and would be freed from competition in continuing to do so. Mrs. Ballinger was still more emphatic that there was no such thing as equal sacrifices (as Dönges had suggested) in compulsory segregation.

> We find it terribly difficult in this country, where only white people sit in Parliament, and where practically only the white man has the vote, to implement the other side of the bargain [she pointed out].[51] The people who were prepared to take away the property rights of the African people have never been prepared to implement the meagre promise of what should be the territorial foundation of their policy.[52]

Although second reading was forced through by the close vote of 69 to 61, the ensuing committee stage was marked by a friendly atmosphere, with the Opposition and the Minister vying with each other in proposing the larger number of amendments. The United Party was particularly proud of an amendment (which they seem to have stumbled on almost by chance) which prevented the Minister from declaring European farms Native territory without permission of Parliament. Its proposer, Bailey Bekker (later a 'rebel',—see p. 293), claimed it proved that the United Party defended rural interests better than the Nationalists. The United Party also took credit for extending the 'privilege of consultation' to local authorities (though this went less far than they desired), reassuring the certainty of land registrations, protecting occupancy rights in Durban until group areas were established and slowing down the implementation of the measure. Natal United Party members tightened certain provisions of the bill, especially referring to visitors, to such an extent that Arthur Barlow (another of the 'rebels') exclaimed in exasperation that:

> The extraordinary thing about our hon. friends from Natal, or some of them, is that they cannot be fair when Indians are discussed.[53]

In all, more than sixty amendments were proposed during Committee stage, and 28 out of 39 clauses amended, many of them through proposals by the Minister himself. The improved parliamentary atmosphere was reflected in the relatively few divisions.

The United Party opposed third reading, however, until 'a commission presided over by a Supreme Court judge' reported on the necessity and practicability of the bill, its financial implications, particularly in regard to vested rights and how they could be compensated, and the provision of alternative accommodation. Strauss also noted that the bill had led India to reject the plans for a round table conference with South Africa. (See p. 397.)

But the Nationalists were adamant. In one of his rare speeches, J. G. Strijdom, subsequently Prime Minister, declared the measure was necessary 'to end friction and its source in contact'; otherwise, he foresaw 'a bloodbath'. It was important to him, too, for maintaining the 'colour sense which is the basis of the purity of the race'. He could not believe that there could be apartheid in one sphere and not in others. Accusing the United Party of being 'actually' in favor of 'mixed social life', he appealed to 'dissidents' in the party 'to speak up and serve South Africa'. Dr. Malan added that United Party opposition was rooted only in their desire to keep the Coloured vote. He declared that:

> Nothing is more desirable than that the European sections of the population should understand each other and cooperate with each other, but they can only cooperate if they think alike on the country's great questions and if they stand together.[54]

Closing the debate, Dönges again struck the note of positive as well as negative apartheid. If further inquiry were necessary, why had the United Party not instituted it after the war?

> They have simply allowed things to develop. They know in their hearts that the non-Europeans will never have a proper chance in a multi-racial society to develop fully unless we have either absolute equality with racial admixture or apartheid . . . we do not believe that the future of South Africa will be that of a mixed population, and this . . . is one of the major measures designed to preserve white South Africa, while at the same time giving justice and fair play to the non-Europeans in this country.[55]

The differences in approach between the Nationalists and the United Party had been obvious—they were not over principle but over methods. The United Party had a 'Royal Commission approach', that there should be careful study of complicated situations by an impartial examining body. It stressed this approach the more because it foresaw that the measure might interfere with the rights of property, vested interests, and the stability of the economy, which it cherished greatly. The Labour Party showed a more forthright humanitarianism, especially regarding compensation and alternative accommodation. The Nationalists were not averse to considering these factors, but ranked them low in comparison with protecting the white population from residential contact with non-Europeans. One Nationalist pointed out justifiably that the most liberal of United Party members lived in the most segregated areas. Afrikaner working-class districts, in contrast, are almost invariably the closest to Native locations. What is surprising, however, is that the Nationalists should have based so much of their argument for segregation on the fear that contact would lead to a loss of color sense.

The United Party does not plan to repeal but only to amend the Group Areas Act if it returns to office. Its proposed changes include offering suitable alternative accommodation before eviction; compensation for loss[55a] (which it foresees to be particularly serious if a European is forced to sell to a non-European); limiting the Minister's powers to essential matters; use of voluntary agreement as far as possible in establishing separate residential areas and, in any case, no use of compulsory powers without full and adequate inquiry, if necessary by a Judicial Commission; annual reports by the Land Tenure Board to Parliament; and restrictions on the right of inspectors to enter private premises. In its customary way, the United Party also assured the public that it would implement the act in a spirit of good-will and justice towards all.

The English-language press, extra-party groups and particularly the non-Europeans were more deeply concerned about the measure. The *Cape Times, Star*, the *Natal Mercury* and the *Rand Daily Mail* stressed the immense concentration of power the bill placed in executive hands.[56] The latter declared on May 31 that it would introduce 'a caste system', and exacerbate racial feelings.[57] The *Star* labelled it on September 13, 1950, 'a mean measure of naked economic discrimination'. In the meantime, the Institute of Race Relations had pointed out that the measure provided no guarantee that overcrowding would not be intensified,[58] and the Christian Council of South Africa urged postponement until consultation could be held with representatives of all racial groups. Subsequently the Methodist Church warned that the act contained possibilities of injustice and hardship.[59]

The most vehement protests came from the non-Europeans, in particular the Indians. On April 28, 1950, *Indian Opinion* wrote that the measure spelled 'economic ruin for the whole Indian community',[60] and on May 19 that it revived 'the ghetto system' for non-whites, and was being put into effect 'without the smallest regard for the feelings or natural rights of the voiceless, non-white majority'.[61] In the face of the emergency, the two rival Indian groups, the South African Indian Congress and the Indian National Organization, united in appealing to the Government, and also to India. Africans, Indians, and Coloured joined together in a rally of protest in Durban on May 29.[62] The African People's Organization reported that the Coloured as a whole were decisively against what they termed a 'venomous' bill,[63] though later a Coloured organization in the Transvaal was said to ask for residential segregation.[64] A general day of non-European protest on June 26 was reported a '95 per cent flop' except in Durban and Port Elizabeth, but the *Star* pointed out that this was a matter for 'thankfulness, not for complacency' and that the real grievances of the non-Europeans remained.[65]

India's official opposition to the Bill met diverse reactions. *Die Transvaler* found its position 'indefensible',[66] but the *Star* termed it 'not unnatural', while the *Cape Times* felt it was the 'inevitable and regrettable results of the Government's maladroit handling'.[67] With no results from its protests, India soon transferred the issue to the United Nations.

While Indians and Coloured remained apprehensive of the impact of the Group Areas Act and occasionally felt its sting, major attention between 1951 and 1954 focused on the Government's concern to remove 'black spots', that is, Native areas within European urban centers. The particular black spot which caused them most concern was known as the 'Western Areas', the three Native townships of Sophiatown, Martindale and Newclare of Johannesburg, which adjoined the European townships of Newlands, Westdene and other suburbs. Among the oldest areas for non-European settlement, having been established between 1905 and 1912, the Western Areas were the only ones in Johannesburg in which Africans could possess land in freehold tenure. Many of its properties were in slum condition but, particularly in Sophiatown, there were also well built houses, schools, long established missions, movies, shops, and the only swimming pool for African children in Johannesburg.

As European living centers stretched out to abut on these Native townships, the pressure for moving the Africans became greater. Yielding to agitation beginning as early as 1939, the Johannesburg City Council passed a resolution in October, 1944, approving a scheme to remove the Africans from the Western Areas to a place adjoining the Native township of Orlando, some eight miles farther outside the city. Nothing further was done, however, until the Nationalist Government officially approached the City Council on the plan in October, 1949; five months later, it was agreed to survey the whole area, as the Orlando site was no longer feasible.

In April, 1951, Dr. H. F. Verwoerd, Minister of Native Affairs, announced forcibly that the black spots in Johannesburg must be moved.[68] The *Bantu World* declared outspokenly that it was an 'iniquitous scheme',[69] and an African Anti-Expropriation Ratepayers' Association and Proper Housing Movement was formed in protest under the leadership of Dr. B. A. Xuma, a distinguished African physician and former President of the African National Congress.[70] Though the *Rand Daily Mail* found the scheme 'impracticable', the Johannesburg City Council agreed in October to accept the responsibility for removing the black spots if the Government would meet the expense. Dr. Ellen Hellmann, of the Institute of Race Relations, opposed the move as 'calamitous on moral, humanitarian and financial grounds', while Father Trevor Huddleston of the Community of the Resurrection (Anglican), warned it would create 'tremendous unrest'.[71] In contrast, *Die Transvaler* welcomed the decision as a Government victory and *Die Vaderland* urged speedy action.[72]

The City Council's plan was to build new townships at Meadowlands, eleven miles from Johannesburg, with the central Government meeting the costs. An *ad hoc* committee recommended declaring the Western Areas a Group area for Native ownership, but European occupancy, with the idea that the Native owners would be forced to sell to the municipality. When the Council adopted the removal scheme in principle it asked for adequate compensation to the dispossessed owners and favored freehold in the new townships. But by selling Meadowlands to the Government in February, 1953, the Council transferred full control to the Government, which was known to be sharply opposed to freehold rights for Africans.

In the Senate, on July 21, 1953,[73] Dr. Verwoerd pointed out persuasively that more land and better facilities would be provided in Meadowlands than existed in the three Native townships. Africans would be able to buy houses there at cost price, or rent or build their own. As a 'basic principle', however, there would be 'no ownership of ground'.

The opponents of the scheme did not deny the need for slum clearance. They took their stand on the fact that there were many good houses in the townships in which their owners, or their families, had lived for upwards of half a century; that the Africans cherished their freehold rights, not only for themselves, but also as a symbol that their people could possess such rights; and that there were worse areas among the shanty towns which should be dealt with first. Above all, African and European opposition centered on the compulsion behind the scheme.[74]

The Government ultimately decided not to use the Group Areas Act for the Western Areas Removal Scheme; instead it introduced new legislation, the Natives' Resettlement Act, published March, 1954, which was not dependent on the cooperation of the local authorities. Under this act the Government accepted responsibility for compensating property owners at purchase price, plus 6 per cent per annum. No compensation was offered, however, for loss of freehold, amenities, or trade.

The Johannesburg City Council opposed the measure, but only because the conditions for removal included grouping the Africans in seven language communities.[75] The Witwatersrand United Party divided sharply over the plan.[76] It could be 'a watershed' in Native policy, wrote the *Star*,[77] while the *Natal Daily News* felt it was 'a test case' on United Party principles of Native urbanization.[78] When the Anglican and Methodist churches protested, Dr. Verwoerd accused the former of doing so because it had 'a vested interest' in the townships, a statement which the Archbishop of Cape Town called 'despicable'. Protest meetings continued but to no avail. In the spring of 1955, the Western Areas Removal Scheme was begun.

Dr. Verwoerd always spoke of the Scheme as 'a pilot project'; during 1956, the Government moved closer towards implementing residential segregation throughout the Union by the Group Areas Act. Group areas in Johannesburg were proclaimed in August, 1956, leading to a storm of protest that they would displace over 100,000 non-Europeans in its western suburbs. Most bitter were the Indians to whom was allocated the township of Lenasia, twenty miles from the city, a move which seemed clearly designed to turn them from a trading to a self-sufficient community. Preliminary inquiries by the Group Areas Committee in Cape Town disclosed still more complicated racial intermixture than in Johannesburg. The Government moves on with its plans for re-designing residential areas into a neat patchwork quilt, but at what a cost!

Bantu Authorities' Act, 1951[79]

Among apartheid measures, the Bantu Authorities' Act assumes special significance as a declaration of intention to reinforce or, perhaps more accurately, to re-establish the authority of the chiefs. The act abolished the already inoperative Natives' Representative Council (see p. 357), a typically Western type of advisory machinery, which had been set up by the Representation of Natives' Act of 1936. At the same time, the Act made provision for a series of local authorities which rested on tribal distinctions. By thus endorsing the traditional basis of authority within the reserves, the Nationalists could argue that they were taking an important step forward toward the kind of positive apartheid which seeks to provide a distinctive type of society for the Bantu.

The new pattern of local administration under the act has at its base a tribal council (consisting of the chief of the tribe and his advisers), which is to administer local affairs of general interest. Above this is a regional council, consisting of representatives appointed or elected by the tribal councils, which has certain limited executive functions in regard to schools, soil conservation, control of stock diseases, afforestation, hospitals, roads, and other matters designated by the Governor-General. It acts also in an advisory capacity, with authority to make representations to the Minister of Native Affairs on questions of general interest. Above this again is to be a territorial council, whose members are similarly chosen from the regional councils of each territory, with powers like those of the regional councils but somewhat wider. On both the regional and territorial councils representatives of the Minister will act in an advisory capacity, and the whole system is to operate (as has always been the case with Native administration in the Union) under the supervision of the Department of Native Affairs.

This new organization, said the Minister of Native Affairs, Dr. Verwoerd, in introducing the second reading of the Bill,[80] was to provide for local self-government in the Reserves when the Bantu themselves wished to make the change from their present system of local councils and, in the Transkei and Ciskei Reserves, of General Councils. It was thus permissive, not obligatory. The Government clearly favored the new system, however, and the Minister spoke of it as 'a restoration of the natural Native democracy'.[81] He declared that:

> The fundamental idea throughout is Bantu control over Bantu areas as and when it becomes possible for them to exercise that control efficiently and properly for the benefit of their own people.[82]

Until then, European assistance through supervision and advice would, of course, be needed. To provide for a Union-wide authority would anticipate too far, but when the Bantu were ready, he declared, they could decide this question for themselves.

To the principle of the three Native authorities provided in the measure, the United Party did not take exception. But Major Piet van der Byl, Minister of Native Affairs under General Smuts, objected to the emphasis on tribal affiliation without regard to 'the growing needs of the vast number of Natives' outside the Native Reserves.

If the more advanced Natives are not given a legal forum where they can express their political views [he declared] (and the important factor is that their political views should be brought to the notice of the Government), we would be living in a fools' paradise.[83]

The United Party thus pointed out the illusion of looking on the Reserves as being separate from the large number of Africans found at any given time outside their boundaries, the more so because the latter necessarily included the most articulate and active among the Bantu. Along this line, then, the United Party urged that there should be a Union-wide authority over both tribalized and non-tribalized Africans. Acknowledging that the Native Representative Council had not been a success, Major van der Byl yet saw dangers in trying

to separate the Natives into small racial or ethnic groups and to prevent them from grouping on a national or natural basis.

Nationalist supporters fought bitterly, however, against this United Party proposal for giving the Africans an opportunity to identify themselves with 'the national interests of the country'.[84] They charged that to give Africans 'their own council in our national life' would be 'definitely one of the most dangerous things we can do'.[85]

Though the Minister spoke of other similar legislation for the Native townships to replace the Native Advisory Boards (see p. 366) this has not yet been brought into being. One of the prime objects of the act seems to have been, in fact, to separate the tribalized from non-tribalized Africans.

The most penetrating attack on the new legislation was by Mrs. Ballinger. Why advocate industry for the Reserves and scientific methods for Native agriculture, she asked, and control them by tribal organization? Moreover, was this new system not a strange hybrid, for regional and territorial authorities were never known in tribal society.

As so often, the United Party was in somewhat of a dilemma over this legislation. It favored building up tribal authority but was afraid it was too late. Unlike Mrs. Ballinger, however, it gave no particular support to the existing General Council systems, though this would have fitted its customary concern for established institutions. The United Party's major objections were summarized by Dr. D. L. Smit at third reading. There had been no consultations with the Africans on this new set-up and thus it lacked prior support from the people it would most deeply concern; it failed to provide for the educated and detribalized Africans; the Natives' Representative Council was being abolished without any replacement; and the bill gave the Minister unlimited right to delegate his authority to members of the Native Affairs' Commission. Once again, it was a negative criticism with nothing concrete to offer as an alternative.

Not until June, 1953, were the first three Bantu Authorities established under this act. These were introduced in the Transvaal, which had eight Councils, all of them established relatively recently and organized largely on a tribal basis both because their people have been in contact with Europeans for a shorter time than have the Africans in the Cape, and because their Reserves are smaller and more scattered.[86] The greatest triumph for the new system came in April,

1955, when the Transkeian Territories General Council, commonly known as the Bunga, unanimously accepted the principle of the Bantu Authorities' Act and established a committee to consider how best to integrate the Council system with the arrangements established under that act.

What this means is apparent when the system provided under the Bantu Authorities' Act is compared with the Council and General Council system as they had developed over the previous sixty years. The Glen Grey Act of 1894 established a District Council for its area which became a pattern for the Council system. In the Transkei, there were twenty-six District Councils, each of which supervised the laying and repairing of roads in its area, the construction of dipping-tanks to free cattle and sheep from ticks, general agricultural improvement, afforestation and public health. Each District Council consisted of the European magistrate for that district, and six Native Councillors. Two of the latter were appointed by the Government, and the other four were elected by the inhabitants, except in Pondoland, where the chiefs nominated two Councillors. Commonly, the magistrates took very much the lead both in discussions and in formulating decisions.

To the Transkeian General Council, known as the Bunga, each district sent three Councillors, one appointed by the Government and the other two nominated by the District Council. Four chiefs were also members: Those of Tembuland, Eastern and Western Pondoland, and of the Galeka. The annual meeting of the Bunga at Umtata, in the center of the Transkei, could discuss any matter affecting the Bantu, and the level of debate was high. Education, agriculture, roads, Native laws and customs, forests, and common grazing grounds were ordinarily considered. Moreover, the Bunga voted all the money needed for work throughout the Transkei, having at its disposal some £185,000 to £200,000 a year, collected through a 10 shilling hut tax, and quitrents from its districts.

If Bunga resolutions referred to a general matter, they were sent to the Government; if they affected the Transkei alone, they were acted on by the General Council's Executive Committee, established in 1932. This body not only carried resolutions into effect, but also administered the Bunga's affairs by supervising the work of the District Councils.

At every level, this system worked under the guidance, or more accurately, the direction of European officials. The Chief Magistrate of the Transkei was the Chairman of the Bunga, and the twenty-six district magistrates were members. The Executive Committee consisted of the Chief Magistrate, three other magistrates whom he selected, and four African members elected by the Council. Nonetheless, over the years, there had been a freer selection of the non-appointed members of the Bunga, and a more outspoken concern with matters of general interest to Africans at large. While the General Council system was far from being true self-government, it provided Africans with experience of local administration, and acted as a useful link between the Government and the people of the Transkei.[87]

The new system provided under the Bantu Authorities' Act is a more tribally-oriented one, and also rests largely on a structure of appointed African officials. Though certain families customarily provide tribal chiefs, the latter are officially appointed by the Government and receive a small salary plus the privilege of collecting certain customary dues in return for carrying out their duties. Under modern circumstances, in fact, the position of the chief and the headmen under him is a dual, and somewhat anomalous one. They must keep the confidence of their people but, at the same time, they are responsible to the European authorities. One of the most dramatic instances of Government pressure was the dismissal, in 1952, of Chief Albert Luthuli from his headship of a small Christian community in Zululand because he refused to give up his membership in the African National Congress, of which he subsequently became President. European magistrates make no secret of the fact that they expect chiefs and headmen to conform to their wishes.

This fact explains why the African National Congress has consistently opposed the Bantu Authorities' Act, and included it among the six laws which they highlighted in the passive disobedience campaign of 1952. On the one hand the African National Congress sees tribalism as the greatest barrier to the sense of African unity for which their nationalistic movement stands. But, beyond this, they feel that the Bantu Authorities' Act is an attempt to reverse the small amount of progress which the African people have made towards self-government on a Western pattern and to reintroduce a more authoritarian African structure which, in turn, is still more under the control of European officials.

Why then did the Bunga vote in 1955 to accept the principle of the Bantu Authorities' Act? Was it because its members hoped that the new territorial authority would be given more responsibilities as it would have greater backing by the Government? Was it, as *Die Burger's* editorial of April 22, 1955, suggested, 'an explicit vote of confidence in the National Government's Native policy'? Or was it the result of governmental pressure on the members of the Bunga, as Opposition members suggested in the House of Assembly?[88] These questions are difficult to answer. It is important to notice, however, that after the principle of the Bantu Authorities' Act was accepted, two of the outstanding figures within the Bunga declared that its stress on tribal units could split the Transkei and that the lack of popular election of the Councillors under the new act was retrogressive. This view served as part of the mandate for the committee, consisting of a quarter of the Bunga's membership and including six magistrates, which was entrusted with the responsibility of integrating the Bunga with the system envisaged by the Bantu Authorities' Act.

Between the Bantu Authorities' Act and the three other laws considered in this chapter took place the general election of 1953, at which the Nationalists gained a greatly increased majority of seats in the Assembly, though not a majority of the votes. With this reinforcement of their parliamentary position, the Nationalists moved into new areas with their apartheid legislation. In combating this program, the Opposition found itself in a weakened position, not only because it had fewer parliamentary seats but also through the 'hiving off' of those who formed the Liberal and Union Federal Parties, and the rumbling of internal revolt against Strauss' leadership, which ultimately led to the formation of the Conservative Party. These facts shaped the parliamentary context in which the next Bills were considered.

The Reservation of Separate Amenities' Act, 1953[88a]

The most obvious feature of South African life is the separation of the facilities used by Europeans and non-Europeans. There are separate entrances to Post Offices, railway stations, and sometimes to buildings (though often the same people provide service to both groups once they are inside); separate carriages on trains; separate buses; separate benches in public parks, most of them marked 'For Europeans only'; and separate beaches. Above all, there are separate hospitals, public pools, and conveniences. The Separate Amenities' Act was not concerned with separation as such, which is too well established to need comment, but with the standard of accommodation provided for both groups. This law embodies the principle of inequality and leaves no discretion to the courts to place limitations on its extent.

Behind the Bill lay a series of court cases on segregation in public places, of which the latest, the so-called Railway Apartheid case, was probably the Nationalists' most effective election propaganda in 1953. (See p. 170.) South African courts have never denied that subordinate law-making authorities, like municipalities, have the right to classify facilities as being exclusively for Europeans or non-Europeans. But for the degree of differentiation between races they adapted the criteria of reasonableness laid down by Lord Russell in a well-known English case, Kruse v. Johnson (1898). Thus in a case in 1943 concerning the use of Cape bathing beaches, the Cape Provincial Division held that the courts could strike down a by-law if the difference in the facilities provided for white and Coloured reflected an inequality of treatment which was in all circumstances 'manifestly unjust or oppressive'.[89]

An extension of this principle appeared in *Rex v. Abdurahman*,[90] in 1950, in which the Appeal Court held unanimously that a regulation which reserved a portion of all trains for Europeans but did not restrict them to these sections led to 'partiality and inequality in treatment', which was not authorized by the Railways Act of 1916. Mr. Justice Centlivres, who subsequently handed down the highly important judgment on the Separate Representation of Voters Act (see p. 128), declared in the Abdurahman case that:

> The State has provided a railway service for all its citizens irrespective of race and it is unlikely that the Legislature intended that users of the railways should, according to their race, have partial or unequal treatment meted out to them.

Fearing a challenge to their policy of racial segregation, the Nationalists amended the 1916 Railways Act in 1949, while the Abdurahman case was still pending. Express powers were given to reserve any railway premises or trains

> for the exclusive use of males or females or persons of particular races or different classes of persons or Natives. . . .

The effect of this amendment was tested in a case which aroused particularly strong feelings among the Nationalists since it concerned an African who entered the European waiting-room in the Cape Town railway station as an act of civil disobedience during the passive resistance campaign. In a decision handed down only three weeks before the 1953 election, the African was acquitted by the Appeal Court on the grounds that the facilities available to him were far inferior to those provided for Europeans.[91] Despite the new section inserted in 1949, the court held again that the administration was not authorized under the Railway Act to show such a degree of partiality and inequality in the facilities provided for different races and classes as existed in this particular railway station.

This time, however, there was one dissent to the verdict which raised a fundamental issue: what had been the intent of the legislature? Mr. Justice van den Heever pointed out that:

> In the last resort the question whether such discrimination must be on a basis of equality depends upon the intention one must impute to the Legislature.[92]

The court's own predisposition was clearly toward the concept of 'separate but equal', and as long as the statute was open to this interpretation, the Appeal Court could maintain what amounted in practice to a decisive civil rights emphasis. But if the legislature affirmed its support for substantial inequality of treatment between races, the court would have to comply.

The Separate Amenities Bill,[93] introduced in the first session after the Nationalists' success in the 1953 election, was obviously intended to legalize unequal facilities for different races in South Africa and thus to make it impossible for the courts to judge the validity of regulation in terms of the degree of discrimination they involved. In moving second reading of the measure on August 6, 1953, C. R. Swart, Minister of Justice, declared that the court's decision that separate facilities must be 'more or less equal' created an 'impossible situation'. The Government's intention was to give each section of the population facilities in accordance with 'its circumstances'.

H. G. Lawrence agreed for the United Party that the Bill 'seeks to crystallize into statutory form the traditional policy of social separation in South Africa'.[94] He added that:

> We realize that, having regard to the set-up of our people, the different racial groups and the circumstances and the extent of development of those groups, it is not practicable or wise or necessary to give exactly the same facilities to every section.[95]

At the same time he maintained that 'partiality must be based on justice', a concept which he left conveniently undefined. He did, however, suggest a number of amendments to the bill to prevent it from resulting in discrimination which was 'capricious or manifestly unreasonable'. To refuse these amendments—which, for example, limited the public places within which violation of a posted regulation created a criminal offense—would be, he declared, to enact 'a cynical apartheid of unrestricted powers'.

At issue between the Nationalists and the United Party was an attitude towards the courts rather than towards unequal separate amenities. Only the Labour and Liberal Parties opposed forcefully the concept of partiality in allotting facilities. But the United Party did not want partiality to go beyond what it considered to be a due regard for the numbers and the standard of civilization of a particular group. Once again it showed itself typically conservative in emphasizing flexibility and varying standards according to the stage of development of those concerned. But the United Party also saw that the only safe way to provide limits to partiality was to make some definitions which the courts could apply in particular cases. Thus, though it could have made the point more clearly, the United Party was trying to maintain the fundamental balance in the constitution of executive, legislature, and judiciary. Only by providing a specific role for the courts as the guardian of certain standards, however defined, could individuals be sure of protection against possible arbitrary action by the executive.

But this was precisely what the Nationalists were determined to avoid.

> We will always find that reasonable amenities are provided for all classes according to their aptitude, according to their standard of civilization and according to their need [said Swart at the end of the second reading debate]. This is our policy; but to leave its interpretation in the hands of courts, to compel people constantly to go to court—that is an impossible task for which we are not prepared.[96]

As for the criteria for limiting partiality and inequality, two Nationalists declared that the highest authority was 'the sense of justice of the people',[97] a standard obviously imprecise even in a society which does not enshrine racial discrimination.

Though the United Party seemed to be going most of the way with the Nationalists, the latter berated them fiercely throughout the second reading debate, accusing them of undermining apartheid by attacks on 'this traditional policy' (Martins) and making 'ineffectual' the Government's efforts to establish social separation. P. W. Botha, Secretary of the Cape Nationalist Party, who levelled the latter accusation, declared that:

> to gain a clear view regarding fair treatment and the rights of non-Europeans, we should first answer another question and that is: do we stand for the domination and supremacy of the European or not? . . . For if you stand for the domination and supremacy of the European, then everything you do must in the first place be calculated to ensure that domination.[98]

He charged that the United Party had never adopted a standpoint on that question, and feared to do so lest it either should become 'too liberalistic', or else too like the Nationalists.

The comment shrewdly focused the difficulties the United Party encountered in trying to combine white domination with their own sense of justice to the non-Europeans. Their broad humanitarianism and dislike of precise rules contrasted sharply with the Nationalist belief in systems and final solutions, and in the Nationalist mission to apply both to particular cases as well as in general. It was not the first nor the last time that the Nationalists scored because of the simplicity and directness of their arguments, or that the United Party showed itself ineffective in capitalizing on its own more legal and practical-minded approach. But there was equal discernment in R. J. du Toit's characterization of the two parties during committee stage.

> We on this side of the house stand for social separation; we have always done so [he said], but we believe that we can bring it about by voluntary means and with the consent and the co-operation of the people themselves, and not by force. That is where we differ radically from this Government. Ever since they have been in power they have tried to force social separation on the non-European people, regardless of what effect it will have, regardless of what economic disabilities may flow from it, regardless of world opinion, but merely to get this power into their own hands so that they can completely control the non-European races in this country.[99]

The most surprising aspect of the Nationalist defense of the Separate Amenities Bill was their assumption that a proper attitude towards color required racial separation rather than being a natural outgrowth of a keen sense of racial differentiation. Thus, in introducing the measure in second reading, Swart declared it was necessary for a nation 'to be educated in color sense in order to maintain proper behaviour'. The liberalistic emphasis on equality led non-Europeans 'to penetrate European facilities in a provocative manner', he declared, and continual contacts would lead 'eventually to racial admixture'. F. E. Mentz reinforced this line by stating forcefully that:

> Come what may, the Nationalist Party will continue to educate the nation along the paths of apartheid, because that is the only guarantee for white South Africa that here in South Africa the white man will remain master. . . .[100]

H. T. van G. Bekker added that:

> it is only in countries where we find two races of different colour and where there is no legislation to bring about apartheid that the European race eventually disappears,[101]

as did the British in Egypt and the Dutch in Indonesia. Thus the Nationalists seemed to fear that social intercourse would breed a familiarity which would blur the sense of color distinctions. They also felt that, if non-Europeans were not kept strictly in their place by apartheid restrictions, they might ultimately oust the European from South Africa.

While the United Party was prepared to plead only for limits to inequality and for equity in its administration, Mrs. Ballinger, now head of the Liberal Party, warned of the inherent dangers of a policy openly based on inequality.

> Part of the justification for our political legislation [she pointed out], is that Europeans and non-Europeans should not be brought into contact at points where they can conflict, yet here the Government is being given enormous powers to increase the points of conflict. . . . It exaggerates the sense of inferiority, and by reaction exaggerates the natural aggressiveness which is the inevitable response to this sort of thing.[102]

It was the most effective counter-argument to the Nationalist position that could be made. It focused, as the Nationalists did, on the danger to white civilization in South Africa, but saw it as far more likely to arise out of repression and its corollary of ultimate violence than from treating each group in the community in terms of its own interests and needs.

The Bantu Education Act, 1953[103]

Of all the apartheid legislation passed by the Nationalist Government, the Bantu Education Act is potentially the most significant. It is also the most controversial. The Act's opponents, inside and outside the country, European and non-European, fear that it will be used to restrict the African permanently to his present subordinate status in South African society. The Nationalists maintain that, on the contrary, the new provisions for Bantu education will not only aid many more Africans than in the past but will also help them to develop more in line with the needs of their community and tradition.

To foresee the consequences of the Act is difficult for its provisions are administrative. It transfers the administrative control of African education from the four provincial administrations to the Union Government. Within the latter, the direction of African education (except university and technical college training but including teacher training) is placed not under the Department of Education, but under a newly created Bantu Education Division of the Department of Native Affairs. If churches wish to retain administrative control of their schools, their State subsidy will be progressively reduced. In all other cases, the local control of African schools is transferred from the missions and given, at least technically, to the African community whose children attend the school. If that community is not advanced enough to take over such direction, the schools become State schools and parent-teacher committees are set up to enable the Africans to take a direct and personal interest in the schools.

These provisions establish a much more coordinated system of education for Africans than formerly; they also bring it under two new centers of authority: the Union Department of Native Affairs and the local African community. How much of a revolution this is becomes apparent from even a brief survey of the history of African education in the Union.

The salient feature of African education in South Africa up to the implementation of the Bantu Education Act was the overwhelming predominance of State-aided mission schools. The missions not only established nearly all the schools for Africans in the Union but originally financed them. At all times they have provided most of the capital equipment and, by 1955, at least 12 to 13 per cent of the cost of educating African children. Gradually, however, public funds were used to supplement mission resources. The Cape and Natal Governments began extending aid to the mission schools about the middle of the nineteenth century; in the Transvaal and Orange Free State, this was not begun until after the Boer War. The system of State-aided mission schools was general, however, by the time the South African Union was established. By 1946, there were 4,567 schools for Africans in the Union, 4,335 of which were State-aided mission schools and only 232 State schools. Of the latter, 216 were in Natal, 15 in the Cape, 1 in the Transvaal and none in the Free State.

Until 1922, the provinces provided the necessary financial aid to the mission schools, over which they also assumed general control. As this burden became too heavy, the central Government took over the financial obligations in this field in 1922, but without disturbing provincial administrative control. At first, the Union Government contributed a lump sum of £340,000 a year for African education. As this was not sufficient to keep abreast of growing needs, a constantly increasing proportion of the Native poll tax was added from 1925 on. By 1943, four-fifths of the latter tax was going to African education. Two years later the Smuts Government agreed that African education should not be restricted by the poverty of the community, and drew the money for this purpose from general revenue. The annual budget for African education increased about 10 per cent a year from then on until it reached over £8 million by 1953.

At the time the Bantu Education Act was introduced, 883,896 Africans were attending school, about 41 per cent of those of school age. Education is not compulsory for Africans, but it is free in the primary grades. African children are normally about two grades below European children of similar age, partly because of tribal responsibilities like cattle herding, partly because of the home background. Half the African children in school are in sub-standard grades as compared with one-fifth of the European children. Only 4 per cent of African students go beyond the primary grades as compared with 24 per cent of European students. Moreover, the facilities for African children are commonly below those for other racial groups in the Union, as is reflected by the fact that, in 1951-52, the State spent an average of £43·88 for each European student, and £18·84 for Asian and Coloured pupils, but only £7·58 for each African in school. All European schools in the Union are, of course, entirely separate from non-European schools.

There has long been a debate about what should be the character of African education and to what degree it is the responsibility or even the right of Europeans to direct it. The early missionaries, particularly those from England, assumed that the best way to Christianize and civilize the Africans was to provide them with a European type of academic education in a European language. On the whole, this has remained the emphasis of the English-speaking churches. The Afrikaners and the Dutch Reformed Church have had many more doubts about the usefulness of academic education for Africans; thus, they have recommended more practical training. The Dutch Reformed Church Congress, in April 1950, for example, declared that Native education should include training for all administrative services, trades, etc.[104] Particularly in recent years, Afrikaners have also stressed the African vernaculars as languages of instruction, and tribal tradition as a basis on which African education should build. The Africans themselves are somewhat suspicious of this latter emphasis (sound as it is according to certain educational theories), and fear lest any attempt to give them a different education from Europeans would handicap their opportunities for development.

In practice, African education at the primary level differed slightly from European education in the same grades. A Bantu language was theoretically the language of instruction to Standard IV though, in fact, English was normally used as a medium much earlier than that. But the syllabus laid down by the provincial authorities differed considerably from that in the European primary schools. At the secondary level, in contrast, the syllabus for Europeans and Africans was the same.

It has been generally acknowledged in the Union that African education was inadequate in many respects and needed far more order and coordination. Thus there was general approval when the Nationalist Government appointed a distinguished Commission on Native Education in 1949 under the chairmanship of Dr. W. W. M. Eiselen, Secretary for Native Affairs. This Commission held hearings throughout the Union, and, on April 18, 1951, presented its findings, which ultimately formed the basis for the provisions of the Bantu Education Act.

The Native Education Commission Report[105] incorporated major criticisms of the existing system of African education. It declared that African education was not 'an integral part of a plan of socio-economic development' of the Bantu people; that it was carried on without the active participation of the Africans as a people, either in their local communities or more widely; that its present financing made planning virtually impossible, and asked almost nothing directly from the Bantu people themselves.[106] The Commission also found that the existing system of inspection and supervision of schools was inadequate, that not enough was being done to 'combat the problem' of stopping school early, that there was an 'inadequate functioning' of teachers in schemes of African development, and that vocational education was not being coupled with economic development.[107]

For all these reasons, the Commission recommended that the Union Government take over control of African education from the provinces, that Bantu communities assume a greater share of administrative and financial responsibility, and that African education should be more closely related to the traditions and distinctive characteristics of its people.

On the last point, however, one member of the Commission, Professor Andrew Murray of Cape Town University, entered a dissent. He declared that:

> The conception that education has a 'social purpose' and that its function is to preserve and propagate the group's 'culture' conflicts with the Christian standpoint that man is an end in himself and his social institutions merely means to aid him to a better life.

This represented a fundamental difference of approach which was to form the rallying point for much of the subsequent opposition to the Bantu Education Act.

When the Commission report was presented, *Die Transvaler* endorsed it with satisfaction on the ground that the educational system must fit the 'character and principles' of the people.[108] On the same day, the *Rand Daily Mail* took the line that the Commission had not been concerned with Native education as such, but with its integration into Government policy.[109] In July 1953, shortly before the bill was introduced, the Natal and Transvaal Teachers' Associations protested against the Report, the former declaring that it was 'terrifying' and 'sinister', while the latter maintained that 'education is education'.[110] Thus opposition to the principle on which the report was based was early as well as persistent.

Though the Bantu Education Act (founded on the Eiselen Report) is largely concerned with administrative arrangements, the details it embodies are not so significant as the spirit in which it is implemented. There is more than ordinary importance, therefore, to the statement made by Dr. H. F. Verwoerd, Minister of Native Affairs, in moving second reading of the measure.[111]

> Racial relations cannot improve if the wrong type of education is given to Natives [he declared]. They cannot improve if the result of Native education is the creation of frustrated people who, as a result of the education they received, have expectations in life which circumstances in South Africa do not allow to be fulfilled immediately, when it creates people who are trained for professions not open to them, when there are people who have received a form of cultural training which strengthens their desire for the white-collar occupations to such an extent that there are more such people than openings available.[112]

The very fact that the measure was piloted through the house by the Minister of Native Affairs rather than by the Minister of Education was suggestive of the Nationalist approach to the subject of African education. That Dr. Verwoerd also emphasized the necessity of aligning educational policy with the general policy of the State showed that the measure was looked on as a part of apartheid policy. When he stressed that those who controlled Native education should not foster wrong expectations, it seemed clear that the education Dr. Verwoerd envisaged for Africans was one which would equip them for that role in South Africa which Nationalist policy outlined.

United Party opposition to the Bantu Education Act, as spearheaded by Dr. Smit, once Secretary of Native Affairs, was comprehensive and emphatic. Constitutionally, he opposed the measure as depriving the provinces of an important function under section 85 of the Constitution, and of doing so without having a petition presented to Parliament as provided for in section 149, as amended in 1934. (The Speaker subsequently ruled that this procedure was not necessary.) Administratively, Dr. Smit sharply opposed placing African education under the Native Affairs Department, which was already 'top-heavy and overburdened' and, moreover, was neither appropriate for this task, nor experienced. Besides, he felt strongly that higher education for Africans should not be based on a curriculum different from that used by Europeans. He pointed out that Africans are being educated 'for good or for evil' by their very contact with European civilization and

> that the interests of the various races of this country are so closely bound up with each other that the backwardness of any section of the community must be a menace to the rest of the country.[113]

In conclusion, Dr. Smit declared that the United Party felt 'that the principles of education are the same for all races', and that the Department of Education was therefore the appropriate body to supervise African as well as European education.[114]

The Labour Party and Mrs. Ballinger were still more insistent that Africans should be provided with the means to develop within the European context in which they necessarily earned their living. The disadvantages of associating African education with Dr. Verwoerd's known aim of 'directing Native life to a particular end and set pattern' was pointed out by Mrs. Ballinger, who declared this was unacceptable to the Africans. Leo Lovell pointed out that

> a tribal society educates its children for a static and fixed position which goes on, so to speak, for ever. Our society is a changing society, both for the Natives and the Europeans. . . .[115]

To the Nationalists, however, these points were either irrelevant or misguided. W. A. Maree, making the major speech for his party, brought out well the Nationalist view of the difference between what he called 'the liberalistic approach and the approach of nationalism' to education. The former was that the individual should be developed as an individual. The latter was that

> the object of education should be to develop the individual as a member of society, so that he can take his rightful place within the society to which he belongs.[116]

It was an instructive distinction not only as far as the African was concerned but also for European education.

The Nationalists were clearly concerned in the main with the great mass of Africans, and particularly with what M. D. C. de Wet Nel called 'the true Bantu community',[117] rather than with the small percentage who went on to higher education. They felt that African schools should be a 'binding element' between tribalized and detribalized Africans, with the emphasis clearly on the former. While the Nationalists did not entirely disregard the point that it was environment rather than race which was decisive, they would never have gone so far as did P. A. Moore when he maintained that:

> There is not such a great difference between the Bantu child in Alexandra township and the boy in Houghton [a wealthy Johannesburg suburb] as there is between the Bantu child in Alexandra township and the Bantu child in the Transkei.[118]

In other words, the Nationalists, perhaps not surprisingly, kept their sights fixed on the Africans that ideal apartheid might some day produce, while the United Party pragmatically concerned itself with the here and now.

This aspect of the Nationalist approach to African education was underlined by their chief whip, J. J. Serfontein, and put in an extreme form by Dr. Albert Hertzog. Serfontein declared that the aim of education should be first to make the African 'family conscious', as a cornerstone of all his social and national life, and then 'community-conscious' in terms of his tribal association. Hertzog pointed out that most Africans get only four years of education and declared that none of these should be 'wasted' by following European standards. In school, he believed, an African should be taught only the most essential things unobtainable elsewhere—hygiene, soil conservation, cattle care—which would make him efficient in his life's work. To detribalize Africans by means of the schools was to make them despise what is their own and to alienate them from their untutored parents. This, he asserted, produced license and lawlessness and consequently a threat to white civilization.

There was much that made sense in the Nationalist arguments. It is obvious that the lack of opportunities in the South African context for Africans with advanced training make them frustrated and bitter. Moreover, it is hard to deny the importance of basing education on the culture of the particular group, both to provide stability and healthy growth, and to permit self-respect. Yet when S. H. Eyssen declared that

> for those who necessarily have to be integrated in the European areas—and these form only a third of the Bantu population—another education curriculum will eventually have to be prescribed to comply with their circumstances,[119]

he was pointing to the essential dilemma of the Nationalist approach. They might believe in a system of education rooted in tribal traditions. They might even hope for an ultimate Bantustan (though it is far from sure that many do hope for this). But the inexorable fact of South African life is that a large number of non-Europeans are in the so-called European areas, and are inevitably accepting their standards. Also, if the Reserves are ever to be made productive through African efforts, it can only be through developing skilled, trained Africans capable of assuming the necessary responsibilities.

That the United Party, as well as the Labour Party and Native representatives, emphasized the need to formulate an educational program which took into account increasing African urbanization and industrialization was attacked by the Nationalists as evidence that the United Party had 'liberalistic' leaders. Verwoerd declared sarcastically that the traditional Smuts view had been replaced by the Smit view.

> . . . the United Party is a new party today [he declared], a changed party, a party which has abandoned its policy of the past. It is a much more leftist party under its present new leadership.[120]

It was the typical Nationalist line in the immediate post-election session when they were trying to detach the United Party's most conservative members.

The Bantu Education Bill aroused bitter feelings both in the House of Assembly and in the country at large, because it impinged on so many sensitive areas. Particularly in Natal, the bill evoked feelings about provincial-Union relations. Beyond this were the emotional and religious sentiments aroused by the threat to the mission schools. Especially during the discussion of the Bantu Education Amendment Bill in 1954, which definitely placed the mission schools under Bantu communities, Senator Verwoerd seemed to go out of his way to antagonize the Opposition and encourage a personal mistrust of the way in which he planned to utilize the legislation.

The fundamental issue was the role of the African in South African life and how to fit him for it. Here the Nationalists themselves desired two conflicting goals: The development of the South African economy, which necessarily demanded African labor above the unskilled level, and the development of the Reserves in a tribal tradition. The Opposition feared that the Bantu Education Act would be used to hamper, if not ultimately prevent, the first objective. At the same time, the United Party had sympathy with the second purpose, provided it did not lead to the sacrifice of the first one. Thus, the difference between the United Party and the Nationalists was a combination of factors: whether to weight most heavily the urbanized or the tribalized African; whether continuity of administration in the schools was important enough to outweigh giving the African community a more decisive role; whether the traditional mission and provincial supervision of African education would not have the interests of the Bantu more at heart than the Department of Native Affairs.

After the Bantu Education Act was passed, the major protests came from those most directly concerned with African education. The Natal Association of European Teachers in African Institutions affirmed its opposition to the legislation, as it had to the Eiselen Report on which the law was based;[121] the Transvaal African Teachers' Association termed the measure 'terrifying'.[122] A Catholic paper, the *Southern Cross*, pointed out that Catholics could not agree with the assumption on which the measure was based, namely, that ordinary education should be a Government monopoly.[123] Early in January 1954, the Native Advisory Board at Orlando township, outside Johannesburg, expressed its opposition to the Act,[124] and the next month the Cape African Parents' Association did likewise, suggesting rather exaggeratedly that it would impose a 'slave system'.[125] The General Assembly of the Bantu Presbyterian Church, in September 1954, expressed the concern so widely felt elsewhere that the new scheme of education seemed to place emphasis on 'preparing pupils for a subordinate role in the country's life rather than giving them the common culture of the Christian West'. It suggested that it would have been more constructive to make provision for the well over half of all African children who were not already in school.[126]

There was still relatively little information, however, about what changes would actually be made in African education. In March 1954, N. C. Havenga, in the budget speech, announced that henceforth the Treasury would contribute only a fixed sum, £6,500,000 a year, to African education, and that anything needed over and above this would have to be found by the Bantu community itself.[127] *Die Volksblad* welcomed this on the next day as 'a healthy attitude'[128] and declared on April 28 that such self-help was necessary since the whites could no longer bear the financial burden of African education.[129] The *East Province Herald*, on the contrary, found it 'pernicious',[130] while the *Star* pointed out that one result of putting Native education on a self-supporting basis would be to lead the Africans to demand higher wages and better conditions.[131]

Another development was to provide double sessions in schools so that twice the number of pupils could be handled, though for shorter periods of time. The Institute of Race Relations reported some of the obvious disadvantages in January 1955: That the teachers were bored by the necessity of repetition; and that the children for the second session tended to come early and create a disturbance. The Institute felt that emphasis was being placed on the small rural schools, and that there was not enough understanding of the needs of African children living in crowded urban areas like the Witwatersrand.[132] The double sessions seemed clearly an expedient, possibly justified under the existing lack of sufficient facilities for the African children seeking education. When it was combined with the new limitation on the contribution to African education from general revenue, it looked less attractive.

The churches, which up to this time had provided the bulk of African education in South Africa, faced particular problems arising not only out of the principle of the Bantu Education Act but also from the necessity of deciding whether to sell or rent their schools to the Government or to continue operating under greatly decreased subsidies. The Dutch Reformed Churches, in fundamental agreement with the Bantu Education Act and the Nationalist philosophy of education, willingly transferred their mission schools to the State. The other churches varied in the degree of their protests and their practical response to the Act.

The Methodist Church, whose schools have provided education for some 200,000 African children, opposed the policy of the Bantu Education Act as 'incompatible with Christian principles' and directed at 'conditioning the African people to a predetermined position of subordination in the State'. At the same time it felt compelled to relinquish its schools to State control so that the immediate educational needs of the Africans could be met. Because of its doubts about how the Act would be implemented, the church limited its agreement with the Government to 'an experimental period'.[133] Watching the development of the school system over a period of time, however, the leading figures in the church, including the President of its Conference, the Rev. J. B. Webb, decided that many of their initial fears were not being realized, and consequently urged that the experiment be given a fair chance.[134]

The Foreign Mission Committee of the Church of Scotland followed a somewhat similar line. It approved the assumption of responsibility for African education by the Government though it regretted that the transition from the existing system was being 'unduly hastened'.[135] It took strong exception, however, to basing educational policy on race. The Committee held that because of their important part in South African economic life the time was past when the Africans should be treated 'as a completely separate community', and it declared that:

> A Christian educational policy must seek to prepare the members of every social group to assume their full share of adult responsibility in the service of the country.

The mission with the longest period of service in Natal, the American Board of Missions, attempted to straddle its dilemma by neither agreeing to relinquish control of its schools nor, at the same time, resisting the assumption of control by the Government. Since it felt it could not continue to operate the schools without the same subsidy that it had depended on before, it thus in effect made way for State control which it declared would take place by 'unilateral action'.[136]

While these three churches ultimately allowed the Government to take over their schools, the Roman Catholic Church decided to finance its own separate schools.[137] The Seventh Day Adventists who, in any case, had never asked for a subsidy, also continued to operate their schools under their own control.

The most difficult position was that in which the Anglican Church found, or placed, itself. On October 23, 1954, the Synod of the Johannesburg Diocese declared that it considered the Bantu Education Act contrary to the will of God because it was based on apartheid, because it attacked the natural rights and dignity of man, and because it was designed to ensure the perpetual domination of one racial group by the intellectual starvation of another. It called on all Christians to work for the repeal of the Act.[138]

Following this resolution, the Bishop of Johannesburg, the Rt. Rev. R. Ambrose Reeves, long an outspoken critic of apartheid policies, took the drastic step of closing all Anglican mission schools in the Southern Transvaal as a protest against the Act.[139] The Archbishop of Cape Town also opposed handing over Anglican schools to the Government. The *Star* felt there could be no doubt about Bishop Reeves' sincerity, but wondered whether his decision was wise.[140] The *Argus* agreed next day, and pointed out that 'the Bantu pays the price'. *Die Burger*, with no intention of flattering them, called the bishops a 'spiritual Torch Commando'.[141] More biting was the reaction of *Die Transvaler* that the most important Anglican clergy were 'imported' from Britain, and were only temporary residents who, to its obvious annoyance, refused 'to die here'.[142] The *Bantu World* declared, however, that:

> Bishop Reeves will go down in history as a man who had principles to which he was determined to stick through thick and thin. The Bishop's faithfulness to his principles and all the hullabaloo caused by the people who dislike the Bantu Education Act may yet be productive of a certain amount of good.[143]

On November 26, 1954, the Department of Native Affairs issued draft syllabi for lower African primary schools, which were to be put into effect in 1956, and subject to criticism in the meantime. The most important changes from the former provincial syllabi were the increased use of mother-tongue instruction and the allocation of more time to Afrikaans. History, geography, and civics were grouped together in a single subject called 'environment studies'. Religious instruction was allotted even more time than previously. P. A. Moore, the United Party expert on education, declared that there was 'nothing inferior' about this new syllabus[144] and other authorities agreed it was 'quite reasonable'.[145] The Institute of Race Relations similarly found the syllabus educationally sound although it felt more time should have been devoted to health and hygiene. It also drew attention to the need for thorough teacher training and refresher courses. An African teacher pointed out that to introduce both English and Afrikaans so early in the syllabus would crowd other subjects, and could possibly lead to confusion. [A. W. Hoernlé, Report, appended comments by W. M. Ngakane.] He also regretted the emphasis on local environment rather than the broad heritage of Western civilization. On the whole, however, the comments on the new syllabus showed that one of the major causes of concern about the Bantu Education Act had been successfully met. Whether the syllabus reflected the plan held from the first for African education or whether it had been shaped by the protests which had been so loudly voiced could not be known.

Well before the draft syllabi were issued, plans were mooted for an African boycott of the schools when they were turned over to State control on April 1, 1955. The African National Congress Executive Committee, in mid-1954, urged the withdrawing of children from school as a protest against the Bantu Education Act.[146] This was followed by a general resolution at the African National Congress annual conference held in Durban in December 1954 'to organize the people in a determination' not to send their children to school on April 1, 1955. In response, Dr. Verwoerd issued a strong warning, in January 1955, that children who participated in such a boycott would not be readmitted to school.

Partly because of pressure by its President, ex-Chief Albert Luthuli, the Executive Committee of the African National Congress decided not to organize a boycott of school children on April 1, although it announced it would demonstrate its opposition to the Bantu Education Act on some other occasion. The Committee also called on Africans not to participate in the elections of school committees. Confusion resulted. While most of the 4,827 State-aided schools affected by the Act were transferred without disturbances on April 1, 1955, there were spasmodic boycotts on the East Rand affecting some 5,000 school children.

Dr. Verwoerd issued an ultimatum that any child who was absent on April 25, 1955, would not be readmitted to school; that if schools or classes were empty that day, teaching posts would be abolished; and that the money earmarked for these institutions would be transferred elsewhere. The African National Congress working committee, apparently much against Luthuli's wishes, called for an intensified boycott on April 25. Some 7,000 children stayed away, or were kept from school that day. They were at once removed from the school registers, and some 116 teachers became surplus and were dismissed with one month's salary. (Some 106 of them subsequently secured other positions.) It was obvious that the Department of Native Affairs held all the cards. Gradually the boycott weakened; on appeal, the Minister agreed to readmit to the schools in 1956 those who had been involved in the boycott if no further trouble occurred. He thus made the future education of these children dependent on the acceptance of the Act both by their communities and by the African National Congress.

The position of the Africans in relation to the Bantu Education Act has been neither an easy nor a clear-cut one. Many Africans have long resented the paternalism of the mission schools and from this point of view could welcome a transition to State control. Yet the fact that this control is vested in the Department of Native Affairs, which is associated in their minds with irksome restrictions, tainted the transfer from the first. Restrained by too heavy penalties from engaging again in passive resistance, the African National Congress envisaged a school boycott on the date of transfer as a means of dramatizing its general opposition to discrimination against Africans. Even when more sober councils within its own ranks tried to call off the gesture, there were still some hot-heads who promoted the boycott. Yet it was not the transfer as such, nor even the Bantu Education Act which was their chief objection, but the whole position of the African in South African society. That the boycott inevitably failed, leaving the Department in a stronger position than ever, is not to say that the symptoms of discontent which promoted the action were not worthy of notice.

At one point in the educational system of South Africa, Africans and other non-Europeans have long shared class rooms with Europeans: in Witwatersrand University in Johannesburg, and in Cape Town University. This has been a source of deep concern to Nationalists, and particularly to Dr. Malan. In

December 1953, he declared openly that action would be taken to make 'just and purposive provision' for the separate education of whites and non-whites.[147] The acting principal of Cape Town University retorted that the evils of educating the two together were 'wholly imaginary'.[148] The Executive Council of the National Union of South African Students (NUSAS), representing the students of English-speaking universities, came out strongly against segregation at the university level. The *Rand Daily Mail* warned also that the expense of enforcing apartheid at the university level would be prohibitive.[149]

To secure the necessary facts on the practicability and financial implications of extending apartheid throughout African education, the Government set up late in December 1953, a Commission of Inquiry on Separate Training Facilities for non-Europeans at Universities. Composed of three outstanding citizens—J. E. Holloway, one-time Secretary of Finance, subsequently South African Ambassador to the United States, and now High Commissioner in London, R. W. Wilcocks, formerly Rector of Stellenbosch University and E. G. Malherbe, Principal of Natal University—the Commission submitted its report in November 1954.[150]

Of the nine universities and one university college in South Africa, only five have admitted non-Europeans and only two of these on a non-segregated basis. The four Afrikaans-speaking universities—at Stellenbosch, Pretoria, Bloemfontein and Potchefstroom—exclude non-Europeans. Of the English-speaking institutions, Rhodes University technically admits non-Europeans to certain graduate courses, but no use is made in practice of this opportunity. Natal University admits non-Europeans, but only to segregated classrooms; the University of South Africa (Pretoria) also has facilities for non-Europeans, but only through correspondence courses, there being no mixed attendance at its lectures. The university college, Fort Hare, is for non-Europeans only. Thus the Commission was only concerned with the effect of closing to non-Europeans the facilities they then enjoyed at Witwatersrand and Cape Town Universities.

Of the 2,327 non-Europeans enrolled at the university level in 1954, 271 were at Cape Town and 214 at Witwatersrand. These universities thus handled about two-thirds the numbers securing their advanced training at Natal and Fort Hare, which had 327 and 370 non-European students respectively. Mainly because it is less expensive, the largest number of non-Europeans (1,145 in 1954) use the University of South Africa's correspondence courses. But of the 1,182 non-Europeans taking classroom work at the advanced level, 485 were at one or the other of the two non-segregated universities.

In the light of this situation, and of the fact that some 60 to 70 per cent of the non-Europeans at Durban and Fort Hare qualify as teachers (the profession offering them the best expectation of a good livelihood), the Commission took a general stand against imposing segregation at the university level. This was because it foresaw that to do so would mean either that non-Europeans would be denied the opportunity for advanced training in specialized fields for which there was little demand, or that the Government would have to embark on a highly costly program of providing these facilities on a separate basis.

Despite these findings, the Minister of Education, Mr. J. H. Viljoen, affirmed that it remained Government policy to establish apartheid at the universities.[151] He declared that this would not be carried into practice until adequate facilities had been provided for African and Coloured students,[152] but National Party members were far from satisfied with this statement, and pressed hard for full educational apartheid.[153]

That segregated education promotes its own problems was illustrated by trouble at Fort Hare which led the authorities of the college to expel the entire student body and close the institution on May 4, 1955. This drastic action was justified on the ground that 'a secret authority' sometimes referred to as 'the Caucus' dominated the students at Fort Hare and had instituted boycotts of college functions, in particular the graduation ceremony on April 29, 1955, which was attended by only 20 students in addition to the graduating class. Subsequently, students were readmitted to Fort Hare if they could prove that they had nothing to do with the boycott. Whether or not the policy of closing the college had been wise, it is difficult to disagree with the comment in the *Star* that the incident raised doubt about the wisdom of establishing entirely separate university facilities for non-Europeans. As it pointed out,

> In the mixed university the non-European, normally in a minority, has the opportunity to learn and practice the arts of civilized conduct which are as important as the acquisition of knowledge and degrees.[154]

It can also be expected that in the South African context segregated education will always be looked on as restrictive, regardless of the facilities offered, and also that its institutions will become hotbeds of nationalism.

Nonetheless the Government has pressed ahead with its plans for segregated university education, though it has had to modify and delay them because of intense criticism and opposition. Part of its plan has been to establish three new universities, one each for the Zulu, Sotho and Xhosa ethnic groups,[155] but the fact that these were to be under the control of the Department of Native Affairs, that Ministers could regulate courses of instruction, and that permanent staff members would be considered guilty of misconduct if they commented adversely on any branch of State administration led to widespread doubts that they would ever deserve to be ranked as institutions of higher learning. The Separate University Education Bill, introduced in mid-March 1957, also provided sweeping powers to the Minister of Education to forbid any university, except the University of South Africa, to admit any non-European student after January 1, 1958, except with the permission of the Minister, and similarly to forbid Fort Hare to admit other than African students without express ministerial permission. So far did its provisions reach that Sir de Villiers Graaff, leader of the United Party, took the unusual step of opposing the introduction of the bill because it provided such serious interference with traditional academic freedom. Already on February 5, 1957, the Minister of Education let it be known that the Government also intended ultimately to replace all the facilities for non-European students at the University of Natal, despite the fact that these are segregated, and that in addition it would transfer the control of its Bantu Medical School. The Medical School staff announced it would resign rather than work under State control, while university students, staffs and administrations maintained vigorous and persistent opposition to the proposed changes.

At one point the Government attempted to meet the criticisms by changing the provision forbidding the 'open' universities to admit non-Europeans to forbidding non-Europeans to attend 'open' universities. In the end it realized more clearly both the strength and the justification of the opposition. Thus it was not without some relief that the measure was withdrawn on a technicality, thereby postponing its final consideration until after the 1958 election.

One of the best commentaries on the whole procedure came from Dawie of *Die Burger*, who drew up a provisional balance sheet on March 16, 1957, of what had been achieved in university apartheid:

1. Embittered non-white feelings against the Nationalists;
2. Agitation throughout the entire overseas academic world;
3. An ultimately 'white' U.C.T. and Wits [University of Cape Town and Witwatersrand]—which will strengthen considerably their competitive position against Stellenbosch and Pretoria.

He asked, 'Are we not granting our opponents unnecessary weapons for agitation by not planning our methods carefully enough?' Coming from a Nationalist it said a lot.

The Native Labour (Settlement of Disputes) Act, 1953[156]

Although male Africans now outnumber all other industrial workers in the Union, they are not allowed to form or participate in a registered trade union under the Industrial Conciliation Act, 1937 (which builds on the 1924 Act of the same name), nor can they use the official machinery for dealing with industrial disputes. This is because a pass-bearing Native is not an 'employee' in the sense in which the term is used in the Act. Thus male Africans have long been in an anomalous position in regard to the highly developed system of industrial councils and conciliation machinery of which other South African workers can make use.

The industrial councils, for which the Industrial Conciliation Act makes provision, can be established in any field except farming, domestic service, Governmental or provincial employment, or certain educational and charitable institutions. They are permanent bodies, composed of representatives of employers and of registered trade unions, with wide powers to make agreements regarding wages, hours and conditions of work. These councils can also fix the wages of male Africans though the latter have no representation apart from a European representative who can speak on their behalf but has no vote. As can be expected both from this fact and from the color bar, these wages are nearly always at a lower level than those of workers protected by the Industrial Conciliation Act.

Oddly enough, African women were not similarly excluded under the 1937 Act, but only because at the time it was drafted there was no expectation that they, too, would be drawn into industry. The Garment Workers' Union, whose membership is predominantly European, but which also includes African and Coloured women workers, was able to register under the Act because African women do not carry passes. Since the Industrial Conciliation Act permits no differentiation on the ground of the race of the employees in any of the matters within the competence of an industrial council, African women were thus in a better position industrially than African males until a 1954 amendment to the Industrial Conciliation Act excluded all Africans from its definition of 'employee'.

Not only were African males unable to share in the advantages of registered unions; under War Measure 145 (which only defined in detail long-existing provisions) they were also compelled to accept compulsory arbitration in disputes, and forbidden to strike. Despite these limitations, however, a long series of African trade unions have operated precariously (see p. 62) outside the system established by the Industrial Conciliation Act. Many of these unions were informally recognized and dealt with by the Departments of Labour and Native Affairs, although they had no official status and therefore could claim no rights.

The unsatisfactory character of this situation has long been recognized. In 1942, the Inter-departmental Committee on the Social, Health and Economic Conditions of Urban Natives[157] reported that the growth of trade unionism among Africans was as inevitable as it had been in other countries, and expressed its belief that it was 'unjust' to refuse them recognition when the unions of other racial groups in the country were statutorily recognized.[158] The Witwatersrand Mine Native Wages Commission of 1943 endorsed this view.[159] It pointed out that under wise direction the activities of such unions would tend to the general advantage of the African people 'whose aspirations would thereby be directed into proper channels, which, uncontrolled, might develop upon wholly wrong lines'.[160]

In line with these suggestions, the Smuts Government drafted an Industrial Conciliation (Natives) Bill in 1947. This measure planned to establish a separate system of conciliation machinery for African males which would have provided them with facilities not far short of those enjoyed under the 1937 Act. The Bill met widespread criticism, however, not only in Parliament, but also from European labor. It had not passed by the time the Smuts Government was defeated in the 1948 elections, and Dr. Malan made it clear that the Nationalists would seek some other means of handling the situation.

To provide a comprehensive review of the whole field of industrial legislation, the Nationalists set up an Industrial Legislation Commission of Enquiry in October 1948, which produced a lengthy report in December 1951. As far as Africans were concerned, this Commission considered three possibilities: admitting them to the machinery of the Industrial Conciliation Act; recognizing African trade unions but providing them with machinery separate from the act; or leaving them uncontrolled and unguided as at present. Since it found that the first and third alternatives involved too many dangers, the Commission unequivocally chose the second. It proposed, therefore, to grant

> recognition in legislation separate from that applicable to other races and to provide special measures for their control and guidance . . . (para. 1637).

These measures, it felt, would be provided by the Department of Labour in consultation with the Department of Native Affairs. The Commission emphasized that African trade unions should not be allowed to indulge in political activities, and must be kept strictly to their economic role. Here they would function like ordinary trade unions. In exceptional cases, where the conciliation machinery was not used properly or Africans were employed in a field or position held 'more suitable' for other races, the Commission even envisaged their right to strike.[161]

The Native Labour (Settlement of Disputes) Act establishes a system very different from that recommended by the Commission. It retains the ban on strikes by Africans, and goes beyond the provisions of War Measure 145 to prohibit people from instigating strikes or engaging in sympathetic strikes related to African grievances. It does not prohibit African trade unions, but it does not legally recognize them. On the contrary, it sets up alternative machinery through which to consider African grievances and bring them to the notice of the authorities.

The machinery established under this Act has at its base a series of regional Native Labour Committees consisting of Africans appointed by the Minister of Labour, who work under the chairmanship of a European called the Native Labour Relations Officer. If a dispute arises in a particular area, the Committee, acting through its European chairman and an inspector of the Labour Department, tries to settle it by dealing directly with the employer. If this fails, the dispute goes to the Central Native Labour Board, which is composed entirely of Europeans appointed by the Minister in consultation with the regional Committees. If this board should also fail, the dispute is referred to the National Board. The latter may call on the assistance of the industrial council if there is one. If the dispute still defies settlement, the National Board can ask the Minister to instruct the Wage Board to make a decision. The ultimate settlement, then, is by the Wage Board.

The National Board can also send representatives to all industrial council meetings where wages and conditions of work of Africans are under consideration to take part in discussions, though they have no right to vote. This is similar to the earlier practice of having a Department of Labour member represent the interests of Africans at industrial council meetings.

The urgency of the problem with which this measure dealt was underlined by the Minister of Labour in introducing its second reading on August 4, 1953.[162] Even leaving out agriculture, domestic service, the railways and Government and provincial services, there were 872,000 Africans in gainful employment by 1946, more than all the Europeans, Coloured, and Indians in these fields. This disparity, he felt, was now much greater. Half a million or so of these African workers belonged under no organized system for the prevention and settlement of disputes.

The debate centered around the advisability of giving official recognition to African trade unions. Despite the Commission's recommendation to do so, the Government felt it would be far too dangerous. It would act as an incentive to their growth, declared Mr. Ben Schoeman, Minister of Labour, and they would be used 'as a political weapon', to create chaos at any given time.[163] Pulling out all the stops, he maintained that 'we would probably be committing race suicide if we give them that incentive'.[164]

Schoeman drew a distinction between what he called the 'microscopically small' number of Africans who 'might' be capable of running a trade union, and the 'hundreds of thousands of illiterate and largely primitive Native workers',[165] who he was convinced had not 'the faintest conception' of the responsibilities of trade unionism.[166] Moreover, he felt that African trade unions were in existence chiefly as a result of the efforts of 'certain European trade unions, and left-wing agitators'.[167] Thus, if this alternative machinery for settlement of disputes was established, he considered that African trade unions 'would probably die a natural death'.[168]

The Opposition was unconvinced. While welcoming the bill as a 'constructive adjustment of this ever-present problem',[169] H. G. Lawrence pointed out for the United Party that it was a 'fundamental defect' not to deal with the Native trade union movement which existed 'whether we like it or not'.[170] Not to do so was to leave the field open to 'any unscrupulous exploiter'.[171] He asked, though unsuccessfully, for a Select Committee.

Labour opposition to the measure was more fundamental and far-reaching. Echoing the new liberalism of its 1953 Native policy, Leo Lovell proposed bringing Africans under the Industrial Conciliation Act. Schoeman had argued that this would end the industrial color bar and be detrimental to the standard of living of European workers. Lovell spoke of Africans as employees, not as a racial group; he pointed out that large numbers of them were in semi-skilled occupations in industry and commerce and foresaw that administrative control over their wages might be used in a way adverse to the interests of white workers, as well as to themselves.

Although the debate started on a high level, and the United Party urged that the question was not a party issue but 'a national one',[172] acrimony mounted quickly. H. G. Lawrence was sent from the Chamber by the Deputy Speaker for complaining about constant interruptions from Nationalist benches and lack of impartiality in dealing with them. Nationalist speakers tried to capitalize on what they suggested was too sympathetic an attitude by United Party speakers towards African trade unions. Under this barrage, the United Party tried to steer a middle way. S. J. Tighy called Labour support for including the Africans under the Industrial Conciliation Act a 'very dangerous' point of view.[173] But if qualified recognition was extended to African trade unions they could be used as an 'instrument of education', argued J. P. Cope.[174] Mrs. Helen Suzman emphasized the rapid increase of industrial Native workers, who were handling semi-skilled work and permanently urbanized. Thus where the Nationalists put their emphasis on the more primitive Africans, the United Party recognized the degree to which the industrial revolution in South Africa had already created an urban industrial African proletariat.

Professor I. S. Fourie, one of the new liberals added to the United Party at the 1953 election, agreed with the Nationalists that Africans must not have the right to strike.[175] But the United Party was not so emotional on this point as Nationalists like B. J. v. d. Walt who spoke of the terrific weapon of the strike[176] and seemed to feel it threatened doom to white civilization in South Africa.

Basic to the division between the two chief parties was a major difference in their approach to the Native question. The United Party's empirical outlook was reflected in its insistence that to ignore the implications of the existence of African trade unions was to act like 'an ostrich', as I. S. Fourie put it. Confronting the growing urbanization and industrialization of a substantial group of Africans, the United Party felt that the best way to preserve white domination was to accept qualified, though not full recognition of African trade unions in industry and commerce. This they coupled with a ban on unions in the mines and agriculture 'at this stage of our economic life and development',[177] and on strikes. It might be a temporary position, but it appeared a tenable one.

The Nationalists were at one and the same time more restrictive, and more radical. Because they feared the potential power of African trade unions, they ignored them, although they would not abolish them. As an alternative, they set up a brand new system which, in J. A. F. Nel's words, made the Minister 'a trustee of Native labour', was adapted 'to the traditions of the Native' (because, in his view, it was similar to their system of chiefs and headmen) and thus fitted in 'with our whole policy'.[178] It was an effort to create a pattern of organization for the industrial African which combined limited representation by Africans with complete European control. It depended for its success, as the Nationalists acknowledged, on finding Europeans who could command the respect and confidence of the African worker, as well as on securing at the regional level Africans who would lend themselves to the system and yet retain the support of their fellows. It was another reflection of the Nationalist belief in systems as an answer to dynamic situations. But its satisfactory working depended on creating a degree of mutual confidence between Europeans and non-Europeans which current conditions could hardly be expected to sponsor.

That the machinery set up under the Native Labour (Settlement of Disputes) Act was less satisfactory than the Nationalists had hoped is suggested by their introduction of an amendment in mid-1955 closing a loop-hole under which 33 Africans had conducted a legal 6-hour protest strike in Port Elizabeth, and imposing still stricter penalties for violating the prohibition on strikes or their encouragement.[179] Opposing this amendment with the same vigor with which she had attacked the earlier measure, Mrs. Ballinger pointed out that despite all restrictions there were more strikes by non-Europeans than by Europeans. Whether harsher penalties will change this situation remains to be seen.

This account, though not exhaustive, has considered the most significant apartheid measures the Nationalists have enacted since 1948 (apart from political apartheid which is dealt with in the next chapter). These measures follow a significant pattern. At first, the spotlight was cast on physical contacts, through the extension to Europeans and Coloured of the long-established ban on marriage and immorality between Europeans and Africans. The next step was the Population Registration Act which will eventually eliminate uncertainty about the race to which a particular person belongs. With this framework established, the Nationalists moved to the far-reaching Group Areas Act under which full residential segregation may some day be established in the Union.

In 1951 was introduced the first major act under which the Nationalists began to shape African society: the Bantu Authorities Act. But it was not until mid-1953, after the election, that this act was first implemented. There followed then in rapid succession the two other most significant laws influencing African development: the Bantu Education Act, and the Native Labour (Settlement of Disputes) Act. The former may or may not be used to train Africans for a subordinate role in South African society; quite possibly not. Its emphasis, however, is on separateness, distinctiveness, differentiation. Both in theory and practice, the African is treated in these laws as being a particular kind of person, largely characterized by his tribal background.

Equally characteristic of all these acts is that they vest tremendous power in the hands of European authorities. It is true that the Bantu Education Act provides an apparently significant role for African parents, that the Native Labour Act has Africans on the committee to which disputes are first referred, and that the Bantu Authorities Act rests on an organization of tribal chiefs. But, in all these cases, the overriding authority is firmly in European hands, and those Africans who are vested with responsibilities have relatively little actual power.

This arrangement is satisfactory to the Nationalists and probably at the moment to many Africans. The Nationalists hope that their new emphasis on tribal authorities, the rural schools, the Bantu community, and the development of the Reserves will maintain the balance which they have established. They even hope that by throwing their weight behind so-called traditional forms and forces, they may shape the African community into a more self-centered group, which in the long run may endorse its exclusion from power in the European areas of the Union because it prefers to concentrate on its own affairs.

In the meantime, the Nationalists are prepared to go to extreme lengths to prevent contact between Europeans and non-Europeans on any social basis. In the spring of 1957 they introduced the Native Laws Amendment Bill, designed to consolidate and extend the many statutes through which the State controls and regulates the lives of Africans in urban areas. The clause around which opposition most fiercely centered was that which enabled the Minister of Native Affairs, by notice in the *Government Gazette*, to 'direct that no Native shall attend any church or other religious service' if he considered his presence created a 'nuisance'. Even the Dutch Reformed Church was concerned and sent a delegation to seek assurance that the freedom and sovereignty of the Church would remain untouched. When Dr. Verwoerd agreed to reword the clause to make it clear that the bill was not intended 'to interfere with the freedom of the individual to worship . . . so long as such freedom was not misused to the disturbance of good order in the community', the Council of the Dutch Reformed Church declared itself satisfied.[180] But the Christian Council, representing all the major Churches in South Africa except the Dutch Reformed Churches and the Roman Catholic Church, found that the redrafts of the clause did not change its principle of state interference with religious freedom and maintained uncompromisingly that:

> We shall be forced to disregard the law and to stand wholeheartedly by the members of the churches who are affected by it.[181]

While Church opposition may well modify the application of this portion of the measure, the measure has far-reaching implications for all organizations like the Liberal Party and the Institute of Race Relations, which have non-European as well as European members and fear the Minister may ban 'mixed' meetings. The Nationalist intention is to control and, if possible, prevent the kind of contacts between Europeans and non-Europeans which might blur their sense of differentness. Rarely has their point of view on this matter been better expressed than by *Die Transvaler* on February 27, 1957, when it wrote:

> It is not so much the overwhelming numbers of the non-Europeans but the destruction of the feeling of difference and otherness which is the great danger for the preservation of the European and his civilization in this multi-racial land. As long as liberalistic bishops and canons, professors, students and politicians can freely attend church and hold meetings and socials together, apartheid will be infringed in its marrow.

In contrast to this Nationalist approach, the United Party has pointed out with increasing decisiveness that the African is becoming so intermeshed into European life and work that it is a fallacy to believe he can be separated from it either in spirit or in practice. While not going nearly as far as the Liberals in accepting the logic of the 1948 Fagan Report, which pointed out that more than half the Africans are out of the Reserves at any given time, the United Party sees clearly the economic dependence of the country on African labor. Thus it has been ready to take a stand in support of a typically Western type of education for Africans; to give limited recognition to African trade unions; and to emphasize the particular needs of urban Africans. Though the United Party joins with the Nationalists in endorsing traditional segregation and discrimination, it also accepts some of the new by-products of African industrialization and urbanization.

Yet neither the United Party nor the Nationalists are facing the full implications of the steadily increasing importance of African labor in the Union's economy, or of the development which such an impact inevitably induces. It remains questionable whether the policy of either party can control the head of steam which is being thus generated.

CHAPTER 4

CONSTITUTIONAL CRISIS, 1951-1956

The issue on which the Nationalist Government and the Opposition most clearly divided was the attempt to ensure full political apartheid by removing the Coloured voters in Cape Province from the common roll. It was not the rights of the Coloured which aroused such deep feeling, however, but the means which the Government used for this purpose, means which most non-Nationalists considered unconstitutional. From their side, the Nationalists claimed that they were acting within the bounds of legality, and deeply resented the criticism levelled at them in South Africa and abroad.

The issue of a non-European franchise was already a controversial subject at the time that South Africans drafted the provisions for their Constitution which the British Parliament subsequently enacted as the South Africa Act, 1909. Neither of the former Boer states—the Orange Free State and the Transvaal—allowed non-Europeans to exercise the franchise. Natal, ostensibly liberal regarding the franchise, was highly restrictive in practice, for a law of 1896 made it impossible for any Asian to be added to the voters' roll, while almost no Africans have ever qualified for the vote in that province. The Cape, however, with its long liberal tradition, maintained a color-blind franchise under which any adult male could vote who could meet literacy and property qualifications.

Long and often difficult discussions took place before the statesmen who formulated the terms of South African union were able to reach a compromise which took these differences into account. To satisfy the sensibilities of the northern states, it was agreed that no non-European could stand for Parliament. As for the franchise itself, it was ultimately decided that each unit should retain its own provisions, subject to subsequent action by Parliament. But to safeguard the color-blind franchise of the Cape, a special guarantee was provided in section 35 of the Act of Union—that no one should be disqualified in that province 'by reason of his race or colour only' unless by a bill passed by both Houses of Parliament sitting together, and by two-thirds of their members at third reading. Thus one of the two so-called 'entrenched clauses' of the South African Act of Union safeguarded the voting rights of non-Europeans in the Cape, a fact reaffirmed in section 152. The other entrenched clause protects the equality of the two official languages, originally English and High Dutch, and now English and Afrikaans.

The number of non-Europeans on the Cape voting rolls has never been high compared to the number of Europeans, except in certain constituencies. Moreover, the balance in the electorate swung still more strongly in favor of Europeans when Hertzog's Nationalist Government gave the vote to adult white women in 1930, and when a year later it removed the need for European males in the Cape to meet the traditional literacy and property qualifications.

The most significant change in the Cape franchise came in 1936 when the Representation of Voters' Act removed registered African voters from the ordinary voters' roll and transferred them to a special Cape Native voters' roll (see p. 32) to elect three Europeans to the House of Assembly as Native representatives. The importance of the measure lay in the principle of communal representation rather than in the numbers it removed from the common roll, for there were only 10,628 Africans on the latter in 1935 as compared with 23,392 Coloured, 1,401 Asiatics (normally listed among the Coloured), and 382,103 whites.

Hertzog had long been concerned, however, with what he saw as the potential danger of a steady increase in the number of African voters to the point where they might outnumber those of European origin. His original proposal in 1926 had been to take all Africans off the electoral roll in the Cape and, as a substitute for this loss of political rights, to give them representation by Europeans in the Senate. In addition, all Africans were to participate directly or indirectly in the election of a Native Representative Council with advisory functions. More land was to be made available for African occupancy in the Native Reserves. When originally proposed, however, various aspects of this plan met sharp criticism from many members of Smuts' South African Party, and Hertzog was unable to secure the two-thirds majority necessary under the Act of Union to change African voting rights in the Cape.

When Hertzog and Smuts fused their parties in 1934 in the United Party, the arrangement ensured support for Hertzog's Native policy, though in a somewhat modified form. In 1936, this agreement was implemented. Legislation provided for the purchase of up to 7¼ million morgen (a morgen of land equals 2·1 acres) for Native occupancy, and the South African Natives' Trust Fund was set up to finance land purchase and to improve Native agriculture and education. The Cape African franchise remained untouched as far as qualifications were concerned, but African voters were placed on a separate roll to elect three European representatives. The legislation also provided that Africans throughout the Union should elect four European Senators through electoral colleges made up of chiefs, local councils, and local advisory boards. In addition, a Natives' Representative Council was established consisting of 12 elected Africans, 4 nominated Africans, and 5 European officials serving under the chairmanship of the Secretary of Native Affairs.

Liberals in the Union were gravely disturbed by this so-called Native settlement, though most South Africans hailed it as statesmanlike. As events were to prove, it was not only difficult to secure the additional land for the Native reserves but this in itself has done little to solve the fundamental problem of their overpopulation, and lack of resources. As the liberals also anticipated, the Natives' Representative Council never acquired the kind of influence which might have satisfied articulate African opinion; thus few Africans mourned its formal demise in 1950. Several of the Native representatives, and in particular Mrs. Ballinger, have played a distinguished role in the Assembly; so have some of the Senators elected by Africans. But the very fact that they stand outside the regular party structure has made their influence only a personal one. Moreover, when Dr. Malan's Nationalists threatened to remove the Native representatives from the House of Assembly and then took steps to remove the Coloured off the common roll, it was obvious that the 1936 Representation of Voters' Act had opened the door to far more radical action in regard to the non-European franchise than Hertzog or the United Party at large had anticipated.

In two significant ways, the attempt to take the Coloured off the ordinary voting rolls and place them on a communal roll differed from the earlier action affecting Cape Africans. In the first place, Hertzog had always spoken of the Coloured as 'an appendage to the white race' and promised at the time of the 1936 franchise legislation that the Coloured would never be taken off the common roll. Moreover, the Nationalists could not command a two-thirds majority to pass the Separate Representation of Voters' Bill in 1951. Thus there were both moral and constitutional reasons to oppose any effort to put the Coloured on a separate roll.

The Government believed, however, that it was legally possible to change the non-European franchise in the Cape by simple majority action. This belief rested on a somewhat complicated legal argument involving the changes in the legal status of the South African Parliament which had resulted from the Statute of Westminster, 1931, and the reaffirmation of its provisions in the Status of the Union Act, 1934, and from the 1937 judgment of the South African Appeal Court in the case of *Ndlwana v. Hofmeyr, N. O.*

The Statute of Westminster, passed by the British Parliament in 1931, made the Parliament of South Africa (like that of the other self-governing Dominions) a sovereign legislature with unlimited legislative power. The Status of the Union Act, enacted by the South African Parliament in 1934, reaffirmed the fact that this body was the sovereign legislative power in and over the Union. Did this mean that the Union Parliament was henceforth in the same position as that of Great Britain, with no legislative or procedural restrictions on its freedom to act? General Smuts had raised this possibility at the time that the Statute of Westminster was being considered, and Prime Minister J. B. M. Hertzog and his colleagues, including some members of Dr. D. F. Malan's 1948 cabinet, had maintained that, whatever the technicalities, the entrenched clauses retained their validity as a matter of honor and good faith. Moreover the resolution of 1930 approving the draft Statute of Westminster and passed by both Houses of the South African Parliament specifically affirmed the understanding that the proposed legislation in no way impaired the entrenched clauses. After the Status of the Union Act, the Speaker, Dr. E. G. Jansen (in 1951, Governor-General) had expressed a similar view.

The Ndlwana judgment of 1937 added in a curious way to the belief of many legal authorities that no South African Act would henceforth be declared unconstitutional by the courts. This case concerned the Native franchise measure of 1936 and questioned its validity on the grounds that the joint session procedure by which that Act had been passed was inappropriate for this legislation. The Appeal Court quickly disposed of this argument by declaring that Parliament could adopt any procedure it wished that was not specifically forbidden by the Constitution. It went beyond this, however, to imply that the Court would not inquire into the validity of an Act of the South African Parliament no matter how it was passed. To the legal advisers of the Nationalist Government, including Professor E. C. S. Wade of Cambridge University, England, who wrote the introduction to the ninth edition of the authoritative legal treatise by A. C. Dicey, *Law of the Constitution* (1939),[1] and to many other constitutional experts,[2] this judgment coupled with the earlier statutes made it possible for the Government to ignore the special legislative procedure of the entrenched clauses if it wished to do so.

Before the Nationalists could introduce their measure to take the Coloured off the common roll, however, they had to overcome the objections of N. C. Havenga, an important member of the governing coalition. Hertzog had always made it clear that he believed the Coloured should never be taken off the common roll. Moreover Hertzog was a strict constitutionalist, and had felt bound to seek the two-thirds' majority procedure laid down in clause 35 when changing the Africans to a separate roll in 1936. Not surprisingly, therefore, Havenga, Hertzog's chief follower, found himself in something of a dilemma. (See pp. 245-7.) With considerable effort, Havenga persuaded the Nationalists to retain the Native representatives in the House of Assembly. Moreover, he restrained Malan from action on the Coloured vote until late in 1950. Finally, however, Havenga agreed that the entrenched clauses were inapplicable on the ground that the provisions of the bill to transfer the Coloured to a separate roll represented no diminution of their political rights.

Long before the Nationalists introduced their Coloured vote legislation in 1951, the press had been canvassing the question of the need for a two-thirds' majority vote. *Die Burger* came out as early as September 3, 1948, in support of action by majority vote on the ground that the election had given the Government a mandate for political apartheid.[3] Soon after, J. G. Strijdom declared that the Coloured must not vote on the same roll as white persons even if action by a bare majority was not legal.[4] The *Forum*, a liberal monthly, found this statement 'shocking', and 'the height of political irresponsibility'.[5] For the most part, the English-language press stressed the moral issue involved in disregarding the special procedure of clause 35. Interestingly enough, *Dagbreek*, the Afrikaans' Sunday paper, also cautioned against doing away with the existing system by a slim majority vote.[6]

In mid-1949, there were reports of articulate Coloured opposition to their removal from the common roll. The *Star* reported on July 16, 1949, that G. J. Golding, commonly more ready to work with Europeans than other Coloured leaders, threatened general 'non-cooperation' if the measure was carried through. The *Sunday Express* called Golding's policy 'dynamite', and the *Rand Daily Mail* saw it as reflecting Coloured bitterness at the franchise proposal. *Die Volksblad*, in contrast, sharply criticized Golding's statement as worsening race relations and maintained that Coloured removal from the common roll would only bring advantages to the Coloured people.[7]

The terms of the Separate Representation of Voters Bill were published on February 6, 1951, a month before the measure was introduced in the House.[8] The proposed bill removed the eligible Coloured from the existing voters roll of the 55 Cape constituencies (54 after the 1952 delimitation), in perhaps half of which they had some considerable influence, and placed them on a separate roll to elect four Europeans to the House of Assembly at regular five-year intervals, not at general elections. The Coloured were also to elect one European to the Senate, instead of sharing in the election of the eight Senators from the Cape, and two Europeans to the Cape Provincial Council, instead of the four for whom they could now vote. The few Coloured already registered in Natal could remain on the common roll, but no Coloured names were to be added after the legislation. On the pattern of the Natives' Representative Council (by then abolished), the bill also provided for a Board of Coloured Affairs, consisting of eleven nominated Coloured under the chairmanship of a European Commissioner, which was to advise on Coloured affairs and to act as an intermediary between the Coloured and the Government.

While recognizing that there would be 'gigantic agitation over this legislation', *Die Transvaler* stressed the benefit for the Coloured of being removed from 'the contaminated atmosphere of opportunist politics'.[9] In contrast, the *Star* called it 'a disgraceful episode' that would deprive the Coloured of a 'valuable and valued right', while the *Argus* was still more vehement in terming it 'an act of moral treachery' which was 'anti-Western, anti-democratic, anti-Christian'.[10] The *Natal Daily News* raised the fear that the legislation might create a common non-European front and the *Friend* felt it would produce a million new enemies for white civilization.[11] The Civil Rights League,[11a] the Christian Council of South Africa, the Transvaal Indian Congress and Golding's Coloured group protested among others. J. G. N. Strauss expressed the United Party's strong opposition, and Colin Steyn, its Free State leader, called it 'a rape of the constitution'.[12] He was answered angrily by J. G. Strijdom, who charged that United Party 'incitement' of the Coloured against apartheid was 'a political crime'. The stage was well set for combat.

On March 8, 1951, Dr. T. E. Dönges asked leave to introduce the Separate Representation of Voters Bill in the House.[13] At once, in a virtually unprecedented move, Strauss objected on a point of order to introducing at a session of the House of Assembly alone a bill which fell within the scope of section 35. He asked for the Speaker's ruling on the matter. In so doing, Strauss cited a wealth of evidence and argument to demonstrate that the entrenched clauses were still binding, that the Ndlwana judgment did not contradict this conclusion, and that entrenchment as such did not impair the sovereignty of Parliament. It was the argument, prepared by D. V. Cowen, Professor of Law at the University of Cape Town,[14] which ultimately convinced the Appeal Court. Strauss was ably supported by John Christie for the Labour Party, who pointed out the possible threat to the equality of the two official languages if the other entrenched clause, section 36, could be changed by majority action.

Oddly enough, it was the Nationalist reply to Strauss and Christie which introduced, however negatively, the issue of the morality of the legislation which proved the central theme of the long debate on the bill. Speaking against Strauss' point of order in his capacity as an ex-Speaker of the House, J. F. T. Naudé argued that the Ndlwana judgment enabled Parliament to use any procedure it wished, that sovereignty involved unlimited legislative power and that no Parliament could bind its successor. This was an analysis in strictly legal terms, he pointed out, adding that 'I am not going into the aspect of whether it is moral or immoral, or right or wrong'.[15] Since legally the Government could pass the measure by majority action, morality was irrelevant: 'Does a larger number render an immoral act moral?'[16] It was only the first of a long series of Nationalist comments on the measure which seemed to discount the importance of morality, and which provided the Opposition with its most potent ammunition.

For a month, action on the proposed measure was held up until the Speaker gave his ruling. The press still debated the issue hotly. The *Rand Daily Mail* accused the Nationalists of belittling the power of precedent,[17] and the *Star* saw the bill as a test of European moral leadership.[18] *Die Burger* agreed that moral issues were more important than legal ones, but found that they favored the Nationalist case.[19] Dawie, its political correspondent, asked on March 17 whether the people were really deeply concerned about the issue, to which the spontaneous protest of the Torch Commando was soon to give a decisive answer. Moreover, deep concern in Natal was reflected in a resolution by its Provincial Council in support of the entrenched clauses which *Die Transvaler,* with insight, found inspired by fear of an Afrikaner republic.[20]

Despite the obvious public concern over the constitutional implications of the legislation, the Speaker's ruling, presented to the House on April 16, rejected Strauss' point of order. In so doing the Speaker was supported by the law advisers of the Government, but rejected the advice of the parliamentary draughtsman. His argument rested heavily on the judgment in the Ndlwana case, and cited authorities who, unlike Cowen, held that the entrenched clauses were no longer binding. To differ from these authorities and the Appeal Court, the Speaker concluded, would be 'an attempt to frustrate this house in expressing its will and in exercising its undoubted rights, powers and privileges'.[21]

Once more, Dönges introduced the bill; once more, Strauss, obviously dissatisfied with the Speaker's ruling, attempted to counter this action. Moving an amendment to require a joint session, Strauss appealed directly to Havenga to support the declarations of good faith of his former leader, Hertzog. Notwithstanding the Speaker's ruling, the path was still open, he declared, 'to follow that sound broad road of nationalism' to which Havenga had 'so often and so eloquently' referred.[22] To which appeal, Strauss received Havenga's blunt answer that he did not believe that separate representation 'in itself encroaches upon the political rights which the Coloured enjoy at this time'.[23]

Not the details of the legislation, however, but the attitude to the Constitution was the basic point at issue. The United Party, and the Torch Commando, which sprang into existence to protect the Constitution, had an unphilosophic but deep feeling for a fundamental document. The entrenched clauses were the outcome of a compact. Moreover one of the entrenched clauses protected the equal position of the two official languages, and those speaking English were already feeling the pressure of Afrikanerdom. But beyond this fact was the instinctive awareness (perhaps still more keenly felt outside than inside the formal ranks of the United Party), that if the concept of constitutionality was to be upheld in South Africa it must be at this point. Moreover, legality must be supported by morality. 'Honour, faith, fidelity to the pledged word are the very soul of white civilization', said Dr. Bernard Friedman, a United Party liberal, when the bill was first introduced. 'How then can you safeguard white civilization by striking a mortal blow at its very soul?'[24]

The Nationalists assumed a totally different attitude. In the first place, they argued that the South Africa Act was 'imposed' by the British, and must not be allowed to stand in the way of those programs which the governing Nationalists determined were best for the country. Mr. J. van den Berg declared that the Act of Union was 'immoral' because it crushed the nationalist Afrikaner school of thought regarding South African development. He felt the 'founding fathers' would have written a very different document 'if they could have imagined the policy of apartheid', and asked the Opposition which came first with them: 'this political argument, or the mould in which you want to cast the future of South Africa? '[25] Dr. Malan reiterated his view that Great Britain was responsible for the entrenched clauses which, in his view, undercut their binding force as a contract. Like Naudé, he asked whether numbers made morality. Yet, in the same speech, Malan declared that 'on great issues' like the establishment of a republic, a special mandate through a more than ordinary majority was necessary.[26]

The only conclusion that can be drawn is that the Nationalists recognized the necessity of a general consensus, or basic agreement in the community for setting up new forms like that of a republic, but refused to acknowledge the binding force of settlements like article 35, entrenching the non-European vote in the Cape, which they maintained they had not shared in making (though Hertzog had participated vigorously) and which currently interfered with their purposes. The Nationalists attempted to justify this latter stand as a higher morality reflecting the people's will, or the 'will of the Lord' (as the Reverend van Schoor maintained) or less exaltedly (as Hertzog and now C. R. Swart did) on the ground that 'self-preservation is the highest principle'. But these rationalizations only raised increasing doubts in the Opposition about the value of any safeguards which the Nationalists were prepared currently to underwrite.

Though presented with so easily exploited a situation, the United Party did surprisingly little with it at first, apart from Strauss' instantaneous and emphatic challenge. The Labour Party and Mrs. Ballinger among the Native representatives were quicker to pick the obvious weaknesses in the Nationalist arguments. When Malan formally admitted that although the Coloured retained their franchise under the new legislation,

> the relative power of the Coloured vote changes, and in that sense the power of the Coloured vote is curtailed and diminished,[27]

Mrs. Ballinger pointed out that the relative value of votes was the essence of party government.

When the Labour Party suggested that the Nationalist attitude to constitutionalism might threaten the position of the English language, W. C. du Plessis (see p. 252) answered that

> the language rights are entrenched by a much higher authority than that of the entrenched clauses and even higher than the authority of this house, because they are entrenched in the sovereign will of the people,[28]

but he did not make clear who 'the people' were or how their will was to be determined.

Though united in general opposition to the Representation of Voters Bill, United Party members had varied reasons for being opposed. Some, like S. F. Waterson, attached morality only to the two-thirds majority procedure, a fact which undercut their opposition to Malan's late-1953 efforts to take the Coloured off the common roll by the procedure laid down in the entrenched clauses. Others, like Dr. Colin Steyn, felt the demands of morality required consultation with the Coloured. Still others went so far as to charge that it was not only the procedure but the purpose of the bill that was immoral. Thus Dr. D. L. Smit, former Secretary for Native Affairs, claimed that the Coloured were a special and unique responsibility of the whites; H. F. Oppenheimer that their interests were identical with those of the whites; and K. Ueckermann that the Coloured had a right to share in the decision-making process.

> We have got to realize [said the latter] that if we accept the peoples of this country, you have got to give them some say in the development of this country. We can only fall back on the forces of tolerance, justice and goodwill if we harbour any wish to save our skins in the future.[29]

A. H. J. Eaton expressed the same slightly equivocal attitude when he declared that:

> We have no right to deprive people of full citizenship, because every human being has a right to progress, and to live a better life, and to become cultured [but added] . . . we do not object to Coloured people—as long as we grow in numbers with them—having the right to vote.[30]

The obvious difficulty for the United Party was that it had no deep concern for the Coloured, or for the way in which they exercised their franchise. It was commonly believed that most of the Coloured voted for the United Party, and were even a decisive factor in swinging some seven Cape constituencies to that party. Even if this were the case—and it was never proved—the Coloured were allowed no significant role within the United Party. Apart from the constitutional issue, the legislation to remove them from the common roll would hardly have awakened deep concern in the United Party. The Nationalists could have made much more capital, in fact, with the question which Swart early levelled at the United Party: Would the Opposition repeal the measure if it were returned to power? On third reading, Strauss denied that he had said the United Party would do so. That question was not completely answered until the United Party special congress in August 1957 pledged the party to replace the Coloured on the common roll from which the Nationalists had removed them in 1956.

Instead of facing this particular question, Strauss produced at second reading the much broader, though less specific proposal of a Bill of Rights to entrench 'the fundamental liberties of the people of South Africa'. These liberties included, in his view, the equality of the two languages; the political rights of the Coloured, freedom of the press, conscience, religion and speech, subject to the necessary safeguards to preserve democracy; the sanctity of the law courts; freedom of movement according to the law of the land; freedom of lawful association; and membership in the Commonwealth and the United Nations.

This proposal, not surprisingly, met two major objections voiced by Dr. Malan: that entrenchment would restrict the sovereignty of Parliament; and that several items in the long list, notably membership in the Commonwealth, were incompatible (presumably in the long run) with Nationalist policy. Dönges called the Bill of Rights proposal 'a red herring' to divert attention from the legislation before the House, and enumerated a long series of problems involved in establishing new constitutional provisions.[31] Partly because of this rather clever attack, but also because Strauss' proposal for a Bill of Rights was over-comprehensive and ill thought out, it never had the effect which might have been hoped from it.

At every stage of the measure, the United Party maintained its opposition, substituting a resounding 'no' for its earlier 'yes but' attitude to apartheid measures, and forcing the Nationalists to keep all their members on hand.[32] Not until third reading, however, did Strauss pull together all the points which different Opposition speakers had made, and unify them into a platform on which the United Party could stand firmly as the defender of the Constitution and the cherished rights of South Africans. Yet even then, Dönges was essentially right that (except for the proposal of a Bill of Rights) the United Party had not offered any practical alternative in the way of a definite color policy.

As the debate went on in an atmosphere of bitterness and recrimination, feelings outside of Parliament were also rising higher. *Die Transvaler* stigmatized the United Party attack on the bill as 'simply criminal',[33] and *Die Vaderland*, Havenga's organ, as 'two-faced'.[34] From the other side, the *Friend* saw the whole affair as 'a struggle for the soul of South Africa'.[35] The *Pretoria News* pointed out shrewdly that a flexible Constitution was 'suited only to a homogeneous population'.[36] Strauss' proposal for a Bill of Rights met mild enthusiasm from the English-language press though *Dagbreek*, which obviously disliked the crisis stirred up by the Nationalists, found it no more than 'an emotional display'.[37]

None of this sparring in the press prepared anyone, however, for the demonstrations of deep public concern which followed the spontaneous organization of the Torch Commando, while the bill was still going through the House. By the time it was passed, torch-light processions, mass meetings and the Steel Commando drive on Cape Town had dramatized (see p. 304) the degree to which wide portions of the South African people were stirred by what they felt was a threat to the Constitution.

Public demonstrations and protests were one means of attempting to change the situation. Court action was another. Strauss had asked Dönges point blank how he would respond to a court decision on the Separate Representation of Voters' Act, 1951, and the latter had replied somewhat equivocally that he would acquiesce in the same sense in which Strauss had accepted the Ndlwana judgment. United Party tactics were to refer the act as quickly as possible to the judicial branch, and the case of *Harris v. Dönges* was soon initiated through the appeal of four Coloured voters. The Cape Provincial Division followed the judgment in the Ndlwana case that a statute could not be questioned in the courts and dismissed the suit. On appeal, however, the case was taken to the highest South African court, the Appellate Division of the Supreme Court, which decided in favor of the plaintiffs on the ground that the act in question had not been passed by the correct procedure.

Few South African cases have awakened such widespread interest, or had such significance as *Harris v. Dönges*.[38] After hearing six days of argument, the court handed down a unanimous judgment on March 20, 1952, which provided an authoritative answer to the legal issues which had been debated in Parliament in the course of the bill. The central question was the effect of the Statute of Westminster (1931) on the entrenched clauses. The court declared unequivocally that it left them fully in force. The Statute of Westminster removed all external limitations on South Africa's exercise of independent sovereign power; it had no effect, the judges held, on the internal procedural arrangements written into the South Africa Act. If the Statute of Westminster had no effect on the entrenched clauses, clearly the Status of the Union Act, 1934, also had no effect on them.

Further, the argument used by the Government's counsel, that the entrenched clauses impaired South Africa's position as a sovereign state, the court found 'a manifest absurdity', since it remained open to the South African Parliament to amend the South Africa Act by a two-thirds majority of both houses in joint session.

> It would be surprising to a constitutional lawyer to be told that that great and powerful country, the United States of America, is not a sovereign, independent country [commented Chief Justice Centlivres in the course of the judgment] simply because its Congress cannot pass any legislation which it pleases.

The most difficult problem for the Appeal Court was the judgment in the 1937 Ndlwana case, which had declared that Parliament could adopt any procedure it thought fit and that the courts would not question an Act of Parliament. Reluctant as the court was to overrule an earlier decision, the judges found that there had been no substantial argument in the Ndlwana case on the constitutional question involved. Moreover, the Chief Justice pointed out that the Ndlwana decision

> enabled Parliament to deprive, by a bare majority in each House sitting separately, individuals of rights which were solemnly safeguarded in the Constitution of the country.

For both reasons, the court declared the earlier judgment in error. Thus on the basis of its reasoning that the entrenched clauses were still in force, the Appeal Court declared the Separate Representation of Voters' Act, 1951, null and void.[39]

That the Nationalists would protest, and attempt to override the verdict of the Appeal Court if it was distasteful to them, had been obvious from the first. Dr. Verwoerd declared openly on June 7, 1951, that if the courts decided against the Government, Parliament would reverse the decision,[40] a statement which the Natal *Witness* pointed out was 'a dangerous attack on the independence of the judiciary'.[41] The *Friend*, next day, felt the country was 'back-sliding into the twilight of political democracy at an alarming rate'.

Immediately the Appeal Court decision was handed down on March 20, 1952, Dr. Malan declared that it created an unacceptable constitutional position. Conflicting court decisions made for uncertainty and instability, he declared, drew the courts into the political sphere and endangered the legislative sovereignty of Parliament which the Government would take steps to ensure. To underline their unity, the four provincial Nationalist leaders—Malan, Havenga, Strijdom and Swart—followed this with a joint statement full of emotional phrases like 'constitutional enslavement', 'the dead hand of the British Parliament', and 'the continuation of the struggle for freedom'.[42] *Die Burger* echoed on March 24 that the decision was 'a threat to freedom and "white-dom"', and *Die Transvaler*, two days later, that 'everything which the Afrikaner has won is threatened'.[43] Already the *Rand Daily Mail* was warning that the Government planned legislation to make Parliament supreme and deprive the courts of the testing power.[44]

The enthusiastic approval of the Appeal Court judgment by the English-language press and its grave concern at the Nationalists' attitude had their counterpart in Parliament. Prevented twice by the Speaker from registering his immediate protest at Malan's statement, Strauss finally succeeded a week later in criticizing it for contributing to unrest and doubt in the country and threatening a grave constitutional crisis.

Beyond this, a full scale attack on the Government through a motion by Strauss to accept the Appeal Court judgment was launched on April 16, 1952, the day of the formal debut of the United Front which joined the United Party, Labour Party and Torch Commando into an alliance to oust the Nationalists from office. (See p. 316.) Rumors, threats, an intense press campaign, the call to action by Kane-Berman, of the Torch Commando, all contributed to the bitter, heated atmosphere in which the debate took place. The United Party concerned itself less with justifying the Appeal Court judgment than with what they rightly felt was their strongest platform: support for the Constitution, the judiciary and the rule of law. Christie of the Labour Party called for the Government's resignation and an appeal to the people to test whether or not the Nationalists had the support they claimed. Government members, in an attempt to counter, called the general public uproar a planned campaign sparked by the press and ready-made telegrams of protest.[45] More positively, they took the offensive against the implications rather than the content of the judgment. Elaborating on Malan's original statement of March 20, they charged that the decision impaired parliamentary sovereignty, majority rule, the will of the people, the clarity of the Constitution and the integrity of the courts.

Though their particular strategy was not disclosed until the High Court of Parliament Bill was introduced, the Nationalists were obviously engaged on a long-range counter-offensive designed to detach wavering members of the Opposition. At one point in the debate on Strauss' motion, Malan appealed directly to 'the more sensible' members of the Opposition to support the Government. It was a tactic repeated consistently thereafter, but resisted relatively successfully by the United Party.

Hardly had this debate ended when Dönges asked permission to introduce the High Court of Parliament bill[46]

> to vest in the democratically elected representatives of the electors, as representing the will of the people, the power to adjudicate finally on the validity of laws passed by Parliament.[47]

This measure provided that a special committee of the Union Parliament, composed of its members, and called the High Court of Parliament, had power to review any judgment or order of the Appeal Court which invalidated a Parliamentary Act. The High Court was expressly declared to be a court of law, whose decisions were final and binding, and to be executed in the same way as those of the Supreme Court.

This new High Court of Parliament, declared Dönges, would be a substitute for the Judicial Committee of the Privy Council (appeals to which had been abolished in 1950),[48] and would relieve the existing South African courts of

> the invidious necessity of becoming involved in constitutional issues which have a party political bias or which impinge on the legislative sphere.[49]

The United Party answer was obvious. Strauss at once opposed leave to introduce the measure which, he said, would undermine the independence of the judiciary, and smash the Constitution which was both the basis of the South African union and the guarantor of liberties. 'This is a bogus court,' he charged, 'set up to express the will of the caucus of the Nationalist Party.'[50] J. Christie, Leader of the Labour Party, seconding Strauss' amendment, called it 'a court of political hacks', and Mrs. Ballinger declared that nothing could be more absurd than to have a Parliament set up a parliament to show that the majority was right. Others compared it to Russian political courts. The United Front was using an effective admixture of ridicule and logic.

The Nationalist line in this debate was to replace their earlier insistence on strict legality with a justification in terms of what they called a higher legality: the necessities of white civilization, particularly as reflected in the *volkswil.*

> I see in it [the bill] the safeguarding and the perpetuation of the white Christian trusteeship in the interests of whites as well as non-Europeans, [said Mr. D. J. Potgieter] in so far as it protects one of the most important foundations of Christian trusteeship, namely the political influence of the whites.[51]

More provocatively, S. M. Loubser declared

> The United Party comes and whines 'the Constitution'. Anyone would think that the Constitution was of greater importance to them than the maintenance of white civilization in our country.[52]

Another Nationalist quoted President Kruger's 'in the voice of the people one also hears the voice of God',[53] perhaps in the back of his mind remembering that the old President of the Transvaal Republic had dismissed Chief Justice Kotzé, when the latter tried to test the legality of a legislative act.

Some Nationalists launched a forthright attack on the Constitution. J. J. Fouché maintained it did not reflect the will of the people.[54] H. J. van den Berg said he would protect a South African Constitution but felt 'a moral obligation' to get rid of the 'imposed' entrenched clauses.[55] At the same time, however, a favorite charge against the United Party was that it had already broken the entrenched clauses in 1946 in passing the Asiatic Land Tenure and Indian Representation Act by ordinary legislation. The fact that no one had suggested at that time that the entrenched clauses were involved, that only two Indian voters were removed from the common roll by the 1946 act and that it would have permitted a great many others to acquire the franchise and, moreover, that the representation provisions of the Act were never used and were repealed by the Asiatic Laws Amendment Act, No. 47 of 1948, did nothing to reduce the barrage of Nationalist attacks on the United Party for its now-revealed 'illegality' of action.

For all their efforts, the Nationalists left themselves open to many searching questions. If every generation must rule itself, as P. O. Sauer maintained,[56] can there be continuity? If the changing make-up of the Appeal Court results occasionally in one bench overriding the judgment of an earlier one, would not a High Court of Parliament, which changed its composition with every election, produce still more uncertainty?

> If the courts should not have the testing right [asked H. G. Lawrence, a United Party frontbencher], then why on earth is the Government giving this High Court of Parliament the testing right?

It was not difficult to show that the device of a High Court of Parliament was intended to deal only with this particular emergency.

Compared to the ragged line of argument of the Nationalists, the Opposition displayed good team work and spirit. From the beginning of the debate, it shifted the focus from the Coloured vote to the demand for an election, the same demand which was being made on public platforms all over South Africa by speakers for the United Front. Moreover, every stage of the measure was combated by words and by votes. As with the original Separate Representation of Voters Bill, Strauss opposed the introduction of the measure, and asked for the Speaker's ruling on the need for a joint session in the light of the Court's decision. Failing to block the measure in either way, Strauss moved to dismiss the bill at second reading, challenging the Prime Minister's refusal to accept the Court's decision and declaring trenchantly

> if he is not prepared to accept the law of the land, then if there is force used by the Government, the people will meet that force with force.[57]

At the committee stage, the Opposition formally refused to participate on the ground that it considered the bill 'a fraud' and wished no part in discussing its details. Though the vote totals were less high for the Opposition on this measure than in the earlier one, the explanation is not that it fought less well, but that many Opposition members were already campaigning against the Government outside the House.

Yet despite what was on total an impressive display of unity, there were also significant signs of differences within United Front ranks over which the Nationalists could take satisfaction. One United Party member, G. N. Hayward, said he would support separate representation if the number of Coloured representatives increased as the Coloured themselves became more numerous. S. J. Tighy said he would support the Nationalists on separate representation for the Coloured if they included a guarantee for language rights.[58] Several United Party members acknowledged that the 1946 Indian legislation had inadvertently broken the entrenched clauses—though legal opinion differs on this. But the most significant points of difference were over consultation and compromise to find an all-party agreement on non-European policy.

During second reading debate, H. Davidoff declared emphatically that the Labour Party was no longer prepared to compromise on non-European policy, not only because it supported the rights of the Coloured but also, more broadly, because the party was critical of the continued white domination over the non-Europeans. It was an open declaration of the more liberal new attitude of the Labour Party on color matters (see p. 342), and a forthright challenge to the Nationalists on the issue over which they felt most keenly.

United Party leadership, in contrast, obviously still hoped to find some ultimate agreement with the Nationalists over non-European policy, and dreaded the prospect of a widening division between the white groups. In a bitter struggle, only white South Africa would lose, warned Colin Steyn, Free State leader of the United Party,

> Let us call a halt and see whether there is not some other solution to this difficult problem we have in South Africa today.[59]

He proposed seeking an agreement with the Coloured who, he felt, were still 'sympathetic' to the whites. 'We will have to come to an agreement', he maintained, 'if we want to preserve white civilization in this country.'[60] This start could then be a bridge to other groups.

Dr. Malan's answer formed his total contribution to the second reading debate. He rejected the idea of discussions with the Coloured since they had 'no representative body'. He had always urged joint cooperation of Europeans to work out a solution to the non-European problem, he declared, but its basic condition must be an acceptance of apartheid. Once again the Nationalists endorsed agreement, but on their own terms. On 'great, serious, vital problems,' said Malan, there could be no compromise. With those members of the United Party who accepted apartheid and disagreed only in its application, the Nationalists could work. 'We do not radically disagree,' he said specifically, 'with the right wing of that side of the House.'[61] With the United Party as a whole, however, the Nationalists could not negotiate because it was not a unit, as shown by its internal differences over color policy. It was an open attempt to split the United Party.

Strauss recognized Malan's appeal for what it was and declared indignantly (perhaps with more emphasis than conviction) that there were no quislings or compromisers in the United Party or the United Front. Once the fight was won, however, the United Party was prepared to lift the whole non-European question out of politics to find 'an all-party solution' which would be 'just and honourable' to the non-Europeans, and which would 'safeguard the maintenance of white civilization in South Africa'. The words were fair, but they left no more concrete impression than earlier ones of what 'solution' the United Party endorsed. Yet the party's support for consultation with non-Europeans as well as Europeans was constructive if it could have been carried out, while its warnings of the danger of creating a non-European bloc might well have been taken with more seriousness on both sides of the House.

Though *Dagbreek* felt that Colin Steyn's speech in Parliament suggested the gulf between the two parties was not as deep as commonly maintained,[62] the mass meetings led by the Torch Commando, and Provincial Council resolutions evidenced sharp divisions. The Free State Provincial Council formally supported the Government on May 8, 1952, in its action on the judgment, and *Die Volksblad* commented that Malan could now know 'the people are behind him'.[63] The Transvaal Provincial Council, in contrast, opposed the 'open violation' of the entrenched clauses implicit in the High Court of Parliament Bill. By far the most disturbed, however, was the Natal Provincial Council, which called openly for a new National Convention to redraft the South African Constitution, a demand subsequently affirmed (see p. 318) by Natal's largest and most impressive of mass meetings.

Even before the High Court of Parliament Bill came into effect on June 3, 1952, Strauss had said the United Party intended to refer it to the courts. On

June 12, the same four Coloured voters who had appealed against the earlier act sought an order against the new measure which *Die Transvaler* declared disapprovingly 'placed the entire constitutional struggle outside the political arena'.[64] Early in August, the Cape Provincial Division temporarily barred the removal of Coloured voters from the common roll pending a judicial decision on the High Court Act. Late in the same month, the High Court of Parliament met in Pretoria and on August 28, 1952, reversed the Appeal Court decision on the Separate Representation of Voters Act. The effect was spoiled, however, both because of the deliberate abstention of United Party and Labour Party members from the High Court session, and because the day afterwards the Cape court declared the High Court of Parliament Act invalid, a judgment unanimously upheld in November 1952 by the Appeal Court.[65]

Though they gave a unanimous decision, each of the five judges of the Appeal Court filed a separate opinion on the High Court of Parliament Act. All of them found that the body given power under this Act did not possess the essential qualities of a court of law because its members had no legal qualifications, and the composition of the tribunal violated the fundamental principle that no one should be a judge in his own case. Moreover, more expressly than in the first Harris case, the judges avowed the right of the law courts to test legislation which they felt came within the entrenched clauses and to strike it down if it did not conform to the provisions of those clauses. Since the High Court of Parliament Act was obviously intended to secure the same ends as the earlier Separate Representation of Voters Act, the validity of the entrenched clauses was again examined. Four of the five judges again used a strict interpretation of the Act of Union to demonstrate the continued binding force of section 152 and 35. Mr. Justice F. P. van den Heever, however, saw the source of their authority in the very fact of their continued existence, and thus implied that the South African Constitution drew its validity not from its enactment by the British Parliament (as Dr. Malan had suggested) but from its local source within South Africa.[66]

What would the Government do this time? While the *Rand Daily Mail* called the now defunct High Court of Parliament a 'sordid and unsavoury stratagem',[67] *Die Transvaler* was declaring that it was 'intolerable' to hold South Africa down by the dead hand of the past, and that the people would be the final arbiters.[68] J. G. Strijdom declared that the Government 'could not—would not—accept the situation caused by the judgment of the Court'.[69] Lawrence countered for the United Party that the Nationalists had an 'infallibility complex', and called it a technique of dictatorship.[70] Finally, on December 6, *Die Burger* reported Dönges as saying that the Government accepted the court's judgment but not the position it created. It would take the case to the people. Otherwise, the Government feared that South Africa could not become a republic, or secede.[71]

'Now the cat is out of the bag,' wrote the *Rand Daily Mail* about Dönges' statement. 'The Coloured vote, *and* membership in the Commonwealth are at stake in the clash with the courts.'[72] From its side, the moderate Afrikaans Sunday paper, *Dagbreek*, deplored the manner in which the constitutional issue was being used for political propaganda.[73]

Everything, however, now pointed to the election. Though, as it turned out, the Nationalists' vastly increased majority fell short of the two-thirds vote necessary to satisfy the requirements of the entrenched clauses, the Coloured vote issue was an important factor in the propaganda on both sides of the political campaign. To the United Front, it demonstrated the unconstitutional behaviour of the Government; to the Nationalists, the issue had still more emotional content, for political apartheid was pictured as the essential foundation of a coherent color policy capable of safeguarding the position of the white minority in South Africa.

Whether or not the Coloured vote had any significant effect in the 1953 election is almost impossible to determine. While Coloured voters are listed separately at the end of the voters' roll for each constituency their votes are not recorded separately. Some of their more radical intellectuals adopted the position that the Coloured should abstain from voting in the 1953 election, but since there were high percentage polls in those constituencies in which many Coloured voters were registered it seems unlikely that their advice had much effect (see p. 216). Those most closely in touch with the Coloured feel that the latter voted solidly for the United Party in the Cape Peninsula constituencies, but that in outlying Cape districts they may well have cast their votes as their employers indicated. Whatever the facts in this regard, few people would disagree with *Die Burger's* assessment that the Coloured vote had not been of decisive significance in any constituency except the predominantly Coloured Cape Flats. The paper suggested that the potential voting power of the Coloured was large enough to enable them to play an important role in several constituencies in the future, but added, probably correctly, that to make this possible the United Party would have to register Coloured in such numbers 'that its own white followers would rise in revolt against it'.[74]

Yet despite the relatively insignificant part played by the Coloured in the 1953 election, the Nationalists retained their determination to remove them from the common roll, and ensure full political apartheid. How should this be done? Though various expedients like packing the Senate or the courts were apparently considered, Dr. Malan carried his point that a constitutional approach should be attempted first. Already, on the morrow of the election, he called for enough voters from the Opposition to enable the Nationalists to meet the two-thirds majority provision of the entrenched clauses. Through two joint sessions, the Nationalists strove to capitalize on the revolt against Strauss' leadership (see p. 293), and to gain the votes necessary to take the Coloured off the common roll. Though in the second joint session they ultimately secured the support of the six United Party 'rebels', or as they called themselves at that time the Independent United Party, the Nationalists failed, however, in their two major and, in a sense, interrelated objectives: securing a two-thirds majority, and further splintering the United Party. Paradoxically, the Nationalists may even have helped to defeat their own purpose of breaking up the United Party by emphasizing the issue over which that party found it most easy to close its ranks.

When Malan announced on July 3, 1953, that the Government would convene a joint sitting to repeal entrenched clause 35 and to provide for separate representation of the Coloured, he seemed to be taking a long step towards meeting the major objection of the Opposition to the earlier attempts to carry out this policy through majority action. The pro-Government press hailed the decision as a generous gesture. The Opposition press was more sceptical. The

Natal Daily News felt that Malan's acceptance of a constitutional approach was a concession of some importance which might yet be a basis for agreement,[75] but the *Rand Daily Mail* saw no merit in the bill, charged that the issues involved were 'elaborately misrepresented', and that the whole formed 'an unacceptable bargain'.[76]

Almost as soon as the newly elected members of Parliament assembled for its mid-year sessions, the joint session was convened, evidence of the high degree of priority the Coloured vote issue retained with the Nationalists. Dr. Malan himself took charge of the bill which he sought leave to introduce on July 14, 1953,

> to amend the South Africa Act, to validate and amend the Separate Representation of Voters Act, 1951, and to define the jurisdiction of the courts of law to pronounce upon the validity of laws passed by Parliament.[77]

The Labour Party, the Liberal Party through Mrs. Ballinger, and the Union Federal Party, opposed the granting of leave; the United Party remained silent. The motion was carried 173-14. The contrast with the first stage of the earlier legislation on the same subject was striking.

At second reading, however, which followed next day, Strauss moved a strongly worded amendment asking for a joint Select Committee to consider the whole multi-racial problem in South Africa with due regard for securing the cooperation of the Cape Coloured and 'the leaders of other responsible and moderate non-European opinion'. It was a variant of his election time proposals for taking the non-European question out of politics (see p. 169). Avowing himself unconvinced of the 'value of separate representation' (a point on which United Party members found great difficulty in agreeing), Strauss made his principal objection on moral grounds. The present proposals would be 'a breach of an undertaking'. Equally,

> they give the citizens of South Africa nothing . . . which they don't already have at the present time, but on the contrary they seek to take away fundamental rights which all sections of our community, both white and black, possess.[78]

At the same time, Strauss took advantage rather cleverly of a definition of apartheid as traditional segregation which had been used by N. C. Havenga on a B.B.C. broadcast in England and said that the United Party would be prepared to use that definition as a basis of Select Committee discussions. Thus he rejected Malan's new approach, despite its use of entrenched clause procedure, and attempted to shift the emphasis away from separate representation to the broad, and safer, path of consultation with everyone on what was obviously everyone's problem.

By offering, in his second reading speech, to entrench language rights, Malan had attempted to forestall one of the United Party's objections. Dönges made a further effort to show Nationalist regard for the English language by ostentatiously using it for his second reading speech. Dönges scoffed, however, at Strauss' Select Committee proposal as 'a device—a sordid stratagem—to preserve the façade of unity' in the United Party. All the way through the Nationalist speeches in this debate ran two approaches: the attempt to keep the United Party from raising a constitutional, language, or rule of law argument which would distract attention from the practical problem of removing the Coloured from the common roll; and the effort to secure support from individual members of that party.

It had been obvious from the first that Labour, Liberals and Union Federalists were completely opposed to the measure. The Nationalists knew, however, that there were United Party members who favored making concessions from the United Party side to match those Malan had wrung from his own more extreme followers. Thus the Nationalists constantly echoed their leader's plea for 'a free vote' on this measure. When Bailey Bekker, leader of the party in the Transvaal (who was expelled from the United Party shortly after for challenging Strauss' leadership), appealed to Malan to provide a sound basis for agreement by leaving out the courts, not touching the Constitution, and promoting the principle of consultation as far as possible, Senator H. F. Verwoerd, speaking immediately thereafter, declared:

> The position is perfectly clear. All that is required is the good will and the sense of independence of those who disagree with the leader of the opposition as regards the definite stand he has made against this bill.[79]

To this Malan added in his concluding speech that Strauss was 'cracking the whip', and that it was 'immoral to curb conscience'. No appeal to dissidents could have been more open.

The effect of the appeal became obvious in the committee sessions. Bailey Bekker openly regretted that the bill was not confined to clause 3 on separate representation and assured Malan that he was not under the party whip, i.e. not committed to vote as the party directed. More dramatic, the United Party's eldest and perhaps most colorful member, Arthur Barlow, suddenly asked Malan if he would be willing to have private talks with some members of the Opposition. In the evening of his life, said Barlow, he was trying to make peace between the two sections of South Africa over South Africa's greatest problem.

From July 17, when the bill was reported without amendment, to the introduction of third reading on September 16, 1953, discussions outside of Parliament were determining not only the fate of the bill before the first joint session, but in a measure also that of the South African party structure. Would a compromise proposal be reached? If so, on what terms? And at what cost? Private approaches to Malan were made by United Party liberals, as well as conservatives. Malan and Strauss engaged in correspondence. The Cabinet was reported divided over the negotiations.[80] The *Argus*, on July 21, condemned the visits to Malan as 'misguided'. Next day, *Die Burger* charged 'sjambok-unity' in the United Party. Yet the *Cape Times*, also writing on July 22, saw the possibility that alternative proposals might be reached which would 'guarantee Western civilization without breaking past pledges',[81] and the *Star* said hopefully, on July 30, that economic pressures might eventually force political cooperation.[82]

There were, in fact, strong arguments both for and against a compromise. No one could suppose that the Nationalists would give up their objective of securing complete political apartheid. If the constitutional means of securing this end should fail, it was easy to foresee that, as ultimately happened, far more dangerous expedients would be used. Was it not better, then, to devise a measure on which agreement could be reached so that the issue could be settled once and for all (if that can ever be done with a non-European issue in South Africa)? It was obvious that pressing economic and social problems needed the combined efforts of South Africa's white minority. Why not free the parties from bitter debates on an issue over which, in fact, few Europeans cared very greatly.

On the other hand, if a compromise were accepted, would the United Party retain any possible basis of unity? If the Nationalists could claim a mandate (as they did) on the basis of increased representation in Parliament, the United Party could justifiably point out (as Strauss did) that it had received a substantial majority of the votes. Should the United Party then yield on the most controversial measure which had divided the parties before and at the election? Should it add to the 'yes but' attitude on most apartheid measures, simply a 'yes' on political apartheid? If it did so, would it retain either the respect and support of the electorate, or enough inner cohesion to continue in existence as the major opposition party?

But if the United Party determined to maintain continued opposition to the Nationalist objectives outlined in the bill, what should be the core of its stand? Earlier debates, and those on the third reading of the bill, made it clear that United Party members were still far from having a common attitude to separate representation as such. H. G. Lawrence, who acted on several occasions as United Party leader in the debates in the second joint session, declared during the first joint session that there was 'nothing *per se* against separate representation', and that the 'immorality' had been in Malan's methods. Sir de Villiers Graaff, leader of the United Party in the Cape, said that the United Party was not in favor of separate representation 'in itself', but was prepared to be convinced if a good case was made out in the Select Committee. What the United Party was holding on to was not a particular program but a method: consultation on the broadest possible scale to reach a general settlement of the non-European problem. With somewhat less unanimity, but considerable fervor in some quarters, the United Party was also basing itself on morality: the morality of 'the pledged word, honour and justice', said Strauss in his third reading speech, from which the parties could be released only by those people in whose favor it had been made.

In an attempt to undercut the United Party argument about consultation, Dr. Malan, in this significant interim period, saw a delegation from the Coloured Peoples' National Union and possibly others. He announced subsequently that Coloured opposition to the franchise change had been much exaggerated.[83] Though the Coloured Peoples' National Union opposed separate representation, as did other Coloured groups like the moderate Coloured Teachers' and Professional Association, the former were strongly criticized as collaborators with the Government. It was fairly obvious that when the extreme left-wing paper *Advance* wrote at this time that

> any African leader who participates in discussion lays himself open to suspicion of trying to make a deal with Europeans,[84]

it could with equal validity have replaced 'African' with 'non-European'. It was, moreover, extremely difficult to secure an accurate expression of Coloured opinion because of the fundamental divisions within that group whose views extended all the way from relative conservatism to Trotskyite Communism.

Despite Malan's attempt to meet one of the major United Party objections to Nationalist action, and the fact that the inter-party negotiations seemed at one time to threaten the very basis of the United Party, the party emerged from this ordeal stronger both in its essential unity and in its opposition to the bill before it. For this both Strauss and Malan were responsible. Strauss retained a stubborn resistance to any proposal which, in his view, took away or diminished rights of the Coloured.[85] Malan, from his side, not only did not yield on the provisions of the bill but allowed third reading to take place under the shadow of a potential threat to the courts. On September 15, 1953, the very day before third reading was introduced, the Nationalists made it known that if the bill failed they proposed to divide the Appeal Court into three sections, one for civil, one for criminal and one for constitutional cases. Instead of weakening United Party resistance and unity, this thinly veiled threat to the integrity of the court system strengthened both. Even the ultra-conservatives, already in the process of an open break with their party, were unwilling to vote for a measure which included an open limitation on the courts, a provision highlighted by the proposal regarding the Appeal Court. When the vote was taken, the total was 122 to 78. The bill had failed by 16 votes to secure a two-thirds majority in joint session.

A bare two weeks later, Malan tried again. This time the measure was obviously tailored to the points raised in the first joint session by Bailey Bekker (whose split with the United Party was now public knowledge) and by Strauss himself. Thus the bill presented to the second joint session on October 2, 1953, was restricted, as Bekker had suggested, to the single point of separate representation of the Coloured. Moreover, Malan announced that before second reading the bill would be referred to a Select Committee to which the Coloured could present their view, and sociologists, demographers, statisticians, etc., bring relevant information. In addition, partly at least in response to a plea by Bekker, the Nationalists had temporarily withdrawn the Appellate Division Bill. 'As far as possible,' said Malan, 'dissension should be eliminated in the interests of this country.'

The new stiffening of United Party resistance to any form of the measure which had already been noticeable in the third reading of the first joint session became still more marked, however, in the second joint session. Instead of remaining silent at first reading as before, Strauss at once introduced an amendment which sought to shift the ground from a strict consideration of separate representation to the broader program of all-party and all-group discussion of the non-European problem as a whole, which he had long held to be the best means of handling the issue. Speaking sharply of the Prime Minister's negotiations with sections of the United Party instead of with the party as a whole, and of the 'sword of Damocles' of the Appellate Division Bill, Strauss refused to make a prior commitment to limit Select Committee discussions to the bill at hand. He asked formally for 'satisfactory assurances' regarding consultation with the Coloured, that the Select Committee would be 'only the first step' towards full consideration of the non-European question, or to taking it out of politics, and that entrenchment would be fully respected. The Labour, Liberal and Union Federal Parties went still farther in objecting to the Select Committee approach under any circumstances, the latter calling it 'supping with the devil'.[86]

With such an inauspicious start, it is hardly surprising that the Select Committee, composed of 11 Nationalists and 7 Opposition members, made little progress. Appointed on the first of February, 1954, it held its discussion and heard its evidence on what the Opposition continued to feel was too limited a basis.[87] Thus, when Malan asked leave, on May 18, 1954,[88] to introduce the bill which came out of the Select Committee, Strauss merely remarked that the measure would be defeated at third reading and that it would be 'an empty gesture' to oppose it at so early a stage.

To Dr. Malan, in contrast, the evidence before the Select Committee had made the problem of the Coloured vote appear a more crucial one than ever. Though there were only 48,000 Coloured voters on the rolls, he declared that the projected increase in their numbers made them as great a potential danger for white control of the franchise as the Africans had been in 1936. Moreover, he now felt convinced that the Coloured desired to be 'recognized as a distinct group', and were not as opposed to separate representation as the United Party imagined.

Strauss responded to this argument by withdrawing to the high plateau of all-out opposition to separate representation. He declared the bill would amount to a 'breach of pledges' that the Coloured would not be segregated politically against their will, that it was a 'diminution of political rights' creating a 'loss of faith in the white man's word' and thus endangering white leadership, and that it would lead to a 'solid anti-European bloc'. When the Nationalists went so far as to introduce a series of amendments in the committee stage to meet compromise proposals by Bekker that Coloured already on the common roll should be allowed to stay there unless they themselves chose to be transferred to the separate roll, Strauss called it 'a vote-getting scheme' to secure the two-thirds majority, and 'separate representation on the instalment plan'. He declared forcefully that the United Party stood for retention of the Coloured on the common roll in the interests of white civilization and of South Africa as a whole.

Why did Strauss take such a determined stand at this time, and what was its significance? For one thing, he was fighting for his leadership of the party. Already the six major dissidents had been excluded from caucus; they were expelled from the parliamentary party during these debates. The most biting attacks on Strauss came from these members who now called themselves the Independent United Party, and who insisted that they, rather than Strauss, were true to the line of United Party policy as it had been manifested over this issue since 1951. The Independent United Party obviously sought an acceptable compromise with the Nationalists, and appreciated the efforts of the latter to come part of the way; in the end, its members voted with the Government. Had Strauss not retreated to another platform and maintained a stubborn resistance, the party might well have split, or sought new leadership.

Strauss was not only concerned with his own position in the party; there is considerable evidence that he was thinking deeply in this period about a broadly conceived and distinctive non-European policy for the United Party.

The separate report of the United Party members of the Select Committee was a coherent statement in support of retaining the *status quo* on the Coloured vote. Moreover, in February 1954, Strauss followed the lead of Professor Fourie, an economist in the liberal wing of the United Party, in endorsing economic integration of Europeans and non-Europeans to meet the needs of the expanding South African economy, and avowed himself ready to face some of the political implications of such a statement. Throughout the year, he was engaged with top-ranking members of his party in hammering out the statement on non-European policy which was considered and accepted by provincial party congresses, and thereafter in November 1954 by the Union Congress of the party. This program (see p. 283) was a more coherent, practical and forward-looking statement of Native policy than the United Party had previously reached, though it fell a little short of what Fourie and Strauss had suggested in Parliament in February. In May 1954, when the bill was before the second joint session, Strauss was deeply involved in the discussions of this policy, and probably as greatly influenced by the liberal wing of his party as at any time in his career. This was perhaps the more so because of all times this was the one in which Strauss needed a stand distinctive from that of Bailey Bekker and the Independent United Party.

Though it was Strauss who resisted Nationalist proposals most trenchantly, much of the burden of leadership in the second joint session debates fell upon Harry Lawrence, United Party frontbencher from the Cape. Lawrence now echoed Strauss' insistence on 'the maintenance of the common roll', but he also gave some of the best statements of basic United Party policy formulated in Parliament. 'There must be a middle way'[89] between apartheid and equality, he argued at one point, but in fact he had enunciated it earlier with reference to Malan's statement about a peaceful solution.

> You can't solve the insoluble [Lawrence declared]. What you can do, at best, is by constant adjustment in the light of changing conditions so to regulate your relationships between the different races either by means of legislative action or by administrative action as to ensure that in the ultimate result there will be a feeling of goodwill and mutual respect and tolerance amongst the various races.[90]

It was a typically conservative approach. It would be difficult to prove that it is not the most promising approach to South Africa's tangled racial problems.

The second joint session failed, as had the first, to secure the necessary two-thirds majority. It was Malan's last attempt to solve the Coloured vote issue. In November 1954, Malan was succeeded as Prime Minister by J. G. Strijdom, to whom a settlement of the issue had always been more important than the means by which it would be done. His tactics were to increase the size both of the Appellate Division and of the Senate.

As a first step, five new judges were appointed in March 1955 to the Appellate Division; in May, a new measure, the Appellate Division Quorum Act (which superseded Malan's Appellate Division Bill) raised the number of judges to eleven whenever the court considered the validity of an Act of Parliament. Mr. Strijdom explained frankly that the purpose behind the bill was to add new judges to the five who had reached the 1952 decision.

The Government then turned its attention to increasing the size of the Senate so as to be able to secure enough votes in joint session to pass a constitutional amendment to take the Coloured off the common roll. On May 11, 1955, the Senate Bill was introduced. Vast numbers of demonstrations throughout the country, including those by a new group, the Black Sash women, seemed temporarily to parallel the great outburst of feeling which marked the Torch Commando. The Opposition fought every stage of the bill in Parliament as destroying the balance of the Constitution, as well as being a subterfuge to achieve the Nationalist purpose of full political apartheid. Most striking of all was the protest by thirteen senior faculty members of the Afrikaans-speaking Pretoria University.[91] Despite all efforts, however, the Senate Bill became law on June 20, 1955.

Under the new Act, the Cape and Transvaal receive more seats than Natal and the Orange Free State, thus overriding the former principle of equal representation. Moreover, the party controlling a province receives all the seats in that province (the Nationalists control the provincial councils in the Cape, Transvaal, and Orange Free State) instead of seats proportionate to their provincial strength. In addition, the number of nominated members in the Senate is increased to 18.[92] The second chamber, selected under this act at the end of 1955, has 89 members instead of the former 48, and the Nationalists control 77 seats in the new body as compared with 30 in the old one.

The final step in completing political apartheid was introduced at a joint sitting of both Houses of Parliament on February 13, 1956: the South Africa Act Amendment Bill, 1956, which re-enacted the provisions of the Separate Representation of Voters Act of 1951. The measure also restricted courts of law from inquiring into or pronouncing on the validity of a law unless it affected section 137 or section 152 of the South Africa Act, which safeguard the equal rights of English and Afrikaans. A motor convoy of Black Sash women from all over the country protested both this bill and the Senate Act. The *Star* declared that when the enlarged Senate voted to provide the two-thirds majority in the last stage of the amendment process it would mark 'the passing of normal parliamentary democracy as South Africa has always known it'.[93] On February 28, 1956, the bill received 173 to 68 votes, a clear two-thirds majority. The Conservative Party (the former Independent United Party) split, with A. G. Barlow, B. Coetzee and A. H. Jonker voting for the Government, and Bailey Bekker, F. H. Waring and V. L. Shearer against it. This marked the beginning of the end of the Conservative Party as well as the end of the parliamentary fight against the expedients for achieving political apartheid.

Even before the introduction of the South Africa Act Amendment Bill, the United Party had announced its intention of testing the validity of the Senate Act in the courts. In the end both Acts were tested together through an appeal by two Coloured. On May 19, 1956, the Cape Supreme Court ruled both acts valid on the ground that

> no limitation can be implied on the scope of powers expressly granted to Parliament as ordinarily constituted so as to preclude Parliament as so constituted from enacting the Senate Act.[94]

Appealed to the highest court, this verdict was upheld on November 10, 1956, by a majority of ten to one. In his dissenting opinion, Mr. Justice O. D.

Schreiner maintained that a Senate constituted *ad hoc* for the purpose of securing a two-thirds majority in a contemplated joint session was not a House of Parliament under a proper construction of the South Africa Act. Chief Justice A. v. d. S. Centlivres declared for the majority, however, that 'the legislative scheme which was adopted is not open to attack by law'.[95] The long struggle was over.

Looking back over the long constitutional crisis, what general judgments can be made about the actions of the Government and the Opposition? Nationalists referred often to the *volkswil* as a major justification for their insistence on ensuring full political apartheid. It is true that Nationalist provincial congresses had asked over and over again for the removal of the Coloured from the common roll. Ideology, and the fear that an increasing number of Coloured would become eligible for the common roll had lain behind this pressure. Nationalist leaders had not attempted, however, to dampen the enthusiasm of the rank and file for political apartheid. To the leaders, in particular to logically minded Mr. Strijdom, an apartheid program which omitted political apartheid was inconceivable.

As for Nationalist tactics, these began with convenience, went through a stage of conservative constitutionalism under the influence of Dr. Malan and Mr. Havenga, and finally ended in the Senate Act, which many South Africans, and almost everyone outside that country, consider far more dangerous than the first attempt to take the Coloured off the common roll, or the slightly ludicrous expedient of the High Court of Parliament. What explains this progression?

There seems no doubt but that Dr. Malan believed sincerely in 1951 that the Separate Representation Bill was legal even if it did not fit fine criteria of moral or constitutional restraint. Much disturbed by the unexpected check from the Appeal Court, he accepted the High Court of Parliament Bill, produced by the too fertile brain of Dr. Dönges, as the easiest means of securing an end of whose need he was convinced. Checked, again by the Appellate Court, Malan waited a few months for a parliamentary mandate. Then, secure in an increased majority, and under heavy pressure from his own extreme wing to secure a settlement of the issue, Dr. Malan used his great personal prestige to persuade the Nationalists to accept the constitutional approach of a joint session, a procedure the more attractive to them because of the possibility of splintering the United Party. The second joint session reached a high-water mark of conciliation by the Nationalists under the spur of Malan's great desire to achieve the purpose of separate representation for the Coloured by means which the courts would hold legal. Yet the fact that a measure tampering with the court system, the Appellate Division Bill, hung over Parliament during the third reading of the first joint session, and was in the background of the second joint session, shows that the constitutional procedure, in its turn, was an expedient rather than a conversion.

If the United Party stand was a more wavering one than that of the Nationalists, it represented at least a clear-cut opposition to what the latter were attempting to do. Moreover, through the apparently shifting grounds on which that opposition rested, there ran a few clear lines: an emphasis on broadly constitutional as well as strictly legal procedures; an insistence at most points on consultation with those most affected by the measure; and an attempt to have this measure seen as part of the whole non-European problem and not dealt with as an isolated matter.

The United Party faced the same major handicaps in dealing with this issue as with other apartheid measures: i.e. its broad acceptance of the same view on the relationship between Europeans and non-Europeans as the Nationalists had, and a lack of deep concern for the Coloured. But there was more which they could exploit in some of the premises of political apartheid than in other apartheid issues. Above all, the initial approach by the Nationalists through means which the Appeal Court ultimately held to be invalid made this issue the one most easy for the United Party to oppose.

The Nationalists created the long constitutional crisis which racked the Union from 1951 on. Was the United Party also to blame that the crisis continued after the 1953 election and finally took the dangerous form of tampering with two of the basic institutions of the country: the Appeal Court and the Senate? In one sense, yes. Prior to the second joint session United Party members had never presented an all-out opposition to removing the Coloured from the common roll. From this point of view, the United Party might have accepted Malan's last measure.

But on a wider view, the opposition to the measure introduced in the second joint session was concerned with what the Nationalists had been doing throughout their long efforts to take the Coloured off the common roll. To give in at that point, simply because the Nationalists had reduced their demand to the measure from which they had started, would have been a capitulation on the issue as a whole. This could be argued convincingly enough to maintain the unity of the overwhelming majority of the United Party.

In these long debates over the varied attempts to remove the Coloured from the common roll, certain basic differences in approach between the Nationalists and the United Party became more obvious than anywhere else. From their side, the Nationalists were impatient with the fetters of a constitutional system which they had not helped to create[96] and which, they felt, thwarted their immediate purposes. They reluctantly accepted a constitutional approach in the joint sessions only because they were determined, if possible, to avoid further uproar in the country. In other words, the Nationalists were directed throughout by the desire to achieve their purpose of full political apartheid by the simplest, most convenient and most practical means possible. Some Nationalists, like J. G. Strijdom, were not even worried about opposition, or by criticism of the methods used. But Dr. Malan, and his close associate, N. C. Havenga, wished at all times to maintain the appearance of legality.

The United Party, in contrast, held a deep feeling for the Constitution and, beyond this, for constitutionality, i.e. the sacredness of fundamental agreements. At the beginning, their position was relatively clear and simple. They opposed action by a simple majority where a two-thirds majority provision had been written into the country's basic document. With time, however, their attitude shifted. In the end, they were enunciating, with a fervor which must have surprised themselves, a belief that there was a fundamental compact with the Coloured, from which only the latter could release them, as well as between the four provinces which formed the South African Union through the Act of Union.

If this late conversion had been expanded and reflected in long-term policy, the division between the Nationalists and the United Party could have become one which divided the major political parties in South Africa on clearly perceived and intelligible grounds. But from the high-water mark of their assertions in the second joint session, and even from the practical-minded statement of non-European policy adopted at its 1954 Union Congress (see p. 284), the United Party receded noticeably as time went on. The second reading debate on the Senate Bill was shot through with bitterness and counter-accusations which find no parallel even in the acrimony of earlier struggles over Nationalist legislation and tactics. But the United Party, perhaps not surprisingly, put greater weight on the potential dangers which this radical tampering with the balance of institutions offered to the language and position of the English in South Africa than on the obvious effect it was going to have for the Coloured vote. The Nationalists even taunted the United Party with the question they had raised already in 1951: Will a United Party Government put the Coloured back on the common roll if we take them off?

To this question, the United Party long gave no final answer. Pressed by one of its liberal wing to face it squarely, the United Party caucus appointed a committee which determined, over the dissent of Dr. Bernard Friedman, that this question could be answered only after the party was returned to power. Under further pressure from its liberal wing, the party issued a statement that:

> All we can promise is that on our return to power, we will, in consultation with the Coloured people, set right the grave injustice done to them in the best way open to us at that time and in a form which will serve the best interests of South Africa as a whole.[97]

Though accepted by seven United Party liberals (who personally pledged themselves, however, to seek the restoration of Coloured voting rights) the statement did not satisfy Dr. Friedman, who resigned his parliamentary seat to put the issue before the voters of Hillbrow, a prosperous Johannesburg constituency for which he had been returned unopposed a number of times. In a straight fight with Dr. Louis Steenkamp of the United Party, Dr. Friedman was defeated. Neither the United Party, nor, it seemed, its electorate, was prepared at that time to bind itself irrevocably to the principle of having the Coloured on the common roll.

Just over two years later, however, at a special congress in mid-August 1957, the United Party pledged itself to restore the Coloured to the common roll when it comes back into political power. Though nothing can wipe out its equivocations on this issue, it is of special importance that this more courageous stand was taken when the 1958 electoral campaign was already in view. Moreover Black Sash women still stand in mourning for the Constitution whose balance was broken by the Senate Act of 1956.[98] The long constitutional crisis is technically over but the issues which gave rise to it have not been forgotten.

Section III: Why the Nationalists Won in 1953

CHAPTER 5
THE ELECTION FRAMEWORK AND RETURNS

Few elections have been so significant in South African history as those of 1948 and 1953. The Nationalist victory in 1948 had not only been a slim one, but also unexpected. Since that time, the Nationalists had increased their parliamentary strength by creating and winning the six seats in South West Africa. But they had also aroused much antagonism within the country, as the progress of the Torch Commando had made obvious. Though the opposition included a wide spectrum of views it was unified by a common desire to turn the Nationalists out of office. Both sides looked on the 1953 election as decisive for the future.

In a very real sense, general elections in South Africa determine the possession of political power. Though the provinces have limited autonomy and exercise a number of important functions, there is no guaranteed, federal division of power in the Union as in Canada, Australia, or the United States. Ultimate legislative power in South Africa resides in Parliament: the Queen, the Senate,[1] and the House of Assembly. Of these three, it is the House of Assembly which possesses by far the greatest influence as the chief seat of executive and legislative authority. General elections concern only the House of Assembly and within this body only the 156 out of its (in 1953) 159 members who are voted for by Europeans. The other three members of the House of Assembly in 1953 were Europeans chosen by qualified African voters in Cape Province at regularly scheduled elections; thus their seats were unaffected by the general election.[2]

Who Could Vote[3]

In South Africa, every white person who is a Union national, 21 years of age or over, and not disqualified because of insanity or conviction of crime, can register as a voter. This uniformity of franchise provisions has existed for Europeans since adult white women were enfranchised in 1930 and the requirement was removed in 1931 for adult white males in Cape Province to meet literacy and economic qualifications.

Although it did not modify this universal franchise for Europeans, the South African Citizenship Act of 1949 (described in Chapter 2) has lengthened the period of residence necessary for British subjects to acquire citizenship, and thus the franchise, and at the time of the 1953 elections the earlier controversy over this act found a mild echo in the English-language press. It pointed out that many post-war immigrants from the United Kingdom would have been eligible to vote except for the Citizenship Act. Dire predictions that the Minister would refuse registration to potential United Party voters could not be substantiated, however, and lethargy about applying for citizenship turned out to be a more convincing reason why some of those who could have been eligible to vote were not.

The non-European franchise was a far more potent cause of controversy in 1953 than the European franchise. Until the Appellate Division handed down its decision on the High Court of Parliament Act, neither the delimitation of constituencies in the Cape, which depended on the numbers on the voters' roll, nor the voters' rolls themselves could be made official. To prevent delay, the voters' rolls for the other three provinces, the Transvaal, Free State and Natal, were actually printed before the Delimitation Commission Report became official on January 8, 1953. Since both the Separate Representation of Voters' Act, 1951, and the High Court of Parliament Act, 1953, were declared unconstitutional, male Coloured and Indians in Cape Province who earned £50 a year or owned fixed property to the value of £75 and were registered on the common roll, were able to vote in the 1953 elections. Along with the small number of male Coloured in Natal who could vote on the common roll if they had an income of £96 a year, or immovable property worth £50, or rental from property of £10 a year, they were the only non-Europeans able to participate in the 1953 general election.

Registration of Voters

South Africa has long been concerned to ensure a high percentage of voting by its white population. Though the Select Committee on Population Registration and Voting, 1935 [S. C., 10, 1935. XI, 77, vi.] under the chairmanship of Leslie Blackwell, endorsed the Australian system of compulsory voting, it felt this practice should not be introduced until the public had a chance to express its views. The Commission's recommendation of compulsory registration, however, was put into effect. The law stated that a white voter who was entitled to be registered as a voter, must apply for registration; similarly the voter must notify the electoral officer of any permanent change of residence. Failure on either count could be punished by imprisonment up to three months or a fine of not more than £25 at the time of the 1953 election.

Despite these provisions for compulsory registration, many Europeans neither registered nor notified the authorities of changes of address. One of the major activities of the Torch Commando in 1952 was to canvass potential voters particularly on the Rand, and around Durban, to see that they registered. It was partly as a result of their activity that the Rand gained two new seats in the delimitations of electoral divisions in 1952, when for the first time the basic quotas for constituencies were calculated on the basis of the number of registered voters.

No such official or unofficial compulsion to register existed in regard to non-Europeans. On the contrary, the Electoral Laws Amendment Act of 1952 made registration the less attractive by requiring non-Europeans to prove their right to do so before an electoral officer, magistrate, or ranking police officer.

Once a voter is registered he remains permanently on the rolls instead of having to re-apply periodically as in the past. Through a master card-index system, notification of change of address leads to an automatic transfer of registration to the electoral officer of the constituency to which the voter has moved.

The Electoral Laws Amendment Act, 1952, provided that a general registration of voters must take place in the future at intervals of not less than two, or more than three years, but not until after the next general election. Thus the voters' rolls used in 1953 were considerably out of date, a matter receiving caustic comment in the English-language press. Moreover the Act specifically stated that, prior to the general registration, supplementary lists were to be compiled every five months, calculated from October 1, 1952, and to come into operation two months later.[4] Thus no one who applied for enrolment as a voter after October 1, 1952, would have been able to vote until May 1, 1953, fifteen days after the general election.

It may be noted that in 1953, as in earlier elections, the South African voting roll was divided into three sections: one for white women; one for white men; and one for non-Europeans. Nationalists pointed out that in a sense this latter provision meant that the Coloured were already on a separate roll in 1953, even though they still voted in the same polling booths and constituencies with Europeans in that year.

Postal Voting

Because of the constant movement of population within the Union, which was particularly marked in the period before the 1953 election, because of the development of the new gold fields in the Orange Free State, postal voting is an important means of ensuring that as many voters as possible exercise their franchise. Application for a postal vote may be made by any registered voter who cannot reach a polling booth because of physical disability, or who will be more than ten miles from the nearest polling booth in his constituency on election day. Such an application can be filed between the day of proclamation, with its official announcement of the date of the general election, and five days prior to the election itself. For the April 15, 1953, election, postal ballot papers were first issued on March 25, 1953, i.e. 21 days before polling day; they could be returned up to 8 p.m. on election day. One substantial restriction, however, is that a postal vote must be cast within the Union, and thus any voter leaving South Africa prior to March 25 would have been unable to vote.

The 1953 election could be called the postal vote election. Though valid postal votes in the 1948 election amounted to 4·26 per cent of the total valid vote, the percentage rose in 1953 to 13·18 per cent of the total valid vote. The actual figures are perhaps even more striking, for the total of 45,597 postal votes counted in the 1948 election swelled to 159,384 in 1953, that is, more than the total possible vote for an average fifteen constituencies. If the number of valid postal votes for the whole Union is averaged, it amounts to 304 per constituency in 1948; and to 1,022 in 1953,[5] when the average constituency had in all only between ten and eleven thousand votes.

In a number of cases the valid postal vote was larger than the majority of the winning candidate. In 1948, there were 19 such cases: 8 in the Cape; 8 in the Transvaal; 2 in Natal; and 1 in the Free State. In 1953, the number of cases rose to 38: 10 in the Cape; 22 in the Transvaal; 1 in Natal, 1 in the Free State; and 4 in South West Africa. While it is not possible to know the distribution of postal votes, since they are mixed with other valid votes on election day, it may be noted that, in 1948, the United Party won 8 seats in this category; the Nationalists 10; and the Afrikaner Party 1. In 1953, the distribution was far less even, as the United Party won only 4 of the seats in which the valid postal vote was larger than the majority of the winner, while the Nationalists won 34.

In the five instances in 1948, and one in 1953, where the majority of the winning candidate was under a hundred, postal votes far outstripped the majority. In Brakpan, which the United Party won by 6 votes in 1948, there were 374 postal votes; in the same constituency, which was won by the Nationalists in 1953, the majority was 47 with 1,466 postal votes. In Victoria West, the majority was 24 in 1948, and the postal vote, 769; in Johannesburg West, 32, and 346; in Kimberley District, 57, and 452; while in North East Rand, the figures stood at 97, and 259. Three of the latter seats were won by the Nationalists. No less interesting are the returns in some of the most hard fought contests in 1953, for example Caledon-Bredasdorp, where the Nationalist majority was 140, and postal votes totalled 1,898; Pretoria City won by 224 votes with 1,451 postal votes sent in; and Randfontein, which was won by a majority of 140, while 1,492 postal votes were cast.

The large number of postal votes in the 1953 election is a tribute to the efficiency of both major parties. Both recognized the potentialities of the postal vote and set up special organizations to handle it. The Nationalists had the advantage of the closely knit character of their community and of an extraordinarily careful coverage of Nationalist voters through the block system on which their party organization is based. Moreover, they carried out a country-wide canvass of voters in the July preceding the election, thus providing themselves with valuable information about the distribution of their strength. The United Party effort was made in the immediate pre-election period when they set up a highly elaborate system operating for the Rand out of its central headquarters in Johannesburg.

In many cases, postal voting was done openly in party headquarters and transmitted from there to the electoral officials. If sent direct, the postal vote was placed in a registered envelope provided for the voters. Since the voter had to swear that he was entitled to a postal vote, the parties made themselves responsible for taking the necessary commissioner of oaths to the voter's home. Most of the tracing of postal voters was done by the party organizations in the constituencies in which the voter then lived. In the electoral district which had the highest percentage of voting, Caledon-Bredasdorp with a 96 per cent turnout, the son of the United Party candidate drove thousands of miles, however, to bring postal vote forms to far scattered former residents.

As the postal votes were received by the returning officer, they were opened at specified times so that the signature on the declaration of identity accompanying the ballot could be compared with that on the application. The candidates, or their representatives, spent many weary hours checking and challenging postal votes. Not surprisingly, the numbers rejected were high compared to those for the election as a whole.[6] In fact, 52·67 per cent of the ballots rejected in 1953 were postal votes whereas in 1948, the proportion was 25·55 per cent. On the other hand, it is a tribute to the care with which the parties handled postal vote arrangements in 1953 that, despite the fact that nearly four times as many postal votes were cast as in 1948, the percentage of postal votes rejected went down from 3·98 per cent to 2·80 per cent.

Not every postal vote was an addition to the total which would have been cast if this opportunity had not been provided. The very activity of the party organizations led some people to vote by post who would otherwise have made the effort to exercise their franchise in person. In De Aar-Colesberg, for example, where the postal vote ran very near the top in both 1948 and 1953, the number on the voters' roll was 76 less in 1953 than in 1948 and the total vote was 25 less, but the number of postal votes increased by 947.

On the other hand, some figures suggest a correlation between the increase of postal votes and of the total vote. In Aliwal, in the Cape, where there was the same number of voters on the roll in both years, the total number of votes polled rose by 313, while the number of postal votes increased by 435. In Potchefstroom, in the Transvaal, the total number on the voters' roll increased by 529, the total vote by 967, and the total postal vote by 1,054. In Krugersdorp, a mining town at the western end of the Rand, where the number on the rolls increased by only 75, the number of votes went up by 972, and the increase in postal votes was 996. Nothing conclusive can be drawn from such random figures, nor indeed from any such calculations, because of the wide changes wrought by delimitation, and the increased party activity in 1953 over 1948, but at least it is clear that the postal vote played a significant role in the outcome of the 1953 election.

Delimitation of Constituencies

Few countries, if any, have carried out such frequent delimitations of constituencies as has South Africa. Between the establishment of Union in 1909 and the 1953 election, no fewer than ten delimitations took place, which left intact only the provincial divisions and, in general, the polling areas. While the reason for these frequent changes lies in history, and may seem to reflect an unusual sense of proportionate justice, one of the unhappy results is vastly to complicate the task of the researcher seeking to discover long range trends in voting.

The South Africa Act, 1909, fixed the number of seats in the first House of Assembly at 121, and arbitrarily divided these between the four provinces so that the two smaller ones, Natal and the Orange Free State, had 17 each, while the Transvaal had 36 seats, and the Cape 51. At the same time, the Act laid down the general principle that seats should be allocated to the provinces in relation to the number of adult white males residing within them. Dividing the total European male population of 349,837 (according to the 1904 census) by the 121 seats would have provided a quota of 2,891·2 per constituency. On this basis, the Cape with 167,546 adult white males would have been entitled to 58 members (and more if its Coloured voters had been taken into account), while Natal, with 34,784 adult white males, would have had only 12 seats, and the Free State with 41,014 only 14. To allay the fear of the smaller provinces that they might be swamped by the larger ones, the Constitution makers guaranteed 17 seats each to Natal and the Free State, and stated further that the number was not to be decreased for ten years, or until the total number of seats in the House of Assembly rose to 150, whichever was the longer period of time.

But despite these initial safeguards for the smaller provinces, the intention was to move as quickly as possible towards a more equitable representation of the provinces by population. Each time the number of adult male Europeans in the Union increased by a full quota unit of 2,891·2, an additional seat was created in the House of Assembly, and assigned where most needed. To secure the necessary data, the South Africa Act provided for a census of the European population in 1911 and every five years thereafter (since 1951, the census will be at ten-year intervals under an Act of 1945). After each census, the representation of the provinces was reconsidered (when women were enfranchised in 1930, the basis became the adult European population), and constituency boundaries redrawn by a delimitation commission. In 1952, Act 55 provided that henceforth the number of seats allocated a province should be in proportion to the registered white voters. The Tenth Delimitation Commission made its decisions on the basis of the voters' rolls as of April 30, 1952.[7]

The original expectation was that the Cape would secure the greatest increase in seats because it had been penalized most in the original allocation. The phenomenal growth of the Transvaal, however, has steadily increased its representation in the House of Assembly. In 1931, when the House reached its upper limit of 150, the Transvaal had 57 seats to 61 for the Cape; at that time, Natal and the Free State each decreased in number of seats to 16. In 1953, the Transvaal had 68 seats, an increase of 2 over 1948; the Cape had 54, and Natal, 15, each having lost one seat since 1948; while the Orange Free State remained constant at 13.[8] When the mandated territory of South West Africa was given parliamentary representation under Act 23 of 1949, it was arbitrarily assigned six seats, and retained the same number in 1953, although its total number of registered voters was only about 24,000.

To determine the number of seats for each province is a purely mathematical calculation, now made by dividing the number of white voters in a province by the Union quota. This quota amounted in 1952 to 10,265·35. Within the provinces, the basic quota per constituency is determined by dividing the number of assigned seats by the total number of persons on the voters' roll, a figure differing somewhat in both the Cape and Natal from that used above, because both had non-European voters on the roll.[9] The number of registered Coloured voters in the Cape on April 30, 1952, was 47,008; in Natal, 1,190.

To draw constituency boundaries is much more complicated, however, than to determine the basic quota of voters. The South Africa Act enumerates five factors which delimitation commissions should take into account in making their decisions: community or diversity of interest; means of communication; physical features; existing electoral boundaries; and sparsity or density of population. In relation to these factors, the Act states that Commissions 'may, whenever they deem it necessary', modify the basic quota of voters per constituency though never by more than 15 per cent in either direction. Thus the maximum difference in the size of constituencies could be 30 per cent.

Delimitation Commissions consist of three judges (four in the original 1910 Commission) selected by the Governor General (in practice, the Prime Minister). It is common, though not invariable, to have one or two members of a former Commission serve on the succeeding one[10] but, possibly because the Nationalist Government was making the selection for the first time, the 1952 Delimitation Commission consisted of three judges who had had no previous experience of this kind. They were C. P. Brink, chairman, J. W. van Zijl, and D. O. K. Beyers.

Of these, Mr. Justice van Zijl was the son of a member of the Commissions for 1928 and 1932. The Chief Electoral Officer, a permanent official, acts as Secretary for the Commission; Mr. van Zijl, the Chief Electoral Officer in 1953, had held this office since 1927.

Over the years, a fairly consistent pattern has developed in the way Delimitation Commissions weight the special factors they may take into account in over- or under-loading constituencies. The most important, and ultimately the most controversial has been the relative weighting of sparsely and densely populated areas, which in practice usually means rural and urban constituencies. The First Commission noted that 'it appeared obvious though not specifically laid down' (Report, p. 11) that it should frame electoral divisions with less than the quota in sparsely populated areas, and with more than the quota in densely populated ones. As the rural population steadily moved into the cities, the drawing of sharp lines between urban and country districts became more difficult. Though the Commissions were frequently besought to leave electoral boundaries constant, they found themselves steadily enlarging rural districts and re-defining urban ones. The 1923 and 1932 Commissions complained of the difficulty, if not impossibility of keeping certain urban constituencies, e.g., East London, Cape Town, and Durban, within the maximum overload, while the 1913 Commission suggested substituting 20 per cent for 15 per cent as the possible variation in load. The 1937 Commission noted the importance of checking the equitability of overloading different urban areas; the 1947 Commission commented that the rural seats were not 'of right entitled to a substantial unload', as had been suggested to them. Nonetheless, the latter Commission imposed very heavy urban loads on Bloemfontein, East London and Durban.

Closely allied to the division between rural and urban areas in some districts is the factor of community of interest. The 1919 Delimitation Commission had already noted that this factor played a large role in its delimitation of the Rand area into which population was constantly flowing because of the gold mines and industry. The 1923 Commission reported at length (Report of Fourth Delimitation Commission, pp. 12-13) its debate as to whether the Rand should have 20 or 21 seats. Though the latter number meant overloading the Rand constituencies only on an average of 2·92 per cent whereas the Cape Peninsula was overloaded on an average of 11·7 per cent, the Rand was finally assigned the 21 seats, since it was the foremost industrial area in the country, supported a heavy burden of taxation and had a 'great under-registration' compared to the country at large. (In several elections the number of votes cast was considerably higher than the registration figures.)

Commissions have not disregarded the other factors mentioned in the South Africa Act. The 1937 and 1943 Delimitation Commissions mentioned means of communication as an important element in their decisions. The 1948 Commission declared, in contrast, that since rural conditions had improved so much this factor need not be stressed so much as community of interest and existing electoral boundaries.

Commissions regulate their own procedure, and may act by majority decision. From the days of the first Delimitation Commission, they have received both general proposals and detailed plans from the political parties, and other interested groups and persons. The final decisions are their own, of course, and need only be justified in general terms.

The Tenth Delimitation Commission, which demarcated the electoral divisions for the 1953 election, was appointed on June 26, 1952. It held a series of public meetings in the capital cities and major towns of all the provinces between July 30 and December 2, at which the political parties and other interested groups presented written proposals through memoranda and maps, and discussed them orally. In Johannesburg, for example, the meetings lasted three days. The procedure was informal, the representatives of the parties putting forward their own points or challenging their opponents with both freedom and gusto. The Commission also toured the larger cities in the company of representatives of the political parties, who were only too eager to point out the particular features supporting their plans for electoral boundary revisions. The Commissioners also made tours of their own areas, not only the urban sections, but also by car throughout the Free State. Their greatest innovation was to take to the air to inspect the cities and rural areas of the Transvaal, Cape and Natal. They reported having found this of great help in tackling their major problem, the division between rural and urban, and industrial and residential areas.

On the basis of all this information, the Commission prepared a provisional delimitation scheme which was made available for public inspection. Further public meetings were then held for criticism of these plans. In Pretoria, for example, the same informal procedure of the earlier meetings led to a fire of comment, almost entirely in Afrikaans, with points illustrated on the delimitation maps hung all over the walls of the meeting room. At this time, only small adjustments are commonly made. The final delimitation report was issued January 8, 1953.

The most comprehensive memorandum[11] presented to the Tenth Delimitation Commission was that prepared by Advocate Arthur Suzman, for the Torch Commando, which presented a wealth of statistics, graphs and histograms designed to show that over the years there had been 'a general though not entirely consistent tendency to weight a rural vote considerably more than an urban one'.[12] The brief pointed out that loading and unloading had increased substantially: in 1923, for example, only 4 per cent of seats were loaded or unloaded between 10-15 per cent,[12a] whereas twenty years later 59 per cent of the seats fell into this category.[13] It claimed that, through loading and unloading under the 1948 delimitation, rural constituencies had gained six seats at the expense of urban constituencies, which meant in effect a difference of twelve seats.[14] In conclusion, the brief declared that the way in which the loading and unloading procedure had been used was responsible for enabling a minority of the electorate to elect a majority in the House of Assembly, and argued that 'a more equitable balance between town and country' would result if the principles of the South Africa Act were 'correctly interpreted and applied'.

The Commission rejected this argument, however, suggesting that its statements 'were often based on a misconception of the delimitation provisions of the South Africa Act', and that the brief itself fell into the same error with which it charged earlier commissions, i.e., of seeing the only basis of comparison between seats to lie in their sparsity or density of population.[15]

The Tenth Delimitation Commission itself points out at the beginning of its report the possibilities of loading and unloading provided by the 15 per cent margin allowed it under the South Africa Act (the figures for 1947 are given in brackets):

	Maximum	*Quota*	*Minimum*
Transvaal	11,721 (10,084)	10,193 (8,769)	8,665 (7,454)
Cape	12,802 (10,934)	11,132 (9,508)	9,462 (8,082)
Natal	12,049 (9,662)	10,477 (8,402)	8,905 (7,142)
Orange Free State	12,085 (10,245)	10,509 (8,909)	8,933 (7,573)

It will be seen that the Cape quota runs consistently higher than that of other provinces, because of the non-Europeans on the voting roll and also because that province covers more than half the Union's total area. For the 1953 election, the Transvaal had the lowest quota of voters per constituency. That the election turned on the Transvaal returns results less from loading, however, than from the Nationalist gains in the vast peri-urban area of the Rand, which makes a diamond, stretching as far north as Pretoria, south to Vereeniging, and east and west along the gold ore ridge from Randfontein to Springs.

While the Commission declared that it did not find the Torch Commando brief of any assistance, it spoke appreciatively of the 'great assistance' of the political parties. It seems, in fact, to have depended very considerably on the party briefs, and attempted to find a middle road between them. In the all-important Transvaal, the Rand was first taken as an area to determine how many seats it deserved in relation to the rest of the province; the next step was to draw the boundaries. While the proposals of the parties for rural areas were fairly similar, they differed considerably for urban constituencies. Indicative of party concern with the areas of greatest importance to them was the fact that the United Party map dealt almost exclusively with consolidated urban areas in and around Johannesburg, while the Nationalist map virtually ignored the central part of the city to concentrate on the peri-urban areas, those most difficult to delimit, and in practice most decisive. Practically all the Nationalist maps extended into the *platteland,* their traditional stronghold.

Except in regard to the more extreme proposals, the Delimitation decisions appeared to follow the Nationalist plans rather more than those of the United Party. But the differences were not strongly marked. Already on November 29, 1952, *The Star* wrote that the provisional proposals of the Commission maintained 'an even balance' between the parties;[16] the *Rand Daily Mail,* also pro-United Party, agreed in an editorial of January 15, 1953, that no political party could claim 'any particular advantage, on balance' from the new demarcation.

The Tenth Delimitation Commission emphasized strongly in its report that it took into account all five factors specified in the South Africa Act, in determining its loading and unloading of constituencies. Regardless of what the 1947 Commission had said about rural means of communication, the Tenth Commission felt they were still an important factor in regard to unloading. It felt justified, on the other hand, in loading the 43 densely populated urban constituencies of the Transvaal (which include about one-third of the voting population of the Union) because the vast majority had 'voters of a homogeneous type'. This criterion is emphasized several times in the report. The most striking instance is in relation to the Cape Flats constituency, which was made to include only 'purely Coloured or mixed areas'. The division of Florida constituency in the Transvaal seemed to suggest a desire to separate English- and Afrikaans-speaking. In so far as there is a distinguishing emphasis in this report, it seems to be upon securing the greatest degree of identity possible amongst the members of a constituency. While the Afrikaner migration to the cities has meant there is less racial difference than in the past between country and city constituencies, the general tendency to live in unilingual districts, plus the Commission's emphasis on homogeneity probably produced some, though not excessive communalism in the electoral delimitation.

The end result of the new demarcation was the elimination of eight constituencies, one each in Natal and the Free State and six in the Cape; the amalgamation of two constituencies in the Free State and two in the Cape; the establishment of ten new constituencies, six in the Cape, two in the Transvaal and two in the Free State; the re-naming of four constituencies; and the re-drawing of many others. Thus the Tenth Delimitation Commission carried out another fundamental demarcation of South African constituencies.

Nominations and Deposits

Dr. D. F. Malan's announcement of the date of the election was made in Parliament on February 12, 1953; on March 4, Parliament was dissolved. Ten days later, on March 14, nomination courts were held throughout the Union for the official selection of candidates. Nomination courts are held by the returning officer for the division between 10 and 11 on the appointed day. Most Rand constituencies hold their nomination courts in the Johannesburg Court House, and on nomination day the ground floor was crowded with interested spectators as well as participants. Each electoral division was assigned a room of its own; the procedure was informal and sometimes difficult to follow because of the buzz of conversation. Each candidate must be nominated by a person enrolled on the voters' list of that division, and similarly seconded. In some instances there were several seconders, to indicate the warmth of party support. Though nomination and seconding may be done in writing, as well as by word of mouth, the latter procedure is almost invariable. The candidate must indicate his consent to nomination within the time limit provided, and also deposit £50, or satisfactory security therefor. This sum is forfeited if the candidate polls less than one-fifth of the votes received by the successful candidate.[17] A tense moment occurred in a Johannesburg nomination court in 1953 as an independent candidate attempted to raise the necessary deposit money, but failed to do so before the court closed.

In 1953, 297 candidates stood for the 156 seats. Of these, 138 stood for the National Party, 148 for the United Party, 6 for the Labour Party, and 5 as Independents. Eighteen United Party candidates were unopposed in 1953 as compared with 12 in 1948; 2 Nationalist seats in 1953 as compared with 1 in 1948. The Nationalist seats uncontested in 1953 were those of Dr. Malan, and the Speaker of the House, Mr. J. H. Conradie, both of whom had had electoral fights in 1948.

Though a larger number of seats were left uncontested in 1953 than in 1948, a feature of the 1953 election was that the Nationalists entered so many more candidates than ever before. Particularly noticeable was the decision to enter 12 candidates in Natal in 1953 whereas in 1948 there had only been 5.[18]

In 1948 and again in 1953, the United Party and Labour Party had an election pact governing the nomination of candidates. Under this pact, Labour fought 6 seats in 1948, 4 in the Transvaal and 2 in Natal, all of which they won; in 1953, they won only five seats. Labour had attempted to secure the same constituencies in 1953 as in 1948, but the United Party reserved relatively safe Edenvale (won in 1948 by Hyman Davidoff) for one of their new candidates, Professor I. S. Fourie, a distinguished economist. Labour was assigned instead the difficult working-class seat of Germiston. Defeated there in a hard fought contest, Davidoff subsequently won a by-election for Johannesburg City, made necessary by the death of the Labour Party leader, John Christie, during the election.

Over the years, many Independents have contested South African seats, but the practice seems to be dying out. In 1948, there were 20 Independents, but in 1953, only 5, none of whom was remotely successful. The Independent contesting the Cape Flats, Dr. R. Bartman, withdrew before the election, leaving it a straight contest between the United Party and Nationalists. The other four Independents, 1 of whom called himself a Liberal, and 2 Independent Nationalists, all lost their deposits. In 1948, 10 of the 20 Independents similarly lost their deposits, and none won a seat. Thus all indications point to the increasing, if not complete elimination of Independents in the future in favor of party-dominated contests.

In view of the stringency of the deposit provision—i.e., that the candidate must receive at least one-fifth of the number of votes polled by the winner—the number of deposits lost is not high. In 1948, 23 candidates lost their deposits: 10 Independents, the 3 Communists, the 4 Centre Group, one C.H.S., one Labour Party, and 4 South African Party. In 1953, the 5 Independents and also 5 Nationalists lost their deposits. Four of the latter were in or close to Durban, Natal, which the Nationalists contested on a wide scale in 1953 for the first time; the fifth was in Johannesburg North, a predominantly English-speaking area of that city. Whether a general rule or not, the National Party paid for the lost deposits in 1953. Interestingly enough, no United Party member lost his deposit in either election, despite the fact that the party contested more seats in both elections than did the Nationalists.

Electoral Expenses

The South African Electoral Act places such rigid restrictions on the expenses which a candidate may incur that, as the standard work on the Constitution points out, they 'are somewhat more honoured in the breach than in the observance'.[19] Numerous conversations with candidates of all parties further confirmed the view that few, if any, find it possible to remain within the limits laid down. The act limits expenditure to voters' lists, printing, advertising, postage, stationery, telegrams, and use of telephones; the hire of one central committee room and one for each polling district, and halls for public meetings; one election agent, four sub-agents, polling agents and clerks; fuel for vehicles bringing voters to the polls; and strictly limited miscellaneous and personal expenses. The total spent by a candidate is not supposed to exceed £350 for 5,000 voters, plus £5 for every additional 100 voters. Thus in a Transvaal constituency with the basic quota of votes for 1953, a candidate would be limited to £605, i.e., $1,694. Personal expenditures are limited to £100.

An examination of three United Party Rand returns, such as are filed with the electoral officer, showed the virtual impossibility of remaining within these limits. Of the expenditures reported, those for fuel alone on election day ran between one-fifth and one-quarter of the total allowed, printing still more, and postage almost as much.[20]

While it was not possible to examine any Nationalist returns, it seems likely that their expenditures for fuel on election day were considerably less. The organization of cars to take United Party workers to the polls was outstanding; so much so, in fact, that late in the afternoon, there were far more cars in the Johannesburg United Party car pool, for example, than could be used. This abundance of cars, especially in the urban areas, reflected the comparatively greater wealth of United Party supporters. This fact makes the prohibition against providing voters with taxis work against the Nationalists. But the latter did not seem to lack transportation for those who needed it, though many more of their voters went to the polls on foot. It seems likely also that United Party cars carried a fair number of Nationalists as well as their own supporters, since they concentrated on getting all available voters to the polls, and had less accurate lists to work from than had the Nationalists.

The Electoral Act provides that candidates and organizations shall file returns of expenditures, and that newspaper proprietors must report to the electoral officials the sums they have received for inserting matter connected with the election. Under the Act, these records are open to inspection for a year. Rather than permit inspection, however, the Chief Electoral Officer in Pretoria preferred to provide a chart of expenditures by parties and other groups, which is printed in Appendix II.

The most noticeable difference between the two elections is the vast increase in expenditures by the National Party. The United Party spent slightly less in 1953 than in 1948, and even the total for the United Front—the United Party, Labour Party and Torch Commando—is only £2,114 12s 5d more than in 1948. In contrast, the National Party spent £23,013 14s 9d more in 1953. Nonetheless its total expenditure in 1953 was £14,688 19s 3d less than that of the United Front.

Significant is the relative emphasis on different types of expenditures. In 1948, the United Party put its greatest amount of money into printing articles, reports, advertisements, notices and other matter not in newspapers; the same year, the Nationalists spent a bare fraction for that purpose, only about one-twentieth of what the United Party did. In 1953, however, while the United Party increased its expenditures in this category by just over £1,100, the Nationalists made it their second largest item, between one-third and one-half of what the United Party spent. The attempt to compare the categories of expenditures is confused, however, by the enormous totals listed under 'miscellaneous'; for the National Party, this figure amounts to more than three-quarters of their total expenditures.

Expenditures for newspaper space show a marked increase in 1953 for all except the Labour Party, as shown by the figures in Appendix II. The United Party more than doubled its amounts; and the Torch Commando spent more than half its total electoral budget in this way. The Nationalists list expenditures seven to eight times as great as in 1948, and apparently spent a great deal more, which is probably included under their 'miscellaneous' heading. A breakdown of the amounts received by particular newspapers, similarly provided by the Chief Electoral Officer, shows that the United Party used virtually all its money on the English-language press, while the Nationalists similarly concentrated on the Afrikaans press. The only exception to this rule is *Dagbreek*, the Afrikaans weekly newspaper, which preserved more independence in the election than did any other Afrikaans newspaper. The United Party actually spent more in *Dagbreek* than did the Nationalists: £350 10s as compared with £263 10s. Apart from this, the United Party put only £7 14s 6d into an Afrikaans newspaper, *Die Volksblad*, in Bloemfontein. The Nationalists spent £254 14s 10d on the same paper in 1953; returns were not received for 1948.

While the Nationalists concentrated on the Afrikaans press, they did not ignore the English press to the same degree as the United Party ignored the Afrikaans press. This was particularly the case in Natal where, as already pointed out, the Nationalists made a big electoral effort for the first time in 1953. In 1948, Nationalist expenditures in Natal newspapers, all of which are in English, amounted to £15 19s 2d; in 1953 they rose to £233 11s 3d. The increase is only for the *Natal Daily News* and *Natal Mercury*, however, for the amount spent in the *Natal Witness* was only half that of 1948. The Nationalists also spent small amounts in *The Friend*, Bloemfontein, *The Star*, Johannesburg, the *Daily Despatch*, East London, the *Cape Times*, the *Cape Argus*, and the *Rand Daily Mail*, Johannesburg,[21] but nothing in the *Sunday Times*. Oddly enough, the Nationalists spent their largest listed amount in 1948 on the *Pretoria News*, £154 8s 6d, but nothing there in 1953.

While the Nationalists list only £745 17s 4d for 1953 under the general heading of 'advertisements or notices in newspapers', the amounts reported by the newspapers themselves soar far beyond this. *Die Transvaler*, Mr. Strijdom's organ, reported receiving £1,730 16s; *Die Vaderland*, which represented Mr. Havenga's point of view, £1,246 3s 3d; and *Die Burger*, which represented Dr. Malan, £169 19s 9d. None of these papers filed returns in 1948; neither did *Dagbreek*, the *Sunday Times*, nor the *Rand Daily Mail*. Total Nationalist expenditures in newspapers in 1953, according to the returns filed by their proprietors, were £4,159 2s 7d. This is far less, of course, than the total in the same category spent by the United Party, which used £3,329 15s in the *Rand Daily Mail* alone.

Election Petitions

While the Electoral Act provides that the results of an election may be challenged because of a corrupt or illegal practice, or some other irregularity, there were no such petitions following the 1953 election. After that of 1948, however, there were three election petitions, all filed before the supreme court in the Transvaal. In Johannesburg West, the election of S. J. Tighy, United Party member, was challenged on grounds of certain irregularities at one of the polling stations, including the absence of secret voting for a brief space of time. In Maraisburg, where B. J. Schoeman, of the National Party, won, irregularities and intimidation were charged. In Brakpan, where A. E. Trollip, of the United Party, had been declared elected by 2 votes, the petition asked that certain votes regarded as spoiled should be counted. In the Brakpan case, a recount of votes actually increased Mr. Trollip's majority to six. In the other two cases, the court held that the elections had been conducted 'in accordance with the principles of the act; and that any mistake or non-compliance did not affect the result of the election'. In the Maraisburg case, where the caretaker had been present in the polling hall when he should not have been, the court pointed out that he would have had to make 40 people an hour change their minds to affect the outcome of the election! The courts thus followed the general practice of not setting aside the results of elections except where there has been deliberate roguery, or where voters have been denied the chance to cast their ballot freely and secretly.

The Election Results

All over the Union on the morning of April 16, 1953, people were learning from the radio that the Nationalists had scored a decisive parliamentary victory. Out of the 156 seats contested, the Nationalists won 94, a marked increase from the 79 which the Nationalist and Afrikaner parties had won in 1948, and the 85 seats they had held in Parliament since the South West Africa elections in 1950. The Opposition had suffered correspondingly. The United Party had gone from 65 to 57 seats, and Labour from 6 to 5. Thus the United Front, now no longer very united in any case, numbered only 62.

The election returns, however, did not reflect with any exactitude the casting of votes on April 15. On no calculation could the Nationalists be said to have polled even 50 per cent of the votes. Because different kinds of calculations are made for the votes which should be allocated for the twenty uncontested seats, estimates vary about the total percentage of votes gained throughout the Union by the Nationalists and the United Front. In the third edition of Henry John May's *The South African Constitution*, figures are given, as noted below, for the votes cast in contested seats, and the estimates for the uncontested seats in what he calls the Nationalist and the United Party press. These figures vary somewhat from the figures used by the author, which are based on the returns of the *Government Gazette*, and the calculation that in uncontested seats 85 per cent of the votes of 85 per cent of the enrolled voters should be allotted to the party conceded the seat, and 15 per cent of the votes of 85 per cent of the enrolled voters to the party conceding the seat. The figure of 85 per cent is used because this is an average poll throughout the Union. May's figures:[22]

	Nationalists	*United Front*
Actual votes cast in contested seats	592,725	620,888
Nationalist press estimate for uncontested seats	43,000	97,000
Total	635,725	717,888
United Party press estimate for uncontested seats	42,192	156,615
Total	634,917	777,503
Author's figures:		
Actual votes cast in contested seats	600,503	616,036
Estimate for uncontested seats	41,066	152,419
85 per cent of 85 per cent of enrolled voters given to winning party		
15 per cent of 85 per cent of enrolled voters given to major opposition party		
Total	641,569	768,455

Thus the Afrikaans-language press estimated that the United Front received 82,163 more votes than the Nationalists; the English-language press that it received 142,586 more; and the author that it received 126,866 more votes.

If the author's figures are reduced to percentages, it appears that the Nationalists received 45·50 per cent of the votes, while the United Front secured 54·40 per cent of them. If seats had been apportioned according to these percentages, the electoral result would, obviously, have been very different. Instead of 94 seats in the House of Assembly, the Nationalists would have received 71; while the United Front, instead of 62 seats, would have gained 85.

How can these results be explained? Partly, of course, they are the outcome of the delimitation which placed more voters in urban constituencies than in rural ones. There is a further explanation, however, which may be still more important, though it seems so far to have escaped the notice of election analysts. The United Party piled up so high a percentage of votes in many of the constituencies it won that, electorally speaking, it wasted a large number of votes. This was partly due to the 1953 delimitation which, in some instances, deliberately demarcated areas in such a way as to include a high percentage of English-speaking, and resulted in fewer close contests in 1953 than in 1948. (Only 4 seats were won by a majority of 2 per cent or under in 1953, as compared with 13 in 1948.) A more accurate and complete explanation must also take into account the concentration of United Party supporters in particular residential areas, for example, the wealthy suburbs of Johannesburg.

Evidence of this latter point comes from a comparison of the size of the majorities by which Nationalist and United Front seats were won, complete figures for which in the 1948 and 1953 elections are given in Chart 2. These contain certain significant facts. In the first place, in 1953 the Nationalists were conceded only 2 seats and the United Front 18. Beyond this, the Nationalists won only 8 of their seats with a differentiation of 50 per cent or more of the votes cast, while the United Front had 21 in this category. If the figures are scanned from the other end, they reveal that 56 Nationalists won their seats by a 25 per cent margin or less, while United Front candidates won only 9 by comparable margins. In 1948, the differences were less great but still marked. The Nationalists were conceded only 1 seat, but the United and Labour Parties 12. In the category of seats in which the majorities were 50 per cent or more, the Nationalists had only 5 while the United Party had 21. As for those seats which were won by less than a 25 per cent margin, the Nationalists had 41 in this category in 1948, while the United Party and Labour had 23.

Thus a major reason why the United and Labour Parties lost in 1948, and the United Front far more decisively in 1953, though in both cases they polled a majority of the votes, is the residential concentration of their supporters. The same fact operates in regard to the Labour Party in the United Kingdom. In other words, so largely urban a party as the United Party, whose supporters are concentrated in particular living centers, needs very considerably more than 50 per cent of the popular votes in order to win 50 per cent of the seats.

Chart 1 shows the relation between the number of seats won and the percentage of popular votes polled in all the general elections from 1910 through 1953 to the present, both in the Union as a whole, and in each of the provinces. Potentially the most significant information included in this chart is the advance made by the Nationalists during the past four elections. This is by far the most striking in the Transvaal, where the Nationalist percentage of the vote has risen from 24·12 per cent in 1938 when only J. G. Strijdom was returned for his party in that province, through 33·18 per cent in 1943, and 38·09 per cent in 1948, to 46·53 per cent of the votes in 1953. Another significant fact is that although the United Front increased its percentage of the vote from 53·14 per cent in 1948 to 54·40 per cent in 1953, the Nationalists made a still larger increase in their share of the popular vote, which rose from 39·96 per cent for the Nationalist and Afrikaner Parties in 1948 to 45·50 per cent of the vote polled for Nationalist candidates in 1953. Thus the evidence of the returns indicated a Nationalist trend in the votes which augured well for its maintenance of office.

CHAPTER 6

THE CAMPAIGN AND THE CANDIDATES

The date of the election was a matter of speculation for more than six months before Dr. D. F. Malan told Parliament on February 12 that it would be April 15. Dire predictions had been made that the Nationalists would hold the election while thousands of United Party supporters were loyally attending the Coronation in June; this rumor ceased when it was announced that Dr. Malan himself would attend the Coronation. The mid-April date seems in fact to have been planned for a long time by the Nationalists, partly because settled dry weather would facilitate rural voting, possibly to ensure use of the old voting roll due to be superseded on May 1.

The South African electoral law, unlike the British, does not specify the exact length of time between the dissolution of Parliament and the general election. It does state the limits of time within which nomination courts must follow the official proclamation—14 to 21 days—and those between nominations and the election. The latter period used to be not less than 63 days nor more than 70; under amendments of 1948 and 1952, this was shortened to between 28 and 35 days. Thus the longest possible time between the dissolution of Parliament and the general election is now 56 days; in 1953, it was 41 days. Dr. Malan's early announcement of the election date, however, provided 61 days of assured election campaigning.

In fact, the campaign may be said to have started with Dr. Malan's broadcast New Year message which made a five-point appeal for national unity in the face of 'natural differences' and 'the gap in the general level of civilization between different sections'.[1] The Prime Minister also asked that the election campaign be conducted 'on a high level, in accordance with the demands of sincerity, honesty and chivalry as it behoves a civilized and Christian nation'. J. G. N. Strauss, leader of the United Party, equally stressed the theme of national unity in his New Year message, but declared that the 'needless constitutional crisis' had cast a 'black shadow' over the country. He proposed that the non-European question be lifted out of 'the turbulent party-political scene'.[2] Thus it was immediately apparent that apartheid would be the key issue in the 1953 campaign, as it had been in 1948.

The following week saw speakers becoming rather more specific in what the press hailed as the first shots of the campaign. J. G. Strijdom, Minister of Lands, and leader of the National Party in the Transvaal, declared that South Africa 'can only be saved for the European if the cooperation of every European is obtained'.[3] Hitting squarely at the Opposition, he accused the United Party, as well as the Communists, of inciting the Natives in the defiance campaign. The National Party stood for the sovereignty of Parliament, subject only to God, he declared, as the people were the highest authority. A week earlier, A. E. Robinson, United Party candidate in Langlaagte, Transvaal, had introduced what became the United Party's most positive theme, that of economic development, racial peace and prosperity. He stressed white immigration, family allowances, a more extensive housing program, improved education, and a tackling of the cost of living problem.[4] The following day, D. E. Mitchell, United Party leader in Natal, challenged that province's Nationalist leader, N. C. Havenga, on the constitutional issue, republicanism, and the Indian problem.[5] The fight was on.

The most sharply defined positions on the non-European problem came not from political sources at this time, however, but non-political ones. Both SABRA, the philosophical proponents of ideal apartheid, and the liberally inclined Institute of Race Relations held their annual meetings in January 1953, thereby providing the public with up-to-date statements on their widely opposed policies. The SABRA sessions voiced the fear that 'planless integration' was proceeding unchecked by the authorities, reaffirmed its belief in the separate development of all groups in their respective areas, and called particularly for steps to combat the dangers of Communist and Indian penetration in Africa.

From the Institute of Race Relations came a grave warning that the continuation of existing discriminatory laws, even without new ones, must lead to mass resistance by the non-Europeans. White domination could continue only on a basis of physical force, warned its President, J. D. Rheinallt Jones. He called for the alternative policy of seeking the cooperation of non-Europeans, though he admitted that this too presented grave difficulties, because most non-Europeans were still unqualified to take 'an effective part in government'.[6] Nonetheless, *Die Burger* declared that the Institute's policy inevitably meant 'economic and social equality, a common citizenship and franchise', with the result that 'the present white domination, as Mr. Jones calls it, will be replaced by the domination of the Black proletariat'.[7] The *Rand Daily Mail*, in contrast, called the appeal for non-European cooperation 'a fair, sensible policy that would in no way jeopardize white leadership; indeed it would become the guarantee of white leadership'.[8]

Not surprisingly, the five-day debate following the Governor-General's Speech at the opening of the brief parliamentary session on January 23 proved a dress rehearsal of the general election campaign. On January 27, J. G. N. Strauss moved the customary vote of 'no confidence' with a vigorous indictment of Government policy. He declared that the Nationalists had destroyed unity between the white peoples of South Africa; caused a state of fear by their apartheid policy: endangered Western civilization by their handling of non-European relations; alienated the sympathy of friendly nations abroad; and violated the law in their effort to remain in power.[9] He and others of the party were more effective, however, in criticizing Nationalist non-European policy than in producing one of their own. Perhaps their most effective point was to bring out the inconsistencies between the Strijdom-Verwoerd line of ultimate complete separation of racial groups and Dr. Malan's view that this was impracticable, and also to contrast Nationalist opposition to economic integration with the fact that non-Europeans were currently entering industry faster than ever before.[10]

Behind the difficulty of the United Party in formulating a distinctive Native policy at this time lay both the naturally conservative attitude of the great bulk of its members, and the alarm caused by the non-European passive resistance campaign of 1952 and, in particular, the Native outbreaks of violence in the predominantly United Party areas of East London, Port Elizabeth and Kimberley. This was demonstrated by United Party reactions to the major legislation of the parliamentary session—the two bills introduced by the Minister of Justice, C. R. Swart, to provide the Government with more power to deal with public emergencies, and a possible renewal of civil disobedience: The Public Safety Bill, introduced January 26, and its complement, the Criminal Laws Amendment Bill, introduced January 30, 1953. The former empowered the Governor-General to proclaim a state of emergency under which virtually all laws could be suspended in any part of the Union where public safety was threatened. The latter provided heavy penalties, including fines, imprisonment and lashes for supporting a campaign of passive disobedience against any law, or for soliciting or accepting help for such a campaign.[11]

When the Public Safety Bill was introduced,[12] the Labour Party and Mrs. Ballinger took the lead in opposing it; Strauss cautiously reserved his attitude. At second reading on February 11, the United Party, through H. G. Lawrence, announced its support for the principle of the measure, though he acknowledged that it was unprecedented in a situation where there was neither war, rebellion nor civil commotion.

Despite this general support, Lawrence charged that the Government was responsible for 'that background of frustration and anxiety against which these events have happened'.[13] When N. C. Havenga asked:

> What are you prepared to give them to root out frustration when they won't be satisfied with less than equal rights?

Lawrence answered 'patience, consultation and thought'. He stressed the United Party line that the race question should be taken out of politics, declared that the Government unnecessarily wounded non-European feelings and susceptibilities, and asserted that there was a middle way between permanent white domination and racial equality, namely:

> accepting the co-existence of Europeans and non-Europeans side by side but recognizing the intrinsic differences between them in legislation and administration.

It was a brave effort to find a distinctive Native policy without leaving themselves open to the charge of obstructionism.

Much the same attitude was maintained by the United Party towards the Criminal Laws Amendment Act[14] which Swart declared was specifically aimed at the defiance campaign. At second reading, the United Party supported the measure, but 'with the contempt which the circumstances which gave rise to this bill necessitates'.[15] The United Party would keep the measure on the statute books with added safeguards, declared Colonel R. D. Pilkington-Jordan, but its future Native policy was based not on restrictive measures but on consultation. He again accused the Government of responsibility for letting disquiet mount to the danger point. The United Party found the first clause of the bill too wide in application and that the second would permit 'gross interference' with the press. Its amendments were rejected, but it still voted for the bill.

Though the United Party offered resistance only in the committee stage, and then without effect, the Labour Party and Mrs. Ballinger opposed both the Public Safety and Criminal Laws Amendment bills through every stage. The *Rand Daily Mail* declared that the Criminal Laws Amendment Bill, read in conjunction with the Public Safety Bill, was 'without question the most shocking measure ever placed before Parliament'.[16] The President of the Christian Council of South Africa, Dr. Geoffrey Clayton, questioned the necessity for such legislation.[17] Most outspoken was the Torch Commando, which in a public statement called the Public Safety Bill 'the request for a blank cheque by a bankrupt government' and 'an insult to the very Parliament—the *volkswil*—which the Nationalists profess to regard as sovereign and supreme'.[18] The Criminal Laws Amendment Bill it considered 'a drastic invasion of fundamental rights'.

Even the Afrikaans press showed concern over the new legislation. *Dagbreek* queried whether the situation had become so serious that the Government had reason 'to ask us to sign away our individual freedom to whatever 14 men may comprise the Cabinet of the Union in the future'.[19] *Die Burger* found it 'regrettable that emergency powers must again be bestowed on a Government' though it drew a sharp distinction between the powers themselves and the use made of them. It declared, however, that in case the defiance campaign was continued and intensified in 1953, 'it is the urgent duty of the State to establish whether it possesses adequate powers to smother a new wave of violence and terrorism in the germ and to protect the lives and property of its citizens'.[20]

That the same view bulked large in the thinking of the United Party was apparent from its decision to vote for both bills despite the fact that only one of its safeguard amendments to the Public Safety Bill was accepted by Mr. Swart. The Minister of Justice did assure the House that he hoped the powers need never be used, though he also went so far as to say in the Senate on February 19 that the measure could and would be put into effect against the Torch Commando if necessary. On the Criminal Laws Amendment Bill, the United Party leader, Mr. Strauss, issued a statement declaring that it was 'in no sense unconstitutional in character'. As to whether the penalties provided were 'improperly severe', the United Party view was that the defiance campaign had created a situation of 'great gravity' which made it difficult to see 'on what possible logical ground' the principle of the measure could be opposed.[21]

The dilemma which the United Party faced was a difficult one. Its members from the Eastern Cape, where the riots had taken place, were pressing for the new legislation in tones at least as urgent as those of the Nationalists. On examination, the legislation appeared less disturbing than when originally introduced, a fact generally acknowledged by the English press. But the very support which the United Party gave the legislation undercut any hope that the party could formulate a Native policy for the election which was essentially different from that of the Nationalists. Whether through design or not, the Nationalists had maneuvered their chief political opponents into public acknowledgement that they feared Native disorders, and accepted stringent penalties as the chief means of preventing them. By so affirming, the United Party not only limited its own freedom of action on the major issue of the election; it also undermined the cohesion of the United Front, and drained much of the fervor for election activities from its most liberal members.

Looked at from another angle, it could be argued that the United Party support of the Public Safety and Criminal Laws Amendment Bills made it difficult for the Nationalists to charge the United Party in the campaign with not being tough enough against Native disorders. The divisions in the United Front on this issue, however, provided considerable ammunition for the Nationalists which they were not slow to use. *Die Burger*, for example, commented on February 12 that the United Party decision to support the Criminal Laws Amendment Bill in principle was a 'right about turn—or is it a deathbed conversion?' The move decreased the division between the major parties, it declared, but caused no dwindling of the distrust of the United Front, whose '"record" in these matters is too damning'.

Economic plans were also debated in the Parliamentary session, which closed on February 24. In this case, the Nationalists took the offensive. The Minister of Finance, N. C. Havenga, claimed during the debate on the Part Appropriation Bill which ended February 10 that the United Party economic platform would cost the country some £20-30 million, and result in higher taxation. To point the contrast, he had already announced on January 26 that there would be a budget surplus for 1952-53; on February 24, he declared the surplus would be £9 million.

With the end of the Parliamentary session, and the Governor-General's proclamation officially announcing April 15 as the election date, the way was clear for the six weeks' election campaign for the 11th Parliament of the Union. The most striking feature from the Nationalist side was the drive they made in Natal for the first time in the party's history. In the English-speaking areas of Cape Town and Johannesburg, in contrast, the Nationalists did virtually no campaigning. From their side, the United Party were slow to organize in the Orange Free State and South West Africa, but ultimately covered all constituencies in the Union except those of Dr. Malan and Speaker Conradie. Both parties concentrated their efforts on the key seats of the Rand.

Though other members of the United Party, notably Sir de Villiers Graaff, Mr. Harry Lawrence and Mr. Harry Oppenheimer attracted considerable attention, it was Mr. Strauss who was by far the chief national figure in the United Party campaign. That he was indefatigable is demonstrated by the vast number of speeches he delivered. He was crisp, optimistic and self-assured. It is doubtful, however, whether he carried as much effect as his efforts deserved. His concentration on the United Party's bread and butter program made less impression than if the country had been less prosperous. Some of Mr. Strauss' speeches included too many points which were rather too imprecise to leave a clear impression on his audiences. In particular, his formulations of non-European policy awakened dissatisfaction. His criticism of Indians in Natal seems to have alienated more liberals than it attracted conservatives; similarly his comments about the immaturity of the Natives in his concluding broadcast is said to have led to the final decision to form a separate Liberal Party. It would be hard to demonstrate that Mr. Strauss' speeches lost the United Party any votes, but they probably also failed to win converts to the United Party cause, if this were still possible. A more serious effect was that they failed to rouse either widespread enthusiasm or a new corporate sense amongst party members.

Although he spoke much less frequently than Mr. Strauss, Dr. Malan succeeded far better in providing the key notes of the campaign. His opening speech on March 3 at Stellenbosch highlighted the first three of four main points around which the election campaign revolved: apartheid, Communism, the sovereignty of Parliament and unity among the white population. He followed this address with two other speeches in the Cape, at Vredendal on March 13 and Piketsberg on March 15. In his one speech in the Transvaal, at Pretoria on March 31, Dr. Malan placed greatest stress on his fourth point of white unity in South Africa. In his final broadcast on the eve of voting, Dr. Malan asked for 'an honest and decisive verdict which cannot be misunderstood here or overseas'.

Carefully focusing his words on major issues, Dr. Malan spoke in each of his public appearances with the deliberate and ponderous solemnity which made him the most impressive figure of the day in South Africa. Thus, he gave a sense of dignity and mission to his party supporters, and wrung a somewhat reluctant admiration from his political opponents.

Apart from Dr. Malan, whose words formed the theme of innumerable editorials in the Afrikaans press, the Nationalist most widely reported was J. G. Strijdom, destined to be Prime Minister on Dr. Malan's retirement. Mr. Strijdom's speeches were straightforward, hard-hitting, and dealt with a number of issues like republicanism, which Dr. Malan preferred to gloss over. Moreover, although Strijdom also stressed the necessity of unity among the whites in South Africa, it was unity in support of Nationalist objectives. 'Thousands of English-speaking people throughout the country', he said in Primrose on February 15, 'are beginning to realize that there can be only one standpoint in South Africa if the European here wants to continue. It is the standpoint that political supremacy (*baasskap*) must remain in the hands of the white man.'[22] He accused the United Party of being 'a hotch-potch of parties and movements, like the mythical dragon with five heads', and said its inability to work out a policy of its own was the natural result of the fact that 'their basis is not national'. He declared that the Republic would come 'when we are economically strong enough, when we have satisfactorily solved the colour problem, and when we have obtained sufficient support for it'. As for the scare stories that a republic would take away the rights of the English-speaking, he maintained that if the Nationalists wanted to do this at all, they could just as well do it at once. Subsequently, he specifically assured the English that the Nationalists would never rob them of their language rights.[23]

Throughout, the campaign remained a straight party fight between the Nationalists and the United Party. Though the United Party's other partners in the United Front, the Labour Party and the Torch Commando, clearly differed from the United Party on significant issues—in particular the Public Safety Act, the Criminal Laws Amendment Act, and Native policy in general—they soft-pedalled these differences in the interests of maintaining the outward appearance of unity. The relatively few Independents played no conspicuous role.

Though Dr. Malan had asked that the campaign be conducted on a high level, there was considerable hooliganism by Nationalist supporters at United Party meetings, particularly on the Rand. As early as January 14, the United Party candidate at Krugersdorp was howled down by Nationalist hecklers. As the campaign became more lively towards the latter part of March, several United Party meetings were broken up in Nationalist strongholds on the Rand and in the Cape. A United Party candidate was injured in Pretoria. Eggs and tomatoes were thrown at Harry Lawrence during a Germiston meeting.[24] Considerable publicity was given to an alleged horsewhipping of United Party canvassers in a Johannesburg suburb. Mr. Strauss' meeting in Uitenhage was badly disturbed.[25] Despite United Party protests, Nationalist spokesmen were only half-hearted in disowning this rowdiness, which, they maintained, was the result of provocation by United Party speakers.[26] The Nationalist candidate in Krugersdorp, Mr. M. J. van den Berg, went so far as to say that the Torch Commando had been sent deliberately into that constituency to stir up the Nationalists.

General tension ran fairly high during the campaign. Towards its end came persistent, if unfounded, rumors from both sides that there would be a 'Reichstag fire'.[27] The Nationalists saw dangerous elements in the United Front—not difficult to identify as the Torch Commando—who, they maintained, spoke of a general strike and cooperation with non-Europeans towards this end. Dr. Malan himself declared at Vredendal on March 13 that this was the reason for keeping the police at full strength.[28] Mr. C. R. Swart affirmed that the cancellation of normal police leaves was on the advice of their chief, General Brink. The Opposition, from its side, charged that police leaves were cancelled only in order to create artificial tension.

Throughout the election campaign, the Native resistance campaign remained dormant. Its funds were exhausted by the end of 1952, perhaps also its supply of volunteers. More important, the outbreaks of violence in East London, Port Elizabeth, and Kimberley (which Native leaders themselves believed were deliberately provoked by Nationalists to provide an atmosphere of fear for the election), had brought the passive resistance movement an unsavoury reputation among Europeans. Further outbreaks would have led to severe retaliation, and the advocacy of passive resistance had itself become subject to heavy individual penalties through the Criminal Laws Amendment Act.

Shortly before election day, Mr. Y. Cachalia, Secretary of the South African Indian Congress, and Mr. Walter Sisulu, Secretary-General of the African National Congress, called on non-Europeans to avoid all forms of provocation.[29] *The Bantu World* underlined their appeal in an editorial which said, 'Let us give no one the opportunity of making our actions an election issue.' Though Dr. Y. M. Dadoo's statement calling for the defeat of the Nationalists was used as Nationalist propaganda, there were no organized non-European activities which could be turned to this purpose. In fact, despite all protestations by non-European nationalist leaders, the passive resistance campaign was dead.

In the next section, the specific issues of the campaign will be analysed in more detail to bring out the points of view expressed on either side. That speeches, or broadcasts, or meetings made much difference to the overwhelming mass of voters is dubious. This was a campaign in which almost everyone knew how he or she was going to vote long before the Prime Minister announced the date of the election. But the issues publicized in the campaign remained important long after the election decision had been made, for they are amongst the most fundamental in South African politics.

Specific Issues of the Campaign

Not surprisingly, the campaign revolved around the efforts of the two major parties to present themselves in the most favorable light possible while showing up their opponents as incompetent, biased and perhaps even dangerous. The Nationalists emphasized the definiteness and concreteness of their program, and its identity with what they had pledged in 1948. They insisted that both theory and experience proved that their program was the only way to handle the immensely complicated multi-racial society of South Africa without allowing it to deteriorate either into Mau-Mauism, or equalitarianism. At the same time the Nationalists pictured the United Party as divided, poorly led, and confused in its thinking, for it should realize, they declared, that the segregation it endorsed should mean active support for Nationalist apartheid policies.

From its side, the United Party presented itself as the true party of national unity, since it included both English- and Afrikaans-speaking. It was also the one best capable of handling the non-European problem, its spokesmen declared, because of its experience and lack of doctrinaire extremism. The United Party called Nationalist apartheid 'a fraud' because so many non-Europeans had been absorbed into industry during their period of office. At the same time, the United Party accused the Nationalists of creating the current tenseness in race relations. They also charged the Nationalists with impairing white unity, and held up the specter of the 'extremist' Mr. Strijdom succeeding Dr. Malan.

In place of the Nationalist emphasis on apartheid, the United Party stressed the cost of living, and its economic plans for improving the condition of many groups like railway workers, smallholders and civil servants. Thus it sought to dispel the stereotype of itself as a party concerned largely with the interests of the wealthy. More effective in the Transvaal was the United Front's attack on the Education Ordinance[29a] proposed for that province which, they claimed, destroyed parents' freedom of action regarding the medium of instruction—English or Afrikaans—for their children's education.

But, despite the efforts of the United Party, apartheid was the central issue of the campaign, as it had been in 1948. In keeping it so, the Nationalists were aided by outside events, in particular the Mau-Mau terror in Kenya and Southern Rhodesian voting on Central African Federation. Even more influential were the Appeal Court decision on railway apartheid, and Dr. Dadoo's endorsement of the United Party. Thus, unlike the Opposition, the Nationalists were able to exploit particular events during the campaign to their own advantage.

Apartheid

The Nationalists presented apartheid in two ways in the 1953 campaign: as a general ideology, and as a program of action in which a number of moves had already been taken. The broader approach was pressed first. Dr. Malan in his opening speech at Stellenbosch on March 5 shrewdly maintained that there were only two courses from which to choose: equality or apartheid. Equality, he defined as 'the removal of all color discrimination' as the liberal desired; apartheid as the Nationalist policy which 'seeks to allow and encourage on both sides of the color line free natural development in accordance with capacity and level of civilization'.[30] Equality and apartheid 'went in directly opposite directions', he maintained, and there was 'no middle path between them' as Mr. Strauss had asserted.

In a clear effort to make apartheid respectable in the eyes of the world, Dr. Malan likened it to national divisions in Europe, and to a wire fence between neighboring farms which separated without eliminating legitimate and desirable contacts in both directions. Apartheid was, in fact, no different in meaning, he said, from segregation. In comparison with what he called the United Party's 'old, impotent, indiscriminate and dangerous' *laissez-faire* policy, however, the Nationalists had a clear-cut definite one which could solve South Africa's problems. In a subsequent speech at Piketberg on March 15, Dr. Malan linked these broad generalities on apartheid to the specific legislative program of the past five years, which he asserted had carried out the pledges of the 1948 manifesto in every regard except abolition of Native representatives, which was no longer necessary since Communists could not now sit in Parliament.

Mr. Strauss' efforts to exploit the differences between the total apartheid which the 1948 election propaganda had promised and the practical apartheid of the Government's legislative program brought responses from both Dr. Malan and Senator H. F. Verwoerd. In his Vredendal speech on March 17, Malan indignantly repudiated the idea that the Government was proceeding towards total apartheid which would take Native labor away from farmers and industry. Even before this, Verwoerd, the champion of ultimate ideal apartheid, had declared that a Government had to follow practical policies. He added that everyone agreed that immediate complete apartheid was impossible, but that a start should be made 'on a long path'.[31] Despite their protestations, this thrust by Strauss, followed up by other United Party speakers, was perhaps the most effective direct attack on Nationalist Native policy developed in the campaign.

Public opinion on both sides responded less to Strauss' proposal for a national, or Peoples' Convention (subsequently said to be composed only of Europeans) to consider the Native problem and formulate proposals which could then be discussed with moderate non-Europeans. Repeated numerous times after its first specific formulation in Strauss' speech at Bredasdorp on February 22, this plan was neither specific nor attractive enough to awaken much interest. Dr. Malan commented at Stellenbosch that such a convention would be only a 'Babel-like gathering' which would lead to nothing but confusion, greater discord and divisions. Even to those more sympathetic to the United Party, Strauss' proposal appeared as more of an excuse for not having a policy on color than as a policy itself. In this sense, the proposal tended to weaken rather than strengthen the party's cause.

The Railway Apartheid Case

These broad generalities on apartheid policy were given sudden precision and urgency by the decision on railway apartheid handed down by the Appeal Court on March 22. The case concerned an African who refused to leave a European waiting-room in the Cape Town railway station when told to do so by a policeman. The charge against the African was dismissed, however, by a Cape Town magistrate, whose judgment was subsequently upheld by the Cape Provincial Division and the Appeal Court in Bloemfontein. The basis for the decision was that the facilities in the non-European waiting-rooms were so far inferior to those of the Europeans as to violate the implications of equal treatment for different races found in the Railways Act of 1914, and the 1949 Amending Act, by which the Railways Administration was bound.

The first shot in a rapid volley of Nationalist attacks on the decision was fired by Dr. Malan. In a statement issued immediately in Cape Town, he declared that the verdict had sent a shock throughout the country, and created a situation which could not be accepted.[32] 'The decision draws a line through the traditional apartheid on the railways as we have always known it,' he maintained, and the Nationalists would rectify the situation without delay if they were returned to office and 'in a way that will leave no doubt about the wishes and intentions of Parliament and the people'.[33] Eight other Cabinet Ministers made statements about the judgment. P. O. Sauer declared that the verdict would encourage non-European defiance of the law. The Afrikaans press also played up the judgment more than any other single issue during the campaign. *Die Transvaler,* in particular, ran front-page reports of instances where non-Europeans were said to have taken advantage of the judgment to violate apartheid regulations.[34]

Dr. Malan also attempted to belabor the United Party with the decision by suggesting that it 'had always been at best indifferent towards this matter'. This accusation Strauss rejected with indignation as 'misleading the people of South Africa because the United Party does not diverge one inch from its policy of segregation on stations and trains'.[35] Subsequently Strauss attempted to turn the tables on the Nationalists by accusing them of making political capital out of its 'horror stories' about African violations of apartheid.[36] It was not the judges who were at fault, he maintained, but the 1949 Amendment which the Nationalists had drafted. If the United Party were returned to office, they would restore the former position by legislation, a pledge which duplicated that of the Nationalists.

Despite United Party efforts, however, the Nationalists exploited the railway apartheid decision so skilfully and incessantly that it became their most effective propaganda weapon. Though H. G. Lawrence called their violent reaction 'a gigantic election bluff' because no such concern had been shown over a similar judgment on post office facilities at Elsies River,[37] the court's verdict had touched Afrikaners, particularly the railway workers, on a sensitive point. All the evidence suggests that both the timing and substance of the Appeal Court judgment helped the Nationalists greatly in whipping up election fervor.

Sovereignty of Parliament v. the Courts

Naturally, the railway apartheid judgment was quickly linked with the Nationalists' general position that the courts should not be able to pass judgment on the validity of legislation. Different as was the railway case from that concerning the Separate Representation of Voters Act (since the former was an interpretation of a statute—not a decision on its constitutionality), the Nationalists grouped the two together as both thwarting apartheid.

In his Stellenbosch speech, Dr. Malan had listed the sovereignty of Parliament as a major issue of the election, and asked the electorate to give the Nationalists power (i.e. presumably a two-thirds majority) to carry through their mandate despite the courts. At Vredendal, on March 13, he went so far as to say that the Nationalists would seek authority to carry out the will of the people without regard for the two-thirds majority provision, a position also affirmed by J. F. T. Naudé in Natal. Strijdom reiterated the same view in Greytown on March 20. Strong criticism from the Opposition seems to have had an effect on toning down this point.

Immediately after the railway apartheid judgment, Dr. T. E. Dönges began to develop a new angle of the 'judges *versus* the people' propaganda. Pointing out that judges had no testing power in Great Britain or Holland, but possessed it in the United States, he maintained that in the latter country Roosevelt had been forced by rejection of his legislation to appoint judges who supported his policy. If the people did not give the Government a sufficient mandate, it might have to make political appointments to the judiciary in order to be able to rule.[38] Again Opposition criticism forced a moderating of the position so that Dr. Dönges subsequently declared that he would not like to see the court packed, though he still felt it was not right that the courts should have the power to test legislation.[39] The Secretary of the Nationalist Party in the Cape, Mr. P. M. Botha, went still further in his comments on the judges, declaring: 'We are sick and tired of legal cunning (*slimmigheid*) in South Africa.'[40]

From the United Party side, the most common points were pledges by Strauss to support the Constitution, maintain the prestige of the courts, and uphold the rights of the Coloured. Though the Opposition was highly critical of Nationalist statements on the so-called sovereignty of Parliament, it did not make as much political capital of Nationalist attempts to override the Appeal Court judgment on the Separate Representation of Voters Act as might have been expected. In so far as the United Party dealt with the issue, it was in constitutional terms, with no attempt to point out the obvious answer to the weighted question raised by Dr. K. Bremer at Goodwood on March 2, 'Do you want the Coloured to dominate in the Cape?'

Communism

In his first campaign speech, Dr. Malan associated Communism with 'the arson and scenes of murder of Port Elizabeth and East London'. All the more telling, therefore, were the attempts to associate the United Party with Communism either by suggesting, as Strijdom did so frequently, that the United Party was as culpable as the Communists in inducing the Native attitudes which led to the riots late in 1952, or by accusing the United Party of being 'soft' to Communists because they had opposed certain aspects of the Suppression of Communism Act.

Forced on the defensive, Strauss first asserted the obvious fact that the party was 'four-square on Communism',[41] and then came out with a proposal that the death sentence should be imposed for Communist agitation if it were proved before an impartial court.[42] The United Party would also eliminate conditions which bred Communism, he said, like malnutrition and bad housing. On the Suppression of Communism Act, Strauss tried to keep clear the distinction between opposition to Communism as such, and the lack of democratic safeguards in the existing Act. It seems unlikely, however, that this distinction was understood widely and Nationalist propaganda on this issue was apparently highly effective both in the *platteland* and Afrikaner working-class suburbs. One of the most spectacular pieces of National Party propaganda luridly dramatized the red hand of Communism.

Still more effective from the Nationalist point of view was the publicity the party gave to Dr. Y. M. Dadoo's appeal to non-European voters to use their franchise to turn the Nationalists out of office.[43] Among the leaders of the South African Indian Congress, Dr. Dadoo was both the best known and the one most closely identified in the public mind with Communism. Far from being disturbed when Dr. Dadoo declared that 'in our struggle for a truly democratic South Africa ensuring full rights and equal opportunities for all' the main task was to defeat 'the most reactionary extreme right wing element in the body politic . . . the *storm-jaers* of Strijdom', the Nationalists gloried in the statement. *Die Burger* declared that the party and Government 'hated and feared' most by the Dadoos was for that very reason 'friend number one and protector of the non-Europeans'.[44] Nationalist speakers similarly drummed in the point that Dr. Dadoo's advice to non-Europeans to vote United Party as the lesser of two evils was proof that the United Party befriended Communism.

Since his statement was so obviously usable in Nationalist propaganda, why did Dr. Dadoo make it? Most other non-European spokesmen emphasized that there was little if anything to choose between the parties. Dr. G. M. Naicker, President of the Natal Indian Congress, told its annual conference in Durban that since all parliamentary parties upheld white domination, the non-Europeans should have no faith in their programs or policies.[45] The able African journalist, Jordan K. Ngubane, commented in *Indian Opinion* on March 6 that it mattered little to the leaders of the African National Congress whether Strauss or Malan were the next Prime Minister. The A.N.C. itself issued a statement that 'freedom, liberty and democracy in South Africa does not depend on which party wins the election but depends on the non-voting masses whose policy is the only road to a happy and prosperous South Africa for all'.[46] Thus the much more common line of unenfranchised non-Europeans was to lump both parties together as equally useless to their cause.

In the Cape there was more division, since the Coloured newspaper, *The Sun*, continued its traditional support of the United Party and on March 20 urged all eligible Coloured to use their votes, as otherwise they would be committing 'political suicide'. *The Torch*, however, declared there was no basic difference between the two sections 'of the ruling class',[47] and the Non-European Unity Movement, of which *The Torch* is the organ, urged a boycott of the election.

On the face of things, then, there was a split between the left-wing leadership in the Cape, and in the Transvaal. Their seemingly divergent policies contributed in practice, however, to the same purpose, i.e. the defeat of the United Party. A boycott of Coloured voters could only work to the advantage of the Nationalists, as did Dr. Dadoo's statement. The reason why left-wing non-European opinion preferred the Nationalists to the United Party seems to be that Nationalist policies sharpen the division between Europeans and non-Europeans, and thus might lead more quickly to the violent outbreak which Communists undoubtedly desire. If this interpretation is correct, it puts Dr. Dadoo's statement in quite the opposite light from that in which the Nationalists presented it, and demonstrates how clever, in fact, the Communist line proved to be.

Cost of Living and Economic Development

The United Party could hardly hope to compete with the Nationalists over apartheid, but it had confidence in its bread-and-butter program, plugged determinedly throughout the campaign. To vote for the United Party is 'a vote for a boom', declared Strauss at the important Rand mining suburb of Krugersdorp on March 10. The Workers' Charter, offer of family allowances, increases for railwaymen and civil servants, etc., were aimed at specific groups which the United Party hoped to detach from the Nationalists. In particular, Sir de Villiers Graaff, United Party leader in the Cape, promised immediate relief to those in need and also an increase in production which would meet the costs of the United Party program.

The long duration of South African prosperity and the very volume of United Party inducements seem, however, to have undercut the appeal of its economic program, particularly to the Afrikaner electorate. The most effective Nationalist answer to this economic program was to insist that its cost would be overwhelming, a charge the United Party never convincingly answered.

Parental Choice and the Education Ordinance

More effective than the economic program was the propaganda of the United Front on the proposed Transvaal Education Ordinance, and its effect on parental choice of the medium of instruction for their children. Credit for dramatizing this issue belongs less to the United Party than to the Education League (see p. 335) through the Education Action Group which sprang into public existence on March 4, and attracted widespread attention in Johannesburg through large and effective posters. The Education Group maintained that the Transvaal Ordinance, supported in the Provincial Council by Transvaal Nationalists, was being used 'to promote a narrow sectional education policy which takes no account of the sacred rights of parents, nor the interests of the children'.[48] 'To get their children back and keep them,' said the Education Action Group's chairman ten days later, meant voting against the Nationalist

Party.[49] Further dramatizing the issue were a quarter of a million strip cartoon pamphlets.

Once it had been raised, the United Party took full advantage of the education issue. The Education Ordinance would establish 'white apartheid', said Strauss. P. A. Moore, in his radio broadcast, said the United Party would respect parental choice of language in the education of their children.

Taken off guard, the Nationalists were less effective in meeting this challenge than the economic one. The Afrikaans press pointed out correctly that South African children had long been educated in that language which inspectors found by testing was their primary one. Dr. Verwoerd insisted the language rights of English children were never in doubt, and that language discrimination in the past had always been against the Afrikaner. In a later statement, he declared, rather less fortunately for the Nationalist case, that 'the fundamental thing about education was not the wish of the parent but the interest of the child'.[50]

Of all the issues raised in the election, this seems to have been the one which detached the largest number of Afrikaner voters, mainly women, from their Nationalist allegiance. Some Nationalists stated after the election that they might have carried five more seats in the Transvaal but for propaganda on the Education Ordinance.

National Unity

Underlying the debate on the Education Ordinance was the broad issue of unity between the English- and Afrikaans-speaking. This was a theme of which the United Party might have been expected to make much since its very composition was testimony to its role as a bridge between South Africa's two European peoples. Rather than stress this feature, however, the United Party tried to exploit fear of an exclusive Afrikaner nationalism. It spoke much of Strijdom 'extremism', and of the danger that the English might be denied rights, including language rights, in an Afrikaner dominated republic. It suggested also that the Nationalists might withdraw South Africa from the Commonwealth.

In part, the Nationalists met this challenge with reassurances. Strijdom insisted, on March 1, that the Nationalists would never deprive the English of their language rights; in two other speeches he emphasized that South Africa needed the unity of its European people. Verwoerd struck another line by maintaining in predominantly English-speaking Johannesburg on March 5 that United Party members would ultimately welcome a republic.

Though Dr. Malan made national unity one of the four points on the Nationalist program, it trailed after apartheid, Communism and the sovereignty of Parliament. In his initial speech in Stellenbosch, Dr. Malan declared that both European language groups were increasingly accepting South Africa as their 'one and only fatherland'. This he termed 'one common Afrikanerhood'. He stressed particularly the unity between English and Afrikaners on foreign policy. In his one major speech in the Transvaal, Dr. Malan accused the United Party of fearing cooperation between English- and Afrikaans-speaking, and of trying to keep the English apart as a solid bloc. One by one the disputes of the past had disappeared; neutrality, the Republic, South African citizenship, Communism and apartheid. The Nationalists were not anti-English, but on the contrary wished to see a strong England and a powerful Europe. On this basis, he called for unity of the Union's European peoples.

English- as well as Afrikaans-speaking may well have viewed this plea for national unity, however, in the way in which *Die Transvaler* interpreted it on March 2. Pointing out that Dr. Malan had always been an uncompromising opponent of unity 'built on sand', the paper declared that 'The National Party is like a big magnet which constantly attracts more and more people towards itself and its firm principles'. Both the history of the National Party, and the emphasis of its speakers could leave little doubt that what the South African English were being offered in all sincerity was a chance to participate in a Nationalist program on Nationalist terms.

The Candidates

Of the 297 candidates for the 156 seats in the House of Assembly, 138 stood for the National Party, 148 for the United Party, 6 for the Labour Party[51] and 5 as Independents. Of these, 94 Nationalists, 57 United Party and 5 Labour Party members were elected.

In an effort to secure as extensive and reliable information as possible, the author sent a questionnaire to each of the candidates with a covering letter making it clear that the survey had the endorsement of top party officials. This questionnaire asked for age, education, occupation, religious affiliation, home language, whether the candidate was bilingual, what language was predominant in his constituency, his length of residence (if any) in his constituency, previous political experience and party experience. About 40 per cent of the candidates replied, a larger percentage from the United Party and Labour Party than of the Nationalists.

For the rest of the candidates, various sources of information were tapped. Both Nationalist and United Party officials were very helpful in providing information about many of those who did not return the questionnaire.[52] A certain amount of additional information was gathered from ordinary biographical sources. The quantity of data secured by these continued efforts compares favorably in many respects with that provided on the candidates in recent British elections by the British series of election surveys sponsored by Nuffield College.[53] Thus it was possible to secure information on the age of all but 37 of the 297 candidates, some details on the education of all but 19, the occupation of all but 11, and the political experience of all but 24. Information on the home language and predominant language of the constituency was secured for all but 8 candidates and on religious preference for all but 11 of the candidates in the Transvaal, Orange Free State and South West Africa. The returns on residence in constituencies were spotty but suggestive.

As far as *age* is concerned, the most striking fact is that in both the major parties, the mean age of candidates was over 50, whereas in Great Britain, for example, it is between 40 and 50. Fifty-three per cent of the 118 Nationalist candidates for whom there are returns were over 50; 47 per cent below that age. The United Party still more obviously drew on older persons as candidates,

57 per cent of the 136 on whom there is information being over 50, and only 43 per cent under it.

The percentage of those over 50 is still higher among those who were successful in the election. Fifty-eight per cent of 86 of the elected Nationalists were over 50 as compared with 42 per cent under that age. The M.P.s of the United Party showed a still higher proportion over 50: 67 per cent of the 55 on whom there is information being above that age, and only 3 per cent below it.

The following breakdown of ages underlines the points already made.

Candidates

	20-29	*30-39*	*40-49*	*50-59*	*60-69*	*70-over*	*unknown*
U.P.	5	16	37	45	27	6	12
Nationalists	2	22	31	40	20	3	20
Labour			3	2			1
Independents				1			4

Successful Candidates

U.P.	2	4	12	22	11	4	2
Nationalists	1	13	22	31	16	3	8
Labour			3	2			

The *educational background* of the candidates of the major parties was also marked by a few significant differences. All but 3 of 115 Nationalists on whom there is this information were educated exclusively at State schools. Two of these 3 went to private schools, and 1 to both a private and a State school. Out of 136 United Party candidates, in contrast, 24 attended only private schools, and 19 others had both State and private education, in addition to the 93 who went exclusively to State schools. For 12 there is no information. Four of 5 Labour candidates went to State schools.

The breakdown for successful candidates shows an even sharper contrast: the 84 successful Nationalists on whom there is information had all attended State schools. Of 47 out of the 57 United Party candidates who were elected, only 23 went to State schools, while 20 went to private schools, and 4 had both private and State education. The contrast may help to explain in part the differences in attitude of the two parties to the Bantu Education Act.

Interesting is the high proportion of Nationalist and particularly of United Party candidates who had received university training in South Africa and/or abroad. One hundred and sixty-one of the 240 candidates on whom there is information had received this kind of advanced training, 67 Nationalists and 94 United Party members. Still more striking is the fact that among the elected members for whom there are such data, 49 of the United Party and 46 of the Nationalists had had university training. The one Labour member who had attended a university was elected.

Notable also is the diversification of training found among the candidates of both major parties. Though the Nationalists all speak Afrikaans as a home language, less than half of the 67 on whom there is information had attended only Afrikaans-speaking universities. Nine of the others had been trained solely at an English-speaking institution in South Africa and 5 at both English- and Afrikaans-language institutions. Eighteen had had some of their training abroad, about half in English-speaking countries, and half on the Continent. Among elected Nationalists, about the same proportions hold.

United Party candidates showed a more even diversification in their advanced training. Twenty-seven had all their training only at an Afrikaans-speaking institution; and an equal number only at an English-speaking university in South Africa. Six went to both English and Afrikaans institutions. Twenty-nine had all or part of their training abroad, 16 wholly at English or Scottish universities. The most noticeable difference among United Party elected members is that 17 were educated at English-language universities and only 9 at Afrikaans ones. A fuller breakdown is given on the following chart.

University Training

Language and place	*U.P. Cand.*	*U.P. Elected*	*Nat. Cand.*	*Nat. Elected*
Afrikaans in S.A.	27	9	31	23
English in S.A.	27	17	9	6
English and Afrikaans in S.A. (none abroad)	6	1	5	4
Corr. course (U. of S.A.)	2	1	2	1
Undesignated S.A. institution	3	3	2	1
English in S.A., U.K.	4	2	2	2
English in S.A., U.K., Continent	1	1	0	0
Afrikaans in S.A., U.K.	1	1	1	1
Afrikaans in S.A., Continent	1	0	6	5
Afrikaans in S.A., U.K., Continent	0	0	3	2
Afrikaans and English in S.A., U.K., and Continent	0	0	1	1
Undesignated S.A. and abroad	2	0	0	0
U.K. only	16	11	1	0
Continent only	0	0	1	0
Both U.K. and Continent (none in S.A.)	2	1	2	0
U.S. only[54]	1	1	1	0
N.Z. only	1	1	0	0
	94	49	67	46

As for the particular institutions, the most widely attended among South African universities were Stellenbosch and Cape Town, and among those abroad Leyden and Oxford. The following chart shows in detail the institutions which any substantial number of candidates attended, either for all their advanced training or part of it. The latter instances are marked 'combined' on the chart.

Universities Chiefly Attended by Candidates

University	U.P. Cand.	U.P. Elected	Nat. Cand.	Nat. Elected
Stellenbosch	9	2	15	10
Combined	4	1	10	9
Pretoria	8	3	5	4
Combined	5	3	1	0
U. of O.F.S. (Bloemfontein)	2	2	5	4
Combined	0	0	5	5
Cape Town	9	5	7	5
Combined	9	4	4	4
Witwatersrand	10	6	0	0
Combined	3	2	1	0
Agricultural College (either alone or combined)	10	3	3	2
Those with University *plus* correspondence course	6	2	8	4
Universities Abroad				
Oxford	1	1	0	0
Combined	5	4	1	1
Cambridge	4	2	0	0
Combined	1	0	2	2
Edinburgh	2	2	0	0
Combined	1	1	2	1
Leyden	0	0	1	0
Combined	2	1	4	3

As is obvious from the two charts, a number of the candidates not only combined two institutions of higher learning in South Africa, but two or more abroad. The broadest combinations were reported by 5 Nationalists: Oxford-Leyden-Amsterdam, Cambridge-Berlin-Copenhagen, London-Berlin, Great Britain-U.S.A.-Germany, and, broadest distribution of all, Great Britain-Holland-Germany-Denmark.

The most striking though hardly surprising fact about the *religious affiliation* of the candidates is the dominant position of the Dutch Reformed Church. In the Transvaal, Free State and South West Africa, 73 out of the 76 Nationalist candidates for whom returns were secured belonged to one or another branch of the D.R.C., only 7 of these tc the Gereformeerde Kerk, and none to the Nederduits Hervormde.[55] The much less complete returns for the Cape and Natal indicate 1 Lutheran and 1 from the Universal Church of God among the Nationalists. For the United Party, 52 from the Transvaal, Free State and South West Africa belonged to the D.R.C., 1 each being listed under its smaller churches. The United Party candidates in those provinces also included 15 Anglicans (Episcopalian), 1 Presbyterian, 2 Christian Scientists, (1 of whom was the party's leader, Mr. Strauss), 6 Jewish, and 1 who wrote 'nil'. The Labour Party included 1 Roman Catholic, 2 Jewish, 1 'Rationalist', and 1 'nil'.

Naturally enough, the D.R.C. also predominated among the successful candidates. All the 73 elected Nationalists on whom there is information belong to that group of churches. The high proportion of D.R.C. members noted among United Party candidates did not persist, however, among those securing election. The 9 among the latter belonging to the D.R.C. were outnumbered by 13 Anglicans (Episcopalian). There were also 6 Jewish, 3 Methodists, 1 Christian Scientist, and 2 Presbyterians. All the Labour Party members noted above were elected, and that group thus had the distinction of containing the only Roman Catholic in the House as far as the author could ascertain.

The most distinctive feature of the South African candidates for the 1953 election was the heavy preponderance of farmers, and of persons who combined farming with some other *occupation*. Despite the Nationalists' hold on the *platteland*, there were more United Party candidates in this category than Nationalists. Twenty-eight Nationalists gave farming as their sole occupation while 36 others combined it with something else. The United Party, however, had 38 who said they were farmers only, while 37 others combined farming with another occupation. Thus 75 United Party candidates had personal knowledge of farming problems, and 64 Nationalists. When it came to the final results, the balance was radically transformed, however, for 55 of the Nationalists in this category were elected to 15 of the United Party, and among the latter only 3 for whom farming was the sole occupation.

Next in line among occupations were the professions. Thirty-five Nationalists and 36 United Party listed one of the professions as their sole occupation; 24 and 15 respectively combined a profession with something else. The number of lawyers was much less high than in most electoral contests—15 Nationalists and 13 United Party—to whom may be added 4 Nationalists and 2 United Party who combined law with another occupation. Eighteen of these professional people were elected for each party, including 13 Nationalist lawyers and 8 United Party. The greatest holocaust was among the educationalists, of whom the Nationalist candidates included 22 and the United Party 13, but only 1 United Party member among all these was successful.

Business was a relatively small category and interestingly enough in the light of the United Party's support by industry and commerce was not much more strongly evident among members of that party than among the Nationalists. While 11 of the United Party and only 2 Nationalists listed business as their sole occupation, the Nationalists numbered 10 directors of companies among their candidates, to 16 among the United Party.

Labour candidates had the most definitely urban occupations, including 2 business men, 2 lawyers and 1 engaged in trade union work. One of the Independent Nationalists was a farmer; the Independent Liberal a business man; and another Independent a dentist.

The following chart gives a fairly complete breakdown of the occupations of the candidates of the major parties and those elected. Noticeable is the number of those who combined two or more occupations. Eleven of those included on this chart noted that they had retired: 8 of these were running for the United Party and 3 for the Nationalists. Three of the former were elected, and all the latter. The most intriguing occupation is not noted on the chart, that of a United Party candidate, alas, not elected, who said he was a rigger ropeman.

Occupations

	Nat. Cand.	*Elected Nats.*	*U.P. Cand.*	*Elected U.P.*
Farming:				
Farmers only	28	22	38	3
Cape	17		18	
Trans.	3		11	
Natal	0		1	
O.F.S.	3		5	
S.W.A.	5		3	
Combined with another occupation	36	33	37	12
Total in Farming	64	55	75	15
Business:				
Business only	2	1	11	2
Combined with farmer	6		10	
Combined with teacher	4		3	
Combined with lawyer	1		1 (also farmer)	
Others	3		3	
Total in Business	16	7	28	7
(Directors of Companies)—included in totals above	(10)	(6)	(16)	(5)
Professions:				
Profession only	35	16	36	17
Combination	24	2	15	1
Total in Professions	59	18	51	18
Lawyers	15	12	13	8
Combination	4	1	2	0
Total	19	13	15	8
Doctors and Dentists	5	3	3	3
Combination	1	0	2	0
Total	6	3	5	3

	Nat. Cand.	Elected Nats.	U.P. Cand.	Elected U.P.
Journalists	1	1	4	3
Combination	3	1	4	1
Total	4	2	8	4
Education:	7	0	7	1
Combination	15	0	6	0
Total	22	0	13	1
Politics	3	0	1	0
Pastors	2	0	2	0
Engineers	1	0	1	0
Mine Experts only	0	0	2	0
Combination	1	0	1	0
Government Servants	1	0	3	2

The overall picture of interests and occupations of the members elected to the 1953 House of Assembly shows a heavy preponderance of those connected with agriculture, especially in the National Party, and a relatively small representation of business experience.[56] The House can therefore hardly be said to provide a true microcosm either of the people who elected it or of the major interests of the country.

In South Africa, it is not necessary to be a *resident* of a constituency in order to be nominated as its candidate. While the returns on this matter were very spotty—only for 107 of the United Party and 80 of the Nationalist candidates—a certain pattern seems to emerge. In the Cape, just over half of those reported were residents of their constituencies and each party had approximately the same proportion: 24 out of 43 for the United Party, and 10 out of 17 for the Nationalists. In the Transvaal, the proportion of resident candidates was much higher: 29 residents out of 38 reported among United Party candidates and 34 out of 38 for the Nationalists. In the Free State, 9 out of 12 United Party candidates, and the 11 Nationalist candidates on whom there is information, were residents. In Natal, 7 of 10 United Party candidates and 4 of 10 Nationalists were residents of their constituencies. In South West Africa the 4 United Party and 4 Nationalist candidates on whom there is information were residents of their constituencies. In the overall totals, the Nationalists had almost three times as many resident candidates as non-resident—63 to 17—and the United Party nearly twice as many: 73 residents to 34 non-residents. Three of the Labour candidates were non-residents, but 2 were long-time residents of their constituencies.

Did residence in constituency make a difference to the result? The outcome seems to suggest that it was not an insignificant factor. Out of 65 of the elected Nationalists, 54 were residents of their constituencies; still more striking is the fact that out of 33 of those elected in the Transvaal, 30 were residents and 26 had lived in their constituencies for more than 5 years. Moreover, out of 37 of those elected for the United Party, 23 were residents of their constituencies. As the chart below shows, the proportion of resident candidates among those for whom there is information was lowest in the Cape.

Residency in Constituency

Province	*U.P. Cand.*		*U.P. Elected*		*Nat. Cand.*		*Nat. Elected*	
	**R*	*NR*	*R*	*NR*	*R*	*NR*	*R*	*NR*
Transvaal	29	9	7	3	34	4	30	3
Natal	7	3	7	2	4	6	1	1
Cape	24	19	9	9	10	7	8	7
O.F.S.	9	3	0	0	11	0	11	0
S.W.A.	4	0	0	0	4	0	4	0
	73	34	23	14	63	17	54	11

*R=resident; NR=non-resident.

The attempt was also made to learn the previous *political and party experience* of the candidates. Nearly one-half of the candidates had previously held national elective office. One hundred and twenty-nine of the 297 candidates had previously been members of the House of Assembly: 72 of the Nationalist candidates, 53 United Party candidates, and 4 Labour candidates. Twenty-eight (that is, almost half) of the Nationalist candidates in the Transvaal had already been in the Assembly, and 26 of those in the Cape, while the respective figures for the United Party were 19 and 24. Eleven of the Free State and all six of the South West Africa Nationalist candidates were former M.P.s, as were 9 of the United Party candidates. One Nationalist and 2 United Party candidates had been members of the Senate.

Moreover, there was a substantial amount of provincial and local government experience represented among the candidates. Thirty-six United Party candidates had previously been members of Provincial Councils, and 23 Nationalists. At the local levels, 12 Nationalist candidates had previously been mayor; 3 deputy mayor; 23 municipal councillors; and 2 on the school board. The United Party had an equally broad distribution with 13 who had previously been mayor; 2 deputy mayor; 18 municipal councillors; and 17 on school, hospital or health boards. At the same time, a considerably larger number of United Party than Nationalist candidates had previously had little or no political experience: 43 as compared with 21.

The final results show a still stronger percentage of ' repeats'. Sixty-one Nationalists, 46 United Party and 3 Labour members had previously been members of the Assembly, making a total of 110 out of the 156 elected. The Nationalist who had been a Senator was elected, but not the two who ran for the United Party. Provincial Council experience also ranked high among successful candidates, as all 23 Nationalist candidates noted as having been M.P.C.s were elected, and also 23 of the 36 United Party candidates with this experience. Eleven of the 12 Nationalists who had served as mayor, 1 of the 3 deputy mayors, and 18 of those who had been municipal councillors were elected. The United Party numbered 4 former mayors and 4 former municipal councillors among its successful aspirants. In the sum total, the Nationalists elected only some 12 members without political experience and the United Party 8, a relatively even proportion when one considers their strength in the House and, in sum, a strikingly small number of novices.

The party experience of the candidate is much more difficult to put in satisfactory categories because of the lack of uniformity in the way the question was answered. Thirteen Nationalist candidates listed themselves as organizers, including 1 who was only part-time, while 16 United Party candidates, including 2 who were volunteers, said they were or had been organizers. Ten Nationalist and 9 United Party said they worked at 'headquarters'. Eight Nationalist and 10 United Party had federal or national party experience; 39 Nationalist and 54 United Party candidates held or had held some party office in the provincial sphere, either as an officer or committee member. At the constituency level, 30 Nationalist and 55, or almost twice as many, United Party candidates had had some working experience; at the branch level, 35 Nationalist and 26 United Party. Seventeen of the Nationalist and 14 of the United Party candidates on whom there is information had little or no party experience. In many instances, of course, the same persons had experience at various levels of the party hierarchy. Nine United Party candidates were members of the Torch Commando, 3 each from the Cape and Free State, 2 from the Transvaal and 1 from Natal.

It is as difficult to get a clear picture of the party experience of the successful candidates as of the group as a whole. Seven of the elected Nationalists and 3 of the United Party had been, or were, party organizers. Seventeen Nationalists had had experience as chairman of a branch; 2 as vice-chairman; 15 on the Executive Committee; 11 at Head Office and Head Committee; 9 on a Divisional Council; 13 as Secretary; 8 in executive positions in the youth organization; 6 as parliamentary whips. Another 20 listed ex-officio experience, while a surprisingly high number—23—said they had 'little or none'. The United Party shows a relatively similar range of party experience among its elected members: 9 chairmen of branches, i.e., almost one-sixth of all their members; 5 vice-chairmen; 7 on the Executive Committee; 6 at Head Office or the Head Committee; 2 Divisional Chairmen and 4 on a Divisional Council; 3 as Secretary; 7 in the youth organization; and 5 as parliamentary whips. Seventeen of the elected United Party members had had little or no party experience.

Little can be deduced from these facts except the relative similarity of party experience represented among the Nationalists and the United Party in the Assembly, coupled with the fact that both major parties include parliamentary members who know from personal experience the workings of the party at every level. It is perhaps noteworthy that, though the National Party is much more highly organized than the United Party, its M.P.s elected in 1953 had a less wide experience and close contact with party organization than those of the United Party.

An overwhelming proportion of the candidates in 1953 were men, 289 of the total of 297. Of the 8 *women* nominated, 6 stood for the United Party and 2 for the Nationalists. Small as is this number compared, for example, to the percentage of women candidates in Great Britain, it marked a considerable advance on earlier South African elections. For the Nationalists it was the first time that women stood as parliamentary candidates.[57]

Both the Nationalist women candidates fought hopeless seats: Mrs. J. T.

Smit at Durban Point, Natal, being defeated by 8,707 votes to 1,039, and Mrs. M. Koster at Port Elizabeth Central by 6,653 to 3,874. The 3 unsuccessful United Party candidates, Miss Gladys E. Steyn (Bloemfontein Central), Miss Jacqueline de Villiers (Vasco) and Mrs. Louise Kerstein (Klerksdorp), were defeated only less decisively. On the other hand, the 3 United Party women candidates who were elected—Mrs. Bertha Solomon (Jeppe), who has held a seat in the House of Assembly since 1938, and 2 newcomers, Mrs. Helen Suzman (Houghton), and Mrs. S. M. van Niekerk (Drakensberg, Natal)—won by substantial majorities or, in the case of Mrs. Suzman, without a contest. These facts provide good evidence that the United Party gives more political opportunities to its women members than do the Nationalists, though the latter seem at last to be realizing the necessity of recognizing in this way the very considerable contribution made to their party by women.

Mrs. Koster, for example, had been district leader in East London, vice-chairman for the Cape Province in 1951, and member of the Nationalist Head Committee in the Eastern Cape, while Mrs. Smit, though less active in party matters, had been city councillor for 13 years in Harrismith, O.F.S., including 2 years as mayor. All the women United Party candidates had also had extensive party experience, suggesting that such activities are looked on, at least for women, as the prerequisite for parliamentary candidacy.

Not unimportant was the obviousness of the outcome in all the contests in which women were candidates. This suggests that party strategists feel that women should be assigned either to safe or hopeless seats, though some of Mrs. Solomon's earlier election fights should have demonstrated that women too can be hard-hitting and effective campaigners.

That much of the old church-induced prejudice against women assuming public positions is dying out is suggested by the fact that 6 of the 8 women candidates belonged to the Dutch Reformed Church, the other 2 being Jewish. In age, 3 of the women were in the mid-thirties, 3 between 45 and 55, and 2 between 60 and 65. The 4 eldest ran for the United Party. More striking is the fact that all 6 women United Party candidates had university education (3 at Cape Town, 1 at Witwatersrand, 1 at Stellenbosch and 1 at the university of the O.F.S.), while neither of the women Nationalist candidates went beyond State school except that 1 had commercial college training. Four of the United Party women candidates were Afrikaans-speaking; all, except 1, bilingual. One of the English-speaking women candidates successfully fought a predominantly Afrikaans-speaking constituency. Both women Nationalist candidates contested English-speaking constituencies, sharing their defeat in such areas with those of their male colleagues.

Few factors are more important in South African political life than *language*, particularly Afrikaans. Though the country is officially bilingual, Afrikaans is increasingly the language of politics as well as of Afrikaner nationalism. Characteristic is the fact that, of the 106 Nationalist candidates for whom this information was secured, only 1 listed English as the home language, while 1 other listed both English and Afrikaans. Both of these candidates ran in predominantly English-speaking Natal. Side by side with this dominance of Afrikaans among Nationalist candidates, however, must be put the fact that all of them were bilingual.

To a marked degree, United Party candidates were also bilingual, though

4 of their English-speaking members reported themselves as not being so while 3 others said they were only partially bilingual. The major difference between the Nationalist and United Party candidates as far as language was concerned was that the latter included a relatively even division between Afrikaans- and English-speaking. Thus, of 134 United Party candidates, 67 listed Afrikaans as the home language, 52 listed English and 15 said both. The Labour candidates were all English-speaking, 2 bilingual, 2 partially bilingual and 1 not bilingual, of the 5 who actually contested seats.

A more complicated calculation is the relation between the home language of the candidate and that of the constituency in which he stands. At this point the dominance of Afrikaans-speaking constituencies becomes apparent. Out of 135 constituencies for which information was secured from candidates or the parties, the United Party considered 86 predominantly Afrikaans-speaking, and 16 as 50-50. Even the 86 predominantly Afrikaans-speaking seats comprise well over 50 per cent of the total of 156 seats contested. All the constituencies in the Free State and South West Africa are Afrikaans-speaking, with the possible exception of 1 Free State seat (Bloemfontein City) which the Nationalists (but not the United Party) listed as 50-50. Of the 59 seats the Nationalists contested in the Transvaal, they cited 38 as predominantly Afrikaans-speaking, 3 as 50-50, and 15 as English-speaking. The United Party saw this most significant of South African provinces as even more strongly Afrikaans-speaking than did the Nationalists, listing 43 constituencies as predominantly Afrikaans-speaking, 3 as 50-50, and only the remaining 22 as English-speaking. The Cape remains more evenly divided but even here the United Party reported 22 out of 47 constituencies as predominantly Afrikaans-speaking, with 11 evenly divided and only 14 predominantly English-speaking. Natal, of course, is almost exclusively English-speaking, with 1 predominantly Afrikaans-speaking constituency among its 15, and 1 (Newcastle) evenly divided.[58] Yet this does little to change the total balance. (For the geographical effect see map p. 446.)

As can be expected, the predominance of Afrikaans-speaking candidates in both parties, coupled with the predominance of Afrikaans-speaking constituencies, makes this combination the most common one. The deviations, however, are the more interesting. Twelve Afrikaans-speaking, bilingual Nationalists contested 12 predominantly English-speaking constituencies. From the other side, 15 English-speaking, bilingual United Party candidates and 1 Labour candidate contested predominantly Afrikaans-speaking constituencies. Of 22 50-50 constituencies (accepting Nationalist estimates), the United Party fought 7 with Afrikaans-speaking bilingual candidates, and 6 with English-speaking bilingual members. Most striking was the valiant but hopeless attempt of 2 English-speaking, partially bilingual United Party candidates to fight Afrikaans-speaking seats in the Transvaal.

When the electoral results are scanned, some significant results appear. The 80 successful Nationalists on whom there is information were all Afrikaans-speaking and bilingual. Of these, 69 won in Afrikaans-speaking constituencies; 10 in constituencies ranked as 50-50;[59] and 1 in a constituency, Pretoria City, which the Nationalists considered mainly English-speaking, though the United Party said it was 55 per cent Afrikaans-speaking.

The picture for the United Party is very different. Out of 52 of those elected in 1953, only 8 were listed as Afrikaans-speaking, while 38 were English-speaking, and 6 regarded both as home languages. All except 1 of these were bilingual. Highly significant is that only 3 (Jeppe, Cape Flats (mainly Coloured) and Hottentots-Holland) Afrikaans-speaking constituencies returned United Party members. One of these was fought by an Afrikaans-speaking bilingual United Party candidate, and 2 by English-speaking bilingual candidates, 1 of whom was a woman. Out of the 22 constituencies listed as 50-50, however, the United Party won 12,[60] 4 with Afrikaans-speaking bilingual candidates, 7 with English-speaking bilingual candidates and 1 with a candidate who listed both languages.

Despite the fact that the United Party must have polled a considerable number of Afrikaner votes in the 50-50 constituencies it won, as well as some in those it lost, the overall pattern of the election follows the language division in the country to a disturbing degree. Thus though the United Party is avowedly a party of national unity, which bridges the two European groups on which the country is founded, only about one-quarter of its parliamentary representatives after the 1953 election were either primarily Afrikaans-speaking or regarded both Afrikaans and English as home languages, while barely a quarter of its constituencies included as many as 50 per cent of Afrikaans-speaking voters. On the other hand, the exclusively Afrikaans-speaking Nationalists won only about one-seventh of their seats in constituencies where there were as many English as Afrikaners and none in predominantly English-speaking constituencies. Thus the division by language in South Africa is reflected all too nearly in politics.

CHAPTER 7
ELECTION PROPAGANDA AND THE PRESS

Neither the Nationalists nor the United Party and Labour Party issued political manifestos to set the stage for their 1953 election campaigns. What the Nationalists called their 'manifesto' was a reprint of Dr. Malan's speech at Stellenbosch on March 4, 1953, which was then issued (for the English version in the wording of the *Cape Times*) as *A Strong Government Necessary for South Africa*. The party also reissued *Common Ground for National Unity*, Dr. Malan's appeal to English-speaking South Africans, delivered to the Natal National Party Congress, September 19, 1950. More particularly, however, the Nationalists made use of nearly a score of topical pamphlets, ranging in size from *The Facts: Replies to Allegations of the United Party*, issued in two parts and 138 pages long (half being the text in Afrikaans, half in English) to *You the Judge*, which was only a large double sheet. More than a third of Nationalist election pamphlets were published only in Afrikaans. Two pamphlets—*Fruits of the National Régime*, some 70 pages long, and *Nothing Better in the World than conditions in South Africa*, only four pages—devoted themselves to facts and figures about Nationalist accomplishments. The rest used all the devices of propaganda to discredit the United Front, and build up the Nationalists.

The Facts presented its material in terms of 'The Story', i.e., United Party allegations against the Nationalists regarding the Republic, the Broederbond (see p. 251), the Transvaal Education Ordinance, decrease in flow of foreign capital to the Union, etc., which were then answered pungently with copious references to Hansard and other sources. Its introductory page accused the United Party of instructing voters in 1948 to 'weed out Nationalism', declared that 'Nationalism means love for what is your own: your own nation, your own citizenship, your own South Africa', and insisted that the people of South Africa must therefore reply to the United Party, 'We refuse. We believe in South Africa First'. The parts of *The Facts* dealing with rights of English-speaking citizens, the Broederbond, the Republic and the Education Ordinance, republished for Natal in English only as *Are You Too Being Misled? Democracy in Danger!* gave the Nationalist argument against the Appeal Court judgment of 1952 on the Coloured vote, ending with 'Save the will of the people. Save Democracy'. Similarly, *Keep your Vote Supreme* (with the choice between 'Torch dictatorship' and 'freedom' pictured on its cover, though there was nothing about the former, or indeed the latter inside), supported the High Court of Parliament and accused the United Party of inconsistency in its court stand.

Other Nationalist pamphlets were still more biting and accusatory. Declaring apartheid to be 'the foundation stone of white civilization', *You the Judge* maintained that the United Party 'vilified segregation' and 'endangered white supremacy' by saying apartheid was 'a danger'. The alternative to apartheid, said the booklet, was 'integration—equality—the end of white civilization'. Three pamphlets printed only in Afrikaans, *The Work of the Nationalist Government, What is the Colour Policy of the United Party?* and *What is the Torch Commando?*, maintained respectively that the United Party had done nothing to make 'black spots' disappear, so 'vote National and get your residential sections white'; that the United Party would give political rights to Coloured, Indians and Natives and thus 'end white domination'; and that the Torch Commando admits 'non-whites' as members, attacks Afrikaner monuments and churches, and has 'cruelly assaulted, kicked and hurt' many Nationalists. *The Menace!!*, with a dramatic red hand imprinted with the hammer and sickle reaching out to engulf South Africa, accused the United Party of blocking Nationalist efforts to deal with Communism. Finally came the so-called 'bombshell' published in screaming red, black and white on the eve of the election, *The United Party Political Plan for Natives and Indians.* This was said to be 'to grant specific political rights to the Native as he develops' which 'might lead' to what is depicted in pictures on the inside of the pamphlet: five African ministers of Nigeria's first cabinet. Below was written 'Save South Africa from this Disaster. VOTE NATIONAL and ensure WHITE DOMINATION!'

While the Nationalists thus obviously placed their greatest emphasis on scare propaganda about the threat to white domination, the United Party plugged along solidly and far less spectacularly with a series of 21 pamphlets, most of which enunciated its policy for particular groups, in the perspective of Nationalist 'inadequacies'. Only a few like *50 Nationalist Failures, The Man of Promises,* and *The People versus D. F. Malan* forthrightly, if somewhat prosaically, assailed their opponents. With the exception of its *Summary of Policy* booklet, which was issued separately in Afrikaans and in English, and one Afrikaans leaflet, *Dr. Malan se Kleurbeleid*, citing Dr. Malan's early interest in giving votes to Coloured women, all the United Party pamphlets were bilingual. They were issued in vast profusion, totalling 3,237,000 copies. (The quantities and the dates are shown on a chart in Appendix III.) Far outnumbering in volume the Nationalist propaganda of this type, it is questionable whether its effect was anything like so great. The Nationalists not only capitalized on fear, but drummed home their most telling points by simple, highly effective presentation, and incessant repetition; against this, the United Party's more moderate appeal to reason and fact seemed somewhat colorless.

Most frequently mentioned in United Party propaganda was the economic issue, where the party's approach was largely positive, detailing its program for workers, smallholders, railwaymen, farmers, etc. Not without significance was the fact that issues of importance to the urban worker received about three times as much prominence as those relating to the farm program. On the rise of the cost of living, and the incorporation of cost-of-living allowances into pensions, the United Party was aggressive, attacking the Nationalists for not taking these matters seriously enough, or keeping its promises to the workers. Pamphlets like the *Workers' Charter* and *50 Nationalist Failures* also stressed the danger to the rights of trade unions offered by Nationalist policy.

In that part of their propaganda in which they dealt with economic problems, the Nationalists seemed on the defensive. They pointed out that the United Party also had been unable to stop the rise in the cost of living, and held (with justification) that costs in South Africa were low compared to those in other countries. Nationalist propaganda pointed to the Government's good record in labor relations, where fewer man hours had been lost in strikes than under the United Party, and to its greater solicitude for the rights of white workers. The color bar in industry, it promised, would protect the worker from the competition of cheap Native labor.

The United Party placed second greatest weight in its propaganda on what it termed 'defence of democracy', including such leaflets as *The U.P.'s Fight Against Communism* (a deliberate effort to counter Nationalist propaganda on this issue), *The Law of Our Fathers*, and *The Railway Waiting Room Case*. On the constitutional issue, 'political courts', and the establishing of 'pass cards' for Europeans under the Population Registration Act, the United Party propaganda was on the offensive, though it could have exploited these questions more dramatically and consistently.

On racial policy, which tailed economic and civil rights issues, the United Party took two lines in its propaganda. The first was its positive program for increasing the white population through children's allowances, immigration, better housing, etc., as well as protection of language rights. It took pains to assure its readers that the nation was wealthy enough in natural resources to sustain increased immigration which would create rather than deprive anyone of jobs. In *The White Policy of the U.P.*, which had a charming picture on the cover of children running home from school, the United Party demonstrated the existence of labor shortages by pointing to the Nationalists' increased employment of non-whites.

In regard to the non-European, the United Party concentrated on the deterioration in race relations, said to be due to Nationalist policy, and on the 'myth' of apartheid, which was called no more than traditional segregation, but with aggressive overtones inflammatory to the Native and Coloured populations. Its own racial policy was said to be the 'traditional' one of developing Native Reserves, maintaining existing segregation and also the representation and rights of the Cape Coloured. Towards Indians, United Party propaganda showed itself still more openly hostile than did the Nationalists, and specifically emphasized a ban on immigration and other restrictions.

Lastly, the United Party attempted to make capital of Nationalist inefficiency, both in the framing of legislation (e.g., the railway apartheid case), and the administration of railways, the police department, the army (where it charged promotion had been by political favoritism) and loss of world confidence which threatened the country's prosperity. The Nationalists tried to make the latter charge boomerang by accusing the United Party in a small pink pamphlet of disseminating the information on which overseas criticism was based. They also produced enough statistics and counter-charges of inefficiency as to leave most readers incapable of deciding where the truth lay.

To other criticisms, the Nationalists replied similarly with counter-attacks. Rather than defend the Broederbond, they cast suspicion on the Torch Commando and the Sons of England. Only on the republican issue were the Nationalists really on the defensive. Here they assured their readers several times that the proposed Republic would be brought about by democratic methods only when the people were ready for it,[1] and 'not merely as the result of a parliamentary majority'.

It is always problematic how much effect election propaganda has, the more so since it is commonly read (if at all) by those already converted. Yet the study of propaganda has one useful function: it shows both the issues on which the parties want to fight the election, and the tone they adopt in presenting them. Broadly speaking, the Nationalist propaganda displayed a concentration on racial issues like that in its official speeches, but with a still greater use of inflammatory words and illustrations. Though the Nationalists also presented a copious array of facts to prove their effectiveness in office, they obviously relied much more on stirring up the European's ever-present fears of being submerged by the numerically preponderant non-European population. In contrast, though the United Party's spokesmen recognized that racial issues are always the most important in South Africa, their propaganda presented hardly anything positive to counteract this Nationalist line on race relations. Their generally well presented material on economic and constitutional affairs lacked the personal appeal of much of the Nationalist propaganda or, indeed, of the striking cartoon sheet of the Education Action Group which dramatically accused the Transvaal Education Ordinance of dangerously handicapping young people in their search for a job by making them unilingual. Astonishingly little was done by the United Party, in fact, with this most promising of all propaganda topics.

Placards

The placards developed by the two parties illustrate in a still more striking way the differences in their use of political propaganda. The United Party placards were relatively small, invariably bilingual, and dealt with a single issue —e.g., 'Vote Nat. and carry a pass', or 'Vote U.P. for the big plan for the smallholder'—and employed few, if any, graphic illustrations. One pictured Strauss with Smuts, Hertzog and Botha behind him. One Nationalist placard, claiming it was the party of national unity, was printed in both languages, but all the rest seen in the Witwatersrand area were in Afrikaans only. More important, the Nationalist placards were in the universal language of cartoons. One of the least sensational showed a smiling workman against a background of industrial South Africa. Another, less innocent, showed the red hand of Communism reaching to take over the country. A third, prominently displayed near several Nationalist polling booths on election day, depicted Strauss with a gun in his hand inscribed 'freedom for the reds', while a *Stürmer*-type, cigar-smoking Hoggenheimer leered in the background.

Letters of Introduction

A personal appeal to each candidate to send the author his letter of introduction to his constituents produced 27 issued by Nationalists, and 38 by United Party candidates, i.e. one-fifth of the former and one-quarter of the latter. Reflecting the high proportion of farmers among the candidates, most of these letters of introduction mentioned personal experience with agriculture as a strong recommendation for support, and stressed farmers' interests far more than was done in official propaganda. Amongst the United Party letters, the interests of civil servants and labor ran a close second to those of farmers; the

Nationalists much more rarely promised economic gain to any group but rather stressed 'the nobility of labour', and 'educational amenities so that the European can hold his own against the non-European'. All but two of the Nationalist letters of introduction emphasized apartheid and the menace of Communism (these two concentrated on economic issues) and all kept close to the official party program.

The United Party candidates' letters showed more individuality and diversity. Economic matters invariably received most frequent mention, however, with special attention, as in the official propaganda, to cost-of-living allowances and housing. Farmers were promised fixed farm prices announced in advance, and help in soil conservation; railwaymen, better pay and shorter hours; civil servants, better conditions. Still more prominently featured in the letters, though less often mentioned, was the United Party's 'white policy': in particular, white children's allowances, maternity benefits and 'selected' immigration. 'White unity', i.e., between the English and Afrikaans sections, which United Party candidates maintained only their party could ensure, received much attention, though less than parents' right to select their children's schools, which was frequently said to be essential for 'white unity' as well as a 'democratic right'.

Apart from education, democratic rights were most frequently interpreted by United Party as well as Nationalist candidates as protection against Communism, no mention being made of any potential threat from a reactionary right. Only three United Party candidates mentioned the Broederbond; only one Nationalist, the Torch Commando. Nearly half the Nationalist as well as United Party candidates mentioned the constitutional issue, the latter talking about 'constitutional sanctity' and 'upholding the rule of law', the former about parliamentary sovereignty.

Apartheid as such was rarely mentioned in the United Party letters, but several suggested that racial issues should be taken out of politics by the United Party's plan for a non-political, impartial race congress. Others contented themselves with advocating residential and social 'segregation' along traditional lines of white trusteeship. One United Party candidate showed himself still more preoccupied with white supremacy than the Nationalists (whom he accused of not being 'true' Nationalists), while another distinguished himself by declaring that 'apartheid will be settled by laws of evolution, not politics'. Among the Nationalists, there were several who not only avowed their belief in God, but also emphasized the compatibility between their Christian principles and non-European policy.

By and large, the letters of introduction of the United Party candidates suggested they were less well known in their constituencies than the Nationalists. Several of the letters provided no indication of the candidate's stand on political issues, giving only a photograph and family details. Wives and children almost as frequently appeared in photographs, in fact, as the candidate himself, and this implication that a sound family life is a desirable attribute of a parliamentary candidate was reinforced in one letter by the declaration that the candidate believed in the sanctity of marriage. Several United Party candidates appeared to have invested more in this type of publicity than did the Nationalists, as they put out several circulars or manifestos on different parts of their program, or directed to different groups in the community. Most United Party letters of introduction were printed in both languages except for Natal constituencies; a number of the Nationalist letters were only in Afrikaans. Lastly, it may be said that both Nationalists and United Party candidates showed a concern to espouse general, fairly non-debatable issues rather than emotional or partisan ones. If on the one hand the United Party candidates quite naturally used far less factual material in their letters of introduction than appeared in the party's official propaganda, the Nationalists, in their turn, avoided almost entirely the inflammatory phrasing of the more lurid Nationalist propaganda in favor of words and concepts which would appeal more generally throughout their communities.

Political Broadcasting

One of the outstanding innovations in the 1953 election campaign was political broadcasting. The suggestion of using the radio in this way was made originally by the head of the South African Broadcasting Corporation—a public corporation which was originally modelled on the British Broadcasting Corporation but subsequently added a commercial channel, the Springbok Radio, to its English and Afrikaans non-commercial channels—and debated at length first by the S.A.B.C.'s board of directors, and subsequently by the political parties. The decision that the Government and the Opposition should each have twelve 15-minute broadcasts, eleven before the election and one following it (each speech being repeated twice, once in each of the official languages, English and Afrikaans) was finally arrived at only a month or so before the opening of the formal election campaign.

Since a very high proportion of South Africans listen almost daily to the radio, the experiment was undertaken by the parties with mingled hopes and apprehensions. The common estimate of the English-speaking papers was that the device would benefit the United Party, whose speakers were expected to be more fluent and eloquent than their opponents. In practice, the contrary seems to have been the case. The Nationalists, all of whose speakers were cabinet ministers, were not only more forceful and persuasive on occasions, but also clearly demonstrated their greater mastery of both languages. All the Nationalists, of course, were primarily Afrikaans-speaking, but their English was well phrased and relatively easy to follow. Apart from Mr. Strauss, who gave the first and last speeches for the United Party during the campaign, and the final speech after election day, four (or, counting Bekker, five) of the United Party speakers were Afrikaans-speaking. One of them, Senator J. G. Carinus, was less easy to understand in English than any of the Nationalist speakers. Of the five others, Douglas Mitchell, leader of the United Party in Natal, made no effort to speak in Afrikaans; his broadcast time in that language was used by the leader of the party in the Transvaal, Bailey Bekker (who subsequently revolted against Strauss' leadership and for a time became part of the Conservative Party). Only one or two of the other English-speaking speakers handled Afrikaans fluently. This was the more unfortunate for the United Party cause since it appeared to confirm the Nationalist stereotype of the English-speaking as predominantly unilingual, a serious handicap in a country which is 70 per cent bilingual, and amongst Nationalist Afrikaners who have an almost fanatical feeling of devotion to their language.

Both parties presented their broadcasts on the same evening, but with the times staggered so that each could be heard by everyone. Thus on the first evening of political broadcasting, March 9, Mr. J. F. T. Naudé spoke from 7.30 to 7.45 p.m. in English, and repeated his speech from 10 to 10.15 in Afrikaans, while Strauss spoke from 7.45 to 8 p.m. in Afrikaans, and from 10.15 to 10.30 in English. Speeches were confined to Monday and Thursday evenings, except that the post-election one was on Saturday following the Wednesday election day.

Naudé, Minister of Education, who said he was primarily responsible for the broadcasts, welcomed them as a better medium for addressing the public than through 'the servile press'. Speaking a little too quickly, but clearly, he introduced the list of Nationalist speakers (whom he called 'the rulers of our country') by picking out United Party charges against them: e.g., the English had been told that Dr. Malan would take away their rights, but they would see how foolish such a charge was; the United Party had tried to coax N. C. Havenga into their fold but he was 'too good a South African, too sincere a patriot'; J. G. Strijdom was held up as an extremist, but 'forcing the Republic' was not an issue. Others were used to illustrate the success of the Government: e.g., Dr. H. F. Verwoerd working to settle 'our greatest problem', the non-European, and Dr. K. Bremer 'to build up a strong and virile people'. In contrast, the United Party was pictured as 'a divided party', full of vacillations, and with a lack of racial program which made it unworthy of political office. Throughout his speech, Naudé exuded confidence that the election results were already a foregone conclusion.

Strauss' opening speech the same evening was delivered in a smooth unhurried manner, but made the same mistake as United Party official propaganda of trying to cover everything, and therefore lacking focus. Moreover, his reference to 'this terrible fear which stalks the land', leading people to lock their doors and teach their wives to fire guns probably alienated more people than it impressed. Nor was his attack on total apartheid—'we shall have to give up a very great deal of our land . . . you might lose *your* farm'—of much importance, since the Nationalists were already emphasizing that it would not come about for perhaps hundreds of years. Better on the United Party's positive economic program, Strauss still propagandized too much when more facts and figures would have backed up his contentions.

The main body of the speeches may be treated more briefly. Dr. Bremer, Minister of Health, made a sober, positive approach which stressed Nationalist accomplishments in housing and health services; C. R. Swart, Minister of Justice, a rather frightening speech which included comments on the Public Safety and Criminal Laws Amendment Acts which reinforced, if anything, the fears expressed at the time this legislation was introduced; Eric Louw, Minister of Economic Affairs, a caustic address accusing the United Party of 'sabotage of their own country' through their criticisms, declaring that Strauss was 'as full of promises as a cheque that bounces', and claiming that the Nationalists had not only saved the Union from its economic difficulties but also aided the United Kingdom; while Paul Sauer, Minister of Transport, who introduced some welcome humor into the series, followed a favorite Nationalist line in defending the management of the railways by attacking the policies of the United Party while it was in office.

More impressive was Dr. Verwoerd, Minister of Native Affairs, who tackled the non-European problem clearly, frankly and with penetration, acknowledging that the Nationalists were alone in the world in their racial policy of inequality, but insisting that their racial policy of progressive segregation offered hope of an ultimate solution (not equated with Bantustan which he called 'a statement of the credulous') while the United Party's Native policy, or lack thereof, would lead to a Native menace. Specifically he warned against immigration, which he believed would only strengthen the 'liberalists', and against the non-party racial congress Strauss had suggested which, he said, would make non-Europeans the real arbiters in the racial question.

In one of the few speeches of the campaign devoted to labor, B. J. Schoeman, Minister of Labour, attacked United Party-endorsed immigration as providing competition for South African workers, and insisted that the Nationalists had protected white labor by such measures as limiting the use of cheap Native labor in building, the Suppression of Communism Act and (still less understandably), the Swart legislation. Positively he offered an overhauling of industrial legislation: machinery to deal with Native disputes which neither permitted Native trade unions nor admission of Natives to the privileges of the Industrial Conciliation Act; an end to 'mixed' trade unions (i.e., those with both Europeans and non-Europeans, like the Garment Workers' Union); maintenance of the color bar in industry; full consultation between employers and employees; and increased productivity. With some justification, he claimed 'ours is the only party which is truly representative of the workers'.

The next speeches, which were given by the three potential successors to Dr. Malan, showed wide differences in approach. N. C. Havenga, Minister of Finance, gave a sound, practical speech full of facts and figures about the country's economy, coupled with a moderate and quite convincing charge that United Party economic proposals would lead to greater taxation particularly at lower income levels. On the constitutional issue, Dr. Dönges followed with an over-simplified and slanted justification of 'parliamentary sovereignty' *versus* what he called the 'despotic power' of the judges. He called on the electorate to make the 'final decision' in the issue. Still more vehement in its attack on the United Party was the speech by J. G. Strijdom, Minister of Lands, who blamed the United Party for the Native resistance movement, and the riots at Port Elizabeth and elsewhere, declared the United Party would be 'dishonest if it did not repeal all discriminatory laws against Natives and give them political rights' and, at the same time, accused Strauss of committing 'political larceny' by endorsing non-European segregation. Notable was his bitterness against Afrikaners like Louis Steenkamp and Marais Steyn for their support of the United Party.

On the same evenings as these speeches were given, United Party spokesmen had been making their appeals and charges. Mitchell in English and Bekker in Afrikaans, emphasized national unity as the keynote of the United Party, in a serious statesmanlike way, though Mitchell made a mistake which he had later to retract when he accused Dr. Malan of saying there were 'radical' and unbridgeable differences between the English and Afrikaans. H. Davidoff, the only Labour candidate to broadcast, made a straightforward attack on Nationalist economic policies, which he blamed for the rising cost of living, and on discriminatory taxation (which penalized the poor), means tests on pensions, and inadequate housing. In particular, he voiced concern over the growing loss of civil rights and interference with labor unions, for creating 'artificial barriers' and 'a land of fear . . .'.

On the racial question, Louis Steenkamp gave an intelligent and unimpassioned speech presenting the United Party's positive program of immigration, family allowances and traditional segregation, followed by an attack on 'the never-never world of total apartheid'. This was followed by P. A. Moore, whose clear and convincing explanation of the education and language issue and of how essential parental choice of schools was for white unity provided one of the best United Party speeches on this issue during the campaign, even though its rather florid style (e.g., his conclusion 'This is the vision splendid; let our children go forward together') did not appeal to some people. The United Party also had one speech by a woman, but, instead of choosing one of their parliamentary candidates, they selected Mrs. Strauss, wife of their leader, who gave a straightforward talk directed to housewives—'your meat bill is twice what it was two years ago'—and ending with a thinly veiled appeal to Nationalist women to switch to the United Party with its concern for human beings rather than ideology.

While Schoeman was speaking of Nationalist labor policy, Senator Carinus, in a homey 'grass roots' speech, dealt with the United Party's agricultural policy in a speech remarkable for its lack of recriminations against his political opponents. He placed United Party priorities on soil conservation, reduction of the price of fertilizers and petrol, speeding up of railroad transport, improved marketing facilities, intensive food production, stabilized prices and farmers' incomes, and ended by stressing the United Party plans for a Smallholders Bank for, in his words, it is 'in our blood to have a plot of land'. More politically slanted was H. G. Lawrence's speech on 'bread-and-butter politics', in which he talked of jobs going to 'the pals of the Broederbond', answered Schoeman in one of the all too rare instances of give and take between the broadcasts, promised the United Party would extend unemployment insurance benefits, raise salaries in the lower ranks of the police (a Nationalist stronghold), and make the railway board non-political.

The last two United Party speeches before Strauss' concluding one were devoted to the economic and racial issues, and primarily to answering Nationalist assertions on them. I. S. Fourie, a professor of economics and a new United Party candidate, in a trenchant, though somewhat over-simplified survey, attacked Havenga ('a good man but he lacks vision'), declared the economy 'not sick in 1948; but certainly ailing now' because of Nationalist mismanagement, and pledged the United Party to do away with unnecessary controls, but also give protection to both industries and workers. 'Remember 1933' (when Smuts and Hertzog joined together to solve the economic crisis), he ended. 'The United Party can do it again. It depends on you.' De Villiers Graaff, leader of the United Party in the Cape, gave a still more convincing and effective speech, asking the voters if they were prepared to give the Nationalists a blank cheque. He termed the Nationalist 'bombshell', their *U.P. Political Plan for Natives and Indians,* 'a complete falsehood', and on the contrary, affirmed United Party racial policy to be identical with that of Smuts and Hertzog in 1936.

Two days before the election, the two leaders—Malan and Strauss—gave the concluding broadcasts for their parties. Once again, Dr. Malan appeared as the most impressive figure of the campaign, with a moving, semi-religious undercurrent running throughout his speech. He contrasted the straightforwardness of the Nationalist approach on race relations with the lack of clarity in policy of the United Party. Already, he voiced his offer to cooperate with all except 'liberalists', an obvious effort to split the United Party's liberal and conservative members. Perhaps the most striking of all was his graphic picture of white South Africa as the only saviour of white civilization in Africa. In contrast, Strauss' expressed suspicions of Native intellectuals and *tsotsis* sounded more like a desperate effort to ingratiate the United Party with race-conscious Afrikaners than a positive approach to South Africa's greatest problem.

While the election broadcasts seem to have had many listeners, the series received numerous adverse comments from newspapers as well as individuals. The *Star* criticized the lack of humor in the speeches; others regretted their acrimonious tone. Unfortunate was the lack of planning so that the two parties could present the same subject on a given evening, or alternatively, answer each other systematically.

Little new was added through the broadcasts. Nationalist speeches mentioned the United Party's lack of a racial policy more than any other single issue. They defended their record in office largely through running down the United Party performance when in power, though some facts and figures were used in presenting their own record. Most of the Nationalist speeches exuded confidence in the result of the election, and assumed a favorable and uncritical audience.

United Party speeches from their side dealt most frequently with economic issues: cost of living, capital inflow, immigration, etc. As in their propaganda, more concern was shown for the urban worker than the farmer, despite Senator Carinus' speech. Race relations ran a close second to economic problems, with most of the United Party fire directed at the nebulous character of apartheid, the economic implications of total apartheid (which the Nationalists were busy disavowing), and the increase of fear and deterioration of relations not only between Europeans and non-Europeans, but also between Nationalist extremists and the others. A deliberate effort was made to equate United Party race policy with that of Hertzog. Three United Party speeches touched on democratic liberties, and one was devoted entirely to the educational issue. Surprisingly enough, the constitutional issue was all but neglected, while the one occasion Communism was mentioned, the United Party seemed on the defensive. On the whole, United Party speakers seemed to be more consciously attempting to influence the floating vote (if there was one) than the Nationalists. But even the United Party speakers resorted to personal attacks and propagandistic charges and claims that could not have aided their cause with any thoughtful voter who was still undecided.

On April 18, when the election results confirmed a greatly increased parliamentary majority for the Nationalists, though a substantial majority of the votes for the United Front, Dr. Malan and Mr. Strauss gave their concluding broadcasts. This time Strauss' dignified, intelligent speech contrasted favorably with that of Malan. The latter chiefly voiced an appeal for 12 to 13 Opposition votes to pass a constitutional amendment to take the Coloured off the common roll. The election was over; the Nationalists were already moving to implement the next stages of their apartheid program.

The Press in the Campaign:

General elections provide the press with one of its greatest opportunities, a ready-made crisis situation in which all voters are interested. In 1953, South African newspapers were still suffering restrictions of newsprint, but increased allowances were granted for the six weeks of the election campaign, the papers being free, of course, to determine whether to use the additional allowance for a greater number of copies or for more news of the election or for other events. In this period, in fact, important international news, like the death of Stalin, and the local sensationalism of the Bettie Smith murder trial, jostled election news for pride of place. There seems little doubt, however, that it was interest in the election which led the circulation of most European dailies and Sunday papers to climb steadily, both up to and throughout the election period (except for the lull of the Easter week-end), and to achieve phenomenal heights on the day when the election returns were announced. The best estimates available suggest that, in March 1953, the major Afrikaans newspapers were averaging 5,000 more copies a day than at the first of the year, that the main English-language papers on the Rand had risen some 7,000 to 10,000, and that the most widely distributed Sunday newspapers were up 9,000 to 12,000.

The handling of the campaign by the South African press underlines many of the points which have been made about its general character. The Afrikaans dailies took their cues from the official Nationalist line as enunciated most authoritatively by Dr. Malan, and reiterated it in varied but not essentially different ways. A high proportion of their space was devoted to the election, and preponderantly to Nationalist achievements and United Party weaknesses. Nationalist meetings, speeches, and activities were reported in great detail as compared with the treatment of the United Party. Only *Dagbreek* made a substantial, and largely successful attempt, to present both points of view on major issues, printing solicited contributions from both parties side by side, as for example by B. J. Schoeman, Minister of Labour, and Colin Steyn, head of the United Party in the Free State, on the respective labor policies of the two parties.

The English-language papers, in contrast, covered Nationalist as well as United Party speeches and meetings, although usually in less detail, and continued up to the last few days to carry a substantial proportion of national and international news and give it prominent position. Their choice of election subjects for editorials reflected an individual interest rather than followed Strauss' speeches or the United Party manifestos. Only late in the campaign did they feel themselves forced to concentrate on the issues on which the Nationalists insisted on fighting in the campaign—in particular Native policy and apartheid—to attempt to answer their arguments and to counter attack. The Natal press and in particular the *Natal Witness*, showed a critical attitude towards the United Party not entirely missing, though more veiled, in the other English-language press. Towards the end of the campaign, however, all the English-language papers, including those in Natal, came out strongly for the United Party.

Where the Afrikaans dailies were jubilant over the electoral victory, seeing it as an endorsement of Nationalist achievements and programs, the English-language press was generally restrained. In Natal, there was some sharp criticism both of the United Party and Mr. Strauss' leadership, which anticipated the support given by the *Natal Witness*, in particular, to the new Union Federal Party. On the whole, however, there was neither recrimination in the English press nor, less helpfully, suggestions for the future. Convinced in general that despite their criticisms of the United Party it offered the best, indeed only, hope of providing an effective opposition to the Nationalists, the English-language press continued to face its permanent dilemma: how to be constructively critical of the United Party without weakening its morale and its strength.

To provide a more careful account of the handling of the 1953 campaign by important segments of the South African press, a detailed analysis was made of the two most important Afrikaans dailies—*Die Burger* and *Die Transvaler*—and of three of the most prominent English-language dailies—*The Star*, the *Rand Daily Mail* and the *Cape Times*—of which the first is an Argus paper, the second belongs to the Bailey group, and the third is independent of either. This examination centered around the amount of space devoted to the election, its division between the Nationalists and the United Party, the topics which the paper emphasized, and the degree to which it followed the line of the party it favored, and the 'slant' given in reports and editorials.

Die Burger continued, throughout the campaign, to print a considerable amount of international and national news; it gave considerable space to the Bettie Smith murder trial. Nevertheless, a great deal of *Die Burger's* attention was devoted to the election: two-thirds of its leading editorials, and many of those in second and third place; full texts of important Nationalist speeches and accounts of their meetings and much lesser coverage of the United Party; daily feature articles, most of which attacked the United Party; the daily political commentaries by 'Dawie', which were written entertainingly but with a sting, and some very effective cartoon comment. All the way through the campaign, every possible device was used to support the Nationalist cause: glowing accounts of the Government's achievements, denigration of the United Party in office, the casting of suspicion on United Party intentions, particularly towards the Natives, Communists, and the Education Language Ordinance, even sharper insinuations about the United Front and its 'liberalist' intentions and, particularly towards the end, warnings of the Mau Mau terror in Kenya, and the partnership concept in Central African Federation as the possible fate of South Africa if the Nationalists were not returned to office. Thus, though *Die Burger* used more restrained language than certain other Nationalist dailies and maintained a broader coverage of news, it missed no chance to provide support for the Nationalist Government and to run down the Opposition.

Throughout the election campaign proper, that is from March 5 to April 15, 1953, *Die Burger* kept color policy as its major theme, intertwining it cleverly with that of national unity. Taking its lead from Dr. Malan's Stellenbosch speech of March 5, and slapping down the United Party's economic program at the same time, *Die Burger* wrote in a leading article of March 6:

> The European of South Africa does not seek his well-being in an extra threepence here and sixpence there. He seeks to ensure his own preservation, in the interests of the non-Europeans as well.

Next day, the paper gave front-page prominence to reports, featured throughout the campaign, that United Party members were 'streaming' over to the National Party because of the United Party's lack of an 'acceptable policy to protect the Europeans'. In a third leader on March 10, *Die Burger* accused Mr. Strauss of attempting to 'don the cloak of apartheid' by equating the latter with segregation. It warned that the United Party had never revoked the policy enunciated by Strauss at Paarl on May 16, 1952, that the party would 'grant political rights gradually to those who show they are able to meet the obligations that go with them', another point plugged effectively throughout the campaign. The following day, the paper cited figures to show that if Coloured women were given the vote it would be only a matter of time till the Coloured could outvote Europeans in the Cape.

From the other side, *Die Burger* argued that a courageous and just apartheid policy contributed importantly to national unity (also following Malan's Stellenbosch speech), and declared in a second leader, on March 6, that the United Party color and immigration policies made it 'the irrevocable enemy of white unity on colour problems'. Another change on the national unity theme came when Malan's speech at Vredendal on March 14 was headlined 'United Party Making English Afraid of Afrikaans', a point dramatized in a cartoon the same day, in which two United Party firemen directed a stream of fear and suspicion at English-speaking voters trying to escape from the United Party's burning house. On April 2, *Die Burger* highlighted in a leading article the national unity part of Dr. Malan's speech in Pretoria the night before, declaring that the charge that Nationalist Afrikaners would oppress the English-speaking was 'the United Party's most important election slogan—a slogan of hate, fear and division'. It concluded:

> The electorate must choose on April 15 between the party which seeks national unity in South Africa's interest and the party which encourages national division in its own interests.

Though apartheid accounted for 8 leading editorials during the election campaign, many more than appeared on any other subject, little that was new on this theme was introduced until the railway apartheid case gave *Die Burger*, like other Nationalist papers, a golden opportunity for scare propaganda. A leading article the day of the judgment referred to its 'shocking implications'. The next day, March 25, a cartoon showed the Appeal Court decision blasting the dam wall of traditional apartheid and people rushing to help a determined-looking Dr. Malan rolling up his sleeves to rebuild the dyke. The day following, in an article entitled 'Where is South Africa Heading Now?', the court was accused of having opened a 'sluice gate' to wash away all apartheid regulations. 'What about apartheid in schools and hospitals, in buses, swimming baths, cinemas and theatres, in restaurants and hotels?' asked *Die Burger*. This new threat to apartheid gave a still greater incentive to return the Nationalist Government with a larger majority.

The other special feature of *Die Burger's* campaign on the color question used Mau Mau activities as its foil. In its second leader, on March 31, *Die Burger* expressed its concern over developments in Kenya, hoped the authorities would not be distracted from enforcing peace by 'pedantic theories thought out in London clubs', and congratulated South Africa on having a Government which 'is not obligated to obey instructions from the outside'. The paper added that it was clear, however, that a 'serious time lies ahead which calls for a strong Government'. According to 'Dawie', the Mau Mau movement, unrest, crime, blood-lust and hostility towards the white man were the fruits of a liberal policy such as the United Party advocated.

Disunity in the Opposition, particularly in color matters, and the dangers of a 'soft' approach both to Natives and Communists were increasingly featured by *Die Burger* as the campaign developed. On March 11, in a leading article, the paper maintained that the 'conservative' section of the United Party was helpless in the company of 'a crowd of defeatists and liberalists' and dependent on the Labour Party 'whose Native policy is very closely akin to that of the British Labour Party with its trend toward abdication'. Following Dr. Malan's attack on 'liberalism' at Vredendal on March 13, *Die Burger* devoted a leader, on March 17, to the United Party's discomfort over its forced alliance with its 'pathetic ally', the Labour Party, which stood for freedom for Communism, return of 'named' Communists to Parliament and trade unions, consultation with leaders of the defiance campaign, extension of non-European political rights and the repeal of the anti-defiance (Swart) legislation. With leftist United Party and Torch Commando support, it would try to put these policies into effect if the Opposition were elected. *Die Burger*, in fact, made somewhat more of Communism as an issue than did Nationalist speakers, casting doubts editorially, on March 10, March 23 and April 1, on the sincerity of the United Party's avowed stand on Communism, and whipping up anti-Communist fervor by reports like that in Dawie's column, on March 18, on Communist penetration in Africa.

It is interesting to notice how little attention *Die Burger* paid to the economic issue which the United Party tried to make such an important part of its program. Comment centered chiefly on the enormous cost of the United Party economic program, and on April 6, United Party promises were termed the 'biggest joke of the election'. Not till March 28 and April 1 did *Die Burger* feature articles on the 'phenomenal growth' of industry and agriculture under the Nationalists, and then not again until the very end of the campaign. It also paid little obvious attention to the workers except that, in commenting on the Nationalists' rare appeals to the trade unions, *Die Burger* called on all workers to support a Government which could not only show an unparalleled record of industrial peace and well-being (reiterated on April 10), but also utterly rejected 'a policy of *laissez-faire* for the disciples of Moscow'.

Not much attention was paid to the Constitution issue. A leading article, on March 9, entitled 'Who is Master?', charged that the United Party was interested only in the right to continue exploiting the Coloured vote for its own advantage. It continued:

> The people, South Africa's master and highest court, must make known their wish on 15th April—whether they are Parliament's master or whether five men in Bloemfontein must have the right to nullify the people's mandate to Parliament.

Speeches by Dr. Malan, Dr. Dönges, Mr. Swart and Dr. Verwoerd on the constitutional question were heavily headlined, but without comment. On March 27, however, the paper published a leading article contrasting the English system of justice, where the courts were outside politics, with what it called the American system of political appointments which the Appeal Court judgment on railway apartheid was said to be foisting on the country.

The United South African Trust Fund (see Chapter 11) also played a minor part in *Die Burger's* campaign. A sub-leader of March 5, with brief comment by Dawie, on March 10, on the hush-hush subsidizing of the so-called democratic United Party by 'big capital' was followed on March 19 by an editorial suggesting the United Party could only be so reticent about how much it was getting from the Fund because it feared popular disapproval. A statement by an obscure United Party candidate that the Trust Fund had given £1 million to the United Party got front-page publicity on April 3, and promoted shocked comment from Dawie as well as editorially on the way in which the United Party had virtually surrendered its independence to a handful of capitalists organized in a body which was not responsible to anyone but themselves.

Far more emphasis was placed on education and mother-tongue instruction than on other minor topics, particularly in the central part of the campaign from March 14-April 6. Both on March 16 and 19, *Die Burger* attacked the United Party for its stand in this area, suggesting that, like Milner, the United Party contemplated aggression against the Afrikaans language. If the United Party opposed compulsory mother-tongue instruction, this could only mean that children would lose their protection against 'foolish' Afrikaans-speaking parents who preferred to send them to English-medium schools.

> It is for these parents that the United Party is fighting, not for English-speaking parents who wish to send their unilingual children to Afrikaans schools—for such parents do not exist.

Further indignant comment came on March 25, *Die Burger* foreseeing a new language and education struggle if the United Party were elected, and hoping such a tragedy would be averted 'in the interests of our children and of national unity'. *Die Burger* also aired another grievance, that English-speaking children could always go to English-medium private schools while Afrikaans children might be forced to go to dual-medium schools, since there were no Afrikaans private schools. These points were reiterated on April 8 and 10, and even found a place in the election day issue.

The dominant issue of color policy, however, completely overshadowed everything else in the last week of the campaign. For the first time the Indian question was introduced when *Die Burger*, in a sub-leader on April 7, not only reiterated its belief that the United Party would gradually extend political rights to non-Europeans, but maintained that the party had never repudiated the policy underlying the 1946 extension of parliamentary representation to

Indians. Three days later, *Die Burger*, commenting on the Nationalist 'election bomb', *The U.P.'s Political Plan For Natives and Indians*, declared that the only way to avert the danger of an eventual Gold Coast government in the Union was to ensure white supremacy by voting for the Nationalists. Dadoo's appeal for the United Party reinforced the point in its opinion. This line was hammered home in a succession of articles, cartoons, and featured speeches. The Mau Mau campaign became almost daily front-page news coupled with prominent photographs of Europeans in Nairobi 'armed to the teeth', and cartoons of the 'Miau-Miau' tiger stalking Strauss and Co. and wearing a 'Vote United Party' placard. On election day, *Die Burger* gave front page prominence to a letter from a leading Afrikaner in Kenya praying that South Africa would be spared a soft Government such as Kenya had, in other words, the United Party with its 'liberalist' supporters.

For the days immediately following the election, *Die Burger* was given over to election results, post-mortems, reports of overseas and local reactions, and election anecdotes. In a jubilant leading article on April 17, entitled 'Our Most Glorious Hour', *Die Burger* attributed the Nationalists' increased strength partly to the youth which had qualified for the vote in the previous years and partly to *platteland* Afrikaners deserting the United Party for the Nationalists. A cartoon showed the river of Nationalism breaking through the wall of urban constituencies with the caption 'The breach becomes ever wider'. Dr. Malan was hailed as the architect of the unity of nationalistic Afrikanerdom which *Die Burger* said had never been so strong and united before. On the other hand, the paper acknowledged, on April 21 and 23, that the English-speaking section had voted in far greater numbers against the Nationalists in 1953 than in 1948. What is to become of them? it asked. Is there to be

> a permanent, frustrated, mainly English-speaking Opposition? a foreign growth with no roots in this country. . . ? or are they going to grasp the outstretched hand of the Afrikaans-speaking Nationalist and allow their political loyalties to be determined by political principles and the consideration that, with regard to Colour matters, everything that belongs together must get together if we are to overcome our Colour problem?

Not without pleasure did *Die Burger* add to this a cartoon, on April 22, depicting the broken United Front with Strauss and Harry Oppenheimer anxiously watching four sizzling time bombs ready to explode: Natal, Liberalism, Arthur Barlow and other dissident United Party right-wingers, and Dr. Malan's request for Opposition votes to pass the constitutional amendment on the Coloured vote.

Die Transvaler, the only Afrikaans morning daily in the Transvaal, is more of a mass paper than *Die Burger*, written less for the professional and business classes than for the urban working class—railway workers, mine workers, etc.—and the small dorps of the *platteland*. It does not match the standard of language and the technical competence of *Die Burger*, but puts its efforts into attracting attention with bold and even sensational headlines and stories.

During the whole of the pre-election period, practically all the space and energies of *Die Transvaler* were devoted to the election: news, comment, editorials, announcements of meetings, photographs, cartoons by 'Etam', and even advertisements. Only two or three such striking events as Stalin's illness and death, and a serious explosion in a school playground in Johannesburg, drove the election into second place in *Die Transvaler's* coverage. Of 70 leaders written between March 2 and April 15, only 2—1 on Stalin, and a religious leader on Good Friday, April 3—did not deal with the election directly or indirectly.

Like *Die Burger, Die Transvaler* divided its energies almost equally between vigorous support of the Nationalist cause, and an equally vigorous campaign against the United Party and the United Front. Nor was there marked difference in the topics on which the two papers concentrated: apartheid, national unity (on Nationalist terms), parliamentary sovereignty, and Communism, in relation to which Dadoo's statement received much prominence. The treatment of the topics varied, however, partly because of the greater proportion of political comment in *Die Transvaler*, and partly because of its more popular approach. Where, particularly in the early part of the campaign, *Die Burger* wrote one editorial on a subject and then did not repeat for some time, *Die Transvaler* hammered at the same point, or a variation of it, or picked out one point after another in a major political speech, and commented exhaustively day after day.

Die Transvaler reported Nationalist election meetings fully, prominently and under bold headlines. Speeches by Cabinet Ministers, almost all of which were extremely long, were reported almost verbatim, with constant references to the size and enthusiasm of the audience. Though *Die Transvaler* has a special and quite natural tenderness for Mr. Strijdom, the paper also accorded Dr. Malan extended and respectful attention. His speech of March 5 was reported under a five-column headline (the paper has seven columns), was carried in full on the inside pages after a synopsis on the first page and illustrated by a double-column photograph. Dr. Malan's audience at Stellenbosch 'of thousands of people' was said to be 'a simmering mass of enthusiasm'. On another occasion, *Die Transvaler* reported 'deafening' applause for Dr. Verwoerd's plan to eliminate the 'black spots' in Johannesburg's western suburbs, announced at a party meeting in Johannesburg's City Hall.

Generous space was also devoted to the organization and progress of the Nationalist campaign. Throughout, *Die Transvaler* displayed complete faith in a Nationalist victory based on Nationalist policy, party organization, and growing enthusiasm and on new support for apartheid as the only way to handle Native disorders like the defiance campaign, and to save white civilization. Nationalist achievements were compared favorably, on March 4, with previous United Party efforts and, on the 17th, a news story lauded the Government for bringing industrial peace, restricting unemployment, raising the national income, increasing educational opportunities for 'our own people', increasing the number of white workers on the railways, and clearing the trade unions of Communists.

Like *Die Burger*, though with greater fanfare and reiteration, *Die Transvaler* regularly reported conversions to the Nationalist cause. An article on March 14 declared that Nationalist policy on the Coloured and Indians had captured thousands of English-speaking people in Natal; the next day, 250 English-speaking people were said to have joined the Nationalists in Durban during the previous three months. Thousands of Jews would vote Nationalist, according to an interview with a Mr. Charles Zeff headlined on March 18. (Zeff also appeared on the platform with the Nationalist candidate in Vereeniging.) Names, statements by and photographs of families which had 'come over' to the Nationalists were interspersed with records of conversions. On April 13, *Die Transvaler* carried the story of a man who declared his life had been threatened over the phone after he had written a letter to the *Cape Times* supporting Parliamentary sovereignty against the courts, and who now announced that he had sent Dr. Malan £100.

Die Transvaler was its most characteristic and effective in exploiting the railway apartheid decision, of which it made more use than any other issue, including Communism. Under a four-banner headline, 'Shocking implications of verdict', its political correspondent declared that non-Europeans could now use station waiting-rooms, tea rooms, lavatories, etc., previously reserved for Europeans. Incidents illustrating apartheid violations—like the story of an African who had tea in a Durban tea room with a white companion in the presence of several Afrikaners—covered the front page in the days following the verdict and the theme was harped on incessantly throughout the rest of the election period. *Die Transvaler* also taunted the United Party for its silence on the judgment.

In general, *Die Transvaler's* campaign against the United Party was one of contempt and denigration rather than opposition. Everything that Nationalist ministers and candidates had to say against the United Party was reported in full, while a fair proportion of *Die Transvaler's* news, comments and about half its editorials were devoted to systematically running down the Opposition and questioning its motives. A permanent feature of the propaganda was a belittlement of Strauss as 'a little man', and 'a political dwarf' not strong enough to hold his party together or, what was more serious, to curb the 'liberalist' elements which dominated the United Party, as the Torch Commando and Labour Party dominated the United Front. The conservative and Afrikaner members of the United Party were called merely an election front for a party full of dissension, financed through the United South Africa Trust Fund by Hoggenheimer (the Nationalist symbol for a capitalist, easily associated with the Oppenheimer family and unpleasantly reminiscent of *Der Stürmer's* Jewish cartoons of Hitler days) and with a sudden conversion to segregation which was mere election hypocrisy.

Reports of United Party meetings in the Transvaal stressed small attendance and many votes of no confidence. Regularly referring to United Party supporters as Saps (harking back to Smuts' South African Party which fused with Hertzog's Nationalists in 1934), a headline on March 18 read 'S.A.P. candidate flees from his own meeting'. Ridicule of Strauss was reflected in headlines like 'Less than 40 motors in escort' (March 5), 'Strauss Mumbles an Answer' (March 11), and 'Only 8,000 of the 100,000 Turned Up' to the Zoo Lake Rally, Johannesburg (April 13).

The United Party's strongest points—its economic program and the Transvaal Education Ordinance—were treated either with ridicule or contempt. Its economic promises were called hopelessly extravagant, or mere election propaganda. Repeated allegations were made that the committee formed to protest against the Transvaal Provincial Council's education policy was an election racket.

Rowdy incidents at United Party meetings led *Die Transvaler* to declare, on March 20, that they were caused by deliberate provocation. Moreover, the paper carried a steady stream of warnings against sinister Sap, and Torch Commando plans. On March 16, the Torch Commando and the Springbok Legion, a left-wing ex-soldiers' association, were said to be preparing a protest demonstration on the constitutional issue; also *Die Transvaler* alleged an election-day plot to empty gasoline (petrol) stations. A story that the Torch Commando had access to confidential information through tapping telephone conversations was published on March 26, and repeated despite denials by the Minister for Posts and Telegraphs. On April 6, a five-column head warned that Nationalists must look after election offices and voting booths, as the United Front was desperate, and 50 organization cards had already disappeared from an office in a Rand town where Dr. Dönges had spoken recently; five days later, the paper announced that the police would guard Rand polling booths. On April 8, *Die Transvaler* reported a cruel attack by Saps on an 'aged man', who turned out to be 52.

Die Transvaler summed up the election campaign in an article on April 7. The central Nationalist line, it said, was to ask the people for a mandate to go forward with apartheid as it had been systematically applied in the last five years. Against this clear policy stood only the promises of the United Party which, moreover, was ashamed of its allies, and frightened of a color policy. The Opposition press was castigated for underestimating the intelligence of the voters, describing every Nationalist seat as marginal, and hiding away or completely suppressing election news. In the two weeks immediately preceding the election, *Die Transvaler* acted as a direct election agent, instructing and exhorting its readers in news items and editorials. Finally, on April 10, *Die Transvaler* warned that the United Party was working very hard, but declared that it lacked the boundless enthusiasm of the Nationalists, who made their efforts not for personal reward but for an ideal and a conception of life.

Even more unrestrainedly jubilant over the election outcome than *Die Burger*, *Die Transvaler* also reacted with the faith that the obvious election trend towards the Nationalists would bring them a majority of the votes by 1958. Confidently expecting the United Party to splinter, and Dr. Malan to get the necessary support to pass the Coloured vote bill, *Die Transvaler* looked forward on the morrow of the election to a highly successful five-year period of Government, during which the fears of the English would steadily diminish, and Nationalist supremacy become still more firmly established.

Die Burger's 'opposite number' among English-language papers is the *Cape Times*, an independently owned paper with a moderately liberal slant. During the election campaign, the *Cape Times* supported the United Party, stating its case in a fairly dispassionate way, and backing up both charge and claims with specific data. At no time did the paper descend to pure propaganda.

The *Cape Times* coverage of the election grew steadily from a little over a dozen reports of major party speeches, and occasional editorials the first week to nearly full front-page handling in the week of the election. Throughout the campaign, however, the *Cape Times* provided a substantial amount of international news, and as late as April 1 allowed hopes for a Korean peace, and the account of Queen Mary's funeral to push election news off the first page.

Both United Party and Nationalist speeches were reported objectively, but in number, extent, and prominence (placing on page and size of headline), the United Party was accorded roughly twice the coverage of the Nationalists. While Dr. Malan's speech at Stellenbosch on March 5 was reported in full, most Nationalist speeches received only a few paragraphs. They included justifications of Nationalist policies, prophesies of victory, and criticisms of the United Party. All candidate 'profiles', which were short biographies usually with a photograph, belonged to the United Party. News stories were treated as such in the first week of the campaign, but increasingly thereafter seemed to be chosen with a view to their propaganda effect, e.g. Nationalist rowdiness at United Party meetings. The headlines emphasized the most challengeable part of Nationalist speeches. At the same time, the paper was scrupulous in reporting votes of no confidence passed at United Party meetings, and evidences of dissent.

While supporting the official United Party program enunciated in the speeches it so faithfully reported, the *Cape Times* put its own particular emphasis primarily on the constitutional question, to which it devoted over ten editorials, and secondarily on problems of race relations and parents' rights under the Transvaal Education Ordinance. During the first and, to a lesser extent, second week of the campaign, though not thereafter, the *Cape Times* paid lavish attention to the Group Areas Act and the Population Registration Act, subjecting them to constant criticism in articles dealing with specific problems these acts created. Special attention was also given to the rising cost of living, which was dealt with in five of the United Party speeches reported the first week of the campaign. The one lead editorial of that week which dealt with the election criticized Malan's Stellenbosch speech for its generalities and deficiencies, specifically attacking the Nationalists' handling of apartheid policy and the consequent deterioration in race relations, and their attitude on the constitutional issue and on Communism. In conclusion, the editorial accused Malan of lack of clarity about what mandate he was requesting, and likened him to a 'recidivist confidence man asking for one more blank cheque to prove how clever he is'.

Indicative of the *Cape Times*' general attitude was an article on March 8, emphasized by a three-column head and two illustrations, which warned voters not to act emotionally but to face realistically South Africa's major problem, the enormous disproportion in numbers between the white and non-European population. At the same time that it emphasized the common needs of Europeans, the paper used a news story on the 6th entitled 'Electioneering in Rand School', which featured Afrikaner exclusiveness, to illustrate the 'reckless, uncooperative' attitude of the Nationalists, of which Mr. Strauss spoke on March 11.

The positive side of the *Cape Times*' support of the United Party came mainly through full reports on United Party speeches, with an increasing amount of editorial and feature article support for the points emphasized in these speeches, like the United Party economic program, protection of civil rights, immigration as a positive answer to the disproportion in numbers between the races, the need to secure better relations between English and Afrikaners and the proposal for a National Convention to secure a better program for non-Europeans. On March 11, the paper described the vast nature of the United Party's organization and its 20,000 volunteer workers, following this up three days later with another story dealing with the party's strength.

Somewhat more effective, and even more wholehearted, however, were the attacks which the *Cape Times* launched at the Nationalists, particularly in the latter part of the campaign. One line of attack, which was pursued from the very start, was the charge that Dr. Malan was merely a front for more dangerous Nationalists like J. G. Strijdom, one of his 'evil counsellors', who might easily become his successor. Reiterated week by week, this concern over Strijdom led to a biography and photograph printed on April 2 under an unusual three-column head. Though written with an anti-Strijdom viewpoint, the article was fairly objective and might even have been found flattering by some of his supporters. Earlier articles on March 20 and 21 had emphasized Strijdom's arbitrary control of party machinery, and his threat against the universities unless social apartheid was enforced.

Prominence was also given consistently to accounts of Nationalist rowdiness at United Party meetings. Rotten eggs and tomatoes thrown at a woman candidate made the front page in the second week of the campaign, as did the sjamboked back of a United Party supporter on March 30. There were six conspicuous news stories of rowdyism the last week of the campaign.

Charges of fraudulence, inconsistency, evasiveness, and inefficiency were systematically made against the Nationalists by the *Cape Times.* The paper declared that Nationalist claims that apartheid policy was new were false and misleading. On March 18, two Nationalist speeches were placed side by side, one of which claimed there was no cause for fear in South Africa and the other reported a speech entitled 'Swart talks of Threats'. This theme of inconsistency in propaganda charges, on the school issue, on republicanism, etc., was played up during that whole week in editorials, special features, United Party speech reports and news stories. Along with this went the twin charge of evasiveness, especially on the constitutional issue, dramatized by a cartoon on March 21 entitled 'That Mandate', in which a hangman with a mask was handing a condemned voter a statement to sign which read 'I bequeath to the Nationalist Caucus unlimited powers'. Another political cartoon of March 12 showed the vulture of nationalism being painted to resemble a 'Little White Dove'.

Three new features introduced during the campaign were 'Under the Nationalists', a single paragraph boxed on the front page which gave unfavorable statistics, e.g. on taxation and civil service dissatisfaction, for which the Nationalists could be blamed; 'The Things They Say', single Nationalist statements of a debatable character illustrated by small drawings, which grew in numbers until election day; and 'Talking Politics', which first appeared on March 28, was witty, frankly partisan and illustrated with Thurberesque cartoons and jingles.

The *Cape Times* countered the Nationalist press outburst on the railway apartheid case by calling it an attempt to confuse issues, cover up the Nationalists' own inefficiency in drafting the legislation (e.g. the story on March 27, 'Nationalists Forget Three Words') and further emotionalize the racial issue.

After the Easter lull, election news was given no greater prominence than before, if indeed so much. The paper commented on the mutual apprehension of the two major parties of last-minute surprises and particularly on the possibility of the Nationalists using a 'red' scare. The voting in Southern Rhodesia on creating the Central African Federation was looked on as a Nationalist weapon, no matter how it turned out. On the whole, the *Cape Times*' approach at this period seemed somewhat defensive, particularly about United Party racial policy, while the paper emphasized that the difference between the Nationalists and the United Party was in approach rather than in ultimate goals. The paper made a conscious effort to concentrate on the more positive and safer elements of the United Party program, like cost of living and other economic matters, the deterioration of the Nationalists' foreign relations and, as earlier, 'Nationalist Threat to Trade Unions'. The paper's Election Survey continued to be impartial in assessing the parties' positions and to offer no predictions, particularly of a United Party victory.

At the very end, however, the *Cape Times* vastly increased its front page election matter, which went from two-thirds on April 14th to practically the whole front page on the 15th and 16th. The more aggressive United Party stand on the racial question received good coverage, and a second-lead story was entitled Strauss' 'Mission to save South Africa'. All the editorials of the last week were devoted to the election, and in full support of the United Party. On the 14th, the *Cape Times* bluntly declared 'Malan is a figurehead . . . and Havenga is a tool. . . . The future is with Mr. Strijdom and the professional politicians'. On election day, the *Cape Times* carried a full-page head, 'Fateful Choice before South Africa Today—Traditional Way of Life or Racial Extremism', and photographs of leading United Party candidates on page 5 were entitled 'Towards a Better Way of Life in South Africa'. The choice before the voters was said to be between the racial, social and economic policies of the United Party and the blind obedience of the Nationalists.

On the 16th, as election results drifted in, the paper ran a full-page headline, 'U.P. Election Hopes Diminishing'. Feature and news stories related 'friendly rivalry' between the parties at the polls. The predominant attitude was one of resignation and conciliation, with appreciative recognition of the efforts of United Party supporters, particularly the women. There was a cautious editorial on the 16th headed 'Judgment is Given'. By the 17th, when the final results were in, an editorial headed 'A Fresh Start?' reminded the Nationalists that though they had won the election they did not have a popular majority, pointed out the dangers of racial division and arbitrary tactics, and tacitly made a plea for statesmanship by the Nationalists in response to their safe parliamentary majority. The editorial on the following day ignored Malan's appeal for Opposition votes to pass the Coloured franchise amendment bill and dealt with the choice which the Nationalists could make between industrial progress based on farmer and worker (non-European as well as European) contentment or the ideological turbulence of the previous five years. Relegating Strauss' charge of 'Despicable Manœuvre' to the third page, the *Cape Times* obviously sought with resignation to make the best of the existing situation.

Moreover, the *Cape Times* printed a certain amount of criticism of the United Party through the medium of reports from the foreign press. The *Manchester Guardian* was cited as criticizing both parties and particularly the United Party for not taking a clearer stand on the racial issue and thus providing the voters with a genuine choice. Rhodesian comment attributed the results of the election to resentment over overseas criticism and reactions to the Mau Mau disturbances. The *Cape Times* itself studiously avoided post-mortems.

In much the same way as *Die Burger* and the *Cape Times* vie for morning readers in and around Cape Town, *Die Transvaler* and the *Rand Daily Mail* compete for them throughout the Witwatersrand and beyond. There is a good deal more difference between the latter two, however, both in circulation and in character, than between the Cape Town morning papers. This is not only because *Die Transvaler* is a more popular and politically oriented newspaper than *Die Burger*, but also because the *Rand Daily Mail* has a broader international, and sometimes a wider national coverage of news than has the *Cape Times*, and is more aggressive in its support of issues like civil rights, for which it has a deep concern.

Throughout the election campaign, the *Rand Daily Mail* gave conspicuous attention to world affairs and a smaller proportion of newspaper space to election material than either the *Cape Times* or the *Star*. Front-page items and election headlines appeared infrequently in the first three weeks of the campaign. Even as late as the sixth week of the election campaign there were three days without any election news whatever on the first page. The major international events of the period—Stalin's death and Malenkov's succession, the Mau Mau disturbances, Queen Mary's illness and death, the Korean peace negotiations, and federation in Rhodesia—competed with and often supplanted election news on the front page and, though to a lesser extent, in the editorial columns of the paper. In general, election meetings received brief handling and speeches were presented only through excerpts except in the case of major addresses by Strauss and Malan.

The *Rand Daily Mail's* editorials, with their occasionally biting sarcasm (as in the 'Alice in Wonderland' comments on March 24 on a statement by Dr. Bremer, Minister of Health), and its almost daily political cartoons left no doubt in any reader's mind about its sympathies in the election. Nevertheless, the paper consistently printed both sides of most issues. This was particularly noticeable in the case of the Transvaal Education Ordinance, where charges by the United Party and United Party-oriented civic groups were placed side by side with Nationalist counter charges. In the election round-up, which gave highlights from political speeches, etc., and in the column on 'Political Broadcasts', both sides were invariably represented, though the United Party received a somewhat greater proportion of space. Moreover, in the straight news stories, there was no admixture of editorial comment and in certain cases, as for example the interview of 'Mr. and Mrs. Average Voter' with a Nationalist candidate, Mr. Fritz Steyn, on April 7, the Nationalist case was presented in a favorable and quite convincing light. Considerable non-partisan election material was printed (e.g. on postal voting), and factual constituency surveys of marginal areas without predictions of how they would ultimately vote. The 'Election Diary' column, however, was reserved for United Party candidates.

Economic matters and civil rights, including the Transvaal Education Ordinance, were the two issues on which the *Rand Daily Mail* concentrated throughout the campaign. For four out of the seven weeks, economic matters held the lead, while in the first and fifth weeks of the campaign, they received nearly twice the space of any other election topic. The paper consistently supported higher cost-of-living allowances (which, it claimed, should be included in calculating pensions), more and improved housing, and decontrol of rent on business property. It also showed persistent concern over railroad mismanagement; retarded industrialization under the Nationalists; and threats to the strength and even existence of trade unions and collective bargaining. Its deepest interest seemed, therefore, in business, the taxpayer, and labor, with relatively much less for the farmer and smallholder. The *Rand Daily Mail* also exhibited considerable sensitivity to overseas opinion and awareness of the Union's need to encourage foreign investments in order to realize its industrial potentialities.

As for civil rights, which was consistently the *Rand Daily Mail's* second most important issue, and rose to top place during two of the seven weeks, about half the references were about the Transvaal Education Ordinance, the rest dealing with the Swart legislation, police tactics, and the general issue of democracy versus dictatorship. Both in editorials and political cartoons, the 'menace' to civil liberties led not only to sharp comments of a general nature but also to personal attacks on C. R. Swart, Minister of Justice, and other Cabinet Ministers. Election rowdyism, including the breaking up of United Party meetings and physical abuse of United Party candidates and supporters, was not stigmatized as an infringement of civil rights, but was reported regularly, and often on the front page.

The racial issue remained in third place in attention until the last week of the campaign, when it rose to the most prominent position. The *Rand Daily Mail* charged on this issue that apartheid was a fraud since it was no more than classic segregation, that Nationalist apartheid regulations and red tape were wasteful of the taxpayers' money and, the aspect most emphasized during the last week of the campaign, that Nationalist racial policy had alienated the Coloured and Bantu populations and created racial tension where previously there had been little or none. Occasionally the racial problem was tied to the economic one, and the *Rand Daily Mail* would point out that, far from having made progress on the road to apartheid, the Nationalists, through their narrow immigration policies, had been forced to introduce non-European labor into previously white areas.

The *Rand Daily Mail's* stand on the racial issue was quite similar to that of the United Party and, in all but two weeks, the number of news stories on this issue roughly paralleled the number of times the racial question was reported in United Party speeches. The closest the *Rand Daily Mail* came to criticizing the United Party was a statement of the London *Daily Telegraph*, reported on the first page on March 26, 'if the United Party approach to the colour problem is somewhat oblique, so are the Nationalist plans for solving the constitutional issue'. The paper did not hesitate, however, either to give full reports of Mau Mau terrorism or, after the election, to publicize an Anglican bishop's comment on racial injustice in South Africa and, less conspicuously, the statement by the President of the African National Congress that both parties were to blame for apartheid and that the defiance campaign would go on (which, in practice, did not happen).

The *Rand Daily Mail* also popularized the idea that the Nationalists were developing 'white apartheid', i.e. separation between English- and Afrikaans-speaking through their stand on single-medium education, and the exclusive Afrikaner composition of the National Party. It vehemently denied the existence of English support for the Nationalists, being more aggressive in this regard than any of the other English-language papers.

The racial issue was also tied to the constitutional question, which commonly received least coverage of the four major issues. The *Rand Daily Mail's* general approach was to print self-incriminating excerpts from speeches of Nationalist Cabinet Ministers and then to underline the points editorially. The paper also attacked the Nationalists for the ambiguity of their constitutional stand—e.g. whether or not a very slim majority would be considered a 'mandate from the people', and how to get around the entrenched clauses 'constitutionally'—and pointed out the dangerous implications of tampering with established legal institutions through experiments like 'the High Court of Parliament' at which it levelled much scorn.

During the fourth week of the campaign, the constitutional question jumped to first billing with the railway apartheid case decision, and received six front-page stories and two editorials which defended the courts and the constitutional system with which they were so intimately connected. Numerous speeches and news stories presented both the Nationalist and the United Party points of view. The *Rand Daily Mail* tried to quell the scare rumors in the Afrikaans press over the decision by stating editorially on March 25, under the title 'The Unwritten Law', that 'We believe that they' (the non-Europeans) 'will simply and patiently wait for better conditions' (though it printed a number of stories of non-European breaches of railway apartheid) as well as insisting that no one had ever intended to provide 'exactly the same facilities in railroad stations . . . for the two classes of passengers'.

Though the 'Reichstag Fire' warning of Strauss' pre-election speech was not exploited by the *Rand Daily Mail*, there was a conspicuous undertone of fear as to Nationalist intentions both in signed articles and in editorials. This was underlined in numerous references in editorials and news stories to Strijdom's 'extremism' and likely succession to Nationalist leadership, as well as personal criticism of other Cabinet Ministers like Swart, especially through cartoons. During the last week of the campaign, the *Rand Daily Mail* warned of the power and 'dark force' of the Broederbond, and cited those Cabinet Ministers influential in the organization.

Unlike the *Cape Times*, the *Rand Daily Mail* showed no noticeable change in the course of the campaign in the degree of its support for or bias towards the United Party. It never made unqualified predictions of United Party success, though it suggested that the party's chances improved during the campaign. Following the election, the *Rand Daily Mail* blamed electoral inequities for the United Party's defeat. Overseas comment on election returns was reported quite fully. Whether by accident or design, the only highly critical comment on the United Party was cited from American papers while that from the English press was largely analytical and relatively impartial.

The *Star* dominates the afternoon press on the Witwatersrand even more than the *Rand Daily Mail* dominates the morning press, partly because of its extensive coverage and also because of its handling of material.

During the election campaign, the *Star* provided a larger overall coverage of election news, and with more special features, than either the *Rand Daily Mail* or the *Cape Times*. From fairly limited general and front-page coverage in the first weeks, election news grew to cover a major proportion of all news in the sixth week, and filled nearly the whole of the front page in the last week of the campaign. At the same time, the *Star* printed all the news of genuine international and national significance during this period, and did not hesitate to relegate election news to back pages when particularly important events took place abroad.

Only Strauss' and Malan's most important speeches were reported in full by the *Star*; for the rest only excerpts were provided. The paper was outstanding, however, in the degree to which it gave equal or nearly equal coverage to the speeches of both the Nationalists and the United Party, and to the way it handled both parties in its general election round up. In the first week, for example, the *Star* reported 9 Nationalist speeches, of which several received two-column heads and Dr. Malan a three-column head. Later, Dr. Verwoerd's speech was illustrated by a photograph. The *Star* also freely reported Nationalist speeches, which included such charges against the United Party as disunity, 'liberalist' and/or business control, and political dishonesty in its promises to workers. Only 'profiles' of United Party candidates, however, were given.

During the first two weeks, election news was largely confined to speeches, and to editorial critique on the issues involved. There was little mixing of views with news. From the third week on, more feature-type articles appeared or 'omnibus' reporting of election speeches with headlines slanted or material selected for its value to the United Party cause. In reports of Nationalist speeches, conflicting stands on major issues, especially the constitutional one, were often printed in the same article, e.g. on March 20, but comment was confined, on the whole, to editorials, special features and political cartoons.

The *Star* accorded most of its references to race relations, but economic matters ran a close second, and were more frequently featured than the other issue. The constitutional issue, which easily ranked third, was treated on the editorial page in a series of scholarly articles by Professor D. V. Cowen, whose insistence that the Statute of Westminster had done nothing to reduce the binding power of the entrenched clauses was an important element in the Appeal Court's decision on the Coloured vote bill. The *Star* also devoted leading or high-ranking position during three of the seven weeks of the campaign to civil rights: the Swart legislation, the cancellation of police leave, and in particular the Transvaal Education Ordinance, which was most often treated from the angle of the civil rights involved and its potential authoritarianism. Thus, like the other English-language papers, the *Star* developed its own list of priorities. Though by and large it accepted the general positions adopted by the United Party, its analyses were often more specific than the party ones, and its proposals more original.

The *Star* made a special point of highlighting the statements of non-party groups and individuals on prominent issues. Thus, the stand against the Transvaal Education Ordinance was presented on the *Star's* front page on March 4 through the statement of the Education Action Group, and two days later by that of the Education League. On March 7, leading non-party individuals voiced fears over the Public Safety Act, and the day before a union official expressed similar anxiety over the Government's attitude on apartheid in trade unions.

More than the other papers examined, the *Star* made a particular effort to appeal both to women and to youth. On March 4, it announced a prize to be given to the best essay written by a woman on 'Why I Shall Vote', a more positive and impartial approach than that of the Torch Commando contest run in the *Sunday Times*, in which the contestants had to list a given number of Nationalists 'sins' in order of their importance. It may be noted that the women listed the education and language issue as the most important in the election, with economic problems, like cost of living, running a close second. A special-feature column initiated during the third week of the campaign provided what was called 'Youth's Political Forum' for those under thirty to express their views on the election, in particular on what the paper pointed out as being of prime importance: race relations, economic affairs and the 'democratic concept'. These turned out to be sober, factual discussions. The *Star* also showed quite conspicuous interest in the Torch Commando, and it is noticeable that a large number of the letters to its editor were from servicemen.

Much attention was paid to matters of concern to labor, more publicity being given to Labour candidates than in other English-language papers, and a fair amount to the needs and difficulties of the trade unions. From the fourth week on, the *Star* featured boxed paragraphs: 'What the election means to the Policemen' (March 25); '. . . the worker in industry' (March 27); '. . . the Public Servant' (March 30); '. . . the Railwayman' (April 1); '. . . the temporary Civil Servant' (April 2); and two in the sixth week on the farmer (who otherwise received relatively little direct attention). A column of answers to voters' questions served general needs, while the almost daily 'Campaign Comment' often provided amusing side-lights on what was going on.

The *Star's* own position on race relations (to which it gave the foremost attention which both parties said it deserved), was relatively conservative in the Burkean sense but far from reactionary. It opposed the Nationalist policy of apartheid not on grounds of abstract justice but as ambiguous and, indeed, unable to achieve the ends it sought. If the goal was 'total' apartheid, it was uneconomic and therefore impossible; if it was 'partial' apartheid, that was nothing more than traditional segregation, which was precisely what the United Party offered, with far less danger of violent Native reaction. In this issue, as on civil rights and the Constitution, the *Star* persistently charged that Nationalist 'extremism' was the most dangerous aspect of its policy.

From its own point of view, the *Star* favored white immigration to redress somewhat the balance in numbers between Europeans and non-Europeans, and for the latter, as stated in its editorial of March 24 on the railway apartheid case decision, facilities which were 'separate but adequate', a happier phrasing than the United Party developed. It may be noted here that the *Star* opposed splitting trade unions along apartheid lines on the ground that it would be a menace to the bargaining power of labor. In general, the *Star* met Nationalist propaganda on the decision with a counter-blast of its own on the Government's 'blundering and incompetence in framing legislation', and Nationalist unscrupulousness in castigating the Opposition and the courts for the Government's own failures. The *Star* also answered Nationalist press charges that the English-language press had not printed violations of apartheid regulations by maintaining that these incidents were isolated ones and had no proved connection to the court ruling.

On the economic issue, the *Star* emphasized cost of living though much more through news stories (e.g. 'State Workers angry over C.O.L.A. Delay' on March 16, followed by six front-page stories that week) than editorials; railway maladministration, on which its article 'S.A.R. wonderful for select few' drew an indignant answer, on March 28, from the General Manager, accusing the paper of misrepresentation; immigration, which it believed would create economic opportunities rather than restrict jobs and, as it declared in its lead editorial of March 23, 'The Open Door', should not be too selective, as numbers were the most important factor; the higher wages which would result from the United Party's program; and foreign capital's lack of confidence in the Union because of Nationalist racial extremism and inefficient administration.

From time to time, the *Star* printed eulogies of Mr. Strauss (e.g. March 6, 'Strauss Puts Life into Political Meeting'); in general it tried to support the strong points of the United Party program without, however, renouncing its right, as it pointed out in a lead editorial of April 13, to criticize the party whenever it found it necessary. The paper's criticism of the Nationalists nearly always had sound factual material behind it, though the *Star* also played up Strijdom's extremism, and the Broederbond, as in 'Sinister Nationalist Plan to Divide School Children' (April 19), and the Dutch Reformed Church's report on the 'Roman Danger' on April 2. A definite effort to appeal to Afrikaner readers was made with the *Star's* special Afrikaans supplement published in the sixth week of the campaign and presenting an assessment of the three major leaders—Malan, Strijdom and Strauss—as well as of the language and educational question, the courts issue, racialism and national unity.

On the eve of the election, April 14, the *Star* contrasted the United Party program, which it presented largely in economic and non-ideological terms, but also as 'respect for law', 'family rights' and 'civil and constitutional rights', with what it foresaw as the result of a Nationalist victory: 'menace to courts', 'threat to freedom of speech and press', 'Transvaal Ordinance sample of racial separation', 'national unity first casualty', and a demand for a 'Nationalist blank cheque' which could lead to 'dictatorship'. Its election headlines were more neutral: 'Women will decide election result' (April 13) and 'South Africa's Destiny in Your Hands Tomorrow' (April 14).

The Nationalist victory led the *Star* to urge restraint on the Government, and to warn it against interpreting the result as a mandate for full-scale apartheid. A lead editorial of April 20 on 'Dr. Malan's Appeal' for United Party votes to pass the constitutional amendment on the Coloured franchise commended it for being at least a constitutional approach to the subject, but condemned the way in which it was directed to one branch of the United Party instead of the whole party.

This balanced, rather than openly hostile approach to the Nationalists was coupled with strong support for the United Party. Unlike several other English-language papers, the *Star* nowhere reported serious criticism of the United Party, as for example from the foreign press. The United Party's failure to win the election was attributed exclusively to Nationalist pre-election maneuvers, constituency delimitation, and to the vigorous pro-Nationalist youth vote. Moreover, the paper placed constant emphasis (as in its lead editorial on April 16, 'The Minority Wins Again') on the fact that the United Party had received a majority of the votes. This United Party majority, coupled with the immigrant vote which could take effect in the next election, still gave the party a position of prominence, and a chance for success. The task of the United Party, maintained the *Star* on April 17, was 'to stand as a solid bulwark against militant nationalism'. Thus the *Star* added to its noteworthy independence, balance and fairness throughout the election campaign a more staunch encouragement to the United Party after its electoral defeat than that accorded by other English-language papers.

How much effect the press, or any particular newspaper has during an election campaign is only a matter for speculation. Most of the voters had made their decisions in any case before the final weeks of the campaign. *Die Transvaler* and the *Rand Daily Mail* seemed to have accepted this view and aimed throughout at the converted. No pro-Nationalist letters appeared in the columns of the *Rand Daily Mail* and its editorials seemed addressed to people already on its own side. This was true to a still greater extent of *Die Transvaler*. In passing, it may be noted that a United Party spokesman told the *Star*, on April 11, that the Nationalist-supporting dailies on the Witwatersrand would not even accept paid United Party advertisements of their meetings.

If any of the English-language papers exercised an influence on the voting of Afrikaners, it was probably the *Star* and the *Cape Times*. The *Star* printed occasional letters criticizing the United Party, and gave full space to a protest by Dr. Verwoerd and a lengthy vindication of himself by Mr. Tothill, a so-called Liberal who finally withdrew after sharp criticism from the *Star* that he might split the vote. The *Cape Times* had a fair measure of pro-Nationalist letters in its columns. These facts suggest that members of the other political camp carefully read these papers, but with how much effect remains problematic.

What is obvious from the detailed analysis of these five dailies is that the English-language press preserved both more balance and greater impartiality in handling election news than did the Afrikaans press. This may well be both a cause and a result of the wider readership which the English-language press commands.

The non-European Press and the Election

Not surprisingly, the attitude of the non-European press to the election was 'a plague on both your houses'. Among non-Europeans, even the small number who could exercise the franchise, the male Coloured and Indians in Cape

Province, were sharply divided as to whether it was better to vote or to boycott the election as a sign of general opposition to European policies. Though Dr. Golding, chairman of the Coloured People's National Union, advised Coloured voters to support the United Party, *The Torch* declared, in its second leader of February 3, 1953, that 'whoever votes for either of them is voting for his own continued enslavement and that of the ten million non-white oppressed'. That the boycott was largely ineffective, however, is suggested by the fact that 75·8 per cent of the voters used their franchise in the almost entirely Coloured Cape Flats constituency.

On April 21, *The Torch* used its undoubted powers of vituperation in a leader entitled 'The Nationalists Retain the Sjambok', which declared that the white man had given the mandate to the party

> which promised him the most ruthless crushing of the *opstandigheid* of the non-whites, the most thorough stamping out of all 'non-national', 'liberalistic', communistic ideas, the most far-reaching kraaling-off of the non-white beast of burden from its master and of each non-white section from the other.

Among the Asiatic press, *Indian Opinion* displayed a consistent interest in the election, coupled with bitterness, and even despair that non-Europeans had no influence on its outcome. On March 20, the leader, probably written by Jordan K. Ngubane, acting as editor in Gandhi's absence, pointed out:

> There is an election fever today throughout the country. A white Parliament will be established by a white electorate. Four times the number of non-whites have practically no say at all. That is why it makes it so convenient for a power-mad minority to disregard the sentiments of voteless and voiceless people and trample under-foot their legitimate rights. Such a 'democracy' may well be called 'mobocracy', which eventually must lead this country and the world to disaster.

Five days before the election *Indian Opinion* had suggested that, between the two parties, the 'lesser evil' was the United Party.

> Under it at least there will be a lease of life for the non-Europeans. Under the Nationalist Party they are given no hope whatsoever. It will be a case of choosing between slavery or death. . . . But what use is it of conjecturing when you have no choice to make?

When the election was over, however, its editor, Manilal Gandhi, wrote:

> With us non-Europeans it is a case of 'better an enemy we know than a friend we do not know'. The Nationalists have won because they were frank and had a definite policy, right or wrong. They meant what they said and did what they said. Truth was on their side. The United Party, who form the bulk of the English-speaking people, were hypocrites. They had no definite policy. What hurt them about the entrenched clauses in the Constitution was the way their own rights and interests were being endangered, not how the non-

> whites were faring. . . . Frankly speaking, this country is doomed to destruction because of the hypocrisy on the part of the English-speaking people and utterly narrow nationalism on the part of the Afrikaans-speaking people. . . .

On the same day, April 24, Ngubane wrote in his section 'African Viewpoint' that the election faced the non-European 'with a major disaster in our life'. Cautiously he suggested that the African National Congress might need to think about 'a broader conception of unity among those who oppose Malanism . . . an all-embracing, non-white unity with a broader outlook than the narrowly political', but also one in which the white minority, 'which is in danger of being as cruelly oppressed as we have been for generations past', is not forgotten.

To this may be added certain points which appeared in the Bantu press. At the annual meeting of the Transvaal branch of the ANC, as reported by *Ilanga lase Natal* on September 25, 1952:

> The fear was privately expressed that a United Party victory would cause the [defiance] campaign to lose impetus without bringing any real amelioration of conditions for the Bantu. . . .

In practice, the campaign was suspended for the three months prior to the election lest it be exploited as an election issue and, despite plans for its continuation, never revived again. At a press conference of A. J. Luthuli, President of the African National Congress, in Johannesburg, at the end of April 1953, a formal statement was issued which explicitly denied, however, that the election had been of any great consequence to the non-European.[2] It read:

> In effect the white electorate as a whole voted for the Nationalist policy because the Opposition also stood for the fundamental policy of denying non-white people full democratic rights; and its belief in segregation is consonant with apartheid and white domination.

Section IV: Nationalist Afrikanerdom

CHAPTER 8
THE NATIONAL PARTY AT WORK

The paradox of the National Party is the apparently loosely knit federal structure of this highly integrated, disciplined organization. The key lies in the interlocking directorate of provincial, federal and parliamentary leaders, and the intense sense of cohesion of the community they represent. Behind the hierarchy described in the provincial Constitutions, and that of the Federal Council, is a finely articulated system of power and control, which is the creation at one and the same time of nationalistic Afrikanerdom, and of the astute leaders who stimulate and direct it.

Its Principles

The preamble of each provincial Constitution lists the common principles of the National Party, which no provincial congress may alter unilaterally. Slightly revised by the Federal Council at the time of formal union with the Afrikaner Party in 1951, and subsequently accepted by each of the provincial congresses, they differ little in form and content from the H.N.P.'s earlier program of principles. This similarity illustrates the consistency with which the party has moved towards its goals and also its essential unity.

As can be expected, the emphasis in the statement of principles is on the national independence of South Africa, economic as well as political. Adequate national defence is to support this independence and, in reflection of the earlier struggle over the flag, the national flag is said to be 'the only and exclusive symbol' of South African nationhood, thus leaving no place for the Union Jack.[1] Using Hertzog's words, the statement declares that the republican form of government 'separated from the British Crown', is the form 'best adapted to the traditions, circumstances and aspirations' of the nation, and 'the only effective guarantee' against South Africa being drawn again into Great Britain's wars. The Republic is to be established, however, only through 'a special and definite mandate from the European electorate'.

These phrases, however, hardly express the intensity of the party's feelings about republicanism. This is deeply rooted in the history of the Boer republics, and felt to be the distinctive form of government for Afrikaners. Moreover, Nationalists frequently maintain that only when a Republic has been declared for South Africa will all its people acknowledge a single loyalty to that country.

The Union Congress of the National Party meeting in Bloemfontein on June 3, 1941, accepted as formal party policy a resolution which demanded

> the re-creation of South Africa into a free independent republic, based on a Christian-National foundation, and incorporating in its nature and character

the best which the Boer Nation in the past devised in this sphere, in accordance with its own national nature and traditions.

This declaration represents Nationalist policy better than the oft cited draft Republican Constitution of 1942,[2] which was prepared by a small group of individuals and published by permission of Dr. Malan, but never submitted to a party congress.

As far as internal arrangements are concerned, the unitary basis of the Constitution is specifically endorsed, though the provincial system is favored for the present. Development should be along 'Christian-national lines, with due regard to the individual's freedom of conscience and religion'. Though 'Christian-national' has a distinctively Afrikaner connotation, equal rights for both Afrikaans- and English-speaking are affirmed the basis of national unity; so, too, is 'mutual appreciation of each other's cultural contributions'. On the touchy point of language, the equality of Afrikaans and English are to be maintained 'in every way in all spheres of South African life where the State itself is concerned or is able to exert influence'. This means bilingualism, of course, and it is to be 'applied faithfully' in the Civil Service, provincial administrations, and all State or State-aided institutions. The one clause about immigration reflects concern lest newcomers might not understand distinctive South African (or Afrikaner?) attitudes. Thus entry should be limited to 'those elements which can readily be absorbed by the South African nation'.

As for the non-Europeans, both Natives and Coloured are recognized as 'permanent parts of the country's population' which should have 'the opportunity to develop themselves, each race in its own field, in both the material and spiritual spheres, in keeping with their natural gifts and abilities'. 'Territorial and political segregation of the Native' is emphasized, as is separation in general between Europeans and non-Europeans, specifically 'in the residential and—as far as is practicable—in the industrial spheres'. Indians are mentioned only in terms of protecting 'all groups of the population' against Asiatic immigration and competition, particularly through 'an effective scheme of segregation and repatriation'.

The most substantial other sections deal with economic, financial and labour policy. Agriculture and mining are said to be the foundations of the country's material well-being, but commerce and secondary industries are necessary 'to perpetuate the progress and independence of the land'. 'Satisfactory protection' will be provided for industries. A certain corporative approach, however, suspicious of the particular interests of both labor and capital, is reflected in the opposition to policies which tend 'to promote class strife', or are calculated to sacrifice the national interest 'for the benefit of organized money powers'.

For white (now predominantly Afrikaner) workers as individuals, the party shows a deep concern. They must be safeguarded against competition from outside the country. Even more important, 'efficient protection' must be given 'the civilized worker in general against replacement by uncivilized labour'. This is especially 'to protect the European worker from being forced out of the sphere which he is entitled to occupy in view of his position and the standard of living expected of him'. Side by side with this concern for urban Afrikaner labor stands the party's basic interest in the *platteland*, reflected in the section on agriculture where 'the existence and welfare of the rural population' is said to be 'the object of particular endeavour and concern'.

Only a few other points are included in the program of principles, though they are far from being unimportant. Section 24 on education urges that 'the Christian-national basis of the State' be taken fully into account in providing sound universal instruction (i.e. for Europeans). Parents are said to have the right to determine the 'direction' of education, but only apparently in regard to 'the ethical and religious development of the child'. The next section speaks of a national health system. Perhaps the most unusual clause is section 26 which refers to public morality, recognizing Sunday 'as a day of rest in the public sphere', opposing 'all unchristian practices in the national life', and asking the authorities 'to maintain a high moral code' though without violating the individual citizen's freedom 'in his own sphere'. Thus is reflected the Calvinist basis of Afrikaner life.

Broad as are these principles, they provide (as the program itself specifically says they must) the framework for the legislative and electoral programs of the National Party. There is little doubt that they are taken with great seriousness by the rank and file of party members. Nor can the unifying effect of common principles be underestimated. It will be remembered that when Dr. Malan rejected the idea of a unitary framework for the National Party, General Hertzog felt that this decision left the way open for the provinces to adopt their own statements of principles[3] (see p. 34). Hertzog's defeat in the Free State Congress in November 1940 meant, among other things, that all provincial organizations must henceforth accept a common program. Thus, at the Nationalists' very core of action, the unitary principle is maintained.

Its Members

Little is more indicative of the importance to the Nationalists of party membership than the solemnity of the pledge the member makes on joining the organization. Not only does he formally accept the principles of the party, and agree to honor them to the best of his ability; in the words of the Transvaal Constitution (which is the one here described except where noted) he also 'voluntarily and sincerely' pledges himself 'to carry out faithfully the obligations' of membership under the Constitution, and to submit 'to the authority and discipline' of the party. At the same time, he affirms that he does not belong to any other political party, or organization with a political purpose. The importance of the latter pledge is underlined in Section 6 of Ch. IV on Membership, which declares that 'in the political field the party demands undivided loyalty from its members', a clause which recalls the bitter struggle with the Ossewa Brandwag (see p. 34).

To become a party member, it is necessary to be a European; resident in the province; eighteen years of age (17 in Natal); a member of a branch except in exceptional cases and then only with the permission of the General Executive; and to sign a membership card with the pledge already described. This pledge is further underlined in Section 7, which states that every member must accept the principles of the party, abide by its Constitution and rules, and also 'actively assist in promoting the growth of the Party, extending its interests and helping it on to victory'

The party has not been free in the past from obvious discrimination in admitting members. Jews were specifically excluded from party membership in the Transvaal until 1951, a reflection of the Hitler-induced anti-Semitism which affected the more extreme wings of the H.N.P. in the thirties. Anti-Jewish feeling continued in some quarters during the war, and the Transvaal Congress asked the Federal Council in December 1940 to persuade the other provinces to follow its example of denying Jews membership.[4] In 1951, however, when the terms of merger with the Afrikaner Party were accepted, Strijdom took the lead in securing the elimination of the discriminatory clause.

A good deal of attention is paid to the process of expulsion from the party, clear evidence of the significance attached to membership. Any part of the organization has the right to expel a member, but the member, in turn, can appeal for reinstatement and the ultimate decision is made by the Committee or Provincial Congress. Within the constituencies of the Witwatersrand, the Rand Controlling Council has the same powers as the Executive Committee.

The most common reason for expulsion is refusal to submit to discipline. A celebrated case was the expulsion of Oswald Pirow from the Transvaal party for publishing booklets on his New Order (p. 34) without first taking them to the Provincial Congress. In 1951, a Port Elizabeth member of the party was ejected for refusing to accept a branch decision; within six months, however, he was reinstated. Such cases, or disputes affecting branches, may be referred in the Cape to a special Judicial Committee of the party consisting of seven barristers resident in Cape Town. They consider one or two appeals a year, and their decision is usually accepted, though there remains the possibility of an ultimate appeal to the Provincial Congress. On the whole, the Cape has fewer expulsions from membership than has the Transvaal.

Compared with the United Party, a high percentage of National Party followers are officially enrolled as members. In the Cape there were 120,000 paid up National Party members in 1953, about one-fifth of the Afrikaans-speaking in the province. Even Natal reported 20,000 enrolled members in 1953 though Nationalist candidates in that province polled only 26,000 votes that year.

Part of the reason why so many people enrol as members of the National Party may be that this is the only route to the party's numerous offices which are prized so much both for prestige and influence. Moreover, in the Cape, no one was allowed to vote in the nominations for a parliamentary candidate for the 1953 elections unless he had been a paid-up member of 18 months' standing. Voting on nominations in the Transvaal was restricted to party members. In Natal the restrictions were not so rigid, but only because its organization is still in an undeveloped stage. On the whole, the Nationalists put a high premium on formal membership in the party, and do everything they can to make it attractive.

Anyone studying the National Party in operation must be struck and indeed deeply impressed by the seriousness with which party membership is accepted, and the extraordinarily hard, devoted work done voluntarily by so high a proportion of its members. The sense of participating in 'a cause', so seldom found outside of Labor Parties these days, is present to a high degree among the Nationalists. Not only is this a drive for power; it reflects also the fervid acceptance of the party as the political representative of 'the *volk*'. Party membership, then, is both a badge of distinction, and a pledge of activity. Under skilled leadership, this spirit transforms party organization from the somewhat lifeless abstraction it can become between elections into a continuous active force.

Its Provincial Organization

In the foreword to the Constitution for the Natal National Party, its provincial secretary, D. J. Potgieter, uses a homely analogy to show the importance of the party machine in reaching the Nationalists' objective. In an exhortation to keep 'continuously going' he writes: 'If you take care that every screw and bolt is tightened up (close unity within the Party relation); that the battery is kept fully charged (the indispensable enthusiasm of our organization), that you grease regularly and change oil (the protection of the watchful eye of the proud owner), and that the tank is full of fuel (the essential funds which must provide the driving force)', then there will be 'decisive victory' in the 'most important battle of our history', the 1953 election. Neither exhortation, nor wording, are meaningless. The sense of urgency and the organization of disciplined effort and teamwork are among the National Party's greatest assets.

In maintaining this spirit and organizing party activity, the key points in the provincial hierarchy are the groups, the divisional committees, and the Steering Committee (*Dagbestuur*). The branches, Executive Committee (*Hoofbestuur*), and Provincial Congress represent mass participation, while the three other units concentrate on direction and discipline.

The groups are the working sub-divisions of the branches, and have provided the smallest, and in a sense, most important units of organization since they were set up by Dr. Malan in mid-1951.[5] Branches exist in every polling district when possible, and may be formed in any other place that the Divisional Committee feels advisable. They must have a minimum of 10 members in the Transvaal, and 25 in the Cape, but are generally much larger. Branch members are then divided, 'with due regard to polling districts, geographical barriers and other common interests' (to quote the Transvaal Constitution), into units of approximately 10, the groups.

At the head of each group is a group leader, elected annually at a branch meeting by his group, or members of the branch. At least once in three months the leader must have personal contact with the members of his or her group, keeping them informed of party activity, distributing pamphlets, and seeing that they are on the voters' roll, and vote at elections. He is 'the shepherd of the herd', as a prominent Nationalist put it, while the group itself is 'a kind of cell' whose members mutually stimulate each other to party activity, and work as a small team under their leader's direction. Beyond this, however, the group leader is officially responsible for ensuring 'that new members are constantly recruited', and must 'canvass persons holding different views'.

Here, in fact, lies the most continuously active propaganda effort of the party. Each group leader covers two, or perhaps three streets in his town or city, paying casual calls on newcomers to determine their political allegiance, winning them over where possible, and at least providing the party with up-to-date information about political support. In addition, a great deal of the election canvassing is done by group leaders, largely on a voluntary basis. Since most of the men work in mines, factories, or offices, this represents a vast amount of night work which cannot be shared with women since the latter cannot be alone after dark because of the large Native population. Women do much of the routine work of organization, particularly at election time, however, and also occasionally act as very efficient group leaders.

The group leaders are not only responsible for their own units; they also normally control the general activities of the branch through the branch committee. Though the Transvaal Constitution states that the chairman, vice-chairman, secretary and treasurer need not 'necessarily' be elected from the group leaders (Chapter VI) the latter usually predominate heavily. The number of committee members varies according to the membership of the branch: in the Transvaal consisting of not less than 5 members, nor more than 15, of whom one-third must be women. When the appropriate time arises, the branch committee works as the election committee, or within it, according to the area of the electoral circuit.

The branches (of which there were 1,200 in the Transvaal in 1952, and 400 in the Free State) raise funds and stimulate party activity. Though they form the basic local units, the center of power within local organization is the constituency, organized under the divisional (or as it is called in the Cape, district) committee. When the constituency is divided into wards, some of the functions of the divisional committee are taken over by ward committees, but the former retains ultimate authority subject to the rulings of the provincial organization. The divisional committee consists of 3 members from each branch, including the chairman and secretary (only the chairman and secretary in the Cape). If there is a ward organization, 5 members of each ward committee, including the chairman and secretary, are on the divisional committee.

Part of the function of the divisional committee is to supervise the branches, and to act as liaison between them and the province. It convenes an annual group leaders' conference, transmits membership fees and the most suitable motions from the branches to the Head Office, sees that the branches have their required meetings after the annual Congress, and holds at least one 'Republican Rally' a year to raise funds.

Beyond this, the responsibilities of the divisional committee are chiefly for the nomination of candidates, and organizing the work for an election. The recognized way of choosing Nationalist candidates is through a party primary. Nominations, or, as they are called, 'requisitions', are handled according to the rules laid down by particular provinces, though nominees must be party members of more than a year's standing. In the Transvaal, nominations must be made by 25 members of more than 3 months' standing; for the April 1953, election, they had to be in by December 15, 1952, and were voted on in direct primaries on January 23. Several of the contests were reported to be 'very hot', especially in the northern Zoutpansberg area.

In the Cape, where only paid-up members may participate in nomination contests, the Provincial Secretary sets the nomination date, and all nomination proposals must be sent to Head Office, with a requisition from a majority of the members of a branch, and a signed statement from the nominee that he accepts the principles of the party. Head Office then circulates the names of all nominees to all branch committees, which subsequently hold a general conference or, as some call it, 'electoral committee' of 150-200 delegates. The objective is to get a unanimous decision on the candidates; voting is by ballot; if one candidate appears to have a substantial majority, the chairman then asks, 'Will you accept him, or shall the question go back to the branches?' If there is not unanimity in the conference, the question is returned to the branches where the ordinary members vote; this happened in only four cases in the Cape before the 1953 election.

Not surprisingly, most sitting members received re-nomination in 1953, but this was not invariable. Four failed to do so in the Cape; 2 in the Free State; and 2 in the Transvaal. In all except one case the decision was made in open contests; in the one instance, which was in the Cape, the sitting member was rejected by the conference because he had no branch support.

Divisional committees also (as the Transvaal Constitution puts it) 'do everything in their power to win elections for the Party and to assist Party candidates in every possible way'. As the campaign approaches, they turn themselves into election committees concerned with everything necessary for the success of their party. Head Office provides them with an organizer, propaganda, circulars and information, while their responsibility is to organize local offices and the 'leg work' of canvassing through group leaders and appropriate volunteers. The Nationalists make a great deal of effort to secure the right person for *huisbesoek* (house visits), e.g. sending railwaymen to call on railwaymen, and organizing a suitably graduated succession of visits which may lead up to a personal call from the organizer and ultimately the candidate. Such strategy is worked out together by the organizer, the chairman of the divisional committee and the candidate; and perhaps because of the tradition of discipline, as well as great party fervor, there seems little of the tension between these three which sometimes affects the holders of those positions among their political opponents.

In areas where there are recognized groupings of urban constituencies, advisory councils (*Beherende Raad*) coordinate activities, and discuss common problems. For the Witwatersrand there is a Rand Controlling Council; the eight Pretoria constituencies are under the Pretoria Council. The Cape Peninsula similarly has a council of its own. These committees meet once in three months, and may formulate suggestions to put before the Executive or Steering Committee. They do not have the same kind of status, however, as the branch, constituency, or Executive Committees, or of their 'opposite numbers' in the United Party.

Finally is the provincial level, the real center of power and organization. Here the supreme executive body is the Executive Committee, composed in the Transvaal of 1 member from each constituency which has a Nationalist organization. In the Cape, election is by geographical areas consisting of 4-5 constituencies, each area electing 2 members, 1 man and 1 woman, plus 6 at large selected by the Provincial Congress since the party came into power; 5 co-opted by the Executive Committee itself; the Cabinet Ministers from the Cape *ex officio*; and the Leader and Secretary of the provincial party. A significant indication of the participation of parliamentary representatives in local party affairs is that 10 M.P.s and 8 M.P.C.s (Member of the Provincial Council) were on the Transvaal Executive Committee in 1952, and that virtually all the Cape Executive Committee members, except the women, were M.P.s. Because the Executive Committee is so large, however, it meets only occasionally. The actual control of provincial affairs lies in the hands, therefore, of the Steering Committee.

The Steering Committee, in fact, provides the continuous direction and control of party organization which is so essential for smooth functioning. Eight of its 14 members are chosen in the Transvaal because of the offices they hold, and include the provincial leader, long J. G. Strijdom, the party leader in the Provincial Council, and the chairman of the Youth Movement; the other 6 are appointed for personal reasons or to represent particular interests. They meet monthly to direct party organization and to check the expenditure of money; they may also appoint and dismiss party officials, and administer party discipline. The Steering Committee passes on the eligibility of candidates for nomination to public office; it also can cancel the membership of an individual or repudiate a branch without giving any reasons. It was the Steering Committee's decision, for example, that Pirow should not have published his booklets on the New Order before submitting them to the Party Congress.

In the Cape, the Steering Committee is organized on a more informal basis, and consists normally of those members of the Executive Committee available for decisions at a given time. For practical details like buying furniture, cars, etc., there is a sub-committee of the Executive Committee called simply the Office Committee. This has its own funds and operates independently in its own sphere in conjunction with the Secretary. During the 1953 election, when quick decisions were necessary, the Office Committee or even its chairman, Mr. D. H. van Gend, together with the secretary and 3 to 4 others living in the vicinity of Cape Town usually formed the Steering Committee.

In every province except the Transvaal there is a chairman of the provincial organization as well as a leader. This used to be the case in the Transvaal also, but in 1943 the Transvaal chairman, the Rev. C. W. M. du Toit, went over to Pirow's New Order, and since his resignation, the leader in the Transvaal has also acted as chairman. At the Congress, however, Dr. H. F. Verwoerd, Minister of Native Affairs, often acted as chairman.

Little mention has been made of the provincial leader, but he wields great authority, in practice, because of his focal position in the Steering Committee, with Head Office, and by commanding the personal allegiance of party members. This has been particularly true in regard to J. G. Strijdom in the Transvaal, and Dr. Malan in the Cape. The former stood alone in the Transvaal for so long that his fervent followers invested him with a special aura. Dr. Malan had vast prestige as the leader of the party in the Cape until 1953. Annual re-elections of the leader in the different provinces have done nothing to shake their continuity of office, but provide enthusiastically received opportunities to affirm the strength of their followers' allegiance.

Somewhat different is the process of choosing a national leader. When Dr. Malan announced his intention, late in 1954, of resigning as National Party leader, there was still doubt as to whether his successor would be the man of his own choice, N. C. Havenga, or whether the leadership would pass at once to 'the Lion of the North', the obvious leader in the long run, J. G. Strijdom. As far as can be determined, the issue was first thrashed out in the Cabinet with the two contestants tactfully absent. The formal decision to select Mr. Strijdom was made in party caucus meeting in Pretoria. Only much later could the selection be confirmed by Party Congresses which had already had their annual meetings. This reinforces the view that the decision on supreme party leadership is looked on as the prerogative of the parliamentary caucus, as is natural, and that its approval by provincial Congresses is a matter of form. In 1958 Dr. H. F. Verwoerd was selected leader by majority caucus vote.

At the same time, the apex of mass participation in party affairs, and, theoretically, the supreme authority, is the provincial Congress. In the Cape, only the divisional councils are represented at the Congress making a body of about 250 members. In the Transvaal, however, every branch has the right to send one or more delegates, and somewhere between 1,000 and 1,200 attend

At a typical Transvaal congress, like that at the City Hall, Pretoria, September 1952, most of the delegates were ordinary branch members, though Dr. Verwoerd had been chosen representative of the Parktown branch, evidence of the desire to keep close touch between Cabinet Ministers and local organization. The *platteland* was heavily represented among the delegates, thin-faced, rangy, and rather tense small farmers being much more in evidence than the better dressed, heavier city people. There were many more men than women; most of the latter were middle-aged and rather worn.

The atmosphere was relaxed and friendly, with a marked sense of general participation, and an easy give-and-take between the platform and the delegates. *Die Stem van Suid-Afrika* was only the first of several songs which everyone sang lustily. Members of Parliament and provincial councillors were called to the platform, and were cheered as they went; there were 40 or 50 of them on the platform by the time all had gathered, the Cabinet Ministers in the front row with Dr. Malan sitting impassively on the chairman's right. A long prayer produced no signs of restlessness. When the meeting got down to business with Strijdom's keynote speech, there were shouts and questions from the floor, which he answered easily and humorously. Yet at all times, there was great attentiveness. Though the hall was relatively bare, except for Nationalist slogans calling for the sovereignty of Parliament, the *baasskap* of the white man, and victory for the party of the workers and farmers, the intensity of party fervor was far greater than that at an American rally, or indeed, at the gatherings of the United Party.

It is commonly said by Nationalist leaders that the provincial congresses produce the big ideas which dominate the party's program. Apartheid, the separate voting roll for the Coloured, and the Transvaal Education Ordinance, have all been voted over and over again by Provincial Congresses. In this sense, they do express the *volkswil* to which any party leader must be sensitive. Yet taken in the whole context of party organization, the provincial Congress seems to be less the supreme authority it is often termed, than a useful sounding board for party leaders, and a necessary outlet for party members. The Afrikaner, especially of the *platteland*, still cherishes his concept of radical, direct democracy. The formal resolutions of Congress, and annual elections of party officers at every level provide a sense of authority, as well as participation by the general party membership. But it is equally true that the all too common divisions within Afrikanerdom in the past, including those that dogged the party between 1939 and 1943, have taught Nationalist Afrikaners that they can be politically successful only by subordinating individual sentiments to a unified party leadership.

Much the same interaction which occurs in the parliamentary party between radical *platteland* members and the small decision-making group of leaders is duplicated within the party organization. The provincial Congress allows for spontaneous expression of the ideas of the rank and file; party leaders implement them only to the degree, and at the time that it appears advisable in the context of the whole political picture. When it was decided, for example, that no further attempt was to be made to remove the Native representatives from Parliament, party Congresses were not consulted. Equally, however, the Transvaal party leadership was immensely strengthened in pressing the Education Ordinance in the provincial council (once the party gained control there) by the frequency with which the Congress had already called for such a measure. Thus the cohesion and strength of a highly disciplined organization receives the additional power of being associated, particularly in the minds of its supporters, with the expressed will of the *volk*.

Its Parliamentary Party

The Nationalist parliamentary party displays the same curious combination of great outspokenness by individual members, and conformity to the decisions of its leaders, which also marks the extra-parliamentary party organization. Caucus (the meeting of the whole parliamentary party) held regularly on Tuesdays during the session, has free and often lengthy debate but well under the control of the whips. In 1953, the presiding office in caucus was its eldest member, but this is not invariable; a sound knowledge of parliamentary procedure is the essential qualification. Whips speak to caucus on impending legislation and tactics on behalf of the party leaders, and consult with the latter at length prior to the meetings. The main purpose of the discussions in the Nationalist caucus is not, of course, to change the Cabinet's decisions, but to inform ordinary party members of Cabinet considerations and strategy and to give them a chance to bring out any points which the latter might have overlooked, such as the effects of certain provisions in proposed legislation.

Where the individual members have freer rein is in the groups into which the parliamentary members divide spontaneously according to their interests: industry, labor, Native affairs, railways, agriculture, and even more limited groups like dairy farmers. These meet at least once, and sometimes as often as three times a week during the session, without either the Minister or a whip commonly present. When a group formulates a policy, or has a question to raise, it sends a delegation to the appropriate Minister, or may ask him to meet with them. If they disagree, one or the other must give in and it is rarely the Minister. Technically a disagreement might be taken to caucus, but this hardly ever happens. Unlike the United Party, the Nationalist parliamentary members did not meet daily as a group when in Opposition, but functioned then, as when their party is in power, through the groups.

The Nationalists have 5 whips, 1 from each province and a fifth from South West Africa, who are elected by caucus for the life of each Parliament. They are always chosen again as whips if their work has been satisfactory, and thus generally serve so long as they are re-elected to Parliament. The whips themselves select a Chief Whip, who had long been J. J. Serfontein[6] of the Free State, a shrewd and unsparing debater who speaks more frequently, though often more briefly, than almost any other Nationalist. The whips meet with the Leader of the House (formerly N. C. Havenga) at least once a week, normally on Friday at noon, to discuss the order of business for the succeeding week.

Nationalist whips are proverbially strict with their members. When the party came into office in 1948, its margins were small, and members were kept constantly on the alert to prevent a reverse through a hastily called vote. Even when their majority increased so greatly, however, the whips remained well in control of attendance. To some extent, this is easier than in the United Party, because fewer Nationalists have important outside demands on their time. It is also a natural result of the general framework of discipline within which the Nationalists work. It is said that, if a bill conflicts with individual sentiment or constituency interest, the whip occasionally excuses a member from voting for the party as long as due notice is given, but both the records and general attitudes suggest that this would be very unusual indeed. The Afrikaans equivalent for the British 'brute vote' is *stemvee* (voting stock or voting cattle), and one sometimes hears members say wearily. 'Here go the *stemvee*.'

The need to apply formal measures of discipline in the Nationalist parliamentary party is rare, both because of the strong sense of basic common purpose infusing all the members even when they differ over details, and because cohesion is accepted as the price of power. If an M.P. transgresses, he is rebuked publicly in caucus by the party leader. For the most serious of offenses, there is expulsion from the caucus, which is considered tantamount to expulsion from the party. The Nationalists cite only one case of such an expulsion, that of Mr. Maartens of Wakkerstroom in 1937, who preached that the Government should underwrite farmers' mortgages. When he ignored warnings to desist, he was expelled from caucus and subsequently disowned by his constituency. In the unlikely event of a constituency insisting on renominating such a person, the National Party is prepared to outlaw the constituency organization, but, with justification, they cannot believe in such a possibility.

One question arising out of the close-knit unity and strict discipline of the Nationalist caucus concerns the possibility, which Dr. Malan used to stress so much, that English-speaking South Africans might join the Nationalists in increasing numbers in the future. At the moment, English-speaking Nationalists are so rare that they are treated with the utmost consideration. So far it is only on their own terms, however, that the Nationalists are prepared to accept any new recruits. Only if they noticeably broaden their rather limited loyalties, or the English-speaking restrict theirs, may the National Party begin to deserve its name.

Its Youth and Women's Organizations

One of the major successes of the National Party is its ability to capture the imagination of young people, and use their services. Every large rally or meeting has its youth guard. Highly significant is the fact that out of the youth groups come most organizers, many of the recruits to branches (as high a proportion as 50 per cent in the Cape), and a number of provincial and parliamentary representatives. In the Transvaal, for example, 5 of those who helped to found the *Nasionale Jeugbond* were in the Provincial Council in 1952; in the

1953 elections, 5 former *Jeugbond* leaders stood for Parliament, and all were elected.

The *Nasionale Jeugbond,* founded in 1938, is closely integrated with the parent political organization. Dr. Malan was official head of the youth organization as well as Leader of the Party, and this personal union at the top finds an echo in the representation of parent and youth groups on each others' committees. The chairman of the *Jeugbond* Executive Committee is always a member of the provincial Executive Committee; more significant, 2 members of the parent organization are permanently on the *Jeugbond* Executive, and the Provincial Secretary generally attends all important meetings. As one prominent Nationalist said, 'we take no nonsense from them.' Far from this supervision being resented, it seems to be welcomed by the *Jeugbond.* It is even said that representatives from the Transvaal parent body have been asked to take a more active share in *Jeugbond* affairs. This contrasts with the more independent attitudes, if less effective work, of the United Party youth groups.

The *Nasionale Jeugbond,* in fact, is both a means of recruiting the services of young people, and of training them. They can become members at 16 in the Transvaal, or 17 in the Cape. Though they can join the parent organization at 21, they often retain membership in both groups until 30 or, in exceptional cases, 35. In the *Jeugbond* they not only have special responsibilities, as, for example, at political rallies, but also carry on propaganda among their own age group. Some university branches of the *Jeugbond* have study groups. Since the highly political *Ossewa Brandwag* youth groups have disbanded, the *Afrikaner Studentebond* has carefully avoided politics. Thus, such political activity as is carried on in Afrikaner universities is through the *Jeugbond.* In the Cape, but not in other provinces, the *Jeugbond* organizes a practice parliamentary election every year.

The pressures to conformity of the close-knit, homogeneous, Afrikaner community help to make Nationalist young people amenable to party discipline, but the fact that they are treated as being more important than are United Party youth groups is also significant. Part of the secret of the Nationalist appeal to youth are the very demands placed on them for disciplined action and responsible behavior. Moreover, the clarity of the Nationalist program of Afrikaner leadership and white supremacy has a sense of immediacy to them which stimulates their idealism and sense of mission. It is perhaps hardly surprising, therefore, that the National Party is attracting more young people than its political opponents.

With women, on the other hand, the National Party has been less successful than the United Party. Though they do a great deal of routine work within the the party, women seldom play the kind of active role there that they do in its rival. While two women stood as Nationalist candidates in 1953, the first to sit in Parliament was Mrs. Koster, appointed to the Senate in 1956. Fundamentally, as a Transvaal Nationalist confessed: 'We old Boers like to keep our women at home, and quiet.' The whole practice of Afrikaner life is against women speaking in a public gathering with men, although their efficiency and drive shows itself in every aspect of life.

A reflection of this apparent paradox is that women have proved less effective in party organization since their separate organization, the *Vroue Nasionale Partie,* was disbanded after women received the vote in 1930. Interestingly enough, the V.N.P. was not an active promoter of female suffrage until shortly before Hertzog introduced the necessary legislation, though at that time the flood of telegrams it organized helped to get the bill through. Its most important function before 1930 had been in raising money, and it was largely because of its effectiveness in this regard that the men proposed mixed branches in 1930, instead of retaining the separate ones. In practice, however, the women have been less effective in fund-raising since the merger, and also have participated relatively little in branch discussions. So much is this the case that some separate women's branches have been started again, though the practice is not general.

Though no Nationalist woman has yet achieved a political office and influence comparable to that of Mrs. Bertha Solomon of the United Party (who has been the spokesman in Parliament for Nationalist as well as United Party women seeking the legislation to remove their legal disabilities, which was finally passed in 1953), women are quite heavily represented on National Party committees under the regulations in force. As already mentioned, one of the two representatives from the Cape areas to the Executive Committee must be a woman; the Transvaal, though no other province, always sends two women to the Federal Council. More women were nominated by the Nationalists in the 1953 election than ever before. The trend, therefore, seems in the direction of giving increasing opportunities to Nationalist women in public life.

Its Professional Organizers

Local leadership and efficient organization play decisive roles in the success of any political party. The Nationalists have evolved a peculiarly effective interaction between the annually elected group leaders and committee members on the one hand, and an ardent young group of professional organizers on the other. The organizer, operating under provincial Head Office, and coordinating the work of three or four constituencies, is a major factor in the efficiency and activity of his area.

It might seem that annual elections of group leaders and committee members would undercut the effectiveness of party organization even though there is a considerable amount of continuity in practice. Nationalists believe that, on the contrary, it keeps them alert, responsible and hard working, a reflection of the prestige attached to office holding. A further advantage is that frequent elections avoid problems which might otherwise arise when the pre-electoral delimitations of constituency boundaries make it necessary to regroup branches, or to change divisional lines.

In any case, the professional organizer provides constant supervision and stimulus to the voluntary organization and office holders. Recruited for the most part from young university graduates, they operate in most constituencies where the Nationalists have a strong organization, or a chance of building one. In the Transvaal, organizers are sometimes appointed only for a year and a half or two years before elections; in the Cape, they are usually constantly at work. They have conferences every two months with the branch committees, advising on organization, and canvassing techniques. Part of their responsibility in the Cape is to prepare monthly reports for the Provincial Secretary, which he presents quarterly to the Provincial Executive. Under the direct control of the Assistant Provincial Secretary, the 40 Cape organizers work constantly with city, provincial and, above all, parliamentary elections in mind. Particularly at election time, their services go far beyond what could be expected in an ordinary job, as they act in every way to supplement the efforts of the candidate. In general, they are concentrated at that period on the doubtful seats, or else those of particularly busy Cabinet Ministers.

The particular importance of party officers and officials is reflected in the special declaration which they, and also any officially nominated candidate, must make on accepting their office:

> I hereby declare solemnly and sincerely that I recognize the sovereignty and guidance of God in the destiny of countries and nations.
>
> That in a spirit of brotherhood with my Party members I shall seek the development of South Africa's national life along Christian-national lines.
>
> That with undivided loyalty I shall maintain the expressed principles of the National Party as the political National Front of the South African nation.
>
> That of my own volition I pledge myself to show undivided loyalty to my Party and to carry out faithfully the obligations attaching to membership of the Party.
>
> That I am not a member of any other political Party or political organization.
>
> That I shall submit myself to the Party's organization in accordance with the Constitution.
>
> May God help me in this my pledge to help towards the achievement of South Africa's national goal of Unity, Freedom and Justice.[7]

One key to the enthusiasm and hard work of the paid organizers is that, unlike the United Party, the Nationalists look on such experience as a stepping-stone to better administrative positions, and subsequently to provincial and parliamentary office. P. W. Botha, for example, now Secretary of the Cape National Party, worked up through the ranks of the organizers, being first responsible for a limited area, then for a 'circle' comprising 6 to 8 constituencies, and subsequently Assistant Secretary. In 1948, he was elected M.P. for George, an office combined with his party work as Secretary. Some 10 Nationalist M.P.s elected in 1953 had been party organizers previously. Senator M. P. A. Malan and Marais Viljoen, who comprise the paid information and propaganda staff of the Federal Council, are now both in Parliament, Viljoen being elected for the safe seat of Alberton, Transvaal, in 1953. This kind of reward for active party work obviously stimulates the efforts of the organizers: it also creates an interesting and, in a sense disturbing, relationship between paid political officials and parliamentary representatives.

Its Provincial Roots

Each of the provinces drafts its own Constitution and, to a degree, has its own form of organization. Some of the major differences have already been indicated. On the whole, however, they are not of sufficient importance to be described in detail. What is important to remember is the distinctive features of the different provinces.

The party is weakest in predominantly English-speaking Natal, which has a substantial proportion of Afrikaners only in its northwest section around Dundee, Newcastle, Vryheid and Ladysmith, where they have been attracted partly by the coal mines. Thus, until shortly before the 1953 election, Nationalist organization in that province was in a very rudimentary state except for those areas. Active party work, coupled with the decision to run candidates in every constituency, had sufficiently encouraging results (the party polled 26,000 votes in 1953 as compared to 14,000 in 1948), however, to persuade the party to move the Head Office from Dundee to Natal's chief city, Durban.

Nationalists feel that their greatest difficulty in Natal in 1953 was the lack of a local Afrikaans newspaper to compete with the province's three English-language papers. Moreover, as long as their membership is so spread out, it is almost impossible to work the group system of organization in Natal. As the number of branches increases (only 3 in Durban in 1948, but 29 by 1953, 17 in Newcastle and 20 in Vryheid), the provincial leadership plans to introduce the smaller units. Nonetheless, though they can capitalize on strong anti-Indian feelings, Nationalists will inevitably find that Natal remains the most difficult area in South Africa on which to make an impression because of its pro-Commonwealth and distinctive local traditions and sentiments.

The Free State, with its long Nationalist tradition, represents the antithesis of Natal. If party organization is sometimes less active in the O.F.S. than the Transvaal, or even the Cape, it is because no other party can hope to make inroads there. The Free State returned only Nationalists in 1953, when even the United Party provincial leader, Colin Steyn, was defeated.[8]

South West Africa, with its great space and small population, is less dominantly Nationalist in votes than is the Free State, but all its M.P.s are Nationalist. It has a much shorter history of organization and activity than the Union's provinces, for no members were elected from that area before 1951.

The most interesting contrasts are provided by the Cape and the Transvaal. The Cape is quieter, steadier, proud of its long and substantial support for Dr. Malan, and somewhat supercilious about the ardor of the Transvaal. Its organization is more hierarchical, and does not include the direct representation of branches in the Provincial Congress. The Cape also has a stronger and more constant system of paid organizers than the Transvaal and operates at a high level of efficiency. The Transvaal is the area, however, where the Nationalists are making their most spectacular advances, particularly in the mining towns along the Rand. What it may lack in consistency is more than made up by intensity. *Die Transvaler* is a less admirable newspaper than *Die Burger*, but considerably more effective as a party and propaganda organ. Something of the same comparison holds for the party activities of the two provinces. The Cape may well continue to provide basic party stability, but the Transvaal makes the more spectacular advances.

Normally, the provinces function quite separately from one another. Occasionally, however, there is joint effort in a particular situation which is seen to be of special significance to the party as a whole. One such occasion was the Wakkerstroom by-election prior to the general election of 1948. As it was regarded as a key opportunity to demonstrate the strength of the party, other provinces sent organizers and financial aid to Wakkerstroom to a degree which made the Nationalist victory there the result of joint effort. Similarly, during the second Wakkerstroom by-election in 1952, again regarded as a trial of strength because of the Torch Commando intervention, Strijdom appealed through the Nationalist press to other provinces for funds.

The greatest amount of aid from one province to another was by the Orange Free State to the Natal organization during the 1953 election. No party workers were sent from the Orange Free State, but those Natal constituencies without a substantial Nationalist organization—in practice, most constituencies—were carried financially by constituencies of the other province, a major factor in stimulating a province-wide Nationalist organization in Natal.

Its National Organization

The only national organ in the National Party is the Federal Council, which, on the surface, appears to have hardly even a coordinating role. Its Constitution begins by stating that the federation exists 'to serve the principles and common interests' of the party in the four provinces and South West Africa, and ends by affirming the principle of 'absolute independence' and 'separate existence' of the provincial organizations. The 'domestic rules' of the Federal Council must not violate either its own constitution, or that of any of the provinces. Also no alteration may be made in the constitution of the Federal Council without confirmation of all the five provincial congresses.

Nor do most of its functions sound impressive. The Federal Council is to take 'the necessary steps' to keep the provincial organizations in touch with one another, keep close touch with the party's parliamentary representatives, forward proposals to the provincial organizations for their consideration, and itself report back annually to the Provincial Congresses. True, section 6 (c) states that the Federal Council shall 'consider all matters of national importance', while two subsequent points vest it with responsibility for political propaganda, and relations with the press. Finally, the Federal Council has the power to convene 'in consultation with Provincial Head Committees', union congresses to consider 'special matters of party concern' or 'national importance'. These union congresses, however, are specifically said to 'function only in an advisory capacity'. In 1938, a union congress considered the problem of Communism; in 1939, the relationship with Hertzog. None have met, however, since those of 1941 and 1942 wrestled with the problems of Afrikaner political unity, and the party's attitude to the war effort.

The Federal Council has no permanent staff except Senator M. P. A. Malan, chief of information for the party, who also acts as the Council's secretary, and Marais Viljoen, also an information officer. There is an office in Bloemfontein, started in 1951, which sends out propaganda and press material. Only in the exceptional case of Natal has the Council concerned itself with party organization and then only until that province began to develop an active organization of its own.

It is the membership of the Federal Council, rather than any specific functions, which provides its importance. It consists of 37 members, 7 nominated by each of the 5 Provincial Congresses, 1 appointed by the Federal Council of the National Youth Movement (in practice, always its chairman), *ex officio*, and the Leader of the Parliamentary caucus, Mr. Strijdom (formerly Dr. Malan). The other provincial leaders are always on the Council and, in addition, 5 or 6 M.P.s. Thus the Federal Council includes an impressive array of parliamentarians, as well as provincial leaders.

Because of its size, the Federal Council usually meets as a whole only a few times a year (it must meet at least once) at which time it takes formal decisions on important issues. Its general operations are carried on through two committees. One is on information, under the chairmanship of Mr. F. C. Erasmus, which concerns itself with issuing pamphlets, propaganda, and *Die Kruithoring*, the one newspaper owned officially by the party. The other is the Steering Committee (*Dagbestuur*), consisting of the four provincial leaders. Here is the real center of power in the Nationalist organization.

The Steering Committee of the Federal Council meets at need, usually monthly, but more or less as often as circumstances direct. Among its official responsibilities, it draws up the general manifesto for the general election, which is then laid before the Federal Council as a whole for approval. Similarly, it draws up the party statement of principles, as, for example, at the time of the fusion of the National and Afrikaner Parties. The principles must be approved by the Provincial Congresses, as indicated, but this is generally automatic. Equally, electoral arrangements with the Afrikaner Party were presented to the provinces as recommendations, and similarly accepted.

The reason why provincial approval of Federal Council proposals is commonly only a matter of form is, of course, because the provincial leaders have already assumed the responsibility. This fact rather than any constitutional provision is what makes the Federal Council's Steering Committee of such vast importance. It can consider any matter of significance to the party. In a real sense, this Steering Committee of provincial and national leaders provides the personal union which turns National Party federalism into centralization.

In some parties, the relation between the party executive and the parliamentary party provides complications. This is not so in the National Party, the more so because here again a personal union exists. The four key members of the Cabinet form the Steering Committee of the Federal Council. Moreover, the Council as a whole rarely considers major policy matters, leaving them to the Cabinet. The only exception to this rule was on the question of taking the Coloured off the common roll. The reasons for referring this question to the Federal Council were said to have been that it was a traditional policy, had been discussed by Congress after Congress in every part of the country, and was an emotional issue of great concern to the Afrikaner people. It seems likely also that the party's problems in securing its desired solution of the issue led it to canvass every conceivable source of strategy, and perhaps, also to publicize its difficulties as widely and directly as possible.

Its Finances

Compared to the United Party, the Nationalists have almost no large sources of financial support. They depend heavily on the fund-raising efforts, and subscriptions of their members. This may well be a source of strength rather than weakness, however, for it increases the sense of personal participation which is one of the party's greatest assets.

The largest source of Nationalist funds are from *stryddaë*, the collection of campaign or, more literally, 'fighting funds'. These are often the result of six weeks or two months of intensive effort in the constituencies. Teas and sales of work bring some money, but most of it is collected at party demonstrations announced well ahead and signalized with speeches by party leaders. In 1951, Transvaal *stryddaë* collected £34,105 according to *Die Kruithoring*. Poor constituencies, of course, can raise only limited amounts, and, for large and relatively well-to-do ones, £1,000 was considered a very high amount for a Transvaal constituency to raise before 1948. In 1952, however, Strijdom's constituency, under his wife's direction, raised the very large sum of £7,400 ($20,720).

Subscriptions form the second largest source of income. In the Transvaal, annual subscription fees amounted to 1/- (15 cents) a member before 1948; after that election, branches were expected to provide a sum equivalent to 6d. for every vote cast for a Nationalist candidate. In the Cape, subscriptions run between 1/6 and 2/6 a year. With 120,000 paid-up members, this amounts to between £7,000 and £8,000 ($19,600-$22,400). All this money, like that from the *stryddaë*, goes to Head Office, the divisional committees being responsible for seeing that it is transmitted.

There are, of course, individual gifts to the party. Nationalist canvassers often ask those they visit to make a contribution to party funds, less to secure money, however, than accurate information about the reliability of their support. Firms, as such, are not allowed to contribute, nor is money accepted with conditions attached. Party leaders say this practice dates back to the unhappy experience of 1933, when interests which had contributed largely to the National Party at an earlier date through Tielman Roos, used their influence to persuade most of the Transvaal group to go into coalition with Smuts. Afrikaner trade unions also do not contribute in a group capacity.

Several funds from which the National Party draws income came into the headlines at the time the Nationalists were attacking the United South Africa Trust Fund, and its support of the United Party. The Federal Council receives £6,000-£7,000 a year (which it devotes to publicity and propaganda work) from a bequest in the estate of Judge Beyers, a member of the first Nationalist Government under Hertzog, who left it to the original National Party. In 1940, when Hertzog and Malan were considering the merger of their two parties, Malan argued against a national unitary organization on the ground that it might jeopardize the Beyers bequest[9] and this apparently continues to be a reason for maintaining the federal form in the party. (Another reason may be that it makes easier the relationship with South West Africa.) Part of the Beyers fund was used, before 1948, to aid the Transvaal organization, and subsequently Natal; the Cape National Party gets £450 a year from the same source. Another much smaller source of income is about £700 a year from the Jannie Marais Fund, the grant being made annually by its trustees to the National Party, as one of several beneficiaries.[10]

More substantial than the Beyers Fund are the Victory Funds collected by the provinces after the 1948, and again after the 1953 elections. After the 1948 election, the Victory Fund amounted to between £27,000-£28,000 in the Cape alone. The Cape also has the D. F. Malan Fund, raised by popular subscriptions particularly from the *platteland* after a wealthy farmer named Nigrini opened it with £4,500, given on condition that the membership raised £100,000 within a year. In 1952, the £100,000 (£75,000 in cash and the rest on paper) was presented to Dr. Malan on his birthday. The interest from this fund is used to finance the Cape office and newspaper.

In general, party units are expected to be self-supporting. Constituencies are only helped by the provinces in exceptional cases, and not consistently. The provinces, in turn, raise their own funds, and meet their own expenses. The Cape budget runs about £20,000 a year; the Transvaal £36,000. The Federal Council helped the latter province before 1948, but it now raises all its own money. Natal is struggling to be self-sufficient, though it still has not enough money to fight elections in constituencies with small Afrikaner populations. The Federal Council finances itself without contributions from the provinces. The general principle holds that aid is extended only for particular purposes which help the general cause of the party.

Nationalists often say that their limited budgets are a handicap. Yet in moments of need, they seem able to tap sufficient resources to carry them through. The stimulus of annual fund raising, and the heavy emphasis on personal contributions make a link between the party and its individual members which should not be underestimated. The longer the party remains in power, the more likely that wealthy individuals from commerce and industry will contribute to it. It is far from certain, however, that this trend, like the marked one towards professionalization of personnel, may not do the party more harm in the long run than good.

Its Strength and Weakness

What kind of people form the backbone of the National Party? What kind of national and provincial leaders do they follow? How much of the striking success of the party can be attributed to such personal factors as compared to those of organization, efficiency, and discipline?

Above all else, the party is an Afrikaner one. Highly illuminating is to compare a language map of the Union with one which plots the political advances of the National Party. Nothing illustrates more accurately the degree to which the Nationalists have become the political standard bearer of the Afrikaner people. This is not to overlook the fact that the United Party still has the support of some 15 per cent of Afrikaners, even in the Orange Free State. But this support now rarely matches that which the Nationalists are able to attract in any given area.

Though the Nationalists insist that they are beginning to attract some English-speaking support, it is still sparse. The more realistic among them say that it may take a hundred years before English South Africans are fully convinced that their political destiny lies with nationalistic Afrikanerdom. That the English-speaking are welcomed, at least theoretically, is sure, but it is to incorporation in a party with a strong sense of its own identity, purposes, and destiny.

English South Africans are severely criticized by Nationalists for their inadequacy in Afrikaans, and it is true that many of them are far less bilingual than are Afrikaners. Afrikaans is the language of the National Party, however, to a far greater extent than English can be said to be the language of the United Party. In 1953, only the Natal branch of the party had its Constitution even translated into English; the others present only the statement of principles in both languages. Hardly a word of English is heard in a National Party Congress, or branch meeting. Moreover, the atmosphere is of a 'family', reflecting Afrikaner ways of the more traditional type. The jokes are difficult to translate into English. It is almost as if the party reflects a way of life.

Among Afrikaners, the party has two great sources of strength: the *dorps*, or villages, which are scattered throughout the *platteland*, and form the nucleus for farm areas; and the urban workers in the mines, industry and commerce. In the *dorps*, Afrikaner nationalism is spread by the most influential people in the community: the *predikant* of the local Dutch Reformed Church, the school teachers, and the school and church committees. Feeling often runs so high in a school that a child whose parents are known to vote United Party may quite literally be fighting constant battles with his Nationalist school-mates, and even victimized by his teachers. Important church offices are denied to United Party supporters. The local hotel keeper may keep his political ideas to himself lest he alienate his preponderantly Nationalist customers. Boycotts of shops owned by United Party supporters are not uncommon in some parts of the Transvaal, and Cape, not to mention the Orange Free State. Every kind of pressure to conformity is used, and often ruthlessly.

In the cities, another kind of pressure operates. Nearly always it has been economic necessity which forced the Afrikaner off the land he loves so well. In the cities, he still finds business and industry predominantly in the hands of English South African or Jewish interests. This helps to counteract the natural tendency of urban life towards a more cosmopolitan attitude, and forces the Afrikaner back amongst his own group. Most of the positions he occupies are in the lower-income level judged by European standards, and he lives in the less wealthy suburbs towards the outskirts of the cities. Here he finds himself perforce near to the Native townships, as he finds himself working close to non-Europeans in the mines, and industry. Often the job he does is not very different from theirs, though his wage scales are much higher. Thus the Afrikaner urban worker is constantly aware of the potential pressure of non-European competition. Also while the wealthier United Party supporter may think of the Bantu only in terms of his own Native servants, the Afrikaner worker still sees them in the mass in adjacent living centers like Sophiatown in Johannesburg, even though the Western Areas Removal Scheme is well under way. [p. 91.]

Small wonder, therefore, that rigidly enforced apartheid appeals to the urban Afrikaner. The kind of segregation traditional in South African life may have served in the past, but the more clear-cut, obvious segregation of the Nationalist program offers the Afrikaner worker not only a more substantial guarantee that his job and his living centers will be protected against the increasing pressures of the urban African, but also that he is regarded as being a different kind of person. Thus, economic security, and an intense sense of racial identity, underlie the Nationalist appeal.

One further point. The Afrikaner who comes from the *platteland* is apt to be rootless and insecure. All the community-building agencies of Afrikaner life help to reincorporate him in Afrikanerdom: the Church with its reinforcement of his sense of separate identity, and destiny, and the practical aid of its welfare program; the Afrikaans-medium school with its strong nationalistic emphasis;

the National Party, which offers him a means of working for the conditions which will protect him. The strength of Afrikanerdom is that every agency within it operates towards the same end.

What kind of men have overcome the separatist tendencies of the Afrikaner people, and welded them into the remarkably cohesive National Party? Foremost among them was Dr. Malan himself, whose prestige went far beyond that of any other single person in the party. His decisiveness, arising out of a deep inner conviction of rightness, was coupled with great dignity and superb oratory. He was unmatched within the party in his ability, even in his late seventies, to make speeches whose majestic ponderousness held his audience in rapt attention for well over two hours. No provincial 'revolt' was ever able to resist his words and presence. Moreover, the party's many distinct personalities owed a personal allegiance to Dr. Malan dating back to the days when the party took form. Thus, his successor, J. G. Strijdom, was the only Nationalist M.P. in the Transvaal to follow Dr. Malan in 1933, while Dr. Dönges, now leader in the Cape, was editor of the party paper.

Serious as he usually appeared in public, Dr. Malan had an easy manner, and a quiet sense of humor in personal contacts. A good chairman, who knew well how to balance conflicting elements, and make them work together, he was, above all, a leader, sure of his judgments, and willing to take responsibility for them. In his inflexibility, dogmatism, and consistency, he provided the rock on which the party was built.

No other man has the same kind of national following in the party as had Dr. Malan. Dönges, with his facile speech, deft intellect, and rather devious tactics, is a Cape man, chosen by Malan himself as his successor as provincial leader. Strijdom was almost his antithesis, sincere, blunt, a radical nationalist who was shrewd enough to choose strategic times for action, but far too determined to be swerved from his goals. Swart, the Free State leader and Minister of Justice, is less impressive than Strijdom, with whom he worked closely, and more vindictive, as his actions towards Hertzog prove. Swart is a man to use a hammer rather than a thrust.

The most brilliant, stubborn and uncompromising of top Nationalist figures is Dr. H. F. Verwoerd, who was chosen party leader and South Africa's sixth Prime Minister on September 2, 1958, following the death of J. G. Strijdom. Dönges and Swart were also candidates for the supreme party office and it took two ballots before Verwoerd was elected, largely, it seems, by the votes of the enlarged Senate. Thus it was not without opposition that the party placed itself under its most rigorous advocate of racial apartheid.

What all of these men and other party leaders, like Eric Louw and Ben Schoeman, possess is determination, ruthlessness, and the ability to appeal to the mass of the party's following. They know how to use organization to secure their objectives, and yet can convince their followers that they are being taken into account in the formulation of those objectives.

The greatest danger to the party leaders is internal rivalries, and/or too great a sense of power. Underneath the cohesiveness of their following lie potential conflicts which could easily flare up in response to personal struggles for party domination. Nor may political success prove so strong an adhesive in the long run as the struggle to get out of the wilderness.

CHAPTER 9

THE AFRIKANER PARTY

The significance of the Afrikaner Party lies in the fact that between 1941 and 1951 it was the only avowedly political group offering nationalistic Afrikanerdom an alternative to Dr. Malan's National Party. At all times the Afrikaner Party had only two strong points, however, its 'pure' Afrikaner membership, and the financial ability and political shrewdness of 'Klasie' Havenga. Though its career was marked more by expediency than principle, the Afrikaner Party, or more accurately Havenga managed for a while with some adroitness to tone down Nationalist extremism in the areas about which General Hertzog had felt most deeply: English-Afrikaner relations, republicanism, and constitutionalism. Yet it is also true that the merger of the two parties in 1951 meant, in practice, the annihilation of the smaller group.

Like its end, the genesis of the Afrikaner Party was forced by the Nationalists. The first step was C. R. Swart's stinging defeat of Hertzog in the Free State Nationalist Congress on November 6, 1940, which led to the latter's resignation as leader in that province. (See p. 34.) A month later the Transvaal Nationalist Congress not only deliberately ignored Hertzog, who was still nominally the national leader, but voted two amendments to the party program—that a majority in parliament could declare a republic, and that other provinces be asked also to exclude Jews from party membership—which no true Hertzogite could accept. Hertzog and Havenga responded to the political extremism of the two Congresses by resigning their Parliamentary seats on December 12, 1940. Those unwilling to withdraw from active politics had the more difficult dilemma of renouncing their principles or their Nationalist membership. Already following the Transvaal Congress, a Transvaal M.P., Mr. S. C. Quinlan, resigned from the National Party, and organized a forum called *Afrikaner Unie* to uphold Hertzog ideals and policies. Towards the end of December, Hertzog supporters in his old Smithfield constituency began to plan a new party to provide themselves with a political home. On January 30, 1941, General Edwin Conroy announced to the House of Assembly that the Afrikaner Party had been formed in all four provinces.

As its statement of principles, the Afrikaner Party adopted, *en bloc*, those which Hertzog had presented, written in his own hand, to the Free State Congress on November 6.[1] Basic to them was the initial declaration that the Party aimed 'at the development of a powerful sense of South African national unity, based on the equal rights of the Afrikaans-speaking and English-speaking sections of the community, coupled with mutual recognition and appreciation of each other's distinctive cultural heritage'. This, of course, was the principle over which Hertzog and the Free State Nationalists had broken.

On the ticklish issue of republicanism, the program specifically denied the doctrine that Parliament was competent to establish a republic, and reaffirmed

Hertzog's traditional stand that this could result only from 'a special and definite mandate from the European electorate'. It was probably on this point, rather than on Afrikaner-English equality, that the Nationalists felt Hertzog to be a serious impediment to their immediate aims, for Great Britain was still in such serious danger at the end of 1940 that many Nationalists wanted to establish a republic at once which would be able to negotiate peace with a victorious Germany.

For all its brave assertions the Afrikaner Party was weak from the first. Only ten of the twenty-nine M.P.s who followed Hertzog in 1939 aligned themselves with the new party; two of these, including S. C. Quinlan, subsequently went over to the United Party. So, too, did the two Senators who originally supported the Afrikaner Party. In the by-elections for Hertzog's and Havenga's former seats, the Nationalists won crushing victories. The crowning blow came when the Afrikaner Party failed to win a single seat in the 1943 elections, and secured only 14,759 votes for the 24 candidates it put forward. Even in the Orange Free State, on which it counted most, the party polled only 10,769 votes, as compared with 49,459 for the Nationalists.

What is remarkable, in the light of this defeat, is that the Afrikaner Party continued to exist. Yet a recognition that it was not an unimportant group came on November 9, 1943, when Malan, in a general appeal for Afrikaner unity at Stellenbosch, specifically invited the Afrikaner Party to join the Nationalists.[2] For the time being, the invitation was rejected but the move was significant, for it formed a backdrop to the Malan-Havenga negotiations of 1947. These discussions led to the Nationalist-Afrikaner election pact which brought Malan into office in March, 1948.

Why did Malan make overtures to the Afrikaner Party when the Nationalists had been so decisively endorsed in the 1943 election as the political representatives of nationalist Afrikanerdom? Part of the reason was to capitalize on that victory to promote an Afrikaner political unity extending well beyond parliamentary representation. No one knew better than Malan how deeply the Afrikaner *volk* felt the compelling urge towards unity. But he knew, too, that the Nationalist struggle with the Ossewa Brandwag was not yet over. The latter entered no candidates in 1943, but it still commanded much of the fervor which had made it the greatest Afrikaner nationalist organization in half a century. If the rivalry with the Ossewa Brandwag for the basic allegiance of Afrikanerdom meant further strife, then it would be well for the Nationalists to have absorbed the Afrikaner Party.

Nor was it difficult at that time to envisage such a reunion. Malan had accepted his severe electoral defeat at Smuts' hands as a sign that it was no longer any use to fight over foreign affairs. The issue of establishing a republic ceased, therefore, to be of such immediate significance. Politically secure within Nationalist Afrikanerdom, Malan had already begun to consider overtures to moderate Afrikaners and even to the English-speaking. The Hertzog tradition could be useful in this effort. At any rate, it would be dangerous to allow Smuts to capture that advantage by luring more Afrikaner Party members to the United Party.

Arthur Barlow maintains indeed that, between the 1943 and 1948 elections, the Afrikaner Party made tentative, though unaccepted overtures to Smuts through Kalie Rood, the United Party member for Vereeniging, who was to resign after the 1948 election when Smuts rebuked him for an attack on 'the liberals' in the party.[3] But the open signs are that the Afrikaner Party felt that its kinship was with the Nationalists, particularly as the latter seemed to moderate the positions which had forced the old Hertzogites into political exile. Thus at the Wakkerstroom by-election in April, 1944, the Afrikaner Party worked on behalf of the official Nationalist candidate, as in fact, did the Greyshirts, Pirow's New Order and, unofficially, many Ossewa Brandwag members.

As long as the war lasted, the issue of formal political cooperation was not so urgent; by 1947, with the election not far away, the situation changed. Havenga was under pressure to run again for Parliament, from which he had excluded himself since his joint resignation with Hertzog in December, 1940. Malan was looking for as broad a basis of support as possible for the coming election. The initiative which led to their *rapprochement* came from the Nationalist member from George, A. J. Werth, who, shortly before his death, persuaded them to meet at his home on March 21, 1947. In a long morning and afternoon session, Malan and Havenga arrived at the mutual understanding which henceforth governed their relations.

In the official statement issued after their meeting, Malan and Havenga declared that they had found 'no differences in principles or in general policy' to interfere with the 'desired and united cooperation', for 'the rejection of the Smuts-Hofmeyr régime', which, they felt, was 'the foremost national interest of South Africa'. Affirming that each party would retain its own identity, they declared that neither had made demands on the other, and that their future relationship would arise out of their 'partnership' in the national service.[4]

Behind these guarded words lay a significant measure of agreement on color policy. On August 17, Malan said that the National Party-Afrikaner Party agreement was based on 'the urgent call to defend white civilization', and denounced the Smuts government for 'running away' on the color question.[5] There seems little doubt that Malan had transmitted to Havenga much of his own sense of the urgency to take a more radical approach to color problems in order to insulate Europeans and in particular Afrikaners from the pressures caused by the growing influx of non-Europeans to the cities. Apartheid might still be a slogan, but it reflected the Afrikaner's greatest fear: the loss of his identity through the sheer pressure of numbers of the non-Europeans. From the Nationalist point of view, the arrangement between Malan and Havenga should also spell the completed unity of Afrikanerdom. Thus, immediately after the initial agreement, *Die Transvaler* advised the Ossewa Brandwag and New Order to dissolve in the interests of 'national unity', in other words to fade away.[6] But desirable as this was from the side of the Nationalists, neither the Ossewa Brandwag nor the Afrikaner Party was yet ready to give up its separate existence, as the struggle over electoral arrangements was to prove.

Further conversations between Malan and Havenga led to a preliminary electoral agreement, subsequently approved by the Federal Council of the National Party, that seats would be divided into three classes: those which each undertook to yield to the party most likely to win; those where the decision rested solely with the party leaders (i.e., Malan and Havenga); and those where neither party would enter a candidate, and both agreed to vote for any independent likely to support the Nationalist color policy.[7] The cooperation during the election was to continue at least during the next session of Parliament, to extend to by-elections, and to be binding both on the parties, and on individual candidates. This arrangement was formally approved by the Transvaal Nationalist Provincial Congress on September 21, 1947, and also accepted by other Provincial Congresses. The Afrikaner Party Congress at Brakpan similarly approved it on February 5, 1948.[8]

It remained to allocate the seats, and nominate the candidates. The Nationalists began by offering one safe, or 'A' seat, to ensure Havenga's sure return to Parliament; the others were in the 'B' or uncertain category. Havenga, from his side, held out for six relatively safe seats.[9] On February 16, Malan and Havenga agreed that the Afrikaner Party should fight 11 seats, but provincial Executive Committees were to determine which ones.[10] A week later, six Transvaal seats—Roodepoort, Brakpan, Potchefstroom, Lydenburg, Pretoria District, and Bethal-Middelburg (amalgamated under the new delimitation)—were assigned to the Afrikaner Party.[11] These were seats in which the United Party majorities had run between 486 and 2,208 in the 1943 election. Nonetheless, the local organization in Potchefstroom protested the Executive Committee's decision, and pressed for a local candidate.[12] The other seats ultimately assigned to the Afrikaner Party were Ladybrand in the Orange Free State, which Havenga contested, and Vryburg, Vryheid, Uitenhage, and Klip River.

In the meantime, tenseness developed over the Afrikaner Party's decision to adopt certain Ossewa Brandwag members as candidates, despite the fact that the Nationalists had been conducting a long and, at some stages, bitter struggle with the Ossewa Brandwag, long its most powerful competitor for the allegiance of nationalistic Afrikanerdom. The original allocation of functions, signalized in the Craddock Agreement of 1940, had been that the Nationalists should form the political, and the Ossewa Brandwag the cultural front of Afrikanerdom. But the ambitions of the Ossewa Brandwag leader, Dr. J. F. van Rensburg, led the Ossewa Brandwag constantly into the political field, particularly while Nazi victory in Europe appeared possible. Malan's determination to maintain political leadership resulted in a mounting series of counter-attacks. In 1941, National Party members were asked to resign from the Ossewa Brandwag. In January, 1942, the Cape Executive Committee forbade party officials to be Ossewa Brandwag members. In September, 1944, the Transvaal Nationalist Congress declared membership in the Ossewa Brandwag to be incompatible with that of the National Party.[13] Even though the policy was never systematically enforced, there was more than enough feeling against the Ossewa Brandwag to make the Afrikaner Party's action almost a deliberate affront.

From the Afrikaner Party side, however, the decision was understandable. By 1948, some 80 per cent of Afrikaner Party supporters were said to be also members of the Ossewa Brandwag,[14] while van Rensburg was on the Afrikaner Party Executive Committee. When Havenga and Malan were discussing allocation of seats, the Ossewa Brandwag deliberately opened a series of party branches in the Cape to strengthen Havenga's bargaining power. While carefully avoiding direct dealings with the Ossewa Brandwag as a group, the Afrikaner Party not only counted on Ossewa Brandwag members and votes, but also on the lingering remnants of the ardor which had made that organization so strong a force. In return, the Afrikaner Party was more than ready to offer them a political forum. Theoretically, they justified adopting Ossewa Brandwag members as candidates on the broad ground of uniting as many Afrikaners as possible; in fact, they were needed to supplement the relatively small number of eligible candidates the Afrikaner Party could propose, while it was necessary to secure Ossewa Brandwag support if the party was to make a showing in the election.

Not surprisingly, a sharp tussle ensued. As late as March 23, 1948, several Afrikaner Party candidates had not yet been announced. John Forster, an Ossewa Brandwag member who was proposed as candidate for Brakpan, was 'vetoed' by the Nationalists; it was said that the seat would revert to the Nationalists if the Afrikaner Party could not find an acceptable candidate shortly.[15] Malan was also said to have vetoed the candidacy of Louis Botha in Roodepoort, though Botha was a member of the Afrikaner Party Executive Committee as well as of the Ossewa Brandwag.[16] Malan himself issued a statement on April 23 declaring that the elimination of these two candidates had not been by 'veto', but because of his agreement with Havenga.[17] Soon after, Malan officially banned local agreements between Nationalist candidates and local Ossewa Brandwag groups, and insisted that neither the National Party nor the Afrikaner Party had any agreement with the Ossewa Brandwag,[18] a point perhaps accurate as far as its organization as a whole was concerned but open to some question in practice.

From the other side, the Ossewa Brandwag newspaper, *Die Ossewa Brandwag*, strongly criticized the allocation of seats between the two parties. It charged that C. R. Swart was keeping the Afrikaner Party out of the Orange Free State, 'in spite of Dr. Malan's promise to Mr. Havenga', and also out of the Eastern Province in the Cape where, in its view, the Afrikaner Party held the balance of power in at least six constituencies. Instead of contesting these obvious places, the Afrikaner Party was being forced to fight in Natal where the Nationalists had never been able to make inroads.[19] Some of this latter comment was justified. The Free State Nationalists had no desire to risk a resurgence of pro-Hertzog sentiment. Above all, the Nationalists were determined to avoid giving the Ossewa Brandwag a parliamentary front. Unity of nationalistic Afrikanerdom they wanted, but on their own terms. Havenga could be useful but it would be better if his group was not a strong one.

From his side, Havenga's objective was to secure six seats in Parliament for his party. That the 1948 election returned nine Afrikaner Party members reflected not only the strong Nationalist swing which so unexpectedly brought Malan into political power but also much hard work by the Afrikaner Party organization, which was refurbished after the 1943 debacle, and given final form on the eve of the election. From the inception of the party, Havenga had been its leader, but he was not in Parliament until 1948. Between 1941 and 1943 the direction of its small group of M.P.s fell to General Edwin Conroy, to whom can be attributed much of the political opportunism of the party in this period. When Conroy was defeated in 1943, along with all other Afrikaner M.P.s, the problem of divided responsibility disappeared. Particularly after he agreed to re-enter active politics as a parliamentary candidate, Havenga had virtually complete control over policy.

After 1943 organization and electioneering details came under the chairman of the party, Harm Oost, a kindly, colorful figure with square shoulders and flowing beard, who had participated in the 1914 rebellion with General de Wet, became the first editor of *Die Vaderland*, and found his happiest years in politics in the period of Hertzog and Smuts' Fusion. It was Oost who was primarily responsible for calling Havenga back into politics, gauging correctly that it was the only way to bring the party any influence.

At the Brakpan Congress, February 5, 1948, the Afrikaner Party formally adopted a Constitution in preparation for the coming election. The program of principles remained that which Hertzog had presented to the Free State Nationalists on November 6, 1940. The formal framework was centralized, and even authoritarian. Any 'white Union citizen' of the age of 16 could become a member by formally accepting the party principles, agreeing to the Constitution and 'decisions of the party organs', and being admitted to a branch. Head Office controlled the branches, though the latter could make their own local rules if they did not conflict with the Constitution. The Central Executive could nominate a provincial or parliamentary candidate without asking for nominations, or reject one chosen by a constituency. Thus, though the annual Congress was declared to be the highest authority, effective control rested quite securely, in practice, in the hands of the national leader, i.e., of Havenga, and of his immediate associates.

The 1948 election, which gave the Afrikaner Party's nine seats the balance of power, placed that group in an unexpectedly strategic position. The United and Labour Parties had 70 seats and they could count on the three votes of the Native representatives; the Nationalists had 65 seats and, with the Afrikaner Party, 74. Thus until by-elections and the 1950 elections in South West Africa combined to give Malan a slight overall majority of his own, he was dependent on Havenga's group for implementing his policy. Even thereafter, the latter could have forced a general election at any time by withdrawing its support.

In the Nationalist-Afrikaner governing coalition, Havenga became Leader of the House of Assembly and also Minister of Finance, the position he had held so long under Hertzog, both in the early Nationalist and United Party Governments. The positions could hardly have been more strategic, but they reflected Havenga's personal usefulness rather than the importance of his party. The Nationalists were weak in financial experience and overseas contacts; Havenga's financial orthodoxy, with no trace of Keynesian theory, suited their rather simple approach to business and commerce. In that field at least, they accepted wholeheartedly the view of Hertzog nationalism that South Africa should industrialize to become as economically independent as possible, and to provide employment for the urban Afrikaner working class. They worried about unbalanced budgets as Havenga did, and were thankful when he was able to secure international credits, so long as they did not limit the party's freedom of action to carry on the policies it saw fit. As Leader of the House, Havenga was also extremely useful because of his long parliamentary experience, his great sense of responsibility for being present through debates (a practice not shared by many of the Nationalist front bench except Malan himself) and his quick tongue.

Even before the Nationalist and Afrikaner Parties merged in 1951, Havenga seemed more a part of the Nationalists than a member of the coalition group. True, he reported to the Afrikaner Party caucus on cabinet policy which was debated there in full freedom. But here too, the Afrikaner Party tended in practice to be Havenga.

Yet in the early days of the coalition, Havenga and the Afrikaner Party stood out against two aspects of the Nationalists' apartheid policy: the elimination of the Native representatives, and the original form of the Separate Representation of Voters' bill to take the Coloured off the common roll in Cape Province. The former had been established as part of the comprehensive Hertzog settlement in 1936 (see p. 120); Havenga argued that to abolish these representatives would be a breach of faith with the Natives. The one notable success scored by the Afrikaner Party was that the Nationalists shelved their plan for getting rid of the Native representatives.

But to remove the Coloured from the common roll was even more specifically to violate pledges which Hertzog had made as Nationalist Prime Minister, and at a time when Dr. Malan was in his cabinet. At Smithfield on March 5, 1938, Hertzog reminded the H.N.P. of those assurances 'that no demarcation in respect of Europeans and Coloured people would be applied other than social separation', and termed the Malan policy of separate representation for the Coloured as 'deliberately conceived to evade the requirement of faith and honour and sincerity'. Nonetheless, Havenga seems to have been less concerned about the principle of separate representation for the Coloured than with the way in which the change would be brought about. Speaking on December 1, 1948, to the Afrikaner Party Congress about the entrenched clauses he reminded them that 'these safeguards had always been respected by General Hertzog'. 'We will not serve the national interests, and in particular, the interests of the whites', he declared, 'if in our zeal and impatience to find an early solution of certain aspects of our colour problem we depart from that old national Hertzog road and follow a road without due regard to the explicit will of the people.' Even if the Ndlwana decision of the Appeal Court (see p. 121) made it juridically possible to disregard the special procedure laid down in the Constitution for the entrenched clauses, Havenga felt it would be better to act 'according to the spirit of those provisions', particularly in the light of the slimness of the Government's majority.[20]

In reply, Malan declared Havenga's statement had caused 'considerable confusion and concern among the Nationalists'.[21] Maintaining that his party had received a 'mandate' for apartheid at the 1948 election, which included full political apartheid, Malan now declared that the Nationalists would consider the 1949 provincial elections a test of the public will on this question.

It was clear that the Nationalists were not only irritated by Afrikaner Party resistance to their plans for political apartheid, but felt that absorption of the minority group was well overdue. Late in August, the rather sensational *Sunday Express* had reported that the Afrikaner Party was making overtures to the United Party as a counter-balance to pressure for amalgamation with the Nationalists.[22] The Afrikaner Party protested publicly shortly thereafter against the whispering campaign against Havenga which was being carried on by Nationalist organizers in constituencies in which both parties had branches.[23] These rumors suggested that Havenga was using Nationalist support as a stepping stone to eventual amalgamation with moderate elements in the United Party. Shortly after, the Nationalists instituted a full scale campaign for a merger. Both Malan and Strijdom made speeches late in October, which urged the end of the Afrikaner Party.[24] On November 2, the Federal Council of the National Party went so far as to pass a resolution which regretted that the 'expected unification' of the two parties had not yet been achieved, declared their unity was 'essential', and urged that it be consummated as quickly as possible. This was supported by a vigorous Nationalist press campaign demanding fusion.

Already, however, the issue of nominations for the 1949 provincial elections was threatening more seriously than at any other time the working arrangement between the National Party and the Afrikaner Party. Within a week of the Federal Council's resolution, Havenga wrote to Malan that 'the necessary good feeling and faith obviously do not yet exist' to make a merger possible. Once again it was a question of nominating Ossewa Brandwag members as Afrikaner Party candidates. The Afrikaner Party had done so for its constituencies of Mossel Bay and Paarl in the Cape; Havenga disclosed that the Cape Nationalist Party had vetoed the nominations. Similarly, the Transvaal party had demanded assurance that no member of the Ossewa Brandwag be nominated to any of the seats assigned in that province to the Afrikaner Party.[25] Moreover, Havenga declared that a 'spirit of ill-will and lack of acknowledgment of our rights' had been revealed in the division of seats in the Orange Free State. Stating that 'I have never been a member of the Ossewa Brandwag and we have no relations with them, and never associated ourselves with their ideals and objects', he maintained that in the interests of unity the Afrikaner Party could not refuse anyone who was honestly prepared to accept their party principles and obligations. 'It is therefore impossible for me to accept the provincial seats which you are prepared to allow us to contest', he concluded, 'under any conditions which would allow interference with candidates.'[26]

No concessions were extended in Malan's reply of November 12, nor by subsequent Nationalist actions. Putting his objection to the Ossewa Brandwag on the ground that 'they preach an ideology and aims' in opposition to those of the National Party and Afrikaner Party, Malan charged that these ideas were openly propagated at Afrikaner Party meetings. He went so far as to say that the National Party might accept members of the Ossewa Brandwag as party members, but not as candidates. Under the circumstances, the 'desired unification' was out of the question at that moment.[27] This the Free State Nationalists made quite sure by refusing to allow the Afrikaner Party a single nomination for the forthcoming provincial elections, even in United Party-held constituencies.[28]

Under this goad, the Afrikaner Party Brakpan Congress affirmed its intention of continuing as 'an independent party', working in cooperation 'with any party or group' which accepted Hertzog principles. A delegate heatedly denounced the Nationalists for their policy in the Orange Free State and against Ossewa Brandwag members. Van Rensburg, still the Ossewa Brandwag leader, spoke at the Afrikaner Congress for the first time, and received a tremendous ovation. On December 7, Havenga formally notified Malan that the Afrikaner Party would take no part in the provincial elections, and that the previous allocation of seats 'must now be considered to have fallen away'.[29] On March 4, 1949, Afrikaner Party supporters were officially asked to ignore the provincial elections to take place five days later.[30]

Yet the trial of strength only proved conclusively how powerful the Nationalists were, and how insignificant was the electoral support of the Afrikaner Party. Malan had said that the response of the provincial elections should show Havenga the feeling for political apartheid; it proved just as conclusively that the Afrikaner Party had no bargaining power outside its immediate parliamentary strength. It is true that United Party members, particularly in Natal, over-optimistically hailed the division between Havenga and Malan, and even talked of Havenga as Smuts' successor. But the links the other way were too strong, if indeed any formal negotiations were undertaken between the United Party and Afrikaner Party. Moreover, the latter's inability to affect the provincial election returns meant that it would be only a question of time before the Afrikaner Party would lose its identity.

A pointed indication of renewed closer relations was the cooperation of the Afrikaner Party and National Party in the Vereeniging by-election, May, 1949;[31] this coincided with persistent comments on a possible merger. Havenga still retained his opposition to the Bill affecting Coloured voters, and Malan promised not to introduce it during the 1949 parliamentary session. The first step in a *modus vivendi* on this issue was announced on December 12, 1949, through a joint statement by Malan and Havenga explaining that the bill on separate representation for the Coloured in Parliament and the Cape Provincial Council would be published for general information and discussion, but that the Afrikaner Party assumed no responsibility for it. It was acknowledged that the parties differed on whether the entrenched clauses were applicable to the measure, and also on the number of representatives the Coloured should have. Still more significant, however, were the assertions that they agreed on the principle of separate representation for the Coloured, and that the need to press ahead with apartheid policy made their continued cooperation essential. The danger or, from the United Party side, hope of a split was over.

But not until the Nationalists virtually freed themselves from dependence on the Afrikaner Party through winning all six seats in South West Africa did Havenga finally agree to terms for taking the Coloured off the common roll. As announced in October, 1950 (barely two months after the South West Africa elections), the Coloured were to have four House of Assembly seats (to be held by Europeans on the pattern of the Native representatives), one in the Senate, and two in the Cape Provincial Council. Havenga had at least won his point that the Coloured should have more seats than the Nationalists were originally prepared to assign them. There were also to be Coloured advisory bodies. Since in his view this arrangement gave the Coloured at least as adequate representation as under existing provisions, Havenga now declared that the procedure for amending the entrenched clauses would be inapplicable. Whatever the rationalization, Havenga's action looked very much like surrender.

The movement towards amalgamation proceeded steadily, if somewhat haltingly, from this point on. Both sides showed concern over the terms of union. Almost immediately after Havenga's acceptance of the Separate Representation of Voters' bill, the Ossewa Brandwag was reported as opposed to the merger on the ground that none but a few Afrikaner Party members would benefit from it.[32] More significant was the conflict behind the scenes with Malan, Havenga, the bulk of the Afrikaner Party and most of the Nationalist Parliamentary caucus urging that the membership of the unified party be thrown open to non-Nationalists, while Strijdom, Louw, Swart and Verwoerd insisted that the party retain its Christian-National character as well as its republican and strict apartheid principles. Important also was the allocation of parliamentary seats in the 1953 election. Most significant of all was the issue of the future leadership of the party. On these last two points, Strijdom apparently won his point that no commitments must be given.

The formal indication that the leaders of the Afrikaner Party and National Party intended to propose a complete unification was given through a carefully worded statement of June 25, 1951. The name, the National (*Nasionale*) Party, was chosen, it was said, because 'that formerly described the political home of both our cooperating parties, and also included all nationally-minded Afrikaners from both white language groups'. Through cooperation, the statement declaimed, 'Afrikanerdom has risen out of the condition of disunity, impotence and mortification in which it found itself . . . regained its self-respect, and has reached a climax of unity and power'.[33]

The actual terms of merger showed a few slight compromises in the interests of gaining unity. All enrolled members of both partes were to be placed on the permanent membership list of the National Party unless they indicated objections within a month. At the same time, new branches were to be formed wherever there were members of both parties.[34] Strijdom agreed to omit the out-dated clause in the Transvaal party's Constitution, which excluded Jews from membership, thereby bringing his provincial organization into line with the rest of the National Party as well as with the former Afrikaner Party. The concession from the Afrikaner Party side went far deeper, for all members of the National Party had to forswear allegiance to any other political organization, including the Ossewa Brandwag.

The formal steps followed quickly. The National Party Federal Council recommended the agreement to the provincial congresses on August 16,[35] and these duly agreed. The Afrikaner Party, at its Bloemfontein Congress, accepted the merger on August 23, though some members refused to join the National Party, notably Mr. Benadé, the former mayor of Bloemfontein.[36] October 22, 1951, was the official day of the merger. More significant, perhaps, was that Strijdom toasted Havenga at a banquet a week before,[37] a fact apparently of such note that it was widely publicized through photographs.

In one sense, the breach between the National Party and the Afrikaner Party had been healed. The end result of the merger, however, turned out to be the elimination of all former parliamentary members of the Afrikaner Party except N. C. Havenga. Thus Harm Oost and others were rejected as Nationalist candidates for the 1953 election despite Malan's expressed wish that all M.P.s and M.P.C.s be renominated.[38] As a former Afrikaner Party member said, 'old bitterness dies hard', and rank and file Nationalists had little reason to look kindly on the Afrikaner Party which had tried to balk their drive towards an immediate republic in the early forties, and for full political apartheid after the Nationalists came into office in 1948. Without bargaining power from assured electoral support, the incorporation of the Afrikaner Party in the Nationalists, and thus its elimination from politics, were inevitable in the long run.

The strangest position was that in which Havenga found himself. He remained titular leader of the National Party in Natal after the 1953 election, though he had been elected for a Free State constituency; he was thus a member of the Federal Council's Steering Committee. He was also Leader of the House of Assembly, and Minister of Finance. But his position rested not so much on these offices as on the fact that he had become a close friend and chief confidant of Dr. Malan.

When Malan decided to retire as leader of the National Party, he desired Havenga to succeed him. Strijdom is said to have agreed to this arrangement as an interim one. But pressures from within the Transvaal Nationalist Party interfered, if indeed Strijdom ever pledged himself temporarily to stand aside. When it became obvious that Havenga could not receive the nomination for leader when Nationalist members of Parliament met in Pretoria in November, 1954, to decide Malan's successor, Havenga bitterly stood aside while P. K. Le Roux nominated Strijdom. Havenga's resignation from Parliament, like that of Dr. Malan, followed soon after.

The refusal to make Havenga leader presaged the new, more drastic line of policy followed by the Nationalists under J. G. Strijdom. That Havenga no longer had influence in the party became strikingly apparent when his public expression of disapproval of the 1955 Senate bill (see p. 141) was ignored. But even when in office he had been a delayer, rather than a shaper of policy. To his credit was the decision not to remove the three Native representatives from the House of Assembly. But he allowed two other and still more important features of the Hertzog heritage to be lost: the special position politically of the Coloured; and strict adherence to constitutional forms. Though Havenga may have slowed the pressures against both, he yielded to them sufficiently to leave him at least partly responsible for the more drastic actions which followed his resignation.

CHAPTER 10

NATIONALIST GROUPS AND INFLUENCES

The cohesion of nationalistic Afrikanerdom comes in part out of the vividness of its memories and grievances: the way in which the British imperial factor pursued the Afrikaners who had trekked North to free themselves from its influence; the Anglo-Boer War; the concentration camps for women and children; the one-time discrimination against Afrikaans. In large part, however, its closely knit unity is the creation of a host of organizations which have more or less consciously sought to overcome the traditional divisions within Afrikanerdom, and develop political, economic and cultural fronts which reflect its common ideals and purposes. The National Party is one of the most influential of these organizations. At the same time, it is only one—though now the most important one—amongst an interacting series of groups covering all aspects of life and knitting nationalistic Afrikanerdom together.

The very fact of describing these groups may, in a sense, exaggerate their importance. Most of them have had, or have, life cycles which reflect the needs or aspirations of nationalist Afrikaners at particular times. Yet they represent something almost unique in modern Western society. Other countries and people, in particular Americans, have developed a network of associations to bridge the divisions caused by shifting populations, and social mobility. But the groups described in this chapter do much more than this. Consciously or unconsciously, they have sought or seek to create out of nationalistic Afrikanerdom an integrated whole which can assume what is looked on as its 'destiny', the direction, if not domination of all other peoples within the Union, and possibly beyond. The intensity of purpose of these groups, and the effectiveness of their actions, provide an essential underpinning for the drive and power of their political spokesman and leader, the National Party.

The most important influence upon the Afrikaner is the Dutch Reformed Church. Its comprehensive philosophy of life, with authoritarian and elitist overtones, provides the conscious or unconscious basis for most courses of action. Though strongly interrelated with Afrikaner nationalism both in concept and actions, the Dutch Reformed Church hardly belongs, however, in the same category as the *Broederbond*, F.A.K. (*Federasie van Afrikaanse Kultuurverenigings*), R.D.B. (*Reddingsdaadbond*), and even the Institute for Christian National Education, all of which have sought, or seek to perform a specific function within the Afrikaner community, not to preach a transcendental truth. More closely related to the Dutch Reformed Church in the sense that it provides a philosophy by which to approach current problems is SABRA (*South African Bureau for Racial Affairs*). The latter two will be considered, therefore, in the latter part of this chapter, and the more specifically oriented organizations first.

The Broederbond

Earliest and probably most influential among the organizations seeking to stimulate nationalistic Afrikanerdom to a realization of its destiny and power is the Broederbond. Some see its beginning in a meeting on June 4, 1918, of 14 Afrikaners who dedicated themselves 'to the good right of the Afrikaner cause', and to establishing a brotherhood of the Afrikaner people. The original aim was to stress 'ideals and not persons', to be non-political, provide mutual support in the economic field, and further Afrikaner art and culture.[1] The group made little progress, however, until December 9, 1919, generally considered the Broederbond's true date of origin, when it was determined that each member must sign a declaration 'affirming his willingness to subject himself to the aim'.[2] A formal Constitution was adopted on September 21, 1920, and from August 1921 the organization began to expand. According to one of its original members, the Broederbond became a secret society in 1922, at which time most of its moderates withdrew, leaving only those who sought to establish a *boere republiek* in which the Afrikaner would predominate.[3]

Because of its secret character, it is difficult to determine the exact nature or significance of the Broederbond. Opponents of Afrikaner Nationalism claim that the Broederbond seeks to dominate all other Afrikaner associations and is, in fact, their governing agency. They quote the last circular issued by the Broederbond, January 16, 1934, in which its chairman, Professor J. C. van Rooy of Potchefstroom University, and secretary, I. M. Lombard of Johannesburg, wrote:

> Let us focus our attention on the fact that the primary consideration is: whether Afrikanerdom will reach its ultimate destiny of domination (*baasskap*) in South Africa. Brothers, our solution of South Africa's ailments is not whether one Party or another shall obtain the whip hand, but that the Afrikaner-Broederbond shall govern South Africa.

Equally, its opponents cite General J. B. M. Hertzog's trenchant attack on the Bond in a speech at Smithfield, November 7, 1935,[4] in which he stigmatized the Broederbond as 'a grave menace to the rest and peace of our social community, even where it operates in the economic-cultural sphere', because they are striving 'by way of domination on the part of the Afrikaans-speaking section to put their foot on the neck of English-speaking South Africa'. Hertzog also accused Dr. D. F. Malan of pursuing 'a course of national division and strife' through his opposition to the Fusion between Hertzog and Smuts, which opposition, he said, resulted from Malan joining the Bond in 1934. In particular, Hertzog declared that the Broederbond had acquired a dangerous domination of Orange Free State education.

> I know of few towns and villages in the Free State where the Broederbond has not established for itself a nest of five, six or more Broers to serve as a focal point for Bond propaganda, and I also know that there is hardly a single nest on which there isn't at least one teacher sitting as a hatcher.

Nine years later, speaking to the Bloemfontein United Party Congress, December 1944, General J. C. Smuts accused the Broederbond of being 'a sort of Gestapo', and declared that it 'is a dangerous, cunning, political Fascist organization of which no civil servant, if he is to retain his loyalty to the State and the Administration, can be allowed to be a member'. In a logical corollary, the Government, on December 15, 1944, then gave Broederbond members of the public services, including teachers, the alternative of resigning from the one or the other. Ironically, W. C. du Plessis (who became South African Ambassador to the United States in 1956) resigned from the Civil Service rather than from the Broederbond, and subsequently defeated General Smuts in his own constituency of Standerton in the 1948 elections.

In response to General Smuts' attack, the Secretary of the Broederbond, I. M. Lombard, wrote a series of four articles in *Die Transvaler*, on December 14, 20 and 30, 1944, and January 3, 1945, explaining in somewhat florid language the purpose and organization of the Broederbond. These articles, together with comments in the House of Assembly at the time of the ban on the Broederbond, and the report of the 1951 committee of inquiry of the Dutch Reformed Churches, form the most authoritative material on which to base a judgment upon the organization.

The keynote of the Broederbond's character is given in the first of the Lombard articles, which quotes from the Constitution to declaim sonorously that:

> Its highest aim is honourable service to Afrikanerdom.
>
> The Afrikaner Broederbond is born out of a deep conviction that the Afrikaner nation was put in this land by God and is destined to continue in existence as a nation with its own nature and calling.[5]

There follows its aim:

> (a) To bring about a healthy and progressive unanimity amongst all Afrikaners who strive for the welfare of the Afrikaner nation.
>
> (b) To arouse the Afrikaner's national self-consciousness, and to implant a love for his language, religion, tradition, country and people.
>
> (c) The furtherance of all the 'interests' of the Afrikaner nation.

Denying that the Broederbond is a subversive organization, undemocratic or Fascist, Mr. Lombard declared that the reasons for the much-criticized secrecy of the Bond's activities are, in part, that publicity would lead its members to be governed by personal ambition rather than selfless service, but more particularly that premature disclosure might result in 'half-baked plans', or 'give competitors or enemies the chance to undermine plans laid in the interest of the people'. Comparing its 'confidential character' to what is found in a meeting of the Cabinet, board of directors of a business, or church committee 'before reaching a decision which it can make known to its members', he wrote that the Broederbond is 'only a deliberative body in which consultations take place on what its members regard as best for the Afrikaner people'.[6]

How then does the Broederbond work to achieve its objectives? Not through party politics, according to Mr. Lombard. The Bond rules specifically in Art. 88 of its Constitution that 'no speaker may play the part of propagandist for one or other existing political party, or for party politics as such', though, of course, almost all, if not all Bond members are also members of the National Party. The Bond lays down, however, a seven-fold 'ideal' for which Broers should strive 'in their political actions'.

> (1) The removal of everything in conflict with South Africa's full international independence.
> (2) The ending of the inferiority of the Afrikaans-speaking and of their language in the organization of the State.
> (3) Separation of all non-white races in South Africa, leaving them free to independent development under the guardianship of the whites.
> (4) Putting a stop to the exploitation of the resources and population of South Africa by strangers, including the more intensive industrial development.
> (5) The rehabilitation of the farming community and the assurance of civilized self-support through work for all white citizens.
> (6) The nationalization of the money market and the systematic coordination of economic policies.
> (7) The Afrikanerization of our public life and our teaching and education in a Christian National spirit while leaving free the internal development of all sections of the nation insofar as it is not dangerous to the State.[7]

Mr. Lombard declares, however, that 'such political considerations are discussed very little at meetings, at which economic, cultural, educational and such-like matters set the tone'.

Naturally enough, the Bond is exclusively Afrikaner. Only those may join

> who are Afrikaans-speaking, of Protestant faith, of good character, and of fixed principles, also with regard to maintaining his Afrikanership, and who accepts S. Africa as his only home-land.

These members are organized in small units of about 20 persons all over the Union, each group a cross-section of the *volk* in its vicinity. In the interests of efficiency, mass membership is not desired; in 1944 total membership was 2,672.

Among the other qualities essential for members, according to Mr. Lombard, are 'zeal and readiness to work for national matters and to contribute regularly in money or otherwise without expectation of reward'.[8] As far as possible, the Bond recruits young men (though at least 35 years of age) who can be trained for this service. But membership is by invitation only, extended by the particular group only after rigid investigation and approval by all local members. Not everyone who identifies himself with the cause of Afrikanerdom is asked to be a member, though this is an essential characteristic of a member. What is particularly in mind in selecting a new member are two questions: what service can he be to the organization? How representative is he of his section of the *volk*? In particular, diversity is sought, so that each group can function as a 'small mutual counselling' body. Thus at the base of the Broederbond organization, and initiating its work, are the cream of the *ware Afrikaner volk*, intelligent, strategically placed, reflecting roughly the distribution of occupations and interests in their area and dedicated to the advancement of Afrikanerdom.

Groups are divided into zones. The General Council (*Algemene Raad*) consists of one representative from each group, plus the Executive Council (*Uitvoerende Raad*), and meets annually unless emergencies dictate more frequent sessions. Every committee of management is said to be chosen yearly by its members, and the highest executive and the chairman by 'elected delegates to a conference by secret ballot once every two years'.[9] The supreme authority is the Executive Council, composed of the so-called Twelve Apostles, each of whom is responsible for a different sphere of life, e.g. labor, religion, education, politics, the press. It is sometimes said that there is also a 'Trinity' of the supreme chief, and two other members of the Executive Council who provide ultimate direction.

According to Mr. Lombard, the Broederbond develops its program through the proposals of individual members. These people, generally experts in their particular field, or 'in a position to make a special study',[10] bring schemes for dealing with some particular problem to their group, where they are thrashed out to develop an effective plan of action. 'Practicability, acceptability and possibility of support from the population' are, of course, particularly important. Among the issues considered, according to the Dutch Reformed Church committee, have been the Native question, immigration, libraries, mother-tongue instruction and usury. Particular proposals are submitted to all other Broederbond groups for comments and criticism. They are then checked with 'all sorts of experts' (presumably only within Nationalist Afrikanerdom). Lastly, the plan goes to the General Council for its final approval.

What is particularly interesting is that the Broederbond itself does not undertake to put such plans into operation, or to publicize sponsorship of them. When they are complete in every detail, it places the plans in the hands 'of those who showed most interest in the matter and had most knowledge of it'.[11] These individuals introduce the project as spontaneously originating with themselves. Examples of such projects, which Mr. Lombard provides, are the establishment of *Volkskas*, originally a people's bank, and the *Federasie van Afrikaanse Kultuurverenigings*, the coordinating body for Afrikaner cultural societies. Once established, Mr. Lombard declares that these organizations become self-operating.

A certain amount of financial assistance has been extended by the Broederbond to the organizations and to the causes it sponsors. Thus the F.A.K. and Reddingsdaadfonds received Broederbond financial help. Other instances cited in *Die Transvaler* articles are £1,000 for the repatriation of Argentine Boers, £3,000 for loan bursaries for the Afrikaner medical faculty at Pretoria, and £3,000 for the Afrikaner Engineering Faculty at Stellenbosch.[12]

All of this may mean very little, or a great deal. There is nothing inherently wrong in a group of people working together for the advancement of causes which they treasure. Supporters of the Broederbond often compare it, to its advantage, with organizations like the Freemasons, which have secret rituals, and the Sons of England, which promote cultural links with a 'foreign' country. Yet it is hard to avoid the conclusion that the purposes of the Broederbond are very different. This is not a voluntary society dedicated either to general benevolent purposes, or to maintaining historic traditions. The Broederbond may well be no more than its adherents claim—a group of devoted individuals whose purpose is service—but it is both a symptom, and a reinforcement of the separatism of nationalistic Afrikanerdom.

Like so much else in Afrikaner life, the significance of the Broederbond lies in its membership. Though the Broederbond maintains a rigid prohibition on disclosing 'one another's membership',[13] any member has the right to make his own membership public. Among those who are known are people of importance, both in themselves, and in their possession of power. Some 80 per cent of Nationalist Members of Parliament are believed to be Broers; so are most, if not all members of the Nationalist Cabinet. The Executive Council of the Broederbond includes Professor L. J. du Plessis and J. C. von Rooy of University College, Potchefstroom (the latter was chairman of the F.A.K. in 1948), Dr. Dönges, Minister of the Interior, and Leader of the Cape Nationalist Party; Dr. Verwoerd, Minister for Native Affairs; and Dr. Albert Hertzog, who was largely responsible for bringing the Mineworkers' Union into the Nationalist camp. Among others said to be Broers are Dr. Malan, Dr. E. G. Jansen, the Governor-General, and Dr. N. Diederichs, formerly Professor at Bloemfontein University, head of the Reddingsdaadbond until 1948, and thereafter Member of Parliament.

The areas in which Broers are most active are those of politics and education. In 1944, Mr. Lombard disclosed that about one-third of its members were teachers.[14] It is commonly held that, as General Hertzog said in 1935, the Free State education system is controlled by Broers, while the Transvaal and Cape educational systems are also strongly influenced by Broederbond conceptions. Basic to these conceptions is the Broederbond's strongly held conviction that education should be single-medium, i.e. that all teaching should be in Afrikaans for those to whom it is the home language.

Because of widespread criticism of the Broederbond, the Dutch Reformed Church set up a special committee in 1949 (to which reference has already been made), to investigate its origin, work and tendencies. As the result of analysing material provided for it by the Executive Committee of the Bond, the Committee reported to the 1951 meeting of the Council of Churches that the Broederbond was 'wholesome and sound'. The report declared further that the Broederbond 'concerns itself only with the Afrikaner people' and 'seeks only to further the best interests of the Afrikaner nation'. It concluded: 'All that the Bond aims for is an undivided loyalty to South Africa'. Is this loyalty to South Africa as a whole, however, or only to Afrikanerdom?

The chance that the Broederbond now holds to the old slogan of 'sweep the Englishman into the sea' is very slim indeed. On the other hand, its emphasis is so pro-Afrikaner (of the Nationalist variety) that it can hardly help but be exclusivist. How much of the welding together, and disciplining of Nationalist Afrikanerdom should be placed to its credit is impossible to gauge. At the least, it provided much of the impetus towards a greater self-consciousness and, by intelligent planning, gave rise to other organizations which have directed and coordinated the activities of national-minded Afrikaners.

Of itself, there is nothing reprehensible about this. On the other hand, the very secrecy of Broederbond activities cannot help but rouse suspicions. Whether or not it is more than a close association of like-minded persons dedicated to the advancement of Afrikanerdom, the Broederbond has contributed strongly, and perhaps dangerously, to the natural isolation of nationalist Afrikanerdom, as well as to its power.

F.A.K.

The chief role in coordinating Afrikaner cultural, religious, educational and economic societies is performed by the F.A.K. (*Federasie van Afrikaanse Kultuurverenigings*), or Federation of Afrikaner Cultural Organizations, which was established December 18, 1929, as the result of Broederbond initiative. Despite some early difficulties, the F.A.K. had over three hundred affiliated organizations by 1937, one-third of them language and cultural associations, while two-thirds were made up of Church Councils, and other Church organizations, charitable groups, student and youth groups, scientific study circles, and educational organizations.[15]

Almost immediately thereafter, the emphasis of the F.A.K. became more strongly economic. The Economic Institute was established in 1939 and has remained under the F.A.K. itself, unlike the R.D.B., the Reddingsdaadbond (described later), which was founded by the F.A.K., but became autonomous. In 1950, the Economic Institute was described as 'the economic policy council of the *volk* as a whole and the R.D.B. in particular'.[16] With due regard for the somewhat exaggerated terminology used in these reports, the close association of cultural and economic developments is unmistakable.

Their interrelation has been, in fact, a constant theme of F.A.K. conferences. In 1937, Dr. N. J. van der Merwe, in opening the annual F.A.K. Congress, declared that 'The F.A.K. is born of strife, and is even a product of a conflict of soul, in which the Afrikaner is searching for a united front against hostile forces which divide him, and smother his soul'.[17] Though he inveighed against the loss of spiritual values, Dr. van der Merwe also pointed out that the F.A.K. could not remain indifferent to the 'economic struggle of the Afrikaner', and declared that 'an enslaved people can only bring to light a slave culture'.[18]

The problem thus high-lighted was indeed a serious one. In the 1920s some 30 to 50 per cent of Afrikaners were in, or close to the category of poor whites; in the 1930s the problem had still not been solved. In comparison, the English-speaking, particularly of the cities, were well-to-do. As a speaker at the 1937 Congress pointed out, the result was that 'the poorer Afrikaner cultural heritage is shamefacedly pushed aside' in favor of English, then and still the dominant language in urban areas. Thus to support Afrikaans language and culture the F.A.K. had almost inevitably to attempt to reinforce the economic position of Afrikaners.

In any case, culture to the Afrikaner has a far broader, more sociological connotation than colloquially given to it in English. As Dr. Dönges (Minister of the Interior after 1948) put it: 'Culture is to the nation what character is to the individual. . . . It is the ideology of a nation as expressed in every sphere of national life and embraces literature, art, religion and customs, social, economic and national aspects of life.'[19] Moreover, the report of the work of the F.A.K. in the significant period of 1934-37 (when so many Afrikaner organizations were withdrawing from close contact with English-speaking ones performing the same functions) challenged the conception that culture 'falls outside politics'. It asked: 'Is the statesman not called upon to act precisely as the guardian of the nation's heritage?' and, in more inflammatory language: 'Does it make no difference to the *volks* culture if a Jewish-imperialist policy regarding our natural resources is applied against Afrikanerdom?'

Taking the broad interpretation of culture, the F.A.K. has sought to stimulate, to coordinate and, where necessary to fill a gap, to create agencies in all aspects of Afrikaner life. Its own organization is relatively small, consisting largely of a central office, and executive committee. These bodies are responsible for making plans, forwarding suggestions to the affiliated organizations, and organizing congresses like the big Economic *Volks* Congresses in 1939 and 1950, and the *Moedertaal* (mother-tongue) Congress in Bloemfontein in 1943, which protested the attempt to reintroduce dual-medium instruction in the schools.[19a]

In addition to its basic structure, several bodies work, or have worked, under the F.A.K., notably the Economic Institute and the *Nasionale Kultuurraad* (National Culture Council) which held its first meeting in Bloemfontein on July 1 and 2, 1936. The latter body was set up to coordinate particular cultural interests. It does not seem to have developed, however, into the hoped-for 'all-embracing advisory cultural organization of the *Boerevolk*'[20] and is little mentioned after the mid-1940s. More important are the Liaison Committees, operating in towns and cities to coordinate local Afrikaner work. Already, in 1937, some 20 Liaison Committees were in existence, many of them established by the Dutch Reformed Church.

The 1952 Report of the Johannesburg Liaison Committee advises the good Afrikaner to attend his Afrikaner church, speak Afrikaans everywhere, read Afrikaans books and papers, send his children to Afrikaans' medium schools, go to Afrikaner *volk* celebrations, buy Afrikaner products, support Afrikaner businesses, and make use of the services of Afrikaner welfare organizations. It also exhorts him to 'fight Communism, and help our own factory workers in their fight against it'.[21]

The Economic Institute, intended for 'the economic uplifting of the Afrikaner',[22] was to bring together Afrikaner financiers, industrialists, businessmen, agriculturalists, and leaders of labor, universities, technical training colleges and the *Armesorg* (poor relief) organizations of the Afrikaner churches. That it had not been entirely successful in getting such a broad representation is suggested by the demand of the 1950 Economic *Volks* Congress for more representation of Afrikaner business, labor and agriculture. Serviced largely by the secretariat of the F.A.K., the Economic Institute carries on economic research, and encourages Afrikaner economic undertakings in so far as this is not done by the R.D.B.

One of the major functions of the Economic Institute has been to control the Reddingsdaadfonds, funds amounting, by 1946, to £150,259 (with interest £183,325), and collected by the R.D.B., which according to its statute[23] were to be used to promote consumers' cooperatives, technical training and economic research. A published record of the allocation of £45,229 of the fund to particular organizations discloses that the largest contributions were £16,548 to the F.A.K. itself; £12,845 to the R.D.B. (which after 1945, when the Fund was closed, was left free to build its own funds); and £6,841 to the National Council of Trustees and other associations for organizing labor.[24] The investment of Fund money is by a committee of three, consisting in 1950 of Dr. M. S. Louw,

Professor L. J. du Plessis (also on the Executive Committee of the Broederbond), and Dr. N. Diederichs (head of the R.D.B. until 1948).

In addition to the bodies directly under its control, the F.A.K. has established at least four organizations which have operated independently although they remain affiliated to the R.D.B. itself: the *Afrikaans Handelsinstituut* (Commerce Institute) which gives information and guidance to Afrikaner businesses (it received £900 from the Fund); the National Council of Trustees, which promotes Afrikaner labor organizations; and the Institute for Christian National Education. The National Council of Trustees, under the chairmanship of Dr. Albert Hertzog, controls the Afrikaner Mineworkers' Union, which did so much to swing Afrikaner mineworkers behind the National Party, but this union is not itself affiliated with the F.A.K. The Institute for Christian National Education, and the educational ideals which it upholds jointly with the F.A.K., are described later in this chapter.

Apart from setting up these bodies, the F.A.K. has performed a number of specific functions of its own. It was largely responsible for organizing the Great Trek celebration in 1938 which gave so much impetus to Afrikaner nationalism. It has sponsored collections of folk songs, a theater association to develop Afrikaans drama, listening groups for Afrikaans broadcasts, an Afrikaner medical faculty, and several publications, including two small historical works with a marked anti-British slant.[25]

The F.A.K. seems less influential now than in the past, and there is less marked enthusiasm for the activities it coordinates. If so, it is probably because the F.A.K. has performed its tasks so successfully rather than any failure to do so. Afrikaners are in a much better economic position now than before World War II. This is for a variety of reasons which include wartime expansion, and general prosperity, as well as the organizations founded to aid them. The Afrikaans language is safe in the hands of the single-medium Afrikaans schools and universities, so much so in fact that there is a growing danger of unilingualism on the part of young Afrikaners. Thus the major needs have been fulfilled for which the F.A.K. was created.

The R.D.B. (Reddingsdaadbond)

One of the most interesting of Afrikaner organizations is the R.D.B., which was founded at the time of the Great Trek celebrations in 1938 to aid and direct the 'second Great Trek' of the Afrikaner people: the first being away from the centers of population out into the wilderness; the second, their return to the settled centers, and the training of the Afrikaner to take his place in industrial society.

Naturally enough, it was the extent to which Afrikaners had sunk into the ranks of the poor white that stimulated this movement to rehabilitate them. At the first R.D.B. Congress, in 1941, Dr. A. J. Stals warned that if the poor whites went under, the Afrikaner nation was doomed.[26] A pamphlet by Fritz Steyn in 1943 declared that 'the Afrikaner nation is the poorest element in the white population of our country, and is even poorer than the Indians'.[27] Steyn estimated that not more than 5 per cent of the total capital in industry was controlled by Afrikaners, and showed that Indians possessed 5,000 more general dealers' licenses than Afrikaners, though they had only one-fifth the numbers.

Dr. Diederichs pointed out in another pamphlet of slightly later date that Afrikaners in the towns worked for others as bus conductors, railway and factory workers, miners and clerks, rather than owning their own shops and businesses.[28]

While the Reddingsdaadbond movement aimed at helping the mass of Afrikaner workers to improve their economic status, it was not only on an individual basis but also through mobilizing, as far as possible, the capital resources of the Afrikaner people. Dr. Dönges claimed that 'We have the purchasing power. We have the capital power. We have the money power. The question is: have we the will power and the power to act?'[29] Equally, the R.D.B. sought to keep the urbanized Afrikaner within his own Afrikaner tradition. 'The foreign influences must be removed from our trade unions,' wrote Dr. Dönges, 'and they must take their place four square on a national basis,' a view reflected in the strongly corporative approach of the National Party. 'It is the task of the R.D.B.', he continued, 'to keep the Afrikaner worker, in the midst of foreign elements, in his Church, language, and *volks* environment.'

The R.D.B. worked in a variety of ways to cope with its problems. One of its biggest tasks was to break down the prejudice against industry and commerce among Afrikaners. A high percentage of them were still on the farms when it began its work; the poor whites were listless and untrained; most Afrikaners were fearful of urban life, afraid of being exploited, and uncertain of how to cope with life in fields so largely controlled by English and Jewish interests. In the initial psychological job, the R.D.B. feels it performed perhaps its most significant tasks.

Especially during the war, the R.D.B. also acted as an employment agency which found places for young Afrikaners to work and get experience. It must be remembered that, although many Afrikaners were in the armed forces, the more extreme Nationalists on the whole were not. Thus they were available for the many jobs opening up in English, and Jewish, as well as Afrikaner firms in response to the tremendous economic stimulus of wartime needs. The R.D.B. reports almost daily calls for personnel in this period, so many, in fact, that its permanent staff was not always able to check everyone they recommended.

Even more important was the aid given to those interested in starting their own businesses. Young Afrikaners were given loans (nearly all of which have been paid back) to take commercial or technical training. The R.D.B. (like the *Afrikaans Handelsinstituut*) also provided counselling on the running of businesses, for Afrikaners, on the whole, knew little at that time about sound business practices. This advice was contributed by experienced persons as a part-time activity. A few businesses were financed through the R.D.B.'s own capital resources, but these did not stretch far.

The greatest success of the R.D.B. was in the smaller towns, or *dorps*, where it organized the people of the community, persuaded them to pool their capital instead of keeping it only for the development of their own farms, and to underwrite Afrikaner business. On the eve of World War II, almost all business enterprise in the dorps was in the hands of English-speaking or Jews; by 1950, it was almost entirely Afrikaner.

In its operation, the R.D.B. depends upon a branch system of organization, coordinated under a National Executive Committee which is assisted by a permanent staff at the central offices in Johannesburg. It holds a bi-annual conference for discussions and to register decisions. In 1953, there were some 275 R.D.B. branches scattered throughout the Union, South West Africa, and those British territories in which there were Afrikaners. Each branch has a part-time, salaried organizer, as well as its own committee, the latter including representatives of local Afrikaner committees as well as branch members.

Each R.D.B. branch is affiliated with the F.A.K. Moreover the members of the R.D.B. Executive Council are elected every two years by the F.A.K.'s Executive Council on the recommendation of its Economic Institute, and the R.D.B.'s full-time organization head is appointed the same way. R.D.B. policy is formulated by an Economic Council, consisting of 40 part-time members, who have strong links with the Economic Institute. Thus, though technically independent, the R.D.B. is virtually a subsidiary of the F.A.K.

Established on an initial basis of £150,000 subscribed through voluntary contributions, the R.D.B. has otherwise financed its activities through membership fees—6d. a month for those over 15, and 3d. a month for those under—which also provide insurance benefits in case of accidents, funeral benefits, recreational facilities, and access to consumers' co-operatives.

Until 1946, as we have seen, the R.D.B. served as the collecting agency for the Reddingsdaadfonds administered by the Economic Institute. Since then, it has kept for its own purposes such money as it has collected, amounting by the end of February, 1950, to £14,267. The R.D.B. works closely with *Volkskas,* the Afrikaner commercial bank, *Sanlam,* the Afrikaner insurance house, and the *Federale Volksbeleggings,* an Afrikaner investment house, all of which antedated it but became more vigorous after the R.D.B. entered the economic field. Probably by now, they have become considerably more important, however, than is the R.D.B.

How much credit can the R.D.B. take for the great spurt by Afrikaners into business and commerce since 1940? This is difficult to calculate. Individual initiative and the opportunities of the war, coupled with the great expansion of secondary industry, may well have been more important factors. But that the advance, however caused, is impressive was illustrated by Dr. Diederichs at the second Economic *Volks* Congress in 1950, when he pointed out that the number of Afrikaner dealers had increased by 150 per cent since 1939, and that Afrikaner businesses now numbered between 9,000 and 10,000. In 1947, he declared that Afrikaners owned over 14 Union-wide financial companies with a joint capital of £7 million and controlled between £20 and 30 million.[30]

At the same time the Afrikaner economic advance seems little more than a relative one. As Professor L. J. du Plessis pointed out in 1945, there was only one Afrikaner company at that time with a capitalization of £1 million, while on the Johannesburg stock exchange alone, 116 companies were quoted with at least that capitalization. The basic lack of Afrikaner capital, coupled with the inability of Afrikaner business to attract capital from abroad, means inevitably that it will be long before it can compete with English or Jewish interests.

Membership figures of the R.D.B. show that it achieved its greatest measure of support in 1946-47, when it had nearly 65,000 members, of whom about 17,000 paid membership fees. The number of branches shrank from 381 in the peak period of 1946 to 26 in 1950; and members sank to 32,757, of whom 9,009 paid fees.[31] Clearly, interest had died down, partly at least because of the feeling, particularly in the dorps, that the R.D.B. had completed its work.

The job of the R.D.B. was an important one for nationalistic Afrikanerdom. Through its activities, the R.D.B. not only helped to adjust Afrikaners to urban industrial and commercial life, but also to wean Afrikaner workers away from the traditional trade unions into Nationalist-dominated unions. Perhaps most significant of all had been its success in developing Afrikaner control of business in the dorps, the centers of the electoral hold of the National Party in the *platteland*.

The Institute for Christian National Education

Potentially still more far reaching than the economic activities on behalf of Afrikanerdom are those to develop a characteristic system of education based on a distinctive educational philosophy. In July 1939, the F.A.K. organized a Christian National Education Conference in Bloemfontein, which reasserted C.N.E. ideals and called for a permanent institute to formulate them more precisely, and ensure their publicity. The F.A.K. immediately established the Institute for Christian National Education, which dedicated itself for nearly ten years to preparing a comprehensive document which would provide a complete formulation of Christian National Education. Drafts of this document were considered not only by the Institute itself, but also by the F.A.K.'s executive organs, and by all the bodies and institutions represented in the F.A.K. and the Institute, which in practice included all the Afrikaner bodies interested in education. In this sense, as Professor J. C. van Rooy, chairman of the F.A.K., points out in his introduction to the basic document of Christian National Education, which was issued February 1948, the policy was approved by 'the whole of Afrikanerdom'. Thus, while Christian National Education is not an official Government policy, it exercises a strong and pervasive influence in the country.

The background of Christian National Education is seen by its sponsors to lie in the struggle to support the Afrikaans language, particularly after the Anglo-Boer war when there was a deliberate policy by the British administration to make English the medium of instruction in the State schools in the Transvaal and Orange Free State. To counteract the potential anglicizing of Afrikaner children, a few C.N.E. schools were started privately though they involved a great financial burden on a war-impoverished people. In 1907, these C.N.E. schools were handed over to the States which by then had acquired responsible government. Thereafter Afrikaans quickly gained a wider official status. In 1914, it was formally recognized as a school subject; in 1920 permitted as a medium of instruction in schools; and in 1925 put on an equal footing with English as one of the two official languages (formerly it had been High Dutch).

Afrikaans-medium schools sprang up everywhere. It became common for a child to receive its primary education in the language which school inspectors determined it understood best. This practice is now compulsory in the Free State and the Transvaal, and since a court decision of June 1951, Afrikaans-speaking parents cannot send their children to a school where the language of instruction is English, unless it is a private denominational, e.g., a Roman Catholic school.

Moreover, of the nine universities in South Africa, of which one, the University of South Africa, is largely a 'correspondence institution', four are Afrikaans-medium; Stellenbosch, Pretoria, Orange Free State (Bloemfontein) and Potchefstroom. This means not only that their students are Afrikaans-speaking, but also that Afrikaans is the language of instruction.

No non-Europeans, it should be noted, are allowed as staff or students in any of the Afrikaner universities. Moreover, since 1933, one after another of the Afrikaner universities has disaffiliated itself from the National Union of South African students, NUSAS, to join a new and separate organization, *Die Afrikaanse Studentebond* (ASB), which refuses to participate in conferences with NUSAS as long as English-speaking universities choose non-Europeans as their representatives.

So far went the trend of separateness in English and Afrikaans education that some educators began to press for dual-medium (i.e., both English and Afrikaans) education at every level, both to foster bilingualism, and to promote the easier intermingling of South Africa's two European peoples. In 1943, a United Party administration in the Transvaal began to establish dual-medium instruction, but the process was reversed, after an all too short and half-hearted effort, by a National Party victory in that province in 1948. The attempt to press single medium education still farther, and to limit the parents' freedom of choice at still higher levels of training, lay behind the draft Transvaal Education Ordinance which was such a hot election issue in 1953 (see p. 173).

It was particularly to counter the movement for dual-medium instruction that the Institute for Christian National Education was founded, whose tenets go well beyond those of the original C.N.E. schools. As its basic document makes clear, Christian National Education asserts that mother-tongue instruction is fundamental and should extend from nursery school through the university. The other official language, English, should be taught, it affirms, but as a foreign though essential language. This concern for basic unilingual instruction rests on the philosophy underlying Christian National Education that every people has a distinctive life of its own which education should not only recognize but also intensify.

At the beginning of the official exposition of C.N.E. policy are defined the words 'Christian' and 'National', as they apply to the education of Afrikaans-speaking children. By Christian is meant a view of life and the world 'based on Holy Scripture and formulated in the Articles of Faith of our three Afrikaans churches'.[32] (A common syllabus is already in existence.) National means 'love for everything that is our own, with special reference to our country, our language, our history and our culture'. The National principle is to be under 'the guidance' of the Christian principle. Thus the Calvinist emphasis on the superiority of Christian doctrine is maintained. More significant and limiting is that the doctrine should be that of the three Dutch Reformed Churches, which is characteristically fundamentalist and authoritarian.

Education is defined as 'the controlling guidance and formation of a child's development into an adult in submission to the Word of God in all things'. Thus 'the spirit and trend in which all subjects are taught' should be Christian and National. This refers not only to religious instruction 'according to the

Bible and our Articles of Faith' which is 'the key-subject at school', but also to the mother-tongue, 'the most important secular subject at school', and to such subjects as civics, geography and history.

Civics aims to 'rear Christian and National citizens'; geography to develop 'a love for our own native country, also in comparison and in contrast with other countries'. For history, C.N.E. holds the view that 'the great antithesis between the Kingdom of God in Christ Jesus and the kingdom of darkness runs through everything'. While accepting the essential unity of history, it also emphasizes that God 'willed separate nations and peoples, and has given to each separate nation and people its special calling and task and talents'. It believes that the successful development of the nation depends on the young obtaining 'through history teaching a true vision' of the nation's origin, cultural tradition and 'the content of the trend in that inheritance'.

That Christian National Education has its own particular approach to subject matters is particularly evident in regard to science, where 'Christian-oriented science' is sharply contrasted with 'non-Christian science'. The statement declares that 'Creator and creation, man and animal, individual and society remain in principle insoluble in each other'. Conversation with Professor Chris Coetzee, one of the foremost exponents of Christian National Education, confirmed the impression that 'Christian-oriented Science' denies the possibility of evolution from animal to man, though not of evolution within a particular species. Here fundamentalism makes its most obvious appearance.

As for control of education, the parents 'as an organized group but not as individuals' should nominate teachers and 'exercise supervision over their teaching'; the church should supervise 'the spirit and trend' of education; and the State should see that academic standards are good, and defray a major part of expenses. While the Christian National school is seen as the ideal, the statement recognizes that present action must be taken through 'the direct leavening of the present State schools by means of our Christian-National spirit and trend'.

Much of this situation is already in operation; thus throughout the Union today, except in Natal, each primary and secondary school has a committee elected by the parents which exercises limited powers of control over the school. In many country districts, the predikant of the local Dutch Reformed Church is also chairman of the school committee. The result, as Leo Marquard points out, is that the appointment of teachers is 'frequently and increasingly made on religious and denominational as well as on party-political grounds'. Though a 'conscience clause' forbids religious tests in the making of appointments, the fact that Afrikaner teachers must submit a testimonial from a predikant commonly nullifies the purpose of the safeguard. In the cities, Marquard declares, 'political rather than religious considerations are a determining factor in appointments'.[33] The resulting lack of intellectual and religious freedom among Afrikaans-speaking teachers too often affects the standards of their professional work.

C.N.E. principles of the appropriate type also apply to the training of non-Europeans. A dúty to christianize both Coloured and Natives (nothing, naturally, is said about Indians) arises from the guardianship of the non-European by the European, and particularly by the Afrikaner. The Coloured should be made 'race-conscious' by applying 'apartness' as strictly in education as in the church. Any system of education for Natives, declares the statement, should follow the three principles of 'guardianship, no levelling, and segregation'. In response to these principles, Native education should be based on 'the life and world view of the European, more particularly that of the Boer nation as the senior European guardian of the Native'. This should not mean slavish acceptance of European or Afrikaner standards, however, but the ultimate development by the Bantu of his own interpretation of Christian and National values. Implicit is the assumption of an ultimate ideal apartheid through which the Native will have a homeland of his own. In the meantime, 'European guardianship' of Coloured and Natives seems to involve less acceptance of responsibility for them than the phrase suggests, for the document declares specifically that the financing of non-European education should not be at the cost of European education.

How influential is Christian National Education? Among the directors of the Institute for C.N.E. in 1948, when the statement was issued, were Dr. T. E. Dönges, about to become Minister of the Interior and subsequently leader of the National Party in the Cape; Dr. E. G. Jansen, subsequently Governor-General; Dr. J. G. Meiring, Professor of Education at Stellenbosch; Professor Chris Coetzee, in 1952, Acting Rector of Potchefstroom University; and Mr. J. H. Greybe, head of the Afrikaner Teachers' Association in the Transvaal.

Still more significant is the degree to which the philosophy of Christian National Education is accepted by Afrikaner teachers throughout the Union. This is particularly the case for those who have been educated at Potchefstroom, the center for the small but potent *Gereformeerde Kerk* which holds the most fundamentalist view amongst the Dutch Reformed Churches. Most of Potchefstroom's graduates go into primary and secondary school teaching so that this university has a greater influence on educational practices and spirit than perhaps any other in South Africa.

Throughout 1949 and to a lesser extent 1950, Christian National Education was vigorously discussed in the South African press. The English-speaking press generally expressed its disapproval. This was partly through recording protests like that of the Education League (discussed on page 334), NUSAS,[34] English-speaking Teachers' Associations, the League of Women Voters,[35] which issued a pamphlet called 'A Case against Christian National Education', and the 17th Biennial Congress of the South African Jewish Board of Deputies.[36] Partly it was through editorial comment as when the *Friend* castigated the 'wide gulf between Christian ideals and the narrow principles of C.N.E.'[37] and the *Eastern Province Herald* declared that C.N.E. would make the people 'half-baked as to intellect and hide-bound as to conscience'.[38] Even the Bantu press entered the fray with a comment by *Inkululeke* that 'C.N.E. is narrow, and intolerant'.[39] P. A. Moore voiced a United Party view in the House of Assembly that C.N.E. was 'a grave offence' against South Africa,[40] while the Labour Party similarly opposed it.[41] *Die Volksblad* retaliated by declaring that the English-speaking were originally responsible for single-medium schools,[42] while SAPA reported 4,000 teachers endorsing C.N.E.[43]

Though Dr. Stals officially denied that the Nationalist Government subscribed to Christian National Education policy or had anything to do with its formulation,[44] the Nationalist press was vocal in support of C.N.E. principles.[45] *Die Burger, Die Volksblad* and *Die Oosterlig* with one accord accused the United

Party of using propaganda on C.N.E. to drive a wedge between Afrikaners and English-speaking.[46] *Die Transvaler* claimed triumphantly that despite attacks on C.N.E. the Nationalists had neither repudiated nor abandoned it and that its essential principles would be realized in the Transvaal.[47] (Education is a provincial matter.) Significantly, *Die Kerkbode*, organ of the Dutch Reformed Church, reported that the Dutch Reformed Church supported C.N.E.[48] Subsequently this publication also noted, however, that the Ecumenical Synod in Amsterdam did not approve the F.A.K. brochure on C.N.E.[49]

The Nationalist press displayed its customary flair for rebuttal as attacks on C.N.E. continued. When the 1949 United Party Youth Congress condemned C.N.E.,[50] *Die Burger* commented caustically that the United Party did not want its youth 'national-minded'.[51] When the Natal Director of Education, Mr. C. M. Booysen, said that no C.N.E. principles would be introduced into any school under his jurisdiction,[52] *Die Transvaler* commented 'poor Natal children', but pointed out sagely that C.N.E. was 'more spirit than system', and thus could work 'outside the orbit of threats and regulations'.[53]

Moreover, there was no slackening of efforts. In August, 1950, *Die Transvaler* reported that the Afrikaner Student Bond had supported C.N.E. in a statement which also emphasized its own irreconcilability with NUSAS, and held out the ideal of separate universities for Europeans and non-Europeans.[54] In September, the F.A.K. Congress asked the C.N.E. Institute to give full practical effect to its policy.[55] At the beginning of 1951, *Die Transvaler* wrote enthusiastically that 'C.N.E. triumphs'. The Afrikaans-medium schools with their Christian-National spirit, it declared, had produced results which other schools could not equal, and without curtailing intellectual development.[56] By the end of that year, the Free State Education Commission recommended that C.N.E. be introduced in the Free State, a move which gave rise to a public meeting of protest in Bloemfontein.[57] Three years later, the Free State Provincial Council passed the Free State Education Ordinance endorsing the cultivation of Christian principles and the maintenance of a national outlook.

Those who support C.N.E. do so with the best of consciences. They point out that it is intended only for the Afrikaans-speaking and that the English are at full liberty to develop their own characteristic philosophy of education, as they feel has been done in large measure in the English-speaking private schools.

The critics of C.N.E. attack it both on philosophical and practical grounds. As a philosophy, they believe it over-emphasizes the differences between peoples at the expense of the similarities; even within a particular group it overstresses tradition and characteristic ways at the expense of individual development. Moreover, they vigorously oppose the notion, so openly held by C.N.E., that subject-matters like science and history should be presented in the light of fixed, preconceived notions.

From the practical point of view, C.N.E. is seen as dangerously dividing Afrikaners from English, partly by encouraging unilingualism, but more particularly by developing widely divergent ideals, conceptions of history and ways of life. The advocates of C.N.E. deny this result, since they feel that school is not the place to bring English and Afrikaners together, but that they can meet on good terms as adults, each secure in his own tradition. For some people this may be true, but the great majority of adult Afrikaners and English see little and know less of each other's ways of life. Moreover, the views inculcated at school, particularly those in history and politics, permeate their future attitudes.

It is always surprising to outsiders to learn how little schools, or indeed universities, teach South African history since 1909, when the Union was established. The common rationale for not doing so is that differences of interpretation are too wide to make it advisable. Attitude formation is left to families, and to the 'slant' given to other material in formal education. Thus the free wind of open inquiry rarely blows into these stuffy corners of prejudice. C.N.E. advocates say that there would be bitterness and fights if the differing attitudes of English and Afrikaners confronted each other in school; to an outsider this is one of the best arguments for letting the process work itself out at that level in the interests of mutual understanding and broadened comprehension later on.

SABRA (South African Bureau of Racial Affairs)

Very different from the Institute for Christian National Education is the South African Bureau of Racial Affairs, commonly known as SABRA, which is the result of the spontaneous efforts of certain Afrikaner intellectuals to evolve a logical and broadly conceived policy of apartheid, or racial separateness, which will provide for the needs and rights of South Africa's non-Europeans as well as Europeans. Yet despite their differences, there is much in common in the view of the two organizations toward the non-European. Each sees the necessity of developing him in terms of his own tradition and capacities. It is a logical inference of Christian National Education views that the African, in particular, must have his own permanent and stable homeland. SABRA rightly deserves the credit, however, for developing the most complete and intelligible statement of the radical doctrine which is known as 'ideal' or 'total apartheid' (see p. 14).

Total apartheid involves the territorial separation from each other of Europeans and Africans as far as basic living areas are concerned. This is no new conception in South African history, for the Native Reserves were set aside to provide for a separate home for the Bantu. But European need for African labor to develop farms and industry, and the pressure on non-Europeans to supplement the scanty output of the Reserves led to an ever-increasing influx of non-Europeans to European areas, until, as the Fagan Report disclosed in 1948, more than half the Africans are outside the Reserves at any given time, and many of them are permanently domiciled outside the European cities. Total apartheid proposes to reverse this trend and ultimately to re-establish the earlier situation of territorial separateness. In this sense, it is a radical doctrine because it goes to the heart of the problem of European and non-European relations.

The conception of total apartheid did not spring full blown from SABRA. Professor R. F. Hoernlé made a tentative consideration of the idea in his *South African Native Policy and the Liberal Spirit* and indicated that many Afrikaners were thinking of total separation as early as 1945. As a political philosophy, the notion seems to have come from a committee of the National Party headed by Paul Sauer, Minister of Transport under Dr. Malan, which was appointed in 1947 to draw up a color policy for use in the coming election. This committee called its policy 'apartheid' and declared that it must be planned so as to 'eventually promote the ideal of complete separation in a national way'. Each race was to develop 'its own national character, aptitude and calling' and the non-European racial groups were to have full opportunity in their own areas

> for complete development in every sphere and will be able to develop their own institutions and social services whereby the forces of the progressive non-Europeans can be harnessed for their own national development.[58]

Some of the most significant early thinking on total apartheid was by Dr. W. W. M. Eiselen, son of a D.R.C. missionary, and Secretary for Native Affairs under the Nationalist Government. To the Witwatersrand Peoples' Forum in 1948, Dr. Eiselen spoke of

> separating the heterogeneous groups from the population of the country into separate socio-economic units, inhabiting separate parts of the country, each enjoying in his own area full citizen rights, the greatest of which is the opportunity of developing such capabilities as its individual members may possess to their optimum capacity.[59]

The theoretical basis for such a policy Dr. Eiselen found in his belief that there are external and possibly spiritual differences between races which no policy can remove. Since differences always lead to discrimination, he declared in an article early in 1949, and

> real development means that the human person will be given the opportunity to unfold to the full extent of his ability the talents and the capacity which the Creator has given him,

the non-European cannot develop fully as long as he has to conform to European South African standards and conditions.

> Apartheid is necessary not because the Native is of lesser potential value than the white, but because he is of another kind or sort (*anderssortig*) and because, under a co-operative system, neither the one nor the other can follow his own nature and fully enjoy (*uitleef*) the wealth of his own culture.[60]

The challenge which brought SABRA into being was the need to develop these positive aspects of apartheid into a coherent doctrine. The genesis of the group was at Stellenbosch, the oldest and most honored of Afrikaans-medium universities, where its headquarters remains. SABRA's first conference was at the beginning of 1950; since then they have been held annually in Cape Town, and serve partly as a forum for discussion, and partly as a means of clarifying and publicizing its ideas. SABRA has a substantial number of influential members (among them Dr. T. E. Dönges, Dr. E. G. Jansen, and Dr. W. W. M. Eiselen), and issues a bilingual scholarly *Journal of Racial Affairs*, almost every month. SABRA has also published a few pamphlets of which the one which most clearly presents its thesis is *Integration or Separate Development?*[61]

SABRA's argument in support of separate development is a mixture of hard facts and moral judgments. To continue with a *laissez-faire* policy of economic integration will result, in 50 years, according to its estimates, in about 12 million

Bantu, that is about twice the European population, being permanent residents of European areas in South Africa. So large a group would inevitably press for a much improved status. In any case, in SABRA's view, it would be 'immoral' to accept Africans as permanent residents in these areas, but refuse them 'political and other rights'.[62] Local separation, such as is practised throughout South Africa today, will only postpone the evil day, in its opinion, since it neither prevents friction nor provides the Bantu with adequate opportunities for development without imperilling the European's position of dominance. The logical conclusion, which SABRA is quite prepared to face, is that there must be territorial separation between Europeans and non-Europeans, and that it must be systematically organized as quickly as possible.

A crucial question which SABRA tries, not too satisfactorily, to answer is: Where can a national home for the Bantu be established? The present Reserves now house less than half the Bantu population at a given time. SABRA itself estimates that not even 10 per cent of the 3¾ million Bantu in the Native Reserves enjoy what they call 'an economic existence'. The residents of the Reserves, as any visitor to them quickly discovers, are chiefly women, children and older people dependent on the earnings of the males between the ages of 16 and 60 who are working in European areas. Thus the Reserves today, which amount to some 11 per cent of the land surface of the Union, are no more than 'sub-economic appendages', exporting their labor forces to make subsistence possible.[63]

A national home for the Bantu, therefore, will require not only a great deal more land than is now available for their use, but also large scale development. Some of these problems SABRA left hopefully to the Commission on the Socio-Economic Development of Native Areas (under the chairmanship of competent and hard-working Professor F. R. Tomlinson, of Pretoria University) which submitted its monumental report to the Cabinet on October 1, 1954, and published it in book-length summary form late in 1955 (see p. 271). In the meantime, though it recognized the difficulties of persuading European farmers to sell their land,[64] SABRA urged the purchase of the 3 million morgen (a morgen equals 2·1 acres) needed to complete the 18 million morgen provided for by Hertzog's Native Trust and Land Act (see p. 120), which would bring the Reserves up to 13 per cent of the Union's land surface. SABRA also favors rearranging areas so that they are no longer a patchwork of interspersed Native Reserves and European holdings as in some parts of the eastern Cape, but this meets the same difficulties.

Looking farther afield, SABRA points out that if the Union's Native Reserves were joined to the High Commission Territories—Basutoland, Swaziland and Bechuanaland—the Bantu share of the combined area of the Union and these territories would be 45 per cent. Beyond this again, it speaks wistfully of the fact that the division of land between European and Bantu is 'a Southern African problem', and should be 'treated as such'.[65] It acknowledges, however, that there is little hope of this being done, at least at the moment, because of the 'fear or suspicion of the Union' held in the European communities farther north. It might also have noted that British public opinion remains adamantly opposed to transferring the High Commission Territories to the Union, because of South African Native policy.

Thus the basic feature of the situation is that the Native Reserves must be made capable of carrying economically a much more substantial proportion of the Bantu population. SABRA sets as its goal a high—most would say, impossibly high—objective. Not only does it envisage developing the Native territories to provide an economic living for those now inhabiting these areas, but 'to accommodate eventually in the Native territories also all the descendants of those Bantu who today have their homes on European farms and in the urban areas'.[66] Still more would it favor a development of the Native areas so rapid that it would also attract in the next ten to twenty years all the Bantu now permanently resident in the European areas. Such a program involves two differing sets of problems: the impact on the European areas themselves, and the scale of development needed to make the Reserves viable for some 9 to 10 million Bantu. SABRA sees a partial answer to both problems in the system of migratory labor. Recognizing, though without any careful examination, the economic and social dislocations inherent in migratory labor, which have already so badly shaken the traditional structure and *mores* of the Bantu, SABRA accepts that such migration should be on a still more extended scale than at present, both to provide for the needs of the European economy and of the Bantu themselves.

SABRA states, it is true, that in its opinion it would be 'preferable for the European community to rely on its own labor resources'.[67] European population increase, more mechanization, efficiency and cooperation particularly on the farms, and planning and coordination of efforts should be sufficient, it says, to provide the European economy 'with all its labour needs at some time in the future'. But it acknowledges that in South Africa 'a situation has developed which has to be accepted for what it is', namely that an essential part of the national life is in the hands of 'the members of another race', the Bantu. It even italicizes its conclusion that:

> It should be clear to any intelligent observer that Bantu labour is not only essential to the country's economy at the present time, but will probably remain so for a very long time to come.

The general character of SABRA's proposal for separate development is radical, but its effect on the European in this regard is to be relatively small.

In essence what SABRA is proposing is that the Native Reserves, enlarged if possible, must become the national home of the Bantu from which they will migrate as necessary to European areas to perform what tasks are dictated by the latter's needs. Within the European areas, the Bantu, naturally enough, will then have no reason to claim those rights to which he would morally be entitled, in SABRA's view, if he were a permanent resident within them. But how are the Bantu areas to be made economically stable so that they can serve as a true national home for the steadily increasing African people?

The most crucial—and many people believe the insurmountable—problem is how to develop the Reserves so that they can support a far vaster Native population than at present, and at a standard of living well above the present meager subsistence. In the first place, SABRA proposes that 'an economic farming class' be brought into being by taking those with a natural aptitude for farming and giving them larger plots of land than the now customary six acres per family. Since this means that many of those still on the land must be removed, the only way to meet their needs and those of the vast numbers who should ultimately secure a stable economic base in the Reserves is through industrialization. This is already being attempted on a very small scale, as with the cotton spinning mill, the Good Hope Textile Factory at Zwelitsha near King Williams Town in the Ciskei, an area in the Eastern Cape where European and Native areas are interspersed. Other small industries[68] are being started also through the efforts of the Industrial Development Corporation, a Government-supported body under the chairmanship of one of the Union's most vigorous personalities, Dr. A. J. van Eck. To meet the needs which SABRA's plan involves, however, would need industrialization on a very large scale indeed.

SABRA, however, calls on the Europeans 'to make the necessary sacrifices' to finance such a development, not only in the interests of 'survival' but also of justice and fairness. Should not a similar expenditure be made for so great a goal as was poured out in World War II? What of the possibility of overseas financial assistance? It also suggests, over-optimistically, that the Bantu themselves might become responsible in due course for the interest payments on such loans. 'Sooner or later', it concludes, 'the Bantu will have to meet their own expenses and carry their own financial responsibilities.'[69]

SABRA points out various compensations for the sacrifices it asks European South Africans to make to establish viable Native areas. The present policy of integration causes European expenditures to aid various services for Native education and social services which, presumably, might ultimately be carried by the Bantu areas themselves. The contributions now made to Native welfare, however, hardly seem comparable to the costs of large scale development of the Native areas. SABRA is on safer ground when it points out that Bantu communities can only maintain their 'organic unity' on a separate basis, though here too the large-scale character of migratory labor it envisages would create serious difficulties. It is also true that, as it says, the Bantu cannot fully bear the cost of their own services in a 'mixed society', and since they are the neediest will inevitably struggle for more aid. Thus SABRA concludes that:

> Only a separation policy, which accepts the organic unity of the Bantu communities as a basis, can create conditions under which the Bantu can determine the rate of their own progress, and which can safeguard the European population against continual accusations of discrimination and neglect.[70]

This does not mean that Europeans will no longer extend aid to the Bantu population, but 'they will not be expected to pay more than they can reasonably afford'.[71]

But what will be the economic and, ultimately, political relationship between the Bantu homeland and European South Africa? SABRA answers the fear that Native industries might undercut those in European areas by maintaining that in the initial stages the former would 'be mainly complementary to', and not in competition with, the latter. Moreover, 'the European and Bantu area should be developed as a single economic unit'. SABRA clearly envisages European control of Bantu industrial development over a long period of time and prefers that it be exercised through a State corporation, i.e., under Government direction.

Politically SABRA is not afraid to face the prospect of Bantu autonomy, or even independence, declaring it to be far less frightening than political demands by the Bantu within a mixed community. But in any case, SABRA minimizes the possibility of what is sometimes called 'Bantustan'. It anticipates that several small Bantu areas will develop rather than a single large one; even more that European control over these areas will persist for a long time to come. Whether the Bantu can eventually gain control over their own affairs is said to depend on 'their cooperation and development'. Moreover a federation might evolve, either of European South Africa and the various Bantu areas, or in 'a broader Southern African Federation'.[72] This clearly is a problem so far distant that it may be left to evolution.

How important is SABRA? Very important indeed. Its doctrine of separate development appeals deeply to Afrikaner intellectuals whose characteristic turn of mind is to seek clear-cut logical solutions based on theoretical conceptions. But beyond this is the fact that 'ideal' or 'total apartheid' offer both a myth for the future, and a rationalization for the present. The myth foresees an ultimately flourishing and happy Bantu homeland, existing side by side with a still more prosperous and happy European South Africa, which can continue to draw on Native labor but without the pangs of conscience induced either by its own standards or those of the outside world. Because separate development will ultimately provide him with a homeland of his own, the rationalization justifies the European in refusing the Bantu a permanent position in the European areas and also such rights and privileges as the African might justifiably demand as the result of that position. On this line of argument, the integration of the Bantu into the European area, as for example by extending him rights, is in fact thwarting the greater good ultimately awaiting him in his own areas.

Is separate development in the full sense of the word more than a myth? If not, will European South Africa accept the price? The best estimates are those of the Commission on the Socio-Economic Development of the Reserves. It believes that primary economic production—agriculture, forestry and mining—can support 2·4 million Bantu in the Reserves,[73] i.e., about half of the present *de jure* population of the Bantu areas. With full scale development in the secondary or industrial, and tertiary or service sectors, which would involve very heavy expenditures, it believes that the Bantu areas in the long run can carry about 10 million Bantu.[74] By the time this is implemented, however, i.e., by about the end of the century, the Bantu population will be about 18 to 20 million. Thus the European areas will have to cater for approximately half of the future Bantu population. This, of course, is on the assumption that South Africa cannot plan for the Protectorates; with them, it could consider a still broader program.

The cost and intention remain the crucial points. Nationalist policy accepts the full implications of the 'differentness' of the Bantu, and apartheid legislation like the Bantu Education Act builds upon this view. Dr. van Eck's Industrial Development Corporation continues to sponsor some industry on the edge of the Reserves. But this is hardly separate development as SABRA outlines it. Far more would need to be done, and to be spent if the recommendations of the Socio-Economic Commission were to be made effective. Even then, it would provide only a limited 'ideal apartheid'.

None the less, SABRA remains important. It provides a spur to the Government and to Nationalist Afrikanerdom to live up to their professions. It provides also a measuring rod by which to estimate their degree of sincerity regarding separate development. Less happily, SABRA's ideal remains one of the myths of nationalistic Afrikanerdom, capable of salving the pangs of conscience which might otherwise be caused by shanty towns, and alleviating the responsibility of coping in a more equitable way with the immediate demands of a multi-racial society.

The Dutch Reformed Churches

No Protestant church in any other country has as strong and pervasive a contemporary influence as has the Dutch Reformed Church on the Afrikaner people. In earlier times, whole families journeyed for days to the *nachtmaal,* the joint communion service which lasted more than a week, and served as a great cementing influence among scattered and isolated Afrikaner settlers. No less of a unifying influence is Sunday observance in a South African country town today. Farmer families and townspeople converge on the open square in front of the local church; the young girls in their white dresses, and boys in dark suits are as conspicuous as older people. Underlying their conformity is a deep-rooted sentiments which accepts the church as a focal point in Afrikaner culture and Nationalist aspirations.

In recent years, two small evangelical churches—the Apostolic Faith Mission, and the Church of the Full Gospel—have attained some prominence with a largely Afrikaans-speaking membership; some few Afrikaners belong to the Methodist, Episcopal or even Roman Catholic Church. The overwhelming bulk of the Afrikaner people accept the Dutch Reformed Church, however, and a remarkably high proportion of them are participating church members.[75]

Though it is common to speak of the Dutch Reformed Church, there are, in fact, three such churches, differentiated by history and also by their interpretation of Calvinism. By far the largest of the three is the *Nederduits Gereformeerde Kerk* (N.G.K.), organized in four provincial, self-governing units coordinated by a federal council. Relatively similar though slightly more liberal in approach, is the *Nederduits Hervormde Kerk,* established in the Transvaal Republic in 1858 to care for the Trekkers with whom the parent church at the Cape lost touch until 1866. The third and smallest[76] of the Dutch Reformed Churches—the *Gereformeerde Kerk*—is the most fundamentalist. It was formed in 1859 as a conscious break-away from the parent church in the Cape, and is centered at Potchefstroom in the Transvaal. Despite its smaller membership, the *Gereformeerde Kerk* has a more potent influence than the other Dutch Reformed Churches partly because its Calvinism is more narrow and rigid, but more particularly because such a high proportion of its members go into education and the ministry. As we have seen, Potchefstroom is the official center for Christian National Education, whose influence spreads steadily as members of the *Gereformeerde Kerk* take over the bulk of the primary schools throughout the Orange Free State and beyond. Moreover, the very rigidity of the dogma preached at Potchefstroom acts as a spur, and sometimes goad, to the other Dutch Reformed Churches.

Throughout the Dutch Reformed Churches, the doctrinal base is that of historic Calvinism, drawn direct from seventeenth-century Holland, and reinfused with fervor by a brilliant, dedicated group of Scottish divines in the nineteenth century. At its core is the doctrine of predestination, held most firmly by the *Gereformeerde Kerk*, from which arises easily the idea of the elect, the chosen people, marked by God for a special destiny. This conception reinforces the sense of racial superiority and distinctive nationalism which springs naturally from the Afrikaner's history, and separate language. Fundamentalism, in relation to the Bible[77] and to personal conduct further intensifies the sense of separateness and of mission with which the Dutch Reformed Church imbues its people.

From the political point of view, it is no less significant that Calvinism is inherently authoritarian. Historically, there has been a great difference in the interpretation of Calvinist doctrines according to whether the members of that faith found themselves in the majority or in the minority. French Huguenots, Scottish Presbyterians and Puritans fought bitterly for freedom of conscience against Catholic or Anglican majorities. Out of these struggles came a religious reinforcement of individual liberties and of self-determination which has been of immense importance for the growth of liberalism. But it was circumstances rather than the doctrine of Calvinism which produced this result. Wherever Calvinists have been undisputedly in the majority, the Church has strongly supported the authority of the State, and of the Government which represents 'the elect'.

Highly significant in this regard are the *Fundamental Principles of Calvinist Political Science* issued by the Council of the N.G.K. following its meeting in Bloemfontein in May 1951 (the same session that received the report on the Broederbond). This statement sees the State 'as born of God and His infallible goodness', and authority as 'God's mercy-gift to a sinful race'. This is not to suggest that the State encompasses life 'universally and totally, as the totalitarian State does'. The task of the State is primarily legal, to protect 'subjects and non-State associations . . . against the aggression of others'. If this function were performed properly there would be no need for trade unions, for the State should 'protect the workers from exploitation by employers', and not leave them to organize and struggle for their rights by economic means as in 'the liberal-democratic State'. This paternalistic approach stands in sharp and avowed distinction to individualism in which 'the sovereign individual with his own interests is the highest good'. Equally, the *Fundamental Principles* maintain that 'the Christian view of society' stands in contrast to universalism, which 'seeks the root of society in a sovereign world-wide relationship which includes all humanity in one whole'.

This emphasis, in the *Fundamental Principles*, on the unique character of each State is coupled with the view that the authority of government within the State is not only 'God-derived' but also 'indivisible'. Thus the N.G.K. statement maintains that 'the Humanistic classification of titular, legal, and political and popular sovereignty is not tenable'. Similarly it rejects the division of State authority between legislative, executive and judicial bodies. While authority may be delegated, the statement holds that there remains responsibility 'to *one* governmental authority'.

At the same time it is not 'unlimited' self-determination but obedience to God's ordinances 'for man and civilization' which brings freedom in its view. Civil freedom results from limits placed on the Government's sphere of action because it is not the State but God's commands which are 'the source of all right'. Political freedom involves political participation, and through his franchise the Christian must 'do everything in his power to get rid of a Government disobedient to God's word'.

Though the statement acknowledges that those who cannot participate in politics are 'politically unfree', it is also apparent that the *Fundamental Principles* enunciate an exclusive, or elitist, concept regarding the franchise. South Africa's greatest problem in regard to the franchise, it states, is the approach 'of the revolutionary democracy of the school of Rousseau', that is, that 'white and non-white must in individual right have the franchise'. It also condemns the view that the 'mass of individuals become the source of the Government's will, authority, and competency'. Out of that view, it declares, 'God's authority-structure of the State on the law side is turned upside down, with subjects above and the authorities under'. This is sternly condemned with the words, 'Here franchise is pure vanity of Sovereignty, rebellion against God'.

The correct approach is to see the 'Christian franchise' as 'a trust', which is to be used 'by the mature with a sense of responsibility towards God'. Using the touchstones of 'maturity' and 'Christianity', the *Fundamental Principles* reject the notion that the franchise 'be given to every man merely because he is a man', and note specifically that its view excludes from voting not only 'the immature communities', i.e. Native Africans, but also those 'in open rebellion against God, as e.g. the Communists'. Though not so stated, it appears also to exclude Jews. Returning in the concluding paragraph of this section to 'our non-whites' the statement maintains that their political participation is through expressing wishes, 'and even criticism', and that anything more would not be 'in *their own* best interests, let alone in the best general interest'.

The theme of Christian control in politics continues in the section on political parties. 'Everyone *must* organize themselves into a party to give expression to their political confession,' the statement declares, defining political party as 'a historical-political creator of power striving after the monopoly of the Government office'. It then states, however, that 'A Christian State depends on a Christian political confession in the hearts of its citizens'. Sounding a warning note, the *Fundamental Principles* declare that 'against this threaten, to a certain degree, Liberalism, more so Democracy and, very dangerously, Communism'. To Communism, it denies as 'anti-Christian' the right to party formation, a view expressed shortly after the passage of the Suppression of Communism Act, 1951. Democracy, it maintains, possesses 'the germ of its own decay' by counting not only votes, but also political principles 'of equal worth'. Against these dangers, the statement declares that 'the Christian must organize and work to see that his political confession of faith will triumph' and gain Government office, warning that 'if he doesn't then *they* surely will instead'.

In the general conclusions of the *Fundamental Principles,* the concept of 'Christian' domination is given its most unequivocal expression. 'Both Scripture and History show that God demands Christian States,' it declares. 'This is only possible with a Christian political confession flowing from a believing heart "aimed" at God.' While 'the details of the definite Christian form of State for our country is not the task of the Church', it is the responsibility 'of the believing citizens'.

The *Fundamental Principles* contain the most clear-cut statement which has been made of the political views of the Dutch Reformed Church. Though it would not be accepted unequivocally by all members of that confession, it represents the prevailing way of thinking about the problems of government and politics. Its authoritarianism about the problems of government and politics, and its exclusiveness and underlying tone of self-righteousness have been reflected from time to time in the actions of the National Party, e.g. the exclusion of Jews from National Party membership in the Transvaal until 1951. At the same time, the *Fundamental Principles* are outspokenly anti-totalitarian. Responsibility, self-restraint and Christian principles, however, rather than any constitutional limitations, provide the curb on the exercise of power in a State called by God to a particular destiny.

Hardly less important than the political attitudes that the Dutch Reformed Churches inculcate are those towards the non-European. No longer, it seems, do Dutch Reformed Church predikants speak of the non-Europeans as 'sons of Ham', who are destined to be eternally 'drawers of water and hewers of wood', though this conception still lingers in the South African *platteland.* Only recently, and gradually, however, has a substantial group in the Dutch Reformed Church rejected the notion that racial segregation rests on theological grounds. In practice, compulsory segregation of church communities and, by implication, in all other areas of life is accepted throughout the Dutch Reformed Church. But there is a sharp and important division between those who still maintain that compulsory color segregation is both theologically and morally justified, and those who see it only as a practical expedient under existing South African conditions, but deny that it has any moral or scriptural basis.

In 1952, Dr. Ben J. Marais, pastor of an important Pretoria church, and subsequently Professor of Theology at Pretoria University, published a significant book entitled *Colour: Unsolved Problem of the West.*[78] Concerned primarily with analysing race relations in the United States and Brazil, Dr. Marais obliquely approaches the South African racial problem on which he ultimately formulates certain conclusions which, by South African standards, may be called advanced, or liberal. Endorsing 'separate ministration and even separate church institutions for the different colour groups in South Africa' as 'sensible and 'expedient', Dr. Marais denounces the attempt to base the policy of segregation on Scripture.[79] The first church to be established on a racial or color basis was in 1787, he points out, and in the United States. Not until 1857, and then only as a concession to 'the weakness of some', did the South African N.G.K. Synod permit separate 'buildings or institutions' for non-European Christians, and then in a declaration which began 'it is *desirable* and *scriptural* that our members from the heathen be admitted to and be incorporated in our existing congregations everywhere where it can be done'.[80] Dr. Marais thus concludes that compulsory church segregation is an outgrowth of slavery, whereas what the Bible teaches is 'not racial apartness but the apartness of sin', that is, the separation of the believer from the unbeliever.[81]

Strongly reinforcing this view are the replies to a questionnaire sent by Dr. Marais to thirteen world-renowned Calvinist and Lutheran Church leaders and theologians. These replies are printed *in toto* in the book as an annexure.[82] All these leaders, who include such persons as Professor Karl Barth and Professor Emil Brunner, unqualifiedly reject the view that there are scriptural grounds for debarring believers on grounds of race or color from a white church or congregation; only one, Professor Samuel Zwemer of Princeton, N.J., goes as far as to state that 'in exceptional circumstances' the Bible might justify such exclusion.

The opposing point of view is perhaps best expressed by Dr. T. N. Hanekom, assistant editor of the N.G.K.'s official newspaper, *Die Kerkbode*, in the review he wrote of Dr. Marais' book, and his lengthy answers to the spirited correspondence which followed it.[83] In substance, Dr. Hanekom argues that the religious color bar is related to racial, cultural and geographical differences, but that it arose more particularly in the Church out of the missionary work of advanced people for immature ones. Church apartheid thus rests on the separateness of 'peoples and races (also classified into white and non-white) as an ordainment of God', and they must 'remain apart, in spite of the unity of faith which exists'. That there must be 'diversity, otherness, and variation' is known, he maintained, 'not only from experience, but from God's revelation in Scripture', both Old and New Testaments.[84]

Finally, in answer to Dr. Marais, Dr. B. B. Keet of the Stellenbosch Theological Seminary, and Professor P. V. Pistorius, noted classical scholar of Pretoria University, who emphasize in the correspondence the importance of seeking universally acceptable interpretations of Scripture, Dr. Hanekom declared that 'until now Afrikaans theology has had too much of the nature of a spiritual protectorate controlled from Europe and England'. World opinion is 'unenlightened about our conditions', he wrote. While not claiming 'that "we alone are right",' Dr. Hanekom maintained 'that we have a right to our own viewpoint about a matter which concerns us *alone*'.[85]

As revealing as Dr. Hanekom's emphasis on the uniqueness of South African conditions, and his implication that this in itself creates a theological justification for Church apartheid, is his attack upon what he called 'the present European and American pattern of integration on a footing of equality'. In his judgment, there was 'no conformity between the spirit of Christ and this spirit of our times'. And he warned that 'the hankering after community of faith, which is also present among our non-white Christians . . . is not separated from the pattern of levelling . . . being forced on the Western world by means of the court of law and other authoritarian means'.[86]

The contrast between the positions taken by Dr. Marais and Dr. Hanekom were underlined in speeches at the important conference of Church leaders convened in Pretoria, November 1953, by the Federal Missionary Council of the Dutch Reformed Churches.[87] In the opening address, Dr. Keet elaborated, in a witty but outspoken manner, on his stand in *Die Kerkbode* correspondence. 'The relation at present existing between white and Coloured Christians,' he declared, 'can well be termed, as the cynic has described it, "Brothers in Christ, Limited"!' a sally greeted with general laughter. There is 'only one apartheid known to Scripture', he maintained, 'and that is separation from sin.' While under present circumstances, apartheid could not be 'unreservedly condemned', he felt it must be 'a temporary measure'. He warned that 'a Church that wants to build on the foundation of gentility is predestined to die'. Going far beyond this, however, Dr. Keet declared that discrimination on ground of color must disappear, however long it might take, and called on 'the Church to lead the State in the direction of unity'.

The opposing point of view was most trenchantly expressed by the Rev. C. B. Brink, Moderator of the Synod of the Transvaal N.H.K.,[88] whose speech immediately followed that of Dr. Keet. Dr. Brink first denied that the Church should enunciate racial policy: 'to demand from the Church of Christ that itself should prescribe rules governing the political relationships of races and groups is to demand too much. . . . Unto Caesar should be left that which belongs to Caesar.' Beyond this, he maintained that there are 'natural differences of rank and status', that God willed 'the separate existence of nations', and that even in the Christian Church 'the Gospel did not abolish the differences in endowment, nature, culture, etc,, between the different racial groups'. To ignore these differences, he maintained, would be to attempt 'to build another Tower of Babel', and he added, 'the products of such attempts in the political field are called "beasts" in the Revelation of St. John'. Thus he concluded that the establishment of separate non-white Churches rests on 'profound Scriptural grounds', and warned that 'the Christian Churches must be careful not to deprive the whole of Africa's Nativedom of the privilege to make its own contribution to the development of the Christian Churches'.

This latter view had infused the discussions of the Federal Missionary Council (representing the four federated N.G.K., and the three Dutch Reformed Mission Churches) at Bloemfontein, in April 1950, when it sought to define a comprehensive policy towards the Native African. The basic statement of mission policy of the Dutch Reformed Church considers 'all segregation as a means of enhancing life and independence'. It also declares that 'The traditional fear of the Afrikaner of "equality" between black and white has its origin in his antipathy to the idea of racial fusion'. While opposed to 'social equality' in the sense of ignoring color differences in daily life, it does not 'begrudge' Coloured or Native as 'honourable' a social status 'as he can reach'. Moreover 'every nation has a right to be itself and to endeavour to develop and elevate itself'.[89]

To this, the 1950 Conference[90] added a good deal. Rather than use the word apartheid, the Conference placed its emphasis on what it called 'distinctive development', that is

> the process of development which seeks to lead each section of the people in the clearest and quickest way to its own destination under the gracious providence of God.[91]

Confronting the disintegration of traditional Bantu society under the impact of Western civilization, the Conference found it 'imperative' that the Reserves be transformed into 'true national homes' for the Bantu, 'with ample opportunity for self expression and self realization'.[92] This made it necessary 'gradually to eliminate the Bantu from European industrial life', and integrate him into a new industrial system in the Native areas. Equally far reaching, the Conference held that 'politically the Bantu should gradually be given the opportunity of self-government in his own territory, and of managing his own affairs'.[93]

It will be noted that this statement goes farther than the official formulation of SABRA policy, particularly in its forthright acceptance that in time there must be Bantu self-government. It echoes the same notes struck in the 1948 statement of Christian National Education, and Dr. Eiselen's article in 1949, namely that the drive for development lies in the particular characteristics and requirements of the Bantu.

By 1952, however, the Mission Council had virtually aligned its policy with that of SABRA, a fact which was hardly surprising since SABRA's chairman, G. B. A. Gerdener, was also chairman of the Action Committee of the Dutch Reformed Church Mission Council. Another reason for the modification, or, as it suggested, elaboration of its earlier statement was the obvious opposition of the Nationalist Government to 'total apartheid' in the terms of the 1950 resolution. This was because the Government had no intention of promoting so far-reaching a revolution in the life of European South Africa as would be involved in rapid withdrawal of Native labor, and because it feared, with justice, that the concept might be used against it in the election campaign.

The Federal Mission Council, meeting at Durban on August 28-31, 1952, issued a statement specifically referring to what it called 'the ideal of total separation between European and non-European eventually', which had been approved by the 1950 Bloemfontein congress. This had supposed a long-term policy, it declared, mentioning '50 or even 100 years'. The political future of the Bantu was also to be considered in such long-range terms. Moreover, the 'ideal', it took pains to note, 'by no means excludes the employment of Native labour for the economic machine of the Europeans for many years to come', and was therefore in 'complete harmony' with the 'realistic presumption' that Bantu labor would be 'indispensable' in European areas 'for many years still'.[94]

Shortly thereafter, the Federal Mission Council held a Union Congress with Bantu Church leaders of the Sotho, Zulu and Xosa groups. This conference recommended replacing State-aided by Government schools as recommended by the Eiselen Report on Native education and implemented in 1953 by the Bantu Education Act. It 'respectfully' asked that all land still available under the Hertzog Land Act of 1936 be purchased for the Bantu, and that industries be created and developed in or near the Reserves. The latter, it said, should be converted into 'a true Bantu national territory' which would be so attractive that people would not 'fall to the lure of the cities'. Going a little further, the Conference declared that it would try to influence the Government 'to initiate consultations between law-abiding Bantu leaders, such as chiefs, teachers and ministers and itself'.[95] It did not go beyond this since the item entitled 'The Political Aspect' was deleted from the agenda 'owing to lack of time'.

Though the Dutch Reformed Church's formulation of 'ideal apartheid' has now conformed to the exigencies of South African life, there are predikants and Afrikaner intellectuals who still hold to the full conviction that territorial separation is essential if the Bantu is to have a true opportunity for self-development. These idealists (in the true sense of the word) find themselves in the unhappy position of being caught between their convictions and the expedients of practical politics. If they are public servants, they necessarily conform to the general policies of Government. Even where they attempt to influence those areas of life for which they have particular responsibility they can do so only within a framework which they reject as inequitable. If they are churchmen, either they presume to instruct the State on racial policy (which

Dr. Brink and many others feel is not the function of the Church), or they accept the continuance of a situation which provides few opportunities for development towards the goal they see to be most desirable.

Writing in the most kindly and tolerant fashion of an ecumenical visit paid to South Africa in April and May 1952, the General Secretary of the World Council of Churches, Dr. W. A. Visser 't Hooft, declares that the real danger in South Africa is not that the Churches interfere in politics but that 'owing to the historical cooperation between Church and nation, the Church is far too much inclined to support uncritically the decisions and policies of the Afrikaner political leaders'.[96]

Part of the reason for the unwillingness of Dutch Reformed Church leaders to maintain a stand distinctively different from that of Nationalist political leaders may lie not only in their attitude to State authority, though this is highly important, but also in their divided counsels. Some, though probably few, predikants hold to the pure milk of 'ideal apartheid'; more see it as a distant goal but are prepared to accept the Nationalist Government's decisions on particular policies and timetable. Both groups, however, give their sanction to racial separation based on color. With all allowances for their sincerity, and even vision, this attitude cannot help but strengthen the division between Europeans and non-Europeans by providing a theoretical justification for it. Yet it is also apparent that there is a small but influential group within the N.G.K. and N.H.K., among whom Dr. Marais and Dr. Keet are prominent, who believe that unity is more important than diversity, and that the weight of the Church should be thrown against color discrimination. They reject ideal apartheid as impractical, although they recognize its theoretical advantages. They are moving, though with great caution, towards the formulation of a theory of race relations which will conform with that of the rest of Western Protestantism. In so doing they have already had considerable influence in their Churches, marked, for example, by the growing disinclination of younger predikants to base their justification of compulsory Church segregation on theological grounds. At the Conference of Church Leaders in Pretoria, one of the older predikants remarked to an observer: 'What Dr. Keet has said is still very much the minority view, but it is the one which is growing.'

If this trend develops, it might have an influence not only on attitudes towards the non-European, but also on relations between the Afrikaans and English-speaking Churches. In the 1920's these Churches maintained cordial relations which were reinforced by frequent meetings and discussions. The Pretoria Conference of 1953 was one of the first in recent times when English and Afrikaner Protestant clerics exchanged points of view. Still more significant was the Inter-Racial Conference of Church Leaders convened in December 1954, to which, for the first time in many years, the Mission Committee of the Dutch Reformed Church invited not only English-speaking clerics, but also African Church leaders from outside its own ranks. This Conference set up a Continuing Committee—composed of 3 members of the Dutch Reformed Church, 1 Anglican, 2 Methodists (of whom 1 is African) and 1 Presbyterian—to arrange for inter-Church consultation on specific issues, and to convene a general conference every three years. In the meantime, it was to examine the proposals of the Conference for practical cooperation and specifically to ask the Government to allow £10 million more annually for non-Europeans. These decisions marked a genuine advance on the road towards cooperation, if not agreement.

Part of the reason for the separation which had developed so markedly in the intervening period lies in the fact that the English-speaking Protestant Churches—Anglican (Episcopalian), Methodist and Presbyterian—as well as the Roman Catholics reject compulsory Church segregation by color, and acknowledge no theological justification for it whatsoever, even though in practice many of their communities are separate. More important as a divisive influence, however, has been the intensity of modern Afrikaner nationalism.

The Dutch Reformed Church has always linked itself closely with this distinctive spirit of the Afrikaner people. Its predikants shared their hardships in the days of the Boer War, and reconstruction; they took an active part in the rise of Afrikaner political nationalism during and after World War I. Dr. Malan, for example, was an N.G.K. predikant until 1915, when he first entered politics as a Nationalist. The vastly intensified Afrikaner nationalism of the thirties and forties led the Afrikaner Churches to withdraw from the earlier cooperation with the English-speaking Churches, just as Afrikaner cultural and fraternal groups isolated themselves. Dutch Reformed Church predikants shared the Nationalist opposition to South Africa's participation in World War II to such an extent that there were not nearly enough of them to minister to the Afrikaner troops. Since Dr. Malan's National Party came into power, the alliance between political nationalism and the Dutch Reformed Church has, if anything, become stronger. Pride, a sense of power, and of mission combine with the Calvinist alliance of Church and State, which is so characteristic when the latter is under the control of 'the elite'. Though the recent moves towards re-establishing cooperation between South Africa's Protestant Churches are promising, they are still small compared with the compulsive force of contemporary Afrikaner nationalism.

Surveying the field of Nationalist Afrikaner organizations and influences, one of the most striking facts is its interlocking directorate of personalities. It is less that any group is consciously trying to influence the others and/or the National Party than that the same people belong to all, or nearly all of them. The most comprehensive associations are the Dutch Reformed Church and the National Party. For many Afrikaners, the one is the religious expression of their nationalism, while the other is the political expression. In between are the institutions devoted to Afrikaner economic advancement, distinctive education, and overall coordinated efforts.

The strength of Afrikaner Nationalists lies in the fact that every institution of the Afrikaner community reinforces it. The schools, the Church, the local officials, storekeepers and farmers, and voluntary societies, all work consciously or unconsciously towards building a remarkable degree of cohesion and single-mindedness in any typical *platteland dorp*. In the cities, the institutions of Afrikanerdom reach out to provide the new urban migrant with a sense of security and 'belongingness'.

Part of this effort is positive in terms of fellowship and responsibility. Part of it arises, however, and expresses itself in opposition to other major influences in the community, in particular to English-speaking South Africans, and the non-Europeans. The fear in relation to the former arises from their powerful economic position, and the strongly entrenched position of their culture and language in South Africa's cities. The fear felt towards the latter is of their overwhelming numbers. In the past, the primitiveness and paganism of the vast majority of the Bantu intensified this fear by raising the danger that they might swamp the Afrikaner's Christian culture. Today, there is added the fear that the rapidly growing group of Bantu with education and technical training may not only offer economic competition to white workers but also claim political privileges which would endanger European and Afrikaner predominance.

The power of nationalist Afrikanerdom in relation to both these rivals is its political control. This is why ultimately every institution of this community has political implications. There seems little reason to suppose that this emphasis will disappear so long as nationalist Afrikanerdom remains convinced of the urgency of its needs.

Section V: The Opposition

CHAPTER II
THE UNITED PARTY AT WORK

Inheritor of the tradition of both Smuts and Hertzog, the United Party is typically conservative in its emphasis on practice rather than theory, its dependence on a leader, and its concern for the nation as a whole rather than one particular group. Before 1948 these characteristics were the bases of its strength. Since then, however, it has confronted a political opponent—the National Party—which, to a remarkable degree, combines the great emotional fervor of a tightly knit community with a highly efficient and disciplined organization. In attempting to meet the challenge of the Nationalists, the United Party developed an overall organization more in keeping with its unitary form than was the loose, personalized structure of its earlier days. But the diverse interests and backgrounds of its broad membership have made it difficult for the United Party to enunciate clear-cut policies, particularly in race relations, which would enable it to compete successfully in this field of policy. Moreover the United Party has been constantly under attack, not only by its opponents but also, though for very different reasons, by both its own ultra-conservative and its liberal wings. Partly as a result, the United Party has yet to demonstrate its ability to reverse the current Nationalist electoral trend.

Its Principles

At first sight, the program of principles of the United Party, or to give its full name, the United South African National Party, is not unlike that of the National Party. This is because the principles of the United Party are founded on the seven points of cooperation agreed to by the South African and National Parties as the basis of fusion in 1934. Despite the similarity of much of the phrasing, however, there are significant differences of emphasis which underline the contrast between the two parties. Less important but worth mentioning is the fact that the Nationalist statement of principles contains almost twice as many words as that of the United Party.

At the outset of its program of principles, the United Party differs slightly from the Nationalists by acknowledging the 'sovereignty and guidance' of God in the destiny of peoples as well as countries, and by adding freedom of thought to that of conscience and religion. Where the Nationalists seek 'vigorous consciousness of national autonomy and independence, as well as a strong sense of national unity', and speak of the 'equal rights' of Afrikaans- and English-speaking, the United Party statement more briefly declares its object to be 'the development of a predominant sense of South African national unity, based on the equality of the Afrikaans-speaking and English-speaking sections of the community'.

On political status and the flag, the United Party endorses the existing relationship between South Africa and the British Commonwealth of Nations (which is nowhere mentioned in the Nationalist statement) and also the place assigned to the Union Jack under the Union Flag Act (abolished in 1957). Equally, it emphasizes the independence of the Union and declares that there shall be no external obligations 'in conflict with its interests', and that the authority of the country shall be symbolized by the South African flag. No mention is made of a republic.[1] On internal constitutional arrangements, the initial statement is the same as in the Nationalist document, but, where the latter cautiously endorses retaining the provincial system 'for the present', the United Party speaks of maintaining the status of the provinces 'with the extension, when necessary . . . of provincial powers and functions' within the framework of the South African Act.

Both parties include a section on equal language rights; only the Nationalists specifically mention bilingualism in the public service. In a brief section on immigration, the United Party encourages 'desirable European immigration with the assurance of equality of treatment in the Union', and displays none of the concern of the Nationalists lest the newcomers lack proper South African attitudes.

The party statements on agriculture are alike except that Nationalists stress 'an independent and prosperous farming community', and urge 'powerful' State encouragement and support for agriculture. On cooperation between employers and employees, the wording is also almost identical except that the United Party speaks of raising wages 'wherever practicable', while the Nationalists use the wording 'where necessary'. Both parties endorse mining and secondary industries, but where the United Party declares that agriculture and mining, 'as the foundations of the country's permanent welfare', are to be 'reinforced by the concurrent development of commerce and manufacturing industry', the Nationalists speak of the State's claim 'to its rightful share in the country's mineral wealth', and stress encouragement of 'the vigorous growth of all secondary industries capable of sound progress'.

In the light of the publicity given to the Transvaal Education Ordinance in the 1953 election, it should be noted that the United Party recognizes the State's duty to ensure a national system of education based on 'sound psychological and educational principles', but also affirms 'the full recognition of the rights of the parents', especially in the moral and religious training of their children. Only the Nationalist program has a section on national health, but the United Party included this subject in its 1954 statement on Native policy.

In its original program of principles, the United Party Native policy seeks 'a satisfactory solution' along lines which give the Native his right of development, but also recognize as paramount 'the essentials of European civilization'. The Nationalist phrases, 'each race in its own field, in both the material and spiritual spheres, in keeping with their natural gifts and abilities', are not found in the United Party statement, nor is the declaration in favor of 'territorial and political segregation'. In reflection of differences of opinion on Native policy at the time of fusion, the United Party statement declares that the political aspect of Native policy, whether involving separate representation of Europeans and Natives, 'or otherwise', should be sought through agreement, and left to the 'free discretion of the individual members' of Parliament. On Asiatics, the United Party statement is less belligerent than is the Nationalist: thus, while recognizing the necessity of protecting other groups from Asiatic immigration and competition, it also affirms the 'existing rights' of Asiatics born or legally domiciled in the Union.

Following widespread criticism after the 1953 election that the United Party's non-European policy was both too vague and too like that of the Nationalists, a far more comprehensive statement of Native policy was drafted by party leaders, taken to each of the 1954 Provincial Congresses, and after vigorous discussion was finally approved by the Union Congress of the party in November, 1954. The statement thus became a part of official United Party policy binding on all members of the party.

While couched in general terms, the detailed United Party program for Natives accepts the African as a part of the South African community as a whole, in sharp contrast to the Nationalists' emphasis on his separate development. Thus it declares that the leadership of the white race can be maintained only on the basis of 'sincere willingness and desire to share Western civilization in practice with all non-whites who have developed the capacity for taking joint responsibility for our future well-being in this sub-continent'. To this it adds that 'the Native should gradually be given a more definite and secure place within the orbit of our Western way of life'. Recognizing that 'a large and permanently detribalized Native urban population' has become 'an integral part of the South African economy', it anticipates the need 'for the better coordination of European and Native interests in the social, economic and political life of the country'.

In its section on economic policy for Africans, the United Party statement declares unequivocally that the party accepts 'economic integration not only as a fact, but also as a necessary dynamic process which will continue', and must be 'regulated, guided and controlled'. Social and residential segregation are endorsed. In the most controversial of all fields, that of political representation, the party treads a careful line between a permanent denial to Africans of all political rights, such as the Nationalists make, and the progressive extension of political rights endorsed by the Liberals. Thus the United Party statement recognizes that political rights are 'an inevitable historical corollary to an increase in economic power', but at the same time stresses the 'long period of training in the ways of democracy and especially in its responsibilities' which lies ahead of the African people. Claims to greater political rights must await 'these lessons', it declares and, still more problematic, the agreement of 'an established and decisive majority of the present electorate'. It proposes, however, a number of small but specific ways in which the Natives can gain more experience of democratic processes and asserts that 'the Europeans dare not close the door to the reasonable aspirations of the Native peoples'.

This statement provides a Native policy distinctive from that of the Nationalists in, at least, two respects: Its endorsement of economic integration, and the opening of the way, however long and difficult, to increased political rights and ultimate influence. Neither African leaders nor the most liberal members of the United Party felt the statement went nearly far enough, while it was attacked by ultra-conservatives as being much too radical. It remains, however, a formulation of a sober, middle-of-the-road Native policy which has commanded the support of the very substantial center group of the party. Moreover it has potentialities not yet exploited for development into an effective alternative to Nationalist apartheid.

Its Organization

Though the United Party has always had a unitary form, it was not until after its electoral defeat in 1948 that it built the strong and well organized central organization necessary for turning its *de facto* federalism and localism into a unitary structure. At a time when the Nationalists had already developed the group system, and highly organized, disciplined provincial party organizations, the United Party still had relatively little branch activity, weak provincial organizations, and almost nothing in the way of a national organization. A quite remarkable extension and tightening of United Party machinery took place prior to the 1953 election, while a new, if temporary, fever of activity at every level of party organization (except perhaps the provincial) contributed markedly to United Party returns. It is this organization which will be described since it remains intact though largely inert between elections.

The United Party chiefly differs in organization from the Nationalists in that its branches are not divided into groups, and that it makes more use of General Councils to coordinate the work of divisional committees. Another contrast is that the United Party provincial structure remains weak, while its central organization is far stronger than the Nationalists' Federal Council, particularly because of the strategic position of the United Party's central office. Within the United Party organization as it had developed by the eve of the 1953 elections, the balance of power still resided with the General Councils, particularly in the Transvaal, but the central office had become influential at every level of party organization.

Each constituency is expected to have at least one branch (a less ambitious goal than the Nationalist target of at least one in each polling district) but many constituencies, of course, have more. There should be not less than twenty members to form a branch, but it is not disbanded if membership falls below this level. Though the Constitution provides for at least two meetings a year, relatively few United Party branches meet regularly, except under the stimulus of a coming election, or a party crisis such as the 'rebellion' against Strauss' leadership late in 1953 (see p. 293). Branch committees consist of the chairman, one or two vice-chairmen, and not less than five members selected at the branch's annual meeting. Each constituency must also have a divisional committee (the name coming from the common designation of 'electoral division' for the voting unit), consisting commonly of the chairman, secretary and one delegate from each branch committee.

The real center of power, however, is the General Council, which has a professional staff and directs the work of the party in the area of the constituencies it coordinates. After 1948, the area under several General Councils was decreased, and their staffs enlarged: e.g., the nine constituencies of the Pretoria area, and those of the *platteland* were separated and each given its own General Council. The Pretoria General Council had three permanent staff members in 1953: an organizing secretary, an assistant and an organizer. Far larger is the Witwatersrand General Council, which has jurisdiction over 38 seats, stretching from Johannesburg to Vereeniging and along the line of the Rand. Its staff of three in 1948 was increased to over 20 prior to the 1953 election.

The United Party Constitution says little about General Councils other than that they are established by the Central Head Committee. The most important of General Councils, the Witwatersrand, has its own Constitution. This provides for a large Council, representative of all party groups in the area.[2] The quorum is fifty, so it is hardly surprising that the direction of the General Council is largely in the hands of the Executive, which also includes representatives of each divisional committee and special groups. More particularly, direction tends to come from the Action Committee members of the Executive and the permanent organizer, who is the Council's Secretary.

While preparing for the 1953 election, the Witwatersrand General Council offices were a constant hive of activity, with the permanent officials supplemented by many volunteers. The Council aided the constituencies under its jurisdiction by providing propaganda, candidates' letters of introduction, and specialized printed matter which supplemented the flood of information and directions coming from central headquarters. It also sent organizers to work with candidates in marginal seats. Moreover, postal votes and car pools were organized under the General Council.

Naturally much of the organization for an election proceeds at the divisional level whether or not the General Council is a particularly active one. Problems arise here from the three-cornered relation between the professional and amateur elements, the party organizer, the chairman of the divisional council, and the candidate. The chairman often feels the organizer should be in the field securing votes, and fails to understand the need for paper work. Particularly if the chairman has been long in his position, the organizer may need a great deal of tact, and if the relationship does not work out satisfactorily, General Councils may have to replace the organizer with another. The Nationalists tend to avoid this problem through frequent election of party officers, and a more consistent pattern of professional direction of amateur party efforts. The United Party has found that organizers and candidates generally get along well but this, too, was not invariable in 1953.

Compared to a General Council, particularly one as powerful as that of the Witwatersrand, the United Party's provincial organization lacks authority and even function. It serves as the regular channel of communication between the General Councils and Union head office, but rarely shapes policy. The annual Provincial Congresses provide for mass participation, but especially in recent years serve as preparations for Union Congresses rather than ends in themselves. The Provincial leaders (Sir de Villiers Graaff, H. Tucker, D. E. Mitchell and H. G. Swart) are important figures in the party organization, but their influence is personal rather than resulting from a cohesive structure or from the popular support of the Provincial Congresses. One of the best illustrations of this fact was that when Bailey Bekker, then United Party leader in the Transvaal, revolted against Strauss' leadership late in 1953, it created a personal rather than a provincial problem.

Only since 1950, however, has the Union organization of the United Party taken on the form and authority which its unitary structure implies. Deeply concerned over the loss of the election in 1948, General Smuts himself gave the initial impetus for transforming the party's previous loose federalism and even localism into a closer knit unity under an efficiently organized central head office. Party officials were sent to England to study the organization of British parties, in particular the Conservative Party, and the re-vamping of party machinery was based in part upon their findings.

While some of the United Party's strongest supporters felt its organization was not brought to as high a pitch of efficiency, particularly in propaganda, as would have been possible, the differences made in overall organization between 1948 and 1953 amounted to a complete transformation. In place of a head office staff of three officials, the United Party developed a series of divisions at the national level for propaganda, fund raising, research, youth organization, etc., each headed by an unpaid 'amateur', generally an M.P., with a paid professional staff working under him. Part of the head office staff is in Pretoria, part in Johannesburg. Since 1951, there has also been a small research office in Cape Town to answer party queries while Parliament is in session.

One consequence of the unitary structure of the United Party (which the Nationalists avoid through their appearance of federalism), is that the United South West Africa party is not an integral part of the organization. This was specifically agreed to by General Smuts, who also arranged that if United Party members were returned from that area (which did not happen in 1950 or 1953) they would have a separate caucus. Moreover, United Party members from the Union who go to South West Africa for campaigning do so as 'guests', while representatives from South West Africa who go to Union United Party Congresses do so on the same basis.

The United Party Head Committee was originally a very large body which included all United Party cabinet members, and ten from each province chosen by the Provincial Head Committees. When Strauss became leader he transformed it into a smaller and more efficient working body by limiting it to the four provincial leaders, the heads of central office divisions, and a number of important individuals co-opted from the party, like Harry Oppenheimer, then director of the United South Africa Trust Fund (see p. 298). In so far as there is one center of power in the United Party, it is the Central Head Committee. Moreover since, as with the Nationalists, the Head Committee includes the top parliamentary members, there are no conflicts between the party organization and the parliamentary caucus.

Officially, the highest authority in the United Party is the biennial Union Congress. It elects the leader and deputy-leader of the party, and passes on important policies like the redrafted Native policy endorsed in November, 1954. The Congress is composed of members of the Head Committee, party members in the Senate, House of Assembly and Provincial Councils, two delegates from each constituency chosen by the Divisional committee and chairmen of the General Councils, Women's Councils, and Provincial and General Councils of the Youth Organizations. While much too large for easy discussions, the United Party Union Congress is, in fact, a good deal smaller than the Transvaal Nationalist Congress.

The most noticeable difference between the 1952 United Party Union Congress and the Nationalists' Transvaal Provincial Congress (see p. 226) was the appearance of the delegates, and the general atmosphere. The United Party delegates were noticeably heavier in build, more smartly dressed, more settled and prosperous in air and with an urban rather than a country look. There were more and younger women and they took a more active share both in open and off-the-floor discussions. Perhaps befitting its public, the atmosphere was more formal, the slogans more sober and the meetings less obviously enthusiastic. There was only one song, 'For He's a Jolly Good Fellow', followed by a rather half-hearted 'hip hip hurrah' for Strauss, and there was none of the easy give and take of sallies from the floor flung at and parried good-naturedly by the leaders. The two meetings are, of course, not quite comparable either in composition (each branch in the Transvaal sends delegates to the Nationalist Provincial Congress) or in functions but the differences are not insignificant. Another contrast was that, while the Nationalist Congress was carried on entirely in Afrikaans, English was the dominant language at the United Party Congress, though some speeches, like that of the party's leader, Strauss, slipped easily from one language to the other. It was obvious, however, that many of the delegates at Bloemfontein did not understand, let alone speak Afrikaans, while all had an easy working knowledge of English.

Since no outsider or newspaper reporter is allowed into the private sessions of the United Party, the most controversial issues and widest divergences of opinion remain unreported. It is common knowledge, however, that sharp differences were expressed over Native policy both in 1952 and 1954. What was remarkable was that so broad a level of agreement was reached at the latter session. This was partly because the statement expressed so well the approach of the large center group of the United Party which endorses white supremacy, but also sees the need to make some (if small) concrete proposals for advancing the status and opportunities of the Natives. Though the statement had been drafted by party leaders, it received careful scrutiny by the delegates to the Union Congress who seemed less intransigent on race relations than in 1952.[3]

It was the National Party parliamentary caucus which selected J. G. Strijdom as Dr. Malan's successor (see p. 225) and J. G. N. Strauss was similarly chosen United Party leader by the U.P. parliamentary caucus after General Smuts' resignation. A very different procedure was followed, however, when Sir de Villiers Graaff succeeded Strauss as party leader. Strauss had been suffering from ill-health for some time and there were important elements in the Party which felt that he should be replaced. The initiative was taken by the four Provincial leaders and the Party's Head Committee, but the final decision was made in a closed session of the United Party's biennial Congress late in 1955. After it was decided that Strauss (who was out of the country) should not be re-elected as leader, Graaff was selected by Congress for that post, a decision approved by caucus when Parliament reconvened.

The United Party leader has great importance, as is common among conservative parties. This importance was specially marked, however, when Smuts was in command. He was a dominant personality with a world-wide reputation, and great political experience. Not only are Strauss and de Villiers Graaff less forceful and magnetic persons than was Smuts, but the United Party has a stronger organization with more channels for discussion than in the earlier period of the party's history.

The United Party's major problem is that its members want to retain the wide variations of views and objectives which come out of their variegated backgrounds and interests and yet, at the same time, to have the power and unity of their far more homogeneous and disciplined political opponents. It may well be, in fact, that only the overriding imperatives of great crises, like depression, war or a Native revolt, can again bring them electoral success by imbuing the party's members with new determination, and capturing fresh adherents.

Its Nomination Procedures

The important function of nominating parliamentary candidates is divided in practice in the United Party between the branches, divisional committees and General Councils. On the *platteland*, which cherishes the spirit of direct democracy, and in certain towns like Pretoria, nominations are decided through primaries. Any party member may be nominated by the simple process of getting several signatures to his nomination petition; in the safe, and particularly in the uncontested seats, no one exercises restraint on the number of those nominated. On the contrary, a free-for-all contest—which is, in effect, the election of the candidate—is thought to encourage general participation. In the *platteland*, 40-50 per cent of the branch members participate in primaries even though they must register their votes in person during branch meetings in order to have them counted. In the cities, the participation is not nearly so high and in two Pretoria constituencies where primaries were held before the 1953 election, only 300 out of the 2,000 eligible voted in the one, and 400 out of a similar number of eligibles in the other.

Though many United Party branches cherish the power involved in direct voting on nominations, party officials are less convinced that it is the wisest and most satisfactory way of choosing candidates. They point to the division which can be created in the party by a bitter fight in a primary, and which has resulted in some defeated nominees standing as independents in their constituencies, thus splitting the vote. Though this has not happened since 1943, they feel that ordinarily the adherents of a defeated nominee do not put their full efforts into working for the election. Another type of criticism of primaries was heard in several quarters in 1953 from young aspirants who tried unsuccessfully to displace well entrenched sitting members. In fact, the United Party less often passes over sitting members than do the Nationalists.

The other method of selecting candidates is an electoral college. The argument in favor of this procedure is that it provides for a more careful selection process, and is more likely to bring in new blood; some criticize it, however, as undercutting the direct contact between party members as a whole and the candidate who is to represent them. But even the Nationalists, who are sometimes caustic about the lack of democracy in the United Party electoral college system, select most of their candidates in the Cape through the branch committees conference which, in practice, is a kind of electoral college. Though disagreement in the Nationalist branch committees conference always throws the final decision to the branches, United Party branches can also demand a primary in areas where the electoral college system is ordinarily in use.

The composition of electoral colleges depends on the desires of the particular area. A variety of different forms are used. In East London, Port Elizabeth and Kimberley, for example, each constituency has its own electoral college consisting of not less than fifteen members made up of one or more from each branch.

In Natal, the electoral colleges consist of expanded divisional committees made up of three delegates from each branch in a rural area and six from each in an urban area. Nominees must be approved by the Provincial Executive,[4] a group of twenty in all, but the final decision is made by the expanded divisional committee. Before the 1953 election, there were four nomination contests in Natal in one of which there were five candidates. In two others, Torch Commando nominees were defeated, leading to much criticism of the system in some quarters. All Natal nominations in 1953 took place, it may be noted, before it was known that Nationalists were going to contest the seats.

One of the most interesting nomination systems is that used by the Witwatersrand General Council. This procedure gives a great deal of influence to a Candidates' Committee, which must approve all aspirant candidates, and has a share, sometimes the decisive one, in making the final choice. The Candidates' Committee consists of an equal number of regular and alternate members. There are six 'ordinary' members who serve at all times and three groups of three 'representative' members, each of the latter groups serving only when the Committee is concerned with aspirants from its own area: Central, East or West Rand. At least five of the committee members must be from the Executive. Members of that body make the nominations for the 'ordinary' committee members and those representing the Central area, and the Executive as a whole elects them by secret ballot. The representatives from the East and West Rand are selected by the Advisory Committees for those areas by whatever means they choose. The Candidates' Committee which acted for the 1953 election had one woman amongst its ordinary members and also one in each group of representative members.

The Candidates' Committee decides the date by which the names of aspirant candidates must be sent to the organizer, and the time of final selection of a candidate. Nominees must normally be members of at least twelve months' standing and must be endorsed by two registered voters of the appropriate constituency who, in turn, must be party members of twelve months' standing. In an unusual procedure, each aspirant candidate must submit a written statement showing why he considers himself worthy of nomination, and deposit £25 with the organizer, which is forfeit to the Council if he receives less than one-fifth of the votes. Highly significant is the fact that the Candidates' Committee has the power of veto on any nominee and may also present names of its own choice for any constituency.

The final stage of selection also remains under the control of the Candidates' Committee. If more than one nominee is approved, the Committee decides, after due consultation with the divisional committee concerned, whether the final choice shall be made through the combined branch committees election meeting, or by a joint committee. The former is made up of not more than six representatives from each branch in the constituency; two persons nominated by the Candidates' Committee attend the meeting, and one of them may act as chairman, though that duty is customarily performed by the chairman of the divisional committee. If there are more than two candidates, there may be several ballots so the weaker ones can be eliminated and the final choice represent a clear majority.

The combined branch committees election meeting is the normal procedure for choosing the candidate, but if there is obvious disagreement between the division and the Candidates' Committee, the alternative procedure of a joint meeting is taken. In this case an equal number of members from the branches and of the Candidates' Committee, as near fifteen of each as possible, meet to make the decision. Since the Candidates' Committee will have had a thorough discussion of the aspirant candidates before the joint meeting takes place, its point of view is likely to dominate. In a sense, of course, the Candidates' Committee and the constituency each have a veto on each other, and neither can completely force its will on the other. It is noticeable that a number of the so-called liberals of the United Party were elected in 1953 from the Witwatersrand area, some of whom, like Helen Suzman, John Cope and 'Sakkie' Fourie, were relative newcomers who subsequently made names for themselves in the House. Their nomination may well have been aided by the Candidates' Committee, a fact criticized as strongly by some members of the United Party as applauded by others.

A nomination irregularity, or an aspirant candidate's complaint, can be referred to an Appeal Court of five members, also chosen by the Witwatersrand Executive. Under all circumstances, however, the Executive of the General Council retains final jurisdiction over nominations, being empowered to disqualify any candidate, however selected, and to order a fresh nomination or even to nominate the candidate itself. But, as can be expected, such a procedure is highly exceptional, and therefore of little or no significance.

Its Parliamentary Party

The United Party, as can be expected, has normally been less rigorous in maintaining discipline in the parliamentary party than are the Nationalists, but it is also noteworthy that between 1953 and 1955 the United Party caucus expelled seven of its members, six of whom temporarily formed the Conservative Party (see p. 353), and one, Dr. Friedman, subsequently ran for office, though unsuccessfully, as an Independent. Moreover, United Party whips have steadily increased their authority in order to match the Nationalists. In particular they seek a stricter formulation of United Party positions in place of the loose, wordy and often divergent attitudes so frequently expressed in past (and sometimes still in present) debates. The caucus itself sometimes asks the whips to be very strict on a controversial measure.

To meet these increasing responsibilities, the three United Party whips of pre-1948 days have expanded to four, with two assistants. The Transvaal, Cape and Natal each have one whip, while there is also a chief whip. There is no whip for the Free State because of lack of representation there. Even if there were United Party members from South West Africa that group would have the right to have their own caucus and whip (see p. 287).

The whips are elected by caucus at the beginning of each parliament. Personal prestige and tact are essential if the whip is successfully to cajole members into attendance and conformity, and the United Party caucus, according to all reports, is not reluctant to debate at considerable length and in all frankness the qualifications of its candidates for this job. Its choice is narrowed, however, by the fact that whips must be thoroughly bilingual.

The United Party tends to be more empirical in the imposition of discipline than are the Nationalists. If the legislation concerns a matter of conscience (in which category both religion and liquor are placed), members are left free to vote as they wish. If it is a matter of special interest to the particular member and his constituency, the party is likely to be lenient as long as the vote does not imperil its position. Under these circumstances, the normal procedure is for the member to go to the whip, explain the circumstances, and ask indulgence. If absolved, the member usually leaves the chamber well in advance of the voting so the abstention is less noticeable. Occasionally in the past, whips have even let members vote with the other side, but this is almost unthought of today when party lines are scanned so carefully both inside and outside the House.

Now that it is in opposition, the United Party is particularly strict about party members supporting its position in the committee stage where it seeks the amendments requisite for its approval to legislation. Since it often accepts the general principle of a Nationalist measure, it may be less insistent on its members' obvious support in second reading than in the committee stage, though it increasingly puts pressure on its members to conform in both.

Like the Nationalists, the United Party parliamentary members divide into special interest groups. At the beginning of the session, a whip specially selected for this purpose asks all persons interested to meet at a special time; he secures nominations for chairman and secretary, and then leaves the groups to run themselves. Each member is entitled to be on any group; he may also attend a group meeting even if he is not officially a member. The groups are on commerce, industry, finance, external affairs, labor, mines, defense, agriculture (with occasionally subsections if a bill affects a particular farming element) and Native affairs, and commonly meet twice a week in the first part of the session when there is still time for the discussion of private members' bills. When the United Party was in office, the groups commonly sent projects or resolutions to the Minister through the whip, or its chairman, and only thereafter to caucus; sometimes, however, a group took its proposals direct to caucus if it found the Minister uncooperative.

Though groups may play this preparatory role, caucus always remains dominant. In fact, it plays a more important role in the United Party than in the Nationalists, even when the United Party is in office. Though the leader has great influence at all times, everyone is looked on as equal in caucus. Even Smuts was sometimes strongly criticized there and he often listened to younger members and took their suggestions into account though, on the other hand, his own definiteness on most subjects, and his cold, clear approach made it difficult to oppose him. Hertzog was still more difficult to deal with in caucus because he hated opposition, but at the same time he had a warm human touch far greater than that of Smuts. Strauss gave caucus definite leadership in certain issues, notably the Native question, but preferred to use conciliation instead of authority. Empirical rather than doctrinaire, Strauss was open to argument but once he reached his decisions he was adamant.

The United Party caucus, like the Nationalist, meets weekly on Tuesday mornings; its chairman is the person who would become speaker if the party came into office. On the chairman's right sits the leader of the party, and on his left, the chief and provincial whips. Normally, the leader opens a subject by giving his views of forthcoming legislation, though he may ask others to speak first. Debate is free and for as long as desired; sometimes, in fact, it goes over into the following day. Here is a major difference from the Nationalist caucus, where debate is more controlled and of narrower scope. This difference is partly a matter of discipline, but it also reflects a basic contrast between the doctrinaire approach of the Nationalists, and the flexible empiricism of the United Party, which prefers to fit policies to particular circumstances rather than embody them in legal forms.

When the party is in opposition, its parliamentary members also meet daily at noon under one of the whips to hear the order of business for the day. When the party is in office, there is no need for such daily meetings, since the Cabinet keeps control of the business of the House.

The United Party parliamentary party has found it far more difficult than the Nationalists to retain a common front because its members differ so sharply over Native affairs. A notable example took place immediately after the 1948 election when Colonel Rood, who had easily won Vereeniging for the United Party, criticized Jan Hofmeyr's approach to Native policy. General Smuts publicly rebuked Rood and he resigned. In the ensuing by-election, Dr. Loock won the seat for the Nationalists by 16 votes, thereby raising the latter's majority in the House from 4 to 6, and seriously damaging United Party morale.

Still more disturbing was the open revolt in the United Party caucus after the 1953 election against Strauss' leadership and over Native policy. As a result, Bailey Bekker, Transvaal leader of the party, and five other members were ejected or, as it is called technically, 'deprived of the service of caucus'. In 1954, these six formed the Conservative Party, dedicated to a middle ground between the Nationalists' aim of territorial apartheid, and the United Party's endorsement of the economic integration of Europeans and non-Europeans. Subsequently, some Conservatives joined the Nationalists. The United Party caucus also expelled one of its liberals, Dr. Bernhard Friedman, early in 1955, because he insisted there was a moral commitment to replace the Coloured on the common roll if the Nationalists succeeded in removing them. Both actions reflected a new insistence by the United Party on caucus unity on major legislation and a determination to maintain a middle-of-the-road position in racial affairs.

Despite its recent use of the extreme penalty of expulsion, the United Party remains a more loosely organized, and less unified group than the Nationalists. This means it provides more freedom for individual members, and more expression of diverse points of view. Its advantages in this respect, however, are more than counter-balanced by lack of ordered effectiveness in debate, and of clear-cut positions on major issues.

Its Youth and Women's Organizations

So far the United Party has had less success with its youth groups than have the Nationalists. The latter's original youth movement, started in 1940 and known as the Youth Front, was militant and nationalistic, campaigning for one South African flag, one anthem, etc., under the direction of its first leader, Japie Basson, who subsequently became Nationalist M.P. for Namab, South West Africa. Cleared of their extreme elements, the youth groups continued to exist in the provinces, but did not acquire a national organization until June, 1951. Then, under the presidency of Ray Swart, of Natal (the second youngest candidate elected in 1953), United Party Youth was established on a national basis with a general secretary and six paid organizers, one in the Transvaal, two in the Cape and two in Natal. Though United Party Youth played less of a role in the 1953 election than did the *Nasionale Jeugbond*, the former was well established by that time with about 30,000 members organized in 195 branches: 84 in the Cape, 70 odd in the Transvaal, about 30 in Natal and 10 in the Free State.

Most active groups in United Party Youth are on the *platteland*, despite the fact that the penalty of being openly United Party may limit young people's chances for school or other offices in what is likely to be a dominantly Nationalist community. In the cities, the multiplicity of existing clubs and organizations undercut the need for special youth groups; on the *platteland*, they serve a definite function as social clubs. Moreover, the very proximity to the Nationalist philosophy in rural areas often makes United Party young people more conscious of their own program than is true on the Rand, where United Party members and Nationalists see far less of each other. It is striking that amongst the youth groups there is a far higher percentage of Afrikaners than in the United Party's support as a whole. Thus some 45 per cent of the members of the United Party Youth Movement in the Transvaal are Afrikaans-speaking and, still more striking, almost 80 per cent of the Cape members. Most members range between 18 and 30 in age, but here, too, the Cape is remarkable in having unusually young members, some no more than 14.

United Party Youth tends to be more liberal, especially on Native policy, than the parent organization. When, in 1954, the Union Congress replaced Ray Swart by a conservative from the Cape, it was widely interpreted as an attempt to secure more alignment of policy between the junior and senior branches of the party. The United Party Youth Executive does not encourage branches in the universities, partly because they fear that the liberal tendencies of college students may be embarrassing to the parent body. United Party Youth has more autonomy, however, than the *Nasionale Jeugbond*, conducts its own annual congresses (of which the first was held in July 1952), and plans its own program.

So far, the chief use made of United Party Youth has been for raising funds, distributing pamphlets and doing election chores. Study groups are rare, though there has been a good one in Durban, and most of their meetings have a social purpose. Both facts help to explain why United Party Youth is not more important in the total United Party organization. Its members can hardly feel that they serve any very significant or highly honored position. Moreover, the more independent their attitude the more likely they are to be rebuffed.

While the United Party has not been noticeably successful with youth, it has done far better than the Nationalists in gaining and using the support of women. Intelligent and efficient women can be found at all except the very top level of United Party organization, and often in positions of much more obvious prestige than is true for the hardworking and also efficient Nationalist women. Moreover, the United Party has rewarded its women with parliamentary candidature and now has three women M.P.s, whereas the Nationalists have only one woman in Parliament, a Senator, appointed in 1956.

United Party women have their own Councils in many places, but also participate in ordinary branch work. Thus they have, in a sense, a dual representation, both as women and as ordinary members. They are particularly active on the Witwatersrand and were represented both among the ordinary and representative members of the Candidates' Committee (see p. 290). Women help with fund raising, do a good deal of canvassing, and much office work, especially at election time. When the English-language press singled out United Party women for special praise in the 1953 election campaign, it was only giving them their due. Broadly speaking, women are one of the greatest assets the United Party possesses.

Its Professional Organizers

Much less than the Nationalists has the United Party made use of professional organizers, particularly outside of election time. Despite pressure to do so, the party set its face resolutely against introducing party agents such as have proved so useful to the British Conservative Party. At the General Council level, there is a nucleus of full-time professionals who can be used as organizers for marginal seats during election campaigns. Apart from these, the party depends on temporary personnel added specially for election purposes. Coupled with the sporadic activity of most branches, this means that United Party campaigning is almost exclusively at election periods, and that there is none of the careful 'nursing' of constituents and voters which works so greatly to the advantage of the Nationalists.

Even for its relatively few professional positions, the United Party finds it difficult to secure people with the right blend of experience, judgment and party ardor. There is still a lack of real permanence in these positions, partly because the party is not yet dedicated to the system, partly because of fear that if people held office too long they might lose their zest and use up their ideas. The United Party is too much wedded to the concept of the amateur in politics (though some of its M.P.s have been re-elected so often that they hardly fit this designation) to give its professionals the chance of parliamentary seats that the Nationalists do. Moreover, up to 1953, there were no pensions for party officials and pay was relatively low. Cape efforts to train young party enthusiasts as organizers ran into difficulties, partly because the *platteland* looked on them as too young and inexperienced, partly because the allure of wealthy farmers' daughters led some to desert the career of organizer (at least after the election) for an easier life. The experiment probably justified itself, however, by developing a small nucleus of professional organizers.

The temporary staff added at election time meets just the opposite objection to the young bloods. Those who are freest to supplement their incomes by such occasional work are generally retired persons drawn from the professional classes, railway workers, post office personnel, etc. They are often elderly, lack spark, and have little idea of canvassing techniques. Not only do they not compete in persuasiveness with the Nationalist organizers; they also lack the intimacy of contact and knowledge possessed by the latter. It is hardly surprising, therefore, that United Party estimates of electoral strength, at by-elections as well as general elections, are far less accurate than those of the Nationalists.

Its Provincial Roots

United Party strength differs less in different parts of the country than does the Nationalist, since it is more widespread, and includes about 15-20 per cent of the Afrikaans-speaking as well as virtually all the English-speaking. Evidence of its ability to command wide support is the fact that the United Party has contested almost every seat in every election without losing an election deposit (which is forfeit if the candidate does not receive one-fifth of his opponent's total). Moreover, despite the hiving off of the Liberals and the Union Federal Party in May 1953, the United Party has not yet lost a provincial contest with either of these parties.

The United Party's greatest strength lies in urban areas, and in Natal. In Natal, its position is relatively recent for, in the 1930s, it was the Dominion Party that flourished there. Moreover, there is perhaps more dissatisfaction with the United Party in Natal than anywhere else. Nonetheless the Natal United Party leader, D. E. Mitchell, has a strong personal hold on the party machinery, and there is too much awareness that the United Party offers the only viable political opposition to the Nationalists to break the party's strength.

In the Free State, the United Party is in a particularly difficult position because its strength is scattered, and provincial organization is weak and relatively unpopular. Having lost its last seat in the Assembly when its provincial leader, Colin Steyn, was defeated in 1953, the Free State seems like a lost cause to many United Party supporters. The party's most ardent supporters, however, make a good show at election times, and continued to pile up some 20 per cent of the votes. In South West Africa, where the Nationalists also hold all the seats, the percentage of United Party votes is higher than in the Free State, and a healthy rivalry continues.

The Cape is the area where the United Party is most strongly entrenched in the *platteland*, apart from Natal. The Liberals have made some slight inroads in Cape Town itself, but not enough to imperil the United Party. (The Liberals, however, have been able to secure Cape Native seats, now that Communists, or those so designated, cannot be candidates.) The Cape United Party is less well organized, however, than parts of the Transvaal, partly because Head Office is in the Rand. For the first time in history, the United Party lost control of the Cape Provincial Council in 1954, a highly disturbing indication of Nationalist electoral inroads.

In the Transvaal, both the Nationalists and the United Party are putting forward their greatest efforts. Probably no area in the country had developed such an efficient United Party organization in 1953 as the Witwatersrand General Council. Its very activity provided an expectation of electoral victory which made the Nationalist gains in the Rand mining towns the more shattering. The Liberals have considerable following in Johannesburg, but not enough for electoral success in any constituency. The major problem for the United Party in Johannesburg and other wealthy cities is that their central areas pile up such high vote totals for the party and thus, in a sense, waste them (see p. 159). Even more than the over-representation of the *platteland* is this wastage of United Party urban votes responsible for the wide disparity between the votes and the seats received by the United Party.

Its Finances

The United Party has the support, tacit if not always active, of a far wealthier group in the community than have the Nationalists. This has its disadvantages as well as its advantages. It leaves the United Party open to the charge, however unfounded, of being subservient to money interests. It also leads to the expectation by ordinary members that large donors will provide for a high percentage of the party's financial needs.

The original and basic sources of party revenue for the United Party, as for the Nationalists, however, are the branches. These raise a good deal of money, especially through combined efforts like fêtes and teas. Branch officers may ask their members for specific contributions, and rural districts sometimes use a collector to aid in bringing in funds, but such contributions are never regarded as a condition of membership. United Party Congresses time and time again have voted down proposals to institute membership fees as such, arguing that to do so would penalize the poorer areas. Though United Party branches agree to raise certain quotas to provide General Council funds, these are not set in the way the Nationalists do, by the number of registered party voters, or the votes cast in the last election, but by ability to pay. The budget is laid before everyone at the General Council meeting and divisional representatives (who in turn represent the branches) are asked what they can afford to contribute. Since apportionment is thus thrashed out publicly, it is likely to be fair. Occasionally, as with the highly successful 'Operation Freedom' (a gigantic fair run at Zoo Lake, Johannesburg, by the Rand General Council, which raised about £5,000 for the 1953 election campaign), divisions join together in a mass fund-raising effort, but normally the branches determine their own ways of raising money.

Some branches, particularly on the *platteland*, salt away much of what they raise, sometimes keeping as much as £300 to use as they see fit. Not surprisingly, the General Councils prefer to have all party funds transmitted to them so that they can redistribute them amongst divisional councils according to need. The Witwatersrand General Council has achieved the greatest amount of success in this regard, partly because it is concerned largely with urban constituencies.

United Party Head Office does not conceal the fact that it would prefer to have all party funds transmitted to itself and then reapportioned to the General Councils on the same system on the national level as that on which the Rand General Council operates. But probably wisely from the point of view of maintaining local interest and responsibility, General Councils insist on preserving their right to control the revenue from below their level except in so far as divisions and branches retain hold of their own resources. General Council budgets are regularly checked by provincial and union offices, and the latter has a still more effective control whenever General Councils have to ask for funds additional to those they can raise from their own sources. Head Office met several General Council deficits prior to the 1953 election and in some instances contributed to a specific purpose like securing an organizer for a marginal seat.

A second source of revenue comes through businessmen's committees, organized on a systematic basis after 1949 in each General Council to secure direct contributions from small businessmen, retailers, etc., who might not be touched by an ordinary fund-raising organization. These businessmen's committees are voluntary groups acting under voluntary chairmen, but they sometimes make use of General Council officials in their actual canvassing. These funds go direct to the General Council and aid in meeting the 'ways and means' part of its budget.

In a way the most interesting, and certainly the most controversial source of revenue of the United Party prior to the 1953 election was the United South Africa Trust Fund. This was established with General Smuts' support in 1949 to raise funds from corporations and wealthy individuals concerned to improve English-Afrikaner relations and, in general, to build a more democratic and cohesive South African community. As the United Party not only included both language groups, but also supported the kind of national unity the Fund endorsed, much of the Fund's money was given to the United Party to improve its national organization and propaganda. While the United Party did not adopt many of the suggestions made for it by the Fund, there is no question that it was largely Fund support which enabled the United Party to build its strong and efficient national organization prior to the 1953 election.

The Fund always faced a dilemma in its relations with the United Party. The U.S.A.T.F. came into existence after big business had withdrawn its support from the party because the United Party prior to the 1948 election, lacked adequate financial accounting and also ran a considerable deficit, in particular through the Conroy party papers, and also because of the very fact that the United Party had lost the election. Efforts to raise a million-pound General Smuts' Fund failed to secure more than a mere fraction of this amount. Recognizing that many people would not give to the United Party as such, it was decided to establish an organization in which people would have faith because of the people who were associated with it. Thus the United South Africa Trust Fund came into being, with Harry Oppenheimer of the Anglo-American Corporation as chairman, a distinguished group of business and professional men as trustees, and a broadly conceived set of objectives. With no specific commitments to the United Party, the Fund had in one sense complete independence about how to use its money. At the same time, the Fund could not make its contributions to the party conditional without imperilling the latter's independence. Thus the Fund increasingly found itself not only acting as a major fund-raising organization for the United Party, but with far less influence on the latter's policies than it would have desired.

The vigorous campaign of innuendos waged by the Nationalist press and politicians against the Fund throughout 1951 and the early part of 1952 contributed to the same end, and did much to destroy the reputation for impartiality which the Fund's sponsors tried to establish. From the first, it was easy to associate the Fund with the United Party, because Harry Oppenheimer, head of the Fund, was a prominent member of the party. The Nationalists cleverly, if somewhat unscrupulously, attacked along two lines. *Die Burger*, on February 23, 1951, accused the United Party of becoming 'a tool of the bosses of the Trust'. *Die Transvaler* declared, on July 24, 1951, that the United Party leadership was 'in Hoggenheimer's pocket, boots and all', and that the people 'who do not receive dividends from the sweat of their own labour' would look with aversion on this 'wedding between capitalism and the United Party'. Dr.

Verwoerd told the Nationalist Congress in South West Africa that 'with the help of the big capitalists, the United Party is trying to crush Nationalism in South Africa with gold'.[5] Equally, the Nationalists used the association between the Fund and the United Party as a stick with which to beat the latter, insisting that the Fund's mild declaration in support of 'the ideals of freedom of speech, language, worship and the fundamental rights of man as recognized by the Member States of the United Nations' was not only 'liberalistic' but implied opposition to the color bar.

Dropping the initial secretiveness about the Fund, Harry Oppenheimer made a forthright speech to his constituents on March 29, 1951, insisting that the Fund was the effort of individuals, not of organized business, commerce, or mining, that there was no truth in the charge that it aimed at the destruction of the industrial color bar, and that the reason it supported the United Party was the similarity in their objectives of national unity. Nonetheless, Nationalist charges, and perhaps industry's fear of being penalized by the Government in power, had an adverse effect on contributions to the Fund. They may also have made the United Party somewhat more reluctant to accept the Fund's suggestions on how to organize its affairs.

The two areas in which the Fund felt most competent to offer advice were the typically business fields of organization and propaganda. In the former, the Fund favored a strong national organization, with professional directors for each division working under party chairmen. It would have liked to have marginal constituencies placed under Head Office and organized by party agents on the model of the British Conservative Party. The Fund felt, too, that more should have been done to make propaganda appropriate and timely, and that press relations could be vastly improved. In practice, none of these suggestions was followed to any great extent, a further reason why enthusiasm for the Fund's work steadily diminished amongst its sponsors.

The United South Africa Trust Fund gave only to the national organization of the United Party, though some of these funds were subsequently passed on to General Councils to help meet deficits, or to provide special services. In the period before the 1953 General Election, the Fund also contributed to the head office of the Torch Commando, the Education Action Committee, which fought the Transvaal Education Ordinance with fire and vigor during the campaign period, Parent and Teachers' Associations and other groups dedicated to overcoming division between the English and Afrikaners. By far the greatest share of its contributions, however, went to the United Party to create its central organization and to strengthen its channels of liaison throughout the party. That the Fund decided, in 1954, to discontinue giving to the United Party is perhaps a mark that it felt its responsibilities had been fulfilled, and that it was henceforth up to the United Party branches to assume the full financial burden of the party's work.

Its Strength and Weakness

The United Party, as a typically conservative party, draws much of its support from the business, commercial and mining interests of the country, from well-to-do farmers, and professional people. Thus, though the economic base of politics is less strongly marked than in countries like Great Britain, Australia and New Zealand, there is a demarcation in South Africa by income and occupation which supplements that by ideology and, to some extent, language.

The strength, yet also the weakness of the United Party is the breadth of the groups it spans. Much of its strength is urban, but it also retains many roots in the *platteland*. Practically all the English-speaking are in its ranks, but its leaders have always been Afrikaners; so also are a fair proportion both of its members and some of its electoral supporters. The party includes Christians and Jews, Protestants and Catholics, deeply religious persons and atheists.

Most difficult of all is that the United Party includes such a wide spectrum of attitudes, ranging from the ultra conservative through a broad center of moderates to confirmed liberals. The touchstone, of course, is race relations, and the United Party has acquired an official policy on this crucial issue. Nonetheless, official affirmations count less than current actions and words and these suggest that the United Party is far from having adopted a single stand on non-European policy. The 1953-54 defections of the six ultra-conservatives and the 1955 resignation of Dr. Friedman, an outspoken liberal, are but the most extreme manifestations of the problem the United Party faces in maintaining its unity.

Yet, for all its difficulties, the United Party has manifest advantages. While the Nationalists keep the initiative with their racial legislation, and create fresh difficulties within the United Party every time they introduce a measure over which that party cannot agree, they also help to maintain the United Party's support in its own areas by constantly stirring up antagonism. It remains obvious that the United Party is the only possible political alternative to the Nationalists. Thus in subsequent national elections, as in 1953, the United Party will secure much support which is more anti-National Party than pro-United Party. Even in the House of Assembly, the Nationalists have had little advantage from the splits in the United Party.

The leaders of the United Party are less persuasive, less ruthless and, in these senses, less effective than the Nationalist leaders. Mr. Strauss is as able as any Nationalist; he could be as obstinate as they. He preferred to work quietly and with conciliation, seeking to hold the party together to the greatest extent possible by finding the middle road which would appeal to the large and uncommitted center. He had less sense of the dramatic, less ability to appeal to the public or to establish easy relations with the press, than was good either for his own position and that of his party. Yet at crucial points, like his presentation of the statement on Native policy to the 1954 United Party Union Congress, Strauss showed qualities of decisiveness and leadership which were undeniable. Wisely Strauss chose to retire from Parliament soon after he was replaced as leader of the party, but it is not yet sure that his political career is permanently over.

More charming and urbane, with an ability to create a personal loyalty far greater than that given to Strauss, is his successor, Sir de Villiers Graaff. More conservative on Native affairs, Graaff finds this no disadvantage in leading his group, or, in mid-1957, in differentiating it from Nationalist policies. Graaff has also shown an ability to take a firm stand when it is essential and, at the same time, to hold his party together.

D. E. Mitchell, leader in Natal, is personable, effective and ambitious, but not particularly successful at ingratiating himself with the rank and file of

United Party members. Colin Steyn, in the Free State, had the fire that Strauss too often lacked, but he represented the older generation of the party, as does Henry Tucker in the Transvaal. Steyn is now replaced by Senator H. G. Swart.

These are men who have more in common with the party they lead than Smuts, with his brilliance, his world-wide view, his vast energy and his frequent detachment from people while his mind explored new lines. Smuts was mistrusted in his own country in his earlier days as being too clever, even too 'slim', as his rapier-like mind played around his slower-witted opponents. Smuts dominated his party, not always to its advantage, for it lost the sense of personal responsibility and touch with the people it existed to serve. Yet Smuts was among the great, as the world always recognized. Perhaps he was never greater than when he turned his back on the book he planned to write (though one must always regret its loss) and plunged into party politics again after the shattering experience not only of defeat at the 1948 General Election, but also in his own constituency at Standerton.

Smuts' heir apparent, Jan Hofmeyr, was no more characteristic of the United Party as a whole than was Smuts. Hofmeyr was a liberal in outlook, as brilliant as Smuts in his own way, but with a mathematical neatness of mind rather than Smuts' breadth of philosophic view. Hofmeyr commanded respect by his ability, his incessant activity, and his adherence to principle, but few people loved him. The party's liberals saw him as their hope, but the conservatives feared and even disliked him.

What would have become of the United Party had Hofmeyr outlived Smuts is anyone's guess. It might have become a party with a more distinctive Native policy and a greater capacity to awaken ideological fervor. For that very reason, however, it might not have commanded so broad a basis of consistent electoral support as does the present United Party.

CHAPTER 12

THE TORCH COMMANDO

Nationalist policies, and in particular the constitutional crises over removing the Coloured from the common roll, have given rise to a series of quasi-political groups of which by far the most important was the Torch Commando. These groups differ sharply from those described under Nationalist Afrikanerdom. Unlike the latter, they have not sought to build a cohesive, ideologically oriented community, but rather to attack Nationalist political control. Partly because their emphasis was thus negative rather than positive, these groups and, in particular, the Torch Commando, neither accomplished as much politically nor had as great an effect on South Africa at large as could have been expected from the extent of their support and their activities.

Other non-Nationalist groups, like the Sons of England, about which the Nationalists make a good deal of propaganda, do more than did the Torch Commando to encourage a positive philosophy similar to that of voluntary Afrikaner organizations. But the similarities are not great. The Sons of England endorse the English heritage of many South Africans, but only mildly. Though, like the Masons, the Sons of England have a closely guarded initiation, they form in no sense a secret society like the Broederbond, nor are they nearly as effective. Nowhere is there an English-oriented or non-Nationalist coordinating group comparable to the F.A.K. (see p. 256).

The Nationalists say, rightly, that there has not been the same need for English South Africans, or for those outside the ranks of Nationalist Afrikanerdom to band together formally to promote their economic well-being, their language, their culture or their conception of life. Most of the wealth of the country has always been in the hands of English or Jewish capitalists. Many Nationalists say, again correctly, that the Chamber of Mines is one of the great influences of South Africa. So too are its rapidly expanding secondary industries. But South African business, commerce and mining are quite ready to work closely with the Nationalists, whether of the Hertzog or Malanite variety. This is the more so, of course, because Afrikaner nationalism has always endorsed those economic developments which make the country independent of outside influences, particularly from Great Britain. English-speaking economic leaders of South Africa no doubt work for the United Party, though with varying degrees of enthusiasm; at the same time they appreciate the independence and support the Nationalists give their enterprises. Thus they neither exert any strongly anti-Nationalist influence nor attempt positively to develop cohesion in non-Nationalist ranks.

Nothing comparable to Christian National Education is found among non-Nationalists. C.N.E. has provoked its own opposition, however, in the Education League, and from the South African Teachers' Association. Moreover, English-language universities have increasingly felt Nationalist pressures. As a result, non-Nationalist education groups have had to formulate more specifically their basic principles of education.

SABRA and the Dutch Reformed Churches can be compared to the South African Institute of Race Relations, and the English-speaking Churches. Yet it is clear that there is no such intimate relationship between these institutions and the non-Nationalist community as exists between SABRA, the Dutch Reformed Church and Nationalist Afrikanerdom. In the first place, almost all non-Nationalist Afrikaners belong to the Dutch Reformed Church. As for other non-Nationalists, it is rare indeed if they take either the findings of the Institute of Race Relations or the exhortations of their Churches with anything like the same seriousness accorded writings and preachings in the other camp.

Particularly in relation to the non-European, the English-speaking Churches enunciate a more liberal attitude than the Dutch Reformed Church, and certainly one which rejects the belief that there is a theological justification for color segregation. Along with the Institute of Race Relations, these Churches also believe that the process of non-European integration in the European areas has gone too far to be reversed in line with the conceptions of 'ideal apartheid'. They are deeply concerned, therefore, to give the non-European more of the opportunities that they feel should be his both as a child of God and as a permanent member of the South African community.

Thus, English-speaking Churches trenchantly oppose the Bantu Education Act which SABRA and the Dutch Reformed Church endorse. The United Party has now pledged itself to repeal the Bantu Education Act if it comes into office. But the difference between the instant opposition to the Act from the Churches and the Institute of Race Relations, and the much more hesitant reactions of the United Party reflects a usual relationship. By and large, non-Nationalist South Africans, like so many people elsewhere, expect their Churches to be well in advance of their own thinking, and particularly of their own actions. But, however slow non-Nationalists are to respond to their Churches and universities when the latter act as a voice of conscience, they do not exert as much pressure on them to conform to current standards of political expediency as does Nationalist Afrikanerdom on its intellectual and religious groups.

This warning should be kept in mind in reading the material at the end of this chapter on the Institute of Race Relations and the English-speaking Churches. In the long run, both do something to inculcate attitudes in non-Nationalist South Africans, but their relation to the political process is far less close than that of their 'opposite numbers' amongst Nationalist Afrikanerdom. The other extra-party groups here described, of which by far the most important was the Torch Commando, were in contrast politically oriented, and sought openly, though without success, to modify Nationalist policies or, in the case of the Torch Commando, to oust the Nationalists from office.

The War Veterans' Torch Commando

Unique in the history of non-Nationalist South Africa was the spontaneous rise and rapid growth of the organization which called itself originally the

War Veterans' Action Committee, but soon broadened to the War Veterans' Torch Commando. Beginning with a knot of people at the time when the Nationalists decided to take the Coloured off the common roll by majority action, instead of the procedure for an entrenched clause laid down in the South Africa Act, the Torch Commando included nearly a quarter of a million members at its height late in 1952. Many of these members were already United Party supporters, but the Torch must be credited with rousing a vast number of people, particularly amongst the English-speaking, to a new sense of concern about politics. That they failed both in their specific objective of turning the Nationalists out of office in 1953 and, more positively, of creating a new sense of unity between English and Afrikaners throughout South Africa, may be due partly to their mistakes but more particularly to the situations which they confronted.

The genesis of the Torch Commando came in April 1951, through the activities of an *ad hoc* committee of ex-servicemen, including Louis Kane-Berman, Ralph Parrott and, by far the best-known name of all, A. G. or 'Sailor' Malan, the South African fighter pilot whose exploits in the Royal Air Force had been a household word in Great Britain as well as in his own country. It was these men and a few others who organized the protest meetings on May 4, 1951, against the Separate Representation of Voters Bill which, to their astonishment, brought 6,000 people out in Port Elizabeth and 15-20,000 in Johannesburg. In the latter city, some 4,000 veterans, men and women, marched eight abreast in a spectacular torch-light procession through the streets, followed by a contingent of students from Witwatersrand University and a column of Coloured veterans.

To the Johannesburg crowd, which responded with tremendous cheers, Sailor Malan, from the steps of the City Hall, assailed 'this latest monstrous act of cynical betrayal known as the Coloured Franchise Bill', adding that, 'when I mention it I feel ashamed to be a South African and a white man'. Declaring that fundamental principles were in danger, such as freedom of speech, religion, movement and others essential to a democratic structure, he maintained that:

> In Abyssinia, at Alamein and a score of bloody campaigns we won the right to a voice in our country's affairs. And we are determined that our voice shall not only be heard but that it shall also be heeded. After all, who has the greater claim to talk about saving white civilization? The moles who now pay lip service to it, or the men who fought for it?[1]

In response, the crowd unanimously accepted four resolutions which protested against the Government's action 'in proposing to violate the spirit of the Constitution', pledged 'every constitutional step in the interests of our country to enforce an immediate General Election', called on other ex-servicemen and 'all democratic South Africans' to pledge themselves to this cause, and decided to transmit these resolutions to the Prime Minister and leaders of other political parties. The fight was on.

Within four days, the War Veterans' Action Committee met not only to implement Sailor Malan's proposal for a nation-wide organization, but to plan the 'steel commando drive' on Cape Town to dramatize their objectives. On

May 11, they issued a manifesto which reaffirmed their intention to use 'every constitutional means' both to oppose

> the attack on the Constitution implicit in the manner in which the Government is seeking to enact the Separate Representation of Voters Bill and its consequent attack on the democratic rights of the people

and to enforce a General Election. In stirring if somewhat flowery words, they concluded:

> We declare our undying opposition to those who would bind the free spirit of men with the chains of bigotry and ignorance and who would prostitute the spirit of democratic Government in South Africa.
>
> We dedicate our skills and our talents and the strength of our hearts, minds and bodies to the concept of free Government and we pledge our alliance with every individual and group engaged in the struggle to maintain the honour of our nation and the security of our democratic heritage.
>
> Within 100 hours of the achievement of our objects we pledge ourselves to dissolve our movement. Until that moment the cause of all free men becomes our cause.
>
> Every home, every street, every village and every city becomes a battlefield.
>
> The battle is engaged.[2]

Four days later, on May 15, an Executive Committee elected at the first meeting of the War Veterans' Action Committee in Cape Town issued its own manifesto which added to the other pledges the declaration that:

> Here in South Africa democracy now stands in need of defence. The present crisis of the Constitution has alarmed all those of us who care about the future of our country.
>
> This is not a matter of party politics; it is a question of fundamental democratic principles. If a breach of the Constitution is committed now, the whole structure of South African democracy may be fatally weakened.
>
> If the political rights of so large a group as the Coloured people are diminished without effective protest, the status and rights of no other group in the community are safe and secure.
>
> Moreover, this attack on their entrenched rights of long standing is sure to embitter the Coloured people, to drive them to extreme courses, and to destroy the hope of future inter-racial cooperation between them and Europeans.[3]

In the light of subsequent developments, this initial and direct concern for the Coloured is worth noting.

No pains were spared by the War Veterans' Action Committee to create a demonstration which would touch the whole country. The petition to the Government to observe the entrenched clauses was carried by motor caravan the thousand miles from Johannesburg to Cape Town. In the leading car of the caravan rode former Senator A. J. de la Rey, affectionately known as 'Oom Dolf', a Boer War veteran, whose presence was only one mark of the effort to accentuate the Afrikaner as well as English character of the demonstration. Two thousand people saw the caravan off from the City Hall in Johannesburg, an equal number received it in Bloemfontein, capital of the Orange Free State, others from as far away as South West Africa and Natal joined the trek. The evening of May 28, a 12-man delegation, supported by a huge procession of some 10,000 ex-servicemen, went to the House of Assembly to present their petitions. Despite long notice, Dr. Malan would not receive them, but J. G. N. Strauss, John Christie, leader of the Labour Party, and Mrs. Ballinger, ranking member of the Native representatives, did so. Strauss declared: 'You are taking part in a resurgence of the spirit of South Africa.' Next day, the petition was handed personally to Dr. Malan and Mr. Havenga in the Prime Minister's private room by Cape members of the veterans' committee.

In the meantime, the impressiveness of the simple ceremony had been marred by serious rioting which broke out shortly after the petition was presented. The *Rand Daily Mail* reported, on May 30, that:

> The crowd taunted the police and some threw their flaming torches at them. . . . The incident which is believed to have set off the riot was when a Coloured man repeatedly pushed his torch into the face of a policeman in Church Square. Within a few minutes the crowd began hurling missiles at the thin police cordons and soon the air was full of missiles and the sound of ambulance sirens.

One hundred and sixty people were hurt. For weeks, the blame for the riot was passed from side to side. The Nationalists, who had belittled the march (e.g. Marais Viljoen in the Transvaal Provincial Council called it 'nothing but a travelling circus and an exhibition of clowning'),[4] now charged that the veterans had started the riot. The United Party, under pressure from the veterans, urged an official investigation; when the Nationalists refused, reports were circulated that Nationalists themselves had incited the riot. The event could hardly have been more unfortunate, both because it distracted attention from the public protest and because it drove a wedge of personal bitterness between the veterans and the Nationalists.

Counter-accusations continued. Dönges insinuated that the Cape Town march had been 'master-minded' by Communists;[5] Sailor Malan retaliated in East London by accusing the Nationalists of 'scheming and plotting for a Fascist Republic', posing as a bulwark against Communism 'when it is in fact the most effective ally of Communism', and as the savior of white civilization; 'but white civilization was never in danger until it came into power'.[6]

The veterans were already developing a nation-wide organization based on the personal activities of those who formed its nucleus. From Port Elizabeth, for example, the region spread as far north as those primarily responsible in that area felt they could reach. Army experience facilitated an easy chain of command. When the first National Congress met in Johannesburg on June 28, 1951, barely two months after the movement had begun, there were 85 delegates from 65 centers throughout the country.

Big questions had to be decided at this point. Would the group form itself into a political party? If not, what should be its relationship with the Opposition parties, in particular the United Party? Should membership remain exclusively ex-service? If civilians were admitted, should it be in auxiliary branches or as full members? What about non-Europeans, particularly Coloured ex-servicemen? What about policy, in particular, policy towards non-Europeans?

From the first, it was agreed that the new organization should be, in the words of Sailor Malan's opening address to the Congress, 'a political pressure group' not a political party or 'an offshoot of any political party'.[7] For the veterans to form themselves into a party seemed tantamount to giving a vote of no confidence in the existing parliamentary Opposition; in any case, as the group's leaders recognized, such a move would split their own ranks. They hoped to support the Opposition parties and yet not become embroiled in party politics. As Sailor Malan pointed out in a private paper before the Congress met, the movement had 'resulted from fundamental political causes and, provided it confines itself to the fundamental issues before the country today, it will remain on firm ground. The moment we get ourselves embroiled in party politics we shall get out of our depth and into serious difficulties.' Yet to be a political pressure group without getting into party politics was more than difficult.

Though the veterans' leaders recognized that the Native question was of paramount importance, they also saw it rightly as the most divisive of all issues because of the vast variety of views on color questions. Their resolution of this problem was to hope that the Government could be persuaded to take color problems out of the political arena. In the meantime, they decided that the organization should take no stand on color matters.

Their objective was numbers. It was this, in the end, which overrode the arguments in favor of keeping the organization a purely ex-service group. Moreover, some felt it would be unfair to exclude those who had been unable to play an active role in the war, while others recognized that an ex-service group would never appeal to Nationalists, of whom so many had been opposed to the war.[8] Sailor Malan had proposed, as early as June 16, that the movement should be open to everyone.[9] The *Rand Daily Mail* protested editorially on June 20:

> This is not a good idea. As an ex-servicemen's organization, the War Veterans have an individuality and a special value of their own; they will lose much of it if they broaden the basis of their organization. This is one of the cases where the right tactics are concentration rather than dispersal.

The majority of those from Natal and the Low Veld agreed with the *Rand Daily Mail*, but were out-argued by the Free State and most of the original leaders. Sailor Malan also favored having separate ex-service and civilian units, at least initially. The final decision was to make no differentiations, or limitations. Membership was opened to all permanent residents of South Africa who had served in the forces in any war, and to all those over 19 who were prepared to assist in carrying out the objects of the movement and were accepted by a branch. In practice, however, most of the leaders, except in the Free State, were always drawn from the ex-service group, and about two-thirds of the membership.

It is easy to criticize the naïveté which looked forward to standing above party politics, hoped to avoid a stand on South Africa's all-pervasive issue of color policy, and saw numbers as more important than conviction. But the leaders of what was now formally named the War Veterans' Torch Commando had both negative and positive objectives in view which needed mass support to carry them through. Numbers would give them influence, they thought, both with the Government and with the Opposition parties. Numbers were essential if they were to help defeat the Nationalists at the next election. This they hoped would come soon, though the more far-sighted recognized that the Torch Commando's very strength might well lead the Government to postpone such a contest as long as possible, i.e. for two years. For their positive objective of developing a stronger sense of national unity, numbers were also important. Thus, they concentrated on broad principles on which agreement was relatively easy.

The five principles of the Torch Commando were both straightforward and potentially far-reaching. They read:

1. To uphold the letter and the spirit of the solemn compacts entered upon at the time of Union as moral obligations of trust and honour binding upon Parliament and the people.
2. To secure the repeal of any measures enacted in violation of such obligations.
3. To protect the freedom of the individual in worship, language and speech and to ensure his right of free access to the Courts.
4. To eliminate all forms of totalitarianism, whether Fascist or Communist.
5. To promote racial harmony in the Union.

These principles were printed on the Torch membership forms. They not only specified opposition to the Separate Representation of Voters Bill but also the positive affirmation of democratic freedoms and way of life. 'Racial harmony' was left undefined.

But what about non-European membership? The movement had started as a moral protest against taking the Coloured off the common roll by what were termed unconstitutional means. Coloured ex-servicemen had marched in the veterans' demonstrations both in Johannesburg and Cape Town. The original draft of the Constitution of the War Veterans' Action Committee, drafted May 23, 1951, had specifically stated one objective to be

> to foster and maintain cooperation amongst the peoples of the Union of South Africa and mandated territories irrespective of race, colour and creed.

In line with this, the veterans' national executive tentatively endorsed separate branches for Europeans and non-Europeans under European leadership.

At the first Congress, considerable division of opinion showed on the matter. Cape members, in particular, wished to establish non-European branches, more or less on the pattern of the separate Coloured ex-servicemen's groups of the British Empire Service League, a benevolent society. The very existence of these groups, and the contacts already established with them on an *ad hoc* basis, would facilitate the establishment of such branches. Others felt it would do neither the Coloured themselves nor the Torch Commando any good to include them as members. The final decision was to avoid mentioning the Coloured in the Constitution, and to leave the matter to be decided by individual branches.

This apparently sensible decision precipitated in practice all the difficulties the Congress had hoped to avoid. Learning that non-Europeans could be admitted as members if local committees decided to accept them, the *Star* publicly applauded the principle of admitting members 'on their merits and not on their colour', which it called striking 'the first direct and courageous blow at the assumptions forced on South Africa by doctrinaire nationalism'.[10] But this was exactly what a great many members and potential supporters of the Torch Commando did not wish to do. A few Coloured branches, and a few mixed branches were set up in the Cape, but the opposition to Coloured membership of some of the movement's leaders not only continued but gained publicity. So too did Nationalist attacks on what Strijdom termed the 'colour-blind policy' of the Torch Commando.[11]

On September 24, 1951, the *Star* reported Louis Kane-Berman, the National Chairman, as saying that the Torch Commando's color policy was still under consideration but 'the generally accepted principle' seemed to be that it should be 'similar to that of the army in the war, where non-Europeans had their own units'. Thus 'non-Europeans will form their own branches, but will be represented on our national bodies by Europeans'. This was further watered down when a National Executive meeting on October 12 and 13 endorsed the principle of separate branches, but only for non-Europeans who possessed the franchise (i.e. the male Cape Coloured who could meet certain literacy and economic qualifications). This limitation was justified on the ground that 'our chief weapon is the vote', to which Kane-Berman added the argument that the present conflict was 'essentially a struggle between the white peoples of the country'. The action committee opposed the admission of Natives, he said, because 'we do not intend to follow in the footsteps of the Government in inflaming Natives against Europeans'.

It was all too apparent that Coloured members were not generally welcome in the Torch Commando. The Northern Cape Region sought a general Cape conference to attempt a solution of the matter; most of the other Cape areas preferred to let the National Executive Committee wrestle with the issue. But the final decision was taken by the Coloured themselves. On November 9, representatives of Coloured ex-servicemen, who had met the action committee of the Torch Commando's Cape Western Branch the night before, issued a statement that Coloured ex-servicemen had 'no desire' to become members of the Commando. With great dignity, they declared that 'the Commando's fight is the white man's fight to re-establish the integrity of his word, and in this work the Coloureds obviously have no part'.[12]

Inevitably, this wavering policy on non-European membership destroyed the initial cordiality of the Torch Commando's relations with the Coloured. Equally, it displayed all too obviously the wide differences in attitude on color matters existing within the movement. Moreover, the fact that there were no Coloured members of the Torch Commando after November 1951 did not save that group from hostile Nationalist election propaganda. *Wat is Die Torch Commando?* (see p. 188) quoted the *Star* article of July 3, 1951, on 'merit is what counts, not colour' in Torch membership. Thus the movement lost all the way round by its equivocations on Coloured membership.

Well before the issue of Coloured membership came to a head, the leadership of the Torch Commando had made it clear that they were not fighting for the rights of the Coloured as such, but against the method the Government was using to take the Coloured off the common roll. An early statement on the purpose of the steel commando march had declared that:

> We are not concerned with the legal aspect of the matter, but we are concerned with the fact that there is a moral obligation on the people in this country to observe the entrenched clauses of the Constitution.[13]

Late in July, the National Executive made their position more explicit when responding to the reply by Dr. Malan and Mr. Havenga to the veterans' petition handed to them in Cape Town on May 29. In their letter, Malan and Havenga had stated that there was no question of 'a repudiation of solemn compact' by changing the Coloured to a separate roll; on the contrary it would be 'a breach of faith with South Africa' if the Government withdrew the legislation for separate representation of voters. They suggested that the protest was 'the result of the partisan propaganda, incitement and misrepresentation conducted by the Opposition and its press'.[14] In their response, the Torch Executive declared that:

> It is abundantly clear from the resolutions that the concern and objection of thousands of South Africans was not the question whether the Coloured man's rights were being altered, but the method by which it was done.

They affirmed the principle 'that if a man makes a promise he is bound by honour to keep it unless absolved by the other party' and pointed out that 'the beneficiaries have not granted absolution from these promises. The Coloured were not even consulted.' If this entrenched clause were altered by simple majority procedure, they foresaw danger also to the clause which safeguarded equal language rights. 'We fear for the future of our country,' the statement concluded, 'and we say that those in power are not fit to govern.'[15] The emphasis was already shifting from the entrenched clauses to the major objective of getting the Nationalists out of office.

The Nationalists were not slow to take up the challenge. J. G. Strijdom[16] and Dr. Karl Bremer[17] imputed totalitarian motives to the Commando. Dr. Malan himself had accused the Torch Commando of being a new incarnation of the Springbok Legion, 'a communistic organization in its make-up and aim', and of acting in the same way by 'dubbing all its opponents as Nazis, pretending to be a protector of democracy, and making no differentiation on the ground of colour'.[18] He declared that, if necessary, the Government would take action against the Torch Commando. Subsequently, at the Cape Nationalist Congress, Dr. Malan criticized the military or semi-military characteristics of the Commando, declaring that private armies would not be tolerated. He also warned that if Torch members made organized appearances at National Party meetings, there would be 'a reaction on the part of the Nationalists'.[19]

To the charge of being dominated by the Springbok Legion, the veterans had a quick and effective answer. The Springbok Legion, formed during the war, was an action group to improve service conditions. Some of its leaders were Communist, and though its membership rose to about 3,000, the organization was never acceptable to the vast majority of servicemen. Naturally enough, Springbok Legionnaires were amongst the earliest supporters of the Veterans' Action Committee. But before they could acquire any substantial influence, a member of the Torch Executive, himself a Legionnaire, proposed that all Springbok members should resign. The motion was carried by a narrow majority, but the decision was made unequivocally. Thus, when Dr. Malan issued his accusation, it was possible for the Torch Executive, by publishing the list of its leading members, to give conclusive evidence that the attack was without foundation.

Not the least of the Torch Commando problems, however, was to determine what should be its next steps. The highly personalized structure of its first three months was giving place to a comprehensive—and thus more cumbersome—national organization. Charles Bekker, senior geologist for Union Corporation, resigned in July 1951, to become national organizer for the Commando; he travelled 30,000 miles and addressed 57 meetings during the succeeding six months. Ralph Parrott became full-time National Director of the Torch Commando's central offices in Johannesburg. Sailor Malan was formally called National President and Louis Kane-Berman, National Chairman. The National Executive now numbered between 50 and 60, being representative of all the regions as well as including the national officers. The size and difficulty of bringing this body together shifted day-to-day decisions to the action committee of some 10 Johannesburg members, who could be joined at will by the chairmen of the areas into which the country was divided. The membership and number of branches continued to grow; late in 1951, there were some 120,000 members in 350 branches. In what direction should their energies be turned so that the momentum would not die down?

In line with the Commando's belief in publicity, and its ambition to heal the gap between English and Afrikaners, the anniversary of one of South Africa's most glorious military exploits, El Alamein Day, October 23, 1951, was signaled out for a Day of Dedication ceremonies 'of service and call to the nation'. In simple, eloquent words, the manifesto read:

> We, veterans of many wars, once more dedicate ourselves to our land.
> In the belief and with the guidance of Almighty God, we shall pursue the truth.
> We shall strive for justice, mutual trust and honour in our affairs.
> South Africans, men have died that you should be free, let no one rob you of your heritage.
> Having met together in a spirit of mutual faith and trust our fathers founded the Union of South Africa. In that same spirit let us go forth together, free men, free from fear, free to worship and free to speak.
> South Africa—awake!

What about the party politics the Torch Commando was so eager to eschew? On August 14, 1951, Kane-Berman said tentatively that though the movement was 'in no way affiliated or identified with the U.P.' the Commando could see no other party that could successfully fight the Nationalists. Torch would also support the Labour Party 'where it was considered advisable'.[20] Six days later, he emphasized that the Commando would take no part in the selection of candidates, nor would it try to influence political parties in their choice of candidates. That should be done from within the parties themselves.[21] A member of the action committee, J. D. Wilson, pointed out a few days later, however, that every Torch member should check his registration as a voter, and encourage others to do likewise, the more so since it was believed (correctly) that the delimitation of constituencies would be based on the number of registered voters rather than, as in the past, on census figures. 'It's up to every alert South African to take this precaution against possible jerrymandering', he declared.[22] Torch had hit on one of its most fruitful activities: to try to make the electoral machinery work as fairly as possible. Along this line was Torch's major effort in sponsoring the Suzman brief on delimitation (see p. 152), and its members' largely successful efforts to get the maximum number of names on the voters' roll and subsequently to bring out the Opposition vote at the 1953 election.

On the more debatable question of liaison with the United Party, there were widely differing points of view. Late in 1951, the Eastern Cape still opposed having an alliance with any party whatsoever; the Cape Peninsula, in contrast, supported either a merger with the United Party or forming a new party; the Transvaal proposed a common anti-Government front; while the Central area favored non-party political assistance for the Opposition parties. In actuality, however, the Torch Commando was steadily moving towards a closer relationship with the United Party as the only means of realizing its major objective of ousting the Nationalists.

At their October National Executive meeting, Torch leaders discussed the movement's possible relationship to Opposition political parties on the basis of various regional resolutions and accepted a broad statement of policy under five headings of which only the first four were intended for publication. They declared

i. That the War Veterans' Torch Commando owes no allegiance and is, and remains, unaffiliated to any political party.
ii. That we can support only those parties or candidates who subscribe to the democratic way of life and to racial harmony.
iii. That the present Government have violated the fundamental freedoms of racial harmony and because of that we oppose them.
iv. That, in so far as the Opposition Parties generally are concerned, we expect they will do all in their power to defend the democratic rights and freedoms and to promote racial harmony.
v. That this meeting views with grave concern the general lack of confidence of the public in the Opposition parties and, in particular, the United Party and urges upon them in the national interest to take immediate and adequate steps to merit the return of that confidence.

In pursuance of a general agreement reached by the Executive, a series of informal, exploratory meetings between the Torch Commando and the United Party were held at different levels between the second and third meetings of the National Executive, i.e., between mid-October, 1951, and the end of January,

1952. Policy discussions were carried on between prominent Transvaal United Party members like Bailey Bekker, Marais Steyn and A. E. Robinson, and Torch Commando leaders like Louis Kane-Berman, Charles Bekker, J. D. Wilson and A. L. Kowarsky. Staff members of the two groups similarly met to consider organizational liaison. At the constituency level, the Torch and United Party joined in some experimental constituency organization in Johannesburg West, with an eye to developing techniques, and also worked together to bring voters' rolls up to date in both urban and rural constituencies.[23] The leaders of both groups issued appeals to their members to cooperate with each other. At the same time, in pursuance of their fifth unpublished resolution, Torch leaders also transmitted to the United Party their criticisms of what they saw as shortcomings both in organization and lack of definiteness in policy.

The Labour Party was not neglected in this period though the illness of its leader, John Christie, slowed negotiations. Labour was keen for an immediate election pact with the United Party, and Torch leaders agreed to urge this closer relationship between the two Opposition parties, although they were aware, as was the United Party, that Labour had little to offer in the way of election strength.

Surveying the position of the Torch Commando at the end of January, 1952, its National Executive still faced serious questions about the future role of the movement. On the one hand was the undeniable fact that its spontaneous, large-scale growth demonstrated dissatisfaction with the Nationalist Government, at least on the constitutional issue, and also the hope that there could be a more broadly based, less partisan governing group and policy. Equally, however, it was clear that the Commando had not appealed to Nationalist Afrikaners, especially on the *platteland*, where many Torch leaders felt the movement had a special mission. Rather than being attracted to it, these people tended to regard the Commando as the English equivalent of the Ossewa Brandwag (see p. 32). Nor had Torch achieved anything positive in its broadest objective of building unity between the English and Afrikaner sections of the community; on the contrary its attacks on the Nationalists, like theirs on the Commando, had probably widened the breach between the two white groups. The impetus of the movement had diminished noticeably with new members joining much more slowly except in certain towns. Moreover, far from all of those who had enrolled were sufficiently enthusiastic to work hard for the movement.

Confronting this situation, the leaders of the Torch Commando divided broadly into two schools of thought. The more conservative, even 'official' line favored concentration on winning the next election, limiting policy to the broad statement of aims in the Constitution, and putting the members' efforts into tasks like the registration of voters. There were others, however, who called for a more dynamic policy to counter current dissatisfaction with the United Party, and the vagueness of its policy. To meet this problem, the latter group urged a political program based on a limited number of vital issues designed for wide general appeal.

A cardinal point of this program was to hold a national convention to revise the South African Constitution to bring it more in line with the country's current economic and social conditions. Special safeguards should be provided for democratic freedoms, they felt, by limiting bureaucratic ministerial powers, and ensuring the right of appeal of all persons at all times to an impartial court of law. Non-European policy should be taken out of the party arena through referring most non-European matters now dealt with in Parliament to a permanent non-party commission. While endorsing social and residential segregation, the sponsors of this program recognized that Europeans might need to make considerable sacrifices in the interest of stable and harmonious relations between Europeans and non-Europeans. In the attempt positively to counteract the gulf widening amongst white South Africans, they proposed a non-political Afrikaner-English Relations Committee with the cultural mission of seeking every means to create better understanding between the two groups. Lastly on 'bread and butter' policy, the group urged special attention to the needs of the average citizen lest the active economic development of South Africa raise too high his cost of living.

Such a program, they hope, would not only bring new members, enthusiasm and financial support to the Torch Commando but provide its members with a platform which they could promote from within any political party. Thus it might not only give fresh direction and strength to the Opposition parties but perhaps even cause a split within the Nationalists between its center group and extremists.

Where this somewhat limited group hoped to invigorate the Opposition by policy proposals, there was strong feeling from Natal that only very drastic measures, such as a threatened withdrawal of financial or Commando support, would bring new spirit, and activity within the United Party. Nationalist strong points were seen to be the emotional appeal of their policy and methods of action, their close contact with the people, and their cooperativeness with business men. The United Party, in contrast, was criticized for the vagueness of its policy, the weakness of its national and provincial leadership, the lack of virility of many of its M.P.s, and the inefficiency and prevalence of cliques in its branch organizations.

None of the Torch leaders was entirely happy about the United Party. Yet the same dilemma confronted them as at the start. If the Commando publicly criticized the Opposition, might it not destroy whatever chances there were of putting the Nationalists out of office? In the end, therefore, the National Executive issued a broadly worded statement of election policy. Reaffirming its principles, it declared that 'the only effective means of achieving a united and democratic South Africa is to remove the present Government from power'. Further, it acknowledged that the Torch Commando 'cannot become a separate political party' and could therefore only defeat 'the opponents of democracy' by the active participation of its members with existing Opposition parties 'with whom we are one in principle'. As a particular responsibility, it pledged efforts to avoid three-cornered electoral contests (in practice there were none in 1953 which might have split the Opposition vote). Lastly, in an effort to meet the criticism of those who felt that the Torch Commando owed more to its members than election activity, the statement ended in all vagueness:

> Any attempt to predict the future of the War Veterans' Torch Commando after the election is premature. The strength and the future of the movement is in the hands of its members. We were formed to fight for our principles and only when those principles are in safe and honourable hands will we relax.

While Torch Commando leaders agonized over their relation with the United Party, the latter from their side also equivocated about the new group. Strauss told the 1951 Transvaal Congress of the United Party that 'we give our blessing to the movement', and added 'They are General Smuts' boys. They are our friends. They are good material, and their program is a good one'.[24] The Congress enthusiastically adopted a motion of appreciation 'of the gallant work' of the Commando 'in fighting the enemies of democracy'. Earlier, Strauss had answered Dr. Malan's half-threat that he took the Commando 'seriously', by declaring 'you dare not touch these men. If you do, you do so at your peril. South Africa will not permit it'. Not surprisingly, Strauss also gave his 'full and emphatic blessing' to the Commando's objective to bring down the Malan-Havenga Government and, in his words, 'to see installed in its place a United Party Government'.[25] Some people chuckled when *Die Volksblad* commented that 'we do not believe that the United Party realizes properly what a dangerous movement it is taking to its bosom'.[26] But the fact that the Government sent C.I.D. (Criminal Investigation Division) personnel to watch Torch meetings,[27] plus charges of liberalism, and 'colour blindness' had almost as much effect on the United Party's ultra-conservatives as on the Nationalists. Thus from the United Party as well as from the Torch side, there was much need to thrash out their relationship.

In mid-February, 1952, Torch leaders went to Cape Town to consult with Strauss and Christie as leaders of the two opposition parties. Rumor was that Strauss had 'sent for' them, and that he warned them against pressing for a United Party-Labour coalition. Kane-Berman insisted that the Torchers had planned to go to Cape Town before Strauss asked to see them,[28] and also that they had 'no intention of dictating to any political party'. They were not urging 'a merger' of the parties, he declared, though they believed it 'imperative' to develop 'a united front to fight the Nationalist Government'.[29] He made it clear that in the belief that there should be 'general and continuous understanding among all Opposition groups', the Torch Commando held 'frequent consultations on routine matters of common interest with the Opposition parties'. On February 25, 1952, Sailor Malan made his first appearance in Johannesburg since the original torchlight procession and declared that the Commando was 'a new democratic spark in the political life of South Africa'. He added significantly:

> but the spark is useless unless it is harnessed to the proper machinery—and that machinery is the constitutional machinery of the present Opposition parties in the House of Assembly. . . . Our role in no way conflicts with that of the parties. We have a common objective—to kick out the Government. We cannot merely stand on the touchlines and cheer on the parties.[30]

The Torch Commando and the United Party were moving closer together.

The Appeal Court decision on March 20, 1952, that the Separate Representation of Voters' Act was unconstitutional (see p. 127), and even more the Government's announcement that it would not accept the implications of the verdict, gave fresh impetus to the Commando. Strauss and Sailor Malan issued a joint statement on March 22 announcing public meetings throughout the country to demonstrate their 'determination to uphold our Constitution'.[31] Huge mass meetings of 20,000 people in Pretoria, and 15,000 in Johannesburg answered the appeal.[32] The Commando had already asked the Prime Minister for an interview, which he refused unless they publicly withdrew the call they had issued for his resignation 'in the interests of democracy', when the Appeal Court decision was announced.[33] Sailor Malan and Ralph Parrott personally took to Cape Town the resolutions passed at the mass meetings, but the Prime Minister refused to see them.[34]

Within three weeks the most far-reaching and most controversial decision in the history of the Torch Commando was made: the formation of the United Democratic Front with the United Party and Labour Party. At a mass rally of some 5,000 people in Cape Town City Hall, Strauss announced dramatically the declaration on which the unity of the three groups was based.

> The United Party, the Labour Party and the Torch Commando, embracing the great majority of the South African people who love liberty and cherish the free institutions of our land, have viewed with growing dismay the immoral and illegal acts and declared intentions of the present Government.
>
> We are determined to uphold the law against lawlessness and to defend the Constitution as our own sacred heritage bequeathed to us by our fathers, both English and Afrikaans-speaking, as the enshrinement of our hard-won liberties.
>
> We declare, with due appreciation of the great responsibility resting upon us, that we have come together freely for the specific purpose of ridding South Africa of its present un-South African Government and to restore the rights of the people, under the rule of law, to our land.
>
> We declare that we will resist any attempted rape of the South Africa Act, no matter how it is disguised, that we will uphold and respect that instrument by which our fathers, on behalf of all South Africa, brought us together in brotherhood and in mutual faith.
>
> We shall see to it that such rights as they extended to the less fortunate shall be defended and that the word of the white man, as given by our greatest patriots and statesmen, shall be honoured.
>
> In forming this alliance of those who love their country before themselves, we extend the hand of friendship to those of our fellow-countrymen who, in the past, may in all good faith have supported the Government, but who are not willing to follow the clique that rule the Government on the road to national ruin.
>
> To them we offer our friendship and our loyal co-operation in the common effort to restore law and honour to the public life of South Africa.
>
> For our struggle is not against those South Africans who have sincerely differed from us in days gone by; our struggle is against self-seeking politicians who are abusing the power they have derived from the support of thousands of honourable men and women in order to pursue the path of political dishonour in a desperate attempt to entrench themselves in power.
>
> From now onwards, acting together in the highest good faith, we dedicate ourselves to work in common devotion for the day when all freedom-loving South Africans will once again be united in peace and security under a government pledged to respect the rights and the dignity of its citizens, to

uphold the Constitution of our Union and to restore South Africa to her rightful place as an honoured member of Western society.

For better or worse, the 'united front' about which Kane-Berman had spoken, was now a reality.

Nothing could be less controversial than the principles of the United Democratic Front, nor were they ever the subject of criticism. But the manner of entering into the United Democratic Front remained a constant source of irritation and even division within the Torch Commando.

How had it come about? Sailor Malan, Louis Kane-Berman and Ralph Parrott had gone to Cape Town in mid-April for more general discussions with Opposition leaders on future policy. Invited to meet with Strauss and Harry Oppenheimer, they were offered a loose arrangement for joint action in fighting the election, to which Christie had already agreed. This arrangement was the more difficult to refuse because the Torch Commando had already urged the Opposition parties to form a common front. Sailor Malan, who undoubtedly had had prior notice from Oppenheimer, was delighted with the idea in any case, as was Parrott; Kane-Berman was more hesitant. But what about the general principles on which such an agreement must rest? These were more difficult to formulate to everyone's satisfaction. When agreement was finally reached on the principles, the Torch Commando members accepted the arrangement on their own responsibility without referring the matter to the action committee in Johannesburg. With Strauss, they felt that the most important thing was to announce the United Democratic Front at once in order to give leadership to the country in the face of the Government's avowed intention to circumvent the Appeal Court decision and thus, in their view, imperil the Constitution.

What the United Democratic Front involved, Sailor Malan tried to make clear at the National Executive meeting held in Cape Town on March 24 and 25. 'The parties to this agreement will retain their separate identities', he said, 'but will work in the closest possible collaboration until sane, democratic government is once more restored in South Africa.' Torch leaders feel that they lived up to the spirit of the agreement and consulted the United Party henceforth on all their decisions. Perhaps inevitably, there was far less consultation in the opposite direction. But this latter fact, coupled with the manner of entering into the United Democratic Front, soured the arrangement for many Torchers.

Yet it was a Torch leader who, by highly injudicious remarks on the very morrow of the announcement of the United Democratic Front, opened the way to a destructive barrage of Nationalist attacks. Speaking in Greenside, Johannesburg, Kane-Berman declared that if the Government went ahead with its plans to circumvent the Appeal Court's decision, the Commando would call a day of protest which would 'bring the country to a virtual standstill'. He continued:

> We will fight constitutionally as long as we are permitted to fight constitutionally, but if this Government are foolish enough to attempt unconstitutional action, then I say, the Torch Commando will consider very seriously its next step.[35]

Immediately, Minister of Justice Swart accused the Commando in Parliament of invoking the aid of non-Europeans in its campaign against the Government.

Die Burger ran a three column headline 'Torchmen Threaten Government', and in a leading article entitled 'A War of Nerves', wrote

> We believe the Torch Commando is prepared to indulge in any irresponsibility and unconstitutional action if its ally, the United Party, does not stop it.[36]

Die Transvaler followed this with accusations, first that the Torch Commando was preparing an armed rebellion against the Government, then that the Commando was arming the Natives in preparation for a revolt, and finally that it was planning a *coup d'état* with the aid of the Freemasons and the Sons of England.[37] Soon after, Dr. Malan himself declared at Porterville that the Torch Commando was 'a most dangerous organization'. Saying that the police had provided information about the Commando 'serious enough for me to stand here today and warn the people' against them, he announced that the Government was taking precautionary measures which included moving some Reserves to Cape Town.[38] It all added up to a very effective counter-attack.

That there was deep concern in the country over the Government's move to establish the High Court of Parliament as a body superior to the Appeal Court, and thus capable of overriding its decision that the entrenched clauses still had their full effect, was reflected by the numbers and deep feeling in Torch Commando protest meetings throughout the country. One of the most impressive was when 6,000 Torchers marched in silent protest through Cape Town streets and were joined from Temple Chambers by 35 members of the Cape Town bar.[39]

Most striking of all was the gigantic torch-lit mass meeting in Durban on June 6, 1952, where 35,000 people pledged themselves to the 'Natal Stand' already formulated in a resolution of June 4 in their Provincial Council.[40] No province in South Africa had a stronger sense of separate individuality, reflected in the past even in distinctive political parties. Nowhere was there a stronger feeling that the Nationalists were imperilling the Constitution by their maneuvers over the Coloured vote. All this lay behind the resolution asking for a new national Convention to reaffirm the Constitution of the Union, and the Covenant pledged unanimously with such feeling that night:

> To preserve the sanctity of the engagements entered upon at the time of Union as moral obligations of trust and honour binding upon the Parliament and the people, and to secure the repeal of any measures enacted in violation of such obligations;
>
> To oppose any attempts to violate the Constitution embodied in the South Africa Act, and more particularly to maintain respect for the Entrenched Clauses of that act;
>
> To maintain the rule of law as the basis of our civil liberties.

When E. G. Ford, chairman of the Coastal Region of the Torch Commando, asked: 'Will you remain in a Broederbond republic if it is declared on the pretext of the *volkswil*?' they shouted 'No!' When he said: 'Are you prepared to take the consequence if Natal is forced to stand on her own?' they roared 'Yes!' No one who attended that meeting is not still stirred by its memory.

The 'Natal Stand' had been affirmed unequivocally; it was to have far-reaching consequences for the Torch Commando and the United Party.

Torch-sponsored meetings demonstrated the depth of public feeling; politically, however, the Commando was less successful. With great fanfare, it moved in on Wakkerstroom on the Transvaal *platteland*, where an important by-election was fought in June, 1952. When the Road Transportation Board refused a permit to transport Torch supplies by road, they were flown in a spectacular air lift from Johannesburg.[41] In a gala send-off, Kane-Berman called the Torch convoy 'a goodwill mission' to show the *platteland* that the Commando were 'determined to promote racial harmony'.[42] For a week, the Torchers lived under canvas near Wakkerstroom seeking to establish relations with the people of the neighborhood and helping the United Party with election activities. Yet for all the Opposition's efforts, the Nationalists not only won the election but gained 850 more votes than before.

The lessons of this experience were amongst the most important considered by the First National Congress of the War Veterans' Torch Commando meeting in Pretoria, July 7-9, 1952.[43] A special 'Side Conference' held on July 8 to consider *platteland* affairs, noted that 'A show of force and publicity campaigns like "Operation Wakkerstroom" frightens *platteland* voters and should not be encouraged'. Instead, it urged that each region, where necessary, form a *Platteland* Advisory Committee and appoint a *Platteland* Organizer; that Torch offices be established in every possible *platteland* town; and that 'huisbesoek' (house visits) be used as widely as possible. Highlighting the lack of channels to the *platteland*, the conference emphasized the importance of bilingualism and declared that 'the importance of an Afrikaans daily newspaper cannot be overstressed'. On the all-important question of coordinating efforts with the United Party, the conference showed a blend of frustration and hope by urging on the one hand that joint committees be established with the United Party and on the other that Strauss be asked to instruct all *platteland* divisional committee chairmen to cooperate 'in view of the present unsatisfactory relationship' existing in many *platteland* constituencies. It urged that the United Party nominate its *platteland* candidates immediately, and that 'all unco-operative United Party organizers or candidates' be reported.

In general, the Congress applauded the formation of the United Democratic Front, but this same concern over United Party-Torch Commando relations showed through the discussions. Great emphasis was placed on a 'master plan' for the organizational aspects of electioneering;[44] at the same time, 'huisbesoek' was endorsed as the most effective means of putting across the program of the United Democratic Front in the marginal areas which were the obvious key to success in the coming election. Grave concern was evidenced at the widespread hooliganism and physical violence at Torch meetings (a broken arm for Charles Bekker, national organizer, was only one example). Even more concern was shown lest the Opposition should break and give the Nationalists enough votes to pass a constitutional amendment on Coloured representation. Thus the Congress, like its side conference, swung between enthusiasm for all out election efforts and fear that their allies, through which they perforce had to work, lacked the organization, spirit and fortitude necessary for their tasks.

Most difficult of the issues faced at the Congress were those arising out of the 'Natal Stand', adopted so dramatically at the Durban mass meeting on June 6.

Natal's delegates to the Congress sought general Torch Commando support for this stand, even if it might lead ultimately to the break-up of the South African Union. The issue was a grave one, and Sailor Malan threw his great personal influence against either a 'blank cheque' resolution supporting Natal, or unilateral action by the Commando apart from its allies in the United Democratic Front.

In the end, the Congress adopted a less drastic resolution than the Natal delegates had proposed at first, but one whose implications were still far reaching. It read:

> This National Congress of the War Veterans' Torch Commando, representing a quarter of a million of South Africans, reaffirms its belief in Union and the spirit in which the Act of Union—our Constitution, was born.
>
> We pledge our full support to Natal in her request for a new National Convention to entrench the basic rights of citizenship.
>
> Furthermore, we regard Natal's stand as an honourable one against a ruling Government which knows no honour.
>
> If, in her efforts to save Union, Natal is forced to stand alone, the Torch Commando throughout South Africa and South West Africa affirms its readiness to support Natal to the full by whatsoever action the National Executive may deem necessary.
>
> The Torch Commando regards any break up of Union caused by the Government's breach of a solemn contract as a purely temporary position until such time as all the people of South Africa can come together once more, in honourable agreement, to build up a greater Union of South Africa.
>
> We, the members of the War Veterans' Torch Commando in all four provinces and South West Africa, pledge ourselves to strive unceasingly for the attainment of our national ideal: the securing of a democratic union of South Africa.
>
> While reserving the right to independent action (on the above) we deem it right to consult our partners in the United Democratic Front at all stages.[45]

For obvious reasons no publicity was given to the resolution. It became public only in January, 1953, when an agreement between the Torch and United Party in Natal made it seem possible to publicize this resolution as well as the bitter differences between these two Natal groups which had marred the latter part of 1952.

Following the Torch Commando Congress, the Coastal and Inland Regions of the Natal Commando formally joined together on July 18, 1952, with the Defenders of the Constitution (see p. 333) and the Natal United and Labour parties, in what was called the Natal Council of the United Democratic Front. This council formally convened for August 25, 1952, the conference of Natal Senators, M.P.s and members of the Provincial Council together with nominated representatives of their own organizations which the Natal Provincial Council had proposed in its resolution of June 19.[46] Already at the opening session of this conference, however, sharp differences appeared. The *Rand Daily Mail* reported:

> Tempers were short, and there was excited, emotional talk between the two groups—the United Party on the one side and the Labour Party, the Torch

Commando and the Defenders of the Constitution on the other. They sat in separate blocks. . . . It is the smaller block that wants Natal to secede, though it does not talk about secession. It wraps up the unpleasant facts in a phrase —Natal should reserve the right to take independent action. Almost every Labour, Torch or Defender speaker began: 'We are not secessionist, but . . . They spoke bitterly of what they called the United Party's appeasement of the Nationalists.[47]

None of the three resolutions passed 'unanimously' by the Natal conference included the word secession,[48] but the matters at issue between the groups were far from settled.

Divisions over policy and personalities existed not only between Natal Torchers and the Natal United Party official group headed by D. E. Mitchell, but also within Torch itself. Early in September, E. G. Ford, chairman of the Commando's Natal Coastal region, returned to the charge with a demand that the United Party should state its policy in regard to the proposed pledge 'to entrench the Constitution, either by national convention or other means', and towards the view that 'by standing alone the province might save the nation'.[49] He also asked specifically for the United Party's attitude on the non-European problem, soil conservation and South Africa's dwindling water supplies. Both Sailor Malan and Kane-Berman answered him sharply. The former declared:

> Surely it is time to stop sniping at our friends, particularly our partners in the United Front, and to concentrate in close harmony with them in the urgent task of defeating the Nationalists in the General Election.[50]

The latter pointed out that 'our members hold many divergent views, but the Commando has never attempted to develop its own policy on matters such as non-European affairs or other questions'.[51] The national leaders were also joined by the vice-chairman of the Commando's Natal Coastal Region, Roy Fenhalls, who pointed out that: 'We cannot win the election by quarrelling and fighting among ourselves. . . . There has been far too much criticism of the working of the United Front'. He also declared that: 'Natal is irrevocably committed to the great Union of South Africa'.[52]

Nonetheless, a bitter personal struggle broke out in October between two Torch leaders, E. G. Ford and the Rev. J. B. Chutter, on the one hand, and D. E. Mitchell on the other. To a large extent it was a clash of personalities. In a sense, also, it was a struggle for power to direct election operations and, in particular, to influence the selection of candidates for the coming election. Mitchell was too strongly entrenched in the United Party organization to be in any great danger, too imperious to be tactful. Ford and Chutter from their side, though under a steady pressure of restraint from both Sailor Malan and Ralph Parrott, were openly critical of the workings of the United Party in Natal. This went so far that late in November there was talk that Torch would enter its own candidates in certain Natal constituencies. Several prominent Torchers resigned in protest from the Commando; from the other side, Chutter publicly resigned from the United Party.

The issue was seething when the United Party Union Congress met at Bloemfontein, November 20, 1952. In an effort to heal the breach in Natal, Strauss declared in his opening speech that:

> The Torch Commando is working with the utmost devotion and enthusiasm and in a harmonious manner with the United Party in order to put forward the maximum united effort to sweep the National Party out of power and put the United Party in its place. There should be no misunderstanding where that is concerned.[53]

At the same time, the Congress adopted a resolution which denied the possibility of unilateral action by any province.

This resolution, passed without consultation with other members of the United Democratic Front, and said to have alienated many people in Natal, led on November 29 to a joint session of the Natal regional executives of the Torch Commando. This meeting decided that there must be a discussion with the top United Party leadership on a number of points: the 'Natal Stand' (i.e., the right of Natal under certain circumstances to take unilateral action); an undertaking that United Party candidates should refrain from racial speeches contrary to Torch principles of racial harmony; the advisability of setting up joint election committees; securing a guarantee from United Democratic Front Parliamentary candidates in Natal that they would not help the Nationalists under any circumstances to gain the two-thirds majority required to put the Coloured on a separate roll; and a proposal to use primaries in Natal for the nomination of candidates.

When the Natal Torch representatives met Strauss and other United Party leaders for a private conference in Johannesburg on December 19, however, only the first of these questions, the 'Natal Stand', was discussed. The 4-man delegation, including Ford and Chutter, insisted that the majority of Natalians upheld the Natal stand, and forcefully put forward their view that the Commando, which had 45,000 members in Natal, could better express opinion in that province than could the United Party with its 20,000 members. They then asked that United Party candidates should make a pledge that if the Constitution was broken or in danger of being broken, or if a Republic was formed or in process of being formed, the Natal M.P.s of the United Party would return to their constituencies to test the feeling of the electorate, and that, if public opinion so demanded, they would release Natal 'from the ruins of the broken contracts' of the Constitution. To this, the United Party leaders would agree only in part, accepting that under special circumstances the M.P.s could return to consult their constituents, but rejecting the possibility of unilateral action.

It is worth noting that, in its reply, the delegation insisted that such an attitude made inevitable the formation of a new political party controlled wholly from within Natal. It was the first mention of what became the Union Federal Party, established May 1953.

Yet however disappointing the immediate results of the meeting, it paved the way for the reuniting of forces in January 1953. By then the situation in Natal had changed, for the Nationalists had decided to enter candidates in their first substantial electoral effort in that province. Faced with this incentive to joint effort, and under continued pressure from top Torch and United Party leadership, an agreement was reached under which D. E. Mitchell and Raymond

Ardé, leaders respectively of the United Party and Labour Parties in Natal, pledged their candidates' support of the Covenant which had been adopted at the June 6 mass meeting in Durban. From its side, the Natal Regional Executive of the Torch Commando, after hearing Mitchell speak on United Party policy, resolved, on January 17, 1953, that it would support United Front candidates if they accepted the 'Natal Stand'.[54] The split was over, at least on the surface and until after the election.

What had caused the split? What significance did it have? Part of the answer to the first question lies in the historical and traditional differences between Natal and the rest of the Union; the strength of the English tradition, amounting at times to a 'little England' view less mature than the approach to the Commonwealth relationship found in Canada or even New Zealand; and a sense of regional difference rising partly out of distinctive climatic and economic conditions. But, more particularly, the 'Natal Stand' embodied both an insistence on the maintenance of high standards of constitutional behavior, and a protest against being overborne either by the numbers or 'alien' tradition of Afrikanerdom.

Just as Natal itself welcomed its place in the Union, from which came its economic prosperity, yet feared the loss of its individuality within a larger community, so had much of the Natal Torch. The ambition of the latter was to mold the whole of the Torch Commando in its own image or, at the least, to secure whole-hearted nation-wide Torch support for its own particular stand. It failed because the sympathetic response it received in many quarters of the Torch Commando never amounted to a wholehearted and unlimited endorsement. It failed particularly because Sailor Malan unswervingly opposed either unilateral action by Natal Torch within the Commando as a whole, or by the Commando within the United Democratic Front.

It may seem odd that Natal separatism expressed itself particularly in a struggle within the ranks of the Opposition itself. Again an explanation can be found in Natal's long-held position as a political fortress virtually free from Nationalist advances except in the mining towns of its northwest frontier. In such a situation, Natal could allow itself the luxury of separate political organization. This was the more so as long as the United Party (or the South African Party before it) held political office in the Union. Whenever that position has been endangered, Natal has rallied to the support of the political party which stood for close English-Afrikaner relations as opposed to militant Afrikanerdom. Thus the Torch separatists, like the Union Federal Party after them, were fighting a losing battle with circumstances. At the same time, both reflected a sentiment that has deep roots in Natal: the desire to base its political action on its own decisions.

The United Party had relatively new and shallow roots in Natal. It was an organization, not a movement. Small wonder, therefore, that Torch, with its widespread membership in the province, should claim a closer affinity to the 'Natal Spirit'. Moreover, much of what Torch was urging, both in organization and in propaganda, was well justified. But in the total picture, as Sailor Malan and others could see so well, Torch could not afford the luxury either of being 'holier than thou' or of sabotaging its political ally. What Natal could no longer afford to do within the Union, Torch could not afford to do within the United Democratic Front.

Yet such arguments, however valid, did not solve the major problem of what should be the relation between Torch and the United Party within the United Democratic Front. The United Party clearly hoped that the Commando would provide it with leg work and their votes. National Torch leaders, with their great vigor, their feeling for organization arising out of army experience, and their deep sense of concern for the outcome of the 1953 election, were eager to influence the United Party not only organization-wise but in policy. Thus, at one point, National Torch leaders explored the possibility of turning the United Democratic Front, or at least the United Party and themselves, into a single political party.

The major argument in favor of forming such a new political party was that it would unify the anti-Nationalist opposition. The Torch Commando would 'come off the fence' politically (if indeed it still occupied that strategic if uncomfortable position), direct its members' efforts into party rather than extra-party activities, and (hopefully) add its 'morality' to United Party politics. Such a union might also solve the problems of Natal and the Free State, where Torch-United Party relations were less than friendly and (though this presented its own difficulties over who should be left out) obviate the double-tier of officers existing in the parallel organizations of Torch and the United Party. Hopefully, also, the announcement of such a union might capture the country's imagination and be a powerful aid to electoral victory.

More wary spirits pointed out that to be anti-Nationalist was not sufficient basis for a cohesive political party. To add fresh groups to the United Party might increase the difficulty of arriving at positive policies. It seemed inevitable also that United Party members would hold most of the important positions in the new party. Was there then so much to gain, especially as compared with the possible loss of support the merger might entail?

Weighing these possibilities, the National Executive agreed, on August 9, 1952, to hold exploratory conversations with United Party leaders on the possibility of an amalgamation. Nine days later, several Torch leaders met with Sir de Villiers Graaff as representative of the United Party Head Committee. As a basis for further discussion a plan was proposed for a new party, perhaps to be called the United National Democratic Party, which would be based on the United Party's seven points of fusion and Torch's five principles. Members of both groups should become members of the new party with the right to contract out within a given period. The structure would be based on that of the United Party with amalgamated branches and enlarged executives. J. G. N. Strauss was to be accepted as leader. If the plan met with general agreement, it should be taken to the National Congress of the Torch Commando, and then of the United Party. If amalgamation were achieved, a mutually accepted statement of policy would be issued before the election.

The basis of such a statement, it was suggested shortly after, might be the reassertion of the unity of English and Afrikaners as opposed to Nationalist sectionalism, the paramountcy of European leadership, immigration from all mother countries so no group need feel endangered, and social and residential segregation for non-Europeans, coupled with development of Native areas and progress in local self-government. Special stress was laid in this proposal on the welfare of urban workers through extended social security, and improved standards of living, provided if necessary by Government-created employment opportunities, and by stimulating output. Healthy agriculture was also emphasized. While Communism was assailed, any law to restrain the movement should be subject to court controls. The possibilities of a Government based on federalism should be explored; in any case, the Constitution should entrench fundamental liberties. Lastly, this proposal highlighted South Africa's need for friends to help guard the Cape, and saw its Commonwealth association as of inestimable value in securing this end. It was a well-rounded program of no small merit though without striking originality. For that very reason, however, it might well have served as a useful election manifesto.

Whatever the reasons—and they probably lay in the basic preference of United Party leaders and perhaps also some Torch leaders for their group's separate existence—the plan for amalgamation went no further. One other effort at closer union—a proposal for a supreme directorate of policy, supported by a unified information, propaganda and policy staff—had no more effect. Henceforth the Torch Commando worked as a partner, a very junior partner as far as influence was concerned, in the United Democratic Front.

Inevitably as the glamor of torch-light processions was replaced by the far more mundane tasks of routine electioneering, many Torchers lost their enthusiasm and no longer contributed their efforts. But to a surprising and impressive degree, others continued up to the very moment of the election to work behind the scenes, or in the streets, taking out postal vote material, checking voters' rolls, protecting United Party meetings in predominantly Nationalist areas, canvassing, translating the information they gained on to vast charts from which to gauge election strength, and then starting out again to seek more information, or to stimulate more political interest, particularly, of course, in the United Party.

The most distinctive single project of the Torch Commando was the Memorandum submitted to the Tenth Delimitation Commission, 1952. Prepared under the direction of Arthur Suzman, Q.C., with the aid of Reuben Sive, the Commando's Honorary Electoral Adviser, the 12-page document, with its 30 pages of Appendices followed by 4 of Histograms, represented a monumental effort. For each of the Provinces in each of the first nine Delimitations the Appendices provided a list of electoral divisions, with the number of voters in each and the percentage load or unload. The Histograms, or frequency distribution graphs, similarly showed the distribution of seats according to the extent of loading and unloading, and also what results would ensue from the United Party and the Nationalist proposals to the Tenth Delimitation Commission. This material, along with other graphs and charts in the body of the document, was designed to prove the argument of the memorandum: that votes in rural constituencies had been given far more weight in relation to those in urban areas than the South Africa Act had intended, and that this was the chief reason why a minority of the electorate was able to elect a majority of the Members of Parliament.

The extensive Torch material on delimitation, which filled one of the largest rooms in its Johannesburg office with detailed colored maps and charts, was fully shared with the United Party. In fact, Torch offered the Suzman brief, as it was often called, to the United Party to use as its own. The United Party preferred, however, to make middle of the road proposals to the Delimitation

Commission which were much more in line with those it had offered in earlier years; the Nationalists, in contrast, made more extreme proposals to their own advantage, though they do not seem to have benefited greatly from them in the final delimitation.

What the Torch memorandum sought, of course, was to equalize the power of urban with rural votes instead of having the latter count for anything from 1·053 to 1·273 as much, or in percentage terms between 5·3 per cent and 27·3 per cent more, as one of its charts proved.[55] Equalization was clearly to the great advantage of the urban-oriented United Party, though it is doubtful whether it would have made as much difference as the memorandum sought to prove, since the United Party will always waste a large number of its votes because it polls such high majorities in certain constituencies. As we have seen (p. 152), the Tenth Delimitation Commission refused to accept the Suzman argument on delimitation, which it said was based on false premises. Thus unaccepted either by the United Party or the Commission, the memorandum is largely of academic interest. What it proves to anyone used to the heavy and disparate overweighting of rural votes in many places in the United States is that South African over- and under-loading is not unusually high compared to practices in other democratic countries, though undoubtedly it has worked to the advantage of the National Party with its strong *platteland* support.

The Suzman brief was only one example of the willingness of the Torch Commando to explore new avenues of possible political significance and, less happily, of its inability to accomplish its ends thereby. Another much smaller project, similarly without effect, was to send the Governor-General a handsomely printed petition on May 12, 1952, requesting that he withhold his assent from the High Court of Parliament Bill.[56] Torch leaders also explored the possibilities of establishing an Afrikaans daily newspaper, over whose policy they would have some influence. They went so far as to consider the possible purchase of an existing weekly, so as to be sure of adequate paper supplies. But in the end the expense was found to be too great, particularly as Torch was already responsible for its own bilingual monthly, *Blikfakkel.*

The Commando had always held aloof from formulating specific policies, though it persistently pressed the United Party to do so. In general, Torch leaders favored broadly constituted expert committees to develop policies in different fields. In an early period, the action committee recommended an Education Advisory Council to study possible policies on finance, defence, education and Native affairs, but the proposal met with such a mixed reception that it was dropped. At the height of the Native defiance campaign, September, 1952, the National Executive debated a proposal to set up a committee on non-European affairs composed of men of great eminence, and went so far as to refer it to the regions, but again without effect.

At that meeting, however, the Executive passed a resolution, transmitted to the Prime Minister, which appealed to the Government 'to meet the non-European leaders in conference and seek to build again "the bridges which should exist between White and Black in South Africa"'.[57] At the same time, the resolution welcomed Strauss' statement that the United Party would follow a policy of consultation with the non-European peoples of South Africa as 'the most significant contribution to the problem in recent times'. In November, when the Native riots broke out in Port Elizabeth and East London, the action committee, like the United Party, called unsuccessfully for an official inquiry. It declared:

> We unreservedly condemn those who pillage, burn and kill with savage indiscrimination, although it must be said the overwhelming majority of non-Europeans are patient, peaceful and good-natured. We fear that even they will reach a breaking-point if the repressive legislation and maladministration by the National Government continues.
>
> Not only do we assert that the Nationalists have created the atmosphere in which extremists have resorted to desperate measures, but also that political capital is being made out of the situation.
>
> If it is the Natives . . . who are wholly to blame for the tragedies, why do the Government refuse an inquiry?[58]

Deepest concern of all arose within the Torch Commando when the National Government introduced in Parliament in January, 1953, what was known as the Swart legislation—the Public Safety Bill, and the Criminal Laws Amendment Bill—which developed a formidable barrier of prohibitions and punishments against a possible recurrence of the Native defiance campaign (see p. 163). When it became apparent that the United Party had decided to support the bills, Sailor Malan, Louis Kane-Berman and Ralph Parrott rushed to Cape Town to try to dissuade its leaders from this course of action. Meeting with Strauss, de Villiers Graaff and Harry Oppenheimer of the United Party, and Christie of the Labour Party, Torch leaders argued that the Criminal Laws Amendment measure could be used against anyone, including Torchers, if the Government trumped up a case. From their side, the United Party put forward the arguments which had finally won over the United Party caucus: that the Nationalists were using the legislation as a trap to 'show up' the United Party reluctance to take necessary action to prevent a further Native defiance campaign; and that the situation where the riots had taken place was far more serious than the country at large realized. They also declared that they had received Nationalist guarantees that the measures would not be used against Torchers, or any European political group. Finally, overborne by warnings that obvious division on this issue in the United Democratic Front might lose the election, Torch leaders reluctantly allowed themselves to be dissuaded from open opposition to the legislation. Some Torchers never reconciled themselves, however, to what they looked on as an unwarranted sacrifice of principle. They felt, too, that in the long run it was a strategic mistake that the United Democratic Front, or at least the Torch Commando, did not fight the legislation by every means at their command.

Already the election was in the offing. All Torch's resources were thrown into the campaign. Ralph Parrott and Charles Bekker, the two chief national officials of the Commando, resigned from their offices to run as United Party candidates, the former in a Nationalist stronghold, Mayfair, and the latter in a more evenly divided constituency, Brakpan. Though neither was elected, both made great efforts, supported loyally and unstintingly by other Torchers. Many other United Party candidates also received volunteer help from Torchers. The Torch Commando pasted placards throughout Johannesburg by night, only to have them torn down or defaced by the Nationalists. Torch also ran an unimpressive contest in the *Sunday Times, Die Landstem* and a few other papers called 'You Be The Judge', in which the contestants placed in a certain order the listed misdeeds of the Nationalists while they had been in office. Some 7-8,000 answers were sent in to compete for the prizes, from £150 to £20, for those who came closest to majority opinion. Perhaps the most interesting feature of the contest was that the rise in the cost of living, and the Transvaal Education Ordinance were widely considered far more serious mistakes than increased bitterness among non-Europeans.

The Nationalist victory on April 15, 1953, shocked the Torch Commando as it stunned the United Party. Like many other South Africans, Torch leaders grasped at one possibility after another at their Executive meeting, May 9 and 10, 1953. Some felt the only hope lay in Natal as a bastion from which the Union might in the distant future be recaptured; others spoke again, as at an earlier meeting, of a federation of the whole of Southern Africa within which South Africa and South West Africa could find a more balanced role. They asked themselves how a more constructive non-European policy could be developed, how English and Afrikaners could be led better to understand each other. But chiefly they had to ask themselves whether or not they should disband, or, if they should continue, for what purposes.

As a movement the Torch Commando had roused many people to an awareness that Nationalist actions involved a potential threat to the Constitution, and to a new concern with politics; as a political instrument, the Commando had been less successful. It had never been satisfied with its role in the United Democratic Front, nor, perhaps, could it have been. If Torch had directed policy, the United Party would have lost its reason for being. Yet without any substantial influence on policy, the Commando had little to offer its members except the possibility of contributing to the United Party's electoral victory.

To some Torchers, the fact that the Nationalists were already calling for Opposition votes to help them pass a constitutional amendment to take the Coloured off the common roll suggested that constitutional crises might come again. Was it not better, therefore, to keep the Commando in existence, ready to mobilize public opinion again if it became necessary? This view gradually won over the Executive as a whole. The press was informed that the Executive would recommend to the National Congress in June that the Torch Commando would remain in existence, and oppose any unconstitutional measures the Government might introduce.[59] Believing, however, that the movement must take a more clear cut stand on what it meant by its 'racial harmony' principle, the Executive declared that:

> it accepts as fundamental in our society that the non-European must be advanced economically, culturally, and politically, so that he is fitted to subscribe to the Western concept of civilization. It is felt that, if this is not done, inevitably he will turn to Communism or other political extremes for the solution of his problems. It accepts that the fundamental principle of democracy cannot be so circumscribed as to exclude from its benefits the ten million non-Europeans who live in our midst.

At long last, Torch Commando leaders were moving towards a clear-cut approach to the non-European question.

For some Torchers, this statement was not strong enough, nor was the United Party an adequate political instrument through which to work for the future. That week-end, the Liberal Party was formed in Cape Town, and several Torchers immediately joined. More immediately significant for the Torch Commando was the formation of the Union Federal Party, publicly joined not only by many Natal members of the Torch Commando but also by its National Chairman, Louis Kane-Berman.

On June 12, 1953, the Second National Congress of the Torch Commando met at Johannesburg to determine the future of the organization. Fifteen resolutions called for disbandment; 9 favored discontinuing activities but remaining in existence in case undemocratic actions were taken by the Government; 12 were for continuing as before. The argument continued for two days. Many were fearful that the Commando might fall under the influence of the Union Federal Party; few spoke strongly for continued liaison with the United Party. The splintering of the Opposition with the two new parties convinced some that it would be better for the Torch Commando to disband. To others, this made the continuance of Torch the more necessary so that there would be a body to uphold its broad general principles, and to act as the watchdog of the Constitution.

The vote was close. Out of 822 votes cast, 399 were for disbandment, 423 for continuation. The Free State, and the Cape South West and *platteland* voted solidly to disband. Cape North, the Border (Transkei and East London), the Northern Transvaal and South West Africa voted equally solidly to continue. The rest were split. Cape East and West and the Southern Transvaal cast substantial majorities against continuation. Central Transvaal, Natal Inland and Natal Coast were as strongly for it. Johannesburg, with its 148 votes, divided almost evenly, 80 for dissolution, 68 against. The 29 individual votes also divided almost evenly, 18 for disbandment, 11 against.

The totals may be broken down in another way. Of the 16 Regions of the Commando organization, 9 voted against continuation. Counted by provinces, the Cape voted 151-142 in favour of continuing; the Transvaal, 187-126 against it; the 28 votes of the Orange Free State went solidly against remaining in being. The great body of support for continued existence thus came from the unanimous 16 votes of South West Africa, and the Natal vote of 118 to 24. The latter was the more decisive because of the absence of its two northern branches, which were expected to cast their 15 votes against continuation.

The very closeness of the vote, and the limited regional support for continuation, indicated that in fact Torch was very nearly, if not quite, dead. There might have been merit in keeping it just alive if its old spirit had remained, but there was little left but a core of organization. It was never again to attain its old vigor or importance even in limited areas, though from time to time efforts were made to revive it. It might have been more dignified, even more constructive, to have disbanded openly after the election, for new crises must throw up their own spontaneous opposition, as the Black Sash Women were to demonstrate (see p. 141).

How does one evaluate such a movement as the Torch Commando? Perhaps first in terms of its independence. How far was it the spontaneous outpouring its leaders claimed? The Nationalists charged that Torch was an instrument of outside interests, though they rather spoiled the effect of their accusations by declaring at one moment that the Commando was a front for what they called the Communist-inspired Springbok Legion and at another that it was a tool of the Oppenheimer capitalist interests working through the United South Africa Trust Fund. The Torch Commando early avoided, as we have seen, the very possible danger of infiltration by Legionnaires. What about the Fund? From where did Torch get the money to finance its activities?

Basically, the Torch Commando depended on its members. Everyone paid a membership fee of 2/6 a year (35 cents); in 1952 a further levy of 10/- a member was put on each branch, which could decide its own way of raising the money. Since at its height, Torch had nearly a quarter of a million members, this brought in a very considerable amount of money. A good deal was also contributed to the Commando in the way of services and equipment, from individuals like Arthur Suzman, who contributed his talents to the preparation of the brief for the Tenth Delimitation Commission, and from mining or other companies.

At the beginning, Torch leaders made a point of assuring the public they were not financed by the United South Africa Trust Fund. Subsequently, however, the heavy pressure of their financial obligations led them to appeal to the Fund. The latter agreed that the Commando was working for the general objective of national unity to which the Fund was dedicated and henceforth contributed to the expenses of the national office, in particular carrying the salary of the National Director. At no time, however, did Fund contributions to the Torch Commando begin to compare with those the United South Africa Trust Fund made to the United Party.

Adequate funds were, in fact, always a problem for the Commando. Appeals to the regions to meet their indebtedness for badges, to consider new ways of raising money, and to provide the Action Committee with the necessary funds for its organizing and publicity programs are dotted throughout the organization's records. *Blikfakkel*, the movement's monthly, ran initially at a loss and the 1952 National Congress was told it would be discontinued unless subscriptions rose to some 10,000, which would make it self-supporting. Publicity, e.g. for El Alamein Day, was the heaviest expense, particularly in the earlier days of the Torch Commando. Subsequently, as the election approached, expenses for organizers and travel increased.

Despite the fact that it experienced most of the difficulties which voluntary organizations face in raising adequate funds through their own efforts, Torch leaders never limited their program on this ground. Some of their publicity may be criticized as flamboyant and exaggerated; the fact remains that the Commando, particularly in its early torch-light procession days, made a deep impression on a large group of South Africans who had not previously taken much interest in politics. Without its publicity devices, Torch could never have made the rapid and deep impression which it did.

The story of Torch's relations with the United Party has been told already in large part. At the lower levels of the movement Torch members, except perhaps in Natal, were frequently also United Party members or at least open supporters. Among the Torch's national leaders, however, there were not more than two or three who had been United Party members. This helps to account for some of the problems of liaison in the United Democratic Front, though, more positively, it may also explain why Torch experimented so freely and sometimes creatively with new techniques of organization and publicity.

One strong link between Torch and the United Party lay in the personal relationship between Sailor Malan and Harry Oppenheimer. The two met in England when Malan was planning to return to South Africa after his brilliant career in the R.A.F. Harry Oppenheimer made Malan his political secretary, a position the latter never enjoyed apart from the personal contacts involved. Before Torch sprang into existence, Sailor Malan had already left this position to farm in the Free State. The close personal feelings and deep respect which Malan and Oppenheimer had for each other made it inevitable, however, that Oppenheimer had a substantial if indirect influence on the Torch Commando. Moreover, Oppenheimer served with de Villiers Graaff as the chief liaison between the two groups, particularly in the period of the United Democratic Front. Sailor Malan's insistence on maximum Torch cooperation in the United Democratic Front may have been reinforced by Oppenheimer. It might well have happened, however, in any case.

Of all the people connected with the Torch Commando, Sailor Malan was the one who most captured public attention inside and outside South Africa. Without his colorful leadership, the Commando might have remained a demonstration rather than become a movement. Yet his role in the organization was an odd one. He did not give the consistent direction and effort of Louis Kane-Berman or Ralph Parrott. He gave keynote speeches both in public and at Torch Congresses, but he took relatively little share in discussions. What was highly significant, however, was that he always looked on himself as the leader of the movement. He believed deeply in democratic operations (a faith which arose out of his experiences in the Battle of Britain rather than being instinctive), but at decisive moments, like the response to Natal Torchers' request for a free hand to support the 'Natal Stand', he was decisive and clear cut. On broad general principles, he was always so.

The Torch Commando movement was curiously like Sailor Malan in this respect. It could rally behind principles of great breadth and obvious significance, in particular in defense of the moral principle to respect the entrenched clauses, but it became confused and divided when it confronted other issues, like the Native question, where so many of its members had deep-seated prejudices rooted in their South African environment. It was perhaps wise tactically to avoid a policy stand on this issue if the movement wanted wide popularity, as it did. But, once its immediate objective of defeating the Nationalists in the general election was no longer before it, there was nothing positive enough to hold its members together.

That the Torch Commando made mistakes is obvious. It rushed all too often into print, particularly at first. It laid itself open to the highly skilful Nationalist propaganda, which frightened the more conservative members of the United Party into feeling that perhaps Torch was 'liberalistic' on the color question. In fact, as its history demonstrates, the Torch Commando was never liberal in the sense in which the South African Liberal Party now understands the word, and certainly not in the English or American sense.

Torch had liberal leaders, however, who felt that the attitude of liberalism should pervade all issues, including the Native question. It was these leaders who faced the most difficult dilemma in deciding how to mobilize most constructively the widely varied group for which they were responsible. In the end, they accepted the defeat of the Nationalists as a more important goal than any positive formulation of policy or stand thereon. Some of them subsequently blamed the capitulation to the United Party on the Swart legislation as their fatal mistake. But Torch's compromises began early, particularly over the issue of Coloured members.

Accepting the basic conceptions of the vast majority of its members, could Torch have done otherwise? Fundamentally, the movement had no quarrel with the characteristic features of South African society; thus its members had no incentive to revolutionary action. On the contrary, Torch sprang into existence to defend the Constitution on the highest possible grounds of moral, rather than legal responsibility. This deep constitutional sense led many of Torch's leaders to feel that their extra-party movement had no place in a democratic society. This concern restrained them from directing Torch towards long-term objectives. It made cooperation with the United Party the more essential even when it became most frustrating.

The story of the Torch Commando is significant not only as a page of South African history but in general. Torch proved that an extra-party movement focused on an issue of grave concern and dramatically presented to the public can secure a wide response from many people previously apathetic to politics. It demonstrated that the appeal can be made as well on idealistic as on self-seeking or purely emotional grounds. It also showed that a fair proportion of those thus awakened to a new concern with politics are prepared to work long and hard at routine political tasks. But it would be hard to prove that such a movement can have an abiding large-scale influence, or great political power.

There were special features to the South African situation which made the influence of the Torch Commando less great than a similar movement in another country. It is difficult to imagine that an American, British, or Canadian Government would not be much more affected than was the South African Nationalist Government by such a demonstration of public sentiment as Torch represented. Moreover, the movement failed in one of its broadest objectives—to build bridges between the English and Afrikaners—at least partly because the existing lines of division were already so deep that Torch activities tended to intensify rather than reduce them. In other words, suspicions already existed on which the National Party could easily capitalize. Moreover, Torch's rather naïve and flamboyant approach did little to overcome these suspicions.

Two final questions may be asked. Is there any place in a democratic country for such a movement as the Torch Commando? Can it usefully exist side by side with the political party structure? Both may be answered in the affirmative for a short time, but not in the long run. A democratic system should welcome public demonstrations of feeling; a democratic Government should take them seriously. Essentially, however, political parties are the instruments through which popular Government must be carried on. But political parties need to take warning when a movement like the Torch Commando springs into existence, and grows apace. The very fact of its existence shows that the political party system is not satisfying the needs of the community. The lesson needs to be heeded both by the friends and the adversaries of the movement: the former because it shows that they are inadequate to their responsibilities for mobilizing opinion and channelling the efforts of their natural constituents; the latter because such a movement is a danger signal that the democratic system is not working well. Nothing is more conducive to the destruction of democracy than a belief on the part of a substantial group in the community that the political system is being used to the disadvantage of conceptions or interests they cherish, and that it does not offer adequate opportunities for self-protection.

One further thing needs to be said. The Torch Commando instinctively demanded the resignation of the Nationalist Government, so the latter would face the verdict of the public over the issue and at the time that public sentiment was most aroused. It might have been possible to put the Nationalists out of office if they had accepted the challenge. Nationalist leaders were too wily, however, either to resign or to press the constitutional issue far enough to outrage public feeling completely. The very outpouring of sentiment in the early days of the Torch Commando's activities drained public energies. Moreover, by the time of the election, divisions over policies like the 'Natal Stand', and the reactions to the Swart legislation, plus problems arising out of participation in the United Democratic Front, had replaced the earlier flush of enthusiasm by something closer to uninspired efforts. The United Democratic Front got their vote out, but it would be hard to prove that they made converts. Torch may well have justified itself politically by making sure that every anti-Nationalist registered his sentiment in the ballot box; it had not, perhaps could not, perform the supreme feat to which it had dedicated itself, that of undermining the Nationalists amongst their own people.

The Defenders of the Constitution

Even before the War Veterans Action Committee sprang into existence, the Defenders of the Constitution had been organized in Natal in response to the decision of the Nationalist Government to change the franchise position of the Cape Coloured by simple majority action instead of the two-thirds majority laid down in an entrenched clause. On March 20, 1951, a mass meeting in Pietermaritzburg, capital of Natal, condemned the threatened breach of the Constitution, and pledged its participants to resist it by every constitutional means at their disposal. To carry out this mandate, it proposed an action committee under the chairmanship of Senator Heaton Nichols (who was not at the meeting but was the senior member of the United Party in the Senate).

Imbued with many of the same ideas as the Torch Commando, the Defenders of the Constitution chose for themselves a different role. Their action committee was composed of senior persons of eminence and wide experience. It was they who drew up the Covenant, which was adopted first by the Natal Provincial Council, by subsequent acclamation of the Durban mass meeting of June 6, 1951, and then personally signed by some 15,000 individuals. Beyond this, however, the Defenders made it their chief responsibility to act as an educational movement through preparing pamphlets on the meaning of the Constitution, and the history of the entrenched clauses.

The Defenders of the Constitution aimed to make South Africans 'Constitution-minded' by establishing study groups for which they would provide the literature. They saw themselves performing for the Torch Commando the task which the Fabian Society had done for the British Labour Party, i.e. furnishing facts and proposing policies. Senator Heaton Nichols told the Torch Commando National Executive Meeting in Johannesburg, on October 13, 1951: 'The Defenders will be the back-room boys whose job it is to think up new arguments as weapons in the campaign.' He urged Torch not to be merely a political pressure group seeking to turn out the Nationalist Government, but to stand for the broad objective of a secure Constitution which would put an end to 'unknown, unpredictable republicanism', and perhaps pave the way for a strong, united Southern Africa.

Compared to the Torch Commando, however, the influence of the Defenders of the Constitution remained small. The study groups hardly materialized. Moreover, it took time to produce the pamphlets around which policy was to center. *Crisis: The Real Issues,* with brief articles on the Constitution, the rule of law and South Africa's constitutional evolution, 1910 to 1952, came out late in 1952; the next two, both by the Hon. R. Feetham—*The High Court of Parliament and the Rule of Law* and *Political Apartheid and the Entrenched Clauses of the South Africa Act*—not before February and March 1953, on the very eve of the election. Useful as these are for the student, their political influence, like that of the Defenders, was never far-reaching.

The Education League

The Education League, like the Torch Commando and the Defenders of the Constitution, came into existence to oppose Nationalist policies, in this case the principles and practice of Christian National Education. Formed in November 1948, the League dedicates itself to opposing 'by all lawful means' any tendency or attempt to introduce a system of education 'based on national racial exclusiveness'. It stands positively for 'freedom of thought and conscience, and intellectual tolerance in all educational institutions'.

These efforts need to be seen against the general background of the educational system in South Africa. At primary and secondary levels are State-supported English-medium schools and Afrikaans-medium schools. There are also a number of excellent private preparatory boarding schools modelled on the English public school system and, like them, independent except as the Government assumes supervisory or directive powers over them by legislation.

At the university level are four English-medium institutions: Witwatersrand in Johannesburg, Cape Town, Natal in Durban and Pietermaritzburg, and Rhodes at Grahamstown in the eastern Cape Province. These universities are largely urban institutions. They draw their staff not only from South Africa, but from Great Britain, other Commonwealth countries and the United States. They maintain the same kind of academic freedom and atmosphere as do these other countries. To a limited extent, they have kept an open door to non-Europeans. Cape Town and Witwatersrand admit non-Europeans to their class rooms; Natal has segregated class rooms but the same staff teaches both groups. Rhodes University acts as examiner for the near-by non-European university college of Fort Hare at Alice. All the English-speaking universities belong to NUSAS (National Union of South African Students), which includes non-European members, who are sometimes elected as representatives to student conferences, which members of the Afrikaner student organization, the Afrikaner Student Bond, refuse to attend for this reason.

Though the officially sponsored Holloway Commission on Separate Training Facilities for Non-Europeans pointed out in 1954 that the expense of instituting them would be overwhelming, the Nationalists introduced legislation in 1957 to force apartheid on the English-medium universities, to place Fort Hare College and the Bantu medical school in Durban under State direction, and to establish a number of tribally oriented institutions of higher learning (see p. 111). Temporarily thwarted by a legislative technicality and a storm of protests from the institutions affected there is no evidence that the Nationalists have given up their objective of educational apartheid.

Thus it is abundantly apparent that there are fundamental differences in educational ideals and policy between the Afrikaans- and English-medium universities in South Africa, and even between Afrikaner and English education in general. The former seeks to reinforce the distinctive aspects of Afrikanerdom where the latter places a broad emphasis on universal values; the former encourages religious conformity of a somewhat fundamentalist type and the latter full academic freedom. Moreover, the English-speaking institutions believe that the non-European should receive the same type of education as the European and at university level in the same or parallel class rooms. The Afrikaner institutions in line with SABRA concepts and the thesis of C.N.E. oppose unsegregated education, and favor a distinctive type of training for the African.

The Education League has concerned itself primarily with attacking the attitudes underlying Christian National Education: the emphasis on Afrikaner nationalism, Christian fundamentalism, and unilingual instruction. More positively, the Education League and the South African Teachers' Association,[60] endorse the multi-racial character of South Africa, vigorously uphold the existing Freedom of Conscience Clause for teachers, and favor parallel medium schools. Above all, they believe that the purpose and end of education is the objective search for truth.

The effectiveness of the Education League is problematic. It had about 1,350 members in 1949, many of these teachers and other professional people. It has published a number of pamphlets, issued both in English and Afrikaans, of which the most widely distributed was *Blueprint for Blackout*,[61] a popularly written attack on C.N.E. It also strongly opposed the draft Transvaal Education Ordinance. The United South Africa Trust Fund endorsed its program as of major importance for the Fund's objective of eliminating racialism and other factors 'tending to the disruption or abandonment of democratic principles', and extended some financial support. With certain other groups the Education League, through the Education Action Committee, promoted the vigorous propaganda on the Transvaal Education Ordinance during the 1953 election campaign, which was the most effective weapon against the Nationalists (see p. 173).

Regardless of the influence of the Education League, strong resistance will be offered to any Nationalist attempt to change the character of non-Nationalist education. But equally the values held widely in English-speaking educational institutions are not likely to spread in the Afrikaans-medium institutions. In other words, the educational system which has been the greatest of unifying forces in the United States is split in South Africa between two systems which have all too little basis for common understanding between them.

Here, as in so many other places, the touchstone may well be the attitude to the non-European. Speaking to the Institute of Race Relations in 1955, Dr. Davie, then Vice-Chancellor of Cape Town University, affirmed his belief that the differences in academic ideals between the English- and Afrikaans-medium universities center largely around the issue of academic equality for non-Europeans. His conclusion was that each group, and indeed each university should be left free to develop its own policy.[62] Paradoxically, the 'two streams' policy which Hertzog sponsored to give the Afrikaner a chance to develop his own individuality is now welcomed as a protection against Nationalist pressures to conformity.

The South African Institute of Race Relations

Founded in 1929, the Institute of Race Relations, with its central office and library in Johannesburg, is primarily concerned with the collection and dissemination of factual information on the non-European. It published the monumental and invaluable *Handbook on Race Relations in South Africa*,[63] which is kept up to date by Annual Surveys. Since its inception, it has also brought out a small monthly called *Race Relations News*, and more occasionally *Race Relations Journal*. In addition, the Institute publishes many useful detailed monographs on different aspects of non-European life and policy, and the annual Hoernlé lecture on an issue of current concern.

Naturally, the Institute keeps close touch with non-European groups and over a long period of time has constituted itself a spokesman for their interests. Broadly liberal and humanitarian in approach, the Institute has accepted the findings of the 1948 Fagan Commission that the process of integration of the Bantu into European life in South Africa has gone too far to be reversed. The Institute favors the development of the Reserves, but as a supplement to, not a substitute for, positive policies to improve the condition of the Africans now in European, and particularly urban, areas.

Thus the Institute of Race Relations stands in sharp and obvious contrast to SABRA both in its general conceptions and the policies it supports. Both organizations perform a valuable service in making information available to the public. Quantitatively, and sometimes qualitatively, the Institute performs by far the greater service in this regard, as is perhaps befitting its much longer experience. It is far from sure, however, that the Institute has proportionately as great an influence on non-Nationalist opinion as SABRA has on the opinion of Nationalist Afrikanerdom.

The Institute, like SABRA, depends basically on private donations. Membership fees and the sale of its publications can hardly support its national office and small field staff, however, let alone its major investigations. Some of the latter have been undertaken on a voluntary basis; others, like the *Handbook*, were underwritten by private individuals. During the year 1953-54, the Institute received £18,929 from ordinary sources, of which £5,000 was from the United South Africa Trust Fund. Only a series of Ford Foundation grants, beginning in 1952-53, have enabled the Institute, however, to maintain its customary scale of operations. Two $50,000 grants were succeeded in 1955 by a three-year grant, totalling $125,000 to be used for research and investigation, publications, the library and, hopefully, a small sum for a campaign organizer to try to raise more funds within South Africa itself.

The English-Speaking Churches

That the English-speaking in South Africa are primarily of English rather than Scottish or Irish descent is well evidenced by the fact that the second largest denomination among the country's Europeans is Anglican (Episcopalian). The 1946 census reports that 16·15 per cent of Europeans are Anglican, 7·17 per cent Methodist, 5·03 per cent Roman Catholic, 3·71 per cent Presbyterian and 0·55 per cent Congregationalist.[64] Thus, where the Dutch Reformed Churches include over half the European population, just about half of the rest belong to another Protestant but English-speaking Church.

Both individually and collectively the English-speaking Churches maintain a much more liberal point of view towards the non-Europeans than does the Dutch Reformed Church. In 1936, the Protestant Churches established the Christian Council to promote inter-Church and inter-racial cooperation. Originally the Christian Council included the two larger Dutch Reformed Churches, but, in April 1941, both withdrew over differences in approach to the relations of Europeans and non-Europeans. The Council now includes some 30 churches and missions, and non-Europeans share in its discussions and serve on its Council. In line with these policies the Council's Rosettenville Conference, in July 1949, asserted the essential multi-racial composition of the Church and repudiated any notions of racial superiority.[65]

Significant too were the attitudes towards the non-European expressed by Protestant leaders in the 1953 Pretoria Conference called by the Dutch Reformed Church (see p. 277). Archdeacon Rouse of the Anglican Church in Johannesburg agreed that 'distinctions of race are part of God's will' but asked pointedly:

> With whom as Christians is our deeper relationship, with Europeans just because they are Europeans, or with Christians because they belong to the Kingdom of God!'[66]

Still more forthrightly, Dr. J. B. Webb, Transvaal chairman of the Methodists, spoke of 'the *laager* (stockade) mentality' represented in European exclusiveness by which 'we have dishonoured the God whom we all profess to love'.[67] The Chairman of the Congregational Union, the Rev. Leonard Heap, asked: 'Is our theory of inevitable segregation founded on principle, not on prejudice?'[68] and denounced expediency, fear and unwillingness to seek the advantage of others (the non-Europeans) rather than oneself. The Right Rev. H. M. Agnes, Moderator of the Presbyterian Church, pointed out that Europeans should remember 'our non-European neighbours are imitative and they draw their conception of God from our daily witness'.[69]

The English-speaking Churches have differed also in practice from the Dutch Reformed Churches. They have far less segregation by color and never justify it theologically. The Anglican and Roman Catholic Churches have refused to accept the provisions of the Bantu Education Act, the former closing their schools in the Transvaal rather than turning them over to the Government, the latter maintaining theirs by private support. Far more vehement, too, were the protests of the English-speaking Churches against the 1957 bill, which would have empowered the Minister of the Interior, at his discretion, to close European Church services to Africans. In this latter situation the Dutch Reformed Church added its pressure to successfully modify the legislation, though at no time was it prepared to go as far as did the Anglican bishops, who affirmed publicly their intention of disobeying such a law if it were enforced.

Very different in character and influence from Nationalist extra-party groups have been those described in this chapter. The most politically oriented of these groups arose out of opposition to Nationalist policies. Nationalist apartheid policies have also forced the English-speaking Churches to clarify their positions towards the non-European. Thus, the initiative has remained in Nationalist hands, though their policies have provoked sharp and often bitter response.

Equally important is the demonstration through the history of the Torch Commando of how rare are the issues on which non-Nationalist sentiment is both unified and forceful. Almost the only one, in fact, has been the constitutional issue, and then in its most obvious terms. When Mr. Strijdom's administration obliquely approached the issue of constitutional change in 1955, through amending the composition of the Appeal Court and of the Senate, the protests inside and outside Parliament were far less widespread than in 1951. That the Black Sash Women long maintained their vigil was a tribute to their own fortitude rather than to the responsiveness of public opinion. University and Church refusals to accept an imposed color segregation in 1957 could have more effect, at least temporarily, because they were defying Government action within their own spheres of life.

The critical problem for non-Nationalist Europeans is to evolve a policy towards non-Europeans at least as logical and coherent as that held by the Nationalists. Economic integration provides a practical basis for such a policy, but its implications are far-reaching. The Labour and Liberal Parties have faced these implications politically, as the next chapter brings out; the United Party and the great mass of non-Nationalists have not. They can point out that the National Party is turning its back on 'ideal apartheid', but in any case the Nationalists can always count on the united support of nationalistic Afrikanerdom. Non-Nationalist Europeans do not possess that same basic sense of fervor and unity. It is all the more serious that they do not have a clearly enunciated policy on the country's most serious issue: What is the future of the non-European?

Unless there is a program as definite and, in a sense, as radical on the non-Nationalist as on the Nationalist side, it is hard to see how a successful resistance can be maintained in the long run to Nationalist policies. This is all too clearly illustrated by the history of the Torch Commando, whose early compromises on Coloured membership inevitably paved the way for its later divisions.

This is not to say that the Nationalist point of view and policies will inevitably encroach on all areas of non-Nationalist South Africa. But only unity and decisiveness can influence official non-European policies. Perhaps only changing convictions within Afrikanerdom itself can influence Afrikaner institutions and attitudes. In the meantime, non-Nationalist Europeans face a gradual process of accretion, the more so because of the tremendous pressures to conformity put upon their Afrikaner members. A few bridges are being built between Nationalist and non-Nationalist Europeans in South Africa, but can they keep pace with the widening gap between the two which threatens to make isolation and even conflict the alternative to absorption?

CHAPTER 13

THE MINOR PARTIES: LABOUR, LIBERALS, UNION FEDERALISTS AND CONSERVATIVES

Minor parties may seem to have been unimportant in South Africa. They have been decisive on the political scene only through enabling major parties to assume political power by merging or acting in coalition with them. Thus the Unionists tipped the scales for Smuts' South African Party in 1921; the Labour Party enabled Hertzog's Nationalists to achieve political office in 1924; and the Afrikaner Party gave Malan needed votes in Parliament in 1948.

Nonetheless, minor parties illustrate some of the most significant features of South African life. They have sprung up to represent a particular group, area, or point of view which the major parties disregard, or threaten. Thus the Labour Party long represented the interests of white labor; the Dominion Party, in an earlier period, and now the Union Federal Party, reflect the anxieties of many Natalians over the position of the English-speaking within South Africa, and of South Africa within the British Commonwealth; while the Liberal Party, formed in 1953, accepts the full implications of the economic interdependence of Europeans and non-Europeans in South Africa. Less stable was the Conservative Party (originally the Independent United Party), which temporarily sought a middle road between Nationalist and United Party Native policies.

A curious cyclical process operates within South African politics. Hertzog's Nationalists first sought to prevent the English influence in South Africa from overwhelming the distinctive life of the Afrikaner; today, it is the English-speaking in South Africa who face the danger of ideological assimilation by militant Afrikanerdom. The Labour Party arose to protect the interests of white labor not only against the capitalist but also against the competition of the vast, unskilled non-European masses; today, its members, now far diminished in numbers, accept the same general assumption as the Liberals, that is, that Europeans and non-Europeans form part of a single South African society and that the country's laws and policies should reflect this fact. Thus the two great themes in South African politics—what should be the relation between English-speaking and Afrikaners, and between Europeans and non-Europeans—are reflected in the history of the minor parties of the country.

The South African Labour Party

Of all the minor parties in South Africa, the Labour Party has had the longest history, and by far the most disturbed one. It has never been able to reconcile its fundamental dilemma: how to live up to its socialist principles of public ownership in the interests of the whole people and at the same time satisfy the demands of the white-worker group. The principles of socialism are universal ones, applying to all workers regardless of their race or color. But South African white workers, not surprisingly, have had a far keener concern for their own privileged position than for the solidarity of labor in their country. Historically (as Chapter 2 points out in detail) the Labour Party left it to the Communists to provide leadership for non-European workers, in so far as the latter and the authorities allowed them to do so.

This compromise with socialist principles was particularly obvious in the response of the Labour Party, and of most trade unions to the urban influx of Afrikaners in the 1920s, who have formed the bulk of the white working class since that time. Some Afrikaners like Johanna Cornelius of the Garment Workers' Union developed an intense sense of loyalty to the working-class group and to socialist principles. But the tendency of white trade unions, like that of the Labour Party (then joined with Hertzog's Nationalists in the Pact Government), was to emphasize the particular needs and purposes of white labor and to adjust their program to the prejudices of the Afrikaners. In the long run, however, the Labour Party could not compete with the Nationalists, for the latter had the appeal both of a more comprehensive and clear-cut color policy and of blood brotherhood.

By 1953, when it was supporting more universal and socialist policies than ever before, the Labour Party had become little more than a head without a body. It had diminished rapidly in strength from its key position in 1924, when the Labour Party virtually put Hertzog into office. It gained less than did the Nationalists from the pro-labor laws passed under the Pact Government. Moreover, dissatisfaction with the number of party offices allocated to Labour at that time, and the feeling that there was favoritism in the allocation of 'jobs for pals', led to a disastrous split within the party in 1928. When Walter Madeley, a Labour member who was Minister of Posts and Telegraphs, disobeyed Hertzog and saw a delegation from Kadalie's I.C.U. (see p. 61), which included William Ballinger, now one of the Native-elected Senators, the Prime Minister used the excuse to secure Madeley's resignation and re-form his Cabinet. Under the view that Labour should act as a unit, the Labour Party convention demanded that all Labour members of the Cabinet should resign. The bitter fight which ensued between Creswell, the party's titular leader, and some of the most vigorous members of its Johannesburg members led the party to break into two groups: the Creswellites, a minority, and the rest, who continued to call themselves the South African Labour Party.

The disastrous effect of the split showed in the election returns of 1929, when the Creswellites and the Labour Party under Madeley each returned only two members. Since that time, Labour has never had more than a handful of members in Parliament and has been increasingly dependent on the United Party even for this degree of electoral success.

In 1941, the Labour Party began some of the thinking on the non-European problem which ultimately worked a revolution in its ideas. When the Labour Party had been organized in 1907 its members were almost exclusively English, since the great Afrikaner exodus from the *platteland* had not yet begun. At first, the party had no color policy at all, being concerned only with the objectives of the English trade unions from which its members came. In 1912, Colonel Creswell, a mine manager, broke with the Chamber of Mines on its policy of using as much cheap non-European, including Chinese (thereafter largely repatriated), labor as possible. Creswell favored using unskilled as well as skilled Europeans in the mines, both because they were more efficient and to provide a secure place for white labor in South Africa. His arguments, and his education and social position weighed heavily with the members of the Labour Party, who enthusiastically followed his lead.

The Labour Party split twice during World War I. The first split was over participation in the war (as recounted in Chapter 2), for which Creswell finally secured support by a small majority. The second and more serious split occurred over whether the Labour Party should continue to be a white workers' party, as it did, or accept the responsibility of leadership for all South African workers, including the non-Europeans, which was then assumed by S. P. Bunting's group, which became the South African Communist Party (see p. 60). Throughout the 1920s, the Labour Party continued to look on itself as the protector of white labor against the competition of non-European labor as well as against the capitalists. By the end of this period, however, and even more during the 1930s, when the Hertzog-Smuts policies and prosperity were satisfying white labor's needs and aspirations, the Labour Party found little on which it could make a distinctive and attractive appeal.

In the early 1940s, liberal-minded members of the Labour Party, like Alex Hepple, later to be its leader, sought, through discussions with Walter Madeley, to formulate the same basic objectives for non-Europeans as for Europeans. But in 1946 (see p. 36), the Labour Party split again over the Asiatic Land Tenure and Separate Representation Bill. Madeley, declaring angrily that he was a white man before he was a socialist, left the party, which then re-formed on a more liberal basis. A landmark in Labour was embodied in its 1946 statement on non-European policy adopted at a special conference on November 10, 1946.[1] This statement formulated a series of 'fundamental rights for all races in the Union'; in a supplementary statement, Labour called on all parties to take the non-European question out of politics by holding a national convention 'for the purpose of framing an agreed Non-European policy'.[2]

Having once taken the decisive step of accepting a liberal non-European policy, the Labour Party moved towards a still more clear-cut statement of what this ought to be. At its forty-second Annual Conference, held in Johannesburg on January 10 and 11, 1953, on the eve of the official 1953 campaign, the Labour Party adopted a restatement of the 1946 position which was by far the most liberal which had been enunciated by a South African political party up to that point.

The 1953 Labour statement on non-European policy[3] opened with an 'earnest appeal' to the electorate to realize that:

> Peaceful cooperation between white and black in South Africa is of such vital importance to every European and Non-European in South Africa, that no effort should be spared to understand what prevents it, and to remove all obstacles to its achievement.

Harking back to Labour's basic socialist objective of overcoming economic exploitation, the statement declared that one of the roots of racial friction was that the Union possessed a social system, fortified by a 'network of repressive laws', designed 'to provide Native labour at the cheapest rate', and 'to keep it cheap and docile'. Not only had this system 'the most shocking social effects', such as

> lack of proper housing, undernourishment, a high infant mortality rate, a low standard of education, a growing prison population and other social evils,

but it also accounted for 'a deep sense of discontent and frustration' among non-Europeans, which was in danger of being 'channelled against Europeans in general' instead of against 'European groups of exploiters'. To overcome these evils, the Labour Party endorsed a series of progressive measures designed to improve the condition of the non-Europeans.

Foremost among these proposals was that non-Europeans should have the right either to join existing trade unions or to form their own. This would necessitate amending the Industrial Conciliation Act so that 'pass-bearing Natives' were included in the definition of 'employees' (see p. 112). In addition, the Labour Party supported training for non-Europeans according to their ability, combining this with the principle of equal pay for equal work, so that white labor should not be undercut by cheap Native labor. A further positive proposal was to abolish all criminal penalties—i.e. under the Pass Laws, Master and Servant Laws, Native Labour Regulation Act, etc.—which prevent Africans 'from selling their labour in the best market'.

As for the general conditions under which Africans live, the Labour Party statement endorsed local residential segregation, but felt it should be made attractive by building 'much needed houses'; stressed the need to rehabilitate the Native Reserves; pointed out that the answer to the shortage of farm labor lay not in further compulsion through farm jails and limitation on the movement of Africans, but through mechanizing the farms and giving African agricultural workers better training; and advocated free and compulsory primary education 'in the large urban centres for the great majority' of non-European children between 7 and 14, and closer integration of vocational education with the regular school program.

On the key issue of political representation, the Labour Party attempted to find a middle way between the existing white monopoly of political power and an indiscriminate extension of the vote. It thus proposed the most advanced program enunciated up to that time, the retention of the existing franchise rights of non-Europeans in Cape Province, plus the extension of the right to vote to all adult male non-Europeans in other provinces, on the basis of a literacy test equal to that of Standard VI. Representation of Africans in Parliament was to be by Europeans, but extended from the 3 elected in Cape Province to a further 3 for the Transvaal, and 2 each from Natal and the Free State. A similar number was recommended for the Provincial Councils. Moreover, in obvious preparation for further responsibilities, the statement recommended 'a qualified direct representation' on town and village councils as was the practice in Cape Province. Pervading the whole statement was the conception that political rights must be extended as non-Europeans gained the experience and training to use them wisely.

> To withhold it [the vote] permanently from all persons, even those fitted to exercise it, merely on the ground of differences in skin colour, is unjust [it declared. Moreover the statement ended with the pledge that] our policy will be subject to such revision which the progress of the African in the cultural and industrial spheres will influence.

Such an advanced statement could be expected to awaken wide interest, and even concern, in South Africa. That it caused little stir reflected the electoral weakness of the party. For some time its ability to return members to Parliament has rested, as we have seen, on the tacit or active support of the United Party. In the 1948 election, Labour contested 8 constituencies and won 6; in 1953, it fought 6 constituencies and won 5. At both times Labour was allowed to fight only those seats which it had a relatively good chance of winning, some of which were in middle-class rather than working-class areas.

The most serious problem for the South African Labour Party today is that it lacks a strong and broad trade-union base.[4] It has only two affiliated unions: the Garment Workers' Union, and the Concession Stores and A.T.A., of which the former was listed in 1953 as representing 1,000 members and the latter 200. Moreover (as Chapter 2 pointed out in detail), the trade union movement as a whole has suffered a series of blows which have impaired even the rather limited strength which it used to possess.

Though the trade union movement tried to strengthen itself, in 1954, by establishing an overall coordinating body, the price paid by the more liberal unions was the exclusion of the non-registered, i.e. the African trade unions. Trade union practices towards the African thus diverged still farther from the policies for him enunciated by the Labour Party. More than ever, therefore, the Labour Party now represents only that relatively small group in the Union which intellectually supports socialist principles.

Another serious problem for the Labour Party is that its branch strength is so localized. On the eve of the 1953 election, 19 of its 28 branches and 485 of its 722 active members were in or close to Johannesburg, where both its affiliated unions also operate. This relative concentration of strength is partly a result of better organization in this area which houses Labour Head Office, but more particularly the result of systematic fighting of local municipal elections. In the Johannesburg municipal election immediately preceding the general election Labour polled a third of the votes though it won none of the seats. In Natal and the Cape, where the Provincial Executives decided not to fight municipal elections, a number of branches have died of inaction. In 1953, there were only 5 branches in Natal, though one of these, Durban Berea, was the largest anywhere, with 100 members, just over half all those in that province; in the whole of the Cape there were only 2 branches, 1 in Cape Town with 15 members, and another in East London with 30 members. It must be said that since all listed Labour Party members are staunch party workers, these members may well have considerably more influence and take a more active role than a comparable number of United Party or even Nationalist members. Nonetheless, the numbers are strikingly small when it is remembered that South Africa is a rapidly industrializing country, which already has substantial secondary industries as well as large-scale primary production.

The pattern of organization of the Labour Party is a common one. Branches are organized by constituency divisions, where numbers make this applicable. Divisions are coordinated by Provincial Executive Councils elected by delegates to a Provincial Congress or, if these are lacking, by the provincial members of the National Executive Council. At the top are the national organizations—the annual conference, the National Executive Council, and Head Office—which possess direct as well as coordinating powers.

The supreme organ is the Annual Party Conference, which is attended by delegates from each branch. The leader of the party is selected annually by this conference as with the other parties, but the party leader has so far always been the same person as the parliamentary leader. Where the Annual Conference exercises its chief power is in its formation of the party's program, as with its non-European policy statements of 1946 and 1953. Between conferences, the party is officially controlled by the National Executive Council, consisting of 25 members elected by the Annual Conference and responsible to it. A small Head Office, with rooms in the Trades and Labour Hall, Johannesburg, keeps the party's records and acts as a central bureau.

The Constitution states that not more than one-third of the National Executive Council may consist of Members of Parliament, an obvious attempt to keep the Council from being overborne by the parliamentary wing of the party. It also declares that the Executive Council, in consultation with the parliamentary candidates, shall define the principal issues for the election. In practice, however, this apparently tightly knit organization operates quite loosely, and the parliamentary caucus is largely independent of Executive control. One rather touchy point in connection with the 1953 election campaign was that, with Labour caucus agreement but over the opposition of the Executive, the United Party checked the broadcast delivered by Labour's H. Davidoff. The incident illustrates the greater awareness of Labour M.P.s than of its militants that the party has relatively little political bargaining power.

With so few active members, the party has little money. Regular members pay four shillings a year; trade union members 2/6. Branches are supposed to keep one-third of their funds, give one-third to the Provincial Executive and one-third to National Head Office. But in a small province like Natal, provincial funds may be almost entirely lacking and the office merely a personal project. Head Office also operates on a slim budget. It issued no party propaganda in 1953. Moreover, it had no funds with which to aid Labour candidates in their constituencies, though during the campaign it had a full-time organizer who helped H. Davidoff in his difficult electoral fight in Germiston. Apart from this, Labour candidates were responsible for their own organizations and meeting their own electoral costs. Neither in 1948 nor in 1953 did the United Party contribute towards expenses in the constituencies which Labour fought, though it was strong pressure from the United Party which finally persuaded Davidoff to move from Edenvale, which he had won in 1948, to Germiston.

Though the branches nominate parliamentary candidates, the National Executive Council must approve them. Ordinarily there is not much competition to become the candidate for a Labour seat, and in 1953 the only nomination contest in a Labour constituency was in Umbilo, Natal. This turned out to be a complicated contest, however, which not only illustrated but also created problems for the party.

The Umbilo Branch nominated ex-Senator S. J. Smith. Other branches and the Natal Provincial Executive added five more names, including that of the sitting member, Mrs. Benson. In accordance with the Constitution of the party, these names were then submitted to the National Executive for a decision. The latter sent down a Commission to investigate, and agreed upon Smith after the withdrawal of a prominent Torcher, Roger Brickhill, who entered the lists late and tied with Smith in the votes of the Executive. By this time, however, Smith had become irritated by Torch criticism and demanded a plebiscite of the United Front in Umbilo as a condition of remaining a candidate: since this was against the rules, the Executive refused to sanction the plebiscite and Smith's name was eliminated. In the meantime, Umbilo had nominated Len Whiteley, once a member of the Natal Provincial Council, as its second choice. In an open ballot Whiteley defeated Raymond Ardé, Chairman of the Natal Provincial Executive of the Labour Party, and subsequently won the seat.

The consequences of this extraordinarily tangled situation were disastrous for the Labour Party in Natal. When the Union Federal Party was organized after the 1953 election, not only Brickhill, but also Ardé and Labour's Natal Senator, E. R. Browne, joined it. The former's action could be expected because of the close relation between the Torch Commando and the new Natal-based party. But the split created by Ardé's and Browne's defections reflected both a lack of conviction about Labour's new policies, and dissatisfaction with its national leadership.

While the Labour Party has not lost any of its members to the Liberal Party, which was also formed in May 1953, many Labourites feel that the latter's existence is the chief reason why Labour is gaining few if any recruits. Though the re-formulation of non-European policy, in January 1953, reflected the convictions of the most influential of Labour members, it was also an obvious bid for the support of the liberals, who were unhappy at the equivocal stand on Native policy of the United Party. But almost at the moment when the Labour Party was openly avowing itself liberal, a new party came into existence which was specifically dedicated to liberal principles. Formally named the Liberal Party, the latter was more attractive to most of the small group of liberally minded Europeans in South Africa than Labour could be, both because the Liberals do not stand for Government ownership of the means of production and because, on the other hand, they can go farther than Labour in support of characteristically liberal ideas.

The most important role that the Labour Party played after the 1953 election was within, rather than outside, Parliament. In Parliament, its leadership presented a stalwart and well-argued front of opposition to Nationalist apartheid policies. Not surprisingly, Labour members worked very well with Mrs. Ballinger, for some time leader of the Liberal Party as well as senior Native representative. But the very fact that Labour's policies are currently so much closer to those of the Liberals than of the United Party makes its electoral future very insecure. In the 1958 election, in fact, Labour failed to secure a seat in Parliament for the first time since the formation of the South African Union.

The Liberal Party

The Liberal Party builds on a long history of liberal approaches to the non-European question and goes farther even than the present Labour Party in endorsing the rights of every group in the community regardless of race or color. The Liberal Party also openly welcomes non-European members.

The terms 'liberal' and 'liberalism' commonly mean something quite different in South Africa than in Great Britain, the United States or Canada. In South Africa, both terms generally refer to a sympathetic attitude to the non-Europeans. The Nationalists sometimes call this 'liberalistic', particularly if the view also supports racial equality, which they see as an open threat to the survival of the whites in South Africa. Thus, they regard as dangerously radical views on the racial question that Americans or British would think of as middle of the road, or slight left of center. But, though few South Africans would subscribe to the view of equality common in the United States, a great many Afrikaners as well as English-speaking have had a warm humanitarianism towards the African, which has been reflected in kindness, consideration and mutual respect. It is largely this attitude which makes life in the Union so much more pleasant in day-to-day affairs than a study of discriminatory policies would lead one to anticipate.

There have always been South Africans, however, who took what anyone would accept as a liberal point of view on the crucial non-European problem. The Institute of Race Relations has been well served by many of them. So have the non-Europeans. The Liberal Party embodies the rigorous type of liberal thinking which the old Cape Liberals maintained so well. In two articles published in its broadsheet, *Contact*, in February and April 1954—'Common Effort for a Common Society' and 'What's in our Name?'—the party declared that the liberal philosophy called for

> the practice of freedom, the recognition of freedom, the acknowledgment of other people's freedom, the fearless acceptance of freedom's responsibilities and rights and disciplines.

Where other parties limited their concern to the enfranchised white group, the Liberals maintain that they 'regard their common humanity as a common possession far more important than the franchise'. Thus the Liberal Party exists not solely to convert white voters and win elections, but more particularly 'to demonstrate that here and now there are South Africans who already belong to a common society'.

This broad approach rests on a careful analysis of existing conditions in South Africa. In particular, it grew out of a series of discussion groups, which met in different parts of the Union, from 1952 to 1953, to grapple with the facts of the South African situation and logically to base a policy upon them. These people felt that the obvious overcrowding of the Native Reserves, coupled with the findings of the authoritative Fagan Report of 1948 that more than half the Africans are outside the Reserves at any given time, indicated the fundamental fallacy of the Nationalists' assumption that the Reserves, even with the addition of the British High Commission Territories—Basutoland, Swaziland and Bechuanaland—can ultimately support the African. Having thus attacked the rationalization of an ultimate ideal apartheid, not on the ground of desirability but of feasibility, they came to the conclusion that there remained no justification for excluding the African, or indeed any non-European, from the rights, including political rights, which should be the concomitant of their economic contribution within the European areas.

How could these radical (for South Africa) conceptions be most effectively promoted? Most if not all the liberals worked hard for the United Front in the 1953 election under the view that the primary need was to turn the Nationalists out of office. Some of them continue to feel that it is better to work within the United Party as the most likely alternative to the Nationalists and to attempt to direct it towards more liberal policies. But other South African liberals became convinced, after the United Party defeat in April 1953, that it was necessary to form a new political party which could provide a clear-cut alternative on Native policy to that of the Nationalists. While it was the young militants of the group who insisted on bringing the Liberal Party into existence so quickly, it secured the immediate support and leadership of people like Mrs. Margaret Ballinger, senior Native representative, and Alan Paton, whose names were best known in the Union and abroad for their liberal stands.

More difficult than securing a roster of distinguished leadership has been the building up of the membership of the Liberal Party. The party has two objectives which are difficult to combine: to stimulate a liberal approach to South African issues, and to provide a model of a cooperative multi-racial community. In both, the Liberals have to combat not only the prejudices of white South Africans but also the suspicions of the non-Europeans.

Inevitably, the crucial point has been the non-European franchise. At its first National Congress, in July 1953, the party built on the Rhodes' tradition of 'equal rights for all civilized men', and proposed that political participation be dependent on education. It asked for compulsory education for all South Africans and the right to the franchise for all who had received such education. In the meantime, it proposed 'the immediate introduction of a qualified franchise' on a common roll for all South Africans over 21. There should be no change in the existing political rights of already enfranchised persons, the statement declared, except that those on the separate African roll should be put back on the common roll. But in an attempt to maintain equality in qualifications, it proposed that all new applicants for the franchise, regardless of 'race, colour, sex or creed', should have to complete Standard VI in school, or have a moderate income (not less than £250 'in cash or kind') or own property worth £500, or, if over 25 years old, be judged worthy of the franchise by 'a judicial tribunal'. Those who could not qualify for the common roll by one of these means were to have indirect representation in the Senate. At the same time, the party proposed abolishing the existing practice of appointing certain Senators to represent non-European interests. Qualifications for election to public offices were to be retained untouched except for the fundamental difference that candidacy for office was no longer to be restricted to white persons.

Far-reaching as were these proposals in a society with a white monopoly of political power, they were greeted with resentment by the more nationalistic among non-Europeans. *Indian Opinion* said the proposal of a franchise 'on a common roll but loaded for the time being' was a step forward, but the Natal

Indian Congress attacked it bitterly. When Miss Ray Alexander, a brilliant trade-union organizer, well known for her Communist associations, fought the Cape Western by-election for Native representative in April 1954 (see p. 70), she polled 3,525 votes to 998 for the Liberal candidate. Under the spur of this non-European lack of trust, and its own hard thinking, the party accepted the ultimate aim of universal adult franchise at its second National Congress in July 1954.

Since it 'may be impracticable' to introduce universal adult suffrage 'immediately', the party agreed, a transition period 'may be necessary' in which it is brought about by stages. These stages will

> have to be determined by interim qualifications for the franchise designed to create an informed electorate and provide opportunity for their obtaining political experience.

The qualifications could be educational, economic or by age groups, whichever circumstances and non-European consultation seemed to indicate would be preferable. But despite this step-by-step approach, the party's Constitution[5] since 1954 has listed at the top of its objects:

> Equal political rights based on a common franchise roll.

In the introduction to the party's Handbook, Mrs. Ballinger writes:

> Today we are the only party in South Africa which really knows where it proposes to go, which has really made up its mind about the type of society it proposes to establish here.

The Liberal Party has, in fact, developed an astonishingly comprehensive program covering all aspects of life, and making clear its stand on a wide range of legislation now in force in South Africa. Though the South African Government has refused to accept the Universal Declaration of Human Rights, the Liberal Party takes this Declaration as its guide post. Calling them infringements of the rule of law, the Party stands for the total repeal of such measures as the Public Safety Act (1953), the Criminal Laws Amendment Act (1953), the Suppression of Communism Act (1950, as amended) and the Natives (Urban Areas) Consolidation Act (1945, as amended) which assumes that Africans are in urban areas only on sufferance. Similarly, it advocates total repeal of the pass laws as infringements of the freedom of movement; the Group Areas Act (1950, as amended) and the Natives Resettlement Act (1954) as infringing freedom of choice of residence and land ownership; and, as violating personal freedom, the Prohibition of Mixed Marriages Act (1949), the Immorality Act (1927, as amended) and the Immigration Regulation Amendment Act (No. 43 of 1953) under which an Indian who is a South African national cannot bring to the country his wife or child of a marriage consummated outside the Union without the consent of the Minister of the Interior. Other recent laws which the party would repeal *in toto* are the Bantu Education Act (1953), the Population Registration Act (1950) as denying the dignity of the individual, and the Reservation of Separate Amenities Act (1953) as discriminatory.

Positively, the Liberal Party declares that 'the raising of the standard of living of all South Africans' should be 'the continuous key objective' of social and economic policy. It endorses the fullest training and use of non-European labor, coupled with adequate housing to provide stable conditions; feels, unlike the Labour Party, that, except in special circumstances, private enterprise is the best means of increasing productivity; sees social services as a means for securing 'an adequate basic standard of living'; believes in the right of all to organize and join trade unions; and supports 'the *objective*' of equal pay for equal work, but not its use to restrict opportunities to certain groups.

On the Native Reserves, the party has a particularly interesting view. It sees them as 'integral parts of an interdependent South African community', and therefore opposes their development as 'separate, isolated and unique economic units'. Recognizing the great need to increase the productivity of the Reserves, the party feels this can best be done through improving agriculture by completely overhauling the existing land-tenure and land distribution systems to create 'economic farming units with a stable farming population', though, where suitable, industry and diversification of economic activity should be encouraged. But in sharp contrast to the Nationalists, the Liberals do not look on the Reserves as a permanent home for the African people in which their tribal structure and traditional ways of life should be bolstered up as much as possible. On the contrary the Liberals hope that the Reserves

> will gradually disappear in the sense of areas in which indigenous peoples continue to live in primitive conditions.

In other words, the Liberals feel that the very existence of the Reserves may offer a two-fold danger to their aim of a unified South African society, i.e., by keeping a large proportion of the population in an outmoded way of life, and by providing an excuse for not extending to Africans the rights and opportunities in other parts of the country which are necessary for their development as members of a community.

At the same time, the Liberal Party is far from wishing to take away from the non-Europeans anything distinctive which they already possess. This is particularly obvious in the party's relations with other organizations. The Liberal Party specifically declares that it regards

> the development of non-European political organizations, under their chosen leaders, as an essential step in this country's advance towards a fuller and more mature democracy.

While recognizing the differences 'of emphasis and methods' between its policies and those of the African National Congress, the Liberal Party not only avows itself eager to cooperate with the African National Congress and South African Indian Congress, but also feels that membership in these organizations is compatible with individual membership in its own organization.

These deliberate overtures to nationalistic non-Europeans have been strikingly reflected in practice. Rather more than a quarter of the Liberal Party's membership in the Cape in 1955 was African, while there was also a small sprinkling of Coloured; in Natal, the proportion of non-European members was almost 50 per cent, divided between Africans and Indians. In the Transvaal, in contrast, non-European membership was extremely small, and there was no organization in the Free State. The Liberals have also openly associated non-Europeans with their campaigning. In Natal, Africans, Coloured and Indians spoke on the same platforms with European Liberal candidates for provincial office in mid-1954; they also worked in the provincial election as transport officers, clerical workers, drivers and even canvassers.

As far as elections are concerned, the Liberal Party's record has not been promising. A vigorous young lawyer fought the South Peninsula (Cape) Provincial Council election for the Liberals in mid-1954 and gained 1,109 votes to 4,621 for the United Party, which has commonly been returned unopposed for the seat. Interestingly enough, the Liberal Party found its greatest support (amounting to over 50 per cent at two polling stations) from the poorest sections among the whites in the constituency. (*Contact*, September 1954.) In Natal, three seats in the Durban-Maritzburg area were contested by excellent candidates who worked hard but secured only a small percentage of the votes. In these and all other similar cases, the United Party won the seat, demonstrating its ability to retain electoral support in the face of challenges from candidates representing a more liberal line.

The only place where the Liberals have elected members to Parliament is as Native representatives. Walter Stanford won the African Transkei seat at the end of 1954 and thus joined Mrs. Ballinger, who was returned again decisively to the Assembly; Leslie Rubin won the nomination contest for the Cape Africans' Senate seat on October 28, 1954, and William Ballinger was returned for the Transvaal and Orange Free State Senate seat. Though Senator Ballinger's majority was considerably reduced from the previous election, he received 593,902 votes to 386,834 for his opponent. (For the method of estimating votes, see p. 356.) Thus by 1955 the Liberals had two representatives in the Assembly and two in the Senate.

The position of the Liberal Party obviously remains problematic. It is organized into provincial divisions with local branches, and a National Committee. The Cape had 8-10 active branches in 1955 and another 4 which were relatively inactive; the most active development in this province was in the eastern areas. The Transvaal reported 10 branches, but the party position there was less clear than in the Cape. Natal showed the most encouraging picture with 14 quite vigorous branches and others in process of formation. Provincial Congresses have been held in these three provinces. There is a Central Office in Cape Town, which is shared by the Cape Division, and permanent offices in Johannesburg, Pietermaritzburg and Durban. This leaves a long way to go to become a political force.

The Party sees its task largely as an educative one. It publishes a small four-page monthly called *Contact*, but this encourages the convinced rather than makes converts. A great difficulty in doing more is lack of money. Larger business interests have found the Liberal program too radical or unpopular to extend support. Thus the Party is dependent on its fees (reduced in 1954 to 2/6 a year) and on canvasses, book sales, etc. This means that a great deal of financial as well as political responsibility falls on the relatively small number of Liberal Party militants.

What is the significance of the Liberal Party? Its lack of electoral success among European South Africans, its inability to command much financial support, the wide unpopularity of its basic ideas and the possibility that the Nationalists will make multi-racial meetings illegal (p. 117) indicate a dim future. Yet there are certain facts which could make the party important. The Nationalists are deliberately trying to maintain and even create conditions in South Africa which run contrary to those stimulated by its economic, and in particular its industrial development. The Liberals, in contrast, accept the full implications of South Africa's industrialization, and build upon it. Historically, liberalism has had its economic underpinning from the expanding secondary industries which depend so much on advances in technical skills. Thus, in countries like the United States and Great Britain, industrialization resulted in universal education, economic advance and social mobility. In South Africa, secondary and primary industry have been unwilling openly to support programs and principles which, in a less race-conscious society, would appear obviously to their interests. Should they ultimately accept the logic of their own needs the Liberal Party might become a political force in South Africa.

In the meantime, the Liberal Party provides a demonstration that a few white South Africans acknowledge their citizenship with non-Europeans in a single society. When G. H. Calpin took the title, *There are no South Africans*, he highlighted the far more common view that South Africa is a white society with non-European problems but not non-European members. It is not even customary in South Africa to use the hyphenated approach so common in the United States of Polish-Americans, Franco-Americans, etc., but rather to speak of South African Indians, Africans and Coloured. Only for Europeans is the term 'South African' commonly used. The Liberals wish to make all the Union's members South Africans.

Beyond this, the Liberals have provided a small but not insignificant demonstration that a multi-racial society can not only exist in South Africa, but be made harmonious and creative. In so far as they are permitted to do so, they provide an alternative to the Communists by holding out welcome and aid to the non-Europeans on a platform of equality. Thus they have made a not insignificant attempt to halt, if not prevent, the dangerous tendency towards polarization of sentiment in the Union which is leading so many whites and non-Europeans to withdraw into their own exclusive groups, reinforced in their fears and dislike of each other by the awareness of growing hostility in the other camp.

The Union Federal Party

Formed in May, 1953, at the same time as the Liberal Party, and similarly out of concern at the Nationalist electoral victory, the Union Federal Party also has a comprehensive view of the direction in which it feels South Africa ought to go. Though it enunciates a moderately liberal program for non-Europeans (thus reflecting its roots in the Torch Commando as well as in Natal), its primary objective is not closer integration of Europeans and non-Europeans but more autonomy for different areas within South Africa. Thus its major aim is to replace the existing unitary structure of South Africa, so obviously under the control of militant Afrikanerdom, by a federal system within which predominantly English-speaking Natal can better promote its own distinctive ways of life. Beyond this, the Union Federalists cherish the still more remote hope that South Africa might become merged in a larger federation of Southern Africa within which the English tradition would be able to hold its own with Afrikanerdom, and the non-European problem be handled on a broader scale.

The opponents of the Union Federal Party charge that it is simply another in the long series of separate Natal parties. Moreover, its failure to win any seats in the 1954 Natal Provincial Council elections demonstrated that it has much less hold in that province than had the Dominion party in the 1930s and, from the other side, that the United Party has a degree of support there, which it always lacked before 1948.

What then is the significance of the Union Federal Party? From a purely theoretical point of view, its position on federalism is almost unassailable. The federal structure which protects French-speaking Quebec could perform the same function for English-speaking Natal. Moreover it is not only the bi-racial character of South Africa's Europeans which suggest the advisability of a federal rather than unitary constitution, but also the vast complexity and variety of its non-European problem. Perhaps, above all, experience suggests that the speed and ease of the operations of the parliamentary system need to be restrained by federalism wherever there is no basic homogeneity of outlook among those operating the system.

But however desirable theoretically, there is no possibility today that a National Convention could draft a new Federal Constitution for South Africa. Natalians called for such a move in the early days of the Torch Commando; the formation of the Union Federal Party reflected this dramatic expression of desire. But Natal is too closely bound by economic ties to the rest of the Union to let sentiment carry it to the extreme measure of threatened secession. Even in the very unlikely case of the province voting for so drastic a move, there seem no good reasons why the Nationalists should accede to this pressure and give up the unitary structure which suits them so well.

Perhaps the chief significance of the Union Federal Party lies along other, less obvious lines. Led first by ex-Senator Heaton Nicholls, formerly senior United Party representative in that body, the Union Federal Party arose partly out of fear that the United Party would not resist strongly enough the Nationalist pressure for a republic and perhaps for ultimately leaving the Commonwealth. Less well, it responded to the sentiment of liberalism by supporting a separate roll for Indians and an eventual transition to the common roll for non-Europeans with educational and property qualifications. Some of its supporters found its most promising feature to be this combination of the traditional views of English-speaking Natal on the English heritage and Commonwealth association with a relatively liberal (for South Africa) attitude to the non-European. On the other hand, this may well have helped to prevent it from becoming an effective force within its own province.

The Conservatives

The third break away from the United Party after the 1953 election arose less out of a division of principle than of opposition to the leadership of J. G. N. Strauss. The group which initially called itself the Independent United Party, and subsequently the Conservatives, came from the right wing of the United Party, and included ultra-conservatives like Bailey Bekker, till then leader of the party in the Transvaal, and traditional non-conformists like Arthur Barlow. Their expulsion from the United Party caucus occurred during Dr. Malan's attempts late in 1953 and during 1954 to remove the Coloured from the common roll by joint session procedure (see p. 136). Two motives seem to have animated the group: their opposition to Strauss, and their desire to find some *modus vivendi* with the Nationalists.

The latter desire ultimately went so far as to lead most of the Conservatives to merge themselves with the Nationalists. But temporarily they differed from the latter on two points: the Nationalists' use of what the Conservatives considered unconstitutional expedients to take the Coloured off the common roll, and the Nationalist belief in an ultimate goal of territorial, or ideal apartheid, and of a republic.

The Conservatives' aim was to become a middle party capable of gaining support from the right wing of the United Party and the more moderate among the Nationalists. Short-lived as they were, the objective they sought remains a major one in South African politics.

Most striking about South Africa's minor parties is that they are seeking a distinctive answer to South Africa's racial problems. The Labour and Liberal Parties go much farther in their affirmations of common citizenship of Europeans and non-Europeans than any other European groups in the country. The Union Federalists have a modified liberalism towards the non-European, though they place their particular emphasis on securing a more balanced relation between English and Afrikaner.

The Nationalists are largely responsible for the fact that there is far more thinking about the non-European problem in South Africa than ever before in that country's history. The Nationalists are not only more clear-cut in their attitude towards the non-Europeans than any previous political party, but they have also gone very much farther towards implementing a rounded and well thought out program. Whether one approves of it or not, it must be respected as a comprehensive one, based on a defined view of what the Nationalists want for South Africa. It is the very definiteness of the mold in which the Nationalists are attempting to hold the dynamic, expanding South African community that has provoked such a wide range of responses in non-Nationalist circles.

Much of the new thinking about what should be the relations between Europeans and non-Europeans arises also from the growing articulateness of the non-Europeans themselves. In 1952, the largest demonstration of non-European sentiment in South African history took place through the passive disobedience campaign against 'unjust laws' directed by the African National Congress and the South African Indian Congress, the most nationalistic but also the more representative organizations within their own groups. For all that the campaign failed to secure sympathetic support for non-European grievances, it impressed many Europeans as well as all non-Europeans. It reinforced the Nationalists in their belief that restrictions must be tightened, leading to such measures as the Public Safety Act and Criminal Laws Amendment Act, both of 1953. It spurred the emergence of the Liberal Party, which seeks not only to abolish discrimination against non-Europeans, but also to establish formal links between Europeans and non-Europeans as parts of a common South African community. But it has yet to be proved that either such overtures, or repressive and apartheid measures can build a viable community in South Africa.

CHAPTER 14

NON-EUROPEAN POLITICAL ORGANIZATIONS

Non-Europeans in South Africa can have almost no direct impact, of course, upon the party structure. The last non-European voters on the common roll—qualified Coloured and Indians in Cape Province—were removed in 1956 to a separate roll to elect four Europeans to the House of Assembly. Since 1936 Africans have had a comparable communal representation by Europeans—three in the Assembly and four in the Senate—whose votes are significant only if the strength of the majority parties is evenly balanced. Apart from these very limited channels of political influence, non-Europeans in South Africa have no constitutional means of expressing their wishes.

Over the years, however, non-Europeans have developed a wide range of politically-oriented organizations which reflect either their opposition to the policies or measures which affect them, or their aspirations towards an effective share in directing their own and the country's destinies. These organizations have nearly always had chequered histories. All too often, restrictions on their growth and actions have kept them from being even as representative as their limited membership might suggest. Nonetheless, they form the spearhead of articulate sentiment in their particular group, sometimes shaping its views even more than reflecting them.

Before describing these political organizations, it is well to consider the constitutional means provided for the expression of African opinion after 1936, since this experience has helped to determine both the demands and the actions of non-Europeans since 1948.

African Political Representation

Seven European members of Parliament—three in the Assembly, and four in the Senate—are elected by Africans and called Native representatives. This communal representation, as we have seen, was the compromise enacted in 1936 when the Africans were taken off the common roll in Cape Province. It is a compromise which has never been satisfactory to anyone despite the fact that the Native representatives have included some of the most distinguished persons elected to Parliament in South Africa. The more the Native representatives have tried to present the needs and views of their constituents, the more they have been disregarded by the other members of Parliament. Not only is their powerlessness frustrating to themselves, but it has also tended to alienate the more extreme of African Nationalist leaders.

To elect the three Native representatives to the House of Assembly, Cape Province is divided into three parts, or circles—Cape Eastern, the Transkei, and Cape Western—each of which elects a member. The qualifications for registering on the Cape Native Voters' Roll and after 1956 on the Coloured Roll are the same which prior to 1936 permitted a male African (and Coloured) to be on the common roll, i.e., ability to write his name in English or Afrikaans, and payment of a dwelling rental of at least £75 per annum or receipt of a wage or salary of £50. Any registered African voter may nominate a candidate, and voting is individual as in any ordinary poll. Elections are held at regular five-year intervals, regardless of the duration of Parliament.

There have been four elections—1938, 1943, 1949 and 1954—and a number of by-elections caused by resignations or, after the passing of the Suppression of Communism Act, by expulsion of the sitting member. Mrs. Margaret Ballinger has been returned four times for the Cape Eastern seat, the first time defeating four male candidates, the second time unopposed, the third time defeating a Nationalist opponent so decisively that he lost his deposit, and the fourth time again unopposed. The Transkei has had four different representatives, of whom the most recent is Walter Stanford of the Liberal Party. The Cape Western seat twice returned Donald Molteno, a liberal lawyer, but after his voluntary withdrawal that constituency was won by a succession of persons who had been associated with the Communist party—Sam Kahn, Brian Bunting and Ray Alexander—each of whom was subsequently expelled from the Assembly. (See p. 70.) Its present member, Len Lee-Warden, publisher of *New Age* (p. 42), was arrested at the time of the treason trials (p. 378).

While the Native representatives are elected to the Assembly by qualified Cape Africans through the casting of direct, individual votes, the Senators are chosen through a cumbersome indirect procedure in four huge constituencies comprising all the Africans in the Union.[1] Two of the districts for senatorial elections are in the Cape, which is divided into the Transkei, the largest of Native Reserves, and the rest of Cape Province; the province of Natal comprises the third; and the fourth includes the vast area of the Transvaal and the Orange Free State. Organs of local self-government, local councils, Native advisory boards, electoral committees and chiefs cast block votes in these elections, with each unit having as many votes as it has taxpayers in its area. *Ad hoc* committees account for the largest number of voting units and chiefs for the second largest. Not only does this system of block voting, i.e., casting all the votes of each unit for a single candidate, curb the expression of minority opinion in heavily populated areas, but the urban vote is strongly restricted by the legal fiction that 95 per cent of the Africans are resident in the countryside although in fact, at any given time, more than half are in urban areas.

Over the years, Native representatives in the Assembly and the Senate have sought to focus attention on the issues of primary concern to their African constituents. They have consistently criticized the pass laws, the cheap labor policy and its perpetuation through the use of convict labor, the unfairness of financing many Native services largely out of Native revenues, the Urban Areas legislation which prevents Native ownership of land and restricts their opportunities for investment, as well as other discriminatory measures. With equal vigor and lack of success, they have urged the recognition of African trade unions, and an extension of the representation of non-Europeans. These positions have been upheld not only during ordinary debates on Bills and other parliamentary business, but also through a series of general resolutions proposing the amelioration or abolition of particular types of economic, social and political discrimination against non-Europeans.

At first, the Native representatives tried to retain their independence within their respective chambers, and to treat every 'voting issue' on its merits:

> supporting in general neither one party nor another, but whatever side represented the more liberal or the less reactionary policy.[2]

Increasingly, however, they found themselves forced towards the United Party by the outspoken anti-liberalism of the Nationalists. On January 22, 1948, shortly before coming into office, Dr. Malan introduced a resolution proposing to curtail Native political representation as part of the policy of apartheid; Mrs. Ballinger opposed this bitterly as 'a promise of a tribal civilization for Europeans and a backyard culture for Africans'.[3] The following year, Senator Brookes directly attacked the Nationalists in a resolution which declared that the relationships between Europeans and non-Europeans 'have deteriorated considerably as a result of the Government's propaganda and politics'.[4] Dissatisfied as the Native representatives were with United Party Native policy, it was at least the lesser of two evils compared to Nationalist apartheid.

The formation in 1953 of the Liberal Party, to which four of the Native representatives belonged in 1955, did little to solve their major problems: the lack of representatives, and of power. It is always difficult to determine how best to provide representation for an advancing but still largely primitive people. India is making the daring experiment of universal franchise with a population whose illiteracy rate is far higher than that of South Africa's Africans. But the situation is vastly more complex when there is an already established representative structure running on Western lines, as in South Africa. To introduce non-Europeans into such a structure is not impossible, as the Federation of Rhodesia and Nyasaland is demonstrating, but representation of this kind does not ensure power. Thus non-European leaders in South Africa and the Native representatives argue that non-Europeans must vote on the common roll if they are to gain an important influence on the policies which affect them.

The same logic underlies Nationalist opposition to non-Europeans on the common roll. In fact, the great majority of European South Africans see their control of politics as the essential means for maintaining their dominant position in the country.

The problem implicit in the position of the Native representatives appeared no less acutely in the history of the Natives' Representative Council, set up in 1936 as part of the substitute for African voting on the common roll. This body consisted of the Secretary of Native Affairs, who acted as chairman, the six Chief Native Commissioners of the Union, known as assessor members, and sixteen full members, all African, of whom four were nominated by the Government and twelve elected through the four electoral areas which choose the Senators. As far as scope of activities was concerned, the Council's field was broad: the estimates of the South African Native Trust Fund, all legislation certified as affecting Africans, and even general issues. But of power it had none. While the reports of its sessions had to be laid before Parliament, its resolutions had no force. In other words, the Natives' Representative Council was a purely advisory body whose effectiveness depended entirely on the weight given its deliberations and proposals by the Government in office.

From the first, African leaders divided over the question of whether or not they should cooperate with the Natives' Representative Council, i.e., stand for election to it. One of the most distinguished of Africans, Professor D. D. T. Jabavu, formed the All-African Convention in 1935 for the specific purpose of fighting the Hertzog Native Bills, and this largely intellectual group refused to have anything to do with the Council. Many other African leaders, like Professor Z. K. Matthews and Dr. J. S. Moroka, were prepared at this time, however, to consider consultation, rather than participation in government, as the major objective. It was in this spirit that they accepted membership of the Council. But they soon became disillusioned at the ineffectiveness of consultation and joined in the rapidly growing demand for a share in the exercise of power.

Matters came to a head following the largest of all African strikes, the walk-out of 50,000 African miners on the Witwatersrand in 1946 (see p. 63). Protesting that the Council had had no opportunity to discuss this matter of urgent and decisive importance, the Council adjourned *sine die* in August, 1946, as a protest against what it called the Government's breach of faith with the African people. Though the Council met again in November, it refused to transact any business. In May, 1947, Prime Minister Smuts tried to break the deadlock by outlining a 'tentative indication of policy', which would make the Natives' Representative Council 'an all-Native elective body' with 'an increasing measure of executive authority in the development of the Native Reserves', though under the final authority of Parliament and the Government.[5] This was rejected by the main body of councillors as involving no constructive departure from traditional Native policy. 'In our view', they declared,

> what is required is a policy which will give the African people a sense of security in the land of their birth, a policy which is flexible and can be readily adapted to changing conditions, in short a policy which recognizes that Africans are citizens of this country and not things apart. . . . The main submission of the Council has been, and continues to be, that the conditions of modern African life demand a reorientation of the whole of our Native policy and not a mere tinkering with the framework of our existing Native policy'.[6]

Thus well before the Nationalist Government abolished the Natives' Representative Council in 1950, Africans had rejected it as a worthwhile means of making their influence felt. Henceforth their activities focused on acquiring some other means of power to make their purposes effective.

Non-European Political Organizations

Non-Europeans in the Union of South Africa obviously confront major difficulties in bringing into being and carrying on political organizations. One great handicap is the wide gap between the educated, highly articulate, but small non-European minority with professional training and the great mass of unskilled workers or peasants. Only recently is this gulf being somewhat bridged by the growing group of semi-skilled in secondary industries, whose emergence into positions of leadership among the non-Europeans is one of the most significant developments in the nationalist movements.

No less of a difficulty than the small number of leaders among the non-Europeans are the barriers to the holding of meetings, particularly for the purpose of organizing non-Europeans into politically oriented associations. When J. B. Marks was organizing the mine workers, for example, he was not allowed into the mine compounds, but had to hold the few meetings permitted outside their bounds. After the resistance movement began to invade the Reserves in 1952, all meetings in the Transkei and Ciskei were banned unless they had the specific approval of European administrators. No less effective in curbing the growth of organization have been the restrictions imposed under the Suppression of Communism Act on African and Indian leaders. Not only are those under ban limited in their movements, but they are also forbidden to attend gatherings of three or more people without the specific permission of the Minister of Justice. Bans may be imposed without warning, thus curbing the effective operation of a meeting. In December 1952, for example, the Secretary of the African National Congress and several other militants were placed under ban just before they were leaving to attend its Annual Congress.

Despite the fact that non-Europeans, and particularly African organizations, always operate perforce on the edge of illegality, there has been a series of African, Indian and Coloured quasi-political groups which reflected their particular purposes. Clement Kadalie's Industrial and Commercial Workers' Union numbered some 100,000 members in the 1920s. No other African organization had so large a membership until the African National Congress swelled to this size following the passive resistance campaign in 1952. But the fate of the Industrial and Commercial Workers' Union,[7] which was split by personal rivalries at the end of the 1920s and is now almost defunct, illustrates further difficulties of non-European organizations: the degree to which these organizations almost inevitably depend on one individual or a few; the tendency of their leaders to become self-seeking, and to put their own interests above those of their group; and the difficulty of developing a systematic program in such a highly restrictive situation as the Union offers.

The longer, and still more chequered histories of the two most nationalistic organizations among non-Europeans—the African National Congress and the South African Indian Congress—reflect a further problem: that moderate leadership is often brushed aside as it proves itself incapable of securing concessions from the Europeans, and is replaced by those who enunciate the extreme demands which despair engenders. Such demands, in turn, create the fear and resistance among Europeans, and in particular the Nationalists, which lead to further restrictions and more severe penalties as in the Public Safety Act and the Criminal Laws Amendment Act. And so the cycle continues.

Non-European Unity Movments

Non-European political organizations fall into two categories: those which include only one of the non-European groups, and those which attempt to bridge these groups to provide for non-European unity. But the two constantly interact.

Non-European unity may be sought, as by the remarkable Coloured leader,

Dr. A. Abdurahman, in 1927, in a single organization to serve the interests of all non-Europeans. This attempt foundered through the opposition of a strong section of African opinion expressed by the now defunct African National Bond. Another more successful effort is represented by the Non-European Unity Movement, organized after the outbreak of World War II on a loose federal basis and without a formal Constitution, in an effort to avoid jurisdictional problems. This movement is led by intellectuals, draws most of its support from the Coloured community, and has strong Communist influences, partly at least of the Trotskyite variety. It believes in non-cooperation with the Government, but not in passive or active resistance until all non-Europeans can be united in a general strike to tie up the whole country.

The Non-European Unity Movement draws its chief support from the Coloured organizations which oppose cooperation with the Government. Much of this sentiment focuses in opposition to the Coloured Advisory Council, which was established in 1943 to advise the Government on current administration affecting the Coloured and assist it in relation to the peculiar problems of the Coloured.[8] It consists of 20 members appointed by the Government, who have pressed consistently for better conditions and an extension of rights for the Coloured. Nonetheless, its inauguration created the sharpest split in the history of the Coloured people. Those opposing the Coloured Advisory Council argued that, regardless of intentions, the body represented a division on racial lines which the Coloured have always tried to prevent, that it presaged further segregation and, that since the social and economic problems of the Coloured were well known, what was needed was not a consultative body but reform.

Events since that time, and particularly since 1948, when apartheid has pressed in on the Coloured, have only confirmed these views. The anti-Coloured Advisory Council Movement not only resists these developments through non-cooperation, but out of its own helplessness has decided that the root of the whole problem is color discrimination, that this must be wiped out for all non-Europeans and that, therefore, all non-Europeans should unite in joint political action to bring this about.

The anti-Coloured Advisory Council group has succeeded in capturing the oldest, and once by far the most impressive movement among non-Europeans: the African Peoples' Organization. Despite its name, the African Peoples' Organization is a Coloured organization, founded in 1902 to work for the extension of the rights of the Cape Coloured to the Coloured in other parts of the Union. It had its heyday under the leadership of Dr. Abdurahman, when it had over a hundred branches in the Cape and a number in the Transvaal. Dr. Abdurahman was always interested in other non-European groups, but the African Peoples' Organization's present part in the Non-European Movement reflects its subservience to anti-Coloured Advisory Council leadership rather than its earlier emphasis on the common interests of all non-Europeans. A further Coloured group associated with the Non-European Unity Movement is the Teachers' League of South Africa, which has marked Trotskyite tendencies.

The Non-European Unity Movement secures some support from African intellectuals, particularly from the All-African Convention (see p. 368), but it is viewed with mistrust by the African National Congress and the South African Indian Congress. The so-called Unity Movement resisted all appeals to join in the resistance campaign, insisting that the latter was premature and therefore useless. Little if any contact exists between the Unity Movement and other non-European organizations. Thus, at the moment, the Non-European Unity Movement has created more disunity than otherwise.

Certainly the Coloured themselves are deeply split between the Anti-Coloured Advisory Council groups and the Coloured People's National Union, which cooperates with the Government. The latter has tried to make itself the distinctive mouthpiece of the Coloured people in contrast to the broader, non-European emphasis of the other Coloured groups. Its president, George J. Golding, principal of a Coloured school, is variously hailed as an important Coloured leader or assailed as a time-server to the Government. In fact, the position of the Coloured People's National Union has been made increasingly difficult by the deliberate extension of apartheid measures to the Coloured group. But even these pressures have not yet overcome the deep divisions within the Coloured community.

Of all the non-European groups, the Coloured are the least unified, and the least effective. They are still torn between their desire to associate themselves with the whites, and their reluctant awareness that the Nationalists are forcing them into the same general category as the Indians and Africans. But while those Coloured in the Non-European Unity Movement accept the logic of this latter development, they refuse to ally themselves with African and Indian Nationalist groups. Thus, at least for the moment, they lack the influence and potential power which they might secure from coordinated efforts with the South African Indian Congress and the African National Congress.

A far more important unity movement amongst South African non-Europeans is the relation which has developed between these latter two most militant and national-minded organizations of the Indians and Africans. This is the more remarkable because there has always been friction between the Indians and Africans in Natal, a friction which flared tragically into widespread violence, in January 1949, in the Durban riots.[9] Arising out of the chance striking of an African boy by an Indian shopkeeper, the riots enveloped most of Durban, as largely tribalized Africans burned many Indian homes, all too often with their families inside. Many Africans were shot by the police in an effort to stop the destruction. The experience of unrestrained African brutality shook European Durban, though no white people were attacked. Beyond this, it roused both Indian and African leaders to the need to develop closer relations both to prevent the repetition of so appalling an event and to work together for their common purposes.

More significant than the riots themselves was the fact that Indian and African leaders together toured the areas of destruction and attempted to stop the violence. They worked together to prepare a brief to the Commission which investigated the riots. The unity welded by this experience took form in the Joint Action Committee of the African National Congress and the South African Indian Congress, which helped to direct the passive resistance campaign of 1952, presented a memorandum to the Indian Government on *The Disabilities of the Non-White Peoples of South Africa*[10] for use by the United Nations in its examination of South African racial policies and, though forced underground after 1953, still attempts to coordinate the activities of these two bodies.

Indian Organizations

Behind these developments lies a chequered history of organization and efforts both by Indians and Africans to improve their condition within South Africa. The parent body among South African Indians is the Natal Indian Congress founded by Mahatma Gandhi in 1894.

Though it was chance which brought Gandhi to South Africa, he quickly realized the particular difficulties of Indians in that country. While many Indians went to foreign countries as indentured labor in the nineteenth century, South Africa was one of the few of these with a settled white population. The plantation owners and industrial managers of Natal, desperate at the uncertainties of Native Zulu labor, encouraged a steady flow of cheap, reliable Indian workers from 1860 to 1911. But when, at the end of their contracts, most of the Indians remained in South Africa rather than accepting free passage home, and other Indians came as traders, the European merchant class complained bitterly of Indian competition. The fear that Indian labor threatened European standards and dominance resulted in a long series of restrictions. Of these, the most important were the Natal law of 1896, under which no Indian could henceforth gain the franchise in that province, and the Transvaal law of 1885, which not only denied citizenship, but restricted Indian living centers and trading to certain areas.

In an effort to ameliorate the discrimination against them, Indian communities in South Africa periodically undertook passive resistance campaigns. The most impressive of these campaigns was carried on intermittently from 1906 to 1914, and culminated in the Smuts-Gandhi Agreement of 1914. This agreement provided some relief for South African Indians, but did not change the basic pattern of discrimination.

Gandhi had hoped that the termination of indentured labor by the Indian Government in 1911, and of free Indian immigration in 1913, would pave the way for an extension of full rights of citizenship to the Indians in South Africa. Instead, European hostility to real and imagined economic and residential penetration by Indians led to proposals for further restrictions. These were climaxed by a measure introduced in 1926 by Dr. Malan, then Minister of the Interior in General Hertzog's Nationalist Government, providing for rigid segregation of Indians. Though the objective was partly to restrict the Indians still further, the primary purpose was to encourage as many Indians as possible to seek repatriation to India.

Concern over this law led to a Round Table Conference between India and South Africa. The resulting Cape Town Agreement, 1927, provided for India's cooperation in a long-term plan for assisting Indians to emigrate from South Africa and thus to reduce the Indian population in that country. From its side, the South African Government agreed to aid the 'upliftment' of Indians remaining in South Africa, a pledge implemented to some extent. The voluntary repatriation provision was seldom invoked, however, since after an initial rush the emigrants returning to India found conditions there unsatisfactory. The Union Government thus resorted to the reservation in the Cape Town Agreement, which authorized it to take what measures it deemed necessary if the emigration plan did not succeed.

Despite several splits in the Natal Indian Congress over what should be the reactions to these developments, it remained concerned only with its own affairs and under the control of moderates until the crisis precipitated by the so-called Pegging Act of 1943. This was largely true also of the South African Indian Congress, formed in 1920 by the Provincial Congresses of Natal, the Transvaal and the Cape. In 1939, however, Dr. Y. M. Dadoo (though still in a subordinate role in the South African Indian Congress) organized joint protests by the Indian, African and Coloured communities against the projected 'Servitude Scheme', under which a three-fourths majority vote of Europeans in a particular community could lead to the exclusion from it of all non-Europeans (i.e., in practice, extending to Indians and Coloured provisions which could already be used against Africans under the Urban Areas Acts). These protests led to the withdrawal of the legislation, and thus strengthened Dadoo's belief in the usefulness of working with other non-European groups. This was the line towards which he turned the South African Indian Congress after he and other militants gained control of that organization in 1946.

Up to 1943, there had been no restrictions on Indian ownership of land in Natal comparable to those in the Transvaal. Accusations that Indians were penetrating European areas led to investigations by Government commissions, the second of which disclosed extended penetration into certain residential areas in Durban between the years 1940 and 1943. Under pressure from Natal, the Smuts Government introduced the Trading and Occupation of Land (Transvaal and Natal) Restriction Act (No. 35 of 1943), which made inter-racial property transactions in Durban illegal, a provision which could be extended to other municipalities if deemed necessary. Shocked by a measure so much more drastic than the situation seemed to demand, Natal Indians objected bitterly and the Indian Government lodged a formal protest. An attempted compromise, the Pretoria Agreement of 1944, which would have relied on self-restraint rather than law to restrict further Indian penetration in Durban, failed because of opposition both by Natal Europeans and the younger, more radical, Indians in that province.

In 1946, General Smuts found himself unable to resist the pressure from within his own party and introduced a new and comprehensive measure, the Asiatic Land Tenure and Indian Representation Act. This had a disturbing impact on the South African party structure, as well as on Indian opinion (see p. 36). This law combined an offer of limited franchise to all South African Indians with provisions under which Natal was demarcated into exempted and unexempted areas. Within the latter, no Indians could henceforth buy or occupy fixed property without a permit from the Minister of the Interior. The measure met a storm of protests from Indians at home and abroad and South African Indians indignantly refused to accept the franchise provisions, since they were combined with such rigorous restrictions on land ownership and occupancy.

Meeting under the shadow of the Smuts legislation, the South African Indian Congress, at its 1946 annual meeting in Cape Town, unanimously passed four resolutions: to request the Indian Government to apply economic sanctions to South Africa; to ask India to refer the treatment of South African Indians to the United Nations; to request the withdrawal of the Indian High Commissioner from the Union; and to wage an 'unrelenting struggle against the 1946 legislation until it was repealed'. A deputation conveyed these resolutions to Prime Minister Smuts and asked him to withdraw the legislation. When he refused to do so, the South African Indian Congress sent its appeal to the Indian Government, which took the three steps which Congress had requested.

The South African Indian Congress and the Natal Indian Congress also considered methods of demonstrating against the 1946 legislation, but divided over the expediency of adopting measures of passive resistance. Defeated in this struggle, the former leaders, A. S. Kajee and Dr. Nather walked out of the Natal Indian Congress, leaving it under the control of the Anti-Segregation group, headed by Dr. G. M. Naicker. At the same time, Dr. Dadoo, also a young, left-wing intellectual, long associated with the Communist Party, acquired control of the South African Indian Congress. The two Indian organizations henceforth embarked on a program of action.

The first step taken by the Natal Indian Congress, under its new leadership, was to organize a campaign of passive disobedience. Some 2,000 Indians, mainly women, and a few Europeans, including the Rev. Michael Scott, deliberately courted jail by squatting on a plot of land in Durban which they were forbidden to occupy. The Passive Resistance Council in the Transvaal had the same purpose of dramatizing Indian grievances. Though it would be difficult to prove that the passive resistance campaign had any constructive effect on European opinion,[11] it had a definite impact on Indian sentiment. Thus the Natal Indian Congress grew in size from a few hundred members to 35,000.

In 1953, the Natal Indian Congress had 27 branches in the province, of which 7 were in Durban. Some of these branches had as many as 300 members. Branches are largely autonomous, have their own officers, and send 1 delegate each to the annual Provincial Congress for each hundred members enrolled. The provincial organizations are also largely autonomous, under a full-time President—Dr. Naicker in 1953—with a secretary and treasurer, a full-time paid organizer, and a Durban office. The Provincial Congress meets annually to discuss policy and to elect provincial officers. There is also a Working Committee composed of 1 delegate for every 300 members, which meets quarterly to supervise the actions of the Executive. At the same time, the officers of the Natal Indian Congress occasionally act in emergency situations on their own authority.

The South African Indian Congress is organized on a federal basis and Head Office spends two years in each of the three provinces in which there is an organization. Thus, it was in the Cape from 1948-50, Durban from 1950-52, and Johannesburg from 1952-54. The Natal and Transvaal organizations see much more eye to eye on policy, however, than with the Cape. Dr. Dadoo, perhaps the most dynamic figure among South African Indians, works virtually full-time as President of the South African Indian Congress, though he also maintains his own medical practice.

The Natal Indian Congress and the South African Indian Congress are action organizations, concerned to maintain contact with the mass of the Indian people. Under existing circumstances only two methods of protest are open to them: passive resistance and a general strike. The lack of results of their own 1946 passive resistance campaign pressed them to associate themselves with other non-European groups, in particular the African National Congress.

While Indian militant leadership endorsed passive resistance and non-European unity, those from whom leadership had been wrested formed their own organization in 1947—the Natal Indian Organization—which expanded, in 1951, into the South African Indian Organization. This group charged that the Natal Indian Congress was under radical Communist influence, was alienating European opinion through the passive resistance campaign, and would thus impair the economic position of the Indian community, especially in Durban. Composed largely of merchants and professional men, though with a small sprinkling of trade unionists, the Natal Indian Organization represents the more wealthy and settled group among the Indians, whereas the Natal Indian Congress appeals to urban and agricultural labor. Another feature of the Natal Indian Organization is that it includes almost all the Moslems in the Indian community while the Natal Indian Congress is a Hindu body.

Naturally, the Natal Indian Organization is much smaller in membership than the Natal Indian Congress, having 13 branches in 1953 with a combined membership of about 10,000. It has a secretary-organizer. Its organization is patterned on that of the original Natal Indian Congress except that, like the present Natal Indian Congress, there are no individual, as opposed to group, members at the biennial congresses to which each branch sends 20 members. A Working Committee, composed of 4 members from each branch, meets 4 times a year, and elects the Executive Committee; the President (Dr. Nather in 1953) is elected by the biennial congress. At least as much as in the Natal Indian Congress, its center of power is its Executive Committee and President. The main difference between the two organizations is that the Natal Indian Organization has no relations with any other non-European group and is ready to cooperate with the Government and other European agencies.

No one can doubt the difficulty of the position in which South African Indians find themselves. Since so substantial a number of them engage in trade, they are peculiarly vulnerable to the restrictions on such activities imposed directly or arising out of laws like the Group Areas Act. The working-class Indian, in turn, may all too easily be replaced by African labor. This insecurity is intensified by the awareness of Indian unpopularity among Europeans, and persistent propaganda that they are an alien element in the country.

On the other hand, Indians in South Africa have had one means of support possessed by no other non-European group: the assured backing of an outside and important country, India, which takes a deep and continuous interest in their position, and gives it world-wide publicity through the United Nations.[12] But this, in turn, has its own disadvantages. The appeal to India embitters European South Africans, who mistrust and fear that country's possible designs on Africa. It reinforces their view that Indians are a 'foreign' group in South Africa. Moreover, it complicates the relations between South African Indians and other non-Europeans in the Union, who often fear that India's interest in them is a selfish one, for furthering its own interests or those of the Indians in South Africa.

Despite any qualms which Africans may have at working closely with Indians, there are marked advantages for both sides. The Africans provide the numerical strength which the Indians lack. The Indians, from their side, have wider experience, greater capacity for organization, more funds, and an open channel to world opinion. Moreover, the Indians have provided the Africans with knowledge of the technique and value of passive resistance, the weapon which Gandhi first forged on South African soil.

African Organizations

The chief problem of African political groups is how to organize. Unlike Indians and Coloured, Africans are spread all over the Union. In the Reserves, where they have most freedom of movement and live in the densest groups, they are under the nominal or actual authority of their chiefs. In European areas, Africans are either under constant supervision, as in the mines, or watched closely by the police, as in the Native townships. Even when completely detribalized, Africans have an impermanence of position which makes them particularly vulnerable to administrative restraints.

Nonetheless, a series of voluntary African organizations have sprung up during the past forty years in response to a particular leader or emergency. All of them have lacked funds and efficient staffs. Among them, only the African National Congress, the oldest and now the strongest among African organizations, is Union-wide in membership.

One other Union-wide organization of Africans—the Congress of Native Advisory Boards—is unique as the only official, non-tribal organization which Africans have possessed since the dissolution of the Natives' Representative Council. The Congress of Native Advisory Boards unites in a loose relationship and mainly through an annual meeting, the Native Advisory Boards of the urban locations. At the time the Bantu Authorities Act was passed, the Nationalist Government planned to supersede these Advisory Boards (which are made up partly of nominated and partly of elected African members) by more tribally oriented bodies. This was partly to reinforce tribalism, partly because the Advisory Boards had become a focus for articulate African opinion on more than local matters. At their Annual Congress in 1951, for example, a resolution was introduced condemning the exclusion of the Rev. Michael Scott from South Africa since his investigations had disclosed conditions in a way clearly to the advantage of the non-Europeans. The resolution was carried unanimously, but the European members of local non-European committees, who were attending the Congress *ex officio*, walked out in protest at the discussion of a motion so obviously political. Though it is thus a vehicle of African urban opinion on political matters, the Native Advisory Board structure has not yet been changed, but every effort is made to keep the Boards purely advisory, and limited to the subjects within their direct range of competence.

Among the voluntary, politically oriented African organizations, only a few are important enough to mention. The Industrial and Commercial Workers' Union is now almost defunct. The All-African Convention is largely a Cape organization, and its role in the non-European Unity Movement is its greatest distinction. The Cape Native Voters' Convention exists to aid the selection of suitable Native representatives, but has only a limited influence. The African Democratic Party is a militant group, centered on the Witwatersrand, which was organized in 1943 after a breakaway from the African National Congress, aims at mass support, and has tried to steer a middle way between the African National Congress and the Communists.

By far the most important vehicle of African nationalist sentiment in recent times is the African National Congress. It was organized at a convention in Bloemfontein, January 1912, by four African lawyers who had returned to the Union after studying abroad. The moving spirit was Dr. P. ka I. Seme, who had taken a B.A. at Columbia University and studied law in England; its first President, the Rev. J. L. Dube, was the founder and principal of the Ohlange Training Institution in Natal, and an editor of *Ilanga lase Natal.*

To the inaugurating convention were invited both the small politically oriented groups of Africans found throughout the country, and tribal chiefs. What was originally called the South African Native National Congress was to be the single political organization within which all the smaller groups, unofficial and official, would be absorbed, or coordinated. Thus, though the character of the organization was clearly national, a great emphasis was placed at first on giving a definite position within it to

> all Kings, Princes, Paramount Chiefs and Chiefs by heritage and other persons of Royal blood in the direct line of succession among the various tribes of the Bantu races in South Africa.[13]

These latter had the right to attend meetings of the association in person or through representatives, and were called Honorary Vice-Presidents. This attempt to bridge national and tribal interests was not successful, however, and the chiefs soon lost any role in the movement. Though reluctant to antagonize the chiefs, the African National Congress openly opposes the Bantu Authorities Act and views tribalism as a barrier to the spread of African nationalism.

The African National Congress was formed because of the underlining of the color bar in the South Africa Act, 1909, particularly in the restricted vote for non-Europeans and their inability to sit in Parliament. A year after the African National Congress came into existence, the Land Act of 1913 added their other most deeply felt grievance by prohibiting Africans from acquiring land outside certain very limited areas. To protest the Land Act, an African deputation went to London in 1914, and another in 1919, since the first one was interrupted by the outbreak of World War I. Out of this experience, African leaders learned to their dismay that Great Britain no longer had any control over South African policies. Their attempt to appeal to an outside source to remedy their disabilities was in a certain sense a forerunner of later appeals to the United Nations.

Like Coloured and Indian organizations, those serving Africans are torn between their desire to protest against their disabilities and their awareness of their almost complete dependence on the Europeans not only for the policies under which they live, but even for livelihood itself. Protests against the pass laws, for example, which culminated at the beginning of the 1930's in pass-burning demonstrations, brought little but suffering to those who participated. But in 1935, the threat to the Native franchise in the Cape gave fresh stimulus to the African National Congress. Its annual meeting in Bloemfontein that year reflected not only a new level of influence and organization among Africans, but also a new interest in the body by Indians and Coloured, some of whose leaders attended the session. But African leaders split, as we have seen, over whether to cooperate with the Government in the Natives' Representative Council, established as part of the 1936 Hertzog Native settlement.

Though Dr. Jabavu and his newly formed All-African Convention refused to do so, practically all the outstanding leaders of the African National Congress served on the Natives' Representative Council at one time or another.

The obvious disadvantage of having different organizations compete for the loyalties of the relatively small number of politically minded Africans led to an attempt, in December 1943, to unify the All-African Convention and the African National Congress. But when a joint committee decided that the All-African Convention should be the supreme African body in the Union, the African National Congress indignantly refused. At its annual convention that year (at which it also re-drafted its Constitution) it passed a resolution which declared that the All-African Convention was a non-European unity organization and that the African National Congress was

> the only premier national organization that can claim to be the true mouthpiece of the African (Bantu) people.[14]

Since that time the African National Congress has amply demonstrated that it is indeed the chief mouthpiece of the African people. Disillusioned by 1943, and completely discouraged by 1946 with the prospects offered by the Natives' Representative Council, the energies of most of its moderates as well as militants were henceforth thrown into organizing a program of action directed toward mass support.

The three aims of the African National Congress, as formulated in its 1943 Constitution, are:

> (a) To protect and advance the interests of the African people in all matters affecting them.
> (b) To attain the freedom of the African people from all discriminatory laws whatsoever.
> (c) To strive and work for the unity and cooperation of the African peoples in every possible way.

To these it added in 1945 a comprehensive 'Bill of Rights', which began:

> We, African people in the Union of South Africa, urgently demand the granting of full citizenship rights, such as are enjoyed by all Europeans in South Africa.[15]

Among the rights enumerated are the vote and election to Parliament, nomination to juries and appointment as judges, freedom of residence, prohibition of police raids on homes 'for tax or liquor or other purposes', free and compulsory education for children and admission to institutions of higher education, equality in social security schemes, collective bargaining, and equal opportunities to engage in any occupation, trade or industry. In the light of the Bantu Education Act of 1953, it is interesting to note that the one italicized clause reads:

> Abandonment of the theory that 'there is a need of a special type of education for Africans as such'. Africans must, therefore, be given the type of education which will enable them to meet on equal terms with other people the conditions of the modern world.

The African National Congress operates on two levels, the provincial and the national; the relation between them varies according to circumstances and leadership. The annual Provincial conference is officially the highest organ within each province, but the degree of organization differs from province to province. The Free State has relatively little organization, though Dr. J. S. Moroka, President from 1949-52, lives in that province; Natal is also not well organized though his successor, ex-Chief Luthuli, resides there. The problem in the Free State has been lack of vigorous local leadership; in Natal that most of the Africans still have strong tribal ties and that Zulu chiefs, in particular, have held aloof from Congress. Traditionally the best organized area has been the Cape where, under the vigorous leadership of Dr. Njongwe, Congress made its greatest advances in the Port Elizabeth area during the passive resistance campaign in 1952. The other area of greatest recent activity is the Witwatersrand in the Transvaal, where most of the dynamic leaders reside.

On the national level, an annual conference determines general policy and program. Even under the official pressures in December, 1952, when the passive resistance campaign was nearly at an end, the annual meeting in Johannesburg included much discussion in its one open session as well as provocative resolutions extending from the pass laws to Korea. The meeting operated under parliamentary procedures and was orderly, though slow at getting under way, partly, however, because at the last moment the Government prevented many of its more active members, including the Secretary, Walter Sisulu, from attending.

The National Conference elects the President, Secretary and Treasurer for three-year terms, and an Executive Committee of not less than fifteen members. While ostensibly the choice is free, ex-Chief Luthuli was one of the few prominent Africans not under ban at the time of his election. At the same time, he was well known for his refusal to give up his African National Congress membership as the price of remaining chief of a small Christian group in Natal. Though the President of the African National Congress is its official spokesman, the real center of power in the organization is in the Working Committee, a body of not less than seven members, appointed by the National Executive Committee from persons living within a fifty-mile radius of National Headquarters in Johannesburg.

The period of greatest activity of the African National Congress coincided with increasingly close links with the South African Indian Congress. In December, 1950, both the African National Congress and the South African Indian Congress passed resolutions supporting an active program of cooperation. This led to a Joint Planning Committee which met in March, 1951, and proposed a nation-wide demonstration against discriminatory laws through a one-day strike on May 1. (The significance of picking May Day, on which Communists now demonstrate all over the world, seems not to have been understood as well by the Africans as by the Indians.) Disturbances arising out of the demonstrations led to eighteen deaths. This loss of life was commemorated on June 26, 1951, at the first national meeting of non-European organizations to consider their future course of action. African Peoples' Organization representatives met at that time with delegates from the African National Congress and the South African Indian Congress. But it was clear that the chief significance of the meeting was the decision to establish the Joint Action Committee of the African National Congress and the South African Indian Congress which was officially set up in March, 1952, and subsequently directed the passive resistance campaign.

Before the campaign was begun, however, there was further consideration and also due notice to the authorities. The African National Congress, meeting in Bloemfontein from December 15-17, 1951, formally adopted a resolution requesting the Government to repeal, by February 29, 1952, six laws: the pass laws, stock limitation (or cattle culling), the Suppression of Communism Act of 1950, the Group Areas Act of 1950, the Bantu Authorities' Act of 1951, and the Separate Representation of Voters' Act of 1951. Failing this, the African National Congress pledged itself to hold protest meetings and demonstrations on April 6, 1952, as a prelude to carrying out their plans for 'the defiance of unjust laws'. Notice of this resolution was formally sent to Prime Minister Malan in a letter of January 21, 1952, to which he replied on January 29, 1952. Shortly after the African National Congress had sent its letter, the South African Indian Congress, meeting in Johannesburg January 25-27, 1952, resolved to support the African Congress in its program of action, a fact of which it notified the Prime Minister in a formal letter of February 20, 1952. The timing was significant, for it showed that the Indians were prepared to allow the Africans to take the initiative.

The exchange of letters[16] between the African National Congress and the Prime Minister illustrates the entirely different points of view out of which each was proceeding. The African National Congress called attention to its long series of efforts 'by every constitutional means', to bring to the Government the 'legitimate demands' of the Africans and, in particular, 'their inherent right' to be directly represented in Parliament and other legislative bodies. It declared that the Government through 'its repressive policy of trusteeship, segregation and apartheid' legislation 'continues to insult and degrade the African people', and refused their offer of cooperation. The consequence, the letter maintained, had been 'a gradual worsening of the social, economic and political position' of the Africans and 'a rising tide of racial bitterness and tension'. Nonetheless, the African National Congress emphasized that the action it now planned was not against any national group or race, but 'against the unjust laws which keep in perpetual subjection and misery vast sections of the population'. With full awareness of the consequences of the decision it had taken, it believed that the action it was about to begin was 'in the interests of all in the country, and will inspire our people for long ages to come'.

In an almost unprecedented step, Dr. Malan, through his Private Secretary, answered this letter point by point. Focusing on the phrase 'inherent right' to direct representation, he took his stand on the typically Nationalist view of the essential dissimilarity of Europeans and non-Europeans.

> You will realize, I think [he wrote] that it is self-contradictory to claim as an inherent right of the Bantu, who differ in many ways from the Europeans, that they should be regarded as not different, especially when it is borne in mind that these differences are permanent and not man-made.

If the Africans did not value their racial characteristics, he added caustically, it was 'an inherent right' of the Europeans to 'take the opposite view', and to adopt 'the necessary measures to preserve their identity as a separate community'.

Relating this view to specific political conclusions, he went on to assert that:

> It should be understood clearly that the Government will under no circumstances entertain the idea of giving administrative or executive or legislative powers over Europeans, or within a European community, to Bantu men and women, or to other smaller non-European groups.

The request that non-Europeans should share political power with Europeans he declared to be 'no genuine offer of cooperation', but an attempt to begin 'supplanting European rule'.

As for the 'differentiating' laws which the African National Congress called 'oppressive and degrading', Dr. Malan insisted that, on the contrary, they were 'largely of a protective character'. The Bantu Authorities' Act, he declared, was designed particularly

> to give the Bantu people the opportunity for enlightened administration of their own affairs in accordance with their own heritage and institutions, adapted to modern conditions.

But beyond all this, Dr. Malan warned of 'the extreme gravity' of pursuing the course of action about which the African National Congress had written. 'Should you in the implementation thereof incite the Bantu population to defy law and order', he declared forcefully,

> the Government will make full use of the machinery at its disposal to quell any disturbance and, thereafter, deal adequately with those responsible for inciting subversive activities of any nature whatsoever.

Dr. Malan's letter was considered at a specially convened meeting of the National Executive of the African National Congress. In its reply of February 11, 1952, the African National Congress refused to modify its stand. It called the rejection of the demand for direct representation 'the kernel of the policy of apartheid'. As for differences, it had not referred to biological ones, it pointed out, but to citizenship rights which were denied to one part of the population by 'man-made laws artificially imposed'. Nothing in the Bantu Authorities' Act 'can be a substitute', it declared, for direct representation 'in the Councils of State'. At the end, not without dignity, it affirmed that 'as a defenceless and voteless people, we have explored other channels without success', and therefore had no alternative to embarking on 'the campaign of mass action'.

Not all Africans were united in support of the campaign of passive resistance. Shortly before the public announcement of the campaign, a former President of the African National Congress, Selope Thema, broke away from the current leaders of that group and formed what he called the National-minded Bloc within the African National Congress. Thema charged that Africans were exploited and oppressed not only by Europeans, but also by Indians[17] and should, therefore, concern themselves only with their own disabilities and aims. Another group, the Bantu National Congress, launched at a meeting of African herbalists in February, 1952, and federated with the Supreme Council of Bantu

Federations, both supported apartheid, and deplored the defiance campaign.[18] But neither the National-minded Bloc nor the Bantu National Congress commanded much active or tacit support. The Bantu National Congress, closely associated with traditional tribal practices, and widely believed to be sponsored by the Government, was shunned by most Africans. The National-minded Bloc had some support from the older, more conservative members of the African National Congress who feared the results of open resistance, but its main role was a negative one: to refrain from endorsing the campaign. Almost the only thing in common between the Bantu National Congress and the National-minded Bloc was their suspicion of the Indians.[19] The African National Congress was prepared to rise above this traditional African sentiment, and to work with the South African Indian Congress in support of what were seen as common objectives.

Even before the demonstrations began, the campaign of passive resistance had become a European political party issue. *Die Volksblad* charged on January 30, 1952, that the campaign was the fault of the liberals for encouraging the Africans to expect too much.[20] In an obvious effort to make it clear that the United Party disapproved of the campaign, J. G. N. Strauss made an open appeal to 'the people of South Africa' to forget their differences during the celebrations of the 300th anniversary of the landing of van Riebeeck.[21]. The Torch Commando followed with a direct appeal to the non-Europeans to abandon their plans for the passive resistance campaign,[22] and later declared it would not condone or encourage law-breaking or civil disobedience.[23] When the African National Congress rejected Strauss' appeal out of hand, *Die Vaderland* chortled that Strauss had got what he deserved, and *Die Transvaler* asked why the Johannesburg English-language press had not publicized this rejection.[24] Throughout the campaign of passive disobedience, in fact, the Nationalist press, as well as party, used every opportunity either to belittle the Opposition's disapproval of the campaign, or to suggest that the Opposition was in some way responsible for it. By so doing, the Nationalists not only secured political advantage for themselves but also made it more difficult for liberal-minded Europeans to express their sympathy with the grievances which lay behind the campaign, even if they opposed this means of publicizing them.

The first move by the African National Congress and South African Indian Congress was a series of protest meetings on April 6, 1952. These took place without incident. The formal campaign of planned acts of disobedience began on June 26, 1952, on the anniversary of the first national meeting of non-European organizations. On that day, some 250 leaders of the African National Congress deliberately infringed regulations governing non-Europeans, thus openly courting arrest and jail. They were followed during the succeeding months of 1952 by over 8,000 volunteers, mostly Africans, who similarly defied the pass laws, the curfew, or an apartheid regulation, and went to jail for the offense. The main centers for these demonstrations were Johannesburg, Cape Town, Port Elizabeth and East London, but they also took place in many other places throughout the Union.

As the campaign increased, so did the punishments. In some instances, volunteers under the age of 21 were whipped. Resisters using the 'for whites only' entrance to the Johannesburg station received two months' imprisonment with hard labor; others who sat on a bench similarly marked 'for whites only' were sentenced to one month imprisonment with hard labor. Moreover, volunteers were sometimes ill-treated by the police either during or after arrest.

The resisters themselves maintained an impressive discipline so that no scenes of violence arose out of their actions. Before any resister was allowed to volunteer for an act of disobedience, he was given a short course of training. He was instructed in techniques of passive disobedience, warned of the treatment he was likely to receive, and took a solemn oath that, regardless of what was done to him, he would not retaliate. This pledge was adhered to throughout.

The primary purpose of the campaign was to publicize opposition to the disabilities of the non-Europeans, and draw attention to their desires. The laws highlighted in the campaign illustrated this fact. Africans resent the pass laws, called by the African National Congress 'perhaps the most hated machinery of oppression',[25] not only because they limit the freedom of movement of male Africans but also as a mark of special indignity, since only Africans must carry passes. The African National Congress opposed stock limitation and cattle culling, not as bad in themselves, but because they were made necessary by the African's lack of land. Opposition to the other four Acts was more theoretical, since only the Suppression of Communism Act was actually in operation. They opposed the Group Areas Act as establishing 'ghettos' for different non-European groups; the Suppression of Communism Act for limiting freedom of organization; the Bantu Authorities' Act for trying to encourage an outworn tribalism and thus dividing the African people in contradiction to the African National Congress's aim of uniting them; and the Separate Representation of Voters' Act because it struck at the only group, the Coloured, still on the common roll. In attacking these laws, the African National Congress and South Africa Indian Congress were publicizing their aims of freer movement, choice of residence, more land, freer opportunities to organize, group unity and the rights of citizenship.

But perhaps still more important than to draw attention to their grievances and demands was the role the defiance campaign played in consolidating African sentiment, and training its Nationalist movement. Each resister became a leader, partly through the fire of his experience, partly because of respect for undergoing it. Each resister became the nucleus of a group for whom he was henceforth responsible. Organization spread so quickly that the African National Congress's 15,000-20,000 members at the beginning of the campaign mushroomed to 100,000 before its end. The growth was particularly noticeable in the Port Elizabeth area, where the fact that most Africans belonged to the Xhosa tribe facilitated the process of communication. Most significant of all, the defiance campaign was spreading into the Reserves, particularly the Ciskei, as it reached its height.

How much effect had the campaign had? In awakening sympathy among Europeans, practically none at all. It is true that, late in November, 1952, Patrick Duncan, the son of a former Governor-General, and a few other Europeans decided to join the campaign. Subsequently, after much publicity, they entered a Native location without proper authorization, stood trial, and chose a jail sentence rather than the alternative fine. Their purpose was to demonstrate that some Europeans other than Communists chose to associate themselves with the non-Europeans in their opposition to discriminatory laws. But most European South Africans ignored the campaign, or resented it.

The English-language press called frequently for a cessation of the defiance campaign lest it destroy, as the *Star* once put it, all possibility of 'bridges of understanding' between whites and non-whites.[26] *Die Transvaler* asked with concern: 'They are united, and we?'[27] *Die Burger* charged that the campaign was the undertaking of 'a limited number of hot-headed educated people',[28] and later warned the English-language press that the campaign aimed at 'absolute equality', and would have taken place just the same if the United Party had been in office. *Die Oosterlig* demanded corporal punishment for the resisters, and joined with *Dagbreek* in proposing that they be 'deported' to the Reserves,[29] without recognizing, apparently, how explosive it would be to have the spirit of the defiance campaign take root in those areas. Commenting on August 31, 1952, *Dagbreek's* editor warned, however, that these developments among the non-Europeans meant that South Africa could no longer afford the luxury of party political differences.[30]

Most concerned of all were the authorities, both at the degree of organization and discipline displayed by the Africans and at the team-work between African and Indian leaders. Thus they struck back quickly at the organizations behind the resisters. In September, 1952, twenty of the outstanding leaders of the African National Congress and the South African Indian Congress were put on trial in Johannesburg. They were convicted under the Suppression of Communism Act of what the judge called 'statutory communism', that is, that between December 15, 1951, and August 13, 1952, they had

> advocated, advised or encouraged a scheme which aimed at the bringing about of political, industrial, social or economic changes within the Union by means which included unlawful acts or omission or the threat of such acts or omission.

The twenty were given suspended sentences under which they were restricted in their movements and attendance at meetings. Similar charges and sentences soon limited the actions of leaders of the resistance movement in the Cape.

Serious as was this handicap, it paled to insignificance with the tragic outbreak of riots in Port Elizabeth late in October. Moreover, these were followed before the end of the year by similar outbreaks of violence in East London and Kimberley. Arising out of the kind of police arbitrariness towards non-Europeans which takes place daily throughout the Union, the riots may have fed on the atmosphere of tension engendered by the resistance campaign, but they were neither stimulated nor condoned by the African National Congress. On the contrary, the African National Congress immediately condemned the Port Elizabeth riots, while its leaders, who were away from the city at the time of the outbreak, did everything in their power to calm them. Nonetheless, when several white persons, most of them long and close friends of the Africans, were killed during the riots which spread into Port Elizabeth's model Native location of New Brighton, it caused a shock of revulsion among European South Africans which was almost inevitably extended to the resistance campaign.

Nationalist Cabinet Ministers openly blamed the campaign for the riots.[31] *Die Transvaler* pointed out, not without satisfaction, that the 'liberal recipe' had failed, for it was precisely where the African enjoyed most freedom that 'murder and arson' had occurred. It called for an 'end to appeasement policy'.[32]

The *Rand Daily Mail* warned on October 21 that 'this extremely ugly incident' had greatly increased the hostility between Europeans and non-Europeans.[33] The *Star* on the same day, declared that the African National Congress should call off 'resistance'.

Strauss asked at once for an inquiry into the riots; so did the non-Europeans themselves and the English-language press.[34] Even *Die Volksblad* felt an investigation was necessary,[35] though *Die Transvaler* declared it was 'premature'. The *Bantu World* reported that seven Africans had been shot before a single European was harmed.[36] The Nationalists refused, however, to authorize an investigation.

To quiet the situation in New Brighton, the Port Elizabeth authorities instituted a curfew. Local leaders of the African National Congress objected and called a one-day strike of protest which *Die Transvaler* called 'totally out of proportion' to the measure proposed.[37] *Die Burger* warned that this spirit could turn to 'violence against all whites',[38] and Dr. Verwoerd spoke of banishing all 'agitators' from 'trouble spots'.[39] When the strike took place, those participating lost their jobs, and had to return to the Reserves where, in any case, tension was rising.

Almost simultaneously occurred the riot in Duncan Village, a Native location outside East London. *The East London Daily Despatch* declared on November 10 that it was an outgrowth of the ban on public meetings, since it sprang out of police interference with an African religious gathering for which permission had been withdrawn at the moment it began. Two days later, however, *Die Burger* charged that the riot was 'barbarism aroused', while Minister of Justice Swart said that 'strict action' was required.[40] The *Star* began to ask whether the National Party did not see some advantage to itself in the disturbances.[41] African National Congress leaders, appealing for restraint,[42] said privately that they believed the riots were deliberately provoked. Strauss again asked unsuccessfully for an inquiry, and a special session of Parliament.

When Parliament met in regular session in January, 1952, the Nationalists soon produced their answer to the situation: the Public Safety Bill and the Criminal Laws Amendment Bill (see p. 163). These measures made it a still more serious offense to advocate as well as to offer passive resistance to a law, and vastly increased the stringency of the penalties imposed for so doing.

Even before these measures became law, the resistance campaign was dying down, partly through lack of funds, partly because the stock of volunteers was running low, partly because of the growth both of European antagonism, and of tension among the non-Europeans. Moreover by January, 1953, it was obvious that the defiance campaign, and even more the riots, would be used effectively by the Nationalists in their election campaign. The African National Congress, under its new President, ex-chief Luthuli, announced it would take no step which might be used for propaganda by political parties, but that resistance would be resumed after the election. In fact, long before then, the campaign was dead.

What had it demonstrated? For one thing, the intensity of the bitterness of educated Africans and Indians at the restrictions under which they live. For another, the quick response of urban, and even many tribal Africans to leaders who formulated easily understood demands for an end to discrimination and a greater share in the country's direction. The Nationalist response was sharper restraints and more severe penalties. The United Party called for 'moderates' to lead the non-Europeans, but few had survived the long demonstration that their attempts at cooperation with Europeans had been fruitless. The *Natal Witness* was on firmer ground when it wrote at the time of the East London riot that while the rule of law had to be asserted with firmness 'the leaders of Native opinion must be granted a status where they could feel self-respect'.[43] It was also necessary for them to be able to show that they could get results.

Two questions asked widely at the time of the passive resistance campaign were: What was the role of the Indians, and of the Communists? It was noticeable that far more Africans participated as resisters than Indians, leading to quips like 'The Indians will carry on the campaign to the last African'. There were several good reasons, however, why the Africans took the lead. The Indians had already had a passive resistance campaign in 1946; they knew the techniques, and also the cost. Indian leaders, with the full endorsement of most African National Congress leaders, saw their major role in the 1952 campaign to supply training, information and funds. The Africans were not only eager for the experience of running a mass campaign; they were also sensitive to charges of being under Indian domination. They were ready to take what advice and aid they wanted from the Indians but preferred to run the campaign in their own way. The largest center of resistance and the best organized area in the African National Congress was in the Eastern Cape, where there are almost no Indians.

The same is largely true of relations with the Communists. Few, if any, African National Congress leaders are ideological Communists, but many have been trained or advised by Communists. Passive resistance, of course, is much more of an Indian than a Communist technique. The appeal of Communists to African organizations is that they have been virtually the only white persons ready to work with Africans on terms of equality, and to endorse their objective of full political rights. But less than either the Indians or Coloured have the Africans been led or permeated by Communists. The African National Congress's passive resistance campaign in 1952 was a nationalist movement.

The overriding question which has confronted non-European organizations since the failure of the passive resistance campaign is whether to continue to work for improved conditions within the existing multi-racial society, or to aim at the ultimate expulsion of Europeans from South Africa as the only means of securing a free and full national life for the African. So far the answer of the most representative of non-European organizations has been consistently in favor of the interdependence of all South Africa's races. Nonetheless, the Government has tended to treat almost all organized expressions of non-European sentiment as anti-European.

The most important of recent non-European conferences was convened in Bloemfontein in October, 1956, by the Interdenominational African Ministers' Federation, a non-political organization whose members are mostly Protestant clergymen. In an effort to get a full and fair consideration of the most workable solution to South Africa's race problem, the Federation invited organized groups and representative figures from every section of African life. The nearly four hundred who attended the three-day conference concentrated their discussion on the Tomlinson Report, which was analysed in detail by persons sympathetic to its recommendations as well as by those who were hostile. What the conference sought to determine was whether the plans proposed in the Report would make for more harmonious relations between the races.

The answer of the Bloemfontein Conference was that the Tomlinson Report did not offer a hopeful road for the future. The logical goal for Africans was seen to be either cooperation with Europeans in an integrating society, or sovereign independence in a separate African State. Since the Tomlinson Report did not envisage this latter development, the conference felt that its type of separation would only create a colonial status for the Reserves which would lead to still more serious strife in the future.

But the Conference looked at more than the Tomlinson Report. Viewing the whole pattern of negative and positive apartheid of the previous eight years, its members found it no workable answer to South Africa's racial problem, but merely the means whereby the Nationalists maintained their undisputed dominance in the country. Nonetheless they called, however fruitlessly, for cooperation with Europeans based on their essential interdependence.

No less significant was the demonstration at the Bloemfontein Conference of the growing solidarity among African groups, with the exception of the relatively small ones represented by the Bantu Congress, the National-minded Bloc, the Africanists (whom the Nationalist leaders call 'confused intellectuals')[44] and the *World* (formerly the *Bantu World*, see p. 43) newspaper. This solidarity did not express itself in pure African nationalism, however, but rather in non-European unity. Moreover, it recognized growing links with other African and Asian people, as at the Bandoeng Conference (attended by Moses Kotane of the African National Congress), in the United Nations and within the Commonwealth. Part of the reason why African leaders at the Bloemfontein Conference could take so broad a view of the South African situation and maintain their emphasis upon cooperation was that they felt that the climate of world opinion supported their aspirations.

The chief expression of these aspirations is found in the Freedom Charter, a finely worded document of fundamental rights (see p. 486), which was officially endorsed at the Congress of the People at Kliptown, near Johannesburg, on June 26-27, 1955, by three thousand delegates from the African National Congress, the South African Indian Congress, the National Union of the Organization of Coloured People, and a European group which calls itself the South African Congress of Democrats (see p. 489) and had 112 members present. Sharply watched by the police, the meeting was forcibly broken up on its second day but not before the Freedom Charter had been adopted phrase by phrase.

Not everyone in the African National Congress, however, had approved participation in the Kliptown meeting. Only in March, 1956, did the African National Congress officially approve the Freedom Charter. The doubts were an indication that the African National Congress was still not settled on a line of non-European unity, and particularly on cooperation with a white group, as compared to a policy which stressed African nationalism.

To the Government, the Kliptown meeting of the Congress of the People in June, 1955, raised two danger signals: non-European solidarity and growing influence by the South African Congress of Democrats. The latter has openly competed with the Liberal Party since 1953 in offering European friendship and leadership to non-Europeans. Unlike the Liberal Party's stress on constitutional procedures and gradual extension of rights, however, the Congress of Democrats attacks the Nationalist Government's 'brand of fascism', and declares that it will work with the African and Indian Congresses 'to forge a mighty, united peoples' alliance',[45] to overthrow it. According to its Constitution, the Congress of Democrats is

> against all forms of inequality and discrimination. It repudiates as false the doctrines of racial inequality, of white supremacy, of apartheid, trusteeship and segregation.

It takes its stand on the Universal Declaration of Human Rights but its emotive language is characteristically Communist.

In December, 1956, the Government moved dramatically against a wide range of persons, European as well as non-European, whom it accused of treason. Among them were Len Lee-Warden, Native representative for the Western Cape; a European Methodist clergyman, and two African Anglican clergymen; Dr. Z. K. Matthews, acting head of Fort Hare College, and Albert J. Luthuli, president of the African National Congress. In all, there were 156 arrests affecting some forty-eight organizations.

Throughout much of 1957 the trial droned on in the Drill Hall in Johannesburg. The evidence for the prosecution seems to have been collected through nearly a thousand police raids in September and October, 1955, and notes taken at many open European and non-European meetings in the past years. But the exact nature of the charges long remained uncertain. What is obvious is that the so-called 'treason trials' are another means whereby the Government is attempting to stop, if not outlaw, joint action between Europeans and non-Europeans.

In the spring of 1957, the spotlight turned from the trials to the bus boycott, a protest against raising the bus fares from the Native townships to Johannesburg. In essence the dispute was an economic one. The income of the average urban African is already below the breadline; increased fares pulled down the level of subsistence. Africans responded by boycotting the buses, 'voting with their feet' as an English paper put it. The Bishop of Johannesburg and, behind the scenes, the Liberal Party, worked hard for a settlement. Committees were appointed representative of all public bodies, including the African National Congress. Many Europeans gave lifts to the weary walkers, some of whom lived six to eight miles from their places of employment. The Government chose to take a strong stand against the boycott, however, calling it 'a dangerous political move'. The United Party refused to commit itself. Only by prolonged and anxious efforts was a compromise ultimately reached whereby through a somewhat complicated refund procedure the Africans could once more ride the buses without additional cost.

What was the lesson of the Johannesburg bus boycott? In the first place that Africans are deeply suspicious of Europeans even when the latter are trying to reach a settlement on their behalf. And moreover that there is a basic solidarity among Africans which enables them to undertake collective effort with little, if any, organization. Neither fact inspires confidence in ultimate developments on the South African scene.

The question most widely asked outside of the Union is: How long can the situation there remain stable? Probably a long time. There is enough tension so that a riot could break out at any time, but the retaliation would be so terrible that every non-European leader will seek to prevent it. Moreover, non-

Europeans are well aware that the country's economy depends on European direction, skill and resources. So far, no responsible non-European leader has openly suggested that the interests of his people would be best served by eliminating the Europeans from South Africa.

The dilemma of non-European leaders in the Union lies precisely in the fact that their aims are not revolutionary, though European South Africans all too seldom seem to recognize this fact. In West Africa, the dynamic is for a political revolution to supersede the control of colonial governments by the political authority of the Africans themselves. In Kenya, the Mau Mau used terror against the Europeans because it wanted to eliminate them and restore tribal control and *mores.* In South Africa, in contrast, non-European political organizations seek changes within the existing system, not its overthrow. They want a share in political power, not to oust the Europeans. They want a fuller return for their contributions to the economy, not to change its character. They want to become more Western, not less.

Most European South Africans would reject the notion that non-Europeans can achieve these aims without, in fact, working a revolution in the way in which the country is organized. They see their monopoly of political and economic power as the necessary safeguard of their particular way of life. They do not believe it is possible to share that power, and to move towards an elimination of racial discrimination without so impairing the character of their society that they feel they would no longer wish to be a part of it. Thus they dam up the process of change with what result no one can foretell.

Section VI: South Africa and the World

CHAPTER 15
INTERNATIONAL REACTIONS

The most vigorous and open opposition to South African racial policies has not been expressed within the Union itself but in the United Nations. Since that international body came into being in 1946, each session of the General Assembly has critically examined some aspect of South African policies. Commonly this is followed by an exhortation to the Union to conform more nearly to United Nations standards of human rights and/or international responsibilities. The issues around which debates have long focused are South Africa's refusal to acknowledge the right of the United Nations to oversee developments in South West Africa, and its treatment of its Indian minority. From 1953 to 1955,[1] however, the United Nations broadened the scope of its concern to include the whole complex of laws and policies which affect non-Europeans in the Union.

The reasons for this concern are not far to seek. The Asian-African members of the United Nations, which commonly spark the debates on racial policy and colonialism, only recently have become free from colonial control. South American and Middle East countries have also experienced economic exploitation and political control. To these countries, the racial issue, particularly in the form of the domination of Europeans over non-Europeans, is surcharged with emotion. It is not surprising, then, that the United Nations, which reflects the great preponderance of people of color throughout the world, should concern itself so persistently and vehemently with issues of this type, or that South Africa, with its explicit assumptions of white domination, should be a constant irritant.

These developments place Western countries, in particular the United States and the older Commonwealth nations—the United Kingdom, Canada, Australia, and New Zealand—in somewhat of a dilemma. South Africa is a charter member of the Commonwealth of Nations whose most jealously guarded principles are mutual support and lack of interference in one another's affairs. The United States, too, out of the experience of two World Wars, and its intimate relations with Commonwealth countries since 1945, has developed some of the same sense of interdependence and also seeks to avoid interference with internal politics. Thus, these countries are reluctant to seem to stand in judgment on South Africa.

Their hesitancy to censure South Africa is shared by other Western countries. Colonial powers know well from their own experience how important are the responsibilities for developing formerly primitive peoples, and how valid may be the justifications for not extending self-rule more quickly. Moreover, the countries of the West appreciate the need for internal stability. They are naturally conservative, both because they have much to conserve, and because they have the perspective of their own long, slow growth towards their contemporary form.

In addition, the Western countries know that they provide the essential balance wheel in current international relations. The new and underdeveloped countries are naturally inexperienced in international as in national politics. They are often politically naïve. They are prone to endorse international ideals of human conduct which they are far from being able to implement at home. They see the United Nations as an instrument for creating conditions which can only be brought about, if at all, by the long, slow processes of education and maturing political consciences. The older, Western powers must hesitate to thwart the impulses towards economic growth, political independence and racial equality which inevitably animate the less fortunate countries of the world, but they must also try to keep these objectives from being used by Communist States for purposes of cynical self-interest, or allowed so to distort the course of orderly international development that they defeat their own purposes.

Moreover, most Western States fall into somewhat the same category as the Union of South Africa. They are countries whose resources are used largely, if not exclusively, for the benefit of white persons. If they are colonial powers, like the United Kingdom, France, Belgium or Portugal, they are subject to many of the same criticisms within the United Nations as is South Africa, that is, that they are acting out of self-interest, or making too slow progress towards the United Nations goal of full development of the indigenous population. These countries often resent, only to a lesser degree than the Union itself, the goads of their United Nations critics, particularly when they involve internal or domestic affairs. Though the United States rarely falls into the category of a colonial power, its own vast color problem leaves it open to biting attacks. To some of the opponents of colonialism and racial domination, it matters little that there is a steady progress, as in British colonies, towards self-government or, as in the United States, towards greater racial equality.

All of this complicates the problem of how Western countries should react to the constant, and sometimes unfair attacks upon South Africa in the United Nations. Their tendency, like that of the Union, is to be legal-minded. In any case, many of the older, Western countries, are seriously concerned lest too loose construction of the United Nations' purposes should lead it to become a virtual Superstate or, still more likely, hamstring its potentialities by demanding that it do too much. Yet, at the same time, they are not unaware of the necessity of yielding to, or even endorsing the new moral claims which have gripped the imagination, and now form the objectives of so many of the formerly dispossessed peoples of the world.

For South Africa, the United Nations is a far less satisfactory international organization than was the League of Nations. The latter was concerned with the *status quo*, rather than human betterment. Its unanimity rule provided safeguards which can never be paralleled by the two-thirds majority necessary in the United Nations on most substantive matters.[2] Moreover, the League of Nations included only a proportion of the underdeveloped countries, and lacked the fervent outspokenness and leadership of countries like India. The United Nations may lack power, but it has never been wanting in the expression of high resolves, or the attempt to implement them, if only by resolutions. Even General Smuts, who helped to draft the Charter as he had contributed to the Covenant in an earlier day, was assailed at the United Nations on both major issues over which South Africa has been put on trial.

South Africa has resigned from UNESCO because of the latter's outspoken views on racial equality, but it remains a member of the United Nations. At times its representatives have walked out of particular discussions of South African policies as a sign of their opposition to the criticisms being levelled at them, or the assumptions on which these discussions are taking place; since 1956 it has refused to attend such sessions. Other countries have walked out, too, when their domestic affairs were brought under consideration, as France did when Algeria was discussed in the autumn of 1955. Yet that uniqueness which South Africa so often claims as a refuge can also be used against it. There is no other country which has had such long and persistent criticism, or which is consistently moving farther away on these issues from the kind of policies the United Nations recommends.

There is a mutual dilemma in this situation which appears still more clearly in the detailed examination of South Africa's relations with the United Nations. Short of using force, which no one is willing to apply, the only way the United Nations can influence a Member State is to appeal to its conscience by marshalling the weight of world opinion against the policies it is pursuing. But in South Africa, this collective pressure has hardened the determination of the ruling National Party to pursue its own line of policy; it has also alienated white South African opinion in general. United Nations members, gradually realizing this fact, have tried from time to time to moderate their approach in the hope of conciliating South Africa and leading it to make concessions. But when this does not happen, opinion hardens again, and more extreme demands are made, or censure passed. Like other cycles in which South Africa is involved, this one also shows little sign of ending.

South West Africa

The first issue to complicate the relations between South Africa and the United Nations concerned South West Africa, a huge territory adjoining the Union with which the latter has long been deeply concerned. Having captured it from the Germans during World War I, General Botha claimed South West Africa at the Peace Conference as a fifth province of the Union. Since President Wilson had set his face against outright annexations, a compromise arrangement was devised, under which South West Africa was placed under the Union as a 'C' mandate. This meant that the territory was administered as an integral part of the Union subject only to a few limitations designed to safeguard the interests of its Native inhabitants, and the duty of reporting annually to the Permanent Mandates Commission of the League of Nations.

South West Africa was unique among mandates not only in sharing a boundary with its mandatory power, but also because it included white inhabitants. Its population structure was, in fact, not much less complicated than that of the Union. Of its over 200,000 non-Europeans in 1919, half lived in tribal conditions in its northern area, only nominally under European control. The other half, divided between half-breeds, Hottentots, and the Hereros of Damara-Namaqualand, occupied Reserves in the southern and central parts of South West Africa. By 1921, the 8,000 Germans still in the territory had been joined by over 10,000 South Africans and other immigrants. The repatriation of the trek Boers from Angola further expanded the white population. The Europeans mostly lived then, as now, on the grassy uplands, or on the tin, copper, marble or diamond mines, or in the chief urban center, Windhoek.

In 1925, the white inhabitants of South West Africa assumed a greater share in the Government of the territory through the establishment of a Legislative Council. Most of the Germans by this time had somewhat grudgingly accepted British citizenship, which was coupled with the right to use their own language in their schools. But during the thirties, there were increasingly strained relations with the German-speaking in the territory, who were constantly reinforced by immigrants from Germany. When Hitler came into office, a German political party was formed in South West Africa which led the non-German Europeans of the United South West Africa Party to petition, in 1934, for immediate incorporation in the Union. This request was finally rejected, but on the eve of World War II the Union Government found it necessary to reinforce the South West Africa police force with armed men lest Nazi groups in that territory attempt a *coup d'état*.

At the end of World War II, South West Africa's legislative body again petitioned for incorporation in the Union. At the first part of the first session of the General Assembly, meeting in London at the beginning of 1946, South Africa formally reserved its position on the future status of South West Africa until it could also conclude consultations with the African inhabitants of South West Africa regarding incorporation.[3] In the second part of the first session, which was held in New York, General Smuts himself proposed that South West Africa 'be internationally recognized as an integral part of the Union'.[4]

The argument on which this proposal was based had three aspects. South Africa stressed the logic of the request because the two areas were so closely integrated geographically, economically and ethnically. It denied that it was legally bound to place South West Africa under trusteeship, interpreting the provisions of Article 77 of the Charter as permissive not obligatory. But beyond this, General Smuts maintained that to conclude a trusteeship agreement, as all other former mandatory powers were doing, would be contrary to the wishes of the inhabitants, and thus to the provisions of the Charter.[5] Emphasizing that the initiative for incorporation had been taken by 'the people of South West Africa', and that the majority of its inhabitants had endorsed the move, the South African delegate declared that he acted as their 'spokesman' in presenting the incorporation proposal.[6]

Only the United Kingdom supported this plan for incorporation; other United Nations members openly opposed it. They differed only on the question of whether South Africa was legally obligated to place South West Africa under trusteeship, as the Assembly resolution of February 9, 1946, had requested all mandatory powers to do. Asian and African States, the Soviet bloc and most of the Latin American countries felt there was a clear legal obligation for the Union to do so; the United States, Western European and the older Commonwealth countries did not agree. Those powers which had placed their former mandates under trusteeship insisted they had acted voluntarily in so doing, though France felt there was a moral obligation to do so. But while the Commonwealth countries remained discreetly silent, other Western delegates expressed their regret that South Africa would not submit a trusteeship agreement for South West Africa. Latin American and Asian states, in particular India, and the Soviet bloc went much farther to voice sharp criticism of the Union's decision and also of the discrimination against its African population at home.

On December 14, 1946, General Assembly resolution 65 (1) requested South Africa not to proceed with the incorporation of South West Africa into the Union, recommended that it be placed under trusteeship, and invited South Africa to submit a Trusteeship Agreement for the territory. In a letter of July 23, 1947, the Union Government replied that it would not proceed with incorporation, but also would not place South West Africa under trusteeship. Reiterating this decision at the 1947 session of the General Assembly, General Smuts declared that South Africa would maintain the *status quo* in South West Africa and continue to administer the territory in the spirit of the mandate. It would also submit annual reports, he said, on the administration of South West Africa.[7]

Behind the divergent positions lay not only an essential difference in attitude between South Africa and most members of the United Nations, but also between the mandate and trusteeship systems. The mandate system had been designed to guard against abuses by the administering power; the Permanent Mandates Commission, composed of representatives of colonial powers, was authorized to examine reports from this somewhat negative point of view. The Trusteeship system, in contrast, is based on the positive principle that it is the duty of the administering authority to advance the indigenous population towards self-government, and of the Trusteeship Council to see that this is done. Thus, the Trusteeship Council, which includes anti-colonial countries like the Soviet Union, examines reports (which are made on the basis of a questionnaire prepared by the Council itself) with a view to determining whether the administering power is stimulating the development of the Native population by 'Westernizing' or 'modernizing' them. This, of course, is far from the primary purpose of South Africa, particularly under the Nationalists, who prefer to advance the indigenous people in terms of their own tribal tradition and who place high priority on the interests of the Europeans in South West Africa and the Union.

There was an obvious shift in emphasis by the Smuts Government between the 1946 and 1947 General Assembly sessions. While H. G. Lawrence reiterated, in 1947, what he called 'the overwhelming desire for incorporation' of the inhabitants of South West Africa,[8] this no longer assumed as important a place as the strictly legal argument that there was no obligation to place the territory under trusteeship. From the other side, even the Asian nations maintained a more moderate, conciliatory attitude. Though they wanted to set a time limit within which South Africa should present a trusteeship agreement it was obvious that everyone desired a settlement. The Netherlands suggested sending the legal question to the International Court of Justice, as was done subsequently. It was becoming apparent, in fact, that some authoritative statement was needed if the deadlock was to be broken.

The legal emphasis by South African delegates increased still further in 1948, the first session after the Nationalists came into power. It was at this time, too, that the submission of annual reports on the administration of South West Africa began to loom as a major issue. The Smuts Government had assured the Assembly it would submit annual reports and chose to do so in a form used by the nations governing non-self-governing territories, i.e., under Article 73e. In accordance with its 1947 statement, the Union Government transmitted a report to the Assembly on conditions in the territory in 1946 and later complied with a request of the Trusteeship Council (which had been authorized by the General Assembly to examine the report on its behalf) that it answer a supplementary questionnaire. It did not respond, however, to the Council's invitation to send a special representative familiar with South West African affairs to answer questions which could not otherwise be clarified, a practice used for trust territories. Moreover, at the Third Session, the Nationalist representative, Mr. Eric Louw, was obviously annoyed at the Trusteeship Council's criticism of the Union's administration and felt the Council was exceeding its authority.[9] He declared that:

> although his Government was willing to supply information, that did not mean that it recognized that the United Nations had any right of supervision over the administration of the Territory.[10]

Though building on the platform already established by the Smuts Government, the Nationalists were prepared to go considerably farther in resisting United Nations supervision of South West Africa. They pointed out that South Africa was in *de facto* control of South West Africa. They categorically denied any legal or moral obligation to submit to United Nations supervision. They openly hinted that if United Nations members continued what they called 'unjust and unwarranted' criticism of South Africa, they would cease sending reports altogether. At the same time, they made known their plans for the closer association of South West Africa with the Union by providing that territory with representation in the Union Parliament.[11] This, they declared, was not incorporation, nor absorption, but rather greater self-government and thus in line with what the authors of the mandate had intended.

Other United Nations members did not accept this interpretation of the move for closer association. They divided only as to the methods which would best underline their opposition to it and induce South Africa to reconsider trusteeship. The Western nations recommended moderation; the Asian-African-Latin American countries, more extreme measures. There was exasperation and frustration in their demands that the United Nations should formally register its disapproval of South Africa on this issue.

Resentful of the criticism to which the 1946 report had been subjected in the Trusteeship Council, and of the reactions in the Fourth Committee, the South African Government not only continued with its plans for closer association of South West Africa with the Union, but also decided to discontinue transmitting reports on South West Africa to the General Assembly. In a letter of July 11, 1949,[12] J. R. Jordaan, Permanent Representative of the Union at the United Nations, informed the Secretary-General of the passage of the South West Africa Affairs Amendment Act, under which the white inhabitants of that territory would henceforth elect six members to the South African House of Assembly, and two to the Senate. The Act also provided for the election of all members of the South West Africa Legislative Assembly, and increased its rather limited legislative power. In addition, the letter provided formal notification that the Union would no longer send reports on South West Africa.

Four reasons were given as to why South Africa had decided to discontinue sending reports. In the first place, the letter stated that

> there appeared to be little understanding in the United Nations of the unique nature of the circumstances governing South West Africa's relationship to the Union.

Moreover, there seemed to be 'little recognition' of South Africa's 'assurances' that it would continue to administer South West Africa 'in the spirit of the mandate'. Beyond this, the letter came to the crux of the matter in stating that the information 'voluntarily furnished' to the United Nations had been used for what South Africa regarded as 'unwarranted criticism' of that Government's administration of South West Africa, and that, in addition, the South African Government

> could not agree that its submission of reports was indicative of its accountability to the United Nations for the administration of the territory.

Behind the legal issue lay a fundamental difference of approach easily apparent through a comparison of the report of the Trusteeship Council[13] and South Africa's detailed reply to its criticisms. The Trusteeship Council pointed out that it was 'opposed as a matter of principle, to any policy involving racial segregation'. It felt that

> great efforts should have been made to eliminate, through education and other positive measures, such apparent reasons [for segregation] as the poor housing and sanitary conditions of the indigenous inhabitants.

Even with a system of urban segregation, the Council held that 'greater attention should have been paid to the well-being of the indigenous inhabitants'.[14]

The South African representative took his stand, in response, on the fact that his Government

> was firmly convinced that the policy of encouraging the separate development of the indigenous population in its own environment was to the advantage of that population.[15]

Segregation, he insisted, was 'not a measure against any particular group'; on the contrary, it was 'the only way' to ensure 'the parallel development of differing groups', and 'quite obviously served to stimulate development'. In an unusually succinct and well-presented statement of the reasons for segregation, he maintained that it was

> to prevent race deterioration, to preserve race integrity and to give the different racial groups an opportunity to build up and develop their own race life; secondly, to protect each community against infiltration by the

other; thirdly, to prevent racial animosity which would inevitably arise if the life of the different races were inextricably mixed up; and fourthly, to prevent unemployment and the overcrowding of urban areas with all their attendant evils.[16]

While this hardly answered the Trusteeship Council's specific criticism of particular conditions in the territory, it did provide an alternative set of principles on which Native policy could be based. Clearly there could be no meeting of minds when such opposing conceptions were at issue.

Still another factor entered into the picture as far as South Africa was concerned: the internal effects not only in South West Africa but also within the Union itself of United Nations discussions. United Nations criticisms, declared Mr. G. P. Jooste,

were used with great effect by agitators to destroy the harmonious race relations upon which successful indigenous administration was inevitably dependent.[17]

Obviously, the Union was concerned lest the views expressed in New York should undermine its authority at home.

Though the position assumed by South Africa in 1949 was hardly new, the refusal to continue sending reports opened a new chapter in the relations between that country and the United Nations on the South West Africa issue. The sharp divergence in fundamental assumptions was obvious, but there were also legal questions involved: Did South Africa have an international obligation to place South West Africa under trusteeship? Was it answerable to some degree to United Nations organs? The Western countries favored legal clarification of the situation. Thus they wholeheartedly endorsed the Assembly resolution (adopted 40-7 with 4 abstentions), which asked the International Court of Justice to give an advisory opinion on the international status of South West Africa, and to decide whether or not South Africa was under an obligation to submit a trusteeship agreement for that territory.

Though the Asian-Latin American countries went along with the Western countries on the need to refer the legal issue to the Court, they differed from them in placing major emphasis on South Africa's move for closer association with South West Africa. This they hinted was *de facto* annexation or would lead to absorption. They also felt strongly that the Assembly should evidence disapproval of, and not merely regret at, South Africa's refusal to submit reports. India, which spoke of the Union's 'defiant attitude', introduced a draft resolution stating that South Africa had 'repudiated' its 1947 assurance to give reports; after debate, this wording was softened to 'withdrawn'; later, on Guatemala's motion, it went back again to 'repudiated', and was adopted in this form by the Fourth Committee over the opposition of the Western countries. But the final phrasing of the resolution was 'withdrawn its previous undertaking', and this was adopted by 33 votes to 9, with 10 abstentions. Thus the more moderate group won the battle of the words.

Those countries whose primary concern was for the indigenous inhabitants of South West Africa, rather than for a settlement, had their way, however, in the Fourth Committee. A number of petitions from the Herero, Nama and Damara tribes had been received prior to the 1949 session. Lengthy debate ensued in the Fourth Committee over whether they should be circulated as official documents. From the 131st to the 134th Meetings, the Fourth Committee also argued hotly over whether the Rev. Michael Scott should be allowed to present an oral petition on behalf of the Hereros of South West Africa. The Western countries strongly opposed hearing him, while the Asian-African-Latin American and Soviet bloc representatives approved. At the 138th Meeting, Scott was allowed to present his petition. At the following meeting, on November 28, 1949, the South African delegate announced that his Government had instructed him to withdraw because the Committee had received the petitions and heard Scott despite its protest. The cycle of counter-actions was under way.

The advisory opinion handed down by the International Court of Justice on July 6, 1950, offered a means, however, to bridge the division between South Africa and the United Nations. On one point, the Court upheld the Union: it decided by a vote of 8 to 6 that South Africa was not obligated to place South West Africa under trusteeship. On the other hand, the Court rejected the South African view that the mandate had lapsed because the original supervisory organ, the Permanent Mandates Commission, had gone out of existence. Since the mandate was still effective, the need for supervision continued, declared the Court, and South Africa was still obligated to present an annual report on South West Africa and to forward petitions from the indigenous inhabitants. The Court also held that the League's supervisory functions had been transferred to the United Nations. To meet these particular circumstances, it suggested that the United Nations should establish a special supervisory system as nearly as possible like that which had existed under the League.

Could this opinion provide an agreed settlement? South Africa refused to give an immediate response and hinted that the tone of the debate, and character of the resolution at the 1950 session would influence its future course of action. It made it clear, also, that, although it had the greatest respect for the Court, it did not consider an advisory opinion to be binding as a judgment would have been.

Every other member nation participating in the debate at the 1950 General Assembly sessions accepted the advisory opinion as the basis on which arrangements for South West Africa should be made. As usual, however, they differed on what should be the next step. The Western Powers, adopting their customary slower, more conciliatory approach, proposed setting up an *ad hoc* Committee to consider jointly with South Africa what kind of supervisory machinery should be set up to receive its reports. They forcefully opposed an Indian-sponsored draft resolution that a committee should be established to examine reports and petitions at once and without first consulting South Africa. While the United States 'deplored' the fact that the matter had not been settled before, it urged keeping the United Nations' objective in mind and adopting the most practical method of attaining it. For the first time, the United Kingdom went so far as to urge that the Assembly adopt a resolution embodying the advisory opinion and recommend that the South African Government conform to it. Thus the Western countries felt that the advisory opinion offered a sound platform for United Nations action and also a solution which South Africa would be willing to accept.

Pursuant to these discussions, the Assembly set up an *ad hoc* Committee to negotiate with South Africa on how best to establish a supervisory system, as suggested in the Court's opinion. This Committee carried on a long, and to all accounts, amicable series of discussions with South Africa. They failed because the latter refused to accept the Court's opinion as a basis of settlement.

Not until the 1953 session of the United Nations Assembly did South Africa spell out the argument with which it justified this refusal. In the 363rd Meeting of the Fourth Committee, its Ambassador, Mr. Jooste, enumerated a series of legal points on the basis of which the Union rejected the obligation to accept United Nations supervision of South West Africa. He reiterated the Union's view that the mandate had lapsed with the disappearance of the Permanent Mandates Commission, and said that it was an 'erroneous' conclusion to hold, as the Court did, that Article 80, para. 1, ensured the continuance of the mandate until trusteeship agreements were concluded. On the contrary, the Union maintained that this clause merely preserved the rights of mandatory powers until another arrangement could be made. Moreover, according to South Africa, the resolution of the final session of the League Assembly on April 18, 1946, did not indicate an expectation that the United Nations would assume responsibility for the supervision of the mandated territories, a view exactly opposite to that held by the Court.

Mr. Jooste also suggested on behalf of his Government that the Court had only declared that the League's supervisory functions had been transferred to the United Nations because it felt that a need for supervision still existed. Moreover, he maintained that if a change involved greater obligations, the law required the consent of the party on whom they were placed, and declared that United Nations supervision necessarily involved obligations greater than those assumed under the League. The United Nations had a different structure and composition, and also acted under majority rule instead of unanimity. Thus, by implication, South Africa was resting part of its objection to the Court's opinion on the increased number of non-white countries in the United Nations as compared with the League and the lack of a veto power with which to protect itself from their attacks.

Little in this South African argument was new. The same points appeared as from the beginning, though a few new supporting ones were added. The argument thus had the advantage of consistency. On the other hand, the International Court of Justice had rejected these interpretations. On the legal issue, then, the South African position was to reaffirm its original stand and to reject the Court's view, partly as a misinterpretation, and partly because it was only an advisory opinion. That this reply was made more than three years after the Court's opinion shows that South Africa had been looking in the meantime for another basis of settlement.

To the *ad hoc* Committee set up to consider with South Africa what kind of supervisory agent might be established by the United Nations, the Union produced, in fact, an interesting, if surprising proposal for a totally new kind of supervision. South Africa offered to negotiate an arrangement with the remaining Principal Allied and Associated Powers of World War I—i.e., the United States, the United Kingdom and France—in which the latter would be principals and not agents of the United Nations. It also proposed to place the administration of South West Africa under the International Court of Justice.

The international supervision was to consist of an agreement by South Africa that any two of the parties to the arrangement could bring evidence of maladministration in South West Africa before the Court. There was, however, to be no submission of annual reports or of petitions from the inhabitants of the territory. This novel plan perhaps deserved more consideration than it secured. It was rejected by the *ad hoc* Committee as being outside its terms of reference both because it was not based on the Court's advisory opinion, and because it did not include the United Nations or any agent of the United Nations as a party to the arrangement.

The *ad hoc* Committee had been empowered to examine whatever reports and petitions were forwarded to it by the South African Government. No report was sent to it, however, and the petitions received from outside were referred to the South African Government for comment in accordance with League practice. The Fourth Committee of the 1951 General Assembly decided therefore by a substantial majority—made up of almost all the Asian, Latin American and African members, plus the Soviet bloc, Sweden and Greece—to hear direct oral petitions from representatives of the Herero tribe. To this, South Africa took the strongest objection. It pointed out that the Hereros were only one tribe among the indigenous peoples of South West Africa, and maintained also that its consultations with the latter showed that the number still opposed to incorporation in the Union was diminishing. Not only did it publicize its feelings through a second 'walkout' from the Committee, but also in a strongly worded letter from the Chairman of the South African delegation to the President of the Assembly.[18]

Nonetheless, United Nations discussions on South West Africa at the 1951 session were characterized on the whole by surprising unanimity plus a moderate conciliatory tone in all the speeches except those from the Soviet bloc, Guatemala and Liberia. For the first time, there was no contest between resolutions reflecting different emphases or points of view. One resolution, sponsored by Cuba, Ecuador, Egypt, India and the Philippines, reiterated earlier ones, and invited South Africa to submit a trusteeship agreement and resume the transmission of information. The Western Powers approved this in principle, but felt it useless in the light of the South African attitude. It was adopted 33—0, with 17 abstentions.

The other, more significant, resolution was sponsored jointly by countries which had previously represented widely divergent points of view: the United States, which had maintained throughout a middle position of disapproval coupled with conciliation; Iraq, which had been quite extreme in its position in the earlier sessions, but had shifted to a more moderate approach as more likely to win South Africa's cooperation; and representatives of the more extreme group. This resolution appealed to South Africa to reconsider its position, and to resume negotiations with the *ad hoc* committee on South West Africa, which was reconstituted. Some countries, like the United Kingdom, Australia and Belgium, felt the wording was too strong and so abstained from voting, though they agreed with its essence. The Soviet bloc alone voted against the resolution, the first time that this group and the Asian-Latin American countries were on opposite sides over this issue. The resolution was adopted 39—5 with 8 abstentions. It marked a major effort to exert the collective pressure of world opinion upon South Africa.

The 1952 Assembly decided to postpone the discussion of South West Africa for another year, and urged the *ad hoc* Committee to continue on the same basis as before and report its progress in 1953. Despite its best efforts, however, the *ad hoc* Committee, now composed of representatives of the United States, Norway, Syria, Thailand and Uruguay, had no more success than in the original discussions with South Africa. Both sides simply reiterated their positions.[19]

When it presented to the 1953 Assembly the justification of its continued refusal to accept United Nations supervision of South West Africa, South Africa declared that it had negotiated with the Committee in the hope of finding a common ground on the basis of the 'sacred trust' of the mandate defined in Article 22 of the Covenant. The Court had held that the trust still existed, the United Nations wanted to ensure its continuance and South Africa was, in fact, carrying it out. Apart from the proposal it had made to the Committee, this was as far as the Union could go.

Faced with this refusal, the Assembly moved to constitute a Committee on South West Africa which was to compile a report on conditions in that area with or without the cooperation of the Union.[20] The resolution providing for this Committee was introduced by Denmark and co-sponsored by 14 other delegations. It was clearly an attempt to ensure United Nations action in the only way which still seemed open to it.

In the debate, a number of delegations, including those of countries like Thailand and Syria, normally ranged among South Africa's harsher critics, pointed out both the psychological difficulties in which South Africa was placed by the South West Africa situation, and the problem of proceeding without its cooperation. It was clear that these countries would have welcomed any overture by South Africa which involved some United Nations supervision of South West Africa. But in addition to this attitude was a new tone of exasperation, and some harsh criticism of South African policy in general as well as on this issue. One of the most outspoken in this regard was the Iraqi delegate, whose sponsorship of the moderate resolution of 1951 had been so notable. He declared forcefully that it was 'deplorable' that a member nation should 'so openly and deliberately flout the authority' of the United Nations. He went on to say that the Union Government was probably the one which had 'most frequently and seriously infringed the principles of the Charter', and ignored resolutions of the General Assembly, and

> had thus incurred the censure of the whole world and had placed its closest allies in a highly embarrassing situation.[21]

The Committee on South West Africa is to stay in existence 'until such time as an agreement is reached' between the United Nations and South Africa. It was composed originally of representatives of Brazil, Mexico, Norway, Pakistan, Syria, Thailand and Uruguay. It began its sessions on January 20, 1954, and by its 36th meeting, on June 25, 1954, had drawn up its report to the Assembly.[22] Failing to secure any help from the South African Government, which found the Committee's terms of reference 'even more inflexible' than those of the *ad hoc* Committee,[23] the Committee on South West Africa drew what information it could from published sources and United Nations specialized agencies.

About half its 1954 report was a factual description of conditions in the territory. It also included a petition from a well-known British authority on Africa, Miss Margery Perham, on behalf of a young Herero, who had been offered a scholarship for study at Oxford but not granted a passport, and a series of communications from the Rev. Michael Scott asking the Committee either to hear him or 'preferably' an authorized Herero regarding conditions and sentiment in South West Africa. The Committee decided to endorse the former petition, but felt that Scott's request fell outside its terms of reference.[24]

Consideration of this report by the 1954 General Assembly embroiled its members in a tricky procedural tangle and an open split over tactics between the more moderate Western countries and the most vigorous opponents of South African racial policies. The Committee itself proposed that voting on South West African matters should be by two-thirds majority precedure as 'an important question' under Art. 18 (2) of the Charter if South Africa would agree; otherwise it suggested seeking a further advisory opinion from the Court of International Justice as to what would be an appropriate voting procedure in the light of South Africa's mandatory obligations. South Africa rejected the two-thirds majority proposal, since the League had operated on the principle of unanimity. The United Kingdom agreed with South Africa that the proposal went beyond the terms of the former mandate; the United States found it an acceptable compromise. Bitter anti-South African sentiments were voiced in the Fourth Committee before both resolutions were accepted.

In plenary meeting, India succeeded in omitting the clause requiring South African approval to the two-thirds majority vote, and thus made unnecessary the appeal to the Court. This ran strongly contrary, however, to the feeling of many representatives. The United States, for example, decided to protest by not participating in the vote on the substance of the report, and refused membership on the Committee. Norway and Thailand withdrew from their Committee membership. In the face of this obvious disapproval, the more extreme members reversed their stand, and a new resolution was carried which referred the question of voting procedures to the International Court. Thailand then agreed to serve again on the Committee, and the United States accepted appointment. Thus, in the end, the breach was healed and the more moderate view prevailed.

Nonetheless, the temporary break in the virtual unanimity previously achieved on this issue undercut the moral force of United Nations action in this session. The very vehemence of the speeches criticizing South Africa and the tendency to refer to domestic policies alienated those holding more moderate views. Moreover, the powers holding trust territories could hardly fail to feel that the supervisory authority of the United Nations was being pushed beyond reasonable bounds. The experience proved to be a warning against pressing the more moderate minority farther than it was prepared to go. It also demonstrated the great difficulties confronted by the United Nations in making its influence effective in an issue on which a Member State is intransigent.

The breach widened irretrievably in 1955. The International Court of Justice handed down an advisory opinion on June 7, 1955,[25] approving a two-thirds majority for voting on South West African matters. Mr. E. H. Louw, Minister of External Affairs, responded by suggesting that 'the Court in this case seems to have been guided by other than strictly legal motives', and declared that:

> We do not care tuppence whether the United Nations observes the two-thirds majority rule or the unanimity rule in dealing with South West African affairs, because we have consistently said the United Nations has no right to concern itself with the affairs of South West Africa.[26]

The Committee on South West Africa presented a further, still longer report to the Assembly.[27] Not only did South Africa retain unchanged its previous attitude of non-cooperation, but it formally withdrew its offer to enter into an agreement with the three remaining Principal Allied and Associated Powers. When the Fourth Committee decided to permit the Rev. Michael Scott to present oral testimony on South West Africa, Mr. Louw declared that it had gone 'out of its way to affront a Member State of the organization', and closed the New York office of its United Nations Delegation in protest.[28] All hope of a compromise was at an end, if indeed there had ever been any.

Already, in 1954, South Africa had transferred the administration of Native affairs from the South West Africa Administrator to the Union Minister of Native Affairs through the South West Africa Native Affairs Administration Act, 1954.[29] Described as a purely administrative arrangement, the Act also placed all Native Reserves in South West Africa under the South African Native Trust. The Union continues to maintain that it has not incorporated South West Africa,[30] but the act marked a further integration which leaves relatively little except local taxation under local control. In any case, there has long been little, if any, essential difference between non-European policies in the Union and in adjoining South West Africa.

On the basis of its investigations, the Committee on South West Africa reported to the 1955 Assembly that:

> after nearly four decades of administration under the Mandates System, the Native inhabitants are still not participating in the political development of the Territory, their participation in the economic development is restricted to that of labourers and the social and educational services for their benefit are far from satisfactory.

It declared also that 'Racial discrimination is prevalent throughout the Territory'. Comparing conditions with those of the year before, it found 'no significant improvement in the moral and material welfare of the Native inhabitants'. Its final conclusion was that:

> the main efforts of the Administration are directed almost exclusively in favour of the European inhabitants of the Territory, often at the expense of the Native population.[31]

The non-European inhabitants of South West Africa numbered 393,700 by 1954, while the European population had expanded greatly to 53,600, of whom about 60 per cent were Afrikaans-speaking, 25 per cent German-speaking and 15 per cent English-speaking.

The South West Africa issue before the United Nations highlights two matters of particular importance: a fundamental disagreement over what should be the policy of an administering country towards the indigenous population; and what means should, and can, the United Nations take to make its views influential. South Africa continued to maintain throughout the negotiations that it was treating South West Africa as 'a sacred trust', and that it was developing the indigenous inhabitants in the way which it felt was best for their interests, i.e., along the path of separate development, and in accordance with their Native institutions. The United Nations, with equal persistence, upheld the position that the political, economic and social development of the indigenous people should prepare them ultimately to assume a full share of the fruits and responsibilities in these areas of life. Behind these two attitudes, of course, lay also a different weight on the interests of the European inhabitants of South West Africa, whom South Africa looked on as by far its most important population element, while the United Nations attempted to weight all the different groups evenly, and had a special concern for the non-Europeans.

These divergent views were further complicated by the persistent refusal of South Africa to accept any United Nations supervision of South West Africa. Those countries which had some sympathy both for the problems arising out of South Africa's huge non-European majority, and its desire to cope with these problems in its own particular way, were alienated by its unwillingness to conform at all to the pressure of world opinion or, still more serious to some of them, to the advisory opinion of the International Court of Justice. Thus, South Africa's intransigence in this regard cost it the express or tacit support of countries like the United Kingdom, which were unwilling to censure South African racial policies as such.

On the other hand, the forthright criticisms of countries like India, coupled with their occasional use of their majority support for declarations or policies which the more conservative minority was unwilling to endorse, caused a certain revulsion which worked to South Africa's advantage. By trying to do too much through the United Nations, these countries tended in fact to undercut what that organization was able to do. Thus the two extreme positions—of South Africa, and of its most hostile critics—both acted to work against their own interests and, of course, against those of United Nations authority in this issue.

The Treatment of Indians in South Africa

Side by side with the discussions on South West Africa have gone the United Nations debates on the treatment of Indians in South Africa. Referred to the United Nations by India when General Smuts' United Party Government passed the Asiatic Land Tenure and Indian Representation Act (as recounted in Chapter 14: see p. 363), this dispute was complicated by the strong emotions it roused both in India and the Union. Moreover, although technically this question was handled separately from that concerning South West Africa, the feelings engendered over the one inevitably reacted upon attitudes assumed in the other issue.

The Indian Government referred the treatment of Indians in South Africa to the Second Part of the First Session of the General Assembly under Articles

10 and 14. In so doing, Madame Pandit, its representative, emphasized that the Asiatic Land Tenure and Indian Representation Act of which it complained had led to badly strained relations between India and South Africa, and also violated human rights in a way contrary to the objects of the Charter. On the latter point, she cited those parts of the Preamble which affirmed 'faith in fundamental rights', and the determination 'to promote social progress and better standards of life in larger freedom'.[32] In this context, the Indian Government maintained that the issue was political, rather than legal, and clearly belonged in the jurisdiction of the United Nations.

Answering for the Union, General Smuts stressed that the issue was purely domestic in nature, and thus outside the competence of the General Assembly. Art. 2 (7), the domestic jurisdiction clause of the Charter, he declared, constituted an 'over-riding principle qualifying . . . all the provisions of the Charter' except enforcement measures, which were not at issue.[33] Although he recognized that certain formal treaty obligations might provide an exception to the limitation of domestic jurisdiction, he denied, with strict legal justification, that the Cape Town Agreement (see p. 362) was a treaty. A further exception, he suggested, 'might be sought in the direction of human rights and fundamental freedoms',[34] but since no internationally recognized formulation of such rights was yet in existence, South Africa had assumed no such specific obligations under the Charter. Moreover, he forcefully denied that South Africa had infringed any 'elementary human rights'.[35]

General Smuts declared that he had no objection to a free discussion of the case in the United Nations, though he refused to admit that the United Nations had a right to intervene in the matter, and held that a General Assembly recommendation on the subject would be intervention. He proposed, however, that the General Assembly seek an advisory opinion from the International Court of Justice concerning the issue of jurisdiction.

Both in the Joint First and Sixth Committee discussions, and the Plenary sessions, United Nations members divided into two groups: those who considered the problem to be primarily political, and therefore within the competence of the Assembly; and those who felt the issue was primarily legal and thus should be referred to the International Court of Justice.[36] Those stressing the moral-political aspects were the Asian-Arab-African countries, several Latin American States, the Soviet Union and its satellites. The core of the second group comprised the United States, and the older members of the Commonwealth: Great Britain, Canada, Australia and New Zealand. Neither group, however, showed any sympathy for South Africa's policies of racial discrimination. Moreover, the division was between those holding the traditional view of international law and those with a broader interpretation of the sphere of international authority, rather than along racial lines. Thus, after the proposal to refer the matter to the International Court was voted down, the resolution accepted by the Joint Committee, and subsequently by a two-thirds vote of the Assembly, was jointly sponsored by France and Mexico.

This resolution, 44 (1), marked a high water-mark in United Nations' pressure in this issue. It declared that the treatment of Indians in South Africa should be in conformity with 'the international obligations under the agreements' between India and South Africa (in particular, the Cape Town Agreement), and 'the relevant provisions' of the Charter. It requested the two Governments to report at the next session of the United Nations 'measures adopted to this effect'. This resolution received 32 votes, those of 11 Latin American, 3 Western European, and 12 Asian-African countries, and the 6 of the Soviet bloc. Opposed were the United States and 4 Commonwealth, 4 European and 6 Latin-American countries. Along with Australia, 3 Latin American, and 3 European States abstained.[37]

Between the First and Second Assemblies, the two Governments exchanged communications[38] following an initial letter from Pandit Nehru to General Smuts offering to enter into discussions. South Africa suggested that India return its High Commissioner to the Union so that the two Governments could enter into direct negotiations through the customary channels. From its side, India proposed a conference between accredited representatives to be held on the basis of the General Assembly's resolution. Smuts rejected this basis for negotiations, however, on the ground that the resolution infringed domestic jurisdiction. Thus no progress was made in reaching a compromise and, on the contrary, the reports of the two Governments to the Second Assembly[39] incorporated mutual recriminations.

The general debate in the 1947 Assembly indicated that a majority of the members considered the treatment of Indians in South Africa a denial of human rights and freedom, and a violation of the Charter which the Assembly was competent to consider. At the same time, the temper of the Assembly was more restrained than during the previous session. A critical Indian resolution failed to receive the necessary two-thirds vote.[40] Preoccupied with other pressing problems, such as the Palestine question, Assembly members urged that the parties to the dispute reconcile their differences through direct negotiations and a round table conference.

Before the Third Assembly met, the Nationalists had come into office, having gained some support perhaps from public irritation over the Indian-South Africa controversy in the United Nations. Despite a vigorous attack by India on what it called the *Herrenvolk* mentality underlying the Nationalists' apartheid policies, the emphasis in the Third Assembly was again on promoting conciliation between the parties. The resolution,[41] adopted by a substantial majority, was couched in the most general terms and merely 'invited' India and South Africa to enter into a round table conference 'taking into consideration the purposes and principles of the Charter of the United Nations and the Declaration of Human Rights'. No mention was made of the 1946 resolution, in order to make it easier for South Africa to participate in such a conference. At the same time, South Africa's own resolution denying Assembly competence in this issue[42] was defeated, while its legalistic arguments were widely criticized as being too narrow an interpretation of the Charter.

More important than the Assembly resolution in advancing the possibility of a round table conference were the personal conversations between Prime Minister Malan and Pandit Nehru at the Conference of Commonwealth Prime Ministers in London in April 1949. From July to September 1949, letters were exchanged on plans for such a conference; in February 1950, preliminary talks in Cape Town led to an agreement to hold a round table conference.

These negotiations had been interspersed, however, with protests by India against further discriminatory legislation affecting South African Indians, such as the withdrawal of the franchise provisions of the 1946 Act (of which the

Indians had refused to make use), and the extension of segregation to trade and business. When the South African Parliament began consideration of the Group Areas Act, India strongly urged postponement of action on this legislation pending the outcome of the conference. Dr. Malan made it clear, however, that the measure would be enacted into law before the conference met. In view of this fact, India informed South Africa, in June 1950, that it would not participate in the round table conference which had been agreed upon in February. At no subsequent point was there so much chance for an Indian-South African round table conference.

These developments deeply disturbed the Fifth Assembly and led it to pass another critical and far-reaching resolution.[43] This held that racial segregation was 'necessarily based on a doctrine of racial discrimination', and called on the South African Government not to implement the Group Areas Act.[44] The Assembly again recommended a round table conference, but decided that, if this did not take place, it would set up a three-member Good Offices Commission to assist in negotiations between South Africa and India, and aid a 'satisfactory solution' in accordance with the principles and purposes of the Charter and the Universal Declaration of Human Rights.

This Commission, established by Assembly resolution 615 (VII) of December 5, 1952, and consisting of representatives of Cuba, Syria and Yugoslavia, had to report to the 1953 Assembly that the Union refused to make use of its services because it did not consider the body constitutional. Out of a hot debate came a controversial resolution which expressed regret not only that South Africa failed to make use of the Good Offices Commission, but also that it was continuing to implement the Group Areas Act, and had proceeded with further legislation 'contrary to the Charter and the Universal Declaration of Human Rights', including the Immigrants Regulation Amendment Act, which virtually prohibited the entry to South Africa of wives and children of South African Indians.[45] The Assembly even went so far as to declare that these actions of South Africa were 'not in keeping with its obligations and responsibilities under the Charter of the United Nations'. Neither this censure nor subsequent efforts of the same kind had any noticeable effect, however, upon South African policies.

Although the Nationalist Government continued to participate in United Nations sessions on the treatment of Indians in South Africa, it assumed a more legalistic attitude than the previous Smuts' Government. The latter had been prepared to discuss the facts of the case, although it challenged the authority of the Assembly to take any action on the issue. In 1950, the representative of the Nationalist Government denied the right of the Assembly even to discuss the question.[46] Moreover, since that session, South Africa has tended to depart from the temperate language of earlier discussions, and to suggest that India brought the case of the treatment of Indians in South Africa to the United Nations for ulterior purposes, possibly reflecting India's own imperialistic aspirations in Africa.

Since the case revolves around the issue of human rights, it is important to consider the South African definition of fundamental rights. Speaking for the Smuts Government at the 1947 Assembly, Mr. Lawrence declared that there are 'certain basic rights with which no one could disagree': the right to exist, freedom of conscience and speech, and free access to the courts.[47] None of these rights, he maintained, had the Union violated. Human dignity was not a human right, according to the South African point of view, because the basis of human dignity had never been clearly defined.

The Nationalist representative, in the 1948 Session, was still less specific. He declared that 'the basic human rights and freedom which had always been recognized in international law had not been denied to any of its citizens, of whatever race, colour or religion'. He also suggested that South Africa's citizens enjoyed 'human liberties and fundamental freedoms perhaps to a greater degree than citizens of many other countries'.[48]

Both in the Third and Fifth Sessions, the South African delegate rejected the view that the Declaration of Human Rights could serve as a basis for United Nations intervention in a case otherwise within domestic jurisdiction. Thus, Dr. T. E. Dönges declared in the 41st Meeting of the *ad hoc* Political Committee of the Fifth Session that the Declaration was 'still very much a counsel of perfection and a declaration of ideals' which 'created no obligations'.[49]

It was apparent that the views of both the Smuts and Malan Governments on this subject were far more limited than those expressed in Resolution 103 (I) 2, on human rights adopted by the First Session of the United Nations General Assembly. This resolution declared that 'it is in the high interests of humanity to put an immediate end to religious and so-called racial persecution and discrimination'. Moreover, it called on Governments and responsible authorities to conform both to the letter and the spirit of the Charter of the United Nations, and to take the most prompt and energetic steps to that end.[50] But despite the obvious disapproval of many United Nations members, the Nationalist Government rapidly implemented apartheid after 1948, as has been described. Thus they extended the type of policies which gave rise to the original dispute and also led to the collapse of plans for the round table conference with India.

As far as direct negotiations were concerned, South Africa maintained that it was still willing to participate in a conference on the basis agreed upon in February 1950. It continued to reject the 1946 resolution, however, and subsequent ones which *inter alia* condemned the Group Areas Act. It also refused to cooperate in the appointment of a Good Offices Commission, or to give it facilities when it was set up.

The Indian Government, from its side, proved no more willing to compromise than did the South Africans. While the Pakistani Government agreed, in 1951, to a round table conference on the basis of the February 1950 agreement, and suggested that it be held in Karachi, India refused to participate unless South Africa suspended the Group Areas Act. Approximately the same sequence of events took place late in 1954. Thus the Indian Government shares responsibility for the fact that such a conference never met.

In its persistent attacks on South Africa in the United Nations, the Indian Government frequently emphasized that racial discrimination in South Africa had deeply disillusioned Asians and Africans and destroyed their faith in Western protestations concerning human rights. During the 1952 Assembly sessions, the Indian delegate described the non-European defiance campaign in South Africa as a symbol of a 'world-wide struggle to maintain the dignity and worth of the human person'.[51] They emphasized to the representatives of South Africa the extent to which world public opinion condemned the actions of their country, and reaffirmed hope that apartheid policies would ultimately be abandoned.

In addition to the pressure it exerted in United Nations debates, India also maintained a boycott on South African goods during this period. In 1954, the South African Government declared that it would not continue to accept the anomalous situation of India having diplomatic relations with the Union at the same time that trade sanctions were imposed against it. On request, India closed its High Commissioner's office in the Union on July 1, 1954.

Most directly concerned over this dispute have been the older members of the Commonwealth—the United Kingdom, Canada, Australia and New Zealand—which are most closely associated with both South Africa and India. Throughout the controversy, these four countries maintained basically similar positions. They doubted the competence of the Assembly to consider the dispute and were convinced that the issue of jurisdiction should be referred for settlement to the International Court of Justice. They felt that direct negotiations between the parties to the dispute were far preferable to Assembly debates. They agreed, as Australia said, that negotiations 'might be more fruitful if undertaken directly by the parties concerned, instead of under conditions imposed beforehand by the United Nations'.[52] Repeatedly they urged South Africa and India to enter into such negotiations, which were the characteristic way of settling disputes within the Commonwealth itself.

The United Kingdom argued for a legal rather than political decision on the ground that it would be 'authoritative', with unquestioned legal validity, which would put it on a stronger basis.[53] The question, it declared, was 'not what are the merits, but what are the powers . . . that we possess in such a matter'.[54] The Canadians also emphasized the need for a Court opinion to get 'a proper determination of the facts, an authoritative exposition of the law, and a judicial application of the law to the facts so determined'.[55] Domestic jurisdiction, they felt, 'should not be given an extensive interpretation which would render other important provisions of the Charter meaningless or insignificant'; at the same time it should be given sufficient scope to maintain a reasonable balance between national and international spheres of action.[56]

Distinctive among these four Commonwealth countries was Australia's stress on protecting domestic jurisdiction against possible United Nations encroachments. It moved from a position of moderate legalism in the First Session to a much more rigorous view in the Fifth Session, when it supported the South African stand that 'the United Nations has no jurisdiction to discuss the question'.[57] In particular, the Australians felt strongly that the Assembly had no right to comment on such specific domestic legislation as the Group Areas Act.

The older Commonwealth countries abstained from voting on the issue of treatment of Indians in South Africa except to support outside means of getting a settlement. In the First Session, all except Australia, which abstained, voted against Resolution 44 (1) because they supported referring the problem of jurisdiction to the Court. In the Third Session, Australia, Canada, and New Zealand endorsed the resolution requesting a round table conference, while the United Kingdom abstained. In the Fifth Session, Australia joined South Africa in voting against United Nations competence in the issue and also against the resolution. Thus, as in the South West Africa issue, the older Commonwealth countries attempted scrupulously to refrain from imposing conditions or criticizing South Africa except in relation to a Court opinion.

The United States supported the view that every effort should be made to promote conciliation and direct negotiations between the parties. As in the South West Africa issue it followed a moderate, middle line of seeking the most practical course of action consonant with upholding the authority of the Assembly. Although, in the First Session, American delegates favored referring the issue of jurisdiction to the International Court of Justice, they later defended the competence of the Assembly to settle a dispute which was 'undeniably moral and political in nature'.[58] This was also because, in contrast to the older Commonwealth countries, the United States believes the Assembly can determine its own competence without resort to a judicial body.[59]

While in the South West Africa issue the United States carefully refrained from commenting on racial conditions, it took a public stand against racial discrimination and segregation during discussion of the treatment of Indians in South Africa. At the same time, it couched its criticism of South African policies in moderate language, and presented its comments in the context of American problems and experience. 'The promotion of respect for human rights throughout the world', its delegate pointed out on May 10, 1949, in the 266th Meeting of the First Committee, 'was an extremely delicate task which required progressive and carefully considered action over a long period of time. . . .'[60]

The Soviet Union was critical of South African discriminatory practices but played a less active role in the debates than might have been expected. It abstained almost completely, for example, in the Third and Fifth Session. The Soviet delegate sharply opposed referring the question of jurisdiction to the International Court of Justice, and argued that this 'diversionary' action was intended to transfer the matter 'from the political to the juridical plane'.[61] Respect for fundamental human rights and freedoms was a basic principle of the Charter, the Soviet delegate maintained, not only obligating all members to abolish racial discrimination within their countries, but also making it the task of the United Nations to uproot such 'social evils'.[62] Its representative, Vyshinsky, interpreted Art. 2 (7) as meaning that 'the Charter does not require Members of the United Nations to submit such matters for examination by the United Nations . . .' but at the same time 'does not forbid . . . [their] submission'[63]; positively, he supported the Assembly's competence to decide its own jurisdiction.

The most violent attacks on South Africa were made by Soviet satellites. While the Soviet delegate refrained from committing himself until the third meeting of the Joint Committee, the Ukrainian delegate, supported by the Byelorussians, spoke immediately after India and South Africa, and stressed the sanctity of international agreements, and South Africa's violation of fundamental rights.[64] The Polish delegate sought to identify South African apartheid policies with the racial practices of Nazism, and to incite anti-Western feeling among the Asians. In the 1946 plenary session, he declared that because he had 'lived under the racial discrimination of the Herrenvolk idea', he could 'not remain indifferent to the similar fate of others'.[65] He then pointed out that discriminatory legislation in South Africa was based on a factor over which no one had control, i.e., color, and added 'it is not only an issue between two Member States of our Organization, but a problem between two continents, Europe and Asia'.[66]

The Soviet bloc used the treatment of Indians in South Africa as a convenient platform for the denunciation of Western countries, particularly the United States and the United Kingdom. The Ukrainian delegate called the Union a 'homeland of neo-fascism', and referred to a statement of the South African delegate as couched in 'slave-owner's language'.[67] The Byelorussian delegate, in turn, accused the United States of 'continuing to support and assist that policy of discrimination'.[68] Fascism, racialism and capitalism were thus combined and jointly attacked.

Following their abstentions in 1950, the Soviet bloc became more temperate in 1951 and 1952, only the Polish delegate maintaining the fascist-capitalist line of attack.[69] Yugoslavia, which had been one of the most vehement critics of South Africa, parted company with the Soviet bloc and thereafter adopted a more conciliatory though still critical attitude towards South Africa.

The attitude of other countries reflected two contrasting points of view. Such nations as Belgium, the Netherlands, Luxembourg, and Argentina generally considered the legal issue of jurisdiction to be paramount. However, a sizable bloc of Member States advocated a broad interpretation of the powers of the United Nations with respect to human rights and freedoms, and consistently supported the cause of India.

It is important to note the voting strength of this coalition composed of certain Asian-African, South American, and Western European nations. On human rights issues they are customarily supported by the Soviet bloc. These States hold a clear majority of the votes and, since 1956, can muster the two-thirds majority required to pass substantive resolutions in the General Assembly.

United Nations consideration of the Indian-South African controversy had no noticeable effect on the racial discrimination policies of the South African Government. If anything, it strengthened the domestic support of the Nationalist Government and intensified anti-Indian sentiment. European South Africans endorse residential segregation and no major political party supports repeal of the Group Areas Act.

In a dispute of this nature the United Nations is limited to formal resolutions expressing international public opinion. A number of countries doubt the wisdom of such solemn, official statements which, in this controversy, have no effect on South Africa's actions and tend to weaken the United Nations by disclosing its lack of effectiveness. These States emphasized the need for direct negotiations between India and South Africa as the only practicable way of securing some change in the treatment of Indians. Yet, as long as the South African and Indian Governments refuse to shift from their basic positions, direct negotiations remain impossible. Thus it may be argued that the only course open to the Assembly is the continued assertion of a moral stand against racial discrimination.

Since discrimination on grounds of race has such a strong emotional impact on non-white peoples throughout the world, it is hardly possible for the United Nations to ignore it. Nor can Western countries be oblivious of the fact that Asian and African States judge them largely on their attitude toward racial discrimination, and that the Soviet bloc exploits this situation whenever possible. In this context, the measures which many European South Africans consider essential to maintain the social structure and internal racial peace of their country provide a serious liability to the Western world.

United Nations Commission on the Racial Situation in South Africa

Still more controversial and far reaching in its implications than the consideration of the positions of Indians in South Africa has been the detailed analysis of the whole racial situation in that country by a Commission set up for this purpose in 1953, and given an annually renewed mandate until December 1955. Not only South Africa but the United Kingdom, for example, considered the Commission 'illegal', as an obvious interference in the domestic affairs of a Member State.[70] Those responsible for establishing it declared, in contrast, that apartheid policies had created a 'dangerous tension' in South Africa, 'with serious consequences for harmony among nations and peace in the world'.[71]

Already, on September 12, 1952, 13 Asian-Arab delegations asked by letter for the inclusion on the General Assembly agenda of 'The question of race conflict in South Africa resulting from the policies of apartheid of the Government of South Africa'.[72] At this time, it will be remembered, the African-Indian passive disobedience campaign was in full progress in the Union. Despite persistent South African protests, and appeals for 'the protection inscribed in Article 2, paragraph 7 of the Charter',[73] and the grave concern of several Western delegations, the item was included on the 1952 agenda by 45 votes (including the United States) to 6, with 8 abstentions. The same numbers rejected a South African motion of incompetence in the *ad hoc* Political Committee. In the vote on the resolution establishing the Commission, however, all the Western and a few Latin American countries abstained, 23 Delegations in all. Thus the 35 votes which set up the Commission came exclusively from Asian, Arab, Latin American and Communist states.

Despite the natural misgivings regarding the Commission, it conducted itself with great sobriety and sense of responsibility. It was composed of three persons who served in their personal capacities, not as representatives of their Governments.[74]

South Africa consistently refused to allow the Commission to enter the Union on the ground that it was unconstitutional. Unable for this reason to study South African conditions at first-hand, the Commission first examined the declarations of Union politicians, studied its principal laws, examined memoranda submitted to it and heard six witnesses, including the Rev. Michael Scott, E. S. Sachs (see p. 71) and John Hatch, author of *The Dilemma of South Africa*. For its second report, the Commission summarized recent developments in the racial situation, brought up to date its analysis of the principal acts providing for differentiation in the treatment of various population groups in the Union, and undertook a detailed study of the South African economy with a view to indicating how economic development might help to improve relations between these groups. The third report concentrated on developments between 1954 and 1955. In the Commission's own words, the first report set out to give 'a clinical picture and diagnosis'; the second, 'proposals for therapy'; and the third, 'a progress report'.[75]

On the basis of its investigations, the Commission concluded in its first report that the situation in South Africa was one of great seriousness, which 'is, to say the least, "likely to impair the general welfare or friendly relations among nations", in the sense of Article 14 of the Charter'. Listing measures of racial discrimination currently in force in the Union, it declared that:

> Four-fifths of the population are thereby reduced to a humiliating level of inferiority which is injurious to human dignity and makes the full development of personality impossible or very difficult.[76]

It seemed 'highly unlikely, and indeed improbable' that the apartheid policy would ever be accepted willingly by the masses 'subjected to discrimination', it declared, or that any efforts by the Government or by South African Europeans would convince them of its justice. Thus, as this policy developed, the Commission felt that the situation 'became daily more explosive and more menacing to internal peace and to the foreign relations of the Union of South Africa'.[77]

Recognizing the very great difficulties of the situation the Union confronted, the Commission foresaw the need for changes along four lines if conditions were appreciably to improve. Foremost it put the economic development of the whole of South Africa; then, 'the actual diminution of the social inequality' now so great; in addition, the opening of 'real' opportunities for individual and group progress; and last, but of decisive importance, 'the sincere wish' of the Government and European population 'progressively to eliminate discrimination'.[78] To aid such a program, the Commission felt that the Union should be offered 'at an opportune moment', all the 'material and intellectual assistance' which an international organization could and should offer one of its members 'in difficulty'. This, it suggested, might include studies, conciliation machinery, and technical, economic, social and financial assistance for the progressive development of all ethnic groups in the South African community.[79]

When this report came before the General Assembly, it met a violent attack from the South African representative, who accused the Commission of being partisan and with an anti-European bias, and declared, but without specifying, that the report was not factual. The United Kingdom, Belgium, Australia, France, Colombia, and Peru, among others, raised doubts about the competence of the *ad hoc* Political Committee to 'intervene' in such clearly domestic issues, and suggested seeking an advisory opinion from the International Court of Justice in the matter. The United States did not agree that the Commission's report constituted 'intervention', but strongly doubted the wisdom of continuing the Commission, seeing no reason for further studies or any prospects of results. They were overborne, however, by 38 Asian-Arab-Latin American-Communist votes, which not only kept the Commission in existence, but instructed it to study the racial situation in South Africa in relation to Article 14 of the Charter, and to suggest measures to alleviate the situation and promote a 'peaceful settlement'.[80]

Against a background of those solutions to the racial problem being currently proposed within the Union itself, and relevant experience with racial issues volunteered by certain other countries, the Commission, in its second report, approached carefully what it called 'The Possibilities of a Peaceful Settlement'.[81] Recognizing that South Africa is 'sociologically and historically unique', it yet found that all the great and promising experiments to develop racial harmony, such as those of Brazil, Haiti, the United States and the Soviet Union, were based on a common principle: 'mutual racial tolerance and a recognition that the different ethnic groups are of equal human dignity'.

To the warnings embodied in its previous report, the Commission added the explicit fear that 'the forces of agitation and subversion' might find the atmosphere of tension in the Union 'an increasingly favorable soil'. It felt, too, that growing non-European resentment against the white groups might create 'a permanent current of conflict and revolt' within the country. This in turn might easily result, it pointed out, in the growth of insecurity on the part of the whites to the point where it would wipe out the minimum of trust and human contact necessary for normal existence.

To prevent such developments, the Commission saw hope in increased interracial contacts such as those sponsored by the Dutch Reformed Church and the Institute of Race Relations. To raise the standard of living of the non-Europeans would also help quickly to reduce internal tension, it pointed out, and asked whether still greater efforts could not be made in this regard. Though this might involve 'painful sacrifices', the Commission reiterated its earlier belief that, under such circumstances, South Africa could well appeal to international cooperation for help. It even went so far as to suggest a committee of technical experts, to be set up at South Africa's request, to catalogue all the forms of assistance the United Nations and Specialized Agencies might supply.

Specifically, the Commission proposed reducing and ultimately abolishing the system of migrant labor; organizing adult and general education for non-Europeans; eliminating the color bar in industry and coupling this with the principle of equal pay for equal work; opening the apprentice system to non-Europeans; allowing the latter to become members of trade unions with full rights to collective bargaining; and 'by rapidly succeeding stages' abolishing the pass laws. Along with this emphasis on economic change, however, the Commission stated its conviction that

> steps to achieve political equality among ethnic groups are of prime importance and cannot be continually deferred without serious danger.

It thus ended its basic ideas for a peaceful settlement by recommending a policy which,

> while being careful to avoid wounding susceptibilities and accepting inevitable delays in implementation, would aim at associating the non-white masses to an ever-increasing extent in the political management of the South African national community, of which they form [it declared] an indispensable, irreplaceable and inseparable part.[82]

The debate on this second report in the *ad hoc* Political Committee of the Ninth General Assembly opened with a fiery exchange between the South African representative and the Chairman of the Commission. The former criticized the Commission's sources of information, and particularly the extensive use it had made of memoranda provided by the African National

Congress and South African Indian Congress, both of which, he maintained, were Communist-dominated. He felt the account given of the Bantu Education Act was especially misleading. As for the Commission's proposed solutions, he declared they had been worked out from 'superficial knowledge of the real situation based on unreliable information'.[83] Mr. Santa Cruz, from his side, defended the Commission's use of material and impartiality.[84] That the latter was the more convincing seemed evidenced by the fact that the resolution which kept the Committee in being was accepted by the largest number of votes—40—which had yet endorsed that body, including, for the first time, Norway, Sweden and Greece.

It was on the issue of competence that the major opposition continued to focus. The United Kingdom, Australia, New Zealand, Belgium, the Netherlands, and France agreed with South Africa that the policies of apartheid were matters of domestic jurisdiction, and these States, together with Canada, Luxembourg and Colombia voted against the resolution. The United States felt the Assembly could justifiably concern itself with situations like that in South Africa, but favored general recommendations in support of the ideals of a multi-racial society rather than singling out a single State for censure. Hence, along with 9 other States, it abstained from voting. The majority maintained its stand, however, that the Preamble to the Charter and articles referring to human rights gave the Assembly competence to consider situations where Governments were moving away from, rather than towards the goals of the Charter.[85]

The 1955 General Assembly witnessed both the sharpest rejection by South Africa of United Nations concern with its affairs, and the most penetrating and sophisticated approach to that country's problems. Speaking in the opening Plenary Sessions, W. C. du Plessis, South African High Commissioner in Canada (later Ambassador to the United States) and its chief delegate, called the annual attacks on his country 'a sort of "Roman holiday"' and declared that the Union was no longer prepared to continue replying to them.[86] The specific recommendations of the Commission on the Racial Situation in South Africa, he declared in particular, had gone 'to the utmost limits in transgressing' Art. 2, para. 7, which safeguarded domestic jurisdiction. Largely supported by the South African press and European South African public opinion, the Union Government has decided henceforth officially to ignore United Nations discussions on its problems, as it has long rejected United Nations competence to hold them.

Yet it was in this year that the third report of the Commission made its most discerning comments on South Africa's need for international solidarity. Calling the Union's situation that 'of a colony without a mother country', it pointed out the sense of insecurity which inevitably grips a white minority which cannot turn for reinforcement to a powerful outside State composed of its own people. While the Union's membership in the Commonwealth helps to reassure the English-speaking in South Africa, the Afrikaners have no such consolation. All the more need, therefore, for South Africa to seek the solidarity which the United Nations tries to create among its members.[87]

This solidarity is not a racial one, it pointed out, but a 'human solidarity'. It is based 'on a common striving towards justice and social progress according to common and generally accepted principles'. In this kind of solidarity, the

Commission saw the most effective guarantee of the security 'so anxiously sought' by minorities such as the white minority in South Africa against the threats which the future seems to hold.

It was paradoxical, in a way, that the body which most ardently endorsed United Nations technical aid and moral support to South Africa if that country was willing to accept them for the purposes defined in the United Nations Charter was the one which South Africa most resented. Yet the very fact that the Commission, like the United Nations, upheld racial equality as an ultimate goal made it inevitable.

South Africans speak often of their desire to be left alone to wrestle with their huge problems in their own terms. Not a few members of the United Nations sympathize with this desire. But the great majority of its members reject the notion that racial discrimination is an internal issue. Regardless of whether South Africa is prepared to cooperate or not, they are determined to press on through whatever channels are open to them to exert whatever influence they can upon the South African situation.

It is true that this increasing concern in the United Nations with the internal affairs of a Member State alienates the more conservative countries, and tends to weaken what is at best a frail instrument of international cooperation. From the other side, it has intensified South African determination to resist the moral exhortations which flow from the General Assembly. It has helped to build a wall between South Africa and the organized international community rather than to bring them closer together.

Yet it is also true that racial discrimination has become a symbol of oppression throughout the world. If the South African Government can handle successfully its vast racial problem along its own lines, it can perhaps afford to flout the opinions of so high a proportion of the world's people. But should it fail at home, to whom will it turn for help when it is in need?

CHAPTER 16

WHERE IS SOUTH AFRICA GOING?

Where is South Africa going? Is it possible for the Nationalists to maintain the kind of apartheid they have been spelling out in legislation in the face of that country's dynamic economic development, which depends so greatly on African labor? In other words, can laws backed by force maintain, and even create a pattern of life in South Africa which is so different from that which would be created by economic forces if they were left free to operate?

Where should South Africa be heading? Today, as we have seen, there are at least four distinctive answers to this question being offered in the Union. They are offered in all sincerity by different groups as means to cope with the basic problem involved in the attempt to combine racial separation with economic integration, and European self-preservation with moral conscience.

Two of these answers are radical ones, in the sense of going to the heart of the problem. They are the answers of ideal apartheid, on the one hand, and of the Liberals on the other. Between them stand the much less clear-cut but politically more important answers being offered by the Union's major political parties: the Nationalists and the United Party.

The proponents of ideal, or territorial apartheid begin with two convincing assumptions: that every racial group should be able to fulfil its own potentialities; and that non-Europeans can never reach their full development under the conditions existing in the European areas. Since, therefore, there will always be discrimination against them in these areas, the answer of ideal apartheid is to build a community—perhaps ultimately, a Bantustan—where the African will be as free to develop himself as are Europeans in the European areas.

Those who support this view are well aware that it would entail major sacrifices for European South Africans. It would mean that ultimately Europeans would have to do the unskilled, and much of the semi-skilled work in the European areas which at the moment is done by Africans. Much of the money necessary to build the Reserves plus, if possible, the High Commission territories, into a viable national home for the Africans would have to come from European pockets. Thus it would mean a lower and less comfortable standard of living for European South Africans than at present, and a better one for Africans. Territorial apartheid, in sum, is an ideal which rests on a keen sense of justice, and is prepared for economic dislocation if this is the only means of securing that justice.

The answer offered by the Liberals is no less fundamental and far reaching. They rest their case, not only on justice, but also on economic necessities. They point particularly to the fact (which no one in South Africa has been able wholly to ignore since the Fagan Report of 1948) that more than half the Africans are outside the Reserves at any given time, a growing proportion of them permanently detribalized and settled in the European areas. They recognize the essential dependence of the South African economy on non-European, and particularly on African labor. They declare that it is necessary to proceed from these facts and to build a theory of right upon them. Thus, in sharp contrast to those who voice the tenets of ideal apartheid, the Liberals take their stand on existing economic conditions and draw the logical conclusions from them: namely that the African should be given the political, economic and personal rights which are the concomitant of his economic contribution to South Africa.

That this stand also involves sacrifices is obvious. It would mean that the European would sacrifice not his material comfort but his present position of undisputed dominance in South Africa. It would mean that the position of the European in the Union would no longer rest on a monopoly of votes, economic power and social prestige but on the ability to provide political and economic leadership which is acceptable to the great mass of non-Europeans.

Either of these approaches to South Africa's problems would require a virtual revolution in the thinking of most European South Africans. In some ways, what the Liberals preach is still more difficult to accept, because it means sharing with the non-Europeans what the Europeans have traditionally enjoyed on an exclusive basis, whereas ideal apartheid would preserve the white society intact, though under much less pleasant conditions.

Yet the Liberals have publicized their answer to South Africa's situation much more loudly and consistently since mid-1953 than have the proponents of ideal apartheid. The latter have been overawed by the difficulties of bringing their plan into being in any foreseeable future, and by the immensity of the changes it would necessitate. Probably only large scale race war would provide the imperative to such a fundamental change in South African society as true territorial apartheid would involve. At the present, therefore, ideal apartheid is less of a fundamental answer to South Africa's problems than a myth. Rather than a solution, it provides a rationalization of what might be an ultimate happy solution to those problems. Thus, except for those who cherish the ideal most dearly, its effect is less to provide an imperative to change than an illusion which tends to relieve people from the necessity of worrying about present inequities.

The Liberals, in contrast, are already practising what they preach. Relatively small though their numbers still are, the Liberals are performing a remarkable, if generally unwelcome service in South Africa by providing a completely logical answer for a badly muddled situation.

Between these two answers, but not wholly uninfluenced by them, lie those to which major political parties are prepared to lend their names. Broadly speaking, the United Party starts from the same premise as the Liberals, but does not draw the same conclusions. It tries to combine the necessary presence of the African in the South African economy with traditional racial segregation. It does not say, as do the Nationalists, that the African can *never* share political power in the Union, but it puts that possibility so far away that it does not disturb the customary functioning of the white South African community. The approach of the United Party is empirical, and where possible conciliatory. It builds on the past rather than being impelled towards a clearly perceived future.

The Nationalists declare that they hold the objective of ideal apartheid as an ultimate goal. But they are not prepared to create major dislocations in contemporary South African society in order to bring it about in the foreseeable future. Proponents of ideal apartheid like Dr. E. G. Jansen, the Governor-General, and Dr. T. E. Dönges, leader of the party in the Cape, now say it will be two or three hundred years before territorial apartheid can be fully brought into being. In the meantime, African labor must be used in developing the European economy not only because the latter cannot function properly without it, but also because the Africans cannot live without this support. But the use of ideal apartheid as an ultimate goal provides the Nationalists with a justification for refusing Africans a position of right within the European community. It also provides the justification for the Nationalists' significant attempts to shape the African community into a more distinctive one and to provide as watertight compartments as possible for non-Europeans within South Africa as a whole.

These broad distinctions between the two major political parties need to be analysed more carefully, however, for they are influenced by other attitudes and directives, and contain nuances which are almost as significant as the sharper outlines of differences.

The United Party stands for traditional racial segregation, and for much of the program of legislative apartheid which the Nationalists have introduced. They would modify some of these laws, for example the Group Areas Act. They are committed to repealing the Bantu Education Act, though they would not necessarily make any decisive changes in the education it provides for Africans. In regard to all apartheid legislation, however, the United Party takes the conservative position that custom is better than administrative regulations, that restrictions should not be made obvious, and that there should be limits to discrimination which are safeguarded by the courts.

On three points, the United Party differs importantly from the Nationalists: in its acceptance of economic integration of Europeans and non-Europeans, though not of all its implications; in its valiant attempt to hold together English- and Afrikaans-speaking in a united front which rests on mutual respect; and in its desire to maintain the balance in the Constitution between executive, legislature and courts.

The first point, it may be argued, springs from the party's particular interest in industry, commerce and finance. It reflects a keen awareness of the degree to which the South African economy depends on African labor and, increasingly, on African skills. When the United Party, though with some hesitation, endorses permanent housing and freeholds for Africans in the Native townships, and vocational training, it does so not out of the goodness of its heart, but because it recognizes that these will make African labor more efficient.

At the same time, the United Party is prepared to extend to Africans the opportunity to use Western style institutions even if not to give the latter a full measure of power. It endorses a revived Natives' Representative Council to which it would entrust slightly more authority than the defunct institution of this name. It is ready to recognize African trade unions though outside the structure established by the Industrial Conciliation Act. It would permit African schools to be more closely coordinated with the European school system through placing the former under the Department of Education. The United Party also seems more willing to give Africans experience of local government and administration along Western lines than are the Nationalists.

Being an empirical, even experimental party, rather than one which looks far ahead to the implications of its actions, the United Party would give these opportunities to Africans without drawing the same kinds of conclusions that the

Liberals have. In other words, while the United Party is prepared to accept the growing integration of urbanized Africans into South African society on more than the purely economic level, it does not feel that it is important, or wise, to analyse what may come thereafter. For one thing, it would almost inevitably split the United Party to do so; for another, its creed suggests that it is better to move slowly, step by step, answering immediate needs and not bothering too much about long range developments. In part this may be escapism, but it also has elements of wisdom, for the future rarely assumes exactly the shape foreseen for it.

The United Party's approach to English-Afrikaner relations is much more incisive. In the first place, the very membership of the party demonstrates the practicability of these two European groups working closely together, without either dominating the other. Though the body of the party is now English-speaking, the titular leadership has always been Afrikaner; its parliamentary candidates are fairly evenly divided between the two peoples; so too are the carrying out of its parliamentary responsibilities.

It is increasingly difficult, however, to keep a representative group of Afrikaners within the United Party fold. The Nationalists have done their best—and with much effect—to stamp United Party Afrikaners as traitors to their own folk, to penalize them outside of Parliament as they jeer at them within it. Moreover, while the liberal Afrikaner is often more forthright in his faith than most English-speaking South Africans, there are insidious influences in the history and environment of the Afrikaner which make it difficult for him to free himself from traditional attitudes towards the African. The Afrikaners who revolted from the United Party to form the ephemeral Conservative Party had an attitude towards Africans virtually indistinguishable from that of the Nationalists. The need to retain its present Afrikaner members helps to hold back the United Party from developing a more liberal non-European policy.

Most clear cut of all United Party attitudes are those towards the Constitution, the courts and democratic ways of acting. Over and over again, as we have seen, the United Party has been antagonized more by the way the Nationalists handled a particular piece of legislation than by the provisions of the Bill. Like any conservative party, the United Party puts special stress on established procedures. It has a strong sense for constitutional ways of acting. Confronting a party which has never hesitated to use the votes at its command to drive through even a measure affecting the Opposition, the United Party is still more convinced than ever of the necessity of proceeding by agreement on those issues which touch the fundamentals of political action. Thus its dismay both at the Senate Act and the fact that the courts found themselves forced to uphold it.

The United Party feels that the courts should play a more distinctive role in the balance of the Constitution. Thus the United Party pleaded for definitions in the Reservation of Separate Amenities' Bill, which the courts could use to check undue discrimination. The difficulty the South African courts face in performing such a function, however, is that they cannot disregard the obvious intent of legislation.

Compared to the United Party ambivalent and pragmatic way of acting, the Nationalists have a precision of aim and directness of approach which are sometimes startling. They are uninhibited by any sense of sacredness of the South African Constitution which, they maintain, they did not share in drafting though, in fact, Hertzog played a very considerable role in doing so. They are far less concerned than the United Party for constitutional ways of acting, for the traditional balance in the Constitution, or for judicial safeguards. They are not prepared to override the courts roughshod but they are determined to gain their ends. They care much less for the constitutional democracy which is marked by established methods of action, and respect for minority and individual rights, than for the much more radical democracy of the *volkswil* of Afrikaner nationalism.

This attitude of the Nationalists towards the Constitution, demonstrated most obviously over the Senate Act, has aroused concern and even action by many of the English-speaking who were previously lethargic about politics. Other factors acerbating English-Afrikaner relations have been the Nationalists' cavalier disregard of English sensibilities, and their obvious intention to possess the key positions, including economic ones, throughout the country.

Moreover, the very exclusiveness of the Nationalist Party has acted as a divisive factor in the country. Political parties which span racial groups as does the United Party, or the Liberal Party in Canada, ameliorate racial tension. Those like the Nationalists which represent one racial group increase it. Thus the National Party by its very nature, as well as by its policies, has widened the divisions between English- and Afrikaans-speaking throughout South Africa.

Yet the Nationalists have a strong trump card in their hands in this particular struggle: their electoral strength. They expect that persistent political defeats will ultimately fragment the United Party. In the long run, therefore, the Nationalists believe that the desire to share in political power will lead to a common white front under their direction, and on their own terms.

A further reason why they expect the moderate Afrikaner and ultimately the English-speaking to be won over to their camp is that the Nationalists believe implicitly that their policies offer the best chance of ensuring both the security and the wellbeing of white civilization in South Africa. To outsiders, their purposes may seem to be directed almost exclusively to the interests of the nationalistic Afrikaner, but few Nationalists would admit that there is an essential difference between the interests of that group and of white society at large. The Nationalists are prepared to welcome into their party any European who accepts their view of life and their political leadership. Confident that their approach to the non-European offers the best and perhaps the only hope of developing a *modus vivendi* in an appallingly complicated racial situation, they feel that ultimately all other Europeans will recognize this also.

Much more than the United Party do the Nationalists know what it is that they want to do with the African. They want to use his labor for the expansion of the South African economy. At the same time, they are determined that Africans shall not gain the right to a substantial foothold in the European areas. The reason why ideal apartheid is so useful to the Nationalists is that it provides what they insist is a long range possibility for giving the African a national home of his own. To the Nationalists, this possibility justifies their refusal to give those Africans who are not already permanently settled in the Native townships the chance to become so.

But in addition to this, the Nationalists are moving steadily along the road of devising institutions for the African which are as distinctively different from those of Europeans as possible. Partly this is, as we have said, to try to make the

African the different kind of person that theory says he is. Partly it is to try to direct his energies away from his desire for more power and a better return for his labor in the European areas. In particular, however, the kind of arrangements provided in the Bantu Authorities' Act, the Bantu Education Act and the Native Labour (Settlement of Disputes) Act seem designed to ensure European, and particularly governmental, control of African development.

Of all the Europeans in South Africa, the Nationalists are the most obsessed with the problem of survival. The Afrikaner fears cultural obliteration almost as much as physical annihilation. Over and over again, the Nationalists warn that the rising black tide may mean the end of white civilization in South Africa. Their rigidity in dealing with the African is a reflection of their fear of being submerged by him.

Among Africans, it is the relatively primitive ones with whom the Nationalists are chiefly concerned, and from whom they draw their stereotype of all Africans. They admit, somewhat reluctantly, that there are more highly developed Africans; they are prepared to continue giving the latter opportunities for higher education and advanced training. But their sights are fixed on the great mass of Africans who still have a foothold in the Reserves, are still affected by tribal tradition, and still moved by primitive instincts. Generalizing from this group, they have evolved their program of apartheid both for European and Bantu areas.

Beyond this, there is something irrational, but none the less compelling, in the Nationalist attitude towards non-Europeans, an instinctive distaste, even horror at the thought of being associated with them on equal terms. It is true that there was a practical motive behind the long efforts of the Nationalists to remove the Coloured from the common roll, the determination not to allow the latter to become an important electoral factor in the Cape, but there was also an emotional urge.

The most extreme example of this sentiment is bound up with the phrase: 'Do you want your daughter to marry a Native? ' Used with great effectiveness in the 1948 election in attacking Jan Hofmeyr's moderate liberalism, this appeal to fear and race consciousness can have a powerful impact. It is likely to be most influential, of course, with those in closest proximity to the non-Europeans, either through their places of residence or conditions of work, i.e., the working class Afrikaners who form so important a part today of the rank and file of the National Party.

One of the most surprising features of Nationalist arguments is the frequency with which they justify apartheid measures on the ground that they are necessary for preserving an acute color sense. In other words, it almost seems as if Nationalists fear that close proximity, rather than intensify distaste, may blur the differences felt between Europeans and non-Europeans.

Yet the two points may not be entirely incompatible. Under normal circumstances, peaceful living side by side in the same district, and cooperative working together may well lead people of different skin color to gain mutual respect, and to learn that a friendly relationship depends on more fundamental factors, like common interests, and attitudes. But the fear of a white minority lest it lose its distinctive identity is a sentiment which may override more mellow considerations based on personal experiences. European South Africans, and Afrikaners in particular, are often devoted to individual Africans with whom they have an easy and mutually satisfactory relationship, but this is very different from the attitude they hold towards Africans in the mass, who somehow tend to take on the worst features of savagery and unreliability of the most drastic stories about Africans they have ever heard. If the former type of experience may blur the sense of color, the latter kind of argument can all too easily re-awaken resentment and fear.

European South Africans are not unique in this regard. The same attitude can be found in any area of Africa where white settlers confront much larger numbers of people of color. Yet South Africa has this major difference: that its colonial people are a part of its society. This has two far-reaching results. On the one hand, as the United Nations Commission on Racial Conditions in South Africa pointed out, white South Africans, and especially the Afrikaners, do not have the reinforcement of their own kind in the home country as do settlers in Kenya or Rhodesia. The other side of this picture, however, is that there is no outside force insisting, as in Kenya, on the development of a more liberal type of Native policy.

The attacks on South Africa in the United Nations recognize that there is a colonial element in the Union's situation. The Western countries, quite naturally, resist United Nations pressure on South Africa because in strict international law the internal affairs of that country should fall under the protection extended to domestic jurisdiction. But this argument can hardly be expected to satisfy those nations newly freed from colonial control which see going on within South African boundaries the same kind of struggle with which they themselves have been so recently involved. These people resent political domination as such, and particularly when it is by those whose skin has a different color.

In much of the world, the new social conscience about colonial responsibility and development has led to major changes in the relationship between people of white skin and those of color. The Commonwealth of Nations, historically British and white, now includes far more Asians than Europeans since the Asian Dominions secured their independence. Oddly enough, this greatest example (apart from the United Nations) of a multi-racial international association includes the country which has been most subject to international criticism for its racial policies.

Basically, the Commonwealth of Nations stands for the traditional liberal view of human worth and progress now being extended to the dependent British Empire. Ghana has become independent; Nigeria is on the threshold. In Kenya, and Tanganyika, with their white settler element, the spur of the British Government has led to the appointment of Africans to legislative and executive positions. In the new Federation of Rhodesia and Nyasaland, Africans are elected to the legislature though they remain in a very junior position as far as political influence is concerned. Thus the multi-racial British colonies begin to move in the direction of the ideal embodied in the multi-racial Commonwealth.

This raises particular problems for South Africa. The pressures within the most intimate association to which South Africa belongs are towards a kind of relationship between Europeans and non-Europeans which neither the Nationalists nor the United Party are prepared to accept. Even on its own borders, South Africa now has a federation—the Federation of Rhodesia and Nyasaland—where Africans are elected to Parliament. Because of the proximity and the similarity to the Union of the Southern Rhodesia racial pattern, this fact is far more disturbing than the thought that an independent African State—Ghana—has become a member of the Commonwealth.

On every count except racial policy, be it noted, South Africa is a model and useful member of the Commonwealth. Its strategic position at the tip of the vast continent of Africa is of primary importance whenever the Suez Canal and Mediterranean route are threatened. Economically, its gold has been of great value in helping the Commonwealth, and particularly the United Kingdom, to meet some of the most difficult of post-war problems of exchange. South Africa has been unfailingly cooperative under the Nationalists as well as under the United Party in all matters of economic and financial policy. Moreover, there are close and satisfactory economic and financial relations between big corporations in the United Kingdom and in South Africa, like the Anglo-American Corporation. Internationally, South Africa commonly follows the lead of the United Kingdom. Moreover, despite all irritation at United Nations criticisms, South Africa, largely because of United Party pressures, contributed troops to the British Commonwealth division in Korea.

All these points can be echoed for South Africa's relations with the United States. The uranium processed from South African gold mine dumps is being exploited through British and American funds; it finds its way for the most part to the United States. Moreover, an increasing number of American firms have close business relations with the Union.

South African racial policy creates significant problems, however, for its companions among the older members of the Commonwealth. They may be sympathetic to its stand on domestic jurisdiction but they are inevitably torn between their desire to support it on this issue and their awareness of the importance of retaining a measure of understanding with the Asian members of the Commonwealth. To Canada, for example, the Commonwealth has taken on new meaning since it provides an insight into Asian ways of thinking and action. Those closest to external affairs in Australia rank good relations with the Asian Dominions much higher than official statements seem to indicate. The United Kingdom retains a greater importance and influence in world affairs because it is the senior member of an association which includes by far the most important non-Communist countries in Asia. But will the Asian members of the Commonwealth stay long within that association if they do not find a strong sense of sympathy with the cause of racial equality to which they have so fervently dedicated themselves?

To South Africa, Commonwealth membership has important advantages. No other Commonwealth country depends so much for defence on the British Navy. Moreover, South Africa must associate strategically with British territories in Africa if it is not to be isolated. South Africa shares to the full some of the interests most significant to the United Kingdom and the Commonwealth, like passage through Suez, the security of the Indian Ocean, and a check to Soviet power creeping into the Middle East and Africa. Economically, South Africa does well out of its close relations with, though not complete dependence on, the sterling bloc.

Moreover, United Kingdom-South African relations are harmonious except for the dispute over the High Commission Territories, which adjoin or are enclosed by South Africa. At the time of South African Union, both South Africans and British anticipated that these three territories—Basutoland, Swaziland and Bechuanaland—would become incorporated in South Africa before long. A provision was even inserted in the Act of Union to facilitate this process, which was to take place after consultation with the Native inhabitants. Not infrequently, South Africa has pressed the United Kingdom to implement what South African Prime Ministers have termed the 'pledge' to transfer the High Commission Territories. But though large numbers of the African inhabitants of the Territories go to the Union to earn their living, they are unenthusiastic about a change in status. Still more important, British public opinion is adamantly opposed to the transfer, the more so since the Nationalists have been implementing their policies of apartheid.

From the Nationalist side, however, it has become of increasing importance to incorporate the High Commission Territories. To plan territorial apartheid with only the present South African Reserves would be a monumental task which requires a scale of investment which is wholly prohibitive. Compared to population, the area is relatively small and at the moment, as we have seen, the Reserves cannot provide a living for even half the Africans of the country. To add the High Commission Territories would change the picture, at least on paper. Basutoland is already overcrowded, though its resources could be better developed. Swaziland is in a much more fortunate condition with a smaller population and a more flourishing economy. Bechuanaland includes a vast area, not unlike that of South West Africa, though similarly without great carrying capacity. Nonetheless, the High Commission Territories are for obvious reasons a major objective of Nationalist policy.

On some issues, a workable compromise can be achieved between British ideals and Nationalist policy. In 1955, an agreement was reached whereby the naval base of Simonstown, near Cape Town, was transferred to South Africa in 1957. At the same time, the British secured an agreement that they would not be forced to impose racial discrimination in their selection or housing of labor. But it would be much more difficult to work out any similarly satisfactory arrangement for the High Commission Territories.

Despite all potential and actual advantages of Commonwealth membership, the Nationalists naturally look on it in a very different way from the predominantly English-speaking United Party. Republicans by tradition, the Nationalists look forward to establishing a republic as soon as this is feasible. Before doing so, they will have to command a majority of the votes in the country, or else the election of a President would be, from their point of view, a dangerous experiment. Though today it is possible to have a republic within the Commonwealth, the Nationalists say openly that they want, ultimately, to have a republic outside of that association.

It is conceivable that the Nationalists might decide almost any time to break this last close tie that South Africa retains. But the chance that they will soon do so is not great. The Commonwealth asks little of its members, and gives richly in return. It provides mutual support, non-interference, and cooperative discussions. There are no major divisions between South Africa and other members of the Commonwealth except over racial discrimination, and these have been handled on the wider forum of the United Nations. Even if South Africa should leave the Commonwealth, its economic, financial and strategic relations would continue in much the same form.

But the Nationalists are right: the most important consequences of South

Africa leaving the Commonwealth would not be external, but internal ones. Dr. Malan used to speak enthusiastically of South Africa following in the path of Eire, meaning, of course, republicanism. Should the Union cut itself off from the Commonwealth, either of its own volition, or through policies which other Commonwealth members are not prepared to accept, it would leave it in an international and intellectual isolation not very different from that of Eire. Despite the economic ties which South Africa has with Great Britain and the United States, the effect of breaking the symbolic bond of Commonwealth association would be to thrust South Africans back upon themselves. Above all, of course, it would weaken the distinctive life of English South Africans and lay them more open to Nationalist pressures. The Nationalists look on this prospect with enthusiasm. But the internal result they desire would be gained at a much greater cost to the richness of South African life than most people seem to realize.

The question still remains: Where is South Africa going? Of all the four answers being offered to its racial situation, it is the Nationalist one which is being implemented most vigorously. Under the spur of Mr. Strijdom and Dr. Verwoerd, efforts are being made to force as rigorous a separation as possible between Europeans and non-Europeans in every segment of life. So drastic and harsh are the provisions under which separation may be forced—e.g., in the universities and in the churches (see p. 111 and p. 117)—that even certain Nationalists have become worried at the doctrinaire rigidity of the conceptions under which regulations are drafted. To the fully dedicated Nationalist, however, the program must be complete in every aspect.

Much less often do references now appear to ideal, or total apartheid as an ultimate goal, a fact not unrelated to the size and scope of the Tomlinson proposals for building up the Reserves. The Government welcomed the Tomlinson Commission's rejection of the policy of integration, but it was not prepared to adopt in large measure either the administrative or financial proposals of the Commission, in particular its long range program of spending £104 million over a ten year period (see p. 421, Note 1). In 1956 £3·5 million were allocated 'as a first instalment', but nothing further the following year, while it was announced, in March, 1957, that not all of the original grant had been spent. It is true that efforts to establish industries in the Reserves still continue but these hardly keep pace with the birth rate of the Africans. Only if there were drastic decisions to divert European capital to build the Reserves into a viable area for large numbers of Africans living in settled, stable communities, and this program were coupled with a consciously directed policy of large-scale European migration to provide the Union with a significantly large white population, could there be any true separation of African and European spheres of life such as ideal or territorial apartheid suggest.

In this perspective, Nationalist apartheid becomes largely restrictive. In other words, the emphasis is mainly on its negative aspect, i.e., on maintaining the European areas of the Union under the exclusive control of white South Africans, rather than the positive one of promoting a distinctive life for the Bantu. This is the more so because the Nationalists owe their foremost allegiance to their own Afrikaner folk, who feel most acutely amongst the Europeans the competition of the Africans. It is not surprising, therefore, that apart from the limited amount which they are doing to develop the Reserves, the Nationalists are concerned primarily with protecting the privileged position of white farmers and white laborers. Thus the inevitable tendency in the future, as in the past, will be to underline and intensify traditional discrimination against non-Europeans, despite the fact that an increasing number of them are living in the so-called European areas.

If European South Africans were living in the kind of community in which they picture themselves, i.e., a self-contained white community wrestling with the problems of a huge non-European population, rather than in a multi-racial society in a multi-racial world, they might still be able to establish a stable balance which reflected within the boundaries of the Union the historic relationship between a dominant white minority and subject peoples of color. But South Africa exists within a world society, however much it may try to separate itself from the assumptions about the relations between races which international society is increasingly accepting. Moreover, not only do non-Europeans within the Union know of the views on racial equality enunciated so forcefully in the United Nations, but also of the halting but steady progress towards more equitable treatment of people of color within the United States, as well as in most African colonial territories. There is a constant interaction between non-European opinion within the Union and these developments outside South Africa which reflect this growth of equalitarianism as between the white and colored races.

Throughout much of the discussion of South African affairs in this book the non-Europeans have been virtually disregarded. This is because, in practice, they have relatively little to say about the political, economic or social policies which affect their lives. Yet in the end, they will be the most important factor of all in determining the future of South Africa.

If the economic development of the country is not to be reversed—and there is no evidence of an attempt seriously to reverse it—then more Europeans, and particularly more Africans will be drawn into primary and secondary industry. With the serious shortage of European skilled labor, non-Europeans will have to take over an increasing number of semi-skilled and even skilled positions.

In one way this will help to relieve the tension building up among non-Europeans. The expansion of economic opportunities, and the rising wages which will almost inevitably follow, will satisfy many of them, at least temporarily. But it is difficult to see that in the long run this can be enough. It is not those who are at the lowest level of subsistence who demand most, but those who have tasted enough of the advantages of an industrial society to know how much is still withheld from them.

Among the non-Europeans, not much action can be expected from the Coloured despite the degree to which they now feel the sting of apartheid. They have not yet made up their minds to throw in their lot with the Indians and the Africans. Despite their resentments, they have been singularly lacking in ability to weld even themselves into a cohesive group. Even their Marxism tends to be Trotskyite.

The Indians are a relatively small but potent group. Their strength is in the intelligence, training and sense of purpose of the more radical group among them; it lies also in the support they receive, implicitly or explicitly, from India. They have a channel to world public opinion which they are not slow to use. This fact creates great bitterness among Europeans against South African

Indians, and is sometimes looked on distrustfully even by Africans. But no non-European would cut off so useful a link with an important outside country.

Significant though the Indians may be through the experience and training which they can provide the Africans, it is the latter who will in the end be the decisive factor by sheer weight of numbers. What is most significant about the African is the rapidity with which his ideas and sentiments can and have changed. In 1948, economic concessions would have been enough to consolidate the moderates in their positions of leadership in Bantu organizations; in 1951, political overtures would have been enough. By now it is doubtful whether any concessions would satisfy the younger, more radical leaders.

Yet it is difficult to evaluate either what the Africans think or how they are going to act. The barriers built by the Nationalists with great skill, the constant police espionage, the immobilization of the relatively few leaders, dam up resentment; there are few clues to how this bitterness can or will express itself. If it is in violence, then the retaliation will be so terrible that it may take years to rebuild a nationalist movement among the Africans. The severe individual retaliation for passive resistance of any obvious sort is a powerful deterrent. Probably only a complete economic boycott could be totally effective, yet the difficulties in the way of organizing it, particularly in the face of current restrictions, are enormous.

What is obvious, and alarming, in the Union is the increasing polarization of sentiment. To a degree, the adoption by the Liberals of universal suffrage as an ultimate objective was a rather desperate attempt to build a bridge between the non-Europeans and at least a small group of Europeans. All too well aware that measures like the Suppression of Communism Act have been used against non-Nationalist trade union leaders in a way similar to their use against non-European leaders, the Liberals have tried to make clear their belief that common problems, needs and aspirations can overbridge the customary divisions of race. But even so far reaching (for South Africa) a declaration as the Liberals have been willing to make seems to have done little to attract non-European leadership. What might have been taken with open hands only a short time ago is now regarded only with suspicion.

This steady tendency of non-European opinion to become more extreme, and estranged from all Europeans, is not only a result of European actions and attitudes; it helps in turn to create them. Thus the United Party has receded from the high water mark of its leaders' outspoken support of economic integration in February, 1954; it is even less assured about freeholds for Africans than some time ago. Far less doctrinaire though it is than the Nationalists on particular measures, the United Party is hesitant to offer concessions unless it is very sure that something specific is going to be gained in return.

Is there anything which can halt this increasing polarization of sentiment which could all too easily bring the Union into the situation of an armed camp in which all non-Europeans are so antagonistic to the whites that the latter feel forced to stand together on all counts as the only hope of self-preservation?

On both sides, there are still factors which restrain so complete and bitter a separation between Europeans and non-Europeans. The non-Europeans themselves are well aware of the contribution the whites make to the growth and development of South Africa. They do not seek to oust the Europeans as the Mau Mau did. For all the intransigence of their more radical leaders, the great bulk of non-Europeans would be willing to accept far less than equality if they gain thereby both a greater return for their contribution to South African development and a greater share in determining their own future.

From the European side, there are those who are working towards a more obviously equitable arrangement between the races. The United Party and the Nationalists avow this purpose even if their policies fall so far short of it so often. The Nationalists' spiritual leaders in the Dutch Reformed Church are moving towards a concept of the relations between races which no longer enshrines inequality but in place emphasizes practicality. The Liberals and Labour Party go all the way to a forthright equalitarianism of treatment between races. There is a movement of thought going on below the surface of European South Africa which, either for theoretical or practical reasons, may lead to concessions to the non-Europeans.

All these signs of flexibility offer hope in an otherwise deteriorating situation. But how long will they continue to do so?

Notes

CHAPTER 1

[1] *Summary of the Report of the Commission for the Socio-Economic Development of the Bantu Areas within the Union of South Africa*, U.G. 61/1955, 213 pp. plus 64 maps and charts. It proposed spending £104 million on a ten-year program of developing secondary and tertiary industries, and estimated that this program would provide the basis for increasing the carrying capacity of the present Reserves, particularly if consolidated, to about 10 million Africans in 25-30 years, of whom some 2 million would be migratory workers. It further estimated that if the same tempo of investment were continued, the Bantu areas would be able to maintain about 70 per cent of the total African population by the end of the century. If the Bantu areas were not developed during this period, the Commission foresaw that the European sector of South Africa would have to accommodate about 17 million Africans by the end of the century. (See also p. 271.)

[2] In May 1956, the Government issued a White Paper on the Development of Bantu Areas, Fact Paper No. 10, 10 pp. It welcomed the Commission's justification of the policy of apartheid but rejected the notion of committing itself to a ten-year program of development, maintaining that funds would be sought annually in accordance with growing needs, plans and the country's capacity to pay. The first grant was for £3·5 million. In March 1957 it was announced that not all this money had yet been spent and that no further grant would be made that year. Specifically Dr. H. F. Verwoerd, Minister of Native Affairs, announced the following decisions on the Commission's estimates: (*a*) the soil reclamation program cut from £27 million to £15 by having the Africans provide the work; (*b*) the £3 million for loan facilities eliminated as superfluous because of the existence of the Trust Fund; (*c*) the allocation of £3 million for forestry and £3.5 million for sugar cane and sisal development and irrigation accepted; (*d*) also accepted was £1 million for mining development but preparatory work must be done first; (*e*) the recommendation for £30 million for the development of industries in the Reserves with the help of white entrepreneurs and the State was rejected as contrary to Government policy; (*f*) £12 million for urgent development in the Reserves were cut to £3 million; (*g*) the estimate of £13 million for basic services like roads, transport and railways to facilitate industrial development cut to a maximum of £5 million; (*h*) health services cut from £5 million to £3 million, welfare services from £3.6 million to £1.5 million, and the £3 million for education eliminated because of the existence of the Bantu Education Act (see p. 100).

[3] As amended, the Urban Areas Act forbids an African to remain in an urban or proclaimed (i.e. designated by law) area for longer than 72 hours unless he has been given permission by a responsible official. Moreover his permit lapses when his period of employment terminates. Exempt from these provisions are those Africans born and permanently resident in the urban areas, or continuously employed in the same area for 15 years, or by one employer for 10 years. Under the Natives (Urban Areas) Amendment Act, 1956, passed on June 18, 1956, however, urban local authorities have the power to order any African to depart from an urban area within a specified period if his presence is held to be 'detrimental to the maintenance of peace and order'. Before this amendment, local authorities could order the departure of an African only if he had been permitted to enter an area to seek work and failed to find it, or if a magistrate so ordered after trial. Despite the foregoing body of legislation, unauthorized movement and settlement of Africans in urban areas still exists on a large scale.

[4] For details about circulation and distribution of South African newspapers, see Appendix I.

[5] Havenga was long Hertzog's chief lieutenant, then leader of the Afrikaner Party, then an important Nationalist Minister. Ultimately defeated by J. G. Strijdom in the struggle for succession to Dr. Malan as supreme party leader, Havenga resigned from Parliament in 1956 when Dr. Malan did. Havenga died in March 1957.

[6] The Hertzog-Brebner Trust is said to have been founded with the money which was sent to General Hertzog by Boer sympathizers after the Anglo-Boer War. See H. Lindsay Smith, *Behind the Press in South Africa*, p. 117.

[7] There are two Afrikaans newspapers in South West Africa: *Die Suidwester*, the Nationalist paper, which concerns itself mainly with local news and follows the *Die Burger* line on national issues: and *Suid West Afrikaner*, the United Party paper, which also concentrates on local news, and carries on a running feud with *Die Suidwester*. Neither circulates outside of South West Africa.

[8] Both the Nationalists and the United Party have published party weeklies from time to time. The Nationalist paper is called *Kruithoring*, of which the not so frequent English version is *National News*, and the U.P.'s is *Challenge*, or in the Afrikaans edition, *Ons Blad*. More important is the Labour Party weekly, *Forward*, which carries a good deal of news on trade union as well as Labour Party activity and attitudes which is generally omitted by the daily press. *Forward* is a non-profit-making enterprise which bears the marks of a good deal of amateur effort but more than justifies itself by its obvious sincerity.

CHAPTER 2

[1] This happened with the Separate Representation of Voters Bill to take the Coloured off the common roll, when discussion centered on the need for a two-thirds vote because the measure affected one of the entrenched clauses.

[2] e.g., Ralph Kilpin, *Parliamentary Procedure in South Africa: A Short Guide to the Rules and Practice of the Union House of Assembly*, Cape Town: Juta, 1950, 190 pp., the standard work on the subject, is by a former clerk of the House.

[3] No. 44 of 1949.

[4] Leave granted to introduce the measure on May 25, 1949, *House of Assembly Debates*, vol. 68, col. 6465; second reading, June 10-15, cols. 7574-8325; motion for guillotine, June 17, cols. 8428-8515; committee stage, June 20-21, cols. 8516-8562 and 8668-8775; report stage, June 22, cols. 8779-8822; third reading, June 23, 8891-8953.

[5] *Ibid.*, col. 7987.

[6] *Ibid.*, col. 8286.

[7] *Ibid.*, col. 7998.

[8] *Ibid.*, col. 8102.

[9] *Ibid.*, col. 8297.

[10] *Ibid.*, col. 7709.

[11] *Ibid.*, col. 7713.

[12] *Ibid.*, col. 7616.

[13] *Ibid.*, col. 7810, S. J. M. Steyn.

[14] *Ibid.*, col. 7951, J. R. Sullivan.

[15] *Ibid.*, col. 7700.

[16] *Ibid.*, col. 7910.

[17] *Ibid.*, col. 7614.

[18] *Ibid.*, col. 8072.

[19] *Ibid.*, col. 8186.

[20] June 14, 1949, *Press Digest* (called hereafter *P.D.*), 24/276/49. This press digest, issued weekly by the Jewish Board of Deputies, Johannesburg, is by far the most useful one for following the South African press.

[21] June 13, 1949, *ibid.*, 277.

[22] June 11, 1949, *ibid.*

[23] *Ibid.*, 25/287/49.

[24] June 17, 1949, *ibid.*

[25] *Ibid.*

[26] *Rand Daily Mail*, July 13, 1949; *P.D.*, 28/324/49.

[27] Series of three articles in *The Star*, August 15-17, 1950, *P.D.*, 35/378/50. See also *Rand Daily Mail*, August 24, 26 and 29, 1950, suggesting 'Afrikaans imperialism' as a contributory motive. The Nationalist press denied this and stressed economic causes. *P.D.*, 35/378-81/50.

[28] *The Friend*, April 6, 1950, *P.D.*, 15/153/50.

[29] *Cape Times*, April 7, 1950, *ibid.*, 162.

[30] *Ibid.*

[31] *Ibid.*, 1/5/51.

[32] *SAPA*, February 20, 1950, *P.D.*, 8/85/51.

[33] *SAPA*, March 7, 1951, *ibid.*, 15/164/51.

[34] *SAPA*, June 9, 1951, *ibid.*, 24/280/51.

[35] June 12, 1951, *ibid.*

[36] November 18, 1951, *P.D.*, *ibid.*, 47/517/51.

[37] November 19, 1951, *ibid.*, 518.
[38] *P.D.*, 10/88/52.
[39] March 3 and 5, *ibid.*
[40] *Star*, September 5, 1952, *ibid.*, 37/364/52.
[41] *Ibid.*
[42] *Ibid.*, 2/18/54.
[43] *Ibid.*, 25/234/54.
[44] June 22, 1954, *ibid.*, 26/239/54.
[45] *Ibid.*
[46] September 7 and 8, *ibid.*, 37/364/54 and 36/352/54.
[47] N.H.K. conference, *Die Transvaler*, March 12, 1954, *ibid.*, 11/10/54, and Transvaal D. R. C. Synod, *Die Transvaler*, May 1, 1954, *ibid.*, 18/165/54.
[48] December 10, 1954, *ibid.*, 50/497-98/1954.
[49] See Chapter 15.
[50] No. 44 of 1950.
[51] The best information on the South African Communist Party is contained in two books by Edward Roux, *S. P. Bunting: A Political Biography*, Cape Town: published by the author, 1944, 160 pp., and *Time Longer Than Rope: A History of the Black Man's Struggle for Freedom in South Africa*, London: Victor Gollancz, 1949, 398 pp. Roux was an early Communist who broke with the party in the mid-thirties over its constant changes in tactics directed from Moscow. He is now Senior Lecturer in Botany at the University of the Witwatersrand in Johannesburg. Another biography with some relevant information is R. K. Cope, *Comrade Bill: The Life and Times of W. H. Andrews, Workers' Leader*, Cape Town: Stewart Printing Co., n.d., 341 pp.
[52] Roux, *Bunting*, p. 89.
[53] *Ibid.*, p. 97.
[54] Roux, *Time Longer Than Rope*, pp. 341-42.
[55] *Ibid.*, p. 340.
[56] *P.D.*, 8/90/49.
[57] *Ibid.*
[58] February 17, 1949, *ibid.*
[59] February 21, 1949, *ibid.*
[60] *Ibid.*, 9/106/49.
[61] African males in the Cape who can meet literacy and property qualifications vote on a separate roll to elect three Europeans to represent them in the House of Assembly and two Europeans for the Cape Provincial Council.
[62] December 8, 1949, *P.D.*, 50/561/49.
[63] December 12, 1949, *ibid.*
[64] March 29, 1950, *ibid.*, 14/145-46/50.
[65] *Dagbreek*, January 8, 1950, *ibid.*, 2/14-15/50.
[66] *Die Vaderland*, August 2, 1949, *ibid.*, 31/352/49.
[67] *SAPA*, March 24, 1950, *ibid.*, 13/140/50.
[68] *Ibid.*, 15/153/50.
[69] *Ibid.*, 13/140/50.
[70] Motion to refer to select committee, *House of Assembly Debates*, Vol. 72, col. 6734.
[71] First reading, June 5, 1950, *House of Assembly Debates*, vol. 73, col. 8014; motion for guillotine, June 13, cols. 8838-8883; second reading, June 14-15, cols. 8909-9183; committee stage, June 17-19, cols. 9314-9490; report stage, June 20, cols. 9496-9529; third reading, June 20, cols. 9529-9590.
[72] *Ibid.*, col. 8855, R. J. du Toit.
[73] *Ibid.*, col. 8850.
[74] *Ibid.*, col. 8858.
[75] *Ibid.*, col. 6158.
[76] *Ibid.*, col. 9135.
[77] *Ibid.*, col. 9170.
[78] *Senate Debates*, Vol. IV, Third Session, Tenth Parliament, col. 6159.
[79] Assembly Debates, col. 8933.
[80] *Ibid.*, col. 8940.
[81] *Ibid.*, col. 8946.
[82] *Ibid.*, col. 9145.
[83] *Ibid.*, col. 8992.
[84] *Ibid.*, col. 8997.
[85] *Ibid.*, col. 8993.
[86] *Ibid.*, col. 8911.
[87] *Ibid.*, col. 9013
[88] *Ibid.*, col. 8914

[89] *Ibid.*, col. 8918.
[90] *Ibid.*, col. 9543.
[91] *Ibid.*, col. 8932.
[92] Boltman and Swart, *ibid.*, cols. 9046 and 9586.
[93] *Ibid.*, col. 9129.
[94] Lovell, *ibid.*, cols. 9321 and 9397.
[95] *Rand Daily Mail*, June 6, 1950, *P.D.*, 23/244-45/50.
[96] *P.D.*, 25/270/50.
[97] *Star*, June 14, 1950, *P.D.*, 24/259-60/50.
[98] *Rand Daily Mail*, June 7, 1950, *P.D.*, 23/244-45/50.
[99] June 12, 1950, *P.D.*, 24/260-61/50.
[100] June 7, 1950, *ibid.*
[101] June 12, 1950, *ibid.*
[102] May 9, 1950, *P.D.*, 19/197/50.
[103] *P.D.*, 25/268/50 and 26/278/50.
[104] May 8, 1950, *P.D.*, 20/213/50.
[105] *Ibid.*, 24/262/50.
[106] *Ibid.*, 25/272-73/50.
[107] *Ibid.*, 26/270-80/50.
[108] *Ibid.*, 18/189-90/50.
[109] *Ibid.*, 25/272/50.
[110] *Ibid.*, 26/281/50.
[111] Clause 5, (1) (d).
[112] The Act to Amend the Suppression of Communism Act, 1950 (Act No. 50 of 1951), signed June 18, 1951.
[113] It was no longer necessary, for example, that their names were on the Liquidator's list or that they had been convicted under the Act. See Swart's explanatory memorandum, tabled February 13, 1951, *SAPA*, February 14, 1951, *P.D.*, 7/78/51.
[114] Both on February 15, 1951, *P.D.*, 8/90-91/51.
[115] D. J. Scholtz, *SAPA*, June 8 and 12, 1951, *P.D.*, 24/271-72/51.
[116] January 23, 1952, *P.D.*, 4/29/52.
[117] January 23, 1952, *ibid.*
[118] *Report of the Select Committee on Suppression of Communism Act Enquiry*, S.C. 6, 1952, 395 pp.
[119] *P.D.*, 21/203-04/52.
[120] *Report of the Select Committee on Suppression of Communism Act Enquiry*, printed September, 1953, Cape Town. S.C. 10, '53, xv, 222, xvi, (in Afrikaans, 237 pp). It includes the minutes of evidence and appendices of Communist Party documents.
[121] *Rand Daily Mail*, November 25, 1950, *P.D.*, 48/522/50.
[122] *Star*, May 23, 1952, *P.D.*, 22/216/52.
[123] May 24, 1952, *P.D.*, 22/217/52.
[124] *Ibid.*
[125] *Rand Daily Mail*, July 1, 1950, *P.D.*, 27/294/50.
[126] *Ibid.*, September 19, 1950, *P.D.*, 38/417/50.
[127] Author of *The Struggle for South Africa*, E. S. Sachs lost the appeal against his ban in December, 1952, and left the Union for England early in 1953. He gave testimony in Geneva in the summer of 1953 to the United Nations Commission on the Racial Situation in South Africa (see p. 402).
[128] May 25, 1952, *P.D.*, 22/210/52.
[129] *Ibid.*, 211-212.
[130] *Rand Daily Mail*, May 29, 1952, *P.D.*, 23/222/50.
[131] *Ibid.*, 223.
[132] See Chapter 12.
[133] *Ibid.*, 224-25.
[134] *Ibid.*, 226.
[135] *House of Assembly Debates*, 1953, July 21, col. 237, and September 18, col. 3674.
[136] *Cape Times*, September 11, 1953, *P.D.*, 36/375/53.
[137] *Cape Times*, September 3, 1953, *ibid.*
[138] Under a 1927 Act, the Governor-General has the power to order an African to go to a particular farm and there were about six such orders, chiefly to African National Congress members, between 1953 and 1956.
[139] *Bantu World*, September 9, 1953, *P.D.*, 36/378/53.

CHAPTER 3

[1] The Coloured Advisory Council and, more recently, the Commissioner for Coloured Affairs are intended to encourage their sense of separate identity.

[2] Act No. 55 of 1949.

[3] *Official Year Book of South Africa*, No. 24 of 1948, p. 1133.

[4] Leave granted to introduce the bill, April 28, *House of Assembly Debates*, vol. 68, col. 4695; second reading, May 19-20, cols. 6164-6206, and May 23-5, cols. 6344-59, 6367-6464; 6471-6513; committee stage, June 8, vol. 69, cols. 7341-7358; report stage, June 23, cols. 9002-3; third reading, June 24, cols. 9065-9071.

[5] *Ibid.*, col. 9060.

[6] Dr. T. W. B. Osborn, *ibid.*, col. 6387.

[7] *Star*, November 22, 1950, *P.D.*, 48/524/50.

[8] Assembly Debates, col. 6192.

[9] May 26, 1949, *P.D.*, 22/253/49.

[10] May 24, 1949, *P.D.*, 22/247/49.

[11] *P.D.*, 3/21/50.

[12] *Ibid.*, 26/303-04/49.

[13] Reported by the *Star*, July 8, 1949, *P.D.*, 28/316/49.

[14] July 12, 1949, *P.D.*, 28/322/49.

[15] *P.D.*, 11/106/50.

[16] *P.D.*, 11/106-08/50.

[17] *SAPA*, March 11, 1950, *P.D.*, 11/109/50.

[18] March 25, 1950, *P.D.*, 12/139-40/50.

[19] *House of Assembly Debates*, vol. 69, col. 6313. The measure was originally introduced on May 20, 1949, but dropped due to the prorogation of Parliament. Leave granted to introduce the measure, January 23, 1950, *House of Assembly Debates*, vol. 70, col. 9; second reading, March 1-2, cols. 2163-2280; committee stage March 28, vol. 71, cols. 3810-3813; third reading, March 30, col. 4005. On April 27, the Assembly agreed to a significant amendment suggested by the Senate: vol. 72, col. 5175.

[20] *Ibid.*, col. 2195.

[21] *Ibid.*, col. 2260.

[22] S. F. Papenfus.

[23] J. E. Potgieter.

[24] *House of Assembly Debates*, vol. 71, col. 2519. Leave was granted to introduce the bill on February 20, 1950, vol. 70, col. 1571. Second reading was from March 8 to 16, 1950, vol. 71, cols. 2498-3159; the Select Committee was appointed March 20, col. 3225; committee stage was from May 4 to 9, 1950, cols. 5666-6100; third reading was on May 16, vol. 72, cols. 6537-6627. On June 16, 1950, the House considered small amendments by the Senate, vol. 73, col. 9245.

[25] *Ibid.*, col. 2534.

[26] J. H. Russell, *ibid.*, col. 3125.

[27] *Ibid.*, col. 3006.

[28] *Ibid.*, col. 3010.

[29] *Ibid.*, col. 2545.

[30] *Ibid.*, col. 2807.

[31] S. J. Tighy, *ibid.*, col. 5834.

[32] *P.D.*, 4/27/50.

[33] February 21, 1950 and February 22, 1950, *ibid.*, 8/78-79/50.

[34] February 24, 1950, *ibid.*, 9/88-89/50.

[35] February 23, 1950 and February 22, 1950, *ibid.*, 88-90.

[36] March 2 and 3, 1950, *ibid.*, 10/102-103/50.

[37] May 9, 1950, *ibid.*, 19/203-4/50.

[38] February 19, 1950, *ibid.*

[39] February 18, 1950, *ibid.*

[40] March 13, 1950 and March 10, 1950, *ibid.*

[41] December 11, 1950, *ibid.*, 50/549/50.

[42] When the Population Register was compiled in the Transvaal from 1955 on, many Coloured found it difficult to keep themselves from being listed as Natives because their skin was dark. European identity cards are not yet, and may never be issued.

[43] No. 49 of 1950.

[44] No. 13 of 1913.

[45] No. 18 of 1936.

[46] No. 21 of 1923, re-enacted, 1945.

[47] No. 28 of 1946.

[48] A relatively simple account of the Group Areas Act and its implications is provided in a pamphlet with this name by Kenneth Kirkwood, published by the Institute of Race Relations, n.d., 43 pp. A more detailed and technical account is in V. G. Hiemstra's *The Group Areas Act*, Cape Town and Johannesburg: Juta, 1953, 147 pp.

[49] Leave granted to introduce the measure on April 24, 1950, *House of Assembly Debates*, vol. 72, col. 4851; motion for guillotine, May 26, 1950, col. 7322ff.; second reading, May 29-31, 1950, vol. 73, cols. 7433-7826; Committee stage, June 6-9, col. 8200ff.; report, June 12, 1950; third reading, June 13, 1950, cols. 8773-8830. Senate amendments approved June 20, 1950. The Group Areas Amendment Bill, given second reading on June 23, 1952, provided for intermediary stages.

[50] Vol. 73, col. 7446, and 7452.

[51] *Ibid.*, col. 7747.

[52] *Ibid.*, col. 7746.

[53] *Ibid.*, col. 8474.

[54] *Ibid.*, col. 8809.

[55] *Ibid.*, col. 8834.

[55a] While no provision for compensation was made in the original Group Areas Act, the Group Areas Amendment Act, No. 69 of 1955, made provision for a Group Areas Development Board which may assist dispossessed persons to sell their lands and buildings and to buy in an appropriate area. Up to mid-1957, the Board had not functioned in this manner and when it does so it is expected to pay amounts much less than the current market value.

[56] *P.D.*, 18/190/50, 19/205/50 and 21/221-23/50.

[57] *Ibid.*, 22/238-39/50.

[58] *Star*, May 5, 1950, *ibid.*, 19/204/50.

[59] *Rand Daily Mail*, October 20, 1950, *ibid.*, 43/472/50.

[60] *Ibid.*, 18/191/50.

[61] *Ibid.*, 21/222-23/50.

[62] *Ibid.*, 23/249/50.

[63] *Rand Daily Mail*, June 5, 1950, *ibid.*

[64] *Die Vaderland*, December 11, 1950, *ibid.*, 50/552/50.

[65] *Star*, June 27, 1950, *ibid.*, 26/285/50.

[66] June 10, 1950, *ibid.*, 24/257-58/50.

[67] June 9, 1950, *ibid.*, 256-57.

[68] *SAPA*, April 4, 1951, *P.D.*, 14/156/51.

[69] April 28, 1951, *P.D.*, 18/208-109/51.

[70] *Rand Daily Mail*, April 14, 1951, *ibid.*, 16/185/51.

[71] *Ibid.*, 40/454/51 and 41/459-61.

[72] *Ibid.*

[73] *Debates*, no. 1, Fifth Senate, col. 84ff.

[74] See *The 'Western Areas' Removal Scheme: Facts and Viewpoints* presented at a Conference convened by the South African Institute of Race Relations at the University of Witwatersrand, 22nd August, 1953, published by the South African Institute of Race Relations, n.d., 35 pp. It recommended substituting slum clearance, and voluntary re-zoning and buffer strips of light industry where non-European and European areas were in close contact.

[75] *Rand Daily Mail*, March 13, 1954.

[76] *Star*, March 9, 1954, *ibid.*, 11/99/54.

[77] *Ibid.*

[78] *Ibid.*, 12/107/54.

[79] No. 68 of 1951.

[80] First reading, June 12, 1951, *House of Assembly Debates*, vol. 76, col. 9255; second reading, June 18, cols. 9807-9905, passed 59-52; committee stage, June 19, cols. 9998-10,060, approved, 49-40; report stage, June 20, col. 10,120; third reading, June 21, cols. 10,256-10,272.

[81] *Ibid.*, col. 9808.

[82] *Ibid.*

[83] *Ibid.*, col. 9822.

[84] *Ibid.*, col. 9834.

[85] Nel, *ibid.*, col. 9845.

[86] There are also two local Councils in the north-western Cape, and two in Natal. The three Reserves in the Free State—Witzieshoek, Thaba 'Nchu, and Seliba—are under Reserve Boards of Management, with European chairmen and vice-chairmen and appointed Bantu members.

[87] The General Council system for the Ciskei, the second largest of the Reserve areas in the Union, was established in 1934. This Council was constituted more on a federal basis and secured its revenue chiefly through contributions of 12½ per cent from the District Councils which, in line with the original Glen Grey system, get the quitrents and levy taxes on land where necessary.

[88] *Debates*, April 18-22, 1955, cols. 4259ff.

[88a] No. 49 of 1953.

[89] (1943) S.A.L.R. 242 (Cape *P.D.*), *Rex v. Carelse.*

[90] (1950) 3 S.A.L.R. 136 (A.D.)

[91] *Rex v. Lusu*, (1953) 2 S.A.L.R. 484 (A.D.)

[92] *Ibid.*, p. 498.

[93] *House of Assembly Debates*, vol. 82. Bill introduced August 3, 1953, col. 756; second reading, August 6, col. 1052ff., August 20, 21, 24, 25, 26, 27, cols. 2064-2401; third reading, September 4, col. 2852. Senate amendment agreed to, col. 4444.

[94] *Ibid.*, col. 2019.

[95] *Ibid.*, col. 2034.

[96] *Ibid.*, col. 2165.

[97] G. F. van L. Froneman and H. E. Martins, *ibid.*, col. 2071.

[98] *Ibid.*, col. 2086.

[99] *Ibid.*, col. 2239.

[100] *Ibid.*, col. 2132.

[101] *Ibid.*, col. 2105.

[102] *Ibid.*, col. 2886.

[103] No. 47 of 1953.

[104] *SAPA*, April 5, 1950, *P.D.*, 14/149/50.

[105] U.G. No. 53/1951.

[106] Para. 752.

[107] Para. 753.

[108] February 13, 1952, *P.D.*, 7/60-61/52.

[109] *P.D.*, 5/42/52.

[110] *Natal Witness*, July 4, 1953 and *The Star*, July 3, 1953, *P.D.*, 26/276/53.

[111] *House of Assembly Debates*. First reading, August 11, 1953, vol. 82, col. 1306; second reading, September 17-23, vol. 83, cols. 3575-4129, accepted 67-35; committee stage, September 25, cols. 4267-4347, clauses voted, 68-41, 67-38, 64-38; report stage, September 28, cols. 4351-60, new clause voted down, 44-76; third reading, September 29, cols. 4396-4426, accepted 79-47. Bantu Education Amendment Act, second reading, June 7, 1954, vol. 86, cols. 6438-52; committee stage, June 8-10, cols. 6605-6672, U.P. amendment rejected 31-64, clause as amended voted 65-30; third reading, June 11, accepted 63-31.

[112] *Ibid.*, col. 3576.

[113] *Ibid.*, col. 3591.

[114] *Ibid.*, col. 3597.

[115] *Ibid.*, col. 3640.

[116] *Ibid.*, col. 3612.

[117] *Ibid.*, col. 4049.

[118] *Ibid.*, col. 3668.

[119] *Ibid.*, col. 4071.

[120] *Ibid.*, col. 4124.

[121] *Natal Witness*, September 28, 1953, *P.D.*, 40/425/53.

[122] *Bantu World*, October 3, 1953, *ibid.*

[123] *Ibid.*

[124] *Star*, January 7, 1954, *P.D.*, 2/17/54.

[125] *Umthunywa*, February 27, 1954, *ibid.*, 10/95/54.

[126] Resolution from its Conference at King William's Town, September 23-29, 1954, cited in *Bantu Education—Oppression or Opportunity?* SABRA, Stellenbosch, 1955.

[127] *SAPA*, March 25, 1953, *P.D.*, 13/118/54.

[128] *Ibid.*

[129] *Ibid.*, 18/168/54.

[130] *Ibid.*

[131] March 25, 1953, *ibid.*, 13/118/54.

[132] A. W. Hoernlé, *Report on the Working of the Bantu Education Act*, South African Institute of Race Relations, 1955.

[133] *Star*, October 22, 1954.

[134] *Star*, April 23 and May 20, 1955.

[135] Communication to the Government, January 4, 1955. Printed in the *South African Outlook*, April 1, 1955.

[136] *Bantu World*, November 13, 1954.

[137] After 1957 there will be no subsidies, nor can school fees be charged. The Catholic schools will only provide for Catholics thereafter, and will depend on voluntary contributions from the parents.

[138] *Star*, October 23, 1954.

[139] *South Africa*, November 27, 1954. Subsequently a former Anglican school in Sophiatown was reopened by Bishop Reeves as a private school but it was denied registration and forced to close early in 1956.

[140] November 22, 1954.

[141] November 23, 1954.

[142] November 29, 1954.

[143] April 9, 1955.

[144] *Star*, December 1, 1954.

[145] *Argus*, November 30, 1954.

[146] *Die Burger*, July 1, 1954.

[147] *Die Burger*, December 12, 1953, *P.D.*, 49/524-25/53.

[148] *Argus*, December 12, 1953, *ibid.*

[149] December 14, 1953.

[150] *Report of the Commission of Inquiry on Separate Training Facilities for Non-Europeans at Universities*, 1954-1955.

[151] *Senate Debates*, weekly edition, May 9-13, 1955, col. 2450.

[152] *Ibid.*, col. 2457.

[153] *House of Assembly Debates*, weekly edition, May 9-14, 1955, col. 5593ff.

[154] May 5, 1955.

[155] Announced in *Dagbreek*, November 18, 1956, *P.D.*, 44/457/56.

[156] No. 48 of 1953.

[157] G.P. 32278—1945.

[158] *Ibid.*, para. 39.

[159] U.G. no. 21 of 1944.

[160] *Ibid.*, para. 466.

[161] Industrial Legislation Commission of Enquiry, *Report*, para. 1820.

[162] *House of Assembly Debates*, vol. 82, 1953, cols. 865-961, 1536-1582, 1587-1644. First reading, July 8, unopposed; second reading, August 4, 13, 14, 1955 accepted, 72-46; committee stage, August 18, 19, 1953, 1817-1932, no divisions; report stage, August 24, col. 2165, no division; third reading, August 26-27, cols. 2355-2401.

[163] *Ibid.*, cols. 869-70.

[164] *Ibid.*, col. 870.

[165] *Ibid.*, col. 866.

[166] *Ibid.*, col. 870.

[167] *Ibid.*, col. 867.

[168] *Ibid.*, col. 872.

[169] *Ibid.*, col. 876.

[170] *Ibid.*, col. 877.

[171] *Ibid.*, col. 880.

[172] Major P. V. G. van der Byl, *ibid.*, col. 1570.

[173] *Ibid.*, col. 950.

[174] *Ibid.*, col. 1577.

[175] *Ibid.*, col. 1622.

[176] *Ibid.*, col. 1549.

[177] Fourie, *ibid.*, col. 1622.

[178] *Ibid.*, col. 1544.

[179] Minister of Labour, *House of Assembly Debates*, May 30-June 3, 1955, cols. 6726-31.

[180] *Rand Daily Mail*, April 9, 1957, *P.D.*, 13/138/57.

[181] *P.D.*, 14/145/57.

CHAPTER 4

[1] He refers to the South African situation, pp. li-liii. The South African Government sought his advice before introducing the Separate Representation of Voters Bill. The reasons why Professor Wade believed the entrenched clauses were no longer binding appear in an article published in the *Cape Times*, March 24, 1952.

[2] See, for example, K. C. Wheare, *The Statute of Westminster* (1931), p. 108; Berriedale Keith, *Governments of the British Empire* (1935), p. 47; W. P. M. Kennedy and Schlosberg,

The Law and Custom of the South African Constitution (1935), p. 100; Ivor Jennings and Young, *Constitutional Laws of the British Empire* (1937), p. 265; H. E. Pollak, 'The Legislative Competence of the Union Parliament', *South African Law Journal*, 269 (1931), p. 286ff.; and Ivor Jennings, 'The Statute of Westminster and Appeals to the Privy Council', 52. *Law Quarterly Review*, 173, p. 187ff.

[3] *P.D.*, 35/258/48.

[4] *Die Transvaler*, October 11, 1948, *ibid.*, 40/293/48.

[5] *Ibid.*

[6] August 22, 1948, *P.D.*, 33/246/48.

[7] *P.D.*, 29/325/49.

[8] *Rand Daily Mail*, February 7, 1951, *P.D.*, 6/62/51.

[9] February 13, 1951, *ibid.*, 7/74/51.

[10] *Ibid.*

[11] *Ibid.*, 8/82-84/51.

[11a] The Civil Rights League organized a nation-wide petition against the Separate Representation of Voters Bill which was signed by 100,000 persons and presented at the bar of the House of Assembly.

[12] *Argus*, January 10, 1951, *ibid.*, 3/29/51.

[13] *House of Assembly Debates*, vol. 74, cols. 2586-2777, March 8-9, 1951. The Speaker's ruling was given on April 16, 1951, vol. 75, cols. 4201-19. Subsequent motion to introduce, April 16, col. 4466ff.; motion for second reading, April 18-19, cols. 5060-80; motion for guillotine procedure, April 24, cols. 5263-5309; second reading, April 25-30, cols. 5381-5705; committee stage, May 8-9, col. 6107ff.; report stage, May 11, cols. 6464-6526; third reading, May 14, cols. 6529-6655; response to Senate amendments, vol. 76, col. 9010ff., June 8 and 11.

[14] See his able pamphlet, *Parliamentary Sovereignty and the Entrenched Sections of the South Africa Act*, Cape Town & Johannesburg, Juta, 1951, 50 pp. and his articles in the *Modern Law Review* cited below.

[15] *Ibid.*, col. 2654.

[16] *Ibid.*, col. 2657.

[17] March 10, 1951.

[18] March 8, 1951.

[19] March 8, 1951, *ibid.*, 11/121-24/51.

[20] March 28, 1951, *ibid.*, 13/144/51.

[21] *Ibid.*, col. 4219.

[22] *Ibid.*, col. 4467.

[23] *Ibid.*, cols. 4493-4.

[24] *Ibid.*, col. 4775.

[25] *Ibid.*, col. 4520.

[26] *Ibid.*, col. 4590ff.

[27] *Ibid.*, col. 4590.

[28] *Ibid.*, col. 4878.

[29] *Ibid.*, cols. 4897-98.

[30] *Ibid.*, cols. 4994-95.

[31] *Ibid.*, col. 5697ff.

[32] The motion to introduce was passed by 77-65; the motion on the date for second reading, over which the Labour Party had not been informed, 76-64; motion for the guillotine procedure, justified by the Government on the ground that an unprecedented 47 hours had already been consumed in debate before second reading was started, 76-58; second reading, 76-69; committee stage, 76-66; report, 77-61; and third reading, 74-64.

[33] April 13, 1951, *P.D.*, 16/179-80/51.

[34] April 12, 1951, *ibid.*

[35] April 12, 1951, *ibid.*

[36] April 13, 1951, *ibid.*, 180-81.

[37] April 29, 1951, *ibid.*, 18/202/51.

[38] 1952 (2) S.A. 428. Also reported in the *Times Law Reports* in (1952), 1 T.L.R. 1245.

[39] Articles on the case include Erwin N. Griswold, 'The "Coloured Vote Case" in South Africa', *Harvard Law Review*, June 1952, pp. 1361-74; D. V. Cowen, 'Legislature and Judiciary: Reflections on the Constitutional Issues in South Africa', Part I and II, *The Modern Law Review*, July 1952, pp. 282-96 and July 1953, pp. 273-98; Edward McWhinney, 'The Union Parliament, the Supreme Court, and the "Entrenched Clauses" of the South Africa Act', *The Canadian Bar Review*, August-September 1952, pp. 692-722 and 'La Crise Constitutionnelle de L'Union Sud-Africaine', extrait de la Revue *Internationale de Droit Comparé*, 1953, no. 3, 22 pp., and Professor G. W. Keeton, 'The Constitutional Crisis in South Africa', *Current Legal Problems, 1953* ed. by G. W. Keeton and G. Schwarzenberger, vol. 6, London: Stevens & Sons, 1953, pp. 22-38.

[40] *SAPA, P.D.*, 24/274-75/51.

[41] June 7, 1951, *ibid.*

[42] *P.D.*, 13/114/52.

[43] *Ibid.*

[44] March 22, 1952, *ibid.*, 113.

[45] *Ibid.*, vol. 78, cols. 3824-26.

[46] Motion to introduce, April 22-23, 1952, vol. 78, cols. 4108-4265, carried 71-58; motion for second reading, col. 4269ff., carried 63-47; point of order and Speaker's ruling, April 30-May 2, 1952, cols. 4668-4864; second reading, May 5-8, cols. 4912-5515, carried 79-65; House in committee, May 12, cols. 5577-98, carried 80-58; third reading, May 14-15, cols. 5776-5922, carried 82-57; motion to adjourn House in protest, May 15, col. 5922ff., defeated, 58-82; Senate amendments accepted, May 29, 1952, 76-47.

[47] *Ibid.*, cols. 4108-9.

[48] Appeals were abolished formally by the Privy Council Appeals Act, no. 16 of 1950. Only in cases raising 'serious' constitutional issues had the Privy Council ever granted leave to appeal from decisions of the South African Supreme Court, and that practice had thus been an infrequent one.

[49] *Ibid.*, col. 4112.

[50] *Ibid.*, col. 4125.

[51] *Ibid.*, col. 5090.

[52] *Ibid.*, col. 5003.

[53] L.M.C. de W. Nel, *ibid.*, col. 5163.

[54] *Ibid.*, col. 5305.

[55] *Ibid.*, col. 5181.

[56] *Ibid.*, col. 5795

[57] *Ibid.*, col. 4939.

[58] *Ibid.*, col. 5422.

[59] *Ibid.*, col. 4955.

[60] *Ibid.*, col. 4954.

[61] *Ibid.*, col. 5134.

[62] May 11, 1952, *P.D.*, 20/195/52.

[63] May 8, 1952, *ibid.*, 190.

[64] *Ibid.*, 24/233/52.

[65] *Minister of the Interior v. Harris* (1952) 4 *S.A.L.R.*, 769 (A.D.), often called Harris case No. 2.

[66] See Edward McWhinney, 'Court versus Legislature in the Union of South Africa: The Assertion of a Right of Judicial Review', *The Canadian Bar Review*, January 1953, pp. 52-64.

[67] November 14, 1952, *P.D.*, 47/472-73/52.

[68] *Ibid.*

[69] *Star*, November 27, 1952, *ibid.*, 49/498/52.

[70] *Argus*, November 29, 1952, *ibid.*, 49/497/52.

[71] *Ibid.*, 50/511/52.

[72] December 9, 1952, *ibid.*, 511-12.

[73] December 28, 1952, *ibid.*, 53/533-34/52.

[74] Quoted by the *Star*, May 26, 1953.

[75] July 8, 1953, *P.D.*, 27/282/53.

[76] July 4, 1953, *ibid.*, 26/270-71/53.

[77] *Joint Sitting of Both Houses of Parliament* (To Amend the South Africa Act, 1909, to Validate and Amend the Separate Representation of Voters Act, 1951, and to Define the Jurisdiction of Courts of Law to Pronounce upon the Validity of Laws passed to Parliament). Bill introduced, July 14, 1953, cols. 10-29; second reading, July 15-16, cols. 32-237, votes, 117-79; committee, July 17, cols. 243-82, votes, 119-80; report, July 17; third reading, September 16, cols. 289-356, votes, 122-78.

[78] *Ibid.*, col. 56.

[79] *Ibid.*, col. 219.

[80] *Landstem*, August 1, 1953, *P.D.*, 30/312-13/53.

[81] *Ibid.*, 29/304-05/53.

[82] *Ibid.*, 30/312-13/53.

[83] *Star*, August 18, 1953, *P.D.*, 32/336/53.

[84] July 23, 1953, *ibid.*, 30/319/53.

[85] *Argus*, July 27, 1953, *P.D.*, 30/312-13/53 report on correspondence with Malan.

[86] *Joint Sitting of Both Houses of Parliament*, 1954, col. 339.

[87] See *The Cape Coloured Vote*: Separate Report by the United Party Members of the Joint Select Committee set up to consider the Separate Representation of Voters Act Validation and Amendment Bill, 1953 (Juta and Co.).

[88] *Joint Sitting of Both Houses of Parliament* (Separate Representation of Voters Act Validation and Amendment Bill 1954), No. 1, May 17-26, 1954; No. 2, June 9-14, 1954. Bill introduced May 18, cols. 5-13, votes 163-14; second reading, May 19-26, cols. 13-384, votes 118-74; committee, June 9-11, cols. 385-563, votes 101-38; report, June 11, cols. 363-66, votes 101-41; third reading June 4, cols. 567-644, votes 129-42.

[89] *Ibid.*, col. 422.

[90] *Ibid.*, col. 268.

[91] In mid-December 1955, a new political party, the South African Bond (*Suid Afrikaanse Bond*), was formed following the declaration of the thirteen professors. Its program of principles concentrated upon eradicating the causes of division between the European population groups. Though never strong, the South African Bond represented one in a series of efforts to establish a political party based on Hertzog principles which could provide an acceptable middle way between the Nationalists and the United Party.

[92] February 13, 1956, *P.D.*, 6/55/56.

[93] *P.D.*, 20/186/56.

[94] *Ibid.*, 43/436/56.

[95] Though it should be emphasized that General Hertzog, first leader of the National Party, took an active part in the discussions which produced the South Africa Act, 1909.

[96] *Sunday Times*, June 19, 1955.

[97] While the United Party Congress approved replacing on the common roll those Coloured voters who had previously voted there, it also proposed that new Coloured registrations should be subject to higher property qualifications.

[98] At its August 1957 congress the United Party also proposed important changes in the composition of the Senate designed both to entrench white leadership and to give more direct representation to non-Europeans.

CHAPTER 5

[1] Prior to the Senate Act of 1955, which so greatly increased the size of the Senate, the latter consisted of 48 members chosen by indirect election. Each of the four provinces selected 8 members through an electoral college consisting of its provincial counsellors and parliamentary representatives, while South West Africa similarly elected two. Of the other 14 members, 10 were nominated by the Governor-General (in practice the Ministry in power) of whom 5 were supposed to have special knowledge of non-European sentiment, and 4 were elected through Native electoral colleges throughout the Union. The latter 4 are chosen for five-year periods (see p. 356); the others were selected for 10-year periods.

Nominated senators must vacate their seats on a change of Government, and the whole Senate (except for the senators elected by the Natives) may be dissolved within 120 days of a general election for the House of Assembly. Though the Senate has equal legislative power with the Assembly, except in financial matters, a deadlock between the two houses is resolved through a joint session. This latter procedure is most significant, as chapter 4 made obvious, when there is a question of amending one of the entrenched clauses.

[2] For details about the election of the Native representatives see p. 355.

[3] The legal framework within which the 1953 election took place was provided by the South Africa Act, 1909, and the Electoral Consolidation Act, 1946, as amended by two Electoral Law Amendment Acts, Act No. 50 of 1948, and Act No. 55 of 1952. The law relating to the franchise, registration of voters and election of members of the House of Assembly is highly detailed, being divided into seven chapters and 188 sections. The same provisions, it may be noted, cover the elections to provincial councils. The latter consist of the same number of members as the province has parliamentary representatives unless, as in Natal and the Orange Free State, this is less than the minimum number of 25 for a provincial council. In the latter cases, a separate delimitation of constituencies must be made for a provincial election; otherwise there are the same constituencies as for a general election.

[4] Normally, supplementary registration takes place three times a year, on the first day of March, July and November, and the new lists of voters are issued on the first day of May, September or January.

[5] The postal vote returns were provided by the Chief Electoral Officer. It is interesting to note that the provinces vary less in percentages of postal votes than might be expected. In 1948, the Cape led with 20,252 valid postal votes or 4.94 per cent of the total vote counted; the Free State came second with 4,717 valid postal votes amounting to 4.72 per cent of the total; while the Transvaal and Natal were very close with 16,822, i.e. 3.69 per

cent for the former, and 3,806, i.e., 3.63 per cent for the latter. In 1953, the Free State had the highest percentage in the Union, 13.53 per cent with 15,785 valid postal votes; the Transvaal came second with 69,479, i.e. 13.27 per cent; Natal had 14,180 valid postal votes, amounting to 12.66 per cent of the valid total vote; while the Cape came last with 54,731, i.e. 12.63 per cent. All the South African provinces were far outstretched by South West Africa, however, which had 22.31 per cent of its total valid vote cast by post, totalling 5,203.

It was in particular constituencies that the postal vote was most striking, and perhaps most decisive. In 1948, Paarl in the Cape led with the highest percentage of valid postal votes to its valid total vote, i.e. 11.28 per cent; De-Aar-Colesberg, also in the Cape, was second with 10.08 per cent; Ermelo in the Transvaal was third with 9.66 per cent, and Kroonstad in the Free State fourth with 9.63 per cent. As might be expected, the percentages in 1953 were very much higher. De-Aar-Colesberg polled the highest percentage, amounting to 20.78; Newcastle in Natal was second with 19.63; Kroonstad third with 18.94 and Potchefstrom in the Transvaal fourth with 18.75.

[6] Of the total of 47,486 postal votes cast in 1948, 1,889 were rejected, i.e. 3.98 per cent as compared with 7,393 ballots rejected of the overall total of 1,077,085 votes cast, i.e. only .69 per cent. In 1953, 4,587 were rejected of the 163,971 postal votes cast, i.e. 2.80 per cent as compared with 8,709 votes rejected of the total of 1,217,637, i.e. .72 per cent.

[7] The numbers of white voters on the rolls on April 30, 1952, were:

Cape Province	554,123
Natal	155,959
Transvaal	693,108
Orange Free State	136,802
	1,539,992

[8] The allocation of seats between the provinces has been as follows:

Delimitation Commission Number	Year	Total	Cape	Natal	Transvaal	Orange Free State
1	1910	121	51	17	36	17
2	1913	130	51	17	45	17
3	1919	134	51	17	49	17
4	1923	135	51	17	50	17
5	1928	148	58	17	55	18
6	1932	150	61	16	57	16
7	1937	150	59	16	60	15
8	1943	150	56	16	64	14
9	1948	150	55	16	66	13
10	1952	150	54	15	68	13

[9] Provincial quotas have been as follows:

Delimitation Commission Number	Year	Cape	Transvaal	Natal	Orange Free State
1	1910	2,791	2,715	1,647	2,131
2	1913	2,913	2,557	1,729	2,342
3	1919	3,655	2,869	1,939	2,793
4	1923	3,863	2,824	2,035	2,884
5	1928	3,381	2,506	2,259	2,641
6	1932	3,526	2,867	2,832	3,141
7	1937	7,077	5,996	5,850	7,321
8	1943	8,905	7,956	7,515	7,846
9	1948	9,508	8,769	8,402	8,909
10	1952	11,115	10,193	10,376	10,508

[10] The delimitation of 1913 was carried out by 3 of the judges who served on the 1910 Commission; there was a complete change in 1919, the quinquennial date having been passed over because of the war; two of the 1923 Commission had served in 1919; two from the 1928 Commission served in 1932; one from the 1937 Commission served in 1943; and two from the 1943 Commission served in 1947.

[11] Memorandum submitted to the Tenth Delimitation Commission, 1952, on behalf of the War Veterans' Torch Commando, 42 pp. plus histograms.

[12] Table Showing Number of Rural Votes at each Delimitation Having the same Voting Strength as 100 Urban Votes.

Year of Delimitation	*Transvaal*	*Cape Province*	*Natal*	*Orange Free State*
1910	89	87	89	92
1913	87	89	85	96
1919	93	88	82	94
1923	91	90	89	94
1928	86	87	86	95
1932	85	86	87	91
1937	81	85	82	93
1943	80	85	79	92
1948	82	87	79	92

[12a] *Ibid.*, p. 9.

[13] *Ibid.*, p. 6.

[14] *Ibid.*, p. 10.

[15] Report, *op. cit.*, clauses 21 and 22.

[16] It is of some interest to note that in the same article The *Star* felt that United Party chances were improved by the new delimitation in 5 Transvaal constituencies—Geduld, Brakpan, Losberg, Florida, and Pietersburg, all of which, except Florida, were lost to the Nationalists in the general election by majorities varying between 47 for Brakpan to 2,271 in Pietersburg. The Nationalists won the five constituencies in which The *Star* felt the delimitation favoured them. The United Party won by 387 votes the new Vereeniging seat which The *Star* felt the Nationalists might take, and also, as expected, the new North Rand seat.

[17] In Great Britain the deposit is £150; and it is lost if the candidate receives less than one-eighth of the valid votes cast.

[18] Though there was no instance of it in 1953, it is possible in South Africa to nominate the same person for two constituencies. Colin Steyn, United Party Leader in the Orange Free State in 1953, won two seats at the same time in 1921; so did Bruckner de Villiers in 1929. The rationale behind the practice is to provide an important party member with both a crucial election fight, and a safe seat. If he wins both, he vacates the safe seat within a week of the election, and a by-election for it is then held. Another, less happy reason for a by-election occurred in 1953 when John Christie, leader of the Labour Party, died during the election campaign for Johannesburg City. No fresh nomination was necessary for his opponent; Hyman Davidoff, a Labour candidate defeated in a tough contest for Germiston during the regular election, was nominated in Christie's place after the election, and won the seat.

[19] Henry John May, *The South African Constitution*, 3rd edition, Cape Town and Johannesburg, Juta, 1955, p. 97.

[20] The detailed figures are as follows: for fuel, £125 2s. od. in one instance, £136 3s. 11d. in another, and £148 14s. 1d. in the third; printing, £185 12s. 6d., £149 2s. 9d. and £236 10s. od. respectively; postage, £101 8s. 1d., £52 13s. 7d., and £46 3s. od. Relatively little advertising was done by these candidates, the cost listed being only £9 12s. 6d., £6, and £23 12s. 9d. The figures were seen under pledge of not naming the constituencies.

[21] For the chart of expenditures see Appendix II. For a more detailed account of the newspapers see p. 457.

[22] May, *op. cit.*, 3rd ed., p. 141.

CHAPTER 6

[1] *Die Burger*, 1/1/53.

[2] *Rand Daily Mail*, 1/1/53.

[3] *Die Transvaler*, 14/1/53.

[4] The *Star*, 9/1/53.

[5] *Natal Mercury*, 10/1/53.

[6] *Cape Argus*, 20/1/53.

[7] *Die Burger*, 21/1/53.

[8] *Rand Daily Mail*, 22/1/53.

[9] *House of Assembly Debates*, Vol. 81, January 27, 1953, cols. 81-137, 139-191, 193-251, 273-356.

[10] A. E. P. Robinson in the House of Assembly, reported in the *Cape Times*, 31/1/53.

[11] Public Safety Act, No. 3 of 1953, and Criminal Laws Amendment Act, No. 18 of 1953.

[12] *House of Assembly Debates*, vol. 81, Leave to introduce, January 26, 1953, cols. 62-71; second reading, February 11-12, 1953, cols. 969-1149, no division; committee stage, February 13, cols. 1160-1210, clauses voted 51-69, 51-67, 47-64; report unopposed; third reading, February 16, cols. 1218-1273, no division.

[13] *Ibid.*, col. 996.

[14] *House of Assembly Debates*, vol. 81. Leave to introduce, January 30, 1953, col. 270ff; second reading, February 19-20, 1953, cols. 1544-1631 no division; committee stage, February 20, 1953, clauses voted, 38-51, 36-54; report stage without division; third reading, February 23, 1953, cols. 1646-1709, no division.

[15] *Ibid.*, col. 1590.

[16] *Rand Daily Mail*, 4/2/1953.

[17] *Ibid.*, 21/2/1953.

[18] *Cape Times*, 9/2/1953.

[19] *Dagbreek*, 1/2/1953.

[20] *Die Burger*, 2/2/1953.

[21] *Cape Times*, 13/2/53.

[22] *Die Transvaler*, 16/2/1955.

[23] *Ibid.*, 2/3/1953.

[24] *Rand Daily Mail*, 27/3/1953.

[25] *Eastern Province Herald*, 25/3/1953.

[26] See *Die Volksblad*, 24/3/1953.

[27] e.g. Mr. Strauss in Port Elizabeth, *Rand Daily Mail*, 26/3/1953.

[28] *Die Transvaler*, 14/3/1953.

[29] Reported in *Pretoria News*, 10/4/1953.

[29a] The Education Ordinance, 1953 embodied the controversial language clauses of the 1949 Education Act (Language) Amendment Ordinance which sought to ensure that children were educated in their home language regardless of their parents' wishes.

[30] *Die Burger*, 6/3/1953.

[31] *Die Vaderland*, 11/3/1953.

[32] *Die Transvaler*, 23/3/1953.

[33] This gave rise to the Reservation of Separate Amenities' Act, passed late in 1953. See p. 96.

[34] *Die Transvaler* e.g. 17/3/1953, 28/3/1953, 30/3/1953, 8/4/1953.

[35] In Port Elizabeth, *Rand Daily Mail*, 26/3/1953.

[36] Statement in Johannesburg, printed in The *Star*, 30/3/1953.

[37] *Cape Times*, 2/4/1953.

[38] *Die Transvaler*, 24/3/1953, and *Die Volksblad*, 23/3/1953.

[39] Speech in Potchefstroom, *Die Volksblad*, 28/3/1953.

[40] *Cape Times*, 27/3/1953.

[41] Barberton, March 8, 1953.

[42] At Newcastle, April 2, *Natal Mercury*, 3/4/1953.

[43] *Advance*, 26/3/1953.

[44] *Die Burger*, 7/4/1953.

[45] *Indian Opinion*, 27/2/1953.

[46] *Bantu World*, 4/4/1953.

[47] *The Torch*, 14/4/1953.

[48] Statement by its Chairman, Dr. S. Wilson, to The *Star*, 4/3/1953.

[49] *Rand Daily Mail*, 14/3/1953.

[50] *Cape Times*, 20/3/1953.

[51] No information was secured on the Labour candidate, John Christie, who died during the campaign. His seat, Johannesburg City, was subsequently contested by Hyman Davidoff, who had been defeated at Germiston.

[52] Particular thanks are due to Senator M. P. A. Malan of the National Party and to Mrs. van den Bos and Miss Jacqueline de Villiers of the United Party.

[53] R. B. McCallum and A. Readman, *The British General Election of 1945* (London, 1947); H. G. Nicholas, *The British General Election of 1950* (London, 1951;) D. E. Butler, *The British General Election of 1951* (London, 1952). As far as possible, the same kind of information was gathered for the South African election as these surveys provide but the author was handicapped by lack of comparable facilities.

[54] Two successful Nationalists and one unsuccessful Nationalist had training in the U.S.A. in addition to other university work.

[55] For the distinction between the three branches of the Dutch Reformed Church see p. 272.

[56] *The Natal Daily News* on April 29, 1953, gave a detailed table of occupations of the newly elected M.P.s which differs considerably from the records compiled by the author. Their table is as follows:

	Nationalists	*United Party*	*Labour*	*N.R.**	*Total*
Farmers	39	11	0	0	50
Lawyers	17	11	1	1	30
Business men	14	14	1	0	29
Politicians	10	—	—	—	10
Medical Practitioners and Dentists	3	6	0	0	9
Writers	1	5	1	1	8
Retired Teachers or Lecturers	5	1	0	1	7

* Native representatives elected at another time.

[57] Nationalists claim that two women who stood earlier as United Party candidates were 'Nationalists' in the true, if not technical sense.

[58] The Nationalists listed it this way; the U.P. said it was 60 per cent Afrikaans.

[59] These were Bloemfontein City, Newcastle, Witbank, Barberton, Brakpan, Langlaagte, Nigel, Randfontein, Roodepoort, Uitenhage.

[60]

Constituency	*Candidate*	*Home Language*
Springs	G. Sutter	English
Turffontein	R. Durant	English and Afrikaans
North Rand	B. Coetzee	Afrikaans
Albany	T. B. Bowker	English
Cape Town Castle	A. Bloomberg	English
Constantia	S. F. Waterson	English
Kingwilliamstown	C. M. Warren	English
Maitland	Z. J. De Beer	Afrikaans
P. E. South	H. O. Frielinghaus	Afrikaans
Queenstown	A. van Stytler	Afrikaans
Roudebosch	R. D. Pilkington-Jordan	English (non-bilingual)
Salt River	H. G. Lawrence	English

CHAPTER 7

[1] e.g. *Common Ground*, p. 10.

[2] *Ilanga lase Natal*, May, 2, 1953.

CHAPTER 8

[1] Early in 1957 the Union Jack ceased to be one of the Union's official flags.

[2] The Republican Constitution was printed as a special supplement of *The British Africa Monthly*, July, 1948, pp. 19-22. It provided for an oddly mixed authoritarian, parliamentary and corporative structure. The State President elected for five years was said to be 'directly and only responsible to God, over against the people'. In carrying out his duties 'he is altogether independent of any vote in Parliament'. All laws were validated by his personal signature and, at his personal discretion, he could relieve the First Minister of his post, or dissolve Parliament. The people were represented by a Parliament of not more than 150 members, and an advisory Community Council representing 'the spiritual, cultural, economic and social interests of the Community and of the groups within the Community'. The Head Minister and Council of Ministers, acting collectively, were to carry on the government of the state as long as they maintained the necessary support and confidence of Parliament, and the President. Special features of the draft constitution were its recognition of the particular position of the 'acknowledged Christian Churches',

presumably the D.R.C.; the fact that English was to be 'a second or supplementary language' though with equal rights with Afrikaans when it was considered to be in the best interests of the State; and that every non-European group was to be segregated in its own areas and spheres of work, though with self-government according to their fitness for it under the central management of the general Government of the country.

Die Transvaler on January 23, 1942, welcomed the draft Republican constitution as 'an indication of the general direction which the Party has already adopted' and felt that a comparison of its terms with those of the Nationalist program of principles showed much similarity.

Though Mr. Strijdom, a strong supporter of an eventual republic, has long said it would not be instituted without a special plebiscite on the issue, he told the O.F.S. National Party Congress on September 11, 1957, that the 1958 election would indicate how far towards a republic the country had gone. Though he declared that the Government could institute a republic by a simple majority, he affirmed that a large majority of votes was necessary and that the Party's present majority of seats in Parliament was insufficient. *The Times*, September 12, 1957.

[3] See also Roberts and Trollip, p. 47.

[4] *Ibid.*, p. 57.

[5] The H.N.P. 'cells' or groups were very like the organization used by the Ossewa Brandwag, though Malan was careful to deny the similarities. Roberts and Trollip, p. 81.

[6] Since November 1954, J. J. Serfontein has been a member of the Cabinet as Minister of Posts and Telegraphs and Social Welfare. He was replaced as Chief Whip by P. K. Le Roux.

[7] This wording is taken from Section 4 of the Transvaal Constitution, but it is more or less similar to the pledge made in other provinces. The Natal Constitution calls the party 'the sole political front of the European sections of the Afrikaner people'.

[8] After his defeat for the Assembly in 1953, Colin Steyn became a member of the Senate. He retired from the latter body because of health in November 1955. The United Party leader in the Free State is now Senator H. G. Swart.

[9] Roberts and Trollip, *op. cit.*, p. 47.

[10] Speech by P. W. Botha, Secretary of the Cape National Party, reported in the *Rand Daily Mail*, September 27, 1951.

CHAPTER 9

[1] These principles became part of the official constitution, Die Afrikanerparty, *Program van Beginsels en Konstitusie*, 1948, 36 pp. The principles are translated into English, pp. 12-17.

[2] *Die Burger*, 10 November 1943.

[3] Arthur G. Barlow, *Almost in Confidence*, p. 320.

[4] *Rand Daily Mail*, March 22, 1947.

[5] *Star*, August 18, 1947.

[6] *Die Transvaler*, March 23, 1947.

[7] *Star*, September 17, 1947.

[8] *Rand Daily Mail*, February 6, 1948.

[9] *Ibid.*, February 16, 1948.

[10] *Ibid.*, February 17, 1948.

[11] *Ibid.*, February 24, 1948.

[12] *Ibid.*, March 8, 1948.

[13] Roberts and Trollip, *op. cit.*, p. 168.

[14] *Rand Daily Mail*, February 16, 1948.

[15] *Die Transvaler*, March 28, 1948.

[16] *Die Volkstem*, March 28, 1948.

[17] *Rand Daily Mail*, April 24, 1948.

[18] *Star*, May 10, 1948.

[19] Quoted in *Rand Daily Mail*, March 6, 1948.

[20] *Star*, December 2, 1948.

[21] Dvorin, p. 72.

[22] *Sunday Express*, August 24, 1948.

[23] *Ibid.*, September 5, 1948.

[24] *Ibid.*, October 24, 1948.

[25] The publication of letters between Jan de Klerk, Organizing Secretary of the National Party in the Transvaal and J. L. V. Liebenberg, M.P. and Organizing Secretary of the Afrikaner Party show that from the beginning the National Party opposed the nomination of members of the Ossewa Brandwag as candidates in any constituency ceded to the Afrikaner Party. Pietersburg, Ermelo, Ventersdorp, Germiston, Losberg and Boksburg were allocated to the Afrikaner Party and it was given the option of nominating candidates for the additional constituencies of Pretoria City, Benoni, Bezuidenhout Valley, Kensington, Troyeville and Houghton. The Nationalist committee under the chairmanship of B. J. Schoeman which met a negotiating committee of the Afrikaner Party in Cape Town declared however that the agreement would bear the desired fruits only if there were a speedy union of the two parties, and no candidate was to be a member of the Ossewa Brandwag.

[26] *Star*, November 9, 1948.

[27] *Ibid*., November 12, 1948.

[28] *Ibid*., November 30, 1948.

[29] *Ibid*., December 7, 1948.

[30] *Ibid*., March 4, 1949.

[31] *Ibid*., May 25, 1949.

[32] *Sunday Times*, October 29, 1950.

[33] *Rand Daily Mail*, June 25, 1951.

[34] *Ibid*., August 2, 1951.

[35] *Star*, August 16, 1951.

[36] *Rand Daily Mail*, August 24, 1951.

[37] *Ibid*., October 15, 1951.

[38] This was contained in the joint statement on membership on August 2, 1951, and was approved by the Federal Council on August 16. *Star*, August 16, 1951.

CHAPTER 10

[1] Report of the Committee on 'Current Problems about the Existence, Aim, and Object of the Afrikaner Broederbond', Addendum B to *The Transaction of the 22nd Council of Churches*, May 16, 1951, Bloemfontein. Subsequently referred to as D.R.C. report.

[2] *Ibid*.

[3] Louis J. Du Plessis, *Letters of a Farmer*, Krugersdorp, privately printed, 1951, 28 pp. Reprinted letters to the *Star*, March 20, 1944, and October 12, 1948. The author maintains that the Broederbond was started in his home on May 24, 1918, that he was a member until 1922, and then resigned.

[4] *Star*, November 7, 1935.

[5] *Die Transvaler*, December 14, 1954.

[6] *Ibid*., December 20, 1944.

[7] *Ibid*., January 3, 1945.

[8] *Ibid*., December 14, 1944.

[9] *Ibid*., December 14, 1944.

[10] *Ibid*., December 30, 1944.

[11] *Ibid*., December 30, 1944.

[12] *Ibid*., December 30, 1944.

[13] *Ibid*., December 20, 1944.

[14] *Ibid*., December 14, 1944.

[15] *Referate en Verslag F.A.K. Kongres*, July 6 and 7, 1937. Nationale Pers Beperk, 130 pp., p. 122.

[16] *Verslag van die Tweede Ekonomiese Volkskongres*, 1950, Voortrekkerpers, Bpk. 176 pp., p. 134.

[17] *Referate, 1937 Kongres, op. cit*., p. 5.

[18] *Ibid*., pp. 7-8.

[19] *Ibid*., p. 10.

[19a] Dual medium instruction means that both English and Afrikaans are used in the classroom for the same students. Parallel medium instruction means that each language group is educated in its own tongue but both in the same school so that there are interchanges on the playing fields and other extra-curricular activities.

[20] *Ibid*., p. 95.

[21] *Die Johannesburgse Skakelkomite Sekretariele Verslag*, November 1951—October 1952, mimeo. 24 pp.

[22] Verslag, 1950 Ekonomiese Volkskongres, *op. cit.*, p. 146.

[23] Section II (c) i, ii, iii.

[24] Verslag, 1950 Ekonomiese Volkskongres, *op. cit.*, p. 151.

[25] J. H. Breytenbach, *Die Betekenis van die Tweede Vryheidsoorlog*, F.A.K., 1949, 69 pp., an account of the 1899-1902 Anglo-Boer War, and G. D. Scholtz, *Die Ondertekening van die Sandrivier Konvensie Herdenk*, F.A.K., 1951, 34 pp., an account of events leading up to the signing of the Sand River Convention, 1852.

[26] *Reddingsdaad en Volksopbou*, speeches at the R.D.B. Congress, Bloemfontein, July, 1941, 68 pp., p. 54.

[27] Fritz Steyn, *Die Bron van ons Ellende*—The Source of Our Misery—16 pp., p. 4.

[28] Dr. N. Diederichs, *Volksverbondenheid van die R.D.B.*, 13 pp., p. 4.

[29] Dr. T. E. Dönges, *Die Toekomsrol van die R.D.B. in ons Ekonomiese Lewe*, 4 pp.

[30] Dr. N. Diederichs, *Sin en Betekenis van die Reddingsdaadbond*, 16 pp., p. 8.

[31] *Report of the Reddingsdaadbond*, 1950, p. 161.

[32] Federation of Afrikaans Cultural Societies, *Christian-National Education Policy*. Drawn up and published by the Institute for Christian-National Education, Johannesburg 1949. English translation by J. Chr. Coetzee, mimeo., 15 pp. This translation is used in the quotations. An abridged translation is included in *Blueprint for Blackout*, issued by the Education League, n.d., 23 pp., which sharply criticizes C.N.E.

[33] Marquard, *Peoples and Policies*, *op. cit.*, p. 179.

[34] *Cape Times*, February 5, 1949.

[35] *Star*, May 14, 1949, *P.D.*, 21/235/49.

[36] June 1, 1949, *P.D.*, 22/255-56/49.

[37] April 14, 1949, *P.D.*, 16/189/49.

[38] April 14, 1949, *P.D.*, 16/189/49.

[39] April 16, 1949, *P.D.*, 16/189/49.

[40] *Star*, May 4, 1949, *P.D.*, 19/222/49.

[41] *Forward*, May 20, 1949.

[42] April 16, 1949, *P.D.*, 16/187/49.

[43] April 13, 1949, *P.D.*, 16/187/49.

[44] *Ibid.*, June 9, 1949, *P.D.*, 24/279/49.

[45] *Star*, May 4, 1949, *P.D.*, 19/220/49.

[46] May 4 and 6, 1949, *P.D.*, 19/220/49.

[47] June 24, 1949, *P.D.*, 26/302/49.

[48] July 20, 1949, *P.D.*, 30/339/49.

[49] October 12, 1949, *P.D.*, 42/470/49.

[50] *Die Suiderstem*, October 6, 1949, *P.D.*, 41, 162/63/49.

[51] October 7, 1949, *ibid.*

[52] *SAPA*, July 20, 1950, *P.D.*, 29/323/50.

[53] July 24, 1950, *P.D.*, 30/328-29/50.

[54] August 8, 1950, *P.D.*, 32/346-47/50.

[55] *Star*, September 5, 1950, *P.D.*, 41/445/50.

[56] January 9, 1951, *P.D.*, 2/19/51.

[57] *Volksblad*, October 16, 1951, *P.D.*, 42/472/51.

[58] *Dr. Malan's Policy for South Africa's Mixed Population*, a pre-1948 election pamphlet.

[59] Subsequently reprinted as an article 'Is Separation Practicable?' in the second issue of *SABRA's Journal of Racial Affairs*, January 1950, p. 13ff.

[60] W. W. M. Eiselen, 'Gedagtes oor Apartheid' (Thoughts on Apartheid), *Tydskrik vir Geesteswetenskappe*, April, 1949, pp. 7-8 (Publication of the University of Pretoria).

[61] *Integration or Separate Development?* issued by the South African Bureau of Racial Affairs (SABRA), Stellenbosch 1952, 35 pp. Another pamphlet, *Apartheid—A Slogan or a Solution* by Professor N. J. J. Olivier, Stellenbosch, 1954, 12 pp., was first printed in the *Journal of International Affairs*, April, 1953 (Columbia University, New York). A third, *Bantu Education: Oppression or Opportunity*, Stellenbosch, 1955, 48 pp., defends the Bantu Education Act.

[62] *Ibid.*, p. 7.

[63] *Ibid.*, pp. 24-25.

[64] These difficulties are the greater because for a sale it is now necessary to get the consent of all the farmers of the area, not merely of an individual. Some who hold land adjacent to present Native Reserves would be ready to sell their holdings but are restrained by their neighbors who wish to keep a barrier between themselves and the Native area.

[65] *Ibid.*, p. 23.

[66] *Ibid.*, p. 24.

[67] *Ibid.*, p. 27.

[68] By May, 1954, industries in or close to Bantu areas included the Foskor works in the Northern Transvaal; the sugar mill at Pongola; the pulp and paper industry in Tugela,

Zululand; and lime works in Taungs District; cf. Dr. Verwoerd's speech to the Federated Chambers of Industry, Cape Town, May 26, 1954, printed in *Bantu: an informal publication of the Department of Native Affairs*, No. 5, August, 1954, pp. 7-24.

[69] *Ibid.*, p. 29.

[70] *Ibid.*, p. 30.

[71] *Ibid.*, p. 31.

[72] *Ibid.*, p. 35.

[73] *Summary of the Report*, p. 179. See also Chapter 1, Note 1.

[74] This estimate has been sharply criticized by L. H. Samuels, Senior Lecturer in Economics at Witwatersrand University, *Rand Daily Mail*, April 30, May 1, and May 2, 1956.

[75] In 1946, when 1,284,135 South Africans declared they belonged to the Dutch Reformed Church, official church records listed as many as 1,066,356 members. In the same census 1,359,691 were recorded as Afrikaans-speaking. In contrast, the Presbyterian Church reported only 19,577 members although 87,905 claimed this affiliation in the census. Eric Gargett, *European Religious Affiliation in South Africa: An examination of Source Material with Particular Reference to the Union Census.* Unpublished thesis submitted for the M.A. degree in the University of Witwatersrand, 1953. 86 pp., p. 72.

[76] While the N.G.K. had 1,078,405 members in 1946 according to the census, and 903,607 on the church rolls, and the N.H.K. had 127,887 in census figures and 96,326 on church rolls, the *Gereformeerde Kerk* had only 77,843 according to the census, and 66,423 by the church records. Eric Gargett, *op. cit.*, p. 72.

[77] In 1930, a minister of the N.G.K., the Rev. J. du Plessis, Professor of Theology at Stellenbosch and the editor of the 'Zoeklight', was excommunicated for heresy for beliefs considered only mildly liberal in most Western Protestant Churches.

[78] Ben J. Marais, *Colour: Unsolved Problem of the West*, Cape Town, 1952, 329 pp.

[79] *Ibid.*, p. 322.

[80] *Ibid.*, p. 292.

[81] *Ibid.*, p. 293.

[82] *Ibid.*, pp. 300-319.

[83] *Die Kerkbode*, 10 December, 1952, vol. LXX, no. 24; 31 December, 1952, no. 27; 14 January, 1953, vol. LXXI, no. 2; 28 January, 1953, no. 4; 4 February, 1953, no. 5.

[84] *Ibid.*, January 14, 1953.

[85] *Ibid.*, February 4, 1953.

[86] *Ibid.*, December 31, 1952.

[87] *Christian Principles in Multi-Racial South Africa: A Report on the Dutch Reformed Conference of Church Leaders*, Pretoria, 17-19 November, 1953, n.d., no publisher listed. 185 pp. The phrasing of quotations is taken from the original mimeograph reports.

[88] The Rev. A. M. Meiring, Assessor of the Synod of the N.H.K., pointed out in his speech that Dr. Brink's point of view was that expressed also by Dr. A. J. van der Merwe, Moderator of the Cape N.G.K. when addressing the Federal Council of the N.G.K. at Cape Town, April, 1953.

[89] Christian Principles, *op. cit.*, pp. 41-45.

[90] *The Racial Issue in South Africa: Being findings on the Native problem of various congresses held under the auspices of the Federal Missionary Council of the Dutch Reformed Mother and Mission Churches* (1950-1952). D.R. Mission Press, Bloemfontein, 1953, 16 pp.

[91] Quoted by Dr. W. A. Visser 't Hooft, *Christianity, Race and South African People: Report on an Ecumenical Visit*, New York, 1952, 33 pp., p. 22.

[92] Racial Issue, *op. cit.*, p. 7.

[93] *Ibid.*, p. 8.

[94] *Ibid.*, p. 15.

[95] *Ibid.*, p. 13.

[96] Visser 't Hooft, *op. cit.*, p. 16.

CHAPTER II

[1] But see clause 2 (d), p. 473, which permits individual members of the Party to 'advocate' their 'honest convictions' regarding 'any change of our form of Government'.

[2] It is composed of the president, one or more vice presidents, the chairman and secretary of each divisional committee, one delegate from each branch within the Council's jurisdiction, ten delegates of the Witwatersrand Women's Council and ten from the central governing body of the Witwatersrand Youth Council, United Party Senators, and

members of the General or Provincial Head Committees resident on the Witwatersrand, M.P.s and M.P.C.s who represent the party in Witwatersrand constituencies, a number of representatives of political clubs in Johannesburg and Krugersdorp, and of local authorities, and up to 25 members co-opted at large by the Council.

[3] The United Party special Union Congress which met in August 1957 made a number of important decisions on non-European policy. It agreed to replace the Coloured on the common roll in Cape Province. (See p. 144 and Note 98, Chapter 4.) It also adopted a moderate proposal for reconstituting the Senate: to reduce its present numbers to about 50, rather less than a quarter of whom would be elected by African and Coloured voters and the rest—except for a few nominated Senators—would be elected by European voters by proportional representation. To become law a Bill, and in particular any measure affecting the Constitution, franchise laws, and fundamental rights to be specified later, would need both an overall majority in the Senate and a majority of the Senators representing Europeans. In this way it was hoped that both the representatives of the Europeans and of the non-Europeans would have a veto on important measures adversely affecting their interests. In other, less fundamental issues, conflicts between the two houses would be resolved by a joint sitting except that in money bills the will of the Assembly would automatically prevail.

The United Party plan for the Senate coupled with its decision to replace the Coloured on the common roll would open the way for a small measure of direct political power to be exercised by non-Europeans, in particular, in defence of their own interests. Moreover the fact that about one-third of those at the Congress were prepared to support the unsuccessful but forward-looking amendments which attempted to secure similar representation in the Senate for Indians to that approved for Africans and Coloured, and to have the latter represented in the Senate by their own people, indicates a significant change in the thinking of a considerable percentage of the United Party which may have important implications for the future.

[4] The Provincial Executive consists of the provincial chairman, and vice chairman, the chairman and four delegates from each of the three General Councils, one representative of the Women's General Council and two of the Youth Organization.

[5] The *Star*, August 1, 1951.

CHAPTER 12

[1] *Rand Daily Mail*, May 5, 1951.
[2] *Rand Daily Mail*, May 12, 1951.
[3] *Cape Times*, May 16, 1951.
[4] *Rand Daily Mail*, May 25, 1951.
[5] *Star*, June 1, 1951.
[6] *East London Daily Despatch*, June 21, 1951.
[7] *Star*, June 29, 1951.
[8] *Die Burger* wrote: 'The protest comes from pro-Opposition servicemen who, by implication or expressly, are calling upon the public to look upon them as fighters for the same freedom they fought for in World War II.

'No approach is conceivable that could more effectively repel the nationally minded population.

'By reminding the nationally minded of what was for so many citizens a period of division and persecution and lack of freedom, the torch bearers assure themselves from the outset of the inexorable opposition of those people.' (*Star*, June 1, 1951.)

[9] *Sunday Times*, June 17, 1951.
[10] *Star*, July 3, 1951.
[11] *Star*, August 9, 1951.
[12] *Star*, November 9, 1951.
[13] *Cape Times*, May 19, 1951.
[14] *Rand Daily Mail*, June 22, 1951.
[15] *Star*, July 23, 1951.
[16] *Star*, August 20, 1951.
[17] *Rand Daily Mail*, August 15, 1951.
[18] *Sunday Times*, August 5, 1951.
[19] *Star*, September 4, 1951.
[20] *Star*, August 15, 1951.
[21] *Star*, August 21, 1951.

[22] *Rand Daily Mail*, August 28, 1951.
[23] *Star*, January 11, 1952.
[24] *Rand Daily Mail*, November 9, 1951.
[25] *Rand Daily Mail*, September 4, 1951.
[26] Quoted in *The Forum*, September 14, 1951.
[27] *Star*, November 12, 1951.
[28] *Star*, February 22, 1952.
[29] *Argus*, February 21, 1952.
[30] *Star*, February 26, 1952.
[31] *Star*, March 23, 1952.
[32] *Rand Daily Mail*, March 25, 1952.
[33] *Star*, March 25, 1952.
[34] *Rand Daily Mail*, March 27, 1952.
[35] *Natal Mercury*, April 18, 1952.
[36] Quoted in the *Star*, April 21, 1952.
[37] Quoted by the *Rand Daily Mail*, April 23, 1952.
[38] *Rand Daily Mail*, May 3, 1952.
[39] *Rand Daily Mail*, June 5, 1952.
[40] This resolution read:

'Now therefore this Council solemnly and earnestly requests and recommends to Parliament, whose sovereign powers we freely acknowledge, to take the necessary legislative steps to call into being a National Convention equally representative of the four Provinces of the Union, and, if deemed advisable, of South West Africa, for the purpose by mutual agreement of reaffirming the Constitution of the Union of South Africa and in so doing to entrench and protect against repeal or amendment (save by the procedure laid down in second proviso to Section 152 of the South Africa Act) the basic principles of the said Act', which basic principles the Council thereupon enumerated: and then expressed 'its belief that the very existence of the Union is now in danger and that unless the Act of Union is honoured both in spirit and in letter the State of Union cannot continue to exist but will dissolve to the detriment of the peoples of South Africa and the destruction of white civilization in our land'.

[41] *Rand Daily Mail*, June 13, 1952.
[42] *Star*, June 13, 1952.
[43] Confusingly, this congress, like that of a year before, was called 'First' on the ground that the earlier one had been an organizing meeting whereas this was the first since the War Veterans' Torch Commando was established as such.
[44] One Torcher had commented earlier: 'We are told the United Party have a master election plan up their sleeve. By the time they produce the rabbit there will be no one left in the hall to applaud the act.'
[45] Published in the *Natal Mercury*, January 17, 1953.
[46] Following the rejection by the Union Government of its resolution of June 4, the Provincial Council had resolved:

'That in spite of the studied insult and the contempt shown to the spirit of goodwill offered by this Province, this Council again reiterates its belief in preserving the state of Union as based on our Constitution; and advocates the immediate calling together of the Members of Parliament, the Senate and the Provincial Council of this Province to consider, in consultation with the representatives of all organizations dedicated to the preservation of the Constitution, what action can be taken to ensure the maintenance of the democratic state of Union and the removal from office of the present Government.'

[47] *Rand Daily Mail*, August 26, 1952.
[48] *Natal Witness*, August 27, 1952.
[49] *Star*, September 11, 1952.
[50] *Rand Daily Mail*, September 13, 1952.
[51] *Star*, September 11, 1952.
[52] *Star*, September 13, 1952.
[53] *Star*, November 21, 1952.
[54] *Natal Mercury*, January 17, 1953, carried the full story.
[55] Memorandum, *op. cit.*, p. 8.
[56] *Petition for the Exercise by His Excellency of his Powers and Discretions in Terms of the Status of the Union Act* (Act No. 69 of 1934) by N. J. de Wet, Patron-in-Chief, A. G. Malan, National President and L. Kane-Berman, National Chairman.
[57] *Star*, September 8, 1952.
[58] *Star*, November 12, 1952.
[59] *Star*, May 9, 1953.
[60] *Christian National Education: A Critical Commentary by the South African Teachers' Association, Cape Province*. Published by the Association, Cape Town, n.d., 20 pp.

[61] *Blueprint for Blackout: A Commentary on the Education Policy of the Instituut vir Christelik-Nationale Onderwys,* with an abridged translation of the recent pamphlet in which the policy is stated. Issued by the Education League, n.d., 23 pp.

[62] T. B. Davie, *Education and Race Relations in South Africa: The Interaction of Educational Policies and Race Relations in South Africa,* South African Institute of Race Relations, Johannesburg, 1955, 31 pp. The Eleventh Hoernlé Memorial Lecture.

[63] Ellen Hellman, ed. by. *Handbook on Race Relations in South Africa,* Oxford University Press, New York, 1949, xii, 778 pp.

[64] Census figures are far higher than the numbers on church rolls. Where the census reported 141,747 for the Methodist church in 1936, church rolls indicated 74,466. The Presbyterians were reported in the 1946 census as having 87,905 members whereas church rolls specified 19,577. 119,389 Roman Catholics were reported in the 1946 census; 79,058 were on church rolls, in fact, more than for the Methodists. The Anglican church does not keep membership records. Like other Protestant denominations, the Anglicans are separate from any overseas control despite their curious name of the Church of the Province of South Africa. Eric Gargett, *European Religious Affiliation in South Africa,* unpublished thesis at Witwatersrand University, 1953.

[65] *The Christian Citizen in a Multi-Racial Society: A Report of the Rosettenville Conference July 1949.* Strand, C.P., n.d., 107 pp.

[66] Christian Principles, *op. cit.,* pp. 25 & 27.

[67] *Ibid.,* p. 60.

[68] *Ibid.,* p. 66.

[69] *Ibid.,* p. 93.

CHAPTER 13

[1] *Non-European Policy,* as adopted by the Special Conference held on 10th November 1946, South African Labour Party, mimeo., 10 pp.

[2] *Supplementary statement to Non-European Policy,* November 13, 1946, South African Labour Party, 2 pp.

[3] Printed in full in *Forward,* January 30, 1953, p. 3.

[4] Paradoxically the party used to fear the trade unions would have too much influence and in 1948 the party's Constitution was formally amended to make sure that the trade union card vote would not be decisive in any issue, a move resulting from the opposition of some of the older trade unions to the progressive Non-European policy adopted in 1946.

[5] See *The Policies of the Liberal Party in South Africa,* n.d., 23 pp. It notes that on February 22, 1955, Mrs. Ballinger, and Walter Stanford, recently elected Native representative, moved for the Liberal Party that Africans now on the separate roll be transferred to the common roll, that all Africans 21 or over who could meet certain education standards be enfranchised, and that educational opportunities be immediately expanded to enable them to meet this qualification.

CHAPTER 14

[1] The best known names among Native Senators are Edgar Brookes and, since 1948, William G. Ballinger, husband of Margaret Ballinger. Of the fourteen persons who acted as Native representatives up to 1953, nine had university education; four studied abroad, three in the United Kingdom and one in the United States; at least four had been connected with institutions of higher learning in a teaching or administrative capacity; six had published. The group included four lawyers, an accountant and a labor leader. At least six had served prominently with the Institute of Race Relations. For this information, the author is indebted to an unpublished paper by Paula Eldot, *Natives' Representatives in the South African Parliament, 1936-1952,* 1953, 53 pp., prepared at Yale University.

[2] Mrs. Ballinger in *Political Representation of the Africans in the Union,* pp. 20-21.

[3] *Journal of the Parliaments of the Empire,* vol. 29, p. 185.

[4] *Ibid.,* vol. 30, pp. 322-23.

[5] See Rene M. de Villiers, 'Politics' in *Handbook of Race Relations in South Africa,* pp. 515-16, published by the S.A. Institute of Race Relations.

[6] *Rand Daily Mail,* November 4, 1947, quoted in Julius Lewin, *The Rise of Congress in South Africa,* reprinted from the *Political Quarterly,* London, 16 pp.

[7] For information on the Industrial and Commercial Workers' Union, see E. Roux, *Time Longer than Rope, op. cit.*, and the unpublished and incomplete autobiography of Clement Kadalie which is in Mr. Roux's possession.

[8] Particularly as disclosed by the epoch-making *Report of the Cape Coloured Commission*, U.G. No. 54, 1937.

[9] See Maurice Webb and Kenneth Kirkwood, *The Durban Riots and After*, Institute of Race Relations, 1949, 22 pp.

[10] Submitted November 4, 1952, mimeo., 30 pp., plus five annexures.

[11] In fact, there was an attempted boycott of Indian traders in the Transvaal in 1947 which the National party tried to use for its own political purposes. 'Politics', *Handbook of Race Relations*, de Villiers, p. 528.

[12] The independence of Ghana in 1957, which will shortly be followed by that of Nigeria, may give Africans the same kind of outside support.

[13] *The Constitution of the African National Congress*, with introductory note, mimeo., n.d., 26 pp. This early Constitution is very detailed, with ten chapters and 166 clauses, many of them with subdivisions. A much simpler Constitution was accepted at Bloemfontein on December 16, 1943, when A. B. Xuma was President General, which consists of 16 sections, many subdivided, but covers only four mimeographed pages.

[14] 'Politics', *Handbook of Race Relations*, de Villiers, p. 517.

[15] *African Claims in South Africa*, Congress Series, No. 11, published by the African National Congress, Johannesburg, reprinted almost in full in *Second Report of the United Nations Commission on the Racial Situation in the Union of South Africa*, General Assembly, Official Records, Supplement No. 16 (A/2719), New York 1954, pp. 60-61.

[16] The letters are reproduced as Annexure B to the *Memorandum on the Disabilities of the Non-White Peoples of South Africa* presented by the African National Congress and the South African Indian Congress to the United Nations, cited above.

[17] *Bantu World*, January 26, 1952, *P.D.*, 5/39/52.

[18] *Die Burger*, October 31, 1952, *P.D.*, 45/449-50/52.

[19] 'The Clarion Call to the Bantu People of Natal', the invitation by the Natal Native Medical Council to the meeting at which the Bantu National Congress was founded, charged that 'the sole Indian aim about the Native' is 'simply the admixture of two races. . . . The Indians insist on miscegenation and immorality with Native womenfolk'. Cited in *The Torch*, February 26, 1952. Quoted by Professor Leo Kuper, in a paper on 'The Background of Passive Resistance', read to the Institute of Race Relations, Durban, 1952. See also his more detailed study, *Passive Resistance in South Africa*, Yale University Press, 1957, 256 pp.

[20] *P.D.*, 6/49-50/52.

[21] *Ibid.*, 10/89/52.

[22] *Rand Daily Mail*, March 10, 1952, *P.D.*, 11/99/52.

[23] *Ibid.*, March 22, 1952, *P.D.*, 13/121/52.

[24] *P.D.*, 11/99/52.

[25] *The Disabilities of the Non-White Peoples of South Africa, op. cit.*, p. 27.

[26] July 8, 1952, *P.D.*, 28/278/52.

[27] June 4, 1952, *P.D.*, 23/229/52.

[28] June 27, 1952, *P.D.*, 27/269/52.

[29] *P.D.*, 31/312/52 and 33/325/52.

[30] *P.D.*, 36/358/52.

[31] *P.D.*, 43/424/52.

[32] October 28, 1952, *P.D.*, 44/426/52.

[33] October 21, 1952, *P.D.*, 43/426/52.

[34] *Ibid.*

[35] *Ibid.*, p. 438.

[36] October 30, 1952.

[37] November 4, 1952.

[38] November 4, 1952.

[39] *Natal Witness*, November 10, 1952.

[40] *Rand Daily Mail*, November 12, 1952, *P.D.*, 46/460/52.

[41] November 10, 1952, *ibid.*, 460-61.

[42] *Star*, November 10, 1952, *ibid.*

[43] November 11, 1952.

[44] The Africanists are an expelled Orlando branch of the African National Congress. They are against the Freedom Charter and white cooperation, and they were critical of the African National Congress boycott of the Bantu Education Act.

[45] *The Threatened People—the Case for a South African Democracy*, South African Congress of Democrats, Johannesburg. Quoted in the *Second Report of the United Nations Commission on the Racial Situation in South Africa*, General Assembly, Official Records, Ninth Session, Supplement No. 16 (A/2719), New York 1954, pp. 61-62.

CHAPTER 15

[1] Though the United Nations Commission on the Racial Situation in South Africa (p. 402) was not continued after 1955, the 1956 General Assembly again expressed its general disapproval of apartheid policies. United Nations General Assembly A/3508.

[2] Only a simple majority is required on matters relating to non-self-governing territories as opposed to trusteeship questions. Though the situation regarding South West Africa is not entirely clear, there are precedents for a two-thirds majority requirement.

[3] U.N.G.A., First Session, First Part, Plenary Meetings, 12th meeting (17 January 1946) p. 185.

[4] *Ibid.*, First Session, Second Part, 4th Committee, 14th Meeting, (4 November 1946) p. 63.

[5] *Ibid.*, First Session, Second Part, 4th Committee, 19th Meeting (13 November 1946) p. 101.

[6] *Ibid.*, First Session, Second Part, 4th Committee, sub-committee 2, set up to consider S.W.A.'s status and the Union's proposal, 9th meeting (28 November 1946), p. 52.

[7] *Ibid.*, Second Session, Fourth Committee, 31st Meeting (25 September 1947), p. 4.

[8] *Ibid.*, Second Session, 4th Committee, 31st Meeting (25 September 1947), p. 3.

[9] *Ibid.*, Third Session, 4th Committee, 76th Meeting (9 November 1948), p. 287.

[10] *Ibid.*, 78th Meeting (11 November 1948), p. 307.

[11] *Ibid.*, 4th Committee, p. 293.

[12] United Nations Document A/929.

[13] *Ibid.*, A/933, 1948.

[14] *Report of the Drafting Committee on the Report on the Administration of the Territory of South West Africa for 1946*, U.N.G.A. Third Session, Supplement, 1948, p. 228.

[15] U.N.G.A., Fourth Session, 4th Committee, 128th Meeting (November 18, 1949), p. 201.

[16] *Ibid.*, p. 202.

[17] *Ibid.*, p. 203. See also Fourth Session, Plenary Meetings, 269th Meeting (December 6, 1949), p. 523.

[18] United Nations Document A/C. 4/L/196.

[19] *Ibid.*, Document A/2261. Report of the *ad hoc* Committee on South West Africa to the General Assembly. Agenda item 36, 55 pp.

[20] General Assembly Resolution, 749 A (VIII) of November 28, 1953, adopted at 460th plenary meeting.

[21] Eighth Session, Fourth Committee, 362nd Meeting (November 11, 1953), pp. 293-94.

[22] Ninth Session, Suppl. No. 14 (A/2666), N.Y. 1955, 39 pp.

[23] *Ibid.*, p. 2.

[24] *Ibid.*, pp. 31-38.

[25] Communique No. 55/32 I.C.J., June 7, 1955.

[26] *South Africa,* June 25, 1955.

[27] Tenth Session, Suppl. No. 12 (A/2913), N.Y. 1955, 50 pp.

[28] *N.Y. Times,* November 15, 1955.

[29] No. 56 of 1954.

[30] *N.Y. Times,* November 1, 1955.

[31] *Report* 1955, p. 30.

[32] U.N.G.A., Second Part, First Session, Joint First and Sixth Committee, p. 2.

[33] *Ibid.*, p. 3.

[34] *Ibid.*

[35] *Ibid.*, p. 4.

[36] See *Ibid.*, pp. 5-51 and Plenary Meetings, pp. 1006-1040.

[37] *Ibid.*, Plenary Meetings, p. 1061.

[38] U.N.G.A., Second Session, First Committee, Annex 5, pp. 539-45.

[39] *Ibid.*, pp. 532-39.

[40] *Ibid.*, Plenary Meetings, Vol. II, Annex 26, Doc. A/492, p. 1616.

[41] U.N.G.A., Third Session, Part II, Resolutions, p. 6.

[42] *Ibid.*, First Committee, p. 321.

[43] 395 (V).

[44] U.N.G.A., Fifth Session, Resolution, p. 24.

[45] *Ibid.*, Eighth Session, Resolutions, p. 5.

[46] *Ibid.*, Fifth Session, *ad hoc* Political Committee, p. 248.

[47] *Ibid.*, p. 474.

[48] *Ibid.*, Third Session, Part II, Plenary Meetings, p. 445

[49] November 14, 1950, p. 251.

[50] U.N.G.A., Second Part, First Session, p. 200.

[51] *Ibid.*, Seventh Session, *ad hoc* Political Committee, p. 36.

[52] *Ibid.*, Sixth Session, *ad hoc* Committee, p. 171.

[53] *Ibid.*, Second Part, First Session, Plenary Meetings, p. 1033.

[54] *Ibid.*, p. 1035.

[55] *Ibid.*, Joint First and Sixth Committee, p. 11.

[56] *Ibid.*

[57] *Ibid.*, Fifth Session, *ad hoc* Committee, p. 256.

[58] *Ibid.*, Second Session, First Committee, p. 448.

[59] *Ibid.*, Second Part, First Session, General Committee, p. 71.

[60] p. 294.

[61] U.N.G.A., Second Part, First Session, Plenary Meetings, p. 1041.

[62] *Ibid.*, Joint First and Sixth Committee, p. 29.

[63] *Ibid.*, Plenary Meeting, p. 1044.

[64] *Ibid.*, Joint First and Sixth Committee, p. 8.

[65] *Ibid.*, Plenary Meetings, p. 1038.

[66] *Ibid.*

[67] *Ibid.*, Second Session, Plenary Meetings, pp. 1140-41.

[68] *Ibid.*, Third Session, Part II, First Committee, pp. 292-93.

[69] e.g., U.N.G.A., Sixth Session, *ad hoc* Political Committee, p. 167, and Seventh Session, same Committee, p. 43.

[70] Letter from the Permanent Representative of the United Kingdom, April 30, 1954, reprinted in the Second Report of the Commission, G.A., Ninth Session, Suppl. No. 16 (A/2719), 1954, p. 8.

[71] First Report of the Commission, Eighth Session, Suppl. No. 16 (A/2505 and A/2505/Add. 1), 1953, p. 4.

[72] *Ibid.*, Annex 11, pp. 121-22.

[73] *Ibid.*, p. 4.

[74] The chairman was Mr. Hernan Santa Cruz, former Permanent Representative of Chile to the United Nations, and one time member of the Economic and Social Council, the Commission on Human Rights, and the Sub-Commission on Prevention of Discrimination and the Protection of Minorities. Mr. Dantes Bellegarde had been Minister of Education for Haiti, Ambassador to Washington, and representative of his country at both the League and the United Nations. Mr. Henri Laugier, the third member of the Commission, was a Professor at the Sorbonne, a member of the Executive board of UNESCO, Honorary President of the International League for the Rights of Men, and formerly Assistant Secretary-General of the United Nations Department of Social Affairs.

[75] Third Report, Tenth Session, Suppl. No. 14 (A/2953, 1955), mimeo., p. 3.

[76] First Report, p. 116.

[77] *Ibid.*, p. 118.

[78] *Ibid.*

[79] *Ibid.*, p. 119.

[80] Second Report, p. 2.

[81] *Ibid.*, Part 2, pp. 87-92.

[82] *Ibid.*, p. 91.

[83] 42nd Meeting, Third Report, mimeo., p. 7.

[84] 43rd Meeting.

[85] 44th to 47th Meetings.

[86] *United Nations Review*, November, 1955, p. 51.

[87] Third Report, (A/2953, 1955), mimeo., 286-7.

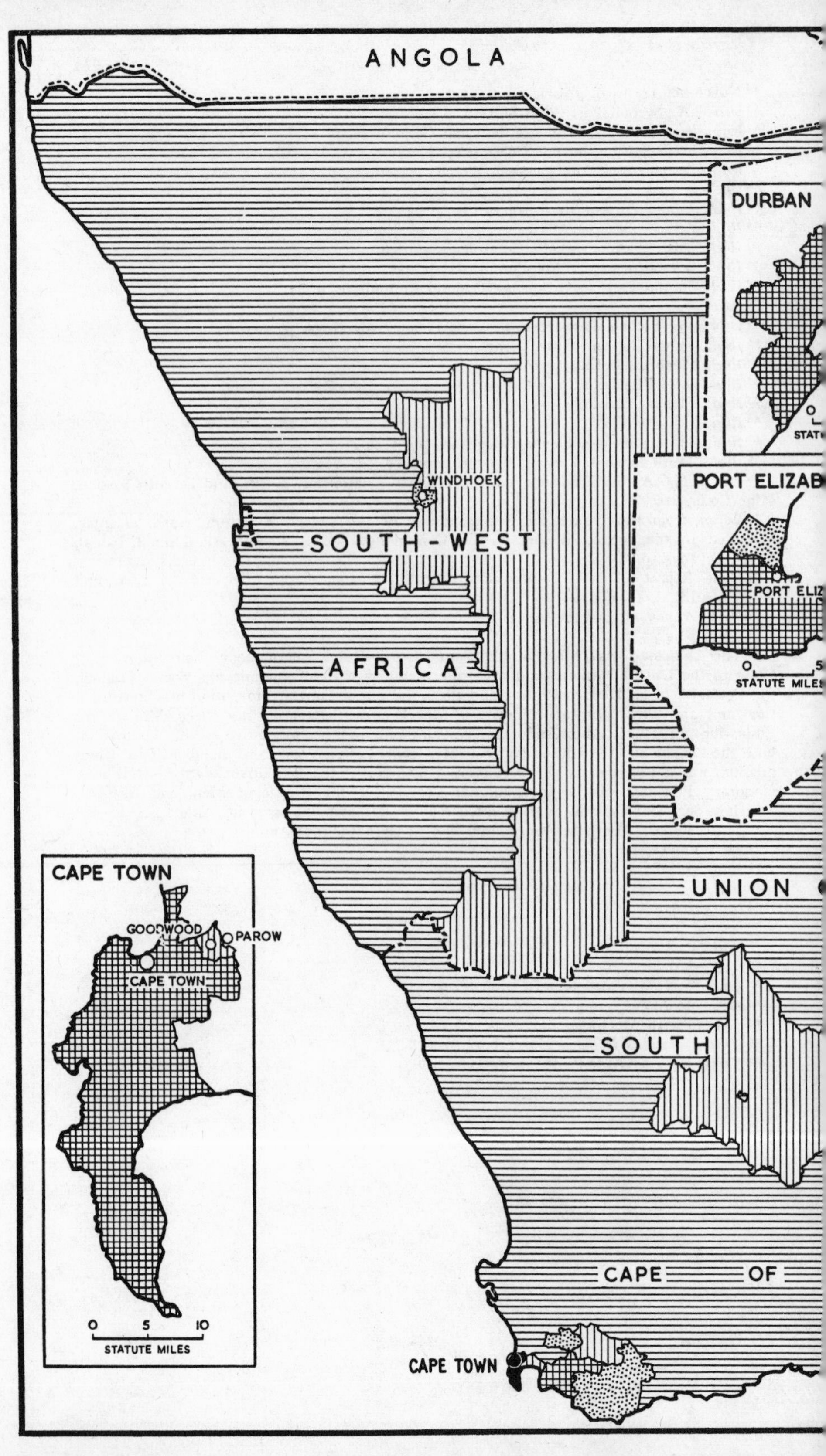
ANGOLA
DURBAN
WINDHOEK
PORT ELIZAB
PORT ELIZ
STATUTE MILES
SOUTH-WEST
AFRICA
UNION
CAPE TOWN
GOODWOOD
PAROW
CAPE TOWN
0 5 10
STATUTE MILES
SOUTH
CAPE OF
CAPE TOWN

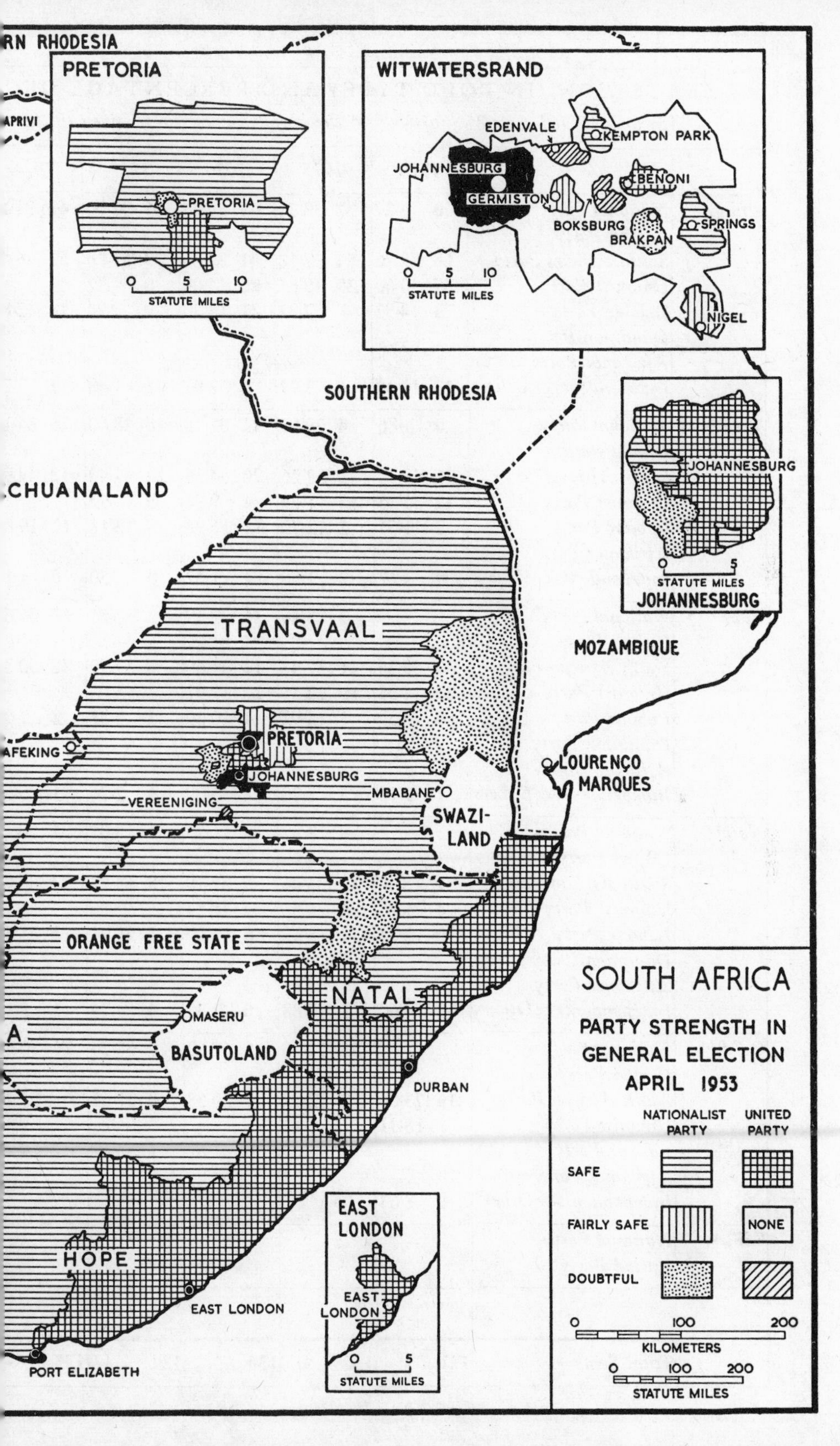

SOUTH AFRICA
PARTY STRENGTH IN GENERAL ELECTION APRIL 1953
NATIONALIST PARTY
UNITED PARTY
SAFE
FAIRLY SAFE
NONE
DOUBTFUL
0 100 200
KILOMETERS
0 100 200
STATUTE MILES
PRETORIA
WITWATERSRAND
EDENVALE
KEMPTON PARK
JOHANNESBURG
BENONI
GERMISTON
BOKSBURG
SPRINGS
BRAKPAN
NIGEL
JOHANNESBURG
EAST LONDON
STATUTE MILES
RN RHODESIA
APRIVI
SOUTHERN RHODESIA
CHUANALAND
TRANSVAAL
MOZAMBIQUE
AFEKING
VEREENIGING
MBABANE
SWAZI-LAND
LOURENÇO MARQUES
ORANGE FREE STATE
NATAL
MASERU
BASUTOLAND
DURBAN
HOPE
EAST LONDON
PORT ELIZABETH

CHART I

SEATS WON (IN BOLD TYPE) AND PERCENTAGE OF

[In uncontested seats 85% of 85% of the enrolled voters were given to the

		1910		*1915*		*1920*		*1921*		*1924*	
Union	*National Party*	**0**	·27	**27**	33·31	**44**	36·93	**45**	37·00	**63**	37·1
	United Party										
	South African Party	**68**	52·76	**54**	37·18	**41**	32·86	**79**	51·26	**52**	46·3
	Unionist Party	**37**	30·60	**39**	19·67	**25**	14·00	**0**	·32		
	Labour Party	**3**	4·92	**4**	7·87	**21**	13·30	**9**	9·94	**18**	12·8
	Dominion Party										
	Afrikaner Party										
	Independents & Others	**13**	11·45	**6**	3·97	**3**	2·91	**1**	1·48	**2**	3·7
Transvaal	*National Party*	**0**	·86	**4**	29·65	**12**	37·18	**16**	38·00	**26**	34·1
	United Party										
	South African Party	**21**	49·26	**22**	37·26	**20**	34·36	**28**	47·40	**12**	44·9
	Unionist Party	**12**	35·25	**15**	18·89	**4**	9·96	**0**	·92		
	Labour Party	**3**	11·51	**2**	12·70	**12**	16·98	**5**	13·18	**12**	19·8
	Afrikaner Party										
	Independents & Others	**0**	3·12	**2**	1·50	**1**	1·52	**0**	·50	**0**	1·1
Cape	*National Party*			**7**	28·40	**16**	33·19	**12**	32·51	**20**	36·6
	United Party										
	South African Party	**30**	56·26	**21**	38·43	**12**	31·60	**36**	57·92	**28**	50·3
	Unionist Party	**20**	34·05	**19**	22·55	**17**	19·91				
	Labour Party	**0**	·59	**1**	4·92	**4**	10·30	**2**	6·81	**2**	7·4
	Dominion Party										
	Afrikaner Party										
	Independents & Others	**1**	9·10	**3**	5·70	**2**	5·00	**1**	2·76	**1**	5·5
Natal	*National Party*			**0**	8·97	**0**	11·75	**1**	13·05	**1**	10·1
	United Party										
	South African Party	**1**	16·38	**11**	36·46	**8**	37·10	**15**	64·27	**12**	56·1
	Unionist Party	**4**	11·28	**4**	26·56	**4**	18·54				
	Labour Party	**0**	12·74	**1**	18·13	**5**	31·29	**1**	21·94	**3**	25·5
	Dominion Party										
	Afrikaner Party										
	Independents & Others	**12**	59·60	**1**	9·88	**0**	1·32	**0**	·74	**1**	8·1
O.F.S.	*National Party*			**16**	61·36	**16**	67·60	**16**	68·76	**16**	70·4
	United Party										
	South African Party	**16**	73·06	**0**	32·52	**1**	30·58	**0**	27·62		25·4
	Unionist Party	**1**	18·31	**1**	6·12						
	Labour Party					**0**	1·82	**1**	3·62	**1**	4·2
	Afrikaner Party										
	Independents & Others	**0**	8·63								
S.W.A.	*National Party*										
	United Party										
	Total Seats	121		130		134		134		135	

POPULAR VOTE FOR THE UNION & FOR EACH PROVINCE

winning party, and 15% *of* 85% *to the major opposing party*]

1929	*1933*	*1938*	*1943*	*1948*	*1950*	*1953*
78 40·37	**75** 39·31	**27** 29·56	**43** 33·66	**70** 36·37	**6** 55·34	**94** 45·50
		111 54·42	**89** 53·18	**65** 50·38	**0** 44·66	**57** 51·62
61 47·54	**61** 32·20					
0 ·45						
1 2·99	**2** 2·61	**3** 5·06	**9** 4·12	**6** 2·76		**5** 2·78
		8 6·08	**7** 3·53			
				9 3·59		
8 8·65	**12** 25·88	**1** 4·68	**2** 5·51	**0** 6·90		**0** ·10
34 40·86	**33** 41·54	**1** 24·12	**11** 33·18	**32** 38·09		**43** 46·53
		57 58·49	**47** 55·42	**26** 48·30		**22** 49·37
14 44·19	**19** 27·38					
1 3·34	**1** 3·99	**2** 9·44	**6** 6·21	**4** 4·62		**3** 3·89
				4 3·92		
6 11·61	**4** 27·09	**0** 7·95	**0** 4·55	**0** 4·85		**0** ·21
26 38·15	**26** 38·35	**20** 34·82	**19** 35·03	**26** 35·69		**30** 44·26
		38 53·71	**35** 59·09	**27** 54·66		**24** 55·73
31 51·39	**30** 38·15					
0 ·97						
2·95	**0** 1·36	**0** 1·75	**1** 1·11			
		1 5·49	**1** 1·36			
				2 2·14		
1 6·54	**5** 22·14	**0** 4·23	**0** 3·35	**0** 6·54		**0** ·01
1 17·26	**1** 5·81	**0** 5·26	**0** 8·79	**1** 6·23		**2** 22·09
		7 43·38	**6** 25·73	**11** 60·97		**11** 66·77
16 65·32	**12** 53·06					
0 4·79	**1** 5·57	**1** 8·91	**2** 13·11	**2** 8·49		**2** 11·14
		7 31·53	**6** 33·72			
				2 6·88		
0 12·63	**2** 35·56	**1** 10·92	**2** 18·65	**0** 11·39		
17 70·64	**15** 71·64	**6** 47·22	**13** 52·79	**11** 62·77		**13** 71·31
		9 52·25	**1** 35·72	**1** 28·84		**0** 28·69
0 24·45						
0 ·28		**0** ·07				
				1 5·15		
1 4·63	**1** 28·36	**0** ·46		**0** 2·24		
					6 55·34	**6** 57·04
					0 44·66	**0** 42·96
148	150	150	150	150	6	156

CHART II

PERCENTAGE OF VOTES BY WHICH SEAT WAS WON OVER MAJOR OPPONENT

	0	3	5	10	15	20	25	30	35	40	45	50	55	60	65	70	
									to								
	2	4	9	14	19	24	29	34	39	44	49	54	59	64	69	up	
Party									per cent								*Unopposed*
									1948								
National	6[a]	4[b]	7[c]	7	10	7	4	6	4	9	0	5	0	0	0	0	1
Afrikaner	0	0	4[d]	3	1	0	0	1	0	0	0	0	0	0	0	0	0
United	7[e]	1[f]	2[g]	3	2	6	2	1	2	4	3	6	0	5	2	8	11
Labour	0	0	0	1	1	0	0	1	1	1	0	0	0	0	0	0	1
									1953								
National	4[h]	6[i]	6[j]	20	8	12	5	9	7	4	3	3	4	1	0	0	2
United	0	2[k]	1[l]	0	2	4	1	4	0	3	3	4	1	6	1	7	18
Labour	0	0	0	1	1	0	0	0	1	0	0	1	0	1	0	0	0

[a] North East Rand, Pretoria West, Bredasdorp, Newcastle, Kimberley District, Victoria West.

[b] Marico, Mayfair, Standerton, Paarl.

[c] Ermelo, Germiston, Krugersdorp, Losberg, Pretoria Central, Bloemfontein District, Worcester.

[d] Potchefstroom, Pretoria District, Uitenhage, Klip River.

[e] Alberton, Brakpan, Johannesburg West, Nigel, Bloemfontein City, Caledon, Vasco.

[f] Durban Pinetown.

[g] Boksburg, Hottentots-Holland.

[h] Brakpan, Pretoria City, Randfontein, Caledon-Bredasdorp.

[i] Langlaagte, Roodepoort, Paarl, P. E. North, Newcastle, Windhoek, S.W.A. (in 1950 by 6 per cent).

[j] Barberton, Nigel, Pretoria District, Priesta, Karas, S.W.A. (in 1950 by 2 per cent), Midlands, S.W.A. (in 1950 by 8 per cent).

[k] Edenvale, Vereeniging.

[l] Boksburg.

CHART III

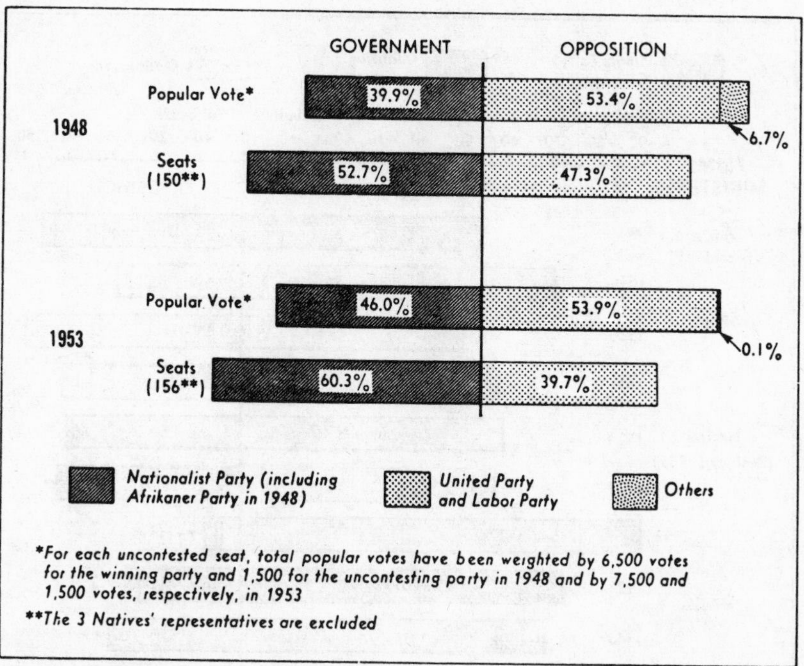

Disparity between popular votes and seats won by political parties in House of Assembly elections, Union of South Africa, 1948 and 1953. (The slight difference in percentages from Chart 1 results from the different weighting for votes in the uncontested seats)

CHART IV

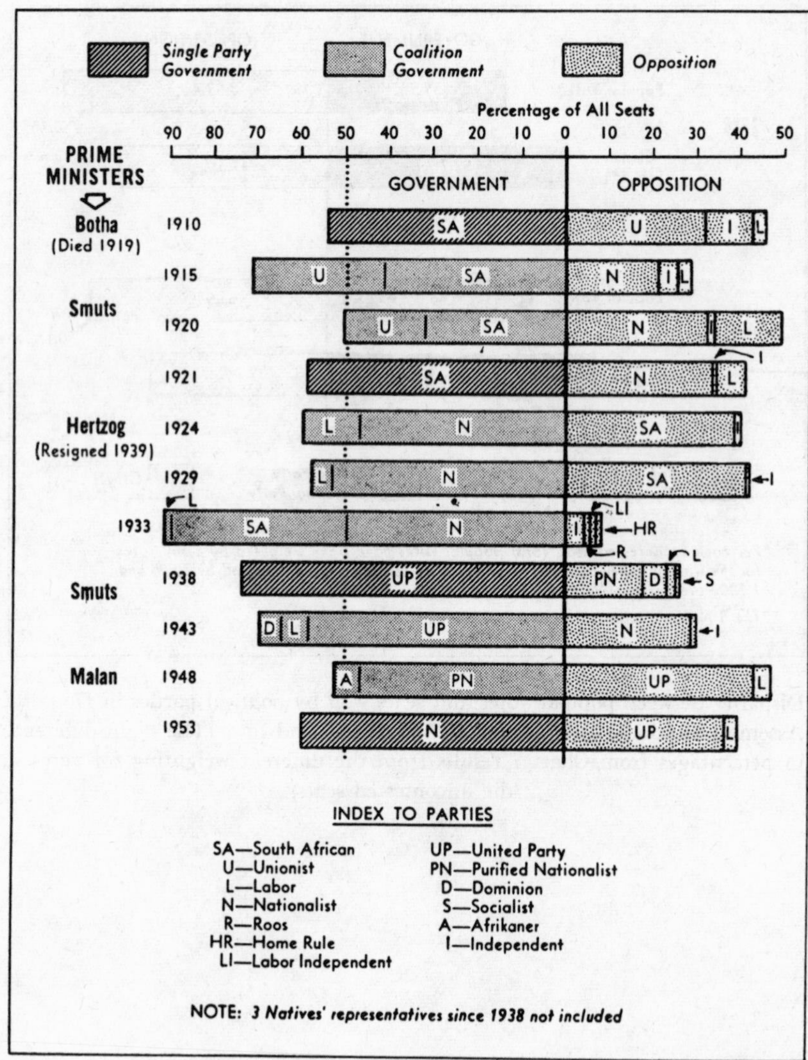

Strength and frequency of one-party and Coalition Governments following general elections, Union of South Africa, 1910-53.

CHART V

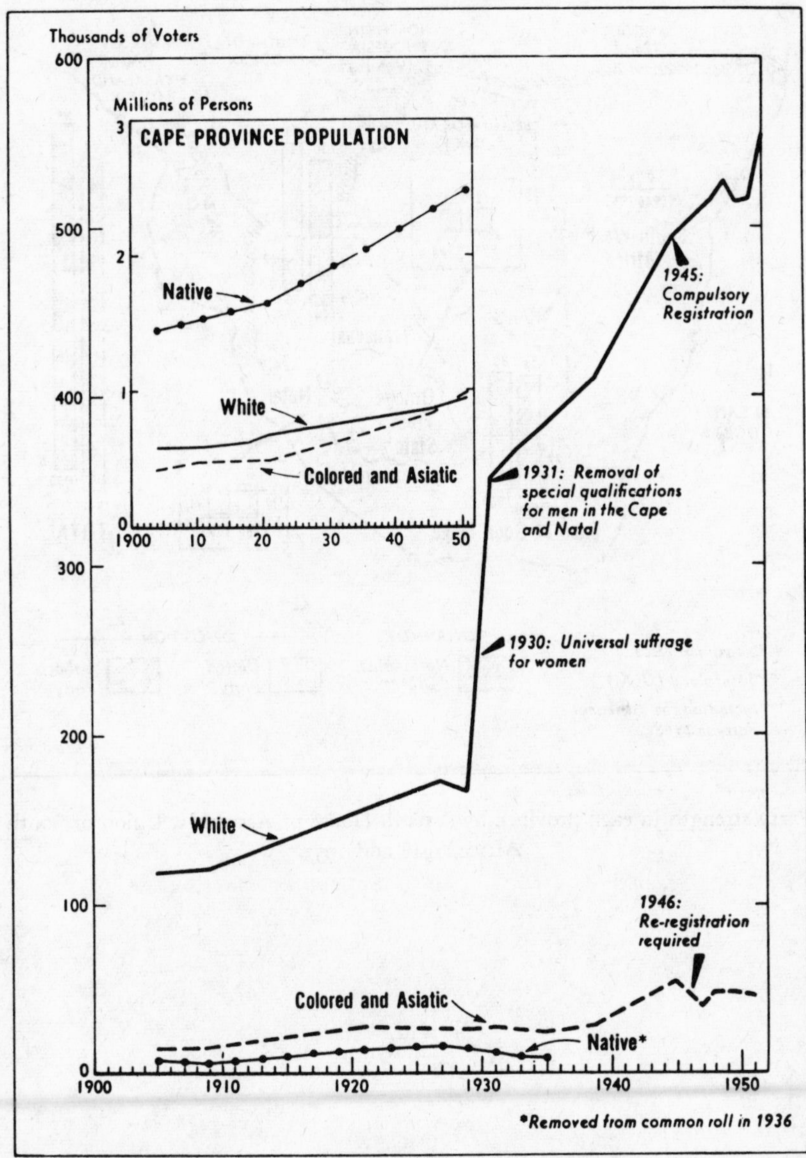

Voters and population in Cape Province, Union of South Africa, by racial groups, 1905-52.

CHART VI

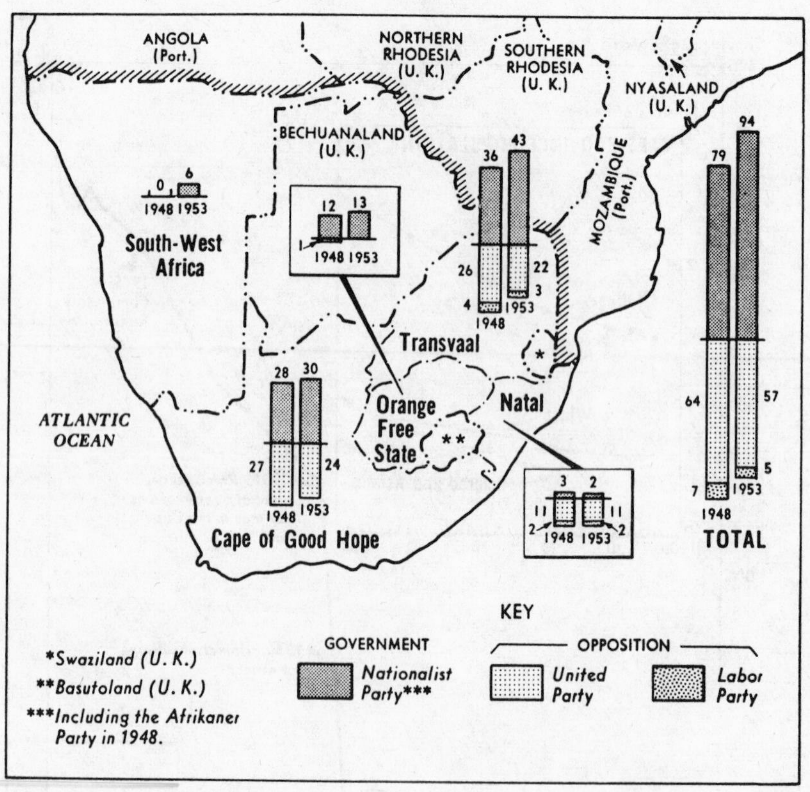

Party strength in each province by seats in House of Assembly, Union of South Africa, 1948 and 1953.

APPENDICES

Appendices

APPENDIX I

CIRCULATION AND DISTRIBUTION OF SOUTH AFRICAN NEWSPAPERS

Unlike the American or British Press, South African newspapers are reticent about their circulation figures, keeping them secret from the public though supplying them regularly for mutual information to an agency known as the Audit Bureau of Circulation in Johannesburg. All estimates of circulation figures, therefore, are approximate. The information about the distribution of certain newspapers which is incorporated in this section comes chiefly from the answers to a questionnaire sent by the author in 1953 to each of the major papers, and from the Fourth Readership survey of the Union of South Africa, January-February, 1951, prepared by the South African Research Services, Ltd., Johannesburg.

None of the Afrikaans dailies has an average circulation of as much as 50,000 and *Die Burger*, a morning paper, probably fluctuates between 34,000 and 40,000, though the figures for its Saturday edition may amount to four or even five times this figure. Predominantly a Cape paper, though some copies circulate to other provinces, to South West Africa and even Rhodesia, *Die Burger* considers that 75 per cent of its copies go to rural areas, and only 25 per cent to urban ones. The 1951 Readership Survey estimated that 20·6 per cent or one-fifth of the adult European population of the whole province reads *Die Burger*; the paper itself feels that the likely division between Afrikaans- and English-speaking readers is about 90 per cent to 10 per cent.

Die Volksblad (Bloemfontein) has a circulation of about 19 to 22,000, almost exclusively in the Free State, and emphasizes local issues. *Die Oosterlig* (Port Elizabeth), which often republishes editorials from *Die Burger*, runs about 8 to 9,000 and is read locally in the Eastern Cape.

Die Transvaler and *Die Vaderland* are both more urban papers than *Die Burger*, a fact partly explained by the extent of the urban concentration on the Witwatersrand as compared with Cape Town. *Die Transvaler*, with a daily circulation of about 36,000 to 39,000, has a 48-52 per cent division between urban and rural areas; *Die Vaderland*, with a somewhat larger circulation of perhaps 41,000 to 43,000, is two-thirds urban in circulation and one-third rural. *Die Transvaler* reported early in 1953 that 87·2 per cent of its circulation was in the Transvaal (8·4 per cent on the West Rand, 13·1 per cent on the East Rand, 9·6 per cent in Johannesburg, and 16·6 per cent in Pretoria), 5·6 per cent in Natal, 4 per cent in the Free State, and 3·2 per cent in the Cape. Its growing distribution in Natal is partly a deliberate effort to compensate for the lack of an Afrikaans daily in that province where the Nationalists are making increasing political efforts. *Die Vaderland* circulates mainly in the Transvaal. Both papers estimate that 99 per cent of their readers are Afrikaans-speaking.

Of the Afrikaans weeklies, *Dagbreek* with a circulation of some 95,000 to 105,000 has a 70 per cent urban distribution and 30 per cent rural. The 1951 Readership Survey estimated that 15·7 per cent of the adult European population had read *Dagbreek* the week before the survey. *Dagbreek's* own staff believes that its readers are about 99 per cent Afrikaans-speaking. *Landstem* is read largely on the *platteland* of the Cape Province, but, by 1953, it also had a Northern edition printed by the Rand Daily Mail Ltd. and had achieved the substantial circulation for a relatively new paper of 65,000-70,000.

The *Cape Times*, also a morning paper, outsells *Die Burger* in the Western Cape by some 20,000 copies, but the Readership survey of 1951 showed that the English-language paper was read in the rural areas by only 10·2 per cent of the people as compared with 30·6 per cent for the Afrikaans paper. In the city, however, the percentages were more than reversed, the *Cape Times* being read by 37·8 per cent of the population as compared with 6·5 per cent reading *Die Burger*. The Argus dailies—the *Cape Argus, The Star* (Johannesburg), *The Pretoria News, The Natal Daily News* (Durban), *The Diamond Fields Advertiser* (Kimberley) and *The Friend* (Bloemfontein)—have a circulation of some 308,000 to 325,000 a day, while the two Sunday papers—*The Sunday Tribune* and the *Sunday Post* (Durban)—run about 96,000. According to the 1951 Readership Survey, the *Cape Argus, The Star, The Friend* and *The Natal Daily News* were read respectively by 26·7 per cent of the people in the Cape, 39·4 per cent of those in the Transvaal, 19·2 per cent of the Free State and 52·1 per cent of those in Natal, while the *Tribune* was read by 9·4 per cent of the Europeans in the Union.

While it was not possible to secure detailed information about all the major English-speaking papers, the following facts are of considerable interest. The *Cape Times* reported that, according to a media research in 1949, 71·3 per cent of its daily edition was read by English-speaking, 26·3 per cent by Afrikaans-speaking, and 2·4 per cent by others. Figures for the weekend edition varied little: 69·8 per cent English, 28·3 per cent Afrikaans, and 1·9 per cent others. The *Rand Daily Mail* quoted figures from the Readership Survey of 1950 which indicated that 65·4 per cent of its readers were English-speaking, 21·8 per cent Afrikaans and 12·8 per cent 'miscellaneous', i.e., mainly non-Europeans. The *Sunday Times* shows a still heavier reading by Afrikaners, with an estimate based on the same source of 58·3 per cent English-speaking readers, 27·6 per cent Afrikaans-speaking readers and 14·1 per cent 'miscellaneous'. The *Natal Mercury* estimated that about 90 per cent of its readers were English-speaking.

The *Rand Daily Mail*, an enterprising, attractive and occasionally tart morning paper, with a daily circulation of some 108,000 to 113,000, makes a particular effort to secure a wide circulation. The bulk of its papers go to the Transvaal and the Northern Free State, where it can place them as early as can the *Friend*. In fact, in 1953 it was outselling the latter in the Northern Free State, where so many people had migrated recently from the Transvaal. The *Rand Daily Mail* also sends papers all the way to Durban, a few to Cape Town and even some by air to Rhodesia. The *Rand Daily Mail* estimates that it has an 88 per cent urban distribution to a 12 per cent rural distribution. Rivalry between the *Rand Daily Mail* and *Die Transvaler* to see which could get into the *platteland* districts earlier once led *Die Transvaler* to print in the late afternoons, so as to get the earliest trains in the morning, but after it missed announcing General Smuts' death, which took place at seven in the evening, it gave up this practice. The 1951 Readership Survey estimated that 16·7 per cent in the Transvaal read *Die Transvaler*, while 34·5 per cent read the *Rand Daily Mail*.

By far the most widely read of afternoon papers throughout the Union is the *Star*, with an estimated circulation of between 138,000 and 145,000. The *Star* also goes throughout the Transvaal, Northern Free State, into Natal, and parts of the Cape and to Southern Rhodesia. It estimates an urban-rural distribution of 84-16 per cent, a *platteland* coverage somewhat higher than that of the *Rand Daily Mail*. The 1951 Readership Survey estimated that 39·4 per cent of the Transvaal read the *Star*, a figure which is more than twice as high as that for *Die Vaderland*, its Afrikaans afternoon competitor.

The *Sunday Times*, a real family paper with a goodly share of sensational stories among its 40 pages but some excellent political comment as well, has by far the largest circulation in South Africa, running between 285,000 and 290,000 copies every Sunday. It is distributed throughout the whole of the Union and sent by air to Southern and Northern Rhodesia. Its distribution is fairly comparable to that of the *Rand Daily Mail* except that it has a wider rural circulation, the distribution being 82 per cent urban to 18 per cent rural. Special vans take the *Sunday Times* to Durban, the Free State, Kimberley, and throughout the Transvaal, for Sunday delivery, but many of the smaller dorps do not receive it until later in the week. As far as readers are concerned, the *Sunday Times* comes closer to being a national paper than any other paper in South Africa; it was estimated in 1951 that 38·6 per cent of the European population read it weekly.

Though Bantu papers are as secretive about circulation as European papers, the *Race Relations Handbook* estimates (p. 484) that in March, 1948, the circulation of publications concerned with the Bantu Press amounted to 83,450 for its weeklies, 5,000 for fortnightlies, 18,400 for monthlies and 6,000 for quarterlies. Among Coloured papers, *The Cape Standard* has a circulation of about 8,000, more than twice that of *The Sun*.

	Dailies	Place	Time	*Approximate Circulation 1952-1953*
1	Die Burger	Cape Town	a.m.	34- 40,000
2	Die Transvaler	Johannesburg	a.m.	36- 39,000
3	Die Vaderland	Johannesburg	p.m.	41- 43,000
4	Die Volksblad	Bloemfontein	p.m.	19- 22,000
5	Die Oosterlig*	Port Elizabeth	p.m. T,F	8- 9,000
6	Cape Times	Cape Town	a.m.	56- 60,000
7	Cape Argus	Cape Town	p.m.	88- 94,000
8	The Star	Johannesburg	p.m.	138-145,000
9	Rand Daily Mail	Johannesburg	a.m.	108-113,000
10	The Pretoria News	Pretoria	p.m.	14- 15,000
11	The Friend	Bloemfontein	a.m.	10- 11,000
12	Diamond Fields Advertiser	Kimberley	a.m.	5- 5,500
13	The Natal Mercury	Durban	a.m.	45- 46,000
14	The Natal Daily News	Durban	p.m.	53- 55,000
15	The Natal Witness	Pietermaritzburg	a.m.	12- 12,500
16	Daily Dispatch	East London	a.m.	17- 18,000
17	Eastern Province Herald	Port Elizabeth	a.m.	22- 23,000
18	Evening Post	Port Elizabeth	p.m.	18- 19,000
	Sunday Newspapers			
19	Dagbreek en Sondagnuus	Johannesburg		100-104,000
20	Sunday Times	Johannesburg		285-290,000
21	Sunday Express	Johannesburg		107-108,000
22	Sunday Tribune & Sunday Post	Durban		95- 96,000

* *Die Oosterlig* is a bi-weekly, appearing on Tuesdays and Fridays.

Readership Survey Jan.-Feb. 1951 Percentage of Adult (over 16) Readers in European Population	*Urban-Rural Distribution 1953*	*Afrikaans, English and Other Readers*				*Group Affiliation*
			A.	*E.*	*O.*	
20·6% in Cape Province	25-75%		90%	10%		Nasionale Pers Beperk
16·7% in Transvaal	48-52%		99%	1%		Independent
18·1% in Transvaal	65-35%		99%	1%		Independent
36·7% in Free State						Nasionale Pers Beperk
						Nasionale Pers Beperk
23·5% in Cape Province		(1949)	26·3%	71·3%	2·4%	Independent
			28·3%	69·8% (weekend)	1·9%	
26·7% in Cape Province						Argus Group
39·4% in Transvaal	84-16%					Argus Group
34·5% in Transvaal	88-12%	(1950)	21·8%	65·4%	12·8%	With Sunday Times & Express
						Argus Group
19·2% in Free State						Partially owned by Argus Group
						Argus Group
51·9% in Natal	66-34%		10%	90%		Independent
52·1% in Natal						Argus Group
13·0% in Natal						Independent
8·0% in Cape Province						Independent
9·7% in Cape Province						With Evening Post
						With Eastern Province Herald
15·7% in Union						Independent
38·6% in Union	82-18%		27·6%	58·3%	14·1%	Same management as Rand Daily Mail
16·5% in Union						Under Sunday Times
9·4% in Union						Argus Group

APPENDIX II

EXPENDITURES BY PARTIES AND OTHER GROUPS IN THE 1948 AND 1953 ELECTIONS[1]

Categories of Expenditure	National Party			United Party			South African Labour Party			War Veterans' Torch Commando			Communist Party			Smaller Parties Including Independents		
	£	s.	d.	£	s.	d.	£	s.	d.	£	s.	d.	£	s.	d.	£	s.	d.
1948																		
1				179	11	0										597	6	4
2																		
3																		
4	99	13	10	6,585	16	6	448	10	0					16	0	770	3	0
5	578	17	4	10,735	9	4	215	10	0				77	0	0	1,064	7	2
6	41	11	0	8,654	16	8	290	5	8				14	1	0	160	9	4
7	427	15	3	9,625	19	10							116	9	10	2,683	2	5
	1,147	17	5	35,781	13	4	954	5	8				208	6	10	5,275	8	3
1953																		
1	218	12	10	2,352	4	4	3	3	1	50	13	0						
2										979	11	0						
3	2	11	0															
4	745	17	4	14,313	3	6	162	1	0	2,038	7	2						
5	4,530	13	1	11,850	7	6	194	5	11									
6	293	16	0	1,298	9	10	146	8	0									
7	18,370	1	11	4,273	11	0	225	12	2	962	13	11						
	24,161	12	2	34,087	16	2	731	10	2	4,031	5	1						

Categories of Expenditure

1 Preparing Articles, Reports, Advertisements, Notices or other Matter.
2 Articles or other Matter in Newspapers.
3 Reports in Newspapers of Speeches or Addresses.
4 Advertisements or Notices in Newspapers.
5 Printing Articles, Reports, Advertisements, Notices or other Matter (other than in Newspapers).
6 Publishing, Issuing, and Distributing Articles, Reports, Advertisements, Notices or other Matter.
7 Miscellaneous Expenses.

[1] Information provided by the Chief Electoral Officer in Pretoria.

Amounts expended by Political Parties at the General Election for the House of Assembly on account of the insertion in certain newspapers of electoral matter, i.e., advertisements, articles and other matter which on the face of it are intended or calculated to affect the result of the election.

Name of Party		*Election in 1948*			*Election in 1953*		
Transvaal:							
DIE TRANSVALER							
					£	s.	d.
The National Party					1730	16	0
DIE VADERLAND							
					£	s.	d.
The National Party					1246	3	3
DAGBREEK EN SONDAGNUUS							
					£	s.	d.
The National Party					263	10	0
The United Party					350	10	0
	Total				614	0	0
THE STAR							
		£	s.	d.	£	s.	d.
The United Party		1253	12	4	1522	7	6
The National Party		12	0	0	24	12	6
The Labour Party		233	5	0	46	7	6
The Torch Commando					178	0	0
Independents and Others		58	10	0			
	Total	1557	7	4	1771	7	6
RAND DAILY MAIL							
					£	s.	d.
The National Party					15	5	0
The United Party					3329	15	0
The Torch Commando					84	10	0
	Total				3429	10	0
PRETORIA NEWS							
		£	s.	d.	£	s.	d.
The United Party		195	15	0	382	13	9
The National Party		154	8	6			
Independents and Others		1	4	6			
	Total	351	8	0	382	13	9

Name of Party	*Election in 1948*			*Election in 1953*		
SUNDAY TIMES						
				£	s.	d.
The United Party				2683	5	0
The Torch Commando				432	0	0
Total				3115	5	0

Cape:

Name of Party	*Election in 1948*			*Election in 1953*		
DIE BURGER						
				£	s.	d.
The National Party				169	19	9
CAPE TIMES						
	£	s.	d.	£	s.	d.
The United Party	404	10	6	743	18	0
The National Party	38	16	0	76	0	0
The South African Party	34	15	3			
The Springbok Legion	36	8	0			
The Communist Party	10	6	0			
The Torch Commando				155	5	0
Independents and Others	43	2	6	165	7	6
Total	567	18	3	1140	10	6
CAPE ARGUS						
	£	s.	d.	£	s.	d.
The United Party	277	15	6	1039	17	6
The National Party	30	0	6	82	12	6
The South African Party	52	0	0			
The Communist Party	16	16	0			
The Torch Commando				332	11	0
Independents and Others	148	17	0			
Total	525	9	0	1455	1	0
DAILY DISPATCH						
	£	s.	d.	£	s.	d.
The United Party	152	0	0	132	11	7
The National Party				36	17	6
The South African Party	64	10	0			
Independents and Others	41	0	0			
Total	257	10	0	169	9	1

Name of Party	*Election in 1948*	*Election in 1953*

Orange Free State:

DIE VOLKSBLAD

		£ s. d.
The United Party		7 14 6
The National Party		254 14 10
Total		262 9 4

THE FRIEND

	£ s. d.	£ s. d.
The United Party	3 12 0	580 6 0
The National Party		40 5 0
Total	3 12 0	620 11 0

Natal:

NATAL DAILY NEWS

	£ s. d.	£ s. d.
The United Party	407 10 11	783 2 6
The National Party	1 2 0	160 4 6
The Labour Party	134 7 6	56 17 0
The South African Party	152 10 0	
The Torch Commando		3 0 0
Independents and Others	29 2 6	2 6 0
Total	724 12 11	1005 10 0

NATAL MERCURY

	£ s. d.	£ s. d.
The United Party	449 0 6	101 8 0
The National Party		66 13 6
The Labour Party	86 7 6	45 9 0
The South African Party	233 19 0	
Independents and Others	92 18 0	23 14 0
Total	862 5 0	237 4 6

NATAL WITNESS

	£ s. d.	£ s. d.
The United Party	174 1 0	220 2 6
The National Party	14 17 2	6 13 3
Independents and Others	59 11 0	
Total	248 9 2	226 15 9

APPENDIX III

PAMPHLETS ISSUED BY THE UNITED PARTY FOR THE GENERAL ELECTION 1953

Pamphlet	*Date of Issue*	*Total Print*
THE MAN OF PROMISES (Cost of Living)	Sept 1952	80,000
50 NATIONALIST FAILURES	Oct 1952	50,000
WORKERS' CHARTER	Oct 30 1952	195,000
THE PEOPLE VERSUS D. F. MALAN	Nov 1952	20,000
WHITE POLICY	Dec 12 1952	31,000
THE NATIONALIST INSULT	Jan 3 1953	130,000
WHAT IS APARTHEID?	Jan 13 1953	165,000
CALL TO ACTION	Sent in advance for release as soon as date of election announced	100,000
CIVIL SERVICE	Feb 20 1953	59,000
WHITE POLICY (Shorter form)	Feb 23 1953	266,000
SMALLHOLDERS' POLICY	Feb 26 1953	70,000
RAILWAYMEN	Feb 26 1953	82,000
DR. MALAN SE KLEURBELIED (Afrikaans only)	Feb 27 1953	142,000
HOUSING	Mar 3 1953	175,000
LAW OF OUR FATHERS	Mar 3 1953	170,000
SUMMARY OF POLICY Afrikaans 258,500 English 176,500	Mar 5 1953	435,000
FARMING	Mar 13 1953	165,000
COST OF LIVING	Mar 18 1953	280,000
THEY PUT SOUTH AFRICA FIRST	Mar 27 1953	190,000
U.P.'S FIGHT AGAINST COMMUNISM	Mar 31 1953	220,000
RAILWAY WAITING ROOM CASE	Apr 2 1953	212,000
		3,237,000

APPENDIX IV

PROGRAMS OF PRINCIPLES AND OBJECTIVES OF SOUTH AFRICAN POLITICAL PARTIES AND GROUPS

The National Party
The United Party
The Labour Party
The Liberal Party
The Union Federal Party
The Conservative Party
The South African Bond
The Natal Indian Congress
The African National Congress
  1919 Constitution
  1945 Bill of Rights
Freedom Charter of the Congress of the People
The South African Congress of Democrats

THE NATIONAL PARTY OF SOUTH AFRICA[1]

I Character and Purpose

1 The Party acknowledges the sovereignty and guidance of God in the destiny of countries and seeks the development of our nation's life along Christian-national lines, with due regard to the individual's freedom of conscience and religion.

2 (a) Its purpose is to promote and to safeguard the welfare of South Africa and her people, in so far as this can be done by political means. It therefore seeks to inculcate and foster a vigorous consciousness of national autonomy and independence, as well as a strong sense of national unity. This unity is to be founded on a common and undivided loyalty and devotion to South Africa and her interests, on mutual trust and on the recognition of the equal rights of both Afrikaans- and English-speaking citizens coupled with mutual appreciation of each other's cultural contributions.

(b) It stands for the just and equal treatment of all parts of South Africa, and for the impartial maintenance of the rights and privileges of every section of the population.

3 The Party strives to realize the national aspirations and convictions of the people of South Africa, under the motto 'South Africa first'. It will also promote a healthy national self-respect based on a full appreciation of the

spiritual and cultural possessions of the nation in all their various forms, and founded on the protection of the rights of each section of the population.

4 With these objects in view the Party seeks to unite in political co-operation all who are prepared to subscribe to its aims and principles and to accept in good faith the obligations arising therefrom, on the understanding that nobody may become a member of the Party unless he is willing to put the interests of South Africa in all circumstances above those of his race or his land of extraction or of any other country.

II Political Status and Future

5 The Party is founded on the unequivocal recognition that South Africa is a sovereign, independent state, which possesses every right, and, on its own authority, can exercise all the functions of a state in the fullest international sense.

6 It undertakes to maintain this independence faithfully and to oppose by every permissible means any interpretation, tendency, action or policy contrary to or threatening such independence, and also to remove any inconsistency hampering the fullest realization of that independence.

7 It will thus ensure that the Government of the country is carried out on the basis of South African national principles and in the spirit of national autonomy as a free, sovereign and independent nation.

8 The unitary basis of a united South Africa, as laid down in the South Africa Act, will be upheld, and no power or right in conflict with or which can be applied in conflict with that basis will be granted to any province. The Party also declares itself in favour of retaining the provincial system, for the present.

9 The Party acknowledges without reservation the right of the nation to change its form of Government or state by constitutional means at any time, if it considers it to be in the country's interests.

10 It is convinced that the republican form of state, separated from the British Crown, is the form best adapted to the traditions, circumstances and aspirations of the South African nation, and is also the only effective guarantee that South Africa will not again be drawn into Great Britain's wars.

11 While the Party thus declares itself in favour of the attainment of this form of state, it recognizes at the same time, however, that a republic can be established only on the broad basis of the national will, and with the faithful observance of the equal language and cultural rights of the two sections of the European population. Accordingly it stipulates that this constitutional change can be brought about only as the result of a special and definite mandate from the European electorate, and not merely by a parliamentary majority obtained as the result of an ordinary election.

III National Flag

12 The Party declares emphatically that it views the national flag as the only exclusive symbol of our own South African nationhood and of the constitutional authority and power of the Union.

IV Economic Independence

13 The Party urges the promotion of South Africa's economic independence and the expansion of her trade relations in all directions, as far as her own interests can be served thereby. It declares itself opposed to any policy or action tending to prevent or retard such development.

V Immigration

14 The Party welcomes the strengthening of the European population by the immigration of desirable persons, provided that the interests of the established population are taken into consideration, but it does not favour a system of immigration at state expense. Furthermore it urges that the state should take the necessary steps to ensure that no undesirable person enters the land, and that immigration be limited to those elements which can readily be absorbed by the South African nation and which cannot be considered a burden or danger to the community.

VI Equal Language Rights and Co-operation Between the European Races

15 The Party desires to foster a spirit of mutual trust and co-operation between the European races. It will thus ensure that equal language rights for the English- and Afrikaans-speaking section of the population are observed in practice and maintained in every way in all spheres of South African national life where the state is concerned or is able to exert influence. The principle of bilingualism will therefore be applied faithfully, not only in the various departments of the Civil Service, but also in all parts of the Provincial Administration and in all public administrative bodies in state or state-aided institutions.

VII Relations with the Non-European Races

16 As a basic principle of its attitude towards Natives and Coloureds the Party recognizes that both are permanent parts of the country's population, under the Christian trusteeship of the European races. It is strongly opposed to every attempt which might lead to the mixing of European and non-European blood, and strives to cultivate a spirit of goodwill and mutual trust between Europeans and non-Europeans, as being in the best interests of South Africa.

In accordance with this principle it desires to give the non-European races the opportunity to develop themselves, each race in its own field, in both the material and spiritual spheres, in keeping with their natural gifts and abilities. Furthermore the Party assures them fair and just treatment under the law and in the administration of the country.

It also declares itself in favour of the territorial and political segregation of the Native, and of separation between Europeans and non-Europeans in general and in the residential and—as far as is practicable—in the industrial spheres. In addition it wishes to protect all groups of the population against Asiatic immigration and competition, among other means by preventing further encroachment on their means of livelihood and by an effective scheme of Asiatic segregation and repatriation.

VIII Co-operation Between Employers and Employees

17 In the economic spheres the Party desires to knit together people of all sections and levels having a right of existence so as to provide security and foster a spirit of mutual trust, solidarity and joint national responsibility. It therefore strives to create economic conditions that will ensure a proper livelihood for each section and which will protect all, particularly the economically weaker section, against exploitation in any form. Accordingly the Party declares itself emphatically opposed to any politics or policy calculated or tending to promote class strife, or to the sacrificing of any national interest for the benefit of organized money powers.

18 In general the Party aims at arousing a true interest in and concern for the interests of the workers, on the part of the Government and the people, with the due consideration for the employers' interests. The worker will be ensured a proper livelihood, and in order to raise his status and standard of living, and to promote his welfare and contentment, the Party will endeavour:

(a) to inspire a feeling of community of interests and mutual regard between employer and employee;

(b) to improve wages where necessary, and working conditions so as to give every citizen the opportunity to enter a suitable, satisfying and assured field of work;

(c) to guard workers in South Africa against competition from labour sources outside the country;

(d) to give efficient protection to the civilized worker in general against replacement by uncivilized labour forces, and in particular to protect the European worker from being forced out of the sphere which he is entitled to occupy in view of his position and the standard of living expected of him.

IX General Economic and Financial Policy

19 General.—The two great primary industries, agriculture and the exploitation of the mineral resources of South Africa, are recognized as the foundation of the country's lasting material welfare. This welfare should also be promoted by an accompanying development of commerce and secondary industry such as to perpetuate the progress and independence of the land.

X Agriculture

20 While the interests of the different sections of the nation will all enjoy equal attention and care from the Government, the existence and welfare of the rural population will be the object of particular endeavour and concern. The application of a progressive settlement policy will aid the healthy introduction of an independent and self-sufficient class of small landowners. The Party envisages an independent and prosperous farming community and thus urges powerful state encouragement and support for the agricultural industry in all spheres, among other means, by satisfactory protection against foreign competition and against exploitation by the middleman, as well as by an efficient system of marketing, farming, credit and agricultural education.

XI *Mining and General Industry*

21 The Mining Industry.—The Party desires to encourage the exploitation of our mineral resources in every way, with due consideration for the welfare of the worker and for the state's claims to its rightful share in the country's mineral wealth.

22 Secondary Industries.—The Party wishes to encourage the vigorous growth of all secondary industries capable of sound progress, among other means by providing satisfactory protection, taking into consideration the interests of the domestic consumer, by an efficient credit system, and by internal and external marketing.

23 Financial Policy.—The maintenance of confidence in South Africa's economic future will be guaranteed by the protection of its finances as well as of the capital assets and resources which aid the progress and development of the country and its people. A healthy and just financial policy, that will take into account the necessity for thrift in the administration, will be pursued. This will be accompanied by a fair division of the burden of taxation, and the employment—as far as possible and in accordance with circumstances—of the country's temporary assets so that they will serve to develop its permanent resources and perpetuate its economic stability.

XII *Education*

24 The Party considers it the duty of the authorities to supervise education and ensure that every child receives instruction in accordance with its talents and opportunities, and based on healthy educational and national principles. It thus urges that in carrying out this duty the Christian-national basis of the state should be taken fully into account, as well as the right of the parent to determine in which direction such education should be given as regards the ethical and religious development of the child.

XIII *National Health*

25 The Party envisages the introduction of a comprehensive and efficient system for the protection and advancement of the nation's health.

XIV *Public Morality*

26 The Party recognizes the duty of the authorities to respect and preserve the Sunday as a day of rest in the public sphere, to oppose all unchristian practices in the national life, and to maintain a high moral code at the same time, taking into consideration the freedom of the individual citizen in his own sphere.

XV *Defence*

27 The Party envisages the maintenance of an adequate system of national defence, drawn up in accordance with the independent status and position of South Africa and with its need for protection against enemy attacks.

XVI Application of Principles

28 In order to apply and defend these principles in practice, among other means by legislation and at election time, the Party maintains itself as an independent political group, organized on a federal basis, and will determine its programme of action from time to time on the basis of its programme of principles. The programme of action must not conflict with any of these principles.

XVII Alteration of Principles

29 This programme of principles contains the common principle of the National Party organizations in South Africa which have joined the federal party, and is not to be altered by their congresses except in consultation with one another through the medium of the Federal Council.

THE UNITED SOUTH AFRICAN NATIONAL PARTY[2]

I The Party acknowledges the sovereignty and guidance of Almighty God in the destiny of peoples and countries, and desires the development of the people of South Africa along Christian-national lines, without prejudice to the right of the individual citizen to freedom of thought, conscience and religion.

Its object is the development of a predominant sense of South African national unity, based on the equality of the Afrikaans-speaking and English-speaking sections of the community, coupled with the recognition and appreciation by either section of the distinctive cultural heritage of the other.

To this end, it seeks to unite in political co-operation all who, whether hitherto members of the Nationalist or South African Parties, or standing outside of both those parties, are prepared to endorse the Party's aims and principles, and to accept in good faith the obligations arising therefrom.

II The Party takes as its starting point the seven points of co-operation between the South African and Nationalist Parties, and on the basis thereof sets forth its aims and principles as follows:

1 *Principles and Spirit of Government*

(a) The Government of the country shall be conducted on a basis of South African national principles and in a spirit of South African national independence in harmony with our sovereign independent status, as confirmed by the Statute of Westminster, and the Status of Union Act, 1934.

(b) It shall be the aim of the Party to ensure, in the Government of the country:

(i) The realization of the national aspirations and convictions of the people of South Africa, with the motto, 'South Africa First';

(ii) The achievement of full national unity in a spirit of devotion to South Africa, and of mutual confidence and goodwill, as the necessary basis of our spiritual and material welfare;

(iii) The promotion of a healthy feeling of national pride, based on the fullest appreciation of the nation's spiritual and cultural heritage in all its bearings, and the protection of the rights of every section of the population therein.

2 *Constitutional Position*

(a) The unitary basis of a United South Africa shall be maintained intact as laid down in the South Africa Act, and no authority or right in conflict therewith, or capable of being applied in conflict therewith, shall be granted to any province or provinces.

(b) The status of the provinces shall be maintained, with the extension, when necessary, and subject to the provisions of sub-section (a) hereof, of provincial powers and functions within the framework of the South Africa Act.

(c) The maintenance is affirmed of the existing relationship between the Union and the British Commonwealth of Nations and co-operation with its members, subject, however, to there being no derogation from the status of the Union, and no assumption of external obligations in conflict with its interests.

(d) While the Party stands for the maintenance of the present constitutional position, no one will be denied the right to express his individual opinion about or advocate his honest convictions in connection with any change of our form of Government.

(e) Without derogating from the provisions of the Union Flag Act, or from the place therein assigned to the Union Jack, the authority and power of the Union shall continue to be symbolized by our National Flag.

(f) The rights and privileges guaranteed to each section of the people by the Constitution shall be impartially maintained and safeguarded.

3 *Equal Language Rights*

Equal language rights in respect of the Afrikaans-speaking and English-speaking sections of the population shall, in practice, in so far as the state is concerned therewith, be exercised and maintained in all respect, and in every part of our national life within the Union.

4 *Agricultural Policy*

(a) While the interests of the various sections of the population will all equally enjoy the attention and the care of the Government, the maintenance and welfare of a healthy rural population will be the subject of special effort and application.

(b) By the application of a progressive land settlement policy, the establishment on a sound basis of an independent, self-maintaining class of small landowners will be promoted.

5 *Social Policy*

A proper standard of living will be assured to the workers, and the existing 'civilized labour' policy will be maintained. The contentment and welfare of the workers will be further promoted by instilling a sense of common interest and mutual goodwill between employer and employee; by stimulating confidence in the Government's impartiality, and in its concern for the interests of the workers; and by improving, wherever practicable, wages and conditions of labour, with a view to raising the workers' status and standard of living.

6 *Native Policy*

(a) An earnest endeavour will be made to arrive at a satisfactory solution of the Native question along lines which, without depriving the Native of his right of development, will recognize as paramount the essentials of European civilization.

(b) It is recognized that a solution of the political aspect of this question on the basis of separate representation of Europeans and Natives, or otherwise, being fundamental in character and not having hitherto been a matter of party division, should as far as possible be sought through agreement and should be left to the free exercise of the discretion of the individual members representing the Party in Parliament.

(c) The recognition of the Natives as a permanent portion of the population of South Africa under the Christian trusteeship of the European race is accepted as a fundamental principle of Native policy, together with the definite avoidance of race intermixture, and the promotion of a spirit of goodwill and mutual confidence between the two races as being in the best interests of South Africa.

7 *General Economic Policy*

(a) The maintenance of confidence in the economic future of the Union will be ensured by the protection of its currency as well as of its capital assets and resources, which serve to promote the progress and development of the land and its people.

(b) The two great primary industries, agriculture and mining, will be recognized as the foundations of the country's permanent welfare, which is to be reinforced by the concurrent development of commerce and manufacturing industry in such manner as will best promote its stability and self-dependence.

(c) A sound and equitable financial policy will be followed, having regard to the necessity for economy in administration, the fair distribution of the burden of taxation, and the application, as far as may be equitable, of the country's wasting assets in such a way as to promote the development of its permanent resources and to ensure its economic stability.

(d) On economic grounds it desires to unite all sections and classes that enjoy the right of existence, into a solid people's union, with a feeling of safety, and in a spirit of mutual trust, solidarity and joint national responsibility.

(e) It therefore endeavours to create such economic circumstances which will ensure to every section a fitting livelihood and that everyone, and particularly the economically weaker sections, shall be protected against any exploitation.

(f) In this spirit the Party declares itself decidedly against any policy which has for its object the tendency to advance class warfare, or to sacrifice any interests of the people in favour of organized capitalism.

III For the furtherance and development of its aims and principles the Party stands for the following :

1 The just and equitable treatment of all parts of the Union.

2 The maintenance by the state of the principle of the public observance of Sunday as a day of rest, with due regard to the liberty of the individual citizen in the domestic sphere.

3 The recognition of the duty of the state to supervise education in a manner which will ensure a national system, based on sound psychological and educational principles; and the full recognition of the rights of parents, more especially in regard to the moral and religious training of their children.

4 The maintenance of public health and of a high standard of public morality.

5 The encouragement of desirable European immigration with the assurance of equality of treatment in the Union, it being understood that a state-financed system of immigration under existing conditions is not desirable.

6 The protection of the European, the Coloured and the Native population against Asiatic immigration or competition, while recognizing and maintaining existing rights of Asiatics born or legally domiciled in the Union.

7 The assurance to all the peoples of South Africa, white, Coloured, and Native, of fair and equal justice, of impartial administration, and reasonable opportunities for material and spiritual progress.

8 The maintenance of an adequate system of national defence, conceived with due regard to the status and situation of South Africa, and to its requirements for protection against hostile attack.

IV Whenever and as often as may be found necessary, the Party shall declare and publish a programme of action which shall contain the demands for practical legislation. These demands shall, in so far as principles are connected therewith, rest on the basis of the foregoing clauses, which constitute the political charter of the Party.

THE SOUTH AFRICAN LABOUR PARTY[3]

Objects

(a) To establish and maintain by means of propaganda and representation on public bodies a Political Labour Party, in order to give effect to the principles from time to time approved by the Party Conference, and to achieve the carrying out of the General and Election Programmes as from time to time adopted.

(b) To secure for the producers by hand or by brain the full fruits of their industry and the most equitable distribution thereof that may be possible, upon the basis of common ownership of the means of production, due regard being had to the presence of an overwhelming Native population and the necessity for maintaining and improving the standards of life: further, to secure the best obtainable system of popular administration and control of each industry or service, with a view to the ultimate achievement of a democratic and socialist commonwealth.

(c) The South African Labour Party acknowledges the religious convictions and aspirations and will safeguard the religious freedom of all sections of our people.

THE LIBERAL PARTY OF SOUTH AFRICA[4]

I The name of the Party is The Liberal Party of South Africa (*Die Liberale Party van Suid-Afrika*).

II *Principles*

(i) The essential dignity of every human being irrespective of race, colour or creed, and the maintenance of his fundamental rights.
(ii) The right of every human being to develop to the fullest extent of which he is capable consistent with the rights of others.
(iii) The maintenance of the rule of law.
(iv) That no person be debarred from participating in the Government and other democratic processes of the country by reason only of race, colour or creed.

III *Objects*

(i) Equal political rights based on a common franchise roll.
(ii) Freedom of worship, expression, movement, assembly and association.
(iii) The right to acquire and use skills and to seek employment freely.
(iv) Access to an independent judiciary.
(v) The application equally to all sections of the population of the principle of compulsory, state-sponsored education.
(vi) The right to own and occupy immovable property.
(vii) The right to organize trade unions and other economic groups and associations.

The Party will employ only democratic and constitutional means to achieve the foregoing objects, and is opposed to all forms of totalitarianism such as communism and fascism.

THE UNION FEDERAL PARTY[5]

I *National Aim*

To create in South Africa opportunities for people of all races to enjoy fullness of life and liberty under the protection of the law, to enable our country to play an honourable and constructive part in world affairs and to promote Western Civilization among the peoples of South Africa.

II *The United States of Southern Africa*

A long-term policy for Southern Africa is essential.

We shall seek ultimately to provide a Constitutional structure and way of life acceptable to neighbouring states, colonies and protectorates as a basis for a future Federal Union of the States and Territories of Southern Africa.

III *To Reshape within the Act of Union the present quasi-Unitary System to one of Federal Union*

To entrench the material elements of the contract of Union and, within that framework to reshape the present quasi-Unitary system to one of Federal Union by redistribution of powers from the Central to Provincial Governments, giving a far greater measure of autonomy to the Provinces, especially in matters which directly concern the life of the citizen, the general principle of which found an earlier expression in the Hollander Memorandum.

IV *The Right of Provinces in given circumstances to determine their own futures*

We shall work for the maintenance and assertion of the right of the people of any Province of the Union, in the face of any actual, attempted or projected violation of the letter or the spirit of the Constitution, to remain a part of the Commonwealth of Nations under the Crown; a Province so as to act in the following amongst other eventualities: A weakening of our allegiance to the Crown; the setting aside of the Entrenched Clauses; the denial of the testing power of the Courts; the abolition of the Provincial Council system or the reduction of Provincial powers; the abolition of full protection or of recognition of the equal rights of both official languages.

V *The State and the Citizen*

The maintenance of a Western democratic form of Government and of Parliamentary institutions; the protection of the basic liberties of the people and the freedom of the individual, and of his right to appeal to the Courts against any arbitrary act of the Executive; the retention by Parliament of direct control over, and the limitation of the Executive's powers; the elimination of all forces of totalitarianism whether Fascist or Communist.

VI *Racial Accord*

The promotion of racial accord among Europeans with unyielding resistance against any attempt at the domination of one group by the other.

Racial harmony between European and non-European is as essential as that between European and European; a progressive rather than repressive non-European policy in line with Western traditions and Christian teachings on race relationships.

VII *Non-European Policy*

The abandonment of fear as the guiding principle, and the adoption in its place of courageous policies, offers the only hope in the field of non-European affairs. The policies that have so far been pursued hold out no genuine prospect of permanently peaceful relationships among the peoples of South Africa.

We believe that the immediate aim in the field of non-European affairs should be the rapid improvement of living conditions, welfare services, education, and economic opportunities; thus striking at the roots of crime, disease and political discontent.

We adhere to the principle that the franchise already extended to the non-European should in no way be curtailed or by any means rendered less effectual. The South African-born non-European should be accorded a right of expression in the organs of Government, commensurate with his degree of civilization as follows:

(a) The present system of limited group representation of Natives to be maintained and an interim period of group representation of Indians on a system similar to that accorded to Natives to be initiated;
(b) Subject always to due safeguards against disproportionate representation of any one section of the non-European population, the long-term policy to be taken in steps over a considerable period of years, is the ultimate placing of those non-Europeans who have passed suitable tests of a high standard, upon the common roll of voters.

We recognize the fact of increasing economic integration of the non-European peoples in the economy of South Africa.

We accept the desirability of residential and social segregation between Europeans and non-Europeans, to be obtained on a fair and equitable basis and wherever possible by the encouragement of voluntary population movements through housing and town planning schemes designed to that end and to the establishment of the foundations of a sound family life.

We believe that those Natives who have attained a high degree of civilization should be entitled to exemption from those laws designed for the protection of backward peoples.

We stand for the recognition of all South African-born people, Coloureds, Bantu and Indians, as members of the greater South African community.

THE CONSERVATIVE PARTY[6]

This Party bases its fundamental principles on a true South Africanism, founded on the sentiments of the moderates of both European language groups in South Africa.

No matter what claims they may make or what desires they may express, the fact remains that the National Party is almost exclusively Afrikaans speaking and Afrikaans dominated. The United Party has progressively become overwhelmingly English speaking and English dominated, with no ability to attract Afrikaans-speaking voters.

For this reason the United Party, as at present constituted and led, cannot hope to regain power, which means that the English-speaking South Africans will be permanently excluded from any effective say in the Government of the country.

This is disastrous, not only for English-speaking citizens, but for South Africa as a whole. South Africa is the home of both language groups and it must be shared and ruled by both.

The Parliamentary leaders of the new party consist of three English and three Afrikaans-speaking men. They aim at:

I *Race Relations*

The bringing together of moderate-thinking men and women of both European language groups in one political party on a basis of true South Africanism, with mutual respect for and protection of the rights, the language and the culture of each group.

II *Constitution*

The preservation of the Constitution of the Union of South Africa, fighting any attempt to change this Constitution except in the manner prescribed by the Constitution itself.

III *Republic*

The maintenance of the position of the Union within the Commonwealth of Nations. They are not Republicans and believe that the republican issue is not in the immediate or best interests of South Africa. Should at some future date the vast majority of South Africans of both language groups decide in favour of a republican form of Government, they will honour and respect the decision as good democrats, but they believe that in this dangerous world in which we are living our association with the Commonwealth of Nations is of vital importance.

IV *Courts*

The maintenance of the independent status and the high prestige of our courts of law. Any attempt to assail this will be opposed most strenuously.

V *Native Question*

The pursuance of the traditional South African principle of *apartheid*—segregation, separation, separate development of Europeans and the Bantu, but the rejection of territorial apartheid as impracticable and unwise.

While they accept that the Bantu will always be in our midst in considerable numbers, they advocate the provision of a national home for the Bantu in his own Reserves, which should be fully developed with European help and funds where the possibilities of full development and political responsibility should exist.

For the Bantu in European areas there should be adequate salaries and wages, housing, medical and educational facilities in separate residential areas, where, under European supervision, the local control and administration should gradually be extended to the Bantu themselves.

VI *Coloured Franchise*

The solution of the Coloured Franchise issue on the basis that those at present on the common roll shall have the option of remaining on the common roll, while new Coloured voters be registered on a separate roll, those on the separate roll to elect four Europeans to represent them in the House of Assembly and two Coloured persons to represent them in the Cape Provincial

Council. As soon as their population increases their representation will be increased.

In addition the proposed Union Coloured Council must, as soon as practicable, be vested with further administrative powers with respect to all matters concerning the Coloured people, with ultimate establishment of a Department of Coloured Affairs with a Minister for Coloured Affairs.

VII *Communism*

The suppression and liquidation of Communism as a dangerous and evil ideology. While whole-heartedly upholding the democratic framework of the Union, they do not believe that Communism can be fought by the ordinary processes of the law and the courts, as has been proved and accepted in democratic countries like the United States of America.

VIII *Immigration*

The furtherance of a vigorous policy of selective immigration, more especially from the homelands of the various European elements of our population, to meet the increasing demands for white skilled labour and to offset the numerical disparity between white and non-white in South Africa.

IX *Education*

The preservation of our traditional educational system of mother tongue instruction in the primary schools, whether they be English, Afrikaans or parallel medium schools, and free parental choice after the primary standards. They believe that both the United Party and the National Party are today going to extremes in the educational field.

THE SOUTH AFRICAN BOND[7]
(SUID AFRIKAANSE BOND)

Principles

The programme of principles of the new party include: the eradication of all causes of division between the European population groups. It will urge people to acknowledge, as symbols of national unity, one coat-of-arms, one flag, and a South African national anthem.

On the question of education the Bond considers that children must attend parallel-medium schools in which they will have the opportunity of getting to know and respect each other.

The Bond will uphold the right of parents in determining the education of their children.

United Nation

The Bond's principles are briefly: the building of a united nation among the white population, a positive policy of guidance and development of the Native races, the raising of the moral tone in the conduct of the state, business and the home, with a guarantee of equal justice for all persons and the development of an economic policy for peace, progress and prosperity in place of the unrealistic political approaches by existing political parties.

Other principles include the elimination of waste, a financial policy to promote private enterprise, sound national defence and active co-operation and friendly relations with the Western nations in general and states comprising the African continent.

The declaration says that, as membership of the Commonwealth of Nations is desirable both in the South African national and international interest, the alteration of the present Commonwealth relationship will only be undertaken if a two-thirds majority of the electorate vote in favour of this by a special referendum.

Undivided Loyalty

The South African Bond declares and demands for its members undivided loyalty to South Africa and its people: It sees, as its first objective, the creation and development of national unity between the European sections of the community.

It accepts that the existing political rights of Natives will not be diminished in any way, and it will undertake the social and economic development of residential areas and settlements for Natives, where freehold ownership of property can be obtained, in those areas where there are natural concentrations of the Native people and where they can develop according to their qualifications and ability.

It accepts the Coloured community as the natural ally of the European.

THE NATAL INDIAN CONGRESS[8]

Objects

(a) To promote and advance the cause of the Indian people resident in the province of Natal; to improve their condition and status economically, politically and socially by the adoption of all necessary means to remove and oppose measures that discriminate on the grounds of race, colour or creed.

(b) To guard vigilantly against any encroachment upon existing rights and privileges.

(c) To work for and to foster co-operation with the nationally representative organizations of the peoples of South Africa on matters of common interest.

(d) To affiliate with the South African Indian Congress.

(e) To promote peace, understanding and goodwill between the various sections and races of the population of South Africa.

(f) To further educational facilities for the Indian community and to work for the removal of discrimination in the field of education.

(g) To work for the improvement of the condition of Indian farmers, especially peasant farmers.

(h) To further the interests of those who depend on wage or salary for their livelihood.

(i) To work for and secure better trading, commercial, professional and industrial facilities.

(j) To work for the extension to Indians of the franchise on the common roll, free from any special qualification.

(k) To work for the removal of existing prohibitions against Indians joining armed units in the Defence Force.

(l) To work for the removal of the Provincial Barriers.

(m) To work for improved social and health services for the indigent and needy and for the community generally.

(n) To help the poor and needy members of the community and to alleviate suffering and hardship of all kinds within such community.

(o) To assist unemployed Indians in securing employment and relief.

(p) To assist in the procuring and extension of civic amenities to all areas where Indians are resident.

(q) Generally to perform all such acts as are incidental to the aforesaid objects.

THE AFRICAN NATIONAL CONGRESS[9]

Objects

The objects for which the Association is established are:

(1) To form a National Vigilant Association and a deliberative Assembly or Council, without legislative pretensions.

(2) To unite, absorb, consolidate and preserve under its aegis existing political and educational Associations, Vigilance Committees and other public and private bodies whose aims are the promotion and safeguarding of the interests of the aboriginal races.

(3) To be the medium of expression of representative opinion and to formulate a standard policy on Native Affairs for the benefit and guidance of the Union Government and Parliament.

(4) To educate Parliament and Provincial Councils, Municipalities, other bodies and the public generally regarding the requirements and aspirations of the Native people; and to enlist the sympathy and support of such European Societies, Leagues or Unions as might be willing to espouse the cause of right and fair treatment of Coloured races.

(5) To educate Bantu people on their rights, duties and obligations to the state and to themselves individually and collectively; and to promote mutual help, feeling of fellowship and a spirit of brotherhood among them.

(6) To encourage mutual understanding and to bring together into common action as one political people all tribes and clans of various tribes or races and by means of combined effort and united political organization to defend their freedom, rights and privileges.

(7) To discourage and contend against racialism and tribal feuds or to secure the elimination of racialism and tribal feuds, jealousy and petty quarrels by economic combination, education, goodwill and by other means.

(8) To recommend, propose and lay before the Government for consideration and adoption laws for the benefit and protection of the Native races. And also to watch Bills introduced in Parliament for proposed legislation as well as in other bodies for legislation affecting Natives and to draft and present amendments thereto.

(9) To agitate and advocate by just means for the removal of the 'Colour Bar' in political education and industrial fields and for equitable representation of Natives in Parliament or in those public bodies that are vested with legislative powers or in those charged with the duty of administering matters affecting the Coloured races;

(10) To promote and advocate the establishment in Parliament and other public bodies of representatives to be under the control of and for the purposes of the Association.

(11) To record all grievances and wants of Native people and to seek by constitutional means the redress thereof, and to obtain legal advice and assistance for members of the Association and its branches and to render financial aid where necessary within the objects hereof.

(12) To encourage and promote union of Churches free from all sectarian and denominational anomalies.

(13) To establish or to assist the establishment of National Colleges or Public Institutions free from denominationalism or state control.

(14) To originate and expound the right system of education in all schools and colleges and to advocate for its adoption by state and churches and by all other independent bodies in respect thereto.

(15) To encourage inculcation and practice of habits of industry, thrift and cleanliness among the people and propagate the gospel of the dignity of labour.

(16) To acquire land by purchase, lease, exchange, gift or otherwise for erections of hall and other public buildings for the use and purposes of the Association.

(17) To sell, dispose, manage, develop, let and deal in any way with all or any part of the property of the Association.

(18) To borrow or raise money by mortgage or charge of all or any part of the property of the Association; and also to grant loans on security of mortgages in the manner hereinafter provided.

(19) To establish a National Fund for the purposes of the Association either by means of voluntary contributions, periodical subscriptions, levies, contribution, charges or other payments; and to hold and manage all funds raised for the objects of the Association.

(20) To all and everything directly or indirectly to maintain and uplift the standard of the race morally and spiritually, mentally and materially, socially and politically.

(21) AND GENERALLY, to do all such things as are incidental or conducive to the attainment of the above objects or any of them:

PROVIDED ALWAYS:

(a) That the Association shall not support with its funds or endeavour to impose on, or procure to be observed by its members or others any regulation, restriction or condition which, if an object of the Association, would make it a commercial or proprietary concern.

(b) The income and property of the Association whensoever derived shall be applied solely towards the promotion of the above objects, and no portion thereof shall be paid or be transferred directly or indirectly by way of interest, bonus or profit to the members of the Association.

(c) Provided nevertheless that nothing herein contained shall prevent the endowment by the Association of any public useful object or the payment in good faith of reasonable and proper remuneration to any officer or servant of the Association or any of its members or other person in return for services rendered to the Association; nor be deemed to prevent the making of a gratuity or honorarium to its officer, servant or member or any other person for special services rendered to the Association voluntarily or otherwise.

BILL OF RIGHTS OF THE AFRICAN NATIONAL CONGRESS[10]

We, African people in the Union of South Africa, urgently demand the granting of full citizenship rights, such as are enjoyed by all Europeans in South Africa. We demand:

1 Abolition of political discrimination based on race . . . and the extension to all adults, regardless of race, of the right to vote and be elected to parliament, provincial councils, and other representative institutions.

2 The right to equal justice in courts of law, including nomination to juries and appointment as judges, magistrates and other court officials.

3 Freedom of residence and the repeal of laws . . . that restrict this freedom.

4 Freedom of movement.

5 Freedom of the press.

6 Recognition of the sanctity or inviolability of the home as the right of every family, and the prohibition of police raids on citizens in their homes for tax or liquor or other purposes.

7 The right to own, buy, hire or lease and occupy land and all other forms of immovable as well as movable property, and the repeal of restrictions on this right. . . .

8 The right to engage in all forms of lawful occupations, trades and professions, on the same terms and conditions as members of other sections of the population.

9 The right to be appointed to and hold office in the civil service and in all branches of public employment on the same terms and conditions as Europeans.

10 The right of every child to free and compulsory education and of admission to technical schools, universities and other institutions of higher education.

11 Equality of treatment with any other section of the population in the state social services, and the inclusion on an equal basis with Europeans in any scheme of Social Security.

[The declaration stresses a number of specific issues connected with industry and labour, commerce, education, public health and medical services and discriminatory legislation.]

A Equal opportunity to engage in any occupation, trade and industry. In order that this objective might be realized to the fullest extent, facilities must be provided for technical and university education of Africans so as to enable them to enter skilled, semi-skilled occupations, professions, Government service and other spheres of employment.

B Equal pay for equal work, as well as equal opportunity for all work and for the unskilled labour workers in both rural and urban areas such minimum wage as shall enable the workers to live in health, happiness, decency and comfort.

C Removal of the Colour Bar in industry, and other occupations.

D The statutory recognition of the right of the African worker to collective bargaining. . . .

E The extension of all industrial welfare legislation to Africans engaged in agriculture, domestic service and in public institutions or bodies.

F The recognition of the right of the Africans to freedom of trading.

G The state must provide full facilities for all types of education for Africans' children.

H Abandonment of the theory that 'there is a need of a special type of education for Africans as such'. Africans must therefore be given the type of education which will enable them to meet on equal terms with other people the conditions of the modern world.

I It is the duty of the state to provide adequate medical and health facilities for the entire population of the country.

J It is fundamental to the establishment of a new order in South Africa to abolish all enactments which discriminate against the African on the grounds of race and colour. . . .

K In short, we demand the repeal of any and all laws as well as the abandonment of any policy and all practices that discriminate against the African in any way whatsoever on the basis of race, creed or colour in the Union of South Africa.

FREEDOM CHARTER
OF THE CONGRESS OF THE PEOPLE[11]

We, the people of South Africa, declare for all our country and the world to know:

that South Africa belongs to all who live in it, black and white, and that no Government can justly claim authority unless it is based on the will of all the people;

that our people have been robbed of their birthright to land, liberty and peace by a form of Government founded on injustice and inequality;

that our country will never be prosperous or free until all our people live in brotherhood, enjoying equal rights and opportunities;

that only a democratic state, based on the will of all the people, can secure to all their birthright without distinction of colour, race, sex or belief;

And therefore, we the people of South Africa, black and white together—equal, countrymen and brothers—adopt this Freedom Charter. And we pledge ourselves to strive together, sparing nothing of our strength and courage, until the democratic changes here set out have been won.

The People shall govern

Every man and woman shall have the right to vote for and to stand as a candidate for all bodies which make laws.

All people shall be entitled to take part in the administration of the country.

The rights of the people shall be the same, regardless of race, colour or sex.

All bodies of minority rule, advisory boards, councils and authorities shall be replaced by democratic organs of self-government.

All national groups shall have equal rights

There shall be equal status in the bodies of state, in the Courts and in the schools for all national groups and races.

All people shall have equal right to use their own languages, and to develop their own folk culture and customs.

All national groups shall be protected by law against insults to their race and national pride.

The preaching and practice of national, race or colour discrimination and contempt shall be a punishable crime.

All apartheid laws and practices shall be set aside.

The people shall share the country's wealth

The national wealth of our country, the heritage of all South Africans, shall be restored to the people.

The mineral wealth beneath the soil, the Banks and monopoly industry shall be transferred to the ownership of the people as a whole.

All other industry and trade shall be controlled to assist the well-being of the people.

All people shall have equal rights to trade where they choose, to manufacture and to enter all trades, crafts and professions.

The land shall be shared among those who work it

Restriction of land ownership on a racial basis shall be ended, and all the land redivided amongst those who work it, to banish famine and land hunger.

The state shall help the peasants with implements, seed, tractors and dams to save the soil and assist the tillers.

Freedom of movement shall be guaranteed to all who work on the land.

All shall have the right to occupy land wherever they choose.

People shall not be robbed of their cattle, and forced labour and farm prisons shall be abolished.

All shall be equal before the law

No one shall be imprisoned, deported or restricted without a fair trial.

No one shall be condemned by the order of any Government official.

The courts shall be representative of all the people.

Imprisonment shall be only for serious crimes against the people, and shall aim at re-education, not vengeance.

The police force and army shall be open to all on an equal basis and shall be the helpers and protectors of the people.

All laws which discriminate on grounds of race, colour or belief shall be repealed.

All shall enjoy equal human rights

The law shall guarantee to all their right to speak, to organize, to meet together, to publish, to preach, to worship and to educate their children.

The privacy of the house from police raids shall be protected by law.

All shall be free to travel without restriction from countryside to town, from province to province, and from South Africa abroad.

Pass Laws, permits and all other laws restricting these freedoms shall be abolished.

There shall be work and security

All who work shall be free to form trade unions, to elect their officers and to make wage agreements with their employers.

The state shall recognize the right and duty of all to work, and to draw full unemployment benefits.

Men and women of all races shall receive equal pay for equal work.

There shall be a forty-hour working week, a national minimum wage, paid annual leave, and sick leave for all workers, and maternity leave on full pay for all working mothers.

Miners, domestic workers, farm workers and civil servants shall have the same rights as all others who work.

Child labour, compound labour, the tot system and contract labour shall be abolished.

The doors of learning and of culture shall be opened

The Government shall discover, develop and encourage national talent for the enhancement of our cultural life.

All the cultural treasures of mankind shall be open to all, by free exchange of books, ideas and contact with other lands.

The aim of education shall be to teach the youth to love their people and their culture, to honour human brotherhood, liberty and peace.

Education shall be free, compulsory, universal and equal for all children.

Higher education and technical training shall be opened to all by means of state allowances and scholarships awarded on the basis of merit.

Adult illiteracy shall be ended by a mass state education plan.

Teachers shall have all the rights of other citizens.

The colour bar in cultural life, in sport and in education shall be abolished.

There shall be houses, security and comfort

All people shall have the right to live where they choose, to be decently housed, and to bring up their families in comfort and security.

Unused housing space to be made available to the people.

Rent and prices shall be lowered, food plentiful and no one shall go hungry.

A preventitive health scheme shall be run by the state. Free medical care and hospitalization shall be provided for all, with special care for mothers and young children.

Slums shall be demolished and new suburbs built where all have transport, roads, lighting, playing fields, creches and social centres.

The aged, the orphans, the disabled and the sick shall be cared for by the state.

Rest, leisure and recreation shall be the right of all.

Fenced locations and ghettoes shall be abolished, and all laws which break up families shall be repealed.

There shall be peace and friendship

South Africa shall be a fully independent state which respects the rights and sovereignty of all nations.

South Africa shall strive to maintain world peace and the settlement of all international disputes by negotiation—not war.

Peace and friendship amongst all our people shall be secured by upholding the equal rights, opportunities and the status of all.

The people of the Protectorates—Basutoland, Bechuanaland and Swaziland —shall be free to decide for themselves their own future.

The right of all the peoples of Africa to independence and self-government shall be recognized, and shall be the basis of close co-operation.

Let all who love their people and their country now say, as we say here: 'These freedoms we will fight for, side by side, throughout our lives, until we have won our liberty.'

THE SOUTH AFRICAN CONGRESS OF DEMOCRATS[12]

Race conflict can be avoided not by suppressing the non-European political movements, but by recognizing their claims. Democracy in South Africa can be entrenched, not by making it more and more exclusive, but by extending it. This is the only alternative to the Nationalist Government, its brand of fascism or any other brand. The 10 million non-Europeans are our natural allies in defence of democracy. We must find the way to build that alliance, by striking out boldly on a new, democratic path.

A genuine opportunity for Europeans to strike out boldly for that alliance is offered by the policy of the Congress of Democrats. Every act of the Nationalist Government abrogating the rights of some section of the South African people has impelled more and more people to the realization that only the united opposition of white and non-white in a mighty political alliance, operating both in the parliamentary field and outside it, can stop the advance of fascism and bring into living reality a democratic society.

The Congress of Democrats has taken its stand firmly on the principles of the Universal Declaration of Human Rights, as adopted by the United Nations General Assembly.

. . . Its Constitution states that the Congress is 'against all forms of inequality and discrimination. It repudiates as false the doctrines of racial inequality, of white supremacy, of apartheid, trusteeship and segregation'.

It works to secure for all South Africans, regardless of race, colour or creed, the rights laid down in the Universal Declaration of Human Rights, with particular reference to:

1 *Equal civil liberties:*

The Freedom of thought, speech and press;
The freedom of movement and assembly;
The freedom of organization and religion.

2 *Equal political rights:*

The right to vote in and to stand for election to state and local law-making bodies on the basis of universal and equal adult suffrage.

3 *Equal economic opportunities without discrimination based on race or colour:*

To qualify for and engage in all trades, crafts, occupations and professions; to acquire and own land and property, and to freely form, join and administer unions.

4 *Equality of social status:*

In every field of state and administration, public activity, education, culture and recreation, and the preservation of family life with no interference which would lead to its disintegration.

Working closely together with the African and Indian Congresses, the Congress of Democrats is helping to forge a mighty united peoples' alliance against fascism. Here is an opportunity for thinking people who realize that only such an alliance and such a force, inspired by a programme of full democracy for all, can defeat the Nationalists. Here is an opportunity for *You* to act for democracy which will have meaning and will bring new life to all the people of our country. It is time for *You* to be with the Congress of Democrats, and in it.

Notes for Appendix Four

[1] Taken from the Constitution for Cape Province, 1952, pp. 11-16. The wording is the same in all provincial constitutions.

[2] *Programme of Principles, Constitution and Nomination Regulations of the United Party*, as amended 1937 and 1944. Issued 1946. pp. 1-4.

[3] Constitution of the South African Labour Party, 1945, p. 1.

[4] *The Policies of the Liberal Party of South Africa*, Cape Town, The Liberal Party, 1955, 23 pp., p. 21.

[5] Issued by the Party's sponsors in Johannesburg, May 1953. *Natal Mercury*, May 11, 1953.

[6] *Fundamental Principles*, mimeo., 2 pp.

[7] *Star*, 17/12/55.

[8] Natal Indian Congress, *Constitution* as amended at first conference, Durban, 1947, pp. 1-3.

[9] *The Constitution of the African National Congress*, 1919, mimeo., pp. 3-6.

[10] *African Claims in South Africa*, Congress Series No. II, published by the African National Congress, Johannesburg. Adopted on December 16, 1945, at the Annual Conference, Bloemfontein.

[11] *Indian Opinion*, July 8, 1955. Adopted at the 'Congress of the People', June 26, 1955, at Kliptown, near Johannesburg.

[12] *The Threatened People—the Case for a South African Democracy*, South African Congress of Democrats, Johannesburg, 1955.

APPENDIX V

THE 1958 ELECTION RETURNS

The general election of 1958 was a Nationalist triumph. For the first time in South African history, a political party was returned to office for the third time in succession, and each time with a stronger majority. The Nationalist percentage of votes continued the steady increase marked since 1938. Still more evident is its powerful majority of members in the House of Assembly: 103 out of the 156 members representing European constituencies, while the other 53 members belong to the United Party.

When the electoral returns are examined more closely, however, the Nationalist electoral victory does not appear so impressive. The National Party has still not succeeded in securing fifty per cent of the votes. Moreover while its share of the votes increased markedly from 36·37 per cent or, with its Afrikaner Party allies, 39·96 per cent of the vote in 1948 to 45·50 per cent in 1953, it did not reach beyond 48·90 in 1958, a considerable slowing up of the pace of advance. The United Party in contrast, despite the defection of the Independent Conservatives, only moved down from 51·62 per cent of the votes in 1953 to 50·36 per cent in 1958. The latter figure is almost identical with the per cent of the votes secured by the United Party in 1948.

In increasing their total of seats from 94 at the time of the 1953 election, and 96 at the moment of dissolution to 103 after the 1958 election, the Nationalists advanced their proportion of the members representing European constituencies from just over 60 per cent to 66 per cent. Since the minority parties were eliminated, the United Party secured the other 53 seats, four less than in 1953 though one more than at the moment of dissolution. In 1953, however, the United and Labour Parties had an electoral pact and the five members of the latter party could be counted on for opposition votes, though they were often sharply critical of United Party as well as Nationalist policy in the period preceding the 1958 election, a factor in the United Party decision not to renew the earlier electoral alliance. Thus the strength of the opposition, apart from the seven representatives of non-Europeans in the House of Assembly, sank from 39·7 per cent in 1953 to 34 per cent in 1958.

These figures, taken in conjunction with the analysis of the vote, indicate still more striking discrepancies than those in 1953. With 47·40 per cent of the vote in Cape Province, the Nationalists won 33 seats while the United Party secured only 19 seats with 51·89 per cent of the vote. In South West Africa, the United Party secured no seats at all despite polling 41·38 per cent of the vote. In the Transvaal, the United Party won only 20 out of 68 seats though it received 48·47 per cent of the vote.

In the 1953 election the discrepancies between votes polled and seats won were largely attributed (on page 159) to the geographical concentration of United Party supporters in the residential sections of the cities. This is still a very influential factor. In addition, however, delimitation, which was again carried out before the 1958 election, accentuated the 'wastage' of United Party votes. Forty of the United Party's 53 seats were won by a majority of fifty or more per cent of the vote while 89 of the Nationalists' 103 seats were won by a smaller majority. As Chart B in this Appendix shows, the Nationalists won 25 seats with a majority of less than 20 per cent of the total vote cast while the United Party had only four in this category. Most striking is the increase in the number of seats uncontested by the Nationalists which rose from 18 to 31, though the seats uncontested by all other parties only moved up from 20 in 1953 to 24 in 1958.

Increasingly, South African delimitations are separating National and United Party supporters into different constituencies so that fewer elections are decided by narrow margins. Only six elections were won by a majority of less than ten per cent of the vote in 1958 whereas there were 19 in 1953 and 31 in 1948. But delimitation appears also to have aided the National Party in specific cases. Of seven seats abolished by the last Delimitation Commission, five were held by the United Party and two by the Nationalists; of the seven new seats which it created, five became Nationalist in 1958 and two United Party. Kimberley North, for example, was formerly compact, largely urban and United Party; the new seat includes a straggling stretch of countryside in its 97 mile length and had a Nationalist majority in 1958.

Despite the heavy majorities by which the United Party won so many of its seats, and the geographical concentration of its urban support, it again contested every seat in the election and demonstrated the breadth of its support throughout the country by failing to lose a deposit (forfeit if a candidate fails to poll one-fifth of the votes received by the successful candidate). Only the small minority parties suffered this indignity; two South African Bond candidates (Hospital and Orange Grove), one Liberal (Orange Grove), one Republican (Lichtenburg), one Independent (Pretoria Central) and one Christian Democrat (Victoria District). It must be remembered, however, that the National Party did not enter candidates in 31 constituencies.

The Labour Party, which for the first time since the formation of South African Union failed to elect a member to the House of Assembly, polled only 2,670 votes and contested no seats outside the Transvaal, though it had elected two members in Natal in 1953. More widespread were the Liberal candidates who electioneered in the Transvaal, Cape and Natal though their total of votes in all three provinces was only 2,934, slightly more than Labour received. The South African Bond, formed in December 1955 following the protest by thirteen professors from Pretoria University against the Senate Bill (page 141) managed to secure 1,086 votes, all in the Transvaal. The Independent Conservatives, all of whom stood in the Cape, polled 1,674 votes. In all, however, minority party and Independent candidates secured only 10,219 votes out of a total (with due allowance for the uncontested seats) of 1,382,405.

Once again the percentage poll was impressive. In the Union as a whole, it reached 89·08 per cent. In two Cape constituencies—one of them Hottentots Holland, a thoroughly redelimited seat in which the leader of the United Party, Sir de Villiers Graaff, was defeated—it went over 96 per cent. The lowest provincial poll was in Natal, the United Party stronghold, and even here it totalled 86·3 per cent. In the Transvaal and Orange Free State, the polls were

89·2 and 89·1 per cent respectively; in the Cape Province and South West Africa, 90·6 and 90·2 per cent respectively. Though the election campaign had not been marked by the vigour and hope displayed in 1953, the electorate turned out on the decisive day to a degree rarely, if ever, matched in the United States or Great Britain.

Far less electoral interest was displayed by the Coloured who voted for the first time on a communal roll, established after they were removed from the common roll in Cape Province by the South Africa Act Amendment Act, 1956 following the long constitutional crisis which racked South African politics from 1951 to 1956 (see Chapter 4, and especially page 141). Only between 41 and 51 per cent of the 29,000 registered Coloured males (who had proved their literacy and owned property worth £75 or earned £50 a year) exercised their franchise in the four new constituencies in which they could vote for Europeans to represent them in the House of Assembly. Twelve candidates were nominated on March 3 for the election held on April 3, thirteen days before the European general election. Though none of the candidates had direct party affiliation, four were supported by the United Party, three by the Nationalists, three by Independents and two by the South Africa Coloured Peoples Organization and the Congress and National Unity movement. The four candidates supported by the United Party polled just over 80 per cent of the votes cast and secured all four seats. They joined the three Native Representatives in the House of Assembly as representatives of non-Europeans, but since the Nationalist Government almost immediately gave notice of its intention to remove the Native Representatives from the House before the next election for their seats in 1960 the position of the new Coloured Representatives lacks any element of strength.

In summary, the 1958 election demonstrated a continued Nationalist trend in the voting which is much exaggerated in their representation in the House of Assembly. The United Party showed widespread strength but failed, as in 1953, to have it reflected equitably in parliamentary representation. Only a split in the National Party or a marked increase in United Party electoral support could overcome the heavy handicaps imposed on the latter by the geographical concentration of so many of its supporters, and the present delimitation of constituencies. There is little in the 1958 electoral returns, therefore, to suggest any alteration of government in the foreseeable future.

CHART A

SEATS WON (IN BOLD TYPE) AND PERCENTAGE OF POPULAR VOTE FOR THE UNION AND FOR EACH PROVINCE

[In uncontested seats 85% of 85% of the enrolled voters were given to the winning party, and 15% of 85% to the major opposing party]

		1958	
Union	*National Party*	**103**	48·90
	United Party	**53**	50·36
	Liberal Party		·21
	Labour Party		·18
	Independents & Others		·31
Transvaal	*National Party*	**48**	50·56
	United Party	**20**	48·47
	Liberal Party		·11
	Labour Party		·43
	Independents & Others		·41
Cape	*National Party*	**33**	47·40
	United Party	**19**	51·89
	Liberal Party		·35
	Independent Conservatives		·36
Natal	*National Party*	**2**	23·55
	United Party	**14**	75·83
	Liberal Party		·42
	Independents & Others		·20
O.F.S.	*National Party*	**14**	73·33
	United Party	**0**	26·55
S.W.A.	*National Party*	**6**	58·62
	United Party	**0**	41·38
Total seats in European Constituencies		156	
Cape Coloured	*Indep. Nat.*		3·66
	Indep. U.P.	**4**	80·40
	Indep. Lib.		3·11
	Indep.		6·53
	SACPO (South African Coloured Peoples Organization)		6·30

CHART B

SOUTH AFRICAN ELECTIONS 1958
PERCENTAGE OF VOTES BY WHICH SEAT WAS WON OVER MAJOR OPPONENT

Party	0 to 2	3 to 4	5 to 9	10 to 14	15 to 19	20 to 24	25 to 29	30 to 34	35 to 39	40 to 44	45 to 49	50 to 54	55 to 59	60 to 64	65 to 69	70 up	Unopposed
	per cent																
National	0	2[a]	2[b]	11	10	16	12	10	10	7	8	5	3	5	2	1	0
United	1[c]	0	1[d]	1	1	1	2	2	0	1	2	5	1	4	1	5	24
Independent United (Coloured)									1			1	1			1	

[a] Kimberley South, Boksberg.

[b] Hottentots Holland, False Bay.

[c] Queenstown.

[d] Pretoria Sunnyside.

Bibliography

A. GOVERNMENT AND UNITED NATIONS PUBLICATIONS

(a) *Official Publications of the Union of South Africa*

The indispensable source for the text of legislation, election returns, appointments, etc., is the weekly *Government Gazette.* Debates in the House of Assembly and Senate are recorded verbatim and issued weekly during the parliamentary session, and in bound volumes annually. Well edited digests of the more significant of these debates are included in the *Journal of the Parliaments of the Commonwealth* but for those seeking insight into party attitudes there is no substitute for reading the debates themselves. The official *Yearbook* is a mine of information, and there is a monthly *Bulletin of Statistics* which keeps its figures up to date.

Many of the most careful and exhaustive studies on various aspects of South African life are embodied in the reports of governmental commissions. Every consideration of the position of the African in that country must be based on the revealing material embodied in the report of the Native Laws Commission, commonly known as the Fagan Report, 1948. The Social and Economic Planning Council issued a series of penetrating analyses which carried forward the pioneering study of the Third Interim Report of the Industrial and Agricultural Requirements Commission. Though the list is far from complete, the most important of these Government documents are listed below in chronological order.

The South African Government also issues a surprising amount of information through weekly, fortnightly or monthly newsletters and press translations emanating from the Public Information Service in Pretoria, London, New York and Ottawa. In addition, its Public Information department prepares and distributes many pamphlets on questions of public concern, as well as beautifully illustrated brochures. A few of the more important of these publications are noted at the end of this section.

Government Gazette. Weekly.

House of Assembly *Debates* (Hansard). Annual.

Senate *Debates.* Annual.

Office of Census and Statistics. *Official Yearbook of the Union of South Africa and of Basutoland, Bechuanaland Protectorate and Swaziland.* No. 27, 1952-53. Pretoria: The Government Printer, 1954. Annual.

South African Reserve Bank. *Bulletin of Statistics.* Quarterly.

Monthly Bulletin of Union Statistics.

Report of the Economic and Wage Commission. U.G. No. 14-1926, 1925.

Report of the Native Economic Commission, 1930-1932. U.G. No. 22-1932.

Board of Trade and Industries. *Establishment of Industries in Native Territories.* Report No. 219. Pretoria: 20th November, 1936.

Report of the Cape Coloured Commission. U.G. No. 54-1937.

Department of Interior. *Report of Asiatic Land Laws Commission.* U.G. No. 16-1939.

Report of the Indian Penetration Commission. U.G. No. 39-1941.

Third Interim Report of the Industrial and Agricultural Requirements Commission, Fundamentals of Economic Policy in the Union. U.G. No. 40-1941.

Report of the Social Security Committee and Report No. 2 of the Social and Economic Planning Council entitled: Social Security, Social Services and the National Income. U.G. No. 14-1944.

Report of the Witwatersrand Mine Natives' Wages Commission of 1943. U.G. No. 21-1944.

Report of the National Health Services Commission. U.G. No. 30-1944.

Board of Trade and Industries. *An Investigation into Manufacturing Industries in the Union of South Africa.* Report No. 282, 1945.

Report of the Interdepartmental Committee on the Social, Health and Economic Conditions of Urban Natives, 1942. G.P. 32278, 1945.

Social and Economic Planning Council. *The Native Reserves and Their Place in the Economy of the Union of South Africa.* Report No. 9 U.G. No. 32-1946.

Office of Census and Statistics. *Industrial Classification of the Economically Active Population, 1946.* Special Report No. 186.

Report of Penal and Prison Reform Commission, 1947. U.G. No. 47-1947.

Report of the Native Laws Commission (The Fagan Report). U.G. No. 28-1948.

Social and Economic Planning Council. *Economic and Social Conditions of the Racial Groups in South Africa.* Report No. 13. U.G. No. 53-1948.

Report of the Department of Social Welfare for the Period 1st October, 1937, to 31st March, 1949. U.G. No. 36-1950.

Report of the Industrial Legislation Commission of Enquiry. U.G. No. 62-1951.

Report of the Department of Social Welfare for the Period 1st April, 1949, to 31st March, 1951, U.G. No. 69-1951.

Bureau of Census and Statistics. *Thirty-second Industrial Census 1948-49 (Provisional).* Special Report No. 191.

Report of the Commission to enquire into the Disturbances in the Witzieshoek Native Reserve. U.G. 26-1951.

Report of the Industrial Legislation Commission of Enquiry. U.G. 62-1951.

Report of the Select Committee on Suppression of Communism Act Enquiry. Cape Town: Printed by Order of the House of Assembly, 1953, 222 pp. S.C. 10.

Report of the Commission of Enquiry on Separate Training Facilities for Non-Europeans at Universities, 1953-1954. G.P.S. 109957-1954.

Report of the Commission to Enquire into the Subject Matter of the Separate Representation of Voters' Act Validation and Amendment Bill, 1953. Part I, U.G. No. 20-1954. Part II (Memoranda and Statistics), U.G. No. 21-1954.

Commission for the Socio-Economic Development of the Bantu Areas. Summary of the Report. Govt. Printer, Pretoria, 1956, 213 pp. (The Tomlinson Report.)

The Government's White Paper on the Development of Bantu Areas, Fact Paper 10, May, 1956 (response to the recommendations of the Tomlinson Report), 10 pp.

Issued by the South African Government Information Office:

Weekly Press Digest (in English and in Afrikaans), Pretoria. Weekly.

South Africa Survey. London. Weekly.

South Africa Reports. New York. Weekly.

Barker, W. E. *What South Africans Earn, European and Non-European Incomes Compared.* 1953.

The Coloured People of the Cape. London: The Public Relations Office, South Africa House, n.d., 51 pp.

Holloway, Dr. John E. *The Problems of Race Relations in South Africa.* New York, 1955, 47 pp. (by the Ambassador to the United States).

Industrial Revolution in South Africa: Its Impact on European and Native Life. South Africa: 1952.

The Indian in South Africa. n.d., 41 pp.

Matheson, Alastair. *The Coloured People of the Cape.* London: 1947, 51 pp.

Southwest Africa and the Union of South Africa: The History of a Mandate. New York, 1946, 108 pp.

(*b*) *United Nations Material on South Africa*

Material on South Africa appears in the records of every session of the United Nations General Assembly. This can be found in the joint First and Sixth Committee, the Fourth Committee, and plenary sessions. No effort has been made to list the extended debates which have been referred to specifically in the text.

Given here are only the small number of special documents issued on South Africa and South West Africa, and an indication of the pamphlet material available from the South African and Indian Governments on their dispute.

General Assembly, *Report of the United Nations Commission on the Racial Situation in the Union of South Africa.* Official Records: Eighth Session, Suppl. no. 16 (A/2505 and A/2505/Add. 1). New York: 1953.

General Assembly, *Second Report of the United Nations Commission on the Racial Situation in the Union of South Africa.* Official Records: Ninth Session, Suppl. no. 16 (A/2719). New York: 1954. 121 pp.

General Assembly, *Third Report of the United Nations Commission on the Racial Situation in the Union of South Africa.* Tenth Session, Suppl. No. 14 (A/2953). New York: 1955. 105 pp.

General Assembly, *Report of the Committee on South West Africa to the General Assembly.* Official Records: Ninth Session, Suppl. No. 14 (A/2666). New York: 1954. 39 pp.

General Assembly, *Report of the Committee on South West Africa to the General Assembly.* Official Records: Tenth Session, Suppl. No. 12 (A/2913). New York: 1955. 50 pp.

Treatment of Indians in the Union of South Africa. Union Government's Statement to the United Nations General Assembly, September 15, 1947. Union of South Africa Government Information Office, 31 pp.

Disabilities of the Non-White Peoples in the Union of South Africa. Government of India: Ministry of External Affairs, 1953, 52 pp.

Treatment of Indians in South Africa: Recent Developments. Government of India Information Services: n.d., 16 pp.

United Nations, International Labour Office. *Report of the Ad Hoc Committee on Forced Labour.* Geneva: 1953, 619 pp. (E/2431). Supplement #13 in the Official record of the 16th session of the Economic and Social Council, and #36 in the Studies and reports (n.s.) of the International Labour Office. (Brief reference to South African system of Native passes.)

(*c*) *United States Government Material on South Africa*

Investment in Union of South Africa: Conditions and Outlook for United States Investors. U.S. Dept. of Commerce: 1954, 149 pp.

B. MATERIAL ISSUED BY PARTIES AND POLITICAL GROUPS

The most difficult of all material to secure in South Africa is that on parties. No detailed systematic study has been made previously either of the party system or of any individual party. The study of political parties does not form part of university offerings. Moreover, party officials themselves seem to have relatively little feeling that their material has any permanent importance. Thus party files are often incomplete, and it is particularly difficult to secure copies of party publications which are not immediately contemporary.

There are other handicaps for the researcher into parties and political groups. The National Party did not even translate its Constitution into English until 1953; much of its other material remains available only in Afrikaans.

Material relating to non-European groups is still more difficult to secure. As with party material, there is no good collection in any library, as far as could be ascertained. Moreover, non-European organizations suffer from lack of stable headquarters, and are subject to police raids and consequent dispersal of material. Most of what the author secured on these groups was from individuals who parted with personal copies.

The party propaganda material distributed during the 1953 election has been analysed in the relevant part of the text and is not cited here. Since that section did not deal with the Labour Party, which issued no substantial propaganda in 1953, a number of earlier Labour leaflets and pamphlets are listed here. In addition, listed below is a brief selection of some of the more important documents of the different parties and political groups.

National Party Programme of Principles and Constitution. 1952, 64 pp. (Each province prints its own program and Constitution. The program of principles is given in English and in Afrikaans, the rest in Afrikaans except for Natal, where it is all in English. This reference is to the program and Constitution of the Cape party.)

Dr. Malan's Policy for South Africa's Mixed Population. A pre-1948 election pamphlet. National Party.

Otto du Plessis. *Separate Representation of Voters.* Pub. by the Information Committee of the National Party, n.d., 68 pp.

Die Afrikanerparty. *Program van Beginsels en Konstitusie* (Program of Principles and Constitution). 1948, 36 pp.

Programme of Principles, Constitution and Nomination Regulations of the United Party. March, 1946, 20 pp.

United South African National Party. Witwatersrand General Council. Constitution and Regulations. Johannesburg: Nov. 1935, 20 pp.

South African 'Nationalism'. A United Party Publication, n.d., 24 pp.

A Guide to Politics for Young and Old. United Party Publication, n.d., 53 pp.

Constitution of the South African Labour Party. Dec., 1945, 16 pp.

Our Common Enemy: A Warning to South African Workers. Johannesburg: Trade Union and Labour Party Representatives on the Committee for Rescue from Nazi Terror, 46, Shakespeare House, Commissioner Street, n.d., 21 pp.

Labour Party's Plan for—A Land and Agriculture Policy for South Africa. National Executive Committee of the Labour Party, n.d., 8 pp.

Labour Stands for Bread and Butter Politics. Johannesburg: 1938, 8 pp.

C. F. Miles-Cadman. *Socialism for South Africa.* Johannesburg: under the auspices of the South African Labour Party, 3rd ed., 1943, 186 pp.

Never Again! 'Labour Bulletin' Victory Supplement, n.d., 23 pp.

Non-European Policy. As adopted by the Special Conference held on 10th November, 1946, South African Labour Party, mimeo., 10 pp.

Supplementary Statement to Non-European Policy, Nov. 13, 1946, South African Labour Party, 2 pp.

Why the Labour Party? n.d., 22 pp.

The Workers' Charter. South African Trades and Labour Council, National Executive Committee, 1944, 15 pp.

Contact. Monthly newsletter of the Liberal Party of South Africa, began publication Jan., 1954.

The Policies of the Liberal Party of South Africa. n.d. (1955) 23 pp. (Includes the Constitution.)

The Liberal Party of South Africa: Summary of Decisions at National Congress, July, 1953. The Liberal Party of South Africa.

Cooperation or Chaos? The Liberal Party of South Africa.

The High Court of Parliament Act and the Rule of Law. A Defenders of the Constitution Publication, Feb., 1953, 20 pp.

Political Apartheid and the Entrenched Clauses of the South Africa Act: Dr. Malan's 'Historical Facts'. A Defenders of the Constitution Publication, March, 1953, 34 pp.

Crisis: The Real Issues. A Defenders of the Constitution Publication, n.d., 28 pp.

Fighting Talk, June, 1953, Vol IX, No. 6. Organ of the Springbok Legion Monthly; began publication 1944.

Democracy and Ex-Volunteers. The Springbok Legion, n.d., 12 pp.

Springbok Legion: The History and Policy. n.d., 36 pp.

Blikfakkel. Torch Commando bilingual monthly. (Discontinued.)

Memorandum Submitted to The Tenth Delimitation Commission, 1952, on Behalf of The War Veterans' Torch Commando. With Pictograms. 42 pp.

The Threatened People: The Case for a South African Democracy. Johannesburg: South African Congress of Democrats, 1953.

The Constitution of the African National Congress. 1919, 36 pp.

Africans' Claims in South Africa. African National Congress Series No. II. Johannesburg: 1945.

The Disabilities of the Non-White Peoples of South Africa. Memorandum by the African National Congress, and the South African Indian Congress, 1952, 30 pp. and annexures.

Natal Indian Congress Constitution. June, 1947, 31 pp.

Why Another Political Body? issued by Natal Indian Congress, Durban, n.d., 3 pp.

Dadoo, Dr. and Molema, Dr. *Onward to Freedom: A Call to the People of South Africa.* South African Indian Congress, 1952, 23 pp.

Pather, P. R. *Seventy Years of Frustration and Unhappiness.* An examination of Land and Trading Rights as they affect Indians in Natal and Transvaal and a criticism of the Group Areas Act, 41, of 1950. South African Indian Organization, n.d., 42 pp.

A Declaration to the People of South Africa From the Non-European Unity Movement. Cape Town: International Printers for the Non-European Unity Movement, n.d., 16 pp.

To the People of Natal: Race Riots and the Nation. The Working Committee Non-European Unity Movement, 1952, 12 pp.

Minutes of the All African Convention. December, 1937, 62 pp.

Tabata, I. B. *The All African Convention: The Awakening of A People* Johannesburg: People's Press, 1950, 161 pp.

Transvaal Council of Non-European Trade Unions. *Memorandum submitted to the Industrial Legislation Commission of Enquiry.* mimeo., 1950.

C. JOURNALS, BOOKS AND PAMPHLETS ISSUED BY NON-GOVERNMENTAL AND NON-PARTY ORGANIZATIONS

(a) *South African Institute of Race Relations, Johannesburg*

Indispensable for keeping abreast of non-European (in particular African) affairs and race relations in South Africa is the wealth of material published by the South African Institute of Race Relations. The monumental *Handbook on Race Relations,* edited by Ellen Hellmann, provides the essential foundation for understanding developments in a wide range of fields like population, politics, press and education. Subsequent developments in these fields as well as of a more general character can be traced through the Institute's annual *Survey of Race Relations, The Race Relations Journal* and *Race Relations News.* Moreover, the Institute publishes a great many excellent pamphlets by experts in particular fields. Those which have been found most useful are listed below. They are grouped roughly by subject, the first group expressing the Institute's own point of view, the second dealing with broad issues, and those thereafter with particular topics.

Hellmann, Ellen (Ed.) *Handbook on Race Relations in South Africa.* New York: Oxford University Press, 1949, xii, 778 pp.

A Survey of Race Relations in South Africa. Annual; began publication 1929.

Race Relations Journal. Quarterly; began publication 1933.

Race Relations News. Monthly; began publication 1938.

Go Forward in Faith (A Statement of the Fundamental Beliefs and Attitudes of the South African Institute of Race Relations).

Whyte, Quintin (Director of the Institute). *The South African Institute of Race Relations' Approach to Racial Problems.*

Clayton, The Rt. Rev. G. H. *Who Pays for Bantu Progress?*

Eiselen, Dr. W. W. M. *The Meaning of Apartheid.*

Frankel, S. Herbert. *Some Reflections on Civilization in Africa.* 1952, 27 pp.

Hellmann, Ellen. *Problems of Urban Bantu Youth*: Report of an Enquiry into the Causes of Early School-Leaving and Occupational Opportunities amongst Bantu Youth in Johannesburg. Johannesburg: 1940, 151 pp.

Hellmann, Ellen. *Racial Laws versus Economic and Social Forces.* 1955, 42 pp.

Horrell, Muriel. *The Group Areas Act: its Effect on Human Beings.* 1956, 156 pp.

Horrell, Muriel. *Non-European Policies in the Union and the Measure of Their Success; A Survey of the Conflict between Economic Trends and Ideological Planning.* 1954, 74 pp.

Horrell, Muriel. *South Africa's Non-White Workers.* 1956, 105 pp.

Houghton, D. Hobart. *Life in the Ciskei.* 1955, 72 pp. [Digest of the Keiskammahook Rural Survey. Pietermaritzburg: Shuter & Shooter, 1952, 4 vols.]

Houghton, D. Hobart. *Some Economic Problems of the Bantu in South Africa.* 1938, 55 pp.

Houghton, D. Hobart. *The Tomlinson Report. A Summary of the Findings and Recommendations in the Tomlinson Commission Report.* 1956, 76 pp.

MacCrone, I. D. *Group Conflicts and Race Prejudice.* Johannesburg, 1947, 31 pp.

Rheinallt-Jones, J. D. *At the Crossroads.* Johannesburg: 1947, 31 pp.

Ross, Emory. *Colour and Christian Community.* 1954, 30 pp.

Suzman, Helen. *A Digest of the Fagan Report.* 1952, 22 pp.

Thompson, L. M. *Democracy in Multi-Racial Societies.* Johannesburg: 1949, 36 pp.

Webb, Maurice, and Kirkwood, Kenneth. *The Durban Riots and After.* 1949,

Whyte, Quintin. *Apartheid and Other Policies.*

Whyte, Quintin. *Behind the Racial Tensions in South Africa.* Johannesburg: 1953, 28 pp.

Bruce, Collins. *The Principle of 'Equal Pay for Equal Work' and its Effects Upon the Employment Opportunities of Non-Europeans.* 1953.

Gibson, Olive. *The Cost of Living for Africans.* 1954, 44 pp.

Hawarden, Eleanor. *Labour and the New Economic Policy: A Commentary on the Third Interim Report of the Industrial and Agricultural Requirements Commission.* 1942, 18 pp.

Hellmann, Ellen. *Sellgoods: A Sociological Survey of an African Commercial Labour Force.* 1953, 68 pp.

Horrell, M. *Economic Developments in South Africa and the Contributions of the Various Racial Groups.* Johannesburg: 1943.

Oppenheimer, Harry. *The Future of Industry in South Africa.* 1950, 8 pp.

Routh, Guy. *Industrial Relations and Race Relations.* 1952, 28 pp.

Routh, Guy. *South Africa's Changing Economy.* 1955, 49 pp.

van der Horst, Sheila T. *Equal Pay for Equal Work.* 1954.

Van Eck, H. J. *Some Aspects of the South African Industrial Revolution.* 1951, 27 pp.

Jones, J. D. Rheinallt. *Native Housing in Urban Areas with Special Consideration of its Social Aspects.* 1951.

Kirkwood, Kenneth. *The Group Areas Act.* Braamfontein: n.d., 43 pp.

Harris, Prof. E. E. *Moral Aspects of the Proposed Western Areas Removal Scheme.* 1953.

The 'Western Areas' Removal Scheme: Facts and Viewpoints. Presented at a Conference convened by the S.A. Institute of Race Relations at the University of Witwatersrand, 22nd August, 1953, n.d., 35 pp.

The Western Areas—Mass Removal? 1953.

Xuma, A. B. *Western Areas Removal Scheme—African Reactions.* 1953.

Davie, T. B. *Education and Race Relations in South Africa.* 1955, 32 pp.

Hartshorne, K. B. *Native Education in South Africa.*

Hoernlé, A. W. *Report on the Working of the Bantu Education Act.* 1955.

Horrell, Muriel. *Standards of Education at Present Attained By the Union's African Population.* 1953.

Summary of the Report of the Commission on Native Education in South Africa, 1949-1951. 1952, 35 pp.

Record of Proceedings of National Conference convened by the Institute in July, 1952, to Study the Report of the Native Education Commission. 32 pp.

Political Representation of Africans in the Union. 1942.

Cape Coloured People's Welfare. 1949.

Thompson, L. M. *The Cape Coloured Franchise.* Johannesburg: 1949, 59 pp.

Burrows, Raymond. *Indian Life and Labour in Natal.* 1952, 64 pp.

Ferguson-Davie, C. J. *The Early History of Indians in Natal.* n.d., 26 pp.

(b) *South African Bureau of Racial Affairs (SABRA)*

Though the South African Bureau of Racial Affairs (SABRA) is much younger and issues much less than the Institute of Race Relations, its publications are of great importance as authoritative statements of Nationalist views on race relations.

SABRA conferences and publications are sometimes used as sounding boards for Government policies, and sometimes include views, particularly on ideal, or total, apartheid which are considerably more extreme than the Nationalist Government would endorse. The articles in SABRA's Journal, and its pamphlets, generally exhibit the same scholarly approach as Institute publications.

Journal of Racial Affairs (*Tydskrif vir Rasse-aangeleenthede*), Articles in English and in Afrikaans. (P.O. Box 238, Stellenbosch.) Bi-monthly; began publication 1949.

Nuusbrief, Articles in English and in Afrikaans. (P.O. Box 238, Stellenbosch.) Bi-monthly; began publication 1949.

The Native Question. First Annual Conference of SABRA (January 1950).

The Native in the Industrial Life of South Africa. Second Annual Conference of SABRA (January 1951).

Group Areas and Residential Separation. Third Annual Conference of SABRA (January 1952).

Integration or Separate Development? Stellenbosch: 1952, 35 pp.

Olivier, N. J. J. *Apartheid—A Slogan or a Solution?* Stellenbosch: 1954: 12 pp. Printed originally as an article in the *Journal of International Affairs*, vol. 7, no. 2 (New York, July 1953).

Bantu Education: Oppression or Opportunity. Stellenbosch: 1955, 48 pp.

(c) *Other non-party groups and individuals*

Other South African organizations, and sometimes individuals, also issue pamphlets or reports on particular topics, but their output is sporadic, and shows much less effort to be comprehensive in the coverage of issues than are the Institute of Race Relations and SABRA. Exception must be made, however, for the invaluable *Press Digest* issued weekly by the Jewish Board of Deputies, which is by far the most helpful source through which to follow the South African press, Afrikaans as well as English. A monthly periodical called 'The Black Sash: *Die Swart Serp*' is published by the Black Sash organization, 92, Westmeath Road, Parkview, Johannesburg. It first appeared in January, 1956.

Among the more significant of the non-party works are those issued by the Churches, which, as the text pointed out, are deeply concerned with and often influential on the Native question. A suggestive approach to South African problems is contained in Keppel-Jones' *Human Relations in South Africa*, while the two pamphlets issued by the Friends' Home Service Committee in London show breadth of view and insight.

It should be noted that, where organizations like the Reddingsdaadbond or F.A.K. are dealt with in the text, the material listed in that section is not repeated in the bibliography.

Press Digest. Johannesburg: Jewish Board of Deputies, weekly (in English).

The Anti-Jewish Movements in South Africa: The Need for Action. South African Jewish Board of Deputies, 1936, 29 pp.

Grant, Edward W. *South Africa: What of the Church?* London: Edinburgh House Press, 1952, 23 pp.

Christian Principles in Multi-Racial South Africa: Report on the Dutch Reformed Conference of Church Leaders. Pretoria, 1953, 185 pp.

The Racial Issue in South Africa: Being findings on the Native problems of various congresses held under the auspices of the Federal Missionary Council of the Dutch Reformed Mother and Mission Churches (1950-1952). Bloemfontein: D.R. Mission Press, 1953, 16 pp.

The Christian Citizen in a Multi-Racial Society: A Report of the Rosettenville Conference, July 1949. The Christian Council of South Africa.

Visser 't Hooft, Dr. Willem Adolph. *Christianity, Race and the South African People:* Report on an ecumenical visit. New York: Department of Racial and Cultural Relations, National Council of the Churches of Christ in the U.S.A., 1952, 33 pp.

Visser 't Hooft, Dr. Willem Adolph. 'A Visit to the South African Churches in April and May, 1952.' *The Ecumenical Review,* Geneva (January 1953), pp. 174-197.

Chaos—or Co-operation?: The meaning of the Malan-Havenga proposals to change the political status of the Cape Coloured People. Summaries of speeches made at the Civil Rights League National Conference, Johannesburg, 9th December, 1950. The Civil Rights League, January 1951, 19 pp.

The Coloured Man Speaks: The Entrenched Clauses. Civil Rights League, Cape Town, n.d., 16 pp.

Report to the Sponsors of a Private Commission of Enquiry Appointed by the South African Trades and Labour Council and the Civil Rights League into Certain Events at Johannesburg on the 24th May, 1952. November 1952, 62 pp.

Bedford, Randolph. *After Victory—What?* Durban: The Knox Publishing Co., in conjunction with the Economic Reform Institute of South Africa, 1944, 27 pp.

Smith, Sidney. *Let Go Our Money.* Durban: The Economic Reform Institute of South Africa, 1945, 40 pp.

Blueprint for Blackout: A Commentary on the Education Policy of the Instituut vir Christelik-Nationale Onderwys. The Education League, n.d., 23 pp.

Christian National Education: A Critical Commentary by the South African Teachers' Association, Cape Province, South Africa. 20 pp.

Tobias, Phillip V. *The African in the Universities:* A memorandum of evidence presented by the National Executive Committee of N.U.S.A.S. to the Commission on Native Education, February 1950. National Union of South African Students, 1951, 30 pp.

Van Schoor, W. P. *The Origin and Development of Segregation in South Africa.* The Teachers' League of South Africa, 1951, 24 pp. (Trotskyite).

Brayshaw, E. Russell. *The Racial Problems of South Africa.* London: Friends' Home Service Committee, 1952, 24 pp.

Racial Problems in South Africa. Report by a Deputation from the Society of Friends (in Great Britain and America) to South Africa, 1938, 28 pp.

Yergan, Max. *Gold and Poverty in South Africa.* International Industrial Relations Institute, 1938, 24 pp.

Van Eck, H. J. *The Potential of Industrial Development in South Africa Bearing in Mind Limitation in Natural Resources.* South African Federated Chamber of Industries, 1952, 16 pp.

Standard Bank Monthly Review (Suppl. Standard Bank of South Africa). Union of South Africa: July 1950.

Transvaal Chamber of Mines. *Annual Reports and Proceedings of the Annual Meeting.*

The Native Workers on the Witwatersrand Gold Mines. Transvaal Chamber of Mines, 1947, 20 pp.

Southern Africa. Seven Articles and a Leading Article Reprinted from *The Times.* London: 1950, 42 pp.

Ballinger, W. G. *Race and Economics in South Africa.* London: Day to Day Pamphlets, No. 21, 1934, 67 pp.

Cilliers, A. C. *Ex Unitate Vires: A Plea for a Grand Political Alliance as a Prerequisite for the Solution of the South African Trilemma* (*Biological, Physiographical and Racial*). 1953, 42 pp.

Duncan, Patrick. *English South Africans Face the Future: The Road Through the Wilderness.* 1953, 17 pp.

Hofmeyr, J. H. *What of the Future?: South Africa's Present-day Problems Analysed.* 1948, 63 pp.

Keppel-Jones, A. *Human Relations in South Africa: Political and Historical.* Johannesburg: St. Benedict's Booklets, No. 2, 30 pp.

Keppel-Jones, A. *Race or Civilization? Who is Destroying South Africa?* 12 pp.

Xuma, A. B. *Reconstituting the Union of South Africa or A More Rational Union Policy.* Address delivered before a Public Meeting of the Bantu Studies Club of the University of the Witwatersrand, May 31st, 1932. 23 pp.

D. PERIODICALS

The most useful of these periodicals for following events in South Africa is *The Round Table*, which ordinarily has a comprehensive section on the Union in each issue. The *Journal of the Parliaments of the Commonwealth* (formerly Empire) provides adequate summaries of the most important debates in the South African Parliament, though, as pointed out above, it cannot carry the full flavor of the verbatim debates. The *Journal* is an indispensable means, however, for covering debates over a considerable period of time, and is, of course, much more easily available abroad than are the debates. Among South African periodicals, the *Forum* is perhaps the most useful for political discussions, though its articles, purposely, do not approach the scholarly level of those in the *South African Journal of Economics.* All the other journals mention South African affairs from time to time though to varying degrees.

Africa: Journal of the International African Institute, London. Quarterly.

African Abstracts: A Quarterly Review of Ethnological, Social, and Linguistic Studies Appearing in Current Periodicals. Quarterly, began publication 1949, pub. by the International African Institute.

African Affairs: Journal of the Royal African Society, London, Quarterly.

Africa Digest. Pub. by the Africa Bureau, London. Bi-monthly.

Africa South. I, 1 Oct.-Dec. 1956, Capetown. Periodicity not announced.

African World. London. Monthly.

Bantu. An Informal Publication of the Dept. of Native Affairs. Monthly, began publication 1954.

Commonwealth Survey: A Record of United Kingdom and Commonwealth Affairs. Fortnightly, began publication 1955.

The Forum. Johannesburg: Bi-monthly, resumed publication 1951 after temporary cessation.

Journal of the Parliaments of the Empire (Subsequently Commonwealth). Quarterly.

The Round Table: A Quarterly Review of British Commonwealth Affairs. Began publication 1920.

South African Outlook: A Journal dealing with Missionary and Racial Affairs. Monthly. Lovedale, Cape Province.

South African Journal of Economics. Quarterly, Johannesburg.

Classified List of South African Annual Publications. Cape Town: South African Public Library Suppl. 1951, 42 pp.

The Index to South African Periodicals. Annual since 1940.

Saul, C. Daphne. *Handlist of South African Periodicals. Current in December 1951.* Cape Town: South African Public Library, 1951, 54 pp. Additions and corrections published every 3 months in the *Quarterly Bulletin of the South African Library.*

Union List of South African Newspapers, November, 1949. Cape Town, 1950, 99 pp. All newspapers issued from 1900 to 1950.

E. BOOKS AND ARTICLES

(a) *General*

There are relatively few analytical studies of South Africa. An excellent introduction is provided by Marquard's *Peoples and Policies in South Africa,* which packs a surprising amount of information into relatively small compass. A still smaller, but meaty book is Brookes' *South Africa in a Changing World.* Calpin's *There are No South Africans* is still well worth reading, as is Dvorin's *Racial Separation in South Africa.* H. Lindsay Smith's *Behind the Press in South Africa* provides the best account available in print of South African newspapers. Scott Haigh's *Strangers May be Present* is a lively and informative account of Parliament in action, by a member of the press gallery. E. S. Sachs' *The Choice Before South Africa* is illuminating on labor. The monumental reports of the Carnegie Commission on the poor-white problem in South Africa deal in great detail with a part of South African life and history which should never be forgotten by anyone studying that country. Henry John May's *The South African Constitution* is the standard work on that subject, but despite the addition of a small section on politics in the third edition remains so factual and loaded with detail that it can be used only for reference. Kilpin's *Parliamentary Procedure* is also authoritative.

Among histories, those by Eric Walker and C. W. de Kiewiet are outstanding, the former for the immense amount of important detail which it includes and the latter for the insight and broad panorama which it presents so smoothly. Leo Marquard and Arthur Keppel-Jones provide shorter, very readable accounts.

Still lacking, however, is a comprehensive and penetrating political history of South Africa since 1910. To learn about the inside story of political moves, it is necessary to go to biographies, autobiographies and reminiscences. Some of these are slight or partisan, others, like those by Deneys Reitz, are first rate, but, taken together, their material helps to provide another level of understanding of South African politics since Union. Outstanding and unique is Roberts and Trollip, *The South African Opposition, 1939-1945,* which is based on first-hand information of the interplay of groups within Nationalist ranks in the very significant period during which Dr. Malan gained undisputed control.

On race attitudes in South Africa, MacCrone's book is helpful. So too is McCord's *South African Struggle*, which presents a picture of developments not always recognizable to one who has learned South African history from more orthodox sources, but characteristic of that held by many Afrikaner nationalists. Neame's *White Man's Africa* performs much the same service.

South Africa's position in the Commonwealth has received more attention from outside than inside the Union. Outstanding for insight and vigor are those sections of Hancock's *Surveys of British Commonwealth Affairs* which deal with South Africa. Mansergh brings the story up to 1939, though in a more matter-of-fact way. Carter treats South Africa in the League, and Wheare is the recognized authority on constitutional issues.

Armstrong, H. C. *Grey Steel (J. C. Smuts): A Study in Arrogance.* Middlesex: Penguin Books, 1939, 280 pp.

Axelson, Eric V. (Ed.) *South African Explorers.* London, New York, Oxford University Press, 1954, 346 pp.

Barlow, Arthur G. *Almost in Confidence.* Cape Town: Juta & Co., Ltd., 1952, 345 pp.

Bate, H. Maclean. *South Africa Without Prejudice.* London: Laurie (T. Werner) Ltd., 1956, 206 pp.

Blackwell, Leslie. *Farewell to Parliament: More Reminiscences of Bench, Bar, Parliament and Travel.* Pietermaritzburg: Shuter and Shooter, 1946, 239 pp.

Blackwell, Leslie, and May, Henry John. *This is South Africa.* Pietermaritzburg: Shuter and Shooter, 1947, 170 pp.

Bond, John. *They were South Africans.* Cape Town, London: Oxford University Press, 1956, 224 pp.

Boydell, Thomas. *'My Luck Was in': With Spotlights on General Smuts.* Cape Town: Stewart, 1948, 370 pp.

Boydell, Thomas. *'My Luck's Still In': With More Spotlights on General Smuts.* Cape Town: Stewart, 1948, 367 pp.

Brady, Alexander. *Democracy in the Dominions: A Comparative Study in Institutions.* Second ed. Toronto: University of Toronto Press, 1952, 604 pp. [Section on South Africa.]

Brand, R. H. *The Union of South Africa.* Oxford: The Clarendon Press, 1909, 192 pp.

Brookes, Edgar Harry. *South Africa in a Changing World.* Cape Town: Oxford University Press, 1953, 151 pp. [A series of public lectures given at the University of Natal in the first semester of 1953.]

Bryce, James (*et al.*) *Briton and Boer: Both Sides of the South African Question.* New York, London: Harper & Brothers, 1900, 250 pp. New and enlarged edition, 309 pp.

Calpin, G. H. *The South African Way of Life: Values and Ideals of a Multi-racial Society.* London: Heinemann Ltd., 1953, 200 pp., and New York: Columbia University Press, 1953.

Calpin, G. H. *There Are No South Africans.* London: Thomas Nelson and Sons Ltd., 1941, 412 pp.

Carnegie Commission of Investigation on the Poor White Question in South Africa. *The Poor White Problem in South Africa, Report of the Carnegie Commission.* Stellenbosch: Pro Ecclesia—Drukkery, 1932. 5 vols.
v. 1. Economic report: Rural impoverishment and rural exodus, by J. F. W. Grosskopf.
v. 2. Psychological report: The poor white, by R. W. Witcocks.
v. 3. Education report: Education and the poor white, by E. G. Malherbe.
v. 4. Health report: Health factors in the poor white problem, by W. A. Murray.
v. 5. Sociological report: The poor white and society, by J. R. Albertyn. The mother and daughter of the poor family, by M. E. Rothman.

Carson, J. J. G. *Emile Solomon, 1858-1939.* Cape Town: Juta & Co., Ltd., 1941, 184 pp.

Carter, Gwendolen M. 'Can Apartheid succeed in South Africa?' *Foreign Affairs,* New York (January 1954), pp. 296-309.

Carter, Gwendolen M. *The Commonwealth and International Security: The Role of the Dominions, 1919-1939.* Toronto: Ryerson, 1947, 326 pp.

Carter, Gwendolen M. 'The Commonwealth in the United Nations.' *International Organization,* IV, No. 2, 1950, pp, 247-260.

Carter, Gwendolen M. 'Union of South Africa: Politics of White Supremacy.' *The Annals* (March 1955), pp. 142-50.

Chadwick, W. S. *Mother Africa Hits Back.* Stellenbosch: The University Publishers, 1948, 219 pp.

Cope, R. K. *Comrade Bill: The Life and Times of W. H. Andrews, Workers' Leader.* Cape Town: Stewart Printing Co., n.d., 340 pp.

Crafford, F. S. *Jan Smuts: A Biography.* London: Allen & Unwin Ltd., 1946, 378 pp.

Curtis, Lionel. *With Milner in South Africa.* Oxford: Basil Blackwell, 1951, 354 pp.

Davidson, Basil. *Report on Southern Africa.* London: Jonathan Cape, 1952, 285 pp.

Davies, Horton and R. H. V. Shepherd. *South African Missions, 1800-1950, An Anthology.* New York: Nelson, 1954, 232 pp.

de Kiewiet, Cornelius W. *The Anatomy of South African Misery*. London, New York: Oxford University Press, 1957, 88 pp.

de Kiewiet, Cornelius W. 'Fears and pressures in the Union of South Africa.' *Africa Today*, ed. by C. Grove Haines. Baltimore: John Hopkins Press, 1955, pp. 203-24.

de Kiewiet, Cornelius W. *A History of South Africa. Social and Economic.* New York: Oxford University Press, 1941, 292 pp.

Dicey, Albert Venn. *Introduction to the study of the Law of the Constitution.* Ninth ed., with introduction and appendix by E. C. S. Wade. London: Macmillan and Co., Ltd., 1939, 681 pp.

Dvorin, Eugene P. *Racial Separation in South Africa: An Analysis of Apartheid Theory.* Chicago: University of Chicago Press, 1952, 256 pp.

Engelenburg, Dr. F. V. *General Louis Botha.* Pretoria: J. L. Van Schaik Ltd., 1929, 352 pp.

Fitzgerald, Walter. *Africa: A Social, Economic and Political Geography of Its Major Regions.* London: Methuen & Co., 1948.

Fortune. *'Gold!'* Vol XXXIV, No. 4 (October 1946), pp. 105-112, 233-246.

Fortune. *Seven Golden Houses.* December 1946, pp. 162-169, 184-199.

Frankel, S. Herbert. *The Economic Impact on Underdeveloped Countries.* Oxford: Basil Blackwell, 1953, 179 pp.

Franklin, N. N. *Economics in South Africa.* Cape Town, London, New York: Oxford University Press, 1948, 1954, 247 pp.

Fuller, Basil. *South Africa—Not Guilty?* London: Jarrolds, 1957, 288 pp.

Geen, M. S. *The Making of the Union of South Africa: A Brief History, 1487-1939.* New York: Longmans, Green and Co., 1946, 227 pp.

Gibbs, Henry. *Background to Bitterness: The Story of South Africa, 1652-1954.* London: Muller, 1954, 255 pp.

Gibbs, Henry. *Twilight in South Africa.* London and New York: Jarrolds, 1950, 288 pp.

Gitsham, Ernest, and Trembath, James F. *A first Account of Labour Organization in South Africa.* Durban: E. P. & Commercial Printing Co., Ltd., 1926, 179 pp.

Gross, Felix. *Rhodes of Africa.* London: Cassell, 1956, 433 pp.

Haigh, Scott. *Strangers May Be Present.* London: George Allen & Unwin Ltd., 1951, 297 pp.

Hailey, Baron William Malcolm. *An African Survey: A Study of Problems Arising in Africa South of the Sahara,* issued by the Committee of the African Research Survey under the auspices of the Royal Institute of International Affairs. London, New York: Oxford University Press, 1938, 1837 pp. (Sections on South Africa.) [Second edition, 1957, 1676 pp.]

Hancock, William Keith. *Survey of British Commonwealth Affairs,* Vol. I, 1937, Problems of Nationality, 1918-39, Vol. II, Part 1 and 2, Problems of Economic Policy, 1939 and 1942. New York: Oxford University Press, 1942, 355 pp.

Hancock, Sir William Keith. *The Smuts Papers.* London: Athlone, 1956, 19 pp.

Hatch, John. *The Dilemma of South Africa.* London: Dennis Dobson Ltd., 1952, 255 pp.

Hattersley, Alan F. *The British Settlement of Natal: A Study in Imperial Migration.* Cambridge: Cambridge University Press, 1950, 351 pp.

Hiemstra, V. G. *The Group Areas Act.* Cape Town: Juta & Co., Ltd., 1953, 146 pp.

Hofmeyr, Jan H. *South Africa.* New York: Charles Scribner's Sons, 1931, 331 pp. (The Modern World.) Rev. ed. by J. P. Cope, Oxford University Press, 1952, 253 pp.

Huddleston, Trevor. *Naught for your Comfort.* Garden City: Doubleday, 1956, 253 pp.

Kennedy, William Paul McClure, and Schlosberg, Herzl Joshua. *The Law and Custom of the South African Constitution,* a treatise on the constitutional and administrative law of the Union of South Africa, the mandated territory of South West Africa and the South African crown territories. London: Oxford University Press, 1935, 640 pp.

Keppel-Jones, Arthur. *Friends or Foes? A Point of View and A Programme for Racial Harmony in South Africa.* Pietermaritzburg: Shuter and Shooter, 1950, 231 pp.

Keppel-Jones, Arthur. *South Africa: A Short History.* London, New York: (Hutchinson's University Library: British Empire History, No. 30), 1949, 212 pp. Second ed., 1953.

Keppel-Jones, Arthur. *When Smuts Goes: A History of South Africa from 1952-2010, First Published in 2015.* Pietermaritzburg: Shuter & Shooter, 1950, 270 pp.

Key, V. O., Jr. *A Primer of Statistics for Political Scientists.* New York: Thomas Y. Crowell Company, 1954, 209 pp.

Kilpin, Ralph. *Parliamentary Procedure in South Africa: A Short Guide to the Rules and Practice of the Union House of Assembly.* Cape Town: Juta & Co. Ltd., 1950, 190 pp.

Kruger, Paul. *The Memoirs of Paul Kruger.* New York: The Century Co., 1902, 444 pp.

Kuper, Leo. *Passive Resistance in South Africa.* London: Jonathan Cape, 1956, 256 pp. New Haven: Yale University Press, 1957, 256 pp.

MacCrone, I. D. *Race Attitudes in South Africa: Historical, Experimental and Psychological Studies.* New York, London, Toronto: Oxford University Press (on behalf of the University of the Witwatersrand, Johannesburg), 1937, 328 pp.

Macmillan, William Miller. *Africa Emergent: A Survey of Social, Political and Economic Trends in British Africa.* London: Faber & Faber Ltd., 1938, 414 pp.

Macmillan, William Miller. *Bantu, Boer and Briton: The Making of the South African Native Problem.* London: Faber and Gwyer Ltd., 1929, 328 pp.

Macmillan, William Miller. *Complex South Africa: An Economic Footnote to History.* London: Faber & Faber Ltd., 1930, 293 pp.

Malan, Daniel F. 'Why South Africans Want Stricter Segregation', *U.S. News and World Report* (April 16, 1954), pp. 60-66. [Interview.]

Malherbe, Ernest Gideon. *Education in South Africa* (1652-1922), A critical survey of the development of education administration in the Cape, Natal, Transvaal and the Orange Free State. Cape Town and Johannesburg: Juta and Co., Ltd., 1925, 521 pp.

Mansergh, Nicholas. *A Survey of British Commonwealth Affairs, 1931-1939.* London, New York: Oxford University Press, 1952, 481 pp.

Mansergh, Nicholas. *The Multi-Racial Commonwealth: A Report on the Fifth Unofficial Conference of the Institutes of International Affairs, Lahore, 1953.* London, New York: Oxford University Press, 1955, 175 pp.

Marais, Dr. Ben J. *Colour: Unsolved Problem of the West.* Cape Town: Howard B. Timmins, 1952, 329 pp.

Marais, J. S. *Maynier and the First Boer Republic.* Cape Town: Maskew Miller, Ltd., 1944, 157 pp.

Marquard, Leo. *The Peoples and Policies of South Africa.* London, New York, Cape Town: Oxford University Press, 1952, 245 pp.

Marquard, Leo. *The Story of South Africa.* London: Faber and Faber Ltd., 1950, 251 pp.

May, Henry John. *The South African Constitution.* Cape Town and Johannesburg: Juta & Co., Second ed., 1949, 447 pp. 3rd ed., 1955, 678 pp.

McCord, Capt. J. J. *South African Struggle.* Pretoria: J. H. de Bussy, 1952, 553 pp.

McKerron, Mrs. Margaretha Emma Martinius. *A History of Education in South Africa 1652-1932.* Pretoria: J. L. van Schaik, Ltd., 1934, 182 pp.

Millin, Sarah Gertrude. *General Smuts.* Boston: Little, Brown & Co., 1936, Vol. 1, 366 pp., Vol. 2, 460 pp.

Millin, Sarah Gertrude. *The People of South Africa.* London: Constable and Co. Ltd., 1951, 324 pp.

Millin, Sarah Gertrude. *Rhodes.* London: Chatto & Windus, 1933, 389 pp.

Molteno, Sir James Tennant. *The Dominion of Afrikanerdom: Recollections Pleasant and Otherwise.* London: Methuen & Co., Ltd., 1923, 257 pp.

Molteno, Sir James Tennant. *Further South African Recollections.* London: Methuen & Co., Ltd., 1926, 236 pp.

Natal University College, Pietermaritzburg. Dept. of Economics. *Natal Regional Survey.* Pietermaritzburg: University of Natal Press.
Vol. 2, Alsop, M. H., *The Population of Natal,* 1952, 144 pp.
Vol. 4, Ringrose, H. G., *Trade Unions in Natal,* 1951, 111 pp.
Additional report no. 2. *The Durban Housing Survey; A Study of Housing in a Multi-racial Community.* 1952, 520 pp.
Small Towns in Natal; A Socio-economic Sample Survey. 1954, 126 pp.

Nathan, Manfred. *The Huguenots in South Africa.* South Africa, Central News Agency Ltd., 1939, 159 pp.

Neame, Lawrence Elwin. *General Hertzog: Prime Minister of the Union of South Africa Since 1924.* London: Hurst & Blackett, Ltd., 1930, 288 pp.

Neame, Lawrence Elwin. *Some South African Politicians.* Cape Town: Maskew Miller, Ltd. 1929, 193 pp.

Neame, Lawrence Elwin. *White Man's Africa: The Problem of a White Nation in a Black Continent.* Cape Town: Stewart, 1952, 105 pp.

Newton, A. P., Benians, E. A., and Walker, Eric A. *The Cambridge History of the British Empire.* Vol. VIII, *South Africa, Rhodesia and the Protectorates.* Cambridge: Cambridge University Press, 1936, 1,005 pp.

Oldham, Joseph Houldsworth. *Christianity and the Race Problem.* New York: George H. Doran Co., 1924, 280 pp.

Patten, J. W. 'Alternatives to Apartheid in South Africa.' *Foreign Affairs* (January 1952), pp. 310-326.

Patterson, Sheila. *The Last Trek: A Study of the Boer People and the Afrikaner Nation.* London: Routledge and Kegan Paul, 1957, 336 pp.

Plessis, Prof. L. J. du. *Problems of Nationality and Race in Southern Africa.* London: The Diplomatic Press and Publishing Co., International Studies, 1949, 16 pp.

Preller, Johann F. (Ed.) *Die Konvensie-Dagboek van sy Edelagbare François Stephanus Malan,* 1908-09. [A diary of the discussions in the National Convention which drafted the provisions of South African union. In Afrikaans and English.] Cape Town: Van Riebeeck Publication, 1951, 284 pp.

Reitz, Deneys. *Commando: A Boer Journal of the Boer War.* Middlesex: Penguin Books, 1939, 373 pp.

Reitz, Deneys. *No Outspan.* London: Faber and Faber Ltd., 1943, 288 pp.

Reitz, Deneys. *Trekking On.* London: Faber and Faber Ltd., 1933, 264 pp.

'The Republican Constitution.' *The British Africa Monthly* (July 1948), pp. 19-22.

Roberts, Michael, and Trollip, A. E. G. *The South African Opposition 1939-1945: an essay in contemporary history*. London, New York: Longmans, Green & Co., 1947, 240 pp.

Rogers, Mirabel. *The Black Sash: The Story of the South African Women's Defence of the Constitution League*. Johannesburg: Rotonews, 1956, 273 pp.

Roux, Edward. *S. P. Bunting: A Political Biography*. Cape Town: The African Bookman, 1944, 160 pp.

Sachs, E. S. *The Choice Before South Africa*. London: Turnstile Press, 1952, 220 pp.

Sampson, Anthony. *Drum: A Venture into the New Africa*. London: Collins, 1956, 256 pp.

Samuels, Leonard H. 'The Changing Economic Structure of the Union of South Africa.' *Africa in the Modern World*, ed. by Calvin W. Stillman, Chicago: Chicago University Press, 1955, pp. 245-263.

Saron, Gustav and Hans Hotz (eds.) *The Jews in South Africa, A History*. Cape Town, New York: Oxford University Press, 1955, 422 pp.

Schumann, C. G. W. *Structural Changes and Business Cycles in South Africa, 1806-1936*. London: P. S. King, 1938, 397 pp.

Smith, H. Lindsay. *Behind the Press in South Africa, Second ed.* Cape Town: Stewart Printing Co., 1947, 172 pp.

Smuts, J. C. *Jan Christiaan Smuts*. London: Cassell & Co. Ltd., 1952, 568 pp. [A biography by his son.]

Smuts, J. C. *Plans for a Better World: Speeches of Field-Marshal the Right Honourable J. C. Smuts*. London: Hodder and Stoughton, Ltd., 1942, 287 pp.

Soward, F. R. *The Changing Commonwealth: A Report on the Fourth Unofficial Conference of the Institutes of International Affairs, Bigwin Inn, Ontario, 1949*. Toronto: Canadian Institute of International Affairs, 1950, 268 pp.

Tingsten, Herbert L. S. *The Problem of South Africa*. London: Gollancz, 1955, 159 pp.

Tinley, James M. *South African Food and Agriculture in World War II*. Stanford, California: Stanford University Press, 1954, 138 pp.

Today's News Today: The Story of the Argus Company. Argus Printing and Publishing Company, 1956, 310 pp.

Toekoms, Jan. *'When Malan Goes': A Progressive Programme for South Africa*. South Africa: Central News Agency, 1953, 141 pp.

U.S. Bureau of Foreign Commerce, Near-Eastern and African Division. *Investment in Union of South Africa Lands and Outlook for U.S. Investors*, by Bernard Blankenheimer. Washington: U.S. Gov. Printing Office, 1954, 149 pp.

van Biljon, F. J. *State Interference in South Africa.* Westminster: King & Staples, 1939, 322 pp.

van den Heever, C. M. *General J. B. M. Hertzog.* Johannesburg: A. P. B. Bookstore, 1946, 299 pp.

van der Horst, Sheila T. 'The Union of South Africa: Economic Problems in a Multi-racial Situation.' *The Annals* (March 1955) pp. 71-83.

van der Poel, Jean. *The Jameson Raid.* London, New York, Cape Town: Oxford University Press, 1951, 256 pp.

Van Rensburg, Hans. *Their Paths Crossed Mine: Memoirs of the Commandant-General of the Ossewa-Brandwag.* Central News Agency, South Africa, 1956, 279 pp.

Walker, Eric Anderson. *The Great Trek.* London: A. & C. Black Ltd., 1934, 389 pp.

Walker, Eric Anderson. *A History of South Africa.* London, New York, Toronto: Longmans, Green and Co., 1928, 1935, 1940, 710 pp.

Walker, Oliver. *Sailor Malan: A Biography.* London: Cassell & Co. Ltd., 1953, 182 pp.

Wellington, John H. *South Africa, a Geographical Study.* Cambridge: University Press, 1955, V. 2. *Economic and Human Geography.*

Wheare, K. C. *The Statute of Westminster and Dominion Status.* London: Oxford University Press, 1953, 4th ed., 347 pp.

Williams, Basil. *Botha, Smuts and South Africa.* London: Hodder & Stoughton, 1948, 216 pp.

Wilson, G. H. *Gone Down the Years.* London: Allen & Unwin Ltd., 1947, 279 pp.

Wolton, Douglas G. *Whither South Africa?* London: Lawrence and Wishart, 1947, 155 pp.

(b) *Native Affairs*

More has been written on Native affairs in South Africa than on any other topic concerning that country. The excellent Government reports on this subject have been listed under official publications. Some of the books and articles in this section provide further detailed information about Native conditions; others are concerned primarily with what has been or should be the policy towards South Africa's African majority. The most illuminating history is E. Roux's *Time Longer than Rope,* which draws on wide research and personal knowledge of African movements. Monica Hunter (now Wilson) has written a superb study of the Pondos. The detailed information in the Natal University investigation into the African factory worker reveals some significant reactions to urbanization and industrialization. Tinley's book remains useful, though now somewhat out of date. Unfortunately there is less written by Africans themselves these days than in the thirties—not an encouraging sign.

Bettison, D. G. *A Socio-Economic Study of East London, Cape Province, with Special Reference to the non-European Peoples.* Grahamstown, C. P.: 1950, mimeo.

Brookes, Edgar Harry. *The Colour Problems of South Africa,* being the Phelps-Stokes lecture, 1933, delivered at the University of Cape Town. Lovedale, South Africa: Lovedale Press. London: K. Paul, Trench, Trubner & Co., Ltd., 1934, 237 pp.

Brookes, Edgar Harry. *The History of Native Policy in South Africa from 1830 to the Present Day.* Second rev. ed. Pretoria: J. L. Van Schaik, 1927, 524 pp.

Dumbrell, H. J. E., and Hooper K. E. L. *African Participation in Government.* New York: Longmans, Green and Co., 1949, 139 pp.

Evans, Ifor L. *Native Policy in Southern Africa: An Outline.* London: Cambridge University Press, 1934, 177 pp.

Hoernlé, R. F. Alfred. *South African Native Policy and the Liberal Spirit.* Johannesburg: Witwatersrand University Press, 1945, 190 pp.

Houghton, D. Hobart, and Walton, Edith M. *The Economy of A Native Reserve.* Pietermaritzburg, Shuter and Shooter, 1952, xii, 194 pp. (Keiskammahook rural survey, v. 2).

Hunter, Monica. *Reaction to Conquest: Effects of Contact with Europeans on the Pondo of South Africa.* With an introduction by General the Right Hon. J. C. Smuts. London: H. Milford, Pub. for the International Institute of African Languages and Cultures by the Oxford University Press, 1936, 582 pp.

Jabavu, D. D. T. *The Black Problem.* Papers and Addresses on Various Native Problems. Second ed., 1921, 173 pp.

Jabavu, D. D. T. *Native Disabilities in South Africa.* Lovedale; Cape Province, South Africa: The Lovedale Press, 1932, 26 pp.

Jabavu, D. D. T. (*et al.*) *Native Views on the Native Bills,* 45 pp.

Joint Council of Europeans and Africans, Johannesburg. *Forced Labour in Africa.* Johannesburg, 1930, 18 pp. (The Council Memorandum No. 6.)

Kahn, Ellison. 'Whither Our War-Time Native Policy?' *South African Journal of Economics,* Vol. X (June 1942), pp. 126-52.

Kirk, John. *The Economic Aspects of Native Segregation in South Africa.* London: P. S. King & Son, 1929, 148 pp.

Lestrade, G. P. 'Some Aspects of the Economic Life of the South African Bantu.' *South African Journal of Economics,* Vol. II (December 1934), pp. 426-43.

Loram, Charles T. *The Education of the South African Native.* London: Longmans, Green and Co., 1917, 340 pp.

Marquard, Leopold. *The Black Man's Burden,* by John Burgar (pseud.). London: Victor Gollancz, Ltd., 1943, 252 pp.

Marquard, Leopold. *The Native in South Africa.* And ed. rev. by Julius Lewin. Johannesburg, Witwatersrand University Press, 1944, 105 pp. (First published in 1939 under the title of *The Southern Bantu.*)

Matthews, Dr. Z. K. 'The African Response to Racial Laws.' *Foreign Affairs* (October 1951), pp. 91-102.

Moore, Wilbert E. 'The Migration of Native Laborers in South Africa.' *The Milbank Memorial Fund Quarterly*, Vol. XXIV, No. 4 (October 1946), pp. 401-419.

Natal University College, Pietermaritzburg, Dept. of Economics. *The African Factory Worker: A Sample Study of The Life of the Urban African Worker.* London: Oxford University Press, 1950, 222 pp. Natal Regional Survey, report no. 2.

'The Native Policy of the Union, 1910-1932.' *The Round Table*, Vol. XXII (June 1932), pp. 658-72.

Phillips, Ray E. *The Bantu in the City, A Study of Cultural Adjustment on the Witwatersrand.* Lovedale, South Africa: Lovedale Press, 1948, 452 pp. (Dissertation, Yale University, 1937.)

Plaatje, Solomon Tshekisho. *Native Life in South Africa, Before and Since the European War and the Boer Rebellion.* Second ed. London: P. S. King & Son, 1916, 352 pp.

Rogers, Howard. *Native Administration in the Union of South Africa*, being a brief survey of the organization, functions, and activities of the Department of Native Affairs of the Union of South Africa. (Bantu Studies, suppl. No. 6.) Johannesburg: University of the Witwatersrand Press, 1933, 372 pp.

Roux, Edward. *Time Longer than Rope, a history of the black man's struggle for freedom in South Africa.* London: Victor Gollancz, 1948, 398 pp.

Schapera, Isaac (ed.) *The Bantu-speaking Tribes of South Africa, An Ethnographical Survey*, ed. for the (South African) Inter-University Committee for African Studies. London, New York: The Humanities Press, 1950, 453 pp.

Schapera, Isaac (ed.) *Select Bibliography of South African Native Life and Problems.* Compiled for the Inter-University Committee for African Studies. London: Oxford University Press, 1941, 249 pp.

South African Native Races Committee. *The Natives of South Africa, Their Economic and Social Condition.* London: John Murray, 1901, 360 pp.

South African Native Races Committee (ed.) *The South African Natives, Their Progress and Present Condition.* A supplement to *The Natives of South Africa, Their Economic and Social Condition.* London: John Murray, 1908, 247 pp.

Sundkler, Bengt G. M. *Bantu Prophets in South Africa.* London: Lutterworth Press, 1948, 344 pp.

Tinley, James M. *The Native Labor Problem of South Africa.* Chapel Hill: University of North Carolina Press, 1942, 281 pp.

Walter, Olivier. *Kaffirs Are Lively.* London: Victor Gollancz, 1948, 240 pp.

(c), (d), (e) These books and articles have been listed separately for the sake of convenience. Calpin's book on the Indians in South Africa forms a good starting point for studying this group, though a good deal has happened since it was written. Patterson's work on the Coloured contains a wide range of information presented in sociological form.

The constitutional issue was handled thoroughly in Chapter 4 and these articles have been referred to there. Some interesting general information on the relation of the courts to legislation is contained in McWhinney's article on 'Race Relations and the Courts'.

The Protectorates form a special issue of particular importance to those who plan to build the Native Reserves into a viable area for a higher proportion of South Africa's Africans. The basic material on the question of transfer is contained in the British and South African official documents on the subject. It is interesting to compare them.

(c) *Other non-European groups*

Aiyar, P. S. *Conflict of Races in South Africa.* Durban: The African Chronicle Printing Works, 251 pp. (1946?).

Appasamy, Bhaskar. *Indians of South Africa.* Bombay: Padma Publications, 1943, 92 pp. (Current Topics Series, No. 12.)

Calpin, G. H. *Indians in South Africa.* Pietermaritzburg: Shuter & Shooter, 1949, 310 pp.

Carter, Gwendolen M. 'The Discrimination Against Indians in South Africa'. *Problems in International Relations,* ed. Andrew Gyorgy and Hubert L. Gibbs. New York: Prentice-Hall, 1955, pp. 184-191.

du Plessis, Izak D. and Carl A. Lückhoff. *The Malay Quarter and Its People.* Cape Town: A. A. Balkema, 1953, 90 pp. [Race relations series of the Sub-Dept. of Coloured Affairs, Dept. of Interior.]

Gandhi, M. K. *Satyagraha in South Africa.* Ahmedabad: Navajivan Publishing House, 1928, 351 pp.

Joshi, P. S. *The Struggle for Equality.* Bombay: Hind Kitabs Ltd., 1951, 304 pp.

Joshi, P. S. *Verdict on South Africa* (*The Tyranny of Colour*). Bombay: Thacker & Co., Ltd., 1945, 365 pp.

Macmillan, W. M. *The Cape Colour Question: An Historical Survey.* London: Faber and Gwyer, 1929, 304 pp.

Marais, J. S. *The Cape Coloured People.* London: Longmans, Green and Co., 1939, 296 pp.

Natal University College, Dept. of Economics. *Natal Regional Survey.* Pietermaritzburg: University of Natal Press. Additional report no. 4, *The Dunn Reserve, Zululand: A Study of a Coloured Community,* 1954, 84 pp.
Vol. 9, Woods, C. A. *The Indian Community: Their Economic Position,* 1954, 112 pp.

Patterson, Sheila. *Colour and Culture in South Africa: A Study of the Status of the Cape Coloured People Within the Social Structure of the Union of South Africa.* London: Routledge & Kegan Paul Ltd., 1953, 402 pp.

Polak, H. S. L., Brailsford, H. N., and Pethick-Lawrence, Lord. *Mahatma Gandhi.* London: Odhams Press Ltd., 1949, 320 pp.

Trollip, Tony. 'The Cape Coloured Franchise.' *Common Sense* (December 1950), pp. 506-509.

Vane, Michael. *The South African Indians: A Plea for Better Understanding.* S. A. Affairs Pamphlets No. 17, n.d., 43 pp.

(d) *The constitutional issue*

The Cape Coloured Vote. Separate Report by the United Party Members of the Joint Select Committee set up to consider the Separate Representation of Voters Act Validation and Amendment Bill, 1953. Juta & Co.

Judgment of Appellate Division in the Separate Representation of Voters Case (With Argument). Cape Town and Johannesburg: Juta & Co., Ltd., 1952, pp. 428-472. (Reprinted from South African Law Reports, May 1952.)

Cowen, D. V. 'Legislature and Judiciary: Reflections on the Constitutional Issues in South Africa: Part I.' *The Modern Law Review* (July 1952), Vol. 15, No. 3, pp. 282-296. Part II (July 1953), Vol. 16, No. 3, pp. 273-298.

Cowen, D. V. *Parliamentary Sovereignty and the Entrenched Sections of the South Africa Act.* Cape Town and Johannesburg: Juta & Co., Ltd., 1951, 50 pp.

Griswold, Erwin N. 'The "Coloured Vote Case" in South Africa.' *Harvard Law Review* (June 1952), Vol. 65, No. 8, pp. 1361-1374.

Keeton, G. W. 'The Constitutional Crisis in South Africa.' *Current Legal Problems,* ed. G. W. Keeton and G. Schwarzenberger, Vol. 6. London: Stevens & Sons, 1953, pp. 22-38.

McWhinney, Edward. *Court Versus Legislature in the Union of South Africa: The Assertion of a Right of Judicial Review.* Reprinted from *The Canadian Bar Review* (January 1953), pp. 52-64.

McWhinney, Edward. 'La Crise Constitutionelle de l'union Sud-Africaine.' Extrait de la *Revue internationale de droit comparé,* 1953, No. 3, 22 pp.

McWhinney, Edward. 'Race Relations and the Courts in the Union of South Africa.' *The Canadian Bar Review* (January 1954), pp. 44-74.

McWhinney, Edward. 'The Union Parliament, the Supreme Court, and the "Entrenched Clauses" of the South Africa Act.' *The Canadian Bar Review* (Aug.-Sept. 1952), Vol. 30, No. 7, pp. 690-722.

(e) *The Protectorates and the Question of Transfer*

Dundas, Sir Charles and Hugh Ashton. *Problem Territories of Southern Africa: Basutoland, Bechuanaland Protectorate, Swaziland.* Cape Town: South African Institute of International Affairs, 1952, 79 pp.

Fitzgerald, Richard C. 'South Africa and the High Commission Territories.' *World Affairs*, London (July 1950), pp. 306-320.

Greaves, Lionel B. *The High Commission Territories: Basutoland, The Bechuanaland Protectorate, and Swaziland.* London: Edinburgh House Press, 1954, 23 pp.

Perham, Margery F. and Lionel Curtis. *The Protectorates of South Africa, The Question of Their Transfer to the Union.* London: Oxford University Press, 1935, 119 pp.

Sheddick, Vernon G. F. *Land Tenure in Basutoland.* London: Her Majesty's Stationery Office, 1954, 196 pp.

Swaziland, A General Survey. Johannesburg: South African Institute of Race Relations, 1955, 48 pp.

Tshekedi, Khama. *Bechuanaland and South Africa.* Introduction by M. Perham. London: Africa Bureau, 1955, 20 pp.

Union of South Africa. *Negotiations Regarding the Transfer to the Union of South Africa of the Government of Basutoland, the Bechuanaland Protectorate and Swaziland, 1910-1939.* G.P.S. 4846-1952-3. Pretoria: The Government Printer, 1952, 52 pp.

United Kingdom. *Basutoland, The Bechuanaland Protectorate and Swaziland: History of Discussions with the Union of South Africa, 1909-1939.* Cmd. 8707. London: Her Majesty's Stationery Office, 1952, 135 pp.

INDEX